HOWARD ROBERTS LAMAR received his B.A. from Emory University and his M.A. and PhD. from Yale University. He joined the history department at Yale in 1949 and was chairman of the department from 1962 to 1963 and director of history graduate studies from 1964 to 1967. Since 1964 he has been professor of American history and the history of the American West.

The Far Southwest
1846-1912
A Territorial History

Howard Roberts Lamar

The Norton Library
W · W · NORTON & COMPANY · INC ·
NEW YORK

For Shirley

Acknowledgments

 The number of individuals and institutions to whom I am indebted for making this study possible is so great that it is impossible for me to express adequate thanks to all.

Among the many officials and staff members of the National Archives who have courteously searched out pertinent materials in the Territorial Papers of the United States I am particularly grateful to the late Clarence E. Carter and to Robert Bahmer. Ray Allen Billington not only provided support and advice but gave me a chance to test several of my conclusions in public meetings. George W. Pierson, as chairman of the Yale History Department, arranged two leaves of absence for me between 1959 and 1961, so that I could give full time to the study. Archibald Hanna, Director of the Yale Western Americana Collection, did all in his power to supply me with needed manuscript materials on the Far Southwest.

A grant from the Henry E. Huntington Library in 1957 permitted the use of the splendid New Mexico Collection of William G. Ritch. In 1959 a fellowship from the American Council of Learned Societies enabled me to visit state archives and historical libraries throughout the Southwest. A subsequent grant-in-aid by the Social Science Research Council allowed me to complete the research in the National Archives and to realize the first draft of the manuscript.

Quite apart from the many services and materials provided me at the New Mexico Historical Society in Santa Fe and the Coronado Library at the University of New Mexico in Albuquerque, I am grateful for many insights into New Mexican history gained from conversations with Myra Ellen Jenkins and Frank D. Reeve. Through Dr. Jenkins' efforts I was able to use the Papers of Governors

Edmund G. Ross and L. Bradford Prince of New Mexico. Officials at the Denver Public Library, the Colorado State Historical Society, and the Colorado State Archives went far beyond the call of duty to chase down obscure newspapers and manuscripts. Among these I am particularly grateful to Laura Allyn Ekstrom, Agnes Wright Spring, Dolores Renze, Maurice Frink, and Alys Freeze.

Similarly, the efficient help and critical comments of Russ A. Mortensen, Everett Cooley, and John James, all of the Utah State Historical Society in Salt Lake City, greatly speeded my research there. In Tucson, Arizona, John A. Carroll, Bernard Fontana, Robert A. Armstrong, and the staff of the Arizona Pioneers Historical Society were of great help in locating papers pertinent to Arizona history. Alice B. Good and Marguerite Cooley of the Arizona State Archives cordially allowed me to use still uncatalogued papers relating to territorial affairs.

In California the officials of the Bancroft Library at Berkeley dragged out many crumbling frontier newspaper files for my use. Amidst the renaissance splendor and courteous ministrations of the staff of the Henry E. Huntington Library, research into New Mexican and Mormon materials housed there became a unique pleasure. I am particularly indebted to John E. Pomfret, Director of the Library, and to Miss Mary Isabel Fry of the staff.

Interviews with a number of Western historians were rewarding. Of these I am delighted to thank Leonard Arrington and S. George Ellsworth of the State University of Utah at Logan, Robert G. Athearn of the University of Colorado, Harold H. Dunham of Denver University, Robert Utley of the National Park Service, and William H. Goetzmann of the University of Texas. The helpful services of Lueva Pfleuger and Robert Oliver of Yale University were many.

For practical assistance in the typing of the manuscript and for constant encouragement and patience when I was "in the rough spots," I shall always be indebted to my wife, Shirley.

H.R.L.

New Haven, Connecticut
July 1965

Contents

Illustrations

Abbreviations

AHR	*Arizona Historical Review*
APHS	Arizona Pioneers' Historical Society, Tucson
ASA	Arizona State Archives, Phoenix
CM	*Colorado Magazine*
CSA	Colorado State Archives, Denver
CSHS	Colorado State Historical Society
DAB	*Dictionary of American Biography*
HEH	Henry E. Huntington Library, San Marino, California
MVHR	*Mississippi Valley Historical Review*
NA	The National Archives of the United States, Washington
NMHR	*New Mexico Historical Review*
NMHS	New Mexico Historical Society, Santa Fe
NMSRC	Archives Division of the New Mexico State Records Center, Santa Fe
OIA	United States Office of Indian Affairs
TP	Territorial Papers of the United States located in the National Archives
UHQ	*Utah Historical Quarterly*
USHS	Utah State Historical Society, Salt Lake City
YWA	The Western Americana Collection in the Beinecke Rare Book and Manuscripts Library, Yale University

Preface to the Norton Library Edition

Since the publication of the first edition of *The Far Southwest* in 1966, many people have contributed to my further education either by helpful criticism or by sharing their own findings about the territorial history of the "Four Corners States." Their comments are reflected in certain factual changes in this paperback edition. Hopefully this time the map will not send the Goodnight-Loving Trail to wander on the wrong side of the Pecos River or any longer permit Laramie to usurp Cheyenne's spot on the Union Pacific line.

I owe special thanks to Harwood P. Hinton, editor of *Arizona and the West*, for his suggestions. Comments by Ray A. Billington, John Porter Bloom, Earl S. Pomeroy, W. Eugene Hollon, John D. W. Guice, Dr. Bert Sacks, Bert Fireman, Kenneth N. Owens, Robert W. Larson, Thomas G. Alexander, William Turrentine Jackson and James Vivian were helpful. And finally the researches, stimulating ideas and irrepressible curiosity of Lewis L. Gould and R. Hal Williams have enriched my own understanding of the history of the American Southwest.

HOWARD R. LAMAR
New Haven, Connecticut
November, 1969

Here two great culture systems have met and
clashed and fused and are still in process of clashing
and fusing. . . . Here, in a truly cultural sense, is
found and may be observed the last frontier. . . .
Here we have a blending of the two Americas, a circumstance which makes the region less "American" in the
sense of the United States than any other, but from
the point of view of the Hemisphere, the most truly
American of all regions.

Howard W. Odum
American Social Problems, 1939

Introduction

In 1956 the late Clarence E. Carter, editor of the Territorial Papers of the United States, lamented that the "Dark Age of American historiography" was territorial history.[1] As its title should indicate, this volume is designed to be a modest excursion into the neglected area of the American past of which Dr. Carter spoke. Specifically, this is a study of the diverse, often turbulent political evolution of four Southwestern territories—New Mexico, Colorado, Utah, and Arizona—from their territorial beginnings to their admission into the American Union. Any history of territories must naturally include some account of national policy, for Congress and the executive branch had direct jurisdiction over these frontier political units. Where it has seemed pertinent, then, the major features of the federal administration of territories between the years 1850 and 1912 have also been treated.

The internal political history of each territory, set in the framework of national policy, forms a more or less complete narrative by itself; yet the future "Four Corners States" had then—and still have—lengthy common boundaries. Historically, they have shared many political, economic, military, and social problems as parts of a single region. Within certain limits, therefore, this volume attempts to comprehend and explain how Anglo-American political institutions and habits took root and flourished in the Spanish Southwest—a region which already possessed a European cultural heritage and established institutions of its own.

American pioneers had confronted imperial Spain and segments of Spanish colonial culture in Florida, Louisiana, Texas, and, later,

1. Clarence E. Carter, "The Territorial Papers of the United States: A Review and a Commentary," *MVHR, 42* (1956), 521–22.

California; but never before had they grappled with such a hardy Spanish-Mexican frontier society as the Rio Grande Valley during the era of the Santa Fe trade. Nor had Americans ever encountered a different culture in as hostile an environment as the Southwest. Between 1821, the year William Becknell inaugurated the Santa Fe trade, and 1879, the year the Atchison, Topeka, and Santa Fe Railroad reached the Southwest, a fundamentally different frontier experience awaited American traders, trappers, and settlers who chose to follow the meandering trails leading into the isolated, rugged Spanish-Mexican borderlands.

Presumably any area called a "region" has common environmental features. If the four territories under consideration are defined in terms of geography, however, it is true that each embraced at least two or more distinct physiographic provinces. On the other hand, they had some features in common; all these provinces had similar soils, surface vegetation, watersheds, and climates. Physical provinces also ignored political boundaries. Both Colorado and New Mexico held within their borders sections of the Upland Trough, the Southern Rockies, and the water courses of the Rio Grande River. The Colorado Plateau spread broken tablelands over areas of all four territories. The magnificent watershed of the Colorado River also reached back into the mountains of every territory. Two, Arizona and Utah, possessed the exclusive but dubious privilege of being part of the arid Great Basin Province. Whatever the larger geographical differences may have been, the entire region had difficult mountains, broken plateaus, deserts, arid or semi-arid climates, and—once whites settled there—similar ranching, mining, and irrigated farming economies. (See Map.)

An historical determinant in the Far Southwest, at times even harsher than physical environment, was a permanent, hostile Indian population. Apache, Navajo, Ute, and Comanche tribesmen occupied lands stretching westward from Texas to the lower Colorado River and southward from Colorado into Sonora and Chihuahua. As excellent fighters and natural raiders the Apaches, in particular, were a constant terror to white colonists. Even the withdrawn, peaceful, Pueblo tribes of the Rio Grande Valley maintained such continuous passive resistance to alien influence that neither their tribal integrity nor their distinct culture was ever suborned by Spain or Mexico. From the day that Juan de Oñate first brought Spanish colonists to the Upper Rio Grande in 1598 until General George Crook brought the majority of the Arizona Apache tribes to heel in 1872, every generation of settlers knew the fear, or the harassment, of savage Indian warfare. What had been a temporary condition on Anglo-American Indian frontiers seemed a constant factor on this Spanish-Mexican Indian one.

For the Southwestern pioneer, whether Spanish, Mexican, or American, the common Indian problem was not simply the old frontier problem of defeating the red man and achieving peace. It was the problem of living with a permanent Indian population of relatively large numbers, which itself was split into tribes as hostile toward one another as they were toward the whites. Edward H. Spicer has aptly observed that historically the Southwest has always been a region where one society did not really conquer another; instead, each society, tribe, or group remained fragmented into disparate cultural enclaves.[2] So disparate was the Indian population, in fact, that even a single tribal group was separated by dialect and language differences, which sometimes prevented one village from communicating with the village next to it. When the United States formally acquired the Southwest in 1848 as a part of the Mexican Cession, the heterogeneous population of wild and peaceful Indians and Spanish-Mexicans had built up actual and psychological walls of resistance to one another and to the intrusion of other peoples and their cultures—walls so strong that they were not to crumble for generations.

Nevertheless, even the most bland conqueror brings his habits and his institutions with him, and these eventually have an impact. Two years after the Treaty of Guadalupe-Hidalgo made the Spanish Southwest American soil, the Compromise of 1850 provided an American territorial system of government for New Mexico and Utah. Within this framework the slow but fascinating process of Americanizing the Southwest began.

The original boundaries of the American territories of New Mexico

2. Edward H. Spicer, *Cycles of Conquest; The Impact of Spain, Mexico, and the United States on the Indians of the Southwest, 1533–1960* (Tucson, Arizona, 1962), pp. 1–4.

and Utah put nearly all of the future state of Arizona and part of
future Colorado under New Mexican jurisdiction; part of western
Colorado and the future state of Nevada were placed under Utah
rule.[3] The creation of huge jurisdictoins over vast areas was far less
important, however, than the fact that three out of the four political
units eventually organized by Congress were to experience long
territorial apprenticeships. New Mexico, conquered by General
Stephen Watts Kearny and his Army of the West in 1846, became a
territory in 1850 and remained one until 1912. Because gold was discovered on Cherry Creek in 1858, Colorado quickly acquired a population and achieved statehood, after being a territory only fifteen
years (1861–76). Though actually settled in 1847 by thousands of
Mormon Latter Day Saints, Utah did not become a territory until
1850; but from that date until 1896 it served a troubled, and often
bitter, territorial apprenticeship. Arizona, created largely to counteract Confederate claims to the Southwest, remained a territory from
1863 to 1912.

Being subject to the same governmental system and sharing common environmental, economic, and Indian problems was far from the
whole story. The fundamental differences between these territory-
states were as remarkable as the similarities. Throughout the territorial
period New Mexico remained stubbornly and overwhelmingly Spanish-American in culture, tradition-directed in habits, and Roman
Catholic in religion. Indeed, Anglo-American citizens remained the
minority ethnic group in New Mexico until 1928.[4] Colorado, on the
other hand, was essentially an American frontier mining society,
which retained close business and social connections with the American East. The settlers of Utah, though partly native American in
origin, felt so persecuted because of their firm belief in the Mormon
religion—and the accompanying doctrine of polygamous marriage—
that they deliberately developed their own unique social and political systems during the territorial period. Their social system has
remained so distinct that anthropologists still identify it as a separate

3. The Gadsden Purchase, now a part of southern Arizona, obviously could not
be put under New Mexican jurisdiction until it was acquired in 1854.

4. James I. Culbert, "Distribution of Spanish-American Population in New
Mexico," *Economic Geography, 19* (1943), 171–76.

American subculture, just as they do Spanish-American society in New Mexico.[5] The diverse pioneer settlers of Arizona Territory, hailing from Mexican Sonora, the Confederate South, the American Northeast, and Mormon Utah, formed a conglomerate American frontier society not quite like any of the other three.

It is not the purpose of this study to dwell on the applicability and completeness of other basic interpretations of the history of the American trans-Mississippi West. Yet such persistent variations in the population origins and in the actual histories of the four territories under consideration would seem to call into question the adequacy of the frontier experience, or of regional factors alone, to explain the growth of American political and social institutions in this area. Clearly, one of the harshest environments within the continental United States did not reduce different cultures to either a composite nationality or a recognizable regional political character. John W. Caughey, in discussing Southwestern regionalism at a conference in 1952, caught the essence of the problem for the frontier and regional historian when he said: "Peculiarly, the inhabitants of this area seem to be relatively innocent of regionalism. Whereas millions proclaim 'I am a Texan' or 'I am a Californian', almost no one boasts, 'I am an Southwesterner.' "[6]

Artificially drawn boundaries of territories and states obviously have a real historical meaning and significance; but again, whether one is discussing Mormon Utah or Spanish-American New Mexico, history from the local or state perspective alone is also inadequate. While no one can doubt the immense value of the regional approach which the late Walter Prescott Webb used so brilliantly in his *The Great Plains,* he himself was to comment later that the nature of the Great Plains environment, and of arid lands generally, meant that such areas would always be sparsely populated regions. In all likelihood, therefore, they could not be self-sufficient regions. This condi-

5. Anthony F. Wallace, in *Culture and Personality* (New York, 1962), p. 103, cites no less than five "cultures" for the American Southwest: Navajo, Zuni, Mormon, Texan, and Spanish-American.
6. John W. Caughey, "The Spanish Southwest: An Example of Subconscious Regionalism," in Merrill Jensen, ed., *Regionalism in America* (Madison, 1951), p. 184.

tion—for the American period at least—implied regional dependence upon other areas of the country—particularly the industrial Northeast. According to Webb many Western regions of the United States must always suffer economically from an unfavorable balance of trade and remain a permanent colonial area.[7] The phrase "colonial area" suggests a necessary and formal relationship to a parent area or a central authority.

From the very beginning of the Anglo-American pioneer movement into the trans-Mississippi West, and particularly into the Far Southwest, the settler had to look for outside help to succeed, even to survive. Help itself came in a great number of ways. Throughout the frontier stages the federal government rendered aid by fighting Indians, protecting colonists and building roads, or it helped in more subtle ways by allowing cattlemen and farmers to abuse the land system. Further, dependence on Eastern and European capital has always been important in the settlement and growth of the entire trans-Mississippi West. In still other cases help came through technical innovations—made possible by the world-wide industrial and transportation revolutions—permitting profitable mining, ranching, and farming economies to exist.

The intractable qualities of the Southwestern environment, persistence of imported cultural beliefs, and dependence on outside support suggest, too, that parts of Frederick Jackson Turner's frontier hypothesis are not applicable to the region. Various of Turner's frontier "stages" are certainly in evidence: there was a distinct trader-trapper period, an era of the miner, a day of the cattleman, and, finally, the farmer-settler. But the classical Turnerian frontier was a forested wilderness which, once conquered, became a garden of abundance. Nature, once tamed, proved to be lavishly beneficent.[8] On the Southwestern frontier, however, nature remained relatively

7. Walter Prescott Webb, "The American West: Perpetual Mirage," *Harper's Magazine, 214* (May 1957), 25–31. For a similar interpretation applied to the history of another area see Robert G. Athearn, *High Country Empire: The High Plains and Rockies* (New York, 1960), pp. 278–333.

8. Frederick Jackson Turner, "The Significance of the Frontier in American History," American Historical Association, *Annual Report for 1893* (Washington, 1894), 199–227.

mean and unproductive, except for periodic mineral discoveries; and another civilized, if colonial, culture already existed there.

Thus the American pioneer deliberately shunned this unattractive region as a place to settle until he was armed with devices to overcome the difficulties. Using military protection, rail transportation, scientific techniques of mining and farming, and machines of all sorts, he conquered frontier conditions with methods far different from those employed in the eighteenth century Appalachian frontier. Something more than the classical frontier hypothesis is needed to explain the history of the American Southwest.

Unfortunately, since Turner has been so closely identified with this most famous of his interpretations of American history, his other provocative ideas and suggestions have been largely ignored by his own defenders. Always openminded and flexible, Turner first urged students of the American frontier to look at history in territorial units. In an early essay written in 1897 he said: "Our colonial system did not begin with the Spanish War; the United States had had a colonial history and policy from the beginning of the Republic; but they have been hidden under the phraseology of 'interstate migration' and 'territorial organization.' "[9]

Here, at least, was a specific geographic and political framework, with a continuous existence, into which one could fit both the chaotic history of American expansion and the story of the maturation of American frontier society and institutions. Using territorial history to relate the local frontier process of evolution to the national scene and policy (therefore explaining the colonial aspects of the Western past) holds as much promise now as it did for Turner in 1897.

It is time to ask: what exactly was this American territorial system, which Dr. Carter insisted was so little understood and which Turner said was nothing less than an internal American colonial system and policy?

The system itself is as old as the present national government, for it was created by the Northwest Ordinance of 1787, became opera-

9. Frederick Jackson Turner, "The Middle West," in *The Frontier in American History* (New York, 1962), p. 127.

tive in the Northwest Territory a year later, and was re-enacted by the Federal Congress in 1789.[10] The Confederation Congress and the interested Ohio Land Company lobbyists who helped draft the original document felt that it would be a constitution for the West: a government for the undeveloped regions that various states with western land claims were then turning over to the central government. Governor Arthur St. Clair, the first administrator of the Ordinance, saw himself as a frontier Washington as he set the wheels of territorial government into motion at Marietta, Ohio, in the summer of 1788.

Constitution for the West seems an apt description of the Northwest Ordinance, since it was an internal colonial system, a device for eventual self-government, a guarantor of property, and a bill of rights rolled into one act.[11] An exceptionally shrewd and comprehensive document, it borrowed the most workable parts of the old British colonial system and formulated a government out of them. The law also guaranteed the sanctity of private property and the inviolability of contracts and provided rules to govern the transference and descent of property. So clearly were these property clauses expressed that the Founding Fathers copied them almost verbatim into the Constitution.[12]

Better known than its economic clauses was a bill of rights promising the territorial citizen freedom of religion, trial by jury, writ of habeas corpus, right of bail, the observance of just fines and punishments, and proportionate representation in a legislative assembly. In

10. The Northwest Ordinance of 1787 has been covered in a number of articles—few of them recent. Among the most useful are John M. Merriam, "The Legislative History of the Ordinance of 1787," *Proceedings of the American Antiquarian Society*, new ser. 5 (1889), 303–47; J. A. Barrett, *Evolution of the Ordinance of 1787* (New York, 1891); Max Farrand, *The Legislation of Congress for the Organized Territories of the United States, 1785–1895* (Newark, N.J., 1896); Beverley W. Bond, Jr., "Some Political Ideas of the Colonial Period as They Were Realized in the Old Northwest," in *Essays in Colonial History Presented to Charles McLean Andrews by His Students* (New Haven, 1931); Milo M. Quaife, "The Significance of the Ordinance of 1787," *Journal of the Illinois State Historical Society*, 30 (1937–38), 415–28; Theodore C. Pease, "The Ordinance of 1787," *MVHR*, 25 (1938–39), 167–80; Merrill Jensen, *The New Nation: A History of the United States during the Confederation, 1781–1789* (New York, 1950), pp. 352–59.

11. For a more detailed summary of the early workings of the Ordinance see Howard R. Lamar, *Dakota Territory, 1861–1889: A Study of Frontier Politics* (New Haven, 1956), pp. 1–27.

12. For the text of the Ordinance see Francis N. Thorpe, *The Federal and State Constitutions* (7 vols. Washington, 1909), 2, 957–62.

short, the ideals of British justice as well as the aims of the American Revolution were guaranteed. Finally, in a burst of liberal sentiment stemming both from the New England experience and Revolutionary zeal, the Ordinance fostered public education by providing lands for its support, denied the right of slavery in the Northwest, and demanded just treatment of the Indian population.

Although the Ordinance has never been fully studied, from the time of its enactment historians have praised it as a brilliant solution to the twin problems of governing colonies while they were growing and of keeping them once they had matured.[13] As many an admiring historian has commented: in the Ordinance the problem of liberty had been reconciled with the problem of empire. Justifiably, much of the praise and attention has centered on the civil rights portions of the act, on the antislavery and public education provisos, and on the happy end result: statehood. Curiously, the actual governmental system which functioned from 1788 until 1954 (when Alaska and Hawaii Territories became the forty-ninth and fiftieth states in the Union) has received much less attention.

Building on the colonial experience of the thirteen colonies, the Ordinance anticipated that government on the frontier would evolve through successive stages. At the beginning of territorial settlement, Congress was to appoint a governor, a secretary, and three federal judges. Each appointee had his separate duties, but during this first stage the officers could act in joint council to write a code for the new political creation by adopting, bit by bit, portions of the laws of older states.

In the second stage, reached when a population of 5,000 male voters could be found within territorial borders, citizens could elect both a legislative assembly and a nonvoting delegate to represent them in Congress. But even then the steps toward local self-government were cautious ones, for the membership of the territorial upper house, or council, had to be approved by Congress. And in the case of the earlier territories the franchise was confined to substantial property holders. Again the similarity to British colonial practice was striking.

The third stage came when the territory could report a population

13. For a laudatory account see Pease, "The Ordinance of 1787."

of 60,000 inhabitants. It was then eligible to hold a constitutional convention, elect a state government, and apply to Congress for admission into the Union on an equal basis with the original thirteen states. Here the Confederation legislators departed from colonial experience and turned to the lessons of the Revolution. They gave the mature territory three things England had denied her colonies: representation, equaltiy with other parts of the Union, and home rule, which meant, in this case, statehood.

Although only Ohio, Louisiana, Michigan, and Florida, of the inland territories of the United States, went through the rather arbitrary first stage of government, all remaining territories passed through stages two and three before they came into the Union. Between 1789 and 1912 no less than twenty-nine American states experienced a territorial period.

Territorial history and policy have been neglected by historians for several very good reasons. If one is to judge by textbook summaries, most historians have assumed that the Old Northwest served as a normal prototype for the history of all subsequent territories. It seemed unnecessary to repeat the story as new territories were formed. Again, American territorial policy obviously did not pass through dramatically different phases such as an era of mercantilism, a period of salutary neglect, or a program of new imperialism, as the British colonies did between 1650 and 1776. Nor was the system run by a colonial office, or a distinct branch of the government. Next, one can argue convincingly that American territorial and state governments have been so similar to one another and territorial periods were often so brief that there has been no need to consider state and territorial history separately. The frontier hypothesis itself stressed environmental factors and private initiative rather than institutional continuity and public action.

All of these assumptions are certainly correct in varying degrees. Nevertheless, the system itself did change over the years. Many territorial periods actually lasted for a quarter century or more, and each territory had an evolutionary history far different from that of the Old Northwest.

Territorial policy appears to have passed through four minor evolutions. In the first phase, lasting from 1789 to 1819, territorial problems were mixed up with international diplomatic disputes, Indian wars, and border intrigues. The major problem was to keep the trans-Appalachian borderlands loyal. As a result the federal government appointed able men to the governorships, while it appeased frontier regions by pressing for speedy Indian removal, by liberalizing public land policy, and by purchasing Louisiana so that frontier products could be shipped down the Mississippi.

After the War of 1812 had ended the British threat to the Northwest, and the Adams-Onis Treaty of 1819 had put a stop to British and Spanish intrigues in the Old Southwest by securing the Floridas for the United States, territorial problems became less burdensome. Congress could now standardize and perfect the system. Even so, internal variations in policy occurred when, for example, Congress reversed its 1787 antislavery stand and allowed slavery to exist in the territories formed out of lands south of the Ohio.

Yet Congress was also engaged in democratizing portions of the Northwest Ordinance.[14] By 1825 all new territories were allowed to skip the first stage of territorial government, and both upper and lower houses of the assembly had become elective. Gradually, property requirements for voting became so nominal that universal male suffrage within a territory was possible. All of these changes and many minor ones were embodied in the Wisconsin Organic Act of 1836. That law replaced the Northwest Ordinance as the model for all future territorial organic acts.[15]

In his excellent history of legislation relating to the territories, Max Farrand has asserted that the Wisconsin Act marked the final democratization and standardization of the American territorial system.[16] While the framework may have become set, attitudes and policies involving the system continued to shift. The states rights ideology, which developed in the thirty years before the Civil War, denied a fundamental assumption of the Ordinance of 1787 by claiming that the states and not the federal government owned the territories.

Stephen A. Douglas' concept of popular sovereignty, which came

14. Farrand, *The Legislation of Congress,* pp. 17–35.
15. Ibid., pp. 34 ff., 45 ff.
16. Ibid.

into national prominence after 1850, also questioned the whole theory of the Ordinance when it claimed that a community was ready for self-government from the moment it was first settled. Thus the evolutionary idea that a new region was unready for self-government until it had passed through three stages of maturation was undermined.

Unhappily, these basic premises came to be debated at the very time the rising slavery issue gave territories—as future slave or free states—political notoriety out of all proportion to their actual importance. Congressional passage of the 1854 act establishing Kansas and Nebraska Territories virtually repealed the theory of the 1787 law. Although the slavery issue prompted most of the ensuing "bloody Kansas" troubles between 1854 and 1857, one of the difficulties was that local Kansans had freedom to do pretty much as they pleased. And while Kansas practiced a mockery of popular sovereignty, Buchanan's government, believing in states rights, denied that the Ordinance gave him the federal power to keep order there. These difficulties illustrate, incidentally, what might have happened in other territories had Thomas Jefferson's more democratic Ordinance of 1784—which embodied states rights and popular sovereignty ideas —been adopted in place of the more conservative 1787 document.[17]

Naturally, territorial policy changed again when the Republican party came into office in 1861.[18] The Lincoln government not only extended the territorial system over the remaining unorganized portions of the Trans-Mississippi West but firmly held that federal rule was paramount in these regions. Anxious to keep the West in the Union, Congress organized Dakota, Colorado, and Nevada Territories in 1861 and Arizona in 1863. By 1870 Congress had organized Wyoming, Montana, and Idaho as well. Only the Indian Territory, part of which was to become Oklahoma Territory in 1890, remained closed to white settlement. Between 1861 and 1888 Congress governed no less than thirteen Western territories, and during that time only four—Kansas, Nevada, Nebraska, and Colorado—were given statehood.

17. Jensen, *The New Nation,* pp. 353–54.
18. Earl S. Pomeroy, *The Territories and the United States, 1861–1890* (Philadelphia, 1947).

Meanwhile, succeeding administrations continued to standardize the rules governing every facet of territorial administration. Every federal appointee had to make reports to his superiors in Washington, secure permission for leaves of absence, and make his public expenditures justifiable to an ever-suspicious treasury comptroller. After 1869 territorial assemblies were told that they could meet only biennially and for only sixty days at a time. Territorial elections had to be reported, and Congress was frequently called on to settle a disputed delegate election.

Besides standardization two other policies, both begun before the Civil War, now became major features of the postwar system. First, the federal government continued to subsidize the territorial economy by paying for its government, maintaining military posts throughout the West, running an elaborate Indian service in the field, building roads, and providing land offices and mail routes in new areas of settlement.[19] In some territories, where the federal government was busily engaged in feeding thousands of Indians, government affairs became so financially important that they became the biggest business there.[20] Second, Congress used territorial offices as political spoils to be divided among interested congressmen of the dominant politcial party.

These two policies together created an unfortunate situation. More often than not, territorial appointees after 1865 were political hacks, defeated congressmen, or jobless relatives of congressmen and cabinet members. These appointees owed their loyalty neither to the territory nor to the branch of government they represented. Thus a territorial judge whose appointment came through a powerful senator could thumb his nose at the Justice Department, which theoretically had jurisdiction over his actions. An unpopular governor with strong congressional backing could stay in office despite a howl of protest from his territorial constituents. There were neither standards of excellence nor any sense of group unity in the federal territorial bureaucracy. Naturally, no civil service or public service traditions de-

19. Pomeroy. William H. Goetzmann, *Army Exploration in the American West, 1803–1863* (New Haven, 1959). William T. Jackson, *Wagon Roads West* (New Haven, 1965).

20. Lamar, *Dakota Territory*, pp. 102–08, 182–88

veloped among such a divisive, individualistic, second-rate set of officials.[21]

Frequently, the office-holding spoilsman wanted the territorial job not for the office alone but because it gave him a chance to take a share of the sizable federal expenditures in each territory. At the same time, he was also interested in milking the territory of whatever funds might become available through land and railroad schemes or business speculations. The presence of cynical, corrupt men holding territorial office was so common after 1865 that Earl S. Pomeroy has called them a breed of Western carpetbaggers, whose sole aim it was to fleece a region and return East with the proceeds.[22] Often the more successful of these men could have their cake and eat it too, by persuading the electorate of a territory to return them to Washington as delegate. Unhappily the corrupt official remained a major feature of the territorial system for the remainder of the nineteenth century.

The presence of corruption and "Grantism" in territorial governments did not go unchallenged. Throughout the 1870s and 1880s both the president and the Congress attempted to reform the Wild West at a number of levels. In 1873 territorial affairs, which had been directed by the State Department since 1789, were turned over to the Department of the Interior. Reform secretaries of the Interior, such as Carl Schurz (1877–81), tried to break up territorial Indian rings; but resistance at the territorial level defeated his crusade more often than not.

Reforms were attempted in other sectors when Grover Cleveland assumed office in 1885. As the first Democrat to occupy the presidency in twenty years, he was under tremendous pressure to oust the powerful Republican machines that had come to control most territorial governments.[23] Under the guise of appointing reform governors and honest land office officials, Cleveland made a vigorous

21. Earl S. Pomeroy, "Carpet-Baggers in the Territories, 1861–1890," *The Historian*, 2 (1939), 53–64.

22. Ibid.

23. See Harold H. Dunham, *Government Handout: A Study in the Administration of Public Lands* (New York, 1941), pp. 180 ff. Lamar, *Dakota Territory*, pp. 107–08, 185–88.

effort to do just this. Most of the machines were too strongly entrenched, however, to be broken in four short years, and many of them returned to power when Benjamin Harrison became president in 1889.[24]

Meanwhile, other Western problems involving territorial administration were coming to the fore. An unrealistic and unsatisfactory Indian policy, punctuated by more than twenty years of intermittent warfare with tribes of the trans-Mississippi West, forced Congress to heed humanitarian cries for reform. As early as 1867 that body had instituted a peace policy, but it had been a notable failure. Finally, in 1887, Congress passed the Dawes Severalty Act, which promised a new deal for the red man. Actually the Indian problem still remained unsolved, but by 1890 the fighting was over, and at least the government had a policy that promised to give the Indians their own lands, a basic education, and the rudiments of Christian civilization.

Another Western problem centered around national land policy. Since the Homestead Act of 1862 did not provide enough acreage for a settler in a plains or arid lands region, Westerners were forced to resort to many schemes to secure holdings large enough for a decent living. Thus both cattlemen and farmers violated land laws in such blatant ways that new laws had to be passed. With the passage of the Timber Culture Act in 1873 as well as two others—the Desert Land Law of 1877 and the Minerals Land Act of 1878—Westerners got some relief. The passage of new laws, however, did not stop abuses. During the first Cleveland administration agents of the Interior Department were busy driving cattlemen off the public domain or cutting the barbed wire fences which the cow men had illegally erected there. At the same time, Cleveland himself tried to foster agricultural settlement by appointing pro-nester governors in the territories, though his efforts accomplished little. Economic law and the wiles of nature accomplished what Cleveland could not, when falling beef prices and the blizzard of 1887 wiped out the open-range industry. This failure coincided with the last great push to settle the West with farmers. Events rather than policy had settled the land question.

24. Pomeroy, *Territories*, pp. 71–72.

The last Western territorial problem that troubled Congress after 1861 was the institution of polygamy in Utah. Ever since 1862 various radical Republican Congressmen had been incensed over the Mormon practice of plural marriage. After passing a half-dozen prohibitory acts—all of which were ineffective—Congress gave Utah federal officials such enormous powers in the Edmunds-Tucker Act of 1887 that Utah by 1890 was reconstructed politically and was monogamous maritally.[25] However sporadic government policy for the West and for its territories had been, all efforts somehow came to a climax in 1890. That year the Census Bureau reported that there were no more great areas of free, unoccupied land; General Nelson Miles fought the last Indian Battle at Wounded Knee, South Dakota; Congress created the last territory, Oklahoma; and President Woodruff of the Church of the Latter Day Saints announced that henceforth its members would not practice polygamy. The frontier and the territorial system that had governed it were drawing to an end.

As the time for statehood and home rule drew closer for the last inland territories, the inevitable reaction to federal or outside authority became greater. Steps toward statehood were like a bloodless reenactment of the American Revolution. Just as Britain had tried to reform its colonial system in 1763, the reform efforts of Carl Schurz, and later, of Cleveland and Congress led local territorial leaders to resent federal interference. At first, territorial citizens, tired of being fleeced by corrupt nonresident appointees, begged that only territorial residents be appointed to office; and after 1890 this became a fairly common practice. But the local politicians proved as adept at corruption as their carpetbagger counterparts. To escape their grasping fingers and, at the same time, to end federal supervision of local affairs, each territory sought escape in statehood. By 1889 every territory in the West was calling its federal officials colonial tyrants and comparing its plight to that of one of the thirteen colonies. Statehood now came to mean freedom, democracy, and home rule.

25. Howard R. Lamar, "Political Patterns in New Mexico and Utah Territories, 1850–1900," *UHQ, 38* (1960) , 384–86.

Relief was not far away. Just before he left office early in 1889 Cleveland admitted North and South Dakota, Montana, and Washington to the Union. The following year Benjamin Harrison approved the admission of Idaho and Wyoming and signed the Organic Act creating Oklahoma Territory. In 1896 during his second term in office, Cleveland declared Utah a state. Only three Southwestern territories, New Mexico, Arizona, and Oklahoma now remained outside the Union.

Before these were to be admitted, however, three final if subtle changes in territorial policy were to occur between 1901 and 1912. As a result of the Spanish-American War the United States had acquired Puerto Rico and the Philippines. These islands were imperial possessions kept more for strategic and economic reasons than for the purpose of becoming states in the American Union. With words like "empire" and phrases like "the white man's burden" being debated and argued daily in Congress and the press, it is not surprising that Theodore Roosevelt and his close friend Albert Beveridge—chairman of the Senate Committee on Territories—appear to have viewed Arizona and New Mexico somewhat as they did the new "empire". They, too, were backward areas which had been stifled by their Spanish heritage.[26] Senator Beveridge's own conviction was so strong, in fact, that he held up the admission of these two states for nearly ten years. His argument was that they were not equal in intellect, resources, or population to the other states in the Union. Nor, said he, were they sufficiently American in their habits and customs. Only the personal intervention of President Taft and a combination of many public pressures forced Beveridge to allow admission bills for these states to pass the Senate in 1910.[27]

Roosevelt himself represented the source of the other subtle change in territorial policy. As a thoroughgoing conservationist he found that many pieces of territorial legislation and much of the substance of territorial politics were related to schemes to grab the remaining

26. Frank C. Lockwood, *Pioneer Days in Arizona* (New York, 1932), pp. 368–78. Marion Dargan, New Mexico's Fight for Statehood, 1895–1912," *NMHR*, *14* (1939), 1–33, 121 ff.; *15*, 133 ff.; *16*, 70–103, 379–400. See also Claude G. Bowers, *Beveridge and the Progressive Era* (New York, 1932), pp. 182 ff.

27. See below, pp. 496–97.

public land, timber, and mineral resources in the West. Prodded by
Gifford Pinchot of the Forestry Service and constantly warned by
Beveridge, Roosevelt kept a close federal scrutiny over Arizona, New
Mexico, and Oklahoma.[28] This very surveillance only increased the de-
sire of each territory to come into the Union as self-governing states.
Beveridge and Roosevelt allowed Oklahoma as the most "American"
of the three territories to become a state in 1907, but it was to take
five more years of lobbying and pressure before New Mexico and
Arizona would achieve statehood in 1912.

It is this final period of territorial policy, lasting from 1861 to 1912,
which has been most neglected by historians. Since the four Southwestern territories generally fall into this time span, their relations
with the national government should throw useful light on the everyday workings of the territorial system. In a way, this study is actually
a second attempt to penetrate and comprehend the history of this
period. In 1956 I published a pilot study under the title *Dakota Territory, 1861–1889.* The cautiously favorable reception of the work by
reviewers and the encouragement of the late Clarence E. Carter,
then editor of the Territorial Papers of the United States, persuaded
me to look at other territories to see if the conclusions reached in the
Dakota volume were applicable elsewhere.

Briefly, these conclusions were: (1) that the territorial period—
lasting in this case some twenty-eight years—was a time when many
basic and distinct political patterns and economic attitudes characteristic of the future states of North and South Dakota were shaped.
Though the evolution from a frontier stage was speedy, and Dakota
political institutions were often imitative of ones found in older
states, nevertheless local patterns did emerge which one could call
Dakotan.

(2) In the process of political growth the scarcity of local wealth
and resources as well as the existence of a Great Plains topography
and climate so hindered normal economic development that settlers,

---

28. This fact becomes apparent from a perusal of the Official Papers and
Letterbooks of Governors M. A. Otero, H. J. Hagerman, and George Curry, now
housed in the Archives Division of the New Mexico State Records Center, Santa Fe.

political leaders, and frontier entrepreneurs necessarily came to hold colonial attitudes. They relied heavily, for example, on the federal government to subsidize both their political and their economic endeavors. Thus federal patronage and federal expenditures for civil government, military installations, and Indian affairs played larger roles in shaping political and economic habits and attitudes than would ordinarily have been the case. Nor did the national party in power ever fail to foster the infant branch of the party in Dakota. (3) These patterns, established in territorial times, continued into the statehood period and help explain the response of the Dakotas to Populism in the 1890s, and their later advocacy of the Non-Partisan League in the twentieth century. (4) Finally, the study did point up the everyday workings—and failures—of the territorial system in the trans-Mississippi West.

Rather than test these conclusions piecemeal on other single territories, it seemed wise to compare the histories of four territories whose geography, population makeup, political patterns, and economic systems were clearly different from those of the Dakotas. The obvious choices were the Four Corners States.

Any exhaustive political history of the Far Southwest could easily run into a score of volumes. To avoid such a formidable task, this study, while telling a narrative history, concentrates on five common American political phenomena. The first concerns the history of the political party system in each area: were there real parties; if so, how did they arise and what was their function? The second concern is for the roles played by the federally appointed territorial officials: the governor, the secretary, the judges, and, occasionally, the surveyor general of public lands. The questions to be answered here are more complex. Were these men hacks or leaders? Did they pursue a recognizable policy, and did they have any impact on the history of a given territory?

Through the appointive officers one can see the role of the federal government in local affairs. On the other side, the territorial delegate was the only popularly elected representative the territory had in Congress. Through him were channeled most of the local demands, and through him federal largess came back to the territory. Given his powerful economic role, the delegate often becomes the key figure in the narrative.

The present study also attempts to understand and analyze the territorial assembly as the locally elected lawmaking body. Its actions reveal local political customs and attitudes, not only toward public issues, but toward the purpose of a legislature as well. Was the legislature a coherent working group or merely a congress of factions? Or was it—as in the case of Dakota—a business-minded set of entrepreneurs, speculators, and promoters? Last of all, where it has been possible, the narrative touches on the role of the office of probate judge, since that role provides a useful yardstick with which to measure the practices and functions of local county government in a territory.

I have also tried to trace local reaction to four basic American political assumptions which became issues in Southwestern politics. They are: separation of Church and State, trial by jury, public maintenance of secular schools, and the custom of monogamous marriage. Where it has seemed politically significant, either as an issue or as the reflection of an unusual set of customs, I have also noted the conflict of the local systems of land tenure with national land policy.

Such guideposts, as imperfect and arbitrary as they may seem, hopefully can lead toward conclusions about the manner in which local, territorial, and regional political patterns and habits evolved. They can also show us what historical impact, if any, the presence of federal authority has had on this evolution. If the territorial narratives which follow succeed in illustrating anew the complicated process by which Americans extended themselves and their democratic political institutions across the continent and into the distant regions of the Spanish Southwest, then the aim of this study will have been fulfilled.

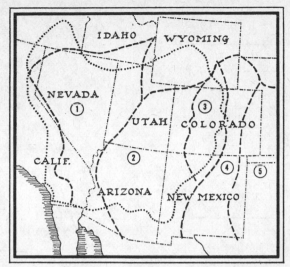

······· Boundaries of State of Deseret   --- Physiographic Provinces
1. Great Basin Province ~ 2. Colorado Plateau Province
3. Southern Rocky Mt. Province ~ 4. Upland Trough   5. High Plains

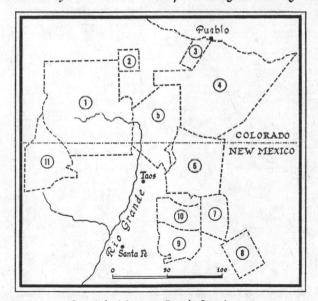

Spanish-Mexican Land Grants

1. Conejos Grant: 2. Luis Maria Baca Grant: 3. Nolan Grant:
4. Vigil & St. Vrain Grant: 5. Sangre de Cristo Grant:
6. Maxwell Grant: 7. Nolan Grant: 8. Montoya Grant:
9. Los Vegas Grant: 10. Mora Grant: 11. Tierra Amarilla Grant.

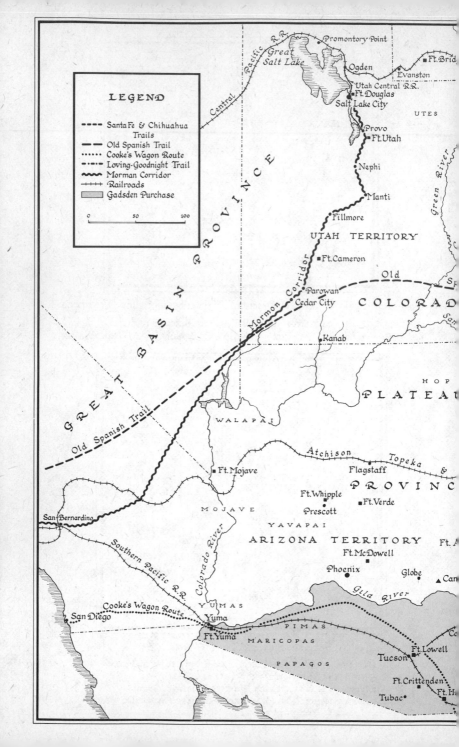

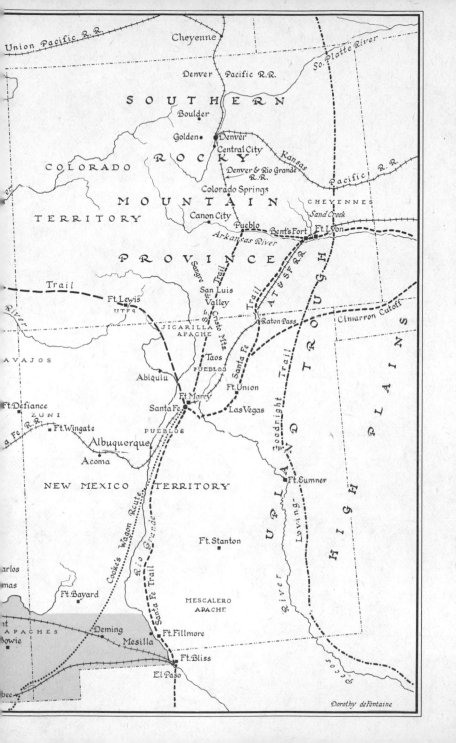

Dorothy deFontaine

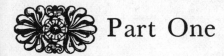 Part One

New Mexico:
Feudal Frontier

Defeated by distance and time, the Rio Grande Spaniards
finally lived as the Pueblo Indians lived—in a fixed, traditional
present.

Paul F. Horgan, *Great River, 1*, 389

Todos dicen que soy un viejo
Yo no sé en que se pueden fundar
Yo me éncuentro tan gordo y robusto
Que tres veces me puedo casar.
"El Viejo," New Mexican folk song

 During the first two weeks of August 1810, small
groups of horsemen could be seen moving along the
rude mountain trails and roads that led to the
City of St. Francis of the Holy Faith, the capital of
New Mexico province. Many of the well-dressed riders were gentry from the fertile Taos Valley on the
northern frontier or *patrons* from the farming villages in the hills
around Santa Fe. Others were *ricos* and *dons* who owned large sheep
herds and farmed irrigated strips of land along the Rio Grande River
south of the capital. As these travelers made their way, they, in turn,
were joined by Catholic priests from the more populated settlements or from the *villas* of Santa Cruz and Albuquerque. Several
horsemen were district alcaldes, second in political rank only to the

provincial governor himself. Obviously an event of great importance was to take place in New Spain's most isolated internal province.

Santa Fe—the capital city toward which the horsemen rode—was then a disorderly motley of low-lying, dun-colored, adobe houses, sprawled along the lifeline of Santa Fe Creek and the irrigation ditches running from the creek. Lying more than 6,000 feet high on the sloping western tablelands of the beautiful Sangre de Cristo range, the straggling community boasted some 4,500 souls of Spanish and Indian blood in 1810.[1] When the horsemen reached the city's environs, they picked their way through narrow crooked streets to the main plaza, a sun-baked expanse where Pueblo and Spanish vendors of farm produce and piñon wood marketed their simple goods amidst shouts of greeting, the babble of voices, and the braying of burros. And over all lay a golden haze of heat and dust which bore the pervasive fragrance of piñon smoke.

On the north side of the plaza was a large, single-storied building fronted by a lengthy wooden shed crudely but stolidly supported by tree trunks. Grandly called the Palace of the Governors, it was the destination of the horsemen, who had come at the call of Governor Jose Manrique to perform a solemn public duty. For the first time since New Mexico had been founded by Don Juan de Oñate in 1598, the province was to send a deputy to the Spanish Cortes.[2]

Three candidates announced themselves for the post, but to avoid harsh feelings the convention resorted to the ancient device of choosing the deputy by lot. The chance winner was Don Pedro Bautista Pino, a public-spirited citizen, son of a leading family, a capable soldier, and, withal, the most learned and scholarly person in this remote province.

The problem remained of financing the new deputy's trip to Spain. Appeals to patriotism—and undoubtedly more informal promise of

---

1. When Zebulon Pike visited Santa Fe in 1806, he estimated that its population was 4,500. Pedro B. Pino in his *Exposicion sucincta y sencilla de la provincia del Nueva Mexico* (Cadiz, 1812) put it at 5,000. In 1831 the census of that year put the figure at 5,275; see Antonio Barreiro, *Ojeada sobre Nueva Mexico* (Puebla, Mexico, 1832) , p. 12.

2. Ralph Emerson Twitchell, *Leading Facts of New Mexican History* (6 vols. Cedar Rapids, Iowa, 1912) , *1*, 470–71.

future services to be rendered—persuaded the convention members
to dip into their own pockets to raise a large purse for Pino. Many of
the more oratorical contributors dramatically declared that in so doing they had been "forced to sacrifice the liberty of their sons." Determined to get their money's worth, the *patrons, ricos,* and churchmen of the province pressed documents, memorials, petitions, and
statistics upon the deputy to take to the Crown authorities in Spain.[3]
Journeying down the *camino real* that October, first to Chihuahua
and then to Vera Cruz for his ship, Pino, with his sheaf of papers,
probably possessed more information on New Spain's northernmost
frontier—the Rio Grande settlements—than any man then living.

Two years later Pino, undoubtedly homesick for the azure hills,
the narrow green canyons, and the lovely gold and blue vistas of his
distant New Mexico, published his collected information in the form
of a memorial to the King. Entitling it *Exposicion sucinta y sencilla
de la provincia del Nuevo Mexico hecho por su Diputado in Cortes,*
Pino gave the historian an intelligent insight into the economic, political, and religious life of his people, and he explained with sincere
eloquence the major problems that harassed them. Since Pino's New
Mexico—in 1810 truly the land of *poco tiempo*—outwardly changed
little between that date and American conquest in 1846, his penetrat-
ing observations still make an excellent primer for those who would
understand Spanish and Mexican New Mexico. Such an understanding is, in turn, a necessary prerequisite to any history of the American period; for the unique internal conditions of this highland Spanish-American frontier not only determined the nature of the Anglo-
American occupation in 1846 but also governed the political, economic, and cultural relations of that region with the United States
for sixty years thereafter.

The New Mexico that Pedro Pino described to his sovereign was
that of an upland, mountainous, and semi-arid country bisected for
more than five hundred miles by the meandering, muddy Rio Grande.
Although the fertile lands along the river had been settled by Spaniards since 1598, the remoteness of the area, the threat of wild In-

3. Ibid., *1*, 470–71.

dians, and the seeming lack of rich mineral deposits dictated that it remain an undeveloped country. The psychological sense of isolation was made more real by a wide east-west corridor, stretching from below Santa Fe to Central Sonora, in which Apache raiders roamed at will.

Given such conditions, it is not surprising that after more than two hundred years only 35,000 Spanish and mixed-blood citizens could be found in the 102 *"plazas de espanoles"* which made up the settled portion of the province.[4] Only three of these plazas—Santa Fe, Santa Cruz de la Cañada at the mouth of the Chama, and Albuquerque— could be called true villas or towns. Many of the remaining villages, missions, and Indian pueblos were located along the Rio Grande and Chama Rivers or along their tributaries northward from Santa Fe to Taos, in what was called the *Rio Arriba* Country. These tiny settlements, focused around a square or plaza, were often dominated by a single large family clan whose members worked together to raise blue maize and chili peppers on small irrigated plots. Other members chose to ranch sheep on common lands fringing the town.[5]

Dotted among the valleys and canyons both north and south of Santa Fe were some twenty-six Pueblo Indian communities whose chief occupation was also irrigated agriculture. But their culture remained distinct from that of the Spanish New Mexicans, although most had been affected by the Christian teachings of the Franciscan fathers. The Pueblos numbered fewer than 10,000 in 1810, but they were, nevertheless, an important, indigenous part of New Mexico's settled population.[6]

In Santa Fe and to the south in the *Rio Abajo* Country life was somewhat different. The ranches and farms were larger and more profitable, and the *rancheros* and *patrons* lived more grandly in rambling whitewashed adobe homes. By risking annual caravans of

4. Pino, *Exposicion*, p. 6.
5. George I. Sanchez, *Forgotten People: A Study of New Mexicans* (Albuquerque, 1940), p. 6. Sigurd Johansen, *Rural Social Organization in a Spanish-American Culture Area* (Albuquerque, 1948), pp. 107–08. John H. Burma, *Spanish-Speaking Groups in the United States* (Durham, N.C., 1954), p. 3. Ernest E. Maes, "The World and the People of Cundiyo, U.S. Department of Agriculture, *Land Policy Review* (March 1941), pp. 8–9.
6. Josiah Gregg, *Commerce of the Prairies* (Dallas, 1933), p. 95, estimated the white creoles to be 1,000, the mestizos, 59,000, and the Pueblos, 10,000.

wool and corn down the Apache-infested camino real to Chihuahua, the Rio Abajo residents were able to secure, in return, supplies and luxuries which raised their level of living to that of rough gentry status.[7] In the Rio Abajo life was easier, wealth was more apparent, and the don or patron with his large herds was virtually the patriarchal dictator of his village. And though his family might be called noble, the lack of education and the great isolation made for a society distinctly different from that of the more populated and accessible provinces of New Spain. Many a New Mexican boasted of his relation to the famed Oñate, or the conqueror De Vargas, or even the fabled Cabeza de Vaca. Yet by 1800 he had so intermarried with local families and with Indian women that the paternalistic society which resulted smacked as much of the frontier as of Spain.

At the same time that the landed or wealthy don occupied a hereditary position at the head of a vast family clan, spreading in concentric circles from his village, his position was further exalted by the rudiments of a peonage system. Crude and often savage attempts to introduce the *encomienda* and *repartimiento* systems into New Mexico had characterized the early Spanish period, but by 1800 the custom of debt peonage had become prominent. Springing from many things, the system worked to keep the servant bound to the master for a lifetime. Many comparisons have been made between the don with his peons and the American pre-Civil War planter with his slaves, but while the don had the powers of his southern counterpart, he moved in a much more primitive, self-sufficient economic system which was more subsistence than commercial. In the unending fight for survival both owner and laborer were bound together by a common race and religion as well as by the common peril of the wild Indian menace.

The peon himself was often related to the patron and was himself a petty entrepreneur, or *partidaro,* who sometimes rented sheep from a patron and shared the profits from the annual increase of the flock.[8] Moreover, with the exception of household lots many lands

7. Max L. Moorhead, *New Mexico's Royal Road: Trade and Travel on the Chihuahua Trail* (Norman, Okla., 1958), pp. 52–60 passim.

8. William J. Parish, *The Charles Ilfeld Company: A Study of the Rise and Decline of Merchant Capitalism in New Mexico* (Cambridge, Mass., 1961), pp. 150–53.

were often held communally, so that a degree of village cooperation and cultural sharing existed which the American plantation owner never knew. The presence of the independent Pueblo Indians, who owned their own lands and farmed in their own way, also made for an enforced toleration between the races which the white and Negro never possessed. In 1810 the wild Indians were still such a constant threat that Pueblo, Spaniard, and mestizo occasionally fought side by side for their lands and their lives.[9]

The internecine war with the local wild tribes—Apache, Ute, Navajo, and occasionally the Comanche—led to still another New Mexican practice: using captured Indians as domestic slaves. This was not slavery in the plantation sense, for in this case the slave was a spoil of war and an item of trade as much as he was the basis for a system of domestic labor.[10] But the practice along with that of peonage did further entrench the economic caste system and lent to the farms and villages the stalemated hierarchical quality that must have characterized life in medieval Europe.[11]

Given such conditions, it was inevitable that a small ruling class comprised of some fifteen of twenty intermarried families would come to dominate New Mexico. By 1810 everyone knew that Peralta was a Chavez bailiwick; it was clear that the Martinez clan dominated some of the Rio Arriba settlements. Similarly, the Archuletas, Pereas, Oteros, Durans, Senas, Montoyas, Ortizes, and Cabeza de Bacas were known as the patrons of the country. And no family was a more distinguished representative of this fortunate group than the Pinos.[12]

If the first loyalty was to the family clan, it was also true that the patriarchal ricos and gentry did not exercise their authoritarian power exclusively. The feudal aspects of village and family life were

9. Burma, *Spanish-Speaking Groups*, p. 13. Johansen, *Rural Social Organization*, p. 124 ff. Olen Leonard, "The Role of the Land Grant in the Social Organization and Social Processes of a Spanish-American Village in New Mexico" (Ph.D. dissertation, Louisiana State University, 1943), pp. 181 ff. Sanchez, *Forgotten People*, p. 6.

10. "Hundreds of Navajo boys and girls by the early 1800s were growing up in Spanish homes as servants." Spicer, *Cycles*, p. 213.

11. Aristide B. Chavez, "The Use of the Personal Interview to Study the Subjective Impact of Culture Contacts" (Master's thesis, University of New Mexico, 1948), pp. 19–22.

12. See Fray Angelico Chavez, *Origins of New Mexican Families* (Santa Fe, 1954), pp. xii–xiii.

in harmony with an equally medieval view of religion and a tradi-
tional Spanish devotion to Roman Catholicism. The New Mexican
Church was represented until 1828 by some twenty or thirty
priests who controlled the spiritual lives of the Spanish residents.
As often as not they also dominated the community or fought the
governor himself. Indeed, the constant and bitter feud between
Church and State in New Mexico was a major factor in shaping
New Mexican history.

In the course of generations local priests had simplified the Church's
elaborate services, while retaining many medieval customs. They had
also allowed many an Indian ritual to mingle with its Christian counterpart. New Mexico was, moreover, still a mission frontier of sorts,
since the nearest bishop lived in Durango. One of Pedro Pino's major
complaints, in fact, was that his people had not looked upon the face
of a bishop for fifty years. The scarcity of priests in residence had
resulted in many common-law marriages, unbaptized children, and
an increasing popular ignorance of proper church teachings and
sacraments.[13]

The continued isolation of the church fathers and the concomitant
lack of a central control allowed them to do as they pleased. Exercis-
ing a supreme authority over simple people who still believed in
miracles, the Evil Eye, and scores of superstitions they assumed an
impressive power in performing the rites of birth, marriage and
death. They exacted fees and labor for the church; they gave advice
in temporal matters and often sat in the provincial Assembly. Given
the easy opportunity, many became corrupt and forsook celibacy to
keep concubines. Before American conquest, wrote one observer, the
priests "kept cocks and fit 'em, had cards and played 'em, indulged
in housekeepers of an uncanonical age, and had more nieces than the
law allowed."[14] The result was a permissive, simplified, decadent
Church that, paradoxically, was quite powerful.

No better illustration of the provincialism in religion could be
found than in the history of a lay group called the Third Order of St.

13. Pino, *Exposicion*, p. 7 ff.
14. Burma, *Spanish-Speaking Groups*, pp. 8, 24–26. James F. Meline. *Two Thousand Miles on Horseback: Santa Fe and Back* (New York, 1867), pp. 189–90.

Francis, which had sprung up in Europe in the fourteenth and fifteenth centuries among men of good faith and high morality. The early conquistadors and priests had founded chapters of the order in New Mexico. There it had become a penitential and flagellant group much preoccupied with pain and death. In the course of time—and particularly in the period 1800-50—the order came to be called *Los Hermanos de los Penitentes,* or the Penitent Brothers. By Pino's time the group had largely rejected any church supervision of its rites. As Easter approached each year, the members of the local chapters would fast and beat one another with cactus whips and reenact the crucifixion with such realism that the brother chosen to play Christ sometimes died from his wounds.[15] Thus at the very moment the ideals of the French Revolution were sweeping South America and New Englanders were moving toward Unitarianism, medieval religious customs and pageants flourished with vigor in the mountain villages of New Mexico. After the American conquest of New Mexico in 1846, the *Penitentes* not only continued their religious practices but became political clubs.

When the first American merchants and trappers came to New Mexico over the Santa Fe Trail between 1821 and 1846, it is not surprising that they fulminated, as did Josiah Gregg, against superstitious ignorant people and a "priest-ridden" country. But Gregg and his fellow traders also discovered a certain spare charm to life in Santa Fe and Albuquerque and in the villages. Although New Mexicans lived in a subsistence economy and often suffered from poverty, an archaic graciousness pervaded their manners. Great hospitality was so basic to the New Mexican character that every visitor found himself overwhelmed by kindness and attention, once he was accepted. In peaceful times the inhabitants moved in a constant round of feast days, marriage celebrations, and fairs. There was always a chance to dance the *raspa* or quadrille at a *baile.* Why bother with the outside world when there was gaming and gambling, and the music of guitars and lutes could be spread on the mountain air?[16]

15. Burma, *Spanish-Speaking Groups,* pp. 188 ff.
16. Gregg, *Commerce,* pp. 128–81, 138–42, 145–46. See also Johansen, *Rural Social Organization,* pp. 122–24, and Leonard, "Role of the Land Grant," pp. 33–35, for a description of the persistence of customs into the twentieth century.

Even the Indian menace and the annual trip to Chihuahua could not interrupt an established family and church-centered life. Unlike the dynamic, individualistic, optimistic society Anglo-American pioneers were creating for themselves in the Shenandoah and Ohio Valleys between 1760 and 1815, here was a stabilized, almost incestuous society existing in nearly total isolation. Stalemated physically, culturally, and economically by the conditions of the land and by the Indian menace, Pedro Pino's country was an arrested frontier society.

As Pino himself observed, New Mexico's political structure also reflected the simplification and even the backsliding of its church and society. The original scheme of government for the Spanish New World and its Indian inhabitants, had been extraordinarily complex and legalistic. By the time such institutions had been hauled overland from distant Mexico City to Santa Fe, however, much had been jettisoned. In contrast to the more elaborate mission government organized for the California Indians after 1760, the New Mexican fathers and governors had tried to impose their authority on existing towns or pueblos of Indians which already had their own form of government. The priest did not create the town; he had to convert an existing one. The Pueblos, however, were never the passive neophytes Spain had encountered in the civilized parts of Mexico and among the primitive California bands. Since the wild Indians remained intractable and could neither be converted nor ruled, control over the Indian population of New Mexico was, in many respects, superficial.

In the regular Spanish towns or villages political authority was centered in an *alcalde* or *alcalde mayor*, who acted as a justice of the peace, a mayor, a probate judge, and sometimes as a militia captain. In turn these local officials came under the jurisdiction of the district *alcaldes* or prefects in New Mexico. The more populated areas of New Spain, large towns or *villas* often had an elaborate municipal council or *ayuntamiento,* but in New Mexico only Santa Fe and Albuquerque appear to have had some form of a regular city government. After 1800 the province did have an Assembly of seven district members who met quadrennially and advised the governor, but contemporaries commented that its powers were *"nulo y insignifi-cante."*[17]

Such an absence of complex local government meant that, by de-fault, the appointive governor was not only the chief official in the province; he was also the executive, the legislator, and the court of appeals rolled into one. He was the head of the provincial military organization as well. And yet for all of these duties, he was provided in New Mexico with only two aides-de-camp and two lieutenants.[18] When a matter of great concern arose, it was the governor, the alcaldes, the prefects, the priests, and the patrons who met in a sort of estates general or junta to make decisions, as they did when Pino was sent to Spain.

By American standards New Mexican government was paradoxi-cally both arbitrary and chaotic, with no division between executive, legislative, and judicial duties. There was no trial by jury, the insti-tution of common law as Anglo-Americans knew it did not exist in the province, and few if any true lawyers could be found there. Certain classes—especially the military and the clergy, were exempt from civil authority. Practically speaking, it was useless to take an appeal beyond the governor unless, as Pino pointed out, one went five hundred leagues to appear before the *audiencia* in Guadala-jara.[19] But there was another side to the rough-cast New Mexican coin. Taxes were nonexistent except for duties on imports and requisi-tions by the Church. There were no schools or bureaucracy to sup-port; and the militia as well as the alcaldes went upaid. Actually, most men could come to terms with this tyranny, subsisting on fees, bribes, and occasional confiscations. They could always expect relief from oppression through periodic rebellions and frequent changes in the governor's office.

What had led to such a stalemate, such a "triste situacion," as Pino put it? Why had New Mexico lagged so far behind? Certain inhabitants dreamed of a new era, for Pino himself had been sent to

---

17. Frank W. Blackmar, *Spanish Institutions of the Southwest* (Baltimore, 1891), (1891), p. 227. Twitchell, *Leading Facts, 1,* 470. Barreiro, *Ojeada,* p. 28.
18. Pino, *Exposicion,* p. 6.
19. Ibid., p. 7

Spain to secure a reformed Church, to find support for a school system, and to bring a court of appeals as close as Chihuahua. He and the patrons also wanted to develop trade with the outside world as well as expand the existing Spanish settlements. The answer lay partly in New Mexico's remoteness from ports and cities, but the major reason was the wild Indian problem.

Surrounding the thin ribbon of settlements stretching for about 240 miles along the watercourses of the Rio Grande were some thirty-three tribes who carried on unending raids against the Spanish and the Pueblos.[20] There had been, Pino reported, "118 years of continuous war" since de Vargas' reconquest of the Province during the 1690s. The war was part of the Spaniards' own making, for they not only had disturbed older Pueblo-wild Indian trade relations but also had been wantonly cruel to the wild Indians.[21] These tribes, made up of the Apaches to the east of the Sangre de Cristo mountains and in the southern part of the province, prevented expansion into the ranching lands of the Pecos River Valley. To the south and southwest still more Apaches hindered both traffic on the Chihuahua trail and the mining of copper and gold at the Santa Rita diggings. To the west and northwest roamed the Navajo, who left their deep canyons to raid right up to the environs of Albuquerque and Santa Fe.

Along the northern frontier, the settlers of the Taos Valley found themselves in an Indian no-man's land, for they were surrounded by Navajos to the west from the wild San Juan country, the Utes from the north, and the Apaches and Comanches to the east. Since all of these Indians together probably equaled the Spanish and Pueblos in number as well as in fighting prowess, they checkmated all Spanish efforts at expansion onto their tribal domains.[22]

To end such a menace, Pino pleaded with Crown authorities to build five new presidios to hold back the "thirty-three heathen na-

---

20. By far the most comprehensive and understanding study of Spanish-Indian relations is to be found in Spicer, *Cycles of Conquest.*

21. Ibid., pp 14 ff. For a new interpretation of Spanish-Indian relations see Jack Forbes, *Apache, Navaho, and Spaniard* (Norman, Okla., 1960).

22. For a treatment of Indian-white relations in the American period see Averam B. Bender, *The March of Empire: Frontier Defense in the Southwest, 1848–1860* (Lawrence, Kans., 1952).

tions" who despoiled the province and also pleaded for a paid,
regularly constituted militia. He would locate the presidios at El
Paso and Socorro, to protect the Chihuahua trade route; on the Pecos
River, to guard the eastern approach to the settlements; and in the
Taos Valley. Only then could New Mexico begin to develop. To make
his case the more urgent, Pino warned the Spanish government that
the United States now owned Louisiana and that American traders
were now supplying ammunition to the wild Indians. He also reminded them that Lieutenant Zebulon Pike—charmingly called "Pay-
kie" by Pino—had been found on their northern frontier in 1806. To
Pino the United States already constituted a palpable menace to New
Mexico's survival. With great prescience he warned Spain that unless
vigorous measures were taken, New Mexico might soon be lost to
the Americans.[23]

Spain was too troubled with larger problems and with the rebellion of her Latin-American colonies for the next ten years to listen
to Pedro Pino's appeals. No schools were opened; the militia continued to be unpaid; the new presidios were not built; no court of
appeals appeared; and the cry for a bishop was only partially answered a few years later when a vicar general came to reside in
Santa Fe. The discerning Santa Feans, with a knowing shrug, placed
the sing-song epitaph on Pino's seven years of labor in Spain with the
delightful phrase: *"Don Pedro Pino fue. Don Pedro Pino vino"*—Don
Pedro Pino went away. Don Pedro Pino came back.[24]

A stalemate could not last forever. The winds of revolution which
swept New Spain and all of Latin America between 1810 and 1821
brought about the independent country of Mexico in the latter year.
In New Mexico itself faint echoes of revolutionary aspirations and
ideals stirred the heart of an able young priest, Jose Antonio Martinez of Taos, with dreams of home rule and turned the mind of a
poor but bright lad, Donaciano Vigil, toward the more abstract goals
of liberty and democracy.

Before New Mexicans could fully grasp the meaning of Mexican
revolution and independence, however, the liberal trade policies of

23. Pino, *Exposicion*, pp. 18–36.
24. Twitchell, *Leading Facts, 1*, 472.

the new nation brought American merchants and trappers from the Mississippi Valley down the Santa Fe trail and across their borders. By 1830 both Taos and Santa Fe had become important trading centers. Meanwhile, even a normally expanding population provided Spanish-American New Mexico with the needed men to wrest new valleys from the Indian and to push unbidden across the Sangre de Cristo range to Mora, Cimarron, and the Pecos River. All too swiftly new ideas from Europe and new invaders from the United States had blundered into remote New Mexico and quickened the pace of life. For feudal New Mexico with her tradition-bound society, subsistence economy, and arbitrary government, the effect was shattering.

2

Taos:
Port of Entry

I believe that . . . the [Turner] thesis may be examined in
other regions and from other points of view. One case that
deserves such study is the meeting of the Spanish-American
frontier in northern Mexico with the westward-moving
American frontier, . . . with reference to social exchanges and
adjustments that occurred.

Silvio de Zavala

 No better example of the rigorous life of the New
Mexicans and later of their American conquerors can
be found than in the history of the frontier communities located in the charming Valley of Taos.
Here, some seventy miles north of Santa Fe, clustered the villages of Rancho de Taos, Ranchitos, and
San Fernandez de Taos, as well as the more ancient adobe pueblo
where the Taos Indians lived.[1] Lying just on the western edge of
the splendid snow-capped Sangre de Cristos and east of the Upper
Rio Grande, Taos was a true Spanish-Mexican frontier community—
one in which all the elements that shaped New Mexican and Ameri-

1. The northernmost of the Indian Pueblos, Taos, appears to have been visited
by Alvarado, one of Coronado's lieutenants, in 1540–42; Juan de Oñate came into
the vicinity July 1598; actual occupation by Spanish colonists dates from the early
seventeenth century. Twitchell, *Leading Facts, 1,* 230, 294–95 n., 319.

can relations before and after the conquest of 1846 could be discerned.

During the first two decades of the seventeenth century, more than a hundred years before American frontiersmen began to thread their pack animals through the narrow defiles of the Cumberland Gap into the wilderness paradise of Kentucky, a few hardy Spanish colonials had struck northward from the recently established towns of Santa Fe and Santa Cruz to occupy the Upper Rio Grande Valley or the Rio Arriba. Some settled around the Indian pueblo of Taos, as much for protection from wild Indian raiders as for the fertile, well-watered lands there.

The devastating Pueblo Indian Rebellion of 1680 drove the Spanish in frontier Taos and in Santa Fe out of the province for twelve years. But after a harsh period of reconquest, climaxed by restoration of Spanish rule under Diego De Vargas in 1693–94, a new generation of New Mexicans went northward to take up where their forebears had left off.[2] By 1723 Taos was important enough to be designated an official trading post, where Indian and Spaniard could swap wares and goods. The awarding of some thirty-seven New Mexican land grants in the period 1715–35 also testified to the pioneers' activity on the northern border.[3]

Slowly these colonists fanned out into the lovely mountain vales, wooded with cedar, piñon, and aspen, following first one and then another clear tributary to the great river. They moved up the main valley itself to found Arroyo Hondo. Some eventually went over Eagle Pass to the northeast to establish themselves on the Cimarron. Still others branched off at Santa Cruz to push northwest up the alternately wide and narrow Chama River valley to Abiquiu, on the borders of Navajo and southern Ute territory.

The conditions the Spanish frontiersmen experienced were like those the Kentucky pioneers were to endure; their difficulties with the Indians were unending. To the wild tribes, however, the Spanish settler was a hostage for barter—as were captured Indians to the

2. Jesse R. Bailey, *Diego de Vargas and the Reconquest of New Mexico* (Albuquerque, 1940).

3. *Report of the Secretary of the Interior for 1855* (Washington, 1856), pp. 433–39.

Spaniard—and his tiny farm and large herd were a source of food. But where the Kentucky frontier was dangerous mainly from 1775 to 1800, the Spanish colonials lived under perennial attack from 1700 to 1865. Since they were steeled by adversity—often pushed back to the larger adobe-walled towns of the Rio Grande Valley—a hardy farming and semi-nomadic ranching population resulted. The harshness of their situation is illustrated by the fact that scarcely a family in the whole of New Mexico passed a decade without the loss of some member to Indian raiders.[4]

Isolated in their mountain communities and preoccupied with the basic problem of physical survival, the culture of these subsistence settlers became even more simplified than that of Santa Fe and the Rio Abajo. In the mountain villages the language became an outdated and unlettered Spanish patois. Through many generations the Indian blood of captured Navajo slaves and Pueblo servants mixed with Spanish. darkening the skin of the average New Mexican. The stern demands of this frontier had, more than elsewhere, atrophied the Spanish heritage, so that by 1821 the residents of the Rio Arriba and Taos were becoming different from the land-rich dons living hacienda-fashion south of Santa Fe.[5]

What were the elements comprising this frontier society living some 7,000 feet above sea level? Typical of the burgeoning Spanish colonial families pushing into northern New Mexico was that of Don Jose Manuel Martinez, who had settled at Abiquiu in the late eighteenth century. Constantly molested by Navajo and Ute Indians sweeping down the Chama Valley to seize his flocks, Don Manuel secured a large grant of land at Tierra Amarilla on the upper Chama, on which he placed four of his sons. While they acted as a buffer settlement to protect their father's holdings, four other sons saw even greener pastures for their herds in the Taos Valley. Two settled at Ranchitos, one at San Cristobal, and the fourth at Arroyo Hondo. Don Manuel's progeny were as prolific as they were able, and by the

4. Twitchell, *Leading Facts, 1,* 445.
5. Gregg, *Commerce,* p. 117, suggests that frontier conditions had given the "yeomanry of the country" a "much higher calibre of moral courage" than the Santa Fe rico or the city dwellers of Chihuahua.

1830s and 1840s the Martinez clan, by virtue of size and holdings, was called the "big family" in Taos.[6]

Sheer isolation had led to such intermarriage with the local Valdez, Vigil, Jaramillo, Lovato, and Trujillo families that by the year of Mexican independence the Martinez tribe stretched throughout the Rio Arriba, knitted together in a complex web of consanguinity more characteristic of an old paternalistic society than of a frontier one. And in true patron tradition they and their relations controlled scores of devoted peons, domesticated Indians, and retainers. Though there were many feuds and personality conflicts between rival families, they felt a common bond of blood and environment which made them truly provincial.

Foremost in the "big family"—and in the history of Taos—was Jose Antonio Martinez. Although born in Abiquiu in 1793, he had gone into the Church after his young wife had died, and Taos had been his choice for a parish. Since he was trained for his priestly duties in Durango, he was, for his community, a well-traveled and learned man. In a land nearly devoid of lawyers, many considered him a legal expert.[7] It was only natural that the first school in Taos was started by Padre Martinez, who carefully picked as students the bright sons of prominent families, thus training at least a dozen future political leaders and priests of territorial New Mexico.[8]

Like many of his family Padre Martinez was not only a shrewd and observant man but a born leader with sizable ambitions. Twitchell calls him "one of the most brilliant men of his time." Possessed of a tremendous physical vitality and verbal eloquence, he was interested in ranching, in opening new lands for occupation, and in politics. He saw that after two centuries of stalemate, the population in the 102 *plazas de espanoles* of New Mexico was suddenly booming; in the ten years from 1835 to 1845 it had increased by 10,000, or nearly 20 per cent. Across the mountains, Las Vegas had sprung up;

6. Cleofas Jaramillo, *Shadows of the Past* (Santa Fe, 1941), pp. 12–15.

7. Twitchell, *Leading Facts*, 2, 337–38 n. A provocative and intelligent new interpretation is to be found in E. K. Francis, "Padre Martinez: A New Mexican Myth," *NMHR*, 21 (1956), 256 ff.

8. For a typical trainee in Martinez' school see the obituary of Pedro Valdez in the *New Mexican Review* for December 3, 1884.

and below Santa Fe, Valverde and Servilleta were still called new settlements in 1822. It was Martinez who appears to have inspired Antonio Barreiro to write his petition of 1832 for aid to the growing Province. Finally, Martinez knew that Mexican rebellion against Spain signified the beginning of a new age. Prophetically, it was he who brought the first printing press into his province and gave his short-lived paper the hopeful name *El Crespusculo de la Libertad* (The Dawn of Liberty).[9]

But the sage of Taos, for all his vigorous qualities, was also a traditionalist, a provincial, and a churchman, who firmly believed that Church and State were one. He did not hesitate to wield local power himself through his priestly offices, his family, or the Taos Indians who slavishly admired the tough, worldly priest. He, in turn, became their spokesman. By usual church standards, moreover, Martinez was not a good defender of the faith. All evidence suggests that he renounced few if any physical pleasures of the world, interfered in politics, charged outrageous clerical fees, and played on the superstitions of his parishoners. The vivid portrayal of the fat, corrupt priest of Taos in Willa Cather's *Death Comes for the Archbishop* is modeled on some of Martinez' less attractive qualities.[10] Ever a localist, he appears to have looked with favor at first on the Texas Revolution in 1836, thinking that New Mexico might also gain autonomy within Mexico.[11] Not one to flinch at violence, he was probably active in the rebellion of the Taos Indians in 1837, when they overthrew the government at Santa Fe. He undoubtedly noted with grim satisfaction the deposition and murder of the unpopular Governor Perez—a nonresident appointee—who was succeeded for a brief time by a Taos buffalo hunter, Jose Gonzales. By such actions Padre Martinez illustrated the active and powerful role that he and many other local church leaders—from the Vicar General at Santa Fe down to the

9. Twitchell, *Leading Facts*, 2, 337–38 n. Barreiro, *Ojeada*, p. 28. Lansing Bloom, "New Mexico under Mexican Administration, 1821–1846," *Old Santa Fe, 1* (1913), 13, 249.

10. Willa Cather, *Death Comes for the Archbishop* (New York, 1927).

11. The 1837 rebellion was another example of the localism that prompted Texans and Californians as well as New Mexicans to rise periodically against outside appointees or unpopular rulings by Mexico City. Twitchell, *Leading Facts, 2,* 53–67.

parish level—played in New Mexican life. Such conditions led Americans to decry this "priest-ridden country," and persuaded Pino to beg for a bishop.[12]

Before Padre Martinez, his family, and their many relations could build the northern half of New Mexico into a parish of their own liking, however, the world intervened. Where cultural and racial frontiers meet, some system of exchange must develop. Taos being virtually a spearhead into Indian country, the Taos Indians, the Spanish settlers, and the nomadic wild tribes stopped their bickering and warfare long enough each July to hold an annual fair. Throughout the eighteenth century it was an event that attracted merchants from distant Chihuahua, and wily French traders all the way from the Mississippi Valley.[13]

This isolation was further impugned in 1803, when the purchase of Louisiana pushed the uncertain boundaries of the United States—once a thousand miles away—to the Arkansas River only 150 miles from Taos. Two years later, James Purcell opened a trail to New Mexico from Missouri; and a year after that, Zebulon Pike crossed the border only to be arrested and hauled off to Santa Fe. Though arrest and imprison they did, the Spanish authorities could not stop a few bold traders from appearing every few years in the hopes of selling goods. In 1821, however, the situation was dramatically reversed when Mexico declared her independence of Spain, threw off the fetters of mercantilism, and declared for free trade. The new era was inaugurated in New Mexico when Captain William Becknell of Franklin, Missouri, set out in 1821 to trade for wild horses on the Great Plains and to engage in Indian barter. Almost by accident he wandered into New Mexico, where, to his amazement, he was favorably received. Quickly he sold his few goods for hard silver dollars and marched back to Missouri with the grand news that trade with Mexico was now possible. Beginning in 1822, annual caravans wound their way over the broad plains and into the mountains to Taos and

12. Gregg, *Commerce*, pp. 161–75. Lewis Hector Garrard, *Wah-To-Yah and the Taos Trail* (Norman, Okla., 1955), pp. 171, 189, 202, comments similarly.

13. Hiram M. Chittenden, *The American Fur Trade of the Far West* (2 vols. Stanford, 1954), 2, 489–500.

Santa Fe, both of which were ports of entry. Not content with these outlets the more bold pushed on to markets in Chihuahua and Saltillo. Everywhere they found that calicoes and fancy wares brought a fine profit from the goods-starved people of the internal provinces. From a few pack animals a year the colorful Santa Fe trade soon expanded into large annual caravans of wagons piled with goods valued in 1843 at $450,000.[14]

In the same years that the Missouri merchants were developing the Santa Fe trade, the prospect of beaver and furs south and west of the Arkansas River lured French-Canadian and American trappers like Antoine LeRoux, the Robidoux brothers, Ewing Young, and Kit Carson to cross the boundary to hunt in the Sangre de Cristo range, the San Luis and San Juan valleys, and all the way to the Gila River. With or without licenses or permission from the authorities at Santa Fe, they came in such increasing numbers that New Mexicans themselves learned the art of trapping in order to share the spoils of their own native land.[15] Taos became a center for trappers and fur expeditions as well as a port of entry.

The dramatic story of the Santa Fe trade and the fur trade has been told elsewhere, but four traders were to advance the Americanization of the Southwest so much by their careers that they merit discussion in depth. The first of these remarkable men was Charles Hipolyte Trotier, Sieur de Beaubien. Born in Trois Riviere, Canada, of a noble family, he had come to the Untied States during the War of 1812. With connections among the French-speaking residents of Missouri, he migrated to that territory; and like many another French-Canadian he was soon engaged in the frontier fur trade. By 1823 Beaubien had visited New Mexico. Attracted by the prospects of keeping a store in Taos, he and several other French-Canadians

14. The classic story of the Santa Fe trade is still Gregg's *Commerce of the Prairies* (2 vols. New York, 1844). The more available 1933 edition has been cited throughout this study, however. R. L. Duffus, *The Santa Fe Trail* (New York, 1930), is a standard account. Moorhead, *New Mexico's Royal Road*, is a thorough recent study.

15. The Southwestern trappers are treated in Robert Glass Cleland, *This Reckless Breed of Men: The Trappers and Fur Traders of the Southwest* (New York, 1952).

settled there. Within a few years this genial, popular, shrewd man had become a Mexican citizen and had married into the prominent Lovato family.[16]

"Senor Carlos Bovian," as the Mexicans called him, was in many ways a transition figure in the history of the Santa Fe trade.[17] He represented the amenable, adjustable eighteenth-century French trader who—familiar with the Spanish in the Mississippi Valley—brought goods to Taos and sometimes settled there. At the same time, he was like the new traders, for he brought goods in bulk and kept a store. During the 1840s he ran a hostelry, owned a ranch, and held office as a justice of the peace. The changes in the community itself were amply illustrated by his children's marriages; through them, Carlos was eventually allied to the Maxwell, Trujillo, Abreu, Clouthier, and Muller families—names reflecting the presence of American, French, Mexican and German born citizens in Taos.[18] By 1846 Carlos Beaubien had established himself through ability, natural charm, and marriage as one of the leading men in New Mexico.

Two years after Beaubien came to Taos, another young trader of French descent appeared. Where Beaubien could boast of a noble past in Canada, Ceran de Hault de Lassus de St. Vrain could point to an equally noble and in many ways tragic family background in France. Ceran St. Vrain's grandfather, Pierre Charles de Hault de Lassus de Luziere, had served on the royal council of Louis XVI until the French Revolution. Unhappy with the new order in France after 1789, he listened eagerly to agents of the Scioto Land Company in Paris. In 1790 he secured from them what he thought was a princely land grant. He came to America only to find that the grant was fraudulent and that the company and its settlements around Gallipolis, Ohio, were a miserable failure. But the great love of the soil was in his blood; and after securing new lands in Spanish

16. Ralph E. Twitchell, *The Spanish Archives of New Mexico* (2 vols. Cedar Rapids, 1914), *1*, 65, Twitchell, *Leading Facts*, 2, 273.

17. William Montgomery Boggs, "Narrative of Adventures in 1844 and 1845," YWA.

18. Twitchell, *Spanish Archives*, *1*, 65.

Louisiana, he settled in Missouri, where he tried to build up his much-shattered estate.[19]

A few years later, two sons of the Chevalier followed him to America. One of them, Charles, became the Lieutenant Governor of Spanish Louisiana, while the other, Jacques, a former naval officer and the future father of Ceran, settled near the old French town of St. Genevieve in 1793–94. Land speculation and dreams of great estates were rife in Louisiana and Missouri in the 1790s, for Spain— pursuing her age-old policy of containment of the foreigner—was trying to turn the Mississippi Valley into a buffer state against the United States by peopling borders there with respectable immigrants loyal to Spain. In Philadelphia the Wharton brothers were persuaded to found the colony of New Madrid. From Virginia, Moses Austin came to Spanish Missouri to exploit a grant of lead mines. And like his father, Jacques St. Vrain caught the fever and speculated. Misfortune after misfortune dogged him, however, until he died a poor man in 1818.

As one of Jacques St. Vrain's ten children, Ceran—then sixteen— was put into the home of a rich Missouri Indian trader and merchant, Bernard Pratte. Excited by the reports of the new Santa Fe trade, Ceran St. Vrain and François Guerin took goods on credit from Bernard Pratte in 1825 and headed west for Taos, by then a thriving outpost and supply center for trappers. A discerning youth, St. Vrain decided to spend the winter in New Mexico—something few Santa Fe traders did—to stake indigent American trappers with supplies in return for a portion of the catch. Retaining connections with Bernard Pratte and Company, he did some trapping on his own and in 1827 actually assumed command of Sylvester Pratte's expedition when the latter died on the hunt.[20] An impressive giant of a man with an open, honest face and great energy, he possessed such natural charm that the admiring Lewis Hector Garrard was to call him a "gentleman in the best sense, his French descent imparting an exquisite, indefinable degree of politeness, combined with the frankness of an ingenuous

19. "Ceran St. Vrain" in *DAB*. David Lavender, *Bent's Fort* (New York, 1954), pp. 49–51.
20. Lavender, pp. 56–62, 73.

mountain man."[21] By 1830 every official in Taos and Santa Fe knew and respected "Senor San Brano."

On one of his fur-trapping expeditions in either 1828 or 1829 St. Vrain met a fellow Missourian whose family he had always known. This was Charles Bent, an intense, able, businessman-trapper, whose own fur business was being ruined by the American Fur Company. Bitterly resentful and highly ambitious, he and his younger brother William, along with St. Vrain and his brother Marcellin, agreed sometime after 1828 to establish their own company and operate south of the Platte River. Thus was born Bent, St. Vrain and Company, the future builders of Bent's Old Fort and the exploiters of a vast Southwestern empire.[22]

To understand the role which Bent's Fort played in the coming of the Americans to the Southwest, one must first see exactly what the Bents and St. Vrain were after. Bent's own bitter experience with ruthless and often senseless competition existing in the fur trade along the Missouri River and beyond persuaded him that operations south of the Platte must not be conducted in this way. To survive, they had to capture or control every aspect of frontier trade in the Southwest. They also had a successful precedent for the control of a frontier area: the career of Auguste Pierre Chouteau. In the late eighteenth century Chouteau had moved to the central plains tribes in Kansas, had constructed a log palace, and had virtually ruled a frontier empire as a king of the Indian trade and arbiter of tribal disputes. The Bents and St. Vrain thus conceived the idea of an equivalent frontier center and bastion at some central spot south of the Platte.

With brilliant strategy they built what is now called Bent's Old Fort or Fort William (in honor of William Bent) on the north bank of the Arkansas River near the mouth of the Purgatory. Unlike any other American outpost Bent's Fort was not only extraordinarily complete but virtually impregnable to Indian attack. Uniquely built of adobe brick made by scores of Mexicans laborers from Taos, it rose

---

21. Garrard, *Wah-To-Yah*, p. 13.

22. Lavender, *Bent's Fort*; also George B. Grinnell, "Bent's Old Fort and Its Builders," Kansas Historical Society, *Collections*, *15* (1919–22), 28–88.

impressively from a barren windy plain like a sentinel in the desert. Its "dun ramparts" were, as Edwin Sabin was to exclaim, "a stronghold and hospice in one."[23]

By the time the fort was completed in 1832, the partners had also worked out an efficient division of labor. Charles Bent, who was the senior partner, would travel back and forth from Missouri with supplies for trade; William Bent, a man who sincerely liked Indians and enjoyed trading with them, would remain at the fort and exchange goods for furs with the Arapahoes, the Utes, the southern Sioux, the Apaches and Comanches, and all other tribes who could be contacted. St. Vrain would remain in Taos with a store, establish a branch in Santa Fe, and periodically send agents to Chihuahua and Sonora. The company would also supply trappers at such cheap rates that no other firm could afford to come into the region, nor could the trappers transport their own supplies from Missouri as efficiently. Bent's Fort thus became the economic capital of the southern fur trade. The plan eventually worked so well that Bent, St. Vrain and Company were second in importance only to Astor's American Fur Company.[24]

The detailed story of that trade has been treated many times elsewhere.[25] Suffice it to say that the Bent brothers and St. Vrain operated one of the most thorough and successful exploitations of an American frontier ever attempted. Not just furs and goods passed through their hands; they were a way station for most caravans going to Santa Fe; they imported Mexican blankets to sell to Plains Indians who did not know how to make their own; they baled buffalo robes by the thousands for the St. Louis market; they caught and traded wild horses, sold Mexican mules, ran ranches, and tried to farm.[26] Through St. Vrain in Taos the firm operated a mill that produced much of the flour consumed by the Colorado goldseekers in the Pike's Peak rush of 1859. As romantic as it seemed, it was a vast and complicated enterprise requiring scores of assistants and enlisting the aid of four Bent brothers and numerous relatives.

23. Edwin L. Sabin, *Kit Carson Days, 1809–1868* (Chicago, 1914), p. 189.
24. Chittenden, *Fur Trade*, 2, 543.
25. See for example, Chittenden, Lavender, and Sabin.
26. George Bent, half-breed son of William, reminisced in a series of letters to George Hyde about the extent of the business. See esp. Bent to Hyde, Seger Colony, Oklahoma, March 19, 1906; April 14, 1908; December 18, 1911 YWA.

By 1840 the more subtle effects of Bent's Fort were being felt. The borderlands of New Mexico were in its economic grip. The Indians, who had once traded with Mexicans, now looked to Bent's Fort for supplies, thus worsening Indian-Mexican relations. Americans owned and dominated much of Taos, and New Mexicans worked by the hundreds either directly or indirectly for the firm. In 1834 St. Vrain was appointed United States Consul in Santa Fe and thus became a diplomatic figure as well. Charles Bent himself became a voice in New Mexico when he moved from the fort down the Taos trail to San Fernandez. By the mid-thirties he had married Maria Ignacia Jaramillo.[27] With Beaubien, St. Vrain, Stephen Luis Lee, and others, Bent became one of the leaders of what Padre Martinez called "the American Party," in Taos.

By far the largest body of Americans in Taos were mountain men like Antoine LeRoux, the Robidoux brothers, François LeCompte, Bill Williams, and Thomas Fitzpatrick. Their finest representative, however, was the famous scout Christopher or "Kit" Carson. As a youth in 1826 Carson had joined a wagon train to Santa Fe and had become a successful independent trapper. Later the Bents hired him as a hunter to supply the hordes of sojourners at Fort William with fresh meat. He, too, was attracted by the blue-tinged hills, the cool climate, and the pure air of Taos. It was at Taos that Carson, as a successful man of the frontier world, married Josefa Jaramillo in 1843, thereby increasing his own happiness, establishing himself socially, and becoming the brother-in-law of Charles Bent in one act.[28]

Such men were the spearheads of the American invasion of New Mexico. In the more subtle and often unconscious process of economic conquest they had compatriot allies throughout New Mexico. In Santa Fe itself former Kentuckian John Scolly owned the "best store" in the province, while Eugene Leitensdorfer's business house there was the "headquarters for all American traders for social and business conversation and for plans for promoting their general interests."[29] Other traveling merchants like James Magoffin penetrated

27. Lavender, *Bent's Fort*, p. 165. Moorhead, *New Mexico's Royal Road*, p. 124 n., says that St. Vrain never assumed his consular duties.

28. Sabin, *Kit Carson Days*, pp. 216–17. Lavender, *Bent's Fort*, p. 216.

29. William J. Parish, "The German Jew and the Commercial Revolution in Territorial New Mexico, 1850–1900," *New Mexican Quarterly, 29* (1959), 308–11.

into Chihuahua, while Dr. Henry Connelly, another Kentuckian, had trading posts at Santa Fe, Peralta, and Albuquerque. Although none of these men at first contemplated doing more than making a good profit and returning some day to a comfortable home in the states, they were engaging in an economic activity that determined the outcome of General Kearny's invasion of the Far Southwest in 1846.

As the Santa Fe trade increased in value, influential Missouri investors, through Senator Benton, persuaded the federal government to improve the trail, build Fort Leavenworth, supply troops occasionally in Indian country, and post consuls in the strategic trade outlets of Santa Fe, Chihuahua, and Saltillo.[30] Mexico herself established a consulate in St. Louis and declared Taos a "port of entry." Slowly the New Mexican economy—primitive though it was—drifted away from that of Chihuahua and into the orbit of the Missouri merchants and traders. The duties paid by the Americans at the border came to constitute the chief source of income for salaries of soldiers and officials of the Department of New Mexico. Unjust customs imposed upon the Americans at Taos and Santa Fe as well as capricious arrests or confiscation of goods by jealous, corrupt officials soon became a major difference between Mexico and the United States.[31]

Nor was this one-way traffic in either commerce or ideas. As early as 1824 some twenty-six Mexican merchants journeyed to Council Bluffs to establish trade relations. By 1840 Mexican merchants such as Don Juan Sena ran the "second-best" store in Santa Fe. A decade before the Mexican War promising young Mexicans were sent to the parochial schools of St. Louis to learn English or were trained in business houses at Westport Landing and Independence.[32] They came home full of knowledge of a different world. Prominent families such as the Chavezes and Oteros, who had once been exclusively in ranching, were now traders. The Armijo brothers, like other men from poorer families, by shrewdness and hard work had become two of the richest men in the province. In a prophetic mood J. Francisco Chavez's father sent his young son off to Missouri in 1841 with the

30. Sister Mary Loyola, "The American Occupation of New Mexico, 1821–1852," *NMHR, 14* (1939), 45. Bloom, *Old Santa Fe, 1*, 13.

31. Loyola, p. 143. Bloom, p. 17.

32. Bloom, pp. 173–74.

admonition: "The heretics are going to overrun all this country. Go and learn their language and come back prepared to defend your people."[33]

Throughout New Mexico business and trade was increasing, and Taos was a symbol of the new dispensation. Although only 700 people lived there in 1844, Edwin Sabin remarked that Taos "was not without the best blood of the west, and as custom place of the New Mexican northern border was a settlement, second only, if at all, to Santa Fe."[34] It was becoming much more than a port of entry for the Santa Fe trade: it was to be a gateway for an empire.

The coming of new settlers and traders to the northern borderlands in 1821–45 coincided with the demise of Spanish rule and the rise of Mexico. Mexico, however, like its parent, feared the expansive nature of the United States, and proceded to revive in the 1820s the parent country's old policy of establishing buffer settlements along her borders to hold back the gringo. Spain had employed the Church, through its missions, to make loyal converts out of the local Indian population and had established presidios of soldiers to keep local order in the northern provinces. In the more secular nineteenth century—and in areas where it seemed impossible to convert wild Indians—Mexico tried the impresario system. Under it the government promised to make a large grant of land to any suitable colonizer who would settle a certain number of trustworthy and loyal families on the tract. Ironically, the first result of this policy was the occupation of Texas by the Americans in such great numbers that Mexico lost the entire province in 1836.

Despite this unexpected turn of events, a lively interest in lands existed all along the borders of Mexico from Texas to California. Historians seem to have ignored the fact that land speculation and fever in the Far Southwest was a Mexican phenomenon as well as an American one between 1821 and 1846. In California local leaders seized the rich and already cultivated monastery lands in the flimsy name of "secularization." Certain ambitious and practical business-

---

33. Dargan, *NMHR, 14,* 181.
34. Sabin, *Kit Carson Days,* p. 200.

men in New Mexico also decided to capitalize on the new land policy. They, too, volunteered to settle the borderlands with loyal colonies to hold back Indians and Americans. Of the 197 land grants made in New Mexico since its founding in 1598, sixty-nine were made in the nineteenth century; twenty-three of these were made in the short period between 1840 and 1847.[35]

Among the first to realize the possibilities were Don Jose Manuel Martinez and his sons, who secured as reward for Indian defense a grant of the beautiful Tierra Amarilla tract on the Chama River.[36] As other grants were made, visions of landed empire also began to haunt the American traders in Taos. But to secure a grant required political connections in Santa Fe. In 1835 they watched with envy as choice lands on the Mora River went to Jose Tapia and seventy-five others who were friends of the presiding governor. Soon thereafter, the influential Baca family was awarded the Las Vegas grant.[37]

Sometime in the late 1830s Carlos Beaubien, Ceran St. Vrain, Charles Bent, and a cooperative Taos prefect, Cornelio Vigil, found Governor Manuel Armijo—also a merchant—receptive to their own request for land grants. Working through the medium of Guadalupe Miranda, former secretary to Governor Perez and Collector of Customs for Armijo, they applied for lands as rewards for Indian defense. With eloquent fervor they declared:

> The welfare of a nation consists in the possession of lands which produce all the necessaries of life without requiring those of other nations, and it cannot be denied that New Mexico possesses this great advantage, and only requires industrious hands to make it a happy residence. This is the age of progress and the march of intellect, and they are so rapid that we may expect, at a day not far distant, that they will reach even us.[38]

35. *Annual Report . . . of the Interior for 1855,* pp. 433–39.
36. Jaramillo, *Shadows of the Past,* p. 13.
37. Ralph Carr, "Private Land Claims in Colorado," *CM,* 25 (1948), 20–21. O. D. Barrett, *The Mora Grant of New Mexico* (Washington, 1884), p. 13, pamphlet, HEH.
38. Twitchell, *Spanish Archives, 1,* 62–65.

The ambitious petitioners promised to raise sugar beets, cotton, wool, and stock. But they also had to pay a price: Miranda and Armijo must share in the spoils as part owners. This was quietly agreed to, and on January 11, 1841, Armijo awarded Beaubien and Miranda a huge tract, which by Mexican law could not be larger than 97,000 acres, but which the holders and their heirs were eventually to stretch into a claim for two million acres. In taking possession of the new empire, which was northeast of Taos, Cornelio Vigil (acting in his capacity as the local justice of the peace) went through the ancient Spanish ritual of joyfully throwing dirt into the air and chanting the magic lines of legal acquisition.[39]

As the land fever increased, Padre Antonio Jose Martinez joined Julian Gallegos and Celedon Valdez in 1842 to petition for a grant in southwestern Colorado. A year later Luis Lee, a Missouri emigré and friend of Beaubien, petitioned with Beaubien's young son, Narciso—who was acting for his father—for a large tract to be called the Sangre de Cristo Grant. Located to the north and west of Taos, it was to be used for colonization purposes. In November 1843 Gervacio Nolan, a French-Canadian by birth, is supposed to have persuaded Armijo to grant him the "Valley of the Rio San Carlos," bordering on the Arkansas River. And a month later the ever-present and cooperative Cornelio Vigil was there to officiate at the formal ceremonies of acquisition.

The fever was now at its height, and Prefect Vigil decided that he, too, might profit from the new industry. In partnership with Ceran St. Vrain and Charles Bent, he asked Armijo for a vast grant south of the Arkansas River but north of the Beaubien-Miranda tract. The generous governor, acting in silent partnership with his petitioners, graciously acceded to their wish.[40] St. Vrain must have thought that through this princely grant the dream of his grandfather, the old Chevalier de Luziere, might come true.

A similar craze for grants was also occurring in the central and

39. Dunham, *Government Handout*, p. 215. LeRoy R. Hafen, "Mexican Land Grants in Colorado," *CM*, *4* (1927), 97.

40. Dunham, *Government Handout*, pp. 215–16 n. Twitchell, *Leading Facts*, 2, 451–81.

eastern counties of New Mexico. Near Las Vegas and Socorro still
other awards were made, and John Scolly, of the "best store" in Santa
Fe, secured a tract in the Mora Valley.[41] Such a lavish give-away
policy and such favoritism were bound to have its critics. Alarmed
at this aggrandizement of a few men—particularly since they encroached upon some of the Taos Pueblo Indian holdings, as well as
his own—Padre Martinez journeyed to Durango, where he secured a
rescission of the Miranda and Beaubien grant in February 1844. But
the Padre's accomplishments were undone when Governor Armijo
returned to power in the spring of 1844 and reinstated the claimants.[42]

Some years before conquest, then, the Americans in New Mexico
had passed beyond furs and trade to that third frontier big business:
land speculation. Thus one of the major issues in Mexican New Mexico was the question of land grants, for it was inevitable that the
land schemes would overlap and that factions would develop. In
Taos, where no less than fifteen grants had been made in six years,
the issue caused a deep split between the "American Party" (of
Beaubien, Bent, Luis Lee, Cornelio Vigil, and St. Vrain) and the Martinez family and their allies. A friendly justice of the peace, prefect,
or governor meant the difference between a confirmed grant and a
rejected one. Consequently, political office became an important
means to economic ends for the two parties. Peace and trade with
the wild Indians meant the difference between colonizing and letting
the grant lie fallow and uninhabited. Thus Indian relations became
part and parcel of this history of the grants. In such a struggle religion and cultural differences were heightened, and hates blossomed
in the small village of San Fernandez de Taos. Faced with these conditions, Charles Bent, Ceran St. Vrain, Carlos Beaubien, and Kit
Carson made a fatal decision: they would fight the "big family" and
particularly Padre Martinez and his brother Pasqual, who were its
leaders.

Some five years before American conquest, Charles Bent began to
send a private newsletter to the American Consul at Santa Fe, Manuel

41. James Josiah Webb, *Adventures in the Santa Fe Trade, 1844–47*, ed. Ralph
P. Bieber, Southwest Historical Series (12 vols. Glendale Cal., 1931), *1*, 74 n.
42. Dunham, *Government Handout*, p. 217.

Alvarez.[43] The central theme of many of the letters—aside from business instructions, for Alvarez was a merchant—was dislike for the Taos priest. In January 1841 Bent sarcastically observed that "the great Literay [sic] Martines" had just returned from Durango, where he reported that he was: "considered by all, as one of the greatest men of the age, as a Literary, an eclesiastic [sic], a Jurist, and a philanthropist . . . If the age of miracles had not gone by, I should expect that God would bestowe some greate blessing on these people, through this great man."[44]

In 1842 Bent opposed Martinez' candidate for justice of the peace. Three years later he reported with relish that the Padre, whom he derisively called "Calf," had become inebriated at a local wedding and had denounced Governor Armijo. Although written to Alvarez, the letter was obviously intended for Armijo's eyes.[45] The hostility between the factions had been greatly heightened by the Texan Santa Fe Expedition of 1841, since it was suspected that the Americans in New Mexico and at Bent's Fort would join the invaders. So great was the tension that the government arrested Charles Bent and imprisoned him in Santa Fe; other Americans sold their belongings in Taos and fled to California; and the United States Consul, Manuel Alvarez, was wounded when a mob invaded his house with the intention of killing him.[46]

Two years later Texans under Colonel A. Warfield attacked the small town of Mora, killing innocent residents and stealing horses. Charles Bent was forced to flee to the Arkansas for safety. Carlos Beaubien, who also wisely left town, had his store looted. To make matters still more difficult, another blustering set of Texans under Colonel Jacob Snively killed and robbed a prominent Mexican merchant and attacked New Mexican militiamen on the Cimarron cutoff of the Santa Fe trail. When the shooting was over, twenty-three Mexicans, many from Taos, lay dead. In Taos itself Padre Martinez often thought that his own life was in danger from the American Party.[47]

43. Moorhead, *New Mexico's Royal Road*, pp. 128–29 n.
44. Charles Bent to Manuel Alvarez, January 30, 1841, Bent Letters, NMHS.
45. Ibid., March 30, 1845; February 26, 1846.
46. Lavender, *Bent's Fort*, p. 202.
47. Bent to Alvarez, February 24, 1846; April 17, 1846; Bent Letters.

On the very eve of American conquest the Taoseños were embroiled in a heated campaign to choose local officials. Bent's friend Beaubien ran against Martinez' brother for justice of the peace. When the Martinez faction won this and other offices, Bent called it an "unfair" election likely to be annulled.[48] A few weeks later, however, the Martinez ranches suffered a large loss of stock from raiders purporting to be Utah Indians. The priest voiced the suspicion that the "Americans" had put the Indians up to it. In breathless excitement Bent scribbled: "I have just learned today that the Priest Martinez and his brother the justice were taking declarations to criminate me for having traded with the Youtahs. . . . The Priest will spare no means to injure me . . . if he can succeed in this there is no telling what he may accomplish."[49]

As rumors of a possible war between Mexico and the United States filtered into the Rio Arriba Country, relations grew so strained that when George Bent and a friend went on a drinking spree one day, a small force of Martinez retainers appeared and beat them up. Roaring with anger, Charles Bent exclaimed to Alvarez that "the servants of the 'big family' (Martinez) had done the whipping and that Pasqual Martinez was behind the attack." And in a hasty postscript he declared: "Whilst this family is in authority, foreigners are not secure."[50]

Curiously, Charles Bent—while very much a temperamental frontiersman, who trusted his own fists—was also a businessman and a believer in the legal process. His early career as a mountain man has obscured the fact that he came from an able family and had gone to college. His father, Silas Bent, was a justice of the territorial supreme court of Missouri.[51] Bent, the businessman and propertied citizen, found the New Mexican government sadly lacking in proper methods of protecting life and property. He dared not appeal to a prefect or justice named Martinez. There was no jury system nor any common law to use as a guide in criminal or property disputes. Appeals to the governor faced the same hazards of family influence and personal

48. Ibid., March 6, 1846.
49. Ibid., April 6, 1846.
50. Ibid., May 3, 1846; and a second letter written at 9:00 P.M. that same day.
51. "Silas Bent" in *DAB*.

caprice, so that Armijo's successor might revoke their princely domain in northern New Mexico. So strongly did he feel this insecurity that in a secret diatribe Bent condemned all New Mexicans:

> Officers and justices particularly, equally ignorant, insolent and avericious are easily bribed, justice is badly administered, and is rendered with extreme delay, caused as much by rangling and subterfuge of advocates as the insufficiency of the law and the ———— ignorant ———— who from their indolence and incapacity and extortion of the justices are always calculated to create delay. Fees are a grevious item—they arc always extracted according to the caprice of the justice. The Mexican character is made up of stupidity, obstinacy, ignorance, duplicity and vanity.[52]

Many a frustrated Taos and Santa Fe merchant and trapper felt the same way when the Mexican government virtually closed the Santa Fe trail in the early 1840s, by imposing excessive traffic duties. In 1843, as a result of the Texan raids on Mexican soil and on the caravan of Mexican merchants, Taos itself was closed as a port of entry. There were ways to get around such arbitrary rulings. One could be naturalized as a Mexican citizen, for example, as were Beaubien and St. Vrain. But it was under such uncertain legal conditions, dilatory reverses of policy, and factional disputes that the Santa Fe traders, the Taos land grant claimants, and the businessmen of Bent's Fort operated. Bent, St. Vrain, Beaubien, and a hundred Missourians were busy in 1846 seeking a way to cut the net enmeshing their various, ambitious enterprises, when Manifest Destiny brought General Kearny to their rescue.

52. MS in Bent's handwriting in Bent Letters which appears to have been written February 1845.

3

A Conquest by Merchants

I chant commerce opening, the sleep of ages
Having done its work—races, reborn, refresh'd.
Walt Whitman
"A Broadway Pageant"

 Probably no state in the Union responded to the outbreak of the Mexican War in May 1846 with more enthusiasm and more caution than Missouri. Since the days of Lewis and Clark, Missouri as territory and state had made the entire West its colonial appendage. Forts Laramie and Union were but Missouri outposts. A hundred miles east of the Rockies the Bents maintained their famous fort with its own string of posts stretching north to the Platte, southeast to Texas, and south to Santa Fe. But their goods came from Missouri warehouses. From Independence, St. Joseph, and Westport Landing had come Josiah Gregg, the Magoffin brothers, James Webb, and a hundred other doughty entrepreneurs in search of the commerce of the prairies, so that by 1843 the Santa Fe trade alone was worth at least $450,000 to Missourians.[1] Missouri am-

1. Josiah Gregg estimated the value of the Santa Fe trade to be $450,000 in 1843, but Max Moorhead, *New Mexico's Royal Road*, pp. 185–86, thinks this figure is extremely conservative. He suggests that it was worth $1,500,000 that year.

bitions did not end there. In Washington Senators Linn and Benton advocated the occupation of Oregon, while Benton's son-in-law, John C. Fremont, engaged in a series of vast reconnaissances of the remaining unknown West from California to Oregon and from the Rockies through the Great Basin region. To Missouri the exploitation of the frontier was a major industry.

The Mexican War promised to increase the already immense area of Missouri's frontier domain, but it also threatened to disrupt the valuable trade with Mexico's border provinces. The problem then was to fight a war against Mexico without disturbing New Mexico. As Senator Benton put it:

> Our first care in this sudden change in our relations with that country (Mexico) was to try and take care of our Santa Fe trade. For this purpose it will be proposed to the people of New Mexico, Chihuahua, and other internal provinces, that they remain quiet and continue trading with us as usual, upon which conditions they shall be protected in all their rights and treated as friends.[2]

To accomplish this delicate task, the Polk Administration chose Colonel Stephen Watts Kearny, a tight-lipped, lanky, professional soldier with a long record of service at the frontier outposts on the American plains. There was little about this blunt officer to suggest that he was fitted to fight a genteel economic war of nerves.[3] Yet in May 1846 Kearny was put in command of the "Army of the West" and ordered to hold the northern provinces of Mexico until peace had been made. Rather than overthrow existing governments, he was to "establish temporary civil governments . . . and as far as possible retain in service those who had held office under the Mexican regime." He was particularly enjoined to see "that trade with the United States was not to be interrupted under the changed conditions."[4]

2. Quoted in George R. Gibson, *Journal of a Soldier under Kearny and Doniphan, 1846–47*, ed. Ralph P. Bieber, Southwest Historical Series (12 vols. Glendale, California, 1935), *3*, 61–62.
3. See "Stephen Watts Kearny" in *DAB*. J. M. Cutts, *The Conquest of California and New Mexico* (Philadelphia, 1847), pp. 34–35.
4. Loyola, *NMHR*, *14*, 159–60.

In addition to a force of some 1,600 soldiers and sixteen pieces of artillery, Polk promised Kearny some unusual instruments of warfare. A "person of Catholic religion and good repute" was to go along, while General Winfield Scott ordered him to add "valuable men at Bent's Fort," and to seek the aid of American citizens abiding in New Mexico. At the same time, a special messenger was sent ahead of Kearny's troops to warn the merchants who had already started out on the annual trek to Santa Fe that hostilities did exist.[5]

The 1,648 men eventually assembled by Kearny at Fort Leavenworth that spring were a curious lot. Besides the regular troops there were rambunctious volunteers—irreverent, disobedient to their officers, and quick to complain when the going got rough. Later a column of Mormons dressed in homespun—sent by Brigham Young to show the Americans that the Latter Day Saints were patriotic—also joined the expedition. Besides soldiering, the Mormon troops could perform the useful task of spying out unknown regions of the Southwest, where perhaps a Mormon retreat could be found. Among the general officers of this motley army there were at least fifty would-be politicians, who needed a war record as an entree to public life. With Kearny rode four future governors and at least a half dozen budding congressmen and delegates.

After an easy march across the Kansas plains, the "Army of the West" stopped at Bent's Fort, where they found 400 merchants resting with their caravans while awaiting news of the war. Observant frank Major Philip St. George Cooke called them "Involuntary Micawbers," hoping for something favorable to turn up.[6] Soon after Kearny's arrival, his sentries spotted a horse-drawn buggy jogging across the plains toward the fort. In it, accompanied only by a driver, was James Wiley Magoffin. Born on one frontier at Harrodsburg, Kentucky, he had drifted across to another and into the Santa Fe trade as a young man. Now the owner of a successful business house in Saltillo, he had served as an American consul there and in the course of his stay had married a cousin of Governor Armijo of New

5. Gibson, *Journal of a Soldier*, pp. 25–26.
6. Phillip St. George Cooke, *The Conquest of New Mexico and California* (New York, 1878), p. 9.

Mexico. Magoffin, in fact, was as well known in the border provinces as any American living there. In the genial and highly convivial Irishman, whom the Mexicans called "Don Santiago," Benton and Polk thought they saw the nearest thing to a "person of Catholic religion and of good repute" who could be found to aid conquest. They had sent him posthaste from Washington to join Kearny on the Arkansas.[7]

It was at Bent's Fort, appropriately enough, that Kearny worked out his pattern of conquest. After catching two Mexican spies hovering about the fort, he let them go to inform Governor Armijo that the Americans came in peace. An army officer, George T. Howard, had already been sent by the Secretary of War to Taos to persuade key persons there—and at Santa Fe—to accept peaceful occupation. Next, a Santa Fe merchant of long standing, Eugene Leitensdorfer, was allowed to ride ahead to urge Armijo not to resist.[8] In a proclamation issued on July 31, 1846, Kearny declared that the Americans had no hostile purpose in mind but came only to occupy. To one Mexican he promised that not "an onion or a pepper would be taken from them without a full equivalent in cash."[9] As the propaganda rolled forth from Kearny's tent, the army itself got under way. Veteran mountain man Thomas Fitzpatrick guided the troops over Raton Pass, while William Bent himself headed a volunteer party of advance spies. As they crossed into enemy territory, Kearny ordered Magoffin, Major St. George Cooke, and a Santa Fe merchant, Juan de Gonzales, to take nine men and ride into the New Mexican capital under a flag of truce and to treat with Armijo in person.[10]

As St. George Cooke's small band nervously made their way toward Santa Fe, Kearny bombarded the alcaldes and padres at Taos and Mora with more proclamations, explaining that he was on a pacific mission. By early August he himself arrived at the small village of Las Vegas, New Mexico, where he climbed on the roof of an adobe house with a reluctant alcalde and priest and proclaimed to the

---

7. Stella M. Drumm, ed., *Down the Santa Fe Trail and into Mexico: Diary of Susan Shelby Magoffin, 1846–1847* (New Haven, 1926 and 1962), p. xii; also "James Wiley Magoffin" in *DAB*. Cooke, *Conquest*, p. 17.

8. Drumm, p. xv.

9. Cutts, *Conquest of New Mexico*, p. 44.

10. Cooke, *Conquest*, pp. 4, 15–16.

astonished citizens: "My government . . . will keep off the Indians, protect you in your persons and property and . . . will protect you in your religion."[11]

The Polk administration had not acted through Kearny alone. Throughout the northern provinces and in California assiduous consuls and commercial agents were busy preparing the way for the American invader. In Santa Fe this task fell to Manuel Alvarez, a participant in the Santa Fe trade since 1824 and now the owner of one of the largest mercantile houses in New Mexico. Alvarez had served as American consul there since 1839, and in 1846 he had been appointed United States commercial agent. An advocate of American rule, he dogged Governor Armijo's steps all that momentous summer, urging him to make a peaceful surrender.[12]

As he paced the puncheon floors of the low adobe Palace of the Governors, Armijo himself was in a state of painful irresolution. The able but notoriously venal governor felt obliged to resist Kearny; yet he was also a businessman whose own fortune had been made from the Santa Fe trade. Ironically, some of Armijo's own wagons now rode in the wake of Kearny's troops. The economic man battled with the political man within Armijo.[13] A month before Kearny's arrival Jose Pablo Gallegos wrote Governor Armijo from Taos that the Americans were on the way and one might as well surrender. How can we resist, observed Armijo's former military secretary, Donaciano Vigil, when our people are armed only with "quivers and slings." Dr. Henry Connelly, a merchant in New Mexico and Chihuahua since 1828, dinned the same theme into Armijo's ears, while other merchants asserted that Kearny's forces were 5,000 strong.[14]

If the New Mexican governor was stalemated by doubts, the ruling classes of New Mexico—the landed families and the Church hierarchy—were equally divided. Those who felt close to higher officials in Chihuahua were joined by the clergy in a real fear of the Ameri-

11. Ralph E. Twitchell, *History of the Military Occupation of the Territory of New Mexico, 1846–51* (Denver, 1909), p. 50.

12. Gibson, *Journal of a Soldier*, pp. 61–62. Webb, *Adventures*, p. 97.

13. Webb, p. 179. Cooke, *Conquest*, p. 17.

14. Jose Pablo Gallegos to Manuel Armijo, July 9, 1846; Donaciano Vigil to Armijo, June 30, 1846, MSS in William G. Ritch Collection (Box 5), HEH.

cans. The Vicar General, Juan Felipe Ortiz, the distinguished Miguel and Nicolas Pino—sons of Pedro Bautista—Thomas Cabeza de Baca of Santa Fe, Manuel Chavez, and most priests argued for a policy of resistance. Young Diego Archuleta breathed defiance and urged an active military campaign. A chance for self-rule, the escape from periodic fleecings by corrupt appointees from Chihuahua, and the vision of an increased American trade led others to accept the idea of a new order. That dissatisfaction existed can be seen from a letter written by Armijo to the Departmental Assembly from Las Vegas that summer. He could not exact more money for defense from the local officers there, he complained, for it would "increase the number of discontented persons and internal enemies at this time when we find ourselves threatened by a very considerable foreign force."[15]

The New Mexican people, traditionally pictured as passively obedient and lacking in patriotic feeling, were greatly excited over the coming of the Americans. Stirred to action by the more conservative dons and by the clergy, an estimated 4,000 volunteers gathered in Santa Fe and declared themselves ready to fight. Diego Archuleta, a former pupil of Padre Martinez and a person with many connections to the central Mexican government, was placed in command, second only to Armijo.[16]

Such was the tense situation when Cooke, Magoffin, and Gonzales arrived at the Palace. Fortunately, Armijo seemed cordial, and a private conference followed in which Kearny's terms were presented. Undoubtedly the Governor was promised some remuneration if he would not resist. But whatever Cooke's and Magoffin's arguments were, they hit their mark. As St. George Cooke climbed on his horse to report to Kearny, he turned to a sullen and suspicious Palace sentry and remarked prophetically: "I'll call again in a week."[17] Meanwhile, in a store near the Palace, a nervous group of American merchants had barricaded themselves, expecting arrest or even death

15. Armijo to the Departmental Assembly [New Mexico], August 10, 1846, Ritch (Box 7), HEH.

16. A remarkably frank account of the events in New Mexico preceding the surrender is to be found in Juan Felipe Ortiz, "People of New Mexico to the President of Mexico, September, 1846;" MS in Ritch (Box 6), HEH.

17. Cooke, *Conquest*, p. 17.

when the fighting should begin. They had no idea that within a few weeks one of their number, Joab Houghton, would become a territorial justice, and several others would hold high political office under Kearny.

As the American army drew near the narrow defile called Apache Canyon—a natural place of defense as well as a pass over the last range of mountains before Santa Fe could be reached—General Armijo with his troops waited on the other side. He had also brought the Departmental Assembly to the Canyon, and there he asked them Hamlet-like: "whether he ought or ought not to defend the Department."[18] Soon it was obvious that there would be no fighting, for Armijo began to excuse men from service if they wished to return home. Always the practical businessman, he charged them from $20 to $100 for their freedom. Leaderless and questioning, an army twice the size of Kearny's began to melt away, while Armijo wrote Kearny a lame explanation of his actions: "we would defend our country, we desire to defend it, but we cannot do so, our general government being hundreds of leagues distant, it is impossible for me to receive the necessary aid to make such a defense."[19]

On August 18 the Americans marched through the last natural barrier to the Rio Grande settlements. The invasion from the north, feared by imperial Spain since the time of LaSalle, had at last become a reality. Armijo fled; and Acting Governor Juan Bautista Vigil y Alarid, himself a descendant of a French trader named Alarie, turned the province over to Kearny. By nightfall the Stars and Stripes waved over the Governor's Palace and the dusty packed earth plaza of Santa Fe. Messengers rode north to Taos and Abiquiu and south toward Bernalillo, Peralta, and Albuquerque to carry the news of peaceful conquest. The blunt General—for Kearny had been promoted by now—could pride himself on accomplishing exactly what Polk, Benton, and all Missourians had wanted. He had taken New Mexico without firing a shot. But he also must have realized that the real conquest had been made over a thirty-year period by traders and merchant-adventurers like James Magoffin, Manuel Alvarez, Henry Connelly, Ceran St. Vrain, and Charles and William Bent.

18. Ortiz, "People of New Mexico."
19. Armijo to Kearny, August 16, 1846, Ritch (Box 6), HEH.

In a superb post-mortem of the whole campaign St. George Cooke remarked:

A colonel's command called an army, marches eight hundred miles beyond its base, its communications liable to be cut off by the slightest effort of the enemy, . . . to conquer 250,000 square miles. . . . (The troops) arrive without food before the capital—a city two hundred and forty years old, habitually garrisoned by regular troops! I much doubt if any officer of rank but Stephen W. Kearny would have undertaken the enterprise. . . . This is the art of War as practiced in America.[20]

St. George Cooke might have made still another observation about the peculiarity of the New Mexican conquest. It was not an expression of land hunger or slavery extension; and it was only partly prompted by that vaguer expansionist sentiment called Manifest Destiny. Rather, American conquest meant regularizing and securing rich trade and safe transportation routes for a previously erratic, uncertain enterprise.[21] It was, in short, a conquest of merchants who worried little about extending the glories of free government to their captive customers.

Having succeeded so admirably at his first task, Kearny was impatient to create a new government and to be on his way to California. Not without ambition, he hoped to take that distant province as well. Captain David Waldo, Private Willard Preble Hall, and Colonel William Doniphan—guided by written suggestions from Polk and the Secretary of State—hastily drafted for the General what has come to be known as the Kearny Code. Compounded of Mexican, Texan, and Coahuila statutes, the Livingston Code of Louisiana, and the organic law of Missouri, it created a governmental structure for New Mexico similar to that envisaged by the Northwest Ordinance of 1787.[22]

20. Cooke, *Conquest*, p. 21.
21. Similar mercantile motives for the acquisition of the Pacific Coast are expounded in Norman A. Graebner, *Empire on the Pacific* (New York, 1955).
22. Cutts, *Conquest of New Mexico*, p. 64.

By the Kearny Code the executive branch was to consist of a governor and a secretary, who corresponded roughly to the *jefe politico* and his assistant of the Mexican period. While the Department of New Mexico had an Assembly, its functions had been more advisory than legislative, so that Kearny's provision for an Assembly was actually something new. Finally, the Code created three district justices, who would periodically meet together to form a territorial supreme court. Perhaps the nearest equivalent in the Mexican period was the custom by which the governor and the district alcaldes or prefects acted as a council to consider appeals, or by which the governor himself, advised by his Assembly, acted as a final judge. Establishment of the offices of solicitor general, marshal, treasurer, and auditor completed the roster of positions under the Code. On the local level, Kearny created counties, retained the district prefect as a sort of probate judge, kept the alcaldes as justices of the peace, and retained the office of constable. To these offices, however, he added the American ones of sheriff and county tax assessor.[23]

Having completed the framework of government, Kearny, with equal dispatch, appointed the "founding fathers" of American New Mexico. For governor he chose the man who had waited so long for "law and order": Charles Bent of Taos. As chief justice he named Antonio Jose Otero, a distinguished native merchant who had been in the Santa Fe trade for many years. And as Otero's associates he appointed Carlos Beaubien of Taos and Joab Houghton. The latter was a Santa Fe merchant, engineer, and jack-of-all trades, who was a friend and confidant of Bent and Beaubien. Houghton's business partner, Eugene Leitensdorfer, became auditor, while still another merchant, Charles Blumner, was appointed treasurer. Two Missourians, Francis P. Blair and Richard Dallam, became solicitor general and marshal.[24]

The Kearny Code has been praised by historians as the legal instrument which brought American government to the Spanish South-

23. *Laws of the Territory of New Mexico* (The Kearny Code) (Santa Fe, October 7, 1846), YWA.

24. An observer wrote of Kearny's judicial appointments: "All the Judges of the Superior Court do not possess the legal knowledge of a justice of the peace in St. Louis." Gibson, *Journal of a Soldier*, p. 242.

west, and for New Mexicans its promulgation did signify a constitutional revolution. Kearny's appointments, however, violated both the spirit of the Code and Polk's orders to retain, so far as possible, the existing native government. Instead Kearny delivered the new creation into the hands of the "American Party" of Taos and the Santa Fe merchants.

Besides Justice Otero, Kearny appointed only one other native New Mexican who could be called a member of the old regime—the affable, intelligent, pro-American Donaciano Vigil, who was made territorial secretary. Like Padre Martinez, Vigil was one of the most unusual men ever to live in New Mexico. From humble Taos origins he had succeeded in becoming a trusted member of the ruling hierarchy. Starting as a private in the war against Spain, by the 1830s he was military secretary to Armijo. A self-educated man full of liberal ideas, he had borrowed Padre Martinez' press for a time to edit a paper called *Verdad*. Vigil also appears to have genuinely welcomed the democratic American system of government, as a means to reform the clergy and to institute public education. For the next twenty years he was in and out of the councils of all who governed New Mexico.[25]

Vigil's appointment was undoubtedly a wise one, but most of Kearny's choices honored the very men who had worked with Armijo to secure grants of land and those who had antagonized the Martinez faction. Kearny's worst mistake was to ignore the ruling Santa Fe families. Nowhere could there be found a Sena, an Archuleta, an Ortiz, a Delgado, or a Pino among the new officers. Nor were many of the influential families of the Rio Abajo—the Pereas and the Chavezes—represented. Instead, Kearny allowed a Missouri and a Taos hegemony to be created, which omitted both the Church and the aristocrats.

Everyone in New Mexico was soon aware that a new order had arrived with the Americans. But it is doubtful whether Kearny or even Charles Bent realized what institutional revolutions the General's young code-makers had introduced. Here was a society with-

25. "Biographical Note on Vigil"; Obituary of Donaciano Vigil"; Ritch (Boxes 25, 26), HEH.

out the tradition of a strong legislature, unfamiliar with both the jury process and common law, unused to voting, or only vaguely aware of the two-party system. Finally, Kearny's Code contained even more revolutionary concepts: the separation of Church and State, the existence of taxes and tax collectors, a standing paid militia, and a system of secular public schools. It was hard for a people whose culture was still medieval in many ways to accept such a thorough and radically different new political constitution.

To Bent, Beaubien, St. Vrain, and the Santa Fe traders, however, the new government seemed a vast improvement over the old. American officials now collected reasonable duties at the border (until New Mexico was officially annexed by the Treaty of Guadalupe-Hidalgo). The American army promised to subdue the wild Apaches and Navajos, who had so long held up New Mexico's frontier expansion and rendered land grants useless.

Immediately after his arrival, Kearny sent Major William Gilpin to fight the Navajos in the Northwest, while Colonel Congreve Jackson marched toward Albuquerque to fight both Navajo and Apache bands. Colonel William Doniphan was dispatched to Navajo country by still another route. Indeed the Indian question seemed so near to solution that within a month after conquest an optimistic group of Taoseños petitioned Governor Bent for revalidation of the Conejos Grant in Ute country.[26]

Not only did Indian affairs seem promising, but the feeding and housing of so many American troops brought to Santa Fe a prosperity never enjoyed before. Lieutenant Abert reported that the streets were laden with burros, bringing in wood from the hills and whiskey from Taos. Labor was at a premium; and wages were high, while the Americans built Fort Marcy on a hill near the city. The soldiers themselves found living quarters so scarce that they were forced to fan out and live in nearby villages.[27]

Underneath this outward show of peace and prosperity many proud New Mexicans bridled with resentment at the loud, pushy

26. Carr, "Private Land Claims," *CM*, 25 (1948), 21.
27. J. A. Abert, *Report and Map of the Examination of New Mexico* (Washington, 1848), pp. 32 ff. Cutts, *Conquest of New Mexico*, p. 56.

Americans. George F. Ruxton, an English traveler in the Southwest, reported that the Americans in Santa Fe were "the dirtiest, rowdiest crew I have seen collected together. Crowds of drunken volunteers filled the streets brawling and boasting but never fighting."[28] The soldiers themselves did not care for Santa Fe or its citizens. One observer complained that it had the appearance of a badly assorted brickyard; another wrote that the population of New Mexico was "almost if not absolutely, impervious to progress."[29]

Rumors also began to float about that if one registered land titles with Secretary Vigil—who was, by a clause in the Kearny Code, to act as a land register—this was but the first step to the confiscation of lands by the Americans. Other rumors hinted that Pueblo lands would soon be seized. Yet another stated that titles were being registered so landowners could be taxed. Another source of discontent, noted by Secretary Vigil himself, was the clergy, "who feared with reason that they would lose their privileges and power, [and] exhorted their parishioners in their confessionals to rebellion. This had its influence among a superstitious and fanatical people."[30] Bent and Beaubien themselves, already deeply involved in Taos feuds, had unwisely antagonized the Taos Indians by trading with their enemies, the Utes, and by encroaching on Pueblo lands. In a region where many a rebellion had succeeded and the last Taos uprising was not yet ten years old, it was not long before certain opponents of American rule began to plot the end of the invader.

In December 1846 Secretary Vigil, who maintained an elaborate political spy system throughout New Mexico, began to hear that Bent and the other leading Americans were to be assassinated. Taos, the more conservative families of Santa Fe, and the clergy seemed to be the centers of dissatisfaction. By taking the necessary precautions, Vigil thwarted an expected uprising on Christmas Eve; Diego Archuleta, who had so wanted to resist at Apache Canyon,

<hr/>

28. George F. A. Ruxton, *Adventures in Mexico and the Rocky Mountains* (New York, 1847), p. 90.

29. John Taylor Hughes, *Doniphan's Expedition; An Account of the Conquest of New Mexico* (Washington, 1914), pp. 48–49. Loomis Morton Ganaway, *New Mexico and the Sectional Controversy, 1846–1861* (Albuquerque, 1944), p. 9.

30. Donaciano Vigil, "History of New Mexico to 1851," Ritch (Box 8), HEH.

and Tomas Ortiz were identified as ringleaders of the still-born rebellion. On January 5, 1847, Governor Bent issued a stirring proclamation condemning these two men for their activities and warning against future acts of treachery. Bent also explained to the public at large that taxes would not be put on land. The registration of land titles served only to make the title more secure, not to despoil men of their property. In the same document Bent reported that Major Doniphan had just won a major victory over Mexican troops at Brazito and tried to show just how futile future resistance to American authority would be.[31]

Satisfied that the rebels had lost heart, Charles Bent—unheedful of the growing anti-American feeling which twice before had endangered his life—journeyed to Taos on business. There on the morning of January 19, 1847, a new set of rebels struck. A band of Taos Indians assaulted Bent's house, battering down the door. While the shrieking women of his household (among them was Mrs. Kit Carson) took refuge in an inner room and dug desperately through a soft adobe wall toward safety, Bent fought off the attackers. The invaders soon wounded Bent fatally, scalped him, and left him to die as they nailed their ghastly trophy to a board and paraded it through the streets.[32]

Other empire builders of Taos were slated for death as well. Sheriff Luis Lee was killed at his door step. The Indians, finding Beaubien away, took instead the life of young Narciso, who was just home from college. Prefect Cornelio Vigil, related both to Mrs. Carson and to Donaciano Vigil and claimant to a princely land grant, also lost his life at their hands. Ranging into the countryside and as far as Mora—though they did not find St. Vrain, now living there—the rebels attacked another symbol of their hatred: Turley's distillery, where the whiskey had been manufactured which had caused trouble with the wild Indians. Before the day was out, Turley lay dead, and his mill and distillery were a smoldering ruin.[33]

The Taos uprising took its bloody toll all over the Rio Arriba, but

31. Charles Bent, "Proclamation" (Santa Fe, January 5, 1847), broadside, HEH.
32. Twitchell, *Military Occupation*, p. 127.
33. Webb, *Adventures*, p. 66.

the rebels in Santa Fe were not so bold or ready. Vigil's spies prevented an outbreak there and saved his own life. When the news of the fighting reached the capital, General Sterling Price, Kearny's successor, force-marched his troops northward along the Rio Grande; after defeating the rebels in several skirmishes along the way, he cornered the remainder in the Taos Pueblo Church. Heavy fighting forced the Indians to surrender and the rebel chieftain, Tomasito, was captured wearing a shirt of Charles Bent's. Although he was made a prisoner of war, Tomasito was soon killed by a guard. The rebellion had been crushed.

Then New Mexicans witnessed a curious example of American justice. The surviving rebels were tried in a civilian court for having borne arms against the United States and for having traitorously attempted to subvert the laws and the Constitution of the Government "and [acted] against the peace and dignity of the Government of the United States." A jury of twelve, with Judge Houghton presiding and St. Vrain as translator, sentenced the ring leader, Jesus Trujillo, and others to be hanged. A witness to the trial, young Hector Lewis Garrard, caught the uncomfortable irony of the situation.

When the concluding words *"muerto, muerto, muerto"*—"dead, dead, dead"—were pronounced by Judge Beaubien [Houghton?] in his solemn and impressive manner, the painful stillness that reigned in the courtroom and the subdued grief manifested by a few by-standers were noticed not without an inward sympathy. The poor wretches sat with immovable features; but I fancied that under the assumed looks of apathetic indifference could be read the deepest anguish. When remanded to jail till the day of execution, they drew their *sarapes* more closely around them and accompanied the armed guard. I left the room, sick at heart. Justice! Out upon the word, when its distorted meaning is the warrant for murdering those who defend to the last their country and their homes.[34]

34. Garrard, *Wah-To-Yah*, pp. 172 73. Twitchell, *Military Occupation*, pp. 140–44.

Even though the trial left many uncertain about its legality, a still larger question remained: exactly who had masterminded this rebellion? The finger of suspicion pointed toward the church leaders and particularly to Padre Martinez. Diego Archuleta, a leader in the Christmas plot, had been one of the Padre's pupils and continued to be a friend. But such men were not to be punished, and the Taos Rebellion quickly became a thing of the past.

The famous anti-American outbreak has usually been called a failure. But it did dramatize to Americans that they had major cultural barriers to overcome before New Mexico could be really theirs. The rebellion also interrupted and complicated the land schemes of the American Party of Taos. Slowly the heirs to Vigil, Lee, Bent, and Narciso Beaubien would collect the torn documents and deeds that lay scattered about the rooms of their dead owners and try to fit the pieces together again.[35] But they would have to wait some twenty years before a lawyer named Elkins and a prophet called Gilpin could begin to make the land-grant business a paying enterprise.

The Taos Rebellion of 1847 also marked the failure of the first American civil government in New Mexico. For the next four years the region was ruled by military commanders so preoccupied with Indian troubles or by nature so autocratic that they showed scant regard for civil rights or the chaotic luxury of elections. To them martial law, warfare against the wild Indians, and obedient federal appointees seemed the first prerequisites to be realized before law and order could be secured. Consequently, the military commanders of New Mexico—who were in fact acting governors—favored either complete military rule or, at best, a territorial form of government with appointive officials.

Resistance and debate over military rule resulted in the birth of the first political parties in American New Mexico. Many an ambitious young American had marched to Santa Fe in 1846 with an eye to a political future there. A reporter described Santa Fe in December

35. The Assembly of 1847 quickly passed a law giving claimants who had lost deeds, leases, or title papers in the Taos Rebellion until 1849 to petition the courts for new title. *Laws of the Assembly of New Mexico, 1847* (Santa Fe, 1848), p. 9.

1847 as "full of lawyers."[36] Texas had just come into the Union with a small population and no territorial apprenticeship. Could New Mexico, with a population of more than 60,000, be denied a similar privilege?

These potential statesmen also realized that the one avenue to success was cooperation with the native population: the vast majority of voters in any electoral process. At the same time, the ever-realistic and flexible New Mexican leaders saw in civil government and statehood the chance to escape military rule, achieve autonomy for their region, and gain local office for themselves. Whether one was anti-American or not, civilian government or statehood seemed preferable to military dictatorship.

After a confused period of military rule under Colonel Sterling Price in 1847, the demand for a civil government became more insistent. The Santa Fe *Republican*, a pioneer newspaper run by James Collins, who had been a merchant in the Santa Fe trade for many years, observed with pointed discontent: "Why call together a legislative body, if its acts may be annulled and made void by the will or caprice of a commanding officer? Why frame laws if the order of a commanding officer is paramount? Why have judges and courts if they can only act at the pleasure of the military authorities?"[37] The sham nature of civil government was made even more apparent when the first Legislative Assembly met in December 1847. Although acting Governor Vigil—who had managed to remain in office through all the military regimes—sent a ringing message to that body, the Assembly's acts were generally disregarded. In February 1848 General Price abolished by proclamation the positions of territorial secretary, district attorney, and marshal and thus assumed direct control over customs. He also assumed the right to levy license fees on gambling houses.[38]

When Colonel John McRae Washington, a bull-headed Scotsman,

36. *Weekly Reveille* [St. Louis], March 1, 1847, YWA.
37. Twitchell, *Military Occupation*, pp. 147–48.
38. Donaciano Vigil, *Governor's Message Delivered to the Senate and House of Representatives* (Santa Fe, December 6, 1847). *Laws Passed by the General Assembly . . . of New Mexico, December, 1847* (Santa Fe, 1848). Headquarters of the Ninth Military District, "Orders No. 10" (Santa Fe, 1848). Ritch, HEH.

became military governor, he continued Price's policies. The opposition to his rule increased so much, however, that on October 10, 1848, a convention met in Santa Fe to consider a course of action. One of the leaders of the protesting group was Padre Martinez, who was made president of the Convention. After some deliberation the delegates petitioned Congress to institute a civilian government, to allow them to appeal cases to the Supreme Court, to elect a local legislature, and to send a delegate to Congress. Martinez' presence at the meeting undoubtedly meant that the conservative anti-American party was represented and that civilian government was chiefly a means of achieving "home rule." Yet among the members was Carlos Beaubien, his enemy, and James Quinn, a lawyer and land speculator. Both men were as interested in land as in civilian rule.[39]

The actions of the 1848 convention unfortunately coincided with the presidential campaign of 1848 and with the broadening national crisis that was developing over the disposal of the spoils of the Mexican War. Guided by James Collins and a number of antislavery Americans in Santa Fe, the convention also took a stand against permitting New Mexico to become a slave state.[40] In the deepening rift between the North and the South over the future of slavery in the Mexican Cession, such a position meant that no help would be forthcoming from Washington, where Polk had declared that the 36° 30' line of the Missouri Compromise should be drawn to the Pacific. For the next two years New Mexico found herself a mere pawn in the bitter Congressional battles, that raged between the end of the war and the Compromise of 1850.

By 1849, in fact, New Mexico's future had become extremely involved with several national questions: the North-South fight over the extension of slavery into the Mexican Cession; the admission of California as a free state—which implied that New Mexico must declare for slavery in order to retain the traditional slave state–free state balance in the Senate; the Texas claim of the Rio Grande for a western border up to and including the Santa Fe district; and, finally, the fate of the Texas debt. For if the United States did not

39. *Petition of the People of New Mexico Assembled in Convention, December 13, 1848* (Santa Fe, 1848), broadside in Bancroft Library, University of California, Berkeley.

40. Ibid.

remunerate Texas bondholders, they in turn would back Texan demands for more territory as a substitute compensation. As is well known, further complications enveloped the issues when it became apparent that the new Taylor Administration differed with both Democrats and moderate Whigs over proposed solutions for these problems.[41]

In national histories of the great crisis of 1848–50, local affairs in the territories concerned have understandably received short shrift. At several stages in the fight over the Mexican Cession, however, activities within New Mexico itself created new problems and deepened the sense of crisis for the government in Washington. Some description of the interplay between the policy-makers in the national capital, the Santa Fe politicians, and the expansionist leaders in Texas is needed to explain the strange sequence of events which eventually resulted in territorial organization for New Mexico.

When Major **Benjamin** Beall succeeded Colonel Washington as the military commander of New Mexico in the summer of 1849, he permitted a new convention to assemble that September. Clearly dominated by Beaubien, St. Vrain, and the American Party, it chose Hugh N. Smith, a Missouri lawyer and close friend of Beaubien's, as delegate to Congress. The success of the convention strongly suggested that by 1849 the military authorities, the remaining territorial officials, and the local prefects and alcaldes had worked out a modus vivendi; a "territorial machine" was actually in operation. Having become used to power, they opposed any sentiment for statehood. Judge Joab Houghton, after an initial brush with the military for ignoring the rulings of the territorial court, appears to have cooperated so completely with the commander and with Governor Vigil that he was pointed out as the leader of the machine. And while these civilian politicians cultivated native sentiment in favor of territorial status, underneath all their public actions lay the constant and growing interest in land grants and their confirmation.[42]

Just as Delegate-elect Smith rode off to Washington, however, a

41. Allan Nevins, *Ordeal of the Union* (2 vols. New York, 1947), *1*, 329 ff.

42. "Journal of the Convention of the Territory of New Mexico" (September 1849), in Territorial Papers of the U.S. Senate, 1789–1873: New Mexico, 1840–1854 (microfilm roll 14), NA. Also Annie H. Abel, ed., *The Official Correspondence of James S. Calhoun* (Washington, 1915), pp. 132–33.

representative of President Zachary Taylor himself appeared in Santa Fe to undercut the territorial movement. Ever since the conquest in 1846, conservative New Mexicans as well as many Missouri merchants and Benton Democrats had wanted immediate admission as a state. Native New Mexicans saw in statehood a chance for home rule, while the Americans were more interested in the federal and state offices that would be created. Ironically, the local statehood schemes fell in with Zachary Taylor's simple but unworkable plan to bypass the slavery issue by admitting New Mexico and California to statehood as soon as possible. To accomplish this, the hero of Monterrey sent agents to both regions to stimulate and guide the local statehood movements.

Taylor's agent in Santa Fe was a former Whig congressman from Georgia, James S. Calhoun. Although his title was Superintendent of New Mexican Indian Affairs, it was soon obvious that his real function was to lobby for statehood. He came to Santa Fe adequately provided with funds and with his two sons-in-law as assistants.[43] Aided by the stand of Senator Benton, who had encouraged the New Mexicans to "meet in convention, provide cheap and simple government, and to take care of yourselves until Congress can provide for you," a dozen Missouri Democrats and Taylor Whigs in Santa Fe stood ready to act.[44] Manuel Alvarez, the former American consul at Santa Fe, saw in statehood a chance to achieve office for himself. Major Richard H. Weightman, an expansive temperamental Washingtonian who had come to Santa Fe with the army, declared himself in favor of statehood. Well versed in the Spanish language, a defender of the Catholic church, and a great favorite of the native New Mexicans, Weightman boasted, drank, and talked his way to the forefront of the statehood forces. Dr. Henry Connelly, long a distinguished resident of New Mexico and now married into the prominent Chavez family of Peralta, lent his name to the new movement.

43. The Taylor administration also sent Colonel George A. McCall to inspect the territory and to write a favorable report for use in Washington. See his *Report to the Secretary of War on the State of New Mexico,* Sen. Ex. Doc. 26, 31st Cong., 2nd Sess. (Washington, 1851) , YWA.

44. Twitchell, *Military Occupation,* pp. 161–62.

Donaciano Vigil and Joab Houghton, seeing the popularity of the statehood cause, began to veer away from the military machine.[45]

The statehood movement formally began when the Calhoun forces started to publish the Santa Fe *New Mexican* in November 1849, a newspaper devoted to the statehood cause. In early December they printed an "Address to the people of New Mexico," in which they not only declared for statehood but used the popular arguments that "as a state we could best resist the encroachments of Texas," and get rid of "anti-Republican and badly administered despotism." Using Taylor's name discreetly, the statehood forces—whom everyone dubbed the "Alvarez faction"—spoke with such persuasion that the territorialists became alarmed enough to issue their own "manifesto." Among its sixty-two signers were nearly all the office-holders under the military government right down to the alcaldes, sheriffs, and clerks of court.[46]

While the statehood forces gathered strength in Santa Fe, Delegate Smith arrived in Washington to find the nation seemingly on the brink of disunion. He must have been shocked to realize how involved New Mexico was with the fate of the country. Taylor in his annual message to Congress and in subsequent notes during the winter of 1849–50 stuck to his original position that New Mexico should be admitted as a state and that the Texas boundary question should then be settled by the Supreme Court as an issue involving the two states.[47] Both Southerners and Texans were unalterably opposed to such a program.

The New Mexican delegate must have been further alarmed to discover that on November 29, 1849, the Texas legislature had passed a "Joint Resolution to Protest the Election of Hugh N. Smith" and that in the debates preceding its adoption, fire-eating Texans had proposed that armed forces be sent "to suppress the existing rebellion in Santa Fe" and to "straighten those rascally traitors into a sense of

45. Richard H. Weightman, "Statehood Memorial, September 11, 1851"; "Manuel Alvarez to U.S. Senate," July 8, 1850; in Territorial Papers of the U.S. Senate: New Mexico, NA.

46. Twitchell, *Military Occupation*, pp. 162–64.

47. *Message from the President*, House Ex. Doc. 17, 31st Cong., 1st Sess. (Washington, 1850), p. 2.

duty." Still another irate Texas legislator had called the convention that elected Smith "renegade white men, and deluded Mexicans and Indians."[48]

Faced with such hostility, Smith—undoubtedly advised by Benton—knew that the territorial cause was for the moment hopeless. He lingered in Washington, nevertheless, to hear the famous eight propositions which the aged Henry Clay laid before the Senate on January 29, 1850, and to listen to the impassioned orators carry on the interminable debate. By April 1850 Smith had come around to the Benton point of view: New Mexico must act for itself. In a public letter sent to his constituents that month, Smith declared that his mission to Washington had failed. Damning all sides, he complained that "the doctrine of the slave-holding states in regard to their domestic institutions is nonintervention, but with regard to yours it is *instant* intervention." The neutrality of the administration, he felt, was actually virtual surrender to Texan demands. "For the present," he concluded, "rely upon yourselves; assert your rights by the establishment of a State government interdicting slavery."[49]

Again it was Delegate Smith's fate to follow rather than guide affairs. Before his message could reach Santa Fe, the statehood party there heard rumors that the Texans were planning to seize all of New Mexico. And to confirm their worst fears, on April 15 a set of Texas commissioners appeared in Santa Fe to organize New Mexico into four Texas counties. Headed by Colonel Robert S. Neighbors, the commission solemnly protested to Colonel John Munroe—Beall's successor—"against any movement in favor of State until Texas has extended her jurisdiction over this portion of her Territory."[50]

Desperate acts were needed to counter this latest invasion, which was a threat to statehood men and territorial party alike. As various Missourians tried to work up a mob spirit of violence against the visiting Texans, both parties persuaded Colonel Munroe as com-

48. "Debate in the [Texas] House of Representatives on the Santa Fe Question," *Southwestern American* (November 29, 1849), pp. 23–31, YWA.

49. *Speech of Hugh N. Smith of New Mexico to the People of that Territory* (Washington, April 14, 1850), p. 20, YWA.

50. *Message from the President . . . June 17, 1850,* Sen. Ex. Doc. 56, 31st Cong., 1st Sess., p. 15.

mander and military governor of New Mexico to issue a call to elect
delegates to a constitutional convention. Fully aware that President
Taylor would approve his action, Munroe issued a call only eight
days after the Texans had arrived. Munroe set May 6 as the date of
election and May 15 for the opening of the convention.

This was a mercurially swift schedule for a frontier community.
Even more whirlwind was the decision of the former territorial party
to capture the statehood movement. The very men who had sent
Delegate Smith to Washington now politicked to be delegates to the
constitutional convention. Temporarily overwhelming the Calhoun-
Taylor forces, they secured a majority of the seats. Their opponents,
the real statehood men, claimed that this surprise victory could not
have occurred without the connivance of Colonel Munroe, who had
asked county prefects to choose the returning boards. As part of the
"territorial machine" the prefects saw to it that the "territorialists"
rather than the statehood men were elected.[51]

Thus the St. Vrain, Beaubien, Houghton, and Vigil faction, posing
as statehood men, dominated the convention, which met on May 15
and in ten days framed an organic act, declared for a free state, and
advocated an American public education system. The document, purporting to come from native New Mexicans, appears to have been
written some months before by Joab Houghton and others, sent to
Washington for approval by certain senators, and returned for use in
the convention.[52]

Much has been written about New Mexico and the antislavery
question. But when all is said and done, the declaration in favor of
a free state was simply a way for New Mexicans, both natives and
former Missourians, to express a bitter anti-Texas feeling. Texas and
the slavery congressmen were allies in the crisis of 1850. This meant
that if New Mexico declared for slavery, the new state might soon
be a Texan New Mexico. Neither St. Vrain, the Missouri merchants,
nor native New Mexicans cared to reroute their trade through Texan
channels or to orient their politics and land-grant troubles toward

51. *R. H. Weightman to the Congress of the United States* (Washington, 1851),
pp. 4–5, YWA
52. Ibid., p. 1.

Austin. Twice before, New Mexicans had turned back a Texan–Santa Fe expedition. The latest invasion by Colonel Neighbors was, in their eyes, but another attempt to subvert their province. What neither abolitionist nor slaveholder ever realized was, first, that New Mexicans were essentially neutral about the slavery controversy but were fiercely anti-Texan; and, secondly, that the business houses of Missouri had no intention of letting Texas get control of their Santa Fe trade. This was the real reason for Senator Benton's suggestion that they "act for themselves." It was these local considerations as much as the dictates of Washington which guided New Mexican affairs during the period 1848–50.

Events were now reaching a painful climax both in New Mexico and in Washington. In May the news reached Taylor via telegraph from Texas not only that the commissioners had gone to Santa Fe but that Texan forces had occupied El Paso and planned to take the rest of New Mexico. Old Rough and Ready was so furious at this latest defiance that he announced his intention to order Colonel Munroe to resist.[53] Now it was the Southern congressmen and the Texans who were angry. Governor Bell of Texas ran out of expletives in his denunciations of Taylor. A moderate Whig like Alexander H. Stephens was so alienated by the President's stand that he roared in print: "the first federal gun that shall be fired against the people of Texas, without the authority of law . . . will be the signal for freemen from Delaware to the Rio Grande to rally to the rescue."[54] Bitter congressmen threatened to impeach the President, and his orders to Colonel Munroe were investigated.

As Congress pondered the latest presidential stand, the date for the ratification of the New Mexican constitution and the election of state officials approached. In Santa Fe the Taylor-Calhoun forces chose Dr. Henry Connelly and Manuel Alvarez as their candidates for governor and lieutenant governor and picked another merchant, William S. Messervy, as a candidate for Congress. To defeat these men, remnants of the old Taos American party—in alliance with the military, the federal judges, the prefects, alcaldes, and the territorial

53. Nevins, *Ordeal of the Union, 1,* 329–30.
54. Ibid., p. 331.

newspapers—went into action. Thomas Cabeza de Baca, a leading New Mexican conservative, was chosen to run for governor, while Ceran St. Vrain was selected for second place.[55] The battle for New Mexican statehood was on.

The intensity of the local fight can be seen in a letter of a young lawyer, Theodore Wheaton, to William Z. Angney. Embroiled in the election at Arroyo Hondo, Wheaton appealed for help. Having heard that Juan Baptiste LeConte was to be arrested so that he would be of no use on election day, Wheaton exclaimed:

This is nothing but a dirty party trick which is of a piece with all their conduct at this election in this district.

You had better have an American of our party at Mora on the day of the election to keep things straight. We have a large majority there if they do not get skeared off the track . . . be sure and send one or two from Santa Fe for we have not got enough here to do the fighting in Taos.[56]

Increasing rumors of Texas invasion, news of the seizure of El Paso, and Taylor's support brought both the St. Vrain and Connelly parties to the realization that, while they might differ on elections to the legislature and local office, they must continue to present a solid front to the world and to Congress. Just before the election both sides appear to have agreed to vote for the constitution. With suspicious solidarity voters went to the poll on June 20 to approve the Constitution 6,371 to 39. At this point even Colonel Munroe—who was greatly disliked—achieved a temporary popularity when he "persuaded" Colonel Neighbors and his commissioners to leave Santa Fe.[57]

The election of the state officials was a less harmonious story,

55. Ibid., pp. 330–31. *R. H. Weightman to the Congress*, p. 7. McCall, *Report*, pp. 10–15.

56. Theodore D. Wheaton to William Z. Angney, June 16, 1850, Ritch (Box 7), HEH.

57. Nevins, *Ordeal of the Union, 1*, p. 329, portrays Colonel Munroe as the instigator of the convention and a pro-state man. New Mexican evidence suggests that Munroe was opposed to statehood, while also opposing Texans. See *Weightman to the Congress*, p. 7.

however. By hard fighting the statehood men—led by Calhoun, Alvarez, and Connelly—got the native vote and defeated Cabeza de Baca, St. Vrain, and the territorialists. When the count was in, Connelly had 4,000 to Baca's 2,000. The personal popularity of St. Vrain merited him 3,465 votes; nevertheless, Alvarez managed to win by a majority of more than a thousand.

For New Mexicans the worst seemed to be over. The "state" legislature met, and although a Munroe faction loyal to the military tried to disrupt affairs by refusing to be seated, the remaining members chose Richard Weightman and Francis Cunningham as senators and petitioned Congress for admission.[58] Yet on the eve of success, hope was again deferred. When Acting Governor Alvarez—in Connelly's absence—sent out circulars of direction to the probate judges, Colonel Munroe, still on the territorialist side, countermanded the orders and declared that the new government must remain inoperative until he could permit it to function.

Furious at this latest evidence of military tyranny, Alvarez dictated a primer on civil rights to the autocratic commander. The people had a sovereign right to form a government without consulting anyone, he declared, and in the absence of congressional legislation they had a duty to do just that. Alvarez warned Munroe that even the President himself could not delegate more powers to the Colonel than he himself had. Munroe's military regime, argued the Lieutenant Governor, was already "suspended by the return of peace." Hard upon Alvarez' note, the legislature adopted a resolution against the "sinking, ineffective and abhorrent system which they had peacefully respected for nearly four years." Echoing Alvarez' and Benton's espousal of sovereignty, they reaffirmed the people's "sacred right" to institute government.[59] Convening side by side, two governments—one military and one civilian—claimed to be the proper authority in New Mexico in the summer of 1850, while in the distance the hovering Texans watched.

58. Twitchell, *Military Occupation*, pp. 181–92 passim. Among the candidates defeated for local office in this election was ex-Governor Armijo, who wrote Vigil somewhat sadly: "I am here as a Saint whose day has passed." Armijo to Vigil, July 16, 1850, Ritch (Box 7), HEH.
59. Twitchell, *Military Occupation*, pp. 190–92.

To end this impossible situation, Governor Alvarez sent the New Mexican constitution and the news of its ratification to President Taylor for approval. As its bearer was coming into the fringe of settlements east of Fort Leavenworth, fate again intervened to delay success. On July 4 President Taylor, after enduring a stiflingly hot day of long-winded patriotic ceremonies and speeches at the base of the unfinished Washington monument, became ill with cholera morbus. By July 9 he was dead, and with him died any chance of statehood for New Mexico in the near future. Although the Santa Fe constitution arrived some hours before Taylor's death, no action could be taken. The new president, Millard Fillmore, proved to be more sympathetic to Clay's compromise measures than to any of Taylor's proposals; consequently he sent the New Mexican document to Congress without any recommendation for action. There it died a formal death when a proposal by Seward that New Mexico be proclaimed a state did not receive a single supporting vote.[60]

With that decisive defeat it was clear that New Mexico would become a territory, as St. Vrain and others had wanted all along. After Clay's proposals failed to pass as an omnibus bill, the separate sections were shepherded through the Senate by Stephen A. Douglas and Senator Pearce of Maryland. Fillmore also applied pressure from the White House for minor amendments here and there.[61] By late August the bills had passed the Senate, and by September 15 all were through the House. The great crisis was over, and Clay, Douglas, Webster, and Fillmore were the heroes of the hour. New Mexicans, looking at the clauses of the Compromise of 1850 which affected their region, found that Texas did gain 33,000 miles of New Mexican territory, but not the 70,000 she had desired. The ten-million debt assumption bill had further quieted the outraged Lone Star solons and the worried New York bondholders. New Mexico itself received territorial organization, as did Utah, without reference to slavery.[62]

60. Frederic Bancroft, *The Life of W. H. Seward* (2 vols. New York, 1900), *1*, 280–81.

61. Robert J. Rayback, *Millard Fillmore: Biography of a President* (Buffalo, 1929), pp. 248–52. Nevins, *Ordeal of the Union*, *1*, 344.

62. For details see Nevins, *Ordeal of the Union*, *1*, 340–43; and Rayback, *Fillmore*, pp. 248–53.

Territorial organization came none too soon in New Mexico; for Colonel Munroe, harassed by Indian problems and badgered by Missouri merchants and lawyers turned politician, had become increasingly arbitrary. In late September, however, the opinionated Colonel learned that Congress had organized a territorial government for New Mexico and that henceforth he was to "abstain from all further interference in civil as well as political affairs of that country."[63] Munroe appears to have withheld news of the Compromise of 1850 from the territory as long as possible; but when Taylor's Indian superintendent, James S. Calhoun, received official notice of his appointment as governor of the new territory, Munroe's day was over.

Thus ended a four-year military rule by a thousand or so Americans over more than 50,000 Spanish-Mexicans. It was a prosperous time for this isolated people with the market of a visiting nonproductive population suddenly thrust in their midst. But it also must have reminded them of the old days of autocratic rule by the *jefe politicos* and of the perennial scrapping between them and the Church. The prefects and alcaldes, backed by American force, also seemed more arbitrary than ever, and even the wild Indians were worse than before.[64] The cooperation of American politicians with the Army to establish a military dictatorship in New Mexico was certainly a poor example of the liberty and democracy General Kearny had promised them in 1846. *Quien sabe?* Perhaps there would not be much change under American rule after all.

63. Twitchell, *Military Occupation*, p. 196.
64. Ibid., pp. 179–80.

4

In Hostile Array:
Civil Government, 1851–1861

> They [the Legislature] do so many foolish things that they
> can hardly be enumerated. The governor and myself are
> almost out of heart in trying to do for this people, and have
> about come to the conclusion that they are past redemption.
> The fools are talking about a state government, when they will
> not be ready for it under twenty-five years. There are good
> men among them but the bad ones [are] much more the
> larger number.
>
> W. W. H. Davis, December 25, 1854

 " 'Let the dead go to the bier, and the living to good
cheer.' Our business is with the future." So spoke the
first governor of territorial New Mexico, James S.
Calhoun, in a ringing inaugural address on March 3,
1851.[1] Having worked faithfully for New Mexican
statehood for two years, he had received the governorship as a compensatory reward from the Whig Administration of
Millard Fillmore, when the Compromise of 1850 made New Mexico a
territory instead of a state. Calhoun was an honorable and intelligent
man, but his career as governor was to be frustrated by so many diffi-

1. James S. Calhoun, "Inaugural Address," March 3, 1851, MS in Journal of
Proceedings, New Mexico, Department of State TP, NA.

culties it could scarcely be praised for its accomplishments.[2] His successors in office: William Carr Lane (1852–53), David Meriwether (1853–57), and Abraham Rencher (1857–61) were baffled by such similar problems that the administrations of the four men can be considered jointly.

Their first task was the delicate one of persuading "the dead" to "go to the bier"; that is, they had to retire certain traditional political habits of the New Mexican populace in order to introduce American customs. When Calhoun took office, for example, he assumed a place that for two hundred years Indian and white alike had looked to as a final court of appeal. To the sprawling Palace of the Governors came scores of petitioners asking redress from an unjust decision by a local alcalde or county prefect. Forty Indians might come in a day, each with a tale of woe about a stolen horse or a lost sheep. John Greiner, Calhoun's secretary, noted wearily in September 1852 that: "14 Jicarillas came in today to see the Tata (Calhoun) with a long story about a horse and a mule which they say a Mexican has taken from them— all as I believe got up for an excuse to get something to eat."[3]

The Pueblos harangued the governor about land disputes with other Pueblos or about the unfair apportionment of water from the main *acequia*. He was swept up in a feud between the Acomas and the Lagunas over land and the possession of certain religious relics, which dragged on for so long it seemed an Indian version of the Hatfields and the Coys.[4] Calhoun's successor, Lane, exclaimed in exasperation that his life was "one eternal round of appeals, written and verbal, from Mexican and Indian, and sometimes from Americans for reparations, of every description of wrongs . . . besides getting at least fifty embraces from Indians and sometimes from Mexicans."[5]

While bracing themselves for the next affectionate onslaught of petitioners, the governors were faced with the task of creating county

2. Abel, *Calhoun*, pp. 1 ff. Twitchell, *Leading Facts*, 2, 282. Will A. Keleher, *Turmoil in New Mexico, 1846–1868* (Santa Fe, 1952), p. 130.

3. Annie H. Abel, ed., "The Journal of John Greiner," *Old Santa Fe, 3* (1916), 243.

4. *Message of His Excellency James S. Calhoun to the First Territorial Legislature, December 1, 1851* (Santa Fe, 1852), p. 7.

5. Ralph P. Bieber, ed., "The Letters of William Carr Lane, 1852–1854," Historical Society of New Mexico, *Publications, 6,* (1928), 187–88.

and local government. In these first years they had the power to appoint prefects—or probate judges—to the nine counties of New Mexico. In certain cases they also appointed or confirmed justices of the peace as well as the county sheriff. By tradition the prefect and alcalde had many powers. And now that under American law landed gentlemen and the clergy were not immune from their jurisdiction, the new appointees—especially in Calhoun's administration—proceeded to settle old personal prejudices, to curb church activities and fees, and to use the high rate of illegitimacy as an excuse to reassign lands to new heirs.[6]

Assuming a political and economic control that smacked of tyranny, the probate judges and the local justices read into their new office the broad powers of an alcalde and were soon trying criminal cases of a sort clearly reserved for the territorial courts. One of the major issues of the first territorial decade was the struggle by federal judges to save some jurisdiction for the federal courts. In 1858 Judge Hezekiah Johnson sarcastically noted that "the District Courts have been *cur*-tailed of much of their jurisdiction, which has been *dove*-tailed into the Probate Courts by [the] Legislative Assembly. I would not be surprised if the next Assembly should pass an act repealing the Organic Act and establishing a Monarchy."[7]

The probate judges also controlled the election machinery, which meant that they had a major voice in determining who should be elected to the Assembly, who would become delegate, and who would succeed to local office.[8] It was no wonder that theirs eventually became the most sought-after of all local political positions in New Mexico.

In choosing these men, Calhoun had to move carefully. With the memory of the Taos Rebellion still vivid in his mind, he adopted the policy of turning local government over to the more conservative and anti-American New Mexicans in an effort to appease this group. The alcaldes and prefects he appointed were those very men who had

6. Donaciano Vigil to Antonio Jose Otero, 1852, Ritch (Box 10), HEH.

7. Hezekiah S. Johnson to William Watts H. Davis, February 27, 1858, Davis Letters, YWA.

8. William Lee Harper, "A History of New Mexico Election Laws" (Master's thesis, University of New Mexico, 1927), p. 8. See also *New Mexican Session Laws, 1851* (Santa Fe, 1852), Chap. 28, Secs. 8–44.

held office under the Mexican regime. Determined not to antagonize the Church, he dealt with what John W. Caughey has alliteratively called "the padre problem in politics" by recognizing that the priests were often the seat of power in a given community and that Church and State had virtually been the joint rulers of New Mexico in the past. Calhoun listened to their counsel and often moved accordingly. To Donaciano Vigil such compromises with the old guard were tragic. He remarked to Antonio Jose Otero that "the miserable Colonel Calhoun" has "united with the vile clergy of the Territory." While "he has been able to quiet the people," it was done through corrupt alcaldes and prefects who willingly stuffed ballot boxes. "The great principle of freedom," sighed Vigil, "has been so quenched out that it is enjoyed only nominally."[9] Whatever principles were lacking, the result was that Calhoun soon had a political machine of sorts in operation.

The discovery that control of local government meant control of elections determined the makeup of the first territorial Assembly of New Mexico. This body and the delegate were the only elective officials provided for on the federal side of the territorial system. The New Mexican legislature proved to be similar to that of other territories in that it was the open cockpit for local factions. Its collective attitude was unusual, however, for early territorial assemblies were made up of the more politically minded members of the native leading families—the "educated gentlemen of the provinces," Colonel Edwin Sumner called them—members of the clergy, and a sprinkling of Americans.[10] The domination of the Assembly by a few families did not mean that they stood as a united body to protect their interests. Family feuds, personal dislikes, and general division over the question whether to cooperate with the Americans or to resist them actually meant that the Spanish-Americans practiced an elaborate and complicated politics of faction and disunity.

The various groups existing in the first New Mexican Assembly, while their differences can be exaggerated, were to be fairly typical

9. John W. Caughey, "Early Federal Relations with New Mexico" (Master's thesis, University of California at Berkeley, 1926), pp. 62–63. Abel, *Calhoun*, pp. 370 ff. Vigil to Otero, 1852, Ritch (Box 10), HEH.
10. *Laws of the Territory of New Mexico . . . 1851–52* (Santa Fe, 1852), p. 422.

of those appearing there for the next decade. Of the thirty-nine
members of the House and the Council, for example, four were priests.
In rank the foremost of these was the Vicar General, the Reverend
Juan Felipe Ortiz. A member of various New Mexican departmental
assemblies since 1825 and the representative of New Mexico in the
Mexican Congress from 1837 to 1841, he was a leading figure in the
territory. Since Governor Armijo felt Ortiz was a man of such persuasive powers, he asked him during the Texas invasion of 1841 to "create
a spirit of opposition" to the Texans among the Mexicans.[11] When
Kearny appeared on New Mexican soil in 1846, Ortiz also urged
resistance; dissatisfied with the outcome of the American invasion
it is likely that he was one of the instigators of the abortive December
1846 uprising. Now in 1851, despite war, rebellion, and a change
of government, the Vicar General appeared as a member of the territorial Council and in its second session was to be its president. At
the same time, this intrepid churchman was judge of probate in
Santa Fe County.

Another member of the conservative church faction in the first
Assembly was Padre Martinez, whose role in territorial affairs though
considerably quieter after the Taos Rebellion, was still important
enough for him to be elected president of the Council in its June
session.

From the haciendas to the South—where most of the *ricos* lived—
came two other factions. There was the stately anti-American don,
Jose Leandro Perea of Bernalillo, who tended to cooperate with the
more conservative members. Opposing him were Francisco Antonio
Otero and the New Mexican merchant, Juan Cristobal Armijo, who
were pro-American in their leaning. From the North, Padre Martinez's brother, Vicente, had been elected to protect the interests of the
big family and the Rio Arriba.

If the Spanish-Americans were faction-ridden, the few Americans
were almost equally so in that they reflected particular economic
interests. Ex-delegate Hugh N. Smith represented the American
merchant and speculator and the St. Vrain and Beaubien interests.

11. Charles F. Coan, *A History of New Mexico* (3 vols. Chicago, 1925), *1*,
312, 318, 321, 363.

A shy young lawyer of slight build but great stamina, Theodore D. Wheaton, also appeared in the Assembly as a friend if not agent of the American party of Taos. It appears that a small but influential German Jewish merchant group, who had come to New Mexico in the wake of Kearny's troops, were represented by George Gold. A burly Texan rancher and lawyer, Spruce M. Baird, who was interested in land grants, completed the roster.

Naturally such an incompatible set of men did not work in harmony. As James L. Collins, editor of the Sante Fe *Gazette,* commented pessimistically, "The legislature is in Session but they are so completely under the influence of party that they are likely to do little."[12] His complaint was amply justified in the second session, when it took three ballots to elect the doorkeeper. The existence of faction, however, did not prevent certain working alliances. Throughout the first Assembly Baird and the New Mexican members of the House outmaneuvered and outvoted a Santa Fe clique of Americans. In the 1853–54 session the land-grant men with Taos connections won both the presidency of the Council and the speaker's chair in the Assembly, while the native New Mexicans took a temporary back seat.[13]

The New Mexicans did not lead in the first years, but they carried many a point by voting no. Never having paid taxes, the Assembly showed a healthy reluctance to tax anyone but grog shops, gambling places, and American merchants—who in turn refused to pay up until the tax laws had been tested in the courts.[14] This meant that the territorial bills had to be paid in warrants or drafts, and speculation over their fluctuating value became a major local business. Governor Lane bluntly told the 1852 solons: "your revenue laws are so defective that sufficient funds are not provided for the ordinary purposes of government." Three years later, Acting Governor W. H. H. Davis complained that "the treasury is without funds and the credit of the territory nearly bankrupt" because of speculation in warrants. "The real wealth is not taxed, but all the burdens are borne by the active

---

12. James L. Collins to Jane M. Edgar, June 30, 1851, Ritch (Box 8), HEH.
13. *Journal of the House of Representatives . . . of New Mexico . . . First Assembly, Second Session* (Santa Fe, 1852). See also *House and Council Journals of the Third Assembly* (Santa Fe, 1854).
14. *House Journal, New Mexico . . . First Assembly, Second Session,* pp. 8–9, 29, 227–28.

business interests of the country," he said.[15] The uncertain joys of speculation in warrants were so attractive, however, that it was 1890 before this expensive and dubious system of public finance was abolished in New Mexico.

Quite used to peonage and Indian slavery, the Assembly members refused to end these two institutions until a federal law in 1867 forced them to do so. On the very eve of the Civil War, Governor Rencher found it necessary to veto a law which declared that all captured Indians were to be slaves of their captors.[16]

A certain quaint charm also attended their criminal legislation. In an act "To Regulate the Proceedings of Judges, Sheriffs, and Constables against Drunkards, Prostitutes and Pimps, in their Various Classes," the pimp was to be "publicly whipped, receiving thirty lashes, and furthermore, shall be carried upon a Jack Ass, upon some feast day, through the streets among the people, in which passage until its conclusion, they shall be followed by a town crier, who shall cry not less than five times the cause of such punishment."[17] An embarrassed Governor Meriwether secured its repeal in 1854.

The Assembly also saw in the American pressure for public schools a threat to religion, the likelihood of taxation, and an unwelcome process of Americanization. The members must have listened in disbelief as their interpreter translated Calhoun's request into Spanish not only for public schools but for female academies as well! Despite constant pressure of the governors, the school bills passed between 1851 and 1861 were suspiciously ineffectual. The real attitude of the New Mexican was revealed in 1856 when an educational tax bill was voted down in a popular referendum by 5,016 to 37. Although the legislature did approve of a bill to create a university, that institution was to remain inoperative until voluntary donors had contributed $7,000 to its upkeep.[18] Despite yearly pleas by the governor, an effective public school law was not passed until 1891.

15. *Message of W. W. H. Davis, Acting Governor of the Territory of New Mexico*, December 3, 1855 (Santa Fe, 1855), pp. 8–9.

16. "Message of Governor Rencher to the Legislative Assembly," in *Council Journal, New Mexico, 1860* (Santa Fe, 1861), p. 15.

17. *Laws of the Territory of New Mexico* (Santa Fe, 1853), p. 97.

18. Calhoun, *Message . . . December 1, 1851.* Caughey, "Early Federal Relations," pp. 64–65. W. W. H. Davis, *El Gringo, or New Mexico and Her People* (New York, 1857), p. 195.

The maintenance of a cultural status quo did not mean that the Assembly resisted other American importations. Guided by experienced American politicians, the members were quick to initiate the habit of requesting appropriations from Congress for territorial projects. In 1853 they asked the federal government to pay $10,000 to James L. Collins, Juan C. Armijo, and Jose Leandro Perea, an amount which the legislature had "borrowed" from these men in 1852 to meet the expenses of the first Assembly. They also petitioned Congress for a penitentiary, for $50,000 to build a wagon road to Taos, and for a mineral and geological survey of the territory. When wells had to be dug in the Jornada del Muerto and $15,000 was needed to retore the "ruined Archives," or money had to be found to pay for volunteers against the Indians, the Assembly turned to Washington with alacrity.[19] "There is much the same system of log-rolling practiced here as elsewhere," wrote Governor Davis, "and the Mexicans show themselves keen, cunning men in politics—quite a match for the Americans."[20]

It was in the field of funds for building a capitol that the Assembly reached a frontier norm for pork barrel handouts. The indefatigable Joab Houghton, now no longer the chief justice, and having become bankrupt as a merchant, suddenly remembered that his first profession had been that of a practical engineer. Why not return to that earlier calling and be of service to the new territory by agreeing to build a suitable capitol building? A cooperative Assembly passed a law permitting the governor to appoint three building commissioners of which Joab Houghton was one. Then they asked Congress for $68,000 —Houghton's estimate of the cost of the construction. At first Washington granted only $20,000, but when the Assembly renewed its plea a year later, $70,000 was forthcoming. Ceran St. Vrain, realizing that there was money in Hougthon's manner of building, secured a lumber contract from the ex-judge, and by 1855 Houghton's own vision had so broadened that he was engaged in plans to build the new penitentiary as well. In his report to Washington he solemnly recom-

19. *Laws of the Territory of New Mexico . . . 1851–52* (Santa Fe, 1852), pp. 215, 224–27. Ibid., 1853–54, pp. 174–78, 180, 182.
20. Robert D. Hepler, "William Watts Hart Davis in New Mexico" (Master's thesis, University of New Mexico, 1941), pp. 66–72 passim.

mended that the prison be constructed of stone and not adobe, for "I am now informed that a visible change has taken place in the climate of New Mexico." The rainfall had become more plentiful. With increased humidity, he warned, an adobe prison soon would "melt."[21]

Four years after Houghton had begun the capitol, Governor Rencher had to ask the Assembly to petition for more money with which to finish it. And in 1859 Congress gave the territory still another $60,000 to complete the state house and penitentiary. A year later Rencher was impertinent enough to ask the practical engineer just how the "new" capitol was coming along. The progress report was not for himself, explained Rencher, but for the Secretary of the Treasury, who was becoming inquisitive.[22] Like Penelope at her web, Houghton seemed unable to bring his task to an end: *manana* was always the deadline. Indeed, the elusive capitol would be nearly twenty years in the building.

Even without a modern building in which to meet, by 1861 the Assembly was an established institution, representing the fifteen or twenty wealthy families of New Mexico. Though riddled with factions, it did act as a check on governors and on any change in the social, religious, and economic status quo. Instead of serving as an instrument through which American law and government might come to New Mexico, it expressed instead the ideas of a conservative and tradition-minded society. The Assembly could do this, since American pioneers did not flood into this part of the Southwest as they did into Texas and California. Thus New Mexico remained basically New Mexican throughout the 1850s. Where there had been eight Americans in the House of Representatives in 1851, there were only two in 1859 and two in the Council. The governors, with their eyes on the future, urged them to learn English and to conduct their sessions in the national language, but to no avail. St. George Cooke, one of the keenest of observers in the Southwest, had predicted all this in the

21. Joab Houghton, "Estimate"; Houghton to Building Commissioners, Santa Fe, May 28, 1853; David Meriwether to Building Commissioners, September, 1853, Ritch (Boxes 10, 11), HEH.
22. *House Journal, New Mexico, 1858* (Santa Fe, 1859), p. 11. *Council Journal, New Mexico, 1860* (Santa Fe, 1861), p .17.

year of conquest. "There will be a territorial government for thirty years—and the language will not change faster than the color of the citizens."[23] The dead would be a long time going to the bier.

The problem of reconciling American and Spanish-Mexican political habits and institutions was complicated by the fact that the governors, until 1857, were saddled with the duties of Superintendent of Indian Affairs. Actually the Indian population probably equaled that of the white inhabitants, so these duties were heavy ones. Between 7,000 and 10,000 were peaceful Indians of the Pueblo, Zuni, and Moquis tribes, who were sedentary agriculturalists. The majority of the Indians, however, were still wild nomads who lived by hunting and raiding. The white settlements of New Mexico could be likened to an attenuated island chain awash in a sea of hostiles stretching from San Cristobal in the north down to El Paso.

To the north and west of Taos roamed the Southern Utes. Their territory overlapped that of the troublesome Navajo, who lived in the northwest quarter of New Mexico and in northeastern Arizona. Some 15,000 of them lived in the canyons and valleys of this wild mountain fastness. South of Albuquerque and westward toward Arizona, the Gila Apaches threatened the few settlers who dared to exploit the Santa Rita Mines or travelers, passing through their domain. On the eastern plains and up the narrow Pecos River past Las Vegas, the Mescalero and Jicarillas rode their ponies, and there, too, bands of Comanche and Kiowas wandered. Occupying nearly four-fifths of New Mexico, the wild Indian population in 1850 numbered between forty and fifty-eight thousand.[24]

At first nearly all the tribes had responded favorably to American occupation, naïvely thinking that any enemy to Mexico must, perforce, be an ally of theirs. This brief illusion was quickly shattered, and soon they were plundering the well-stocked wagon trains of the newcomers, picking off isolated travelers, and taking advantage of the confusion accompanying the transfer of power from Mexican to American authorities. Kearny, almost immediately after his arrival,

23. Cooke, *Conquest,* pp. 32–33.
24. Bender, *March of Empire,* pp. 11–13.

had been forced to send troops into the field to overawe the Navajo, Ute, and Apache tribes. Hastily made treaties were soon broken, and a second expedition under Colonel Washington in 1849 failed to accomplish any satisfactory settlement between Indians and whites.[25]

Having served as Indian superintendent for two years before becoming governor, Calhoun had formulated an Indian policy by 1851. His first problem was to persuade the federal government to distinguish between the Pueblo and wild Indians, to give the former property rights, and if possible to let them vote.[26] After a period of confusion lasting into Governor Meriwether's administration, the Pueblos' property rights were confirmed, but they were denied the vote. In dealing with them, it was really a question of granting legal and civil privileges; but with the wild Indians it was a question of curbing their raids, transforming them into peaceful agriculturalists, and changing their entire way of life.

Calhoun's program for these wild tribes was an intelligent one. Subdue them, he argued, give them an agent, and secure "compulsory enlightenment . . . enforced at the point of a bayonet." "Spend your millions now," he pleaded, "and it will cost little in the future, whereas if you spend little now expensive wars will be the result."[27] Calhoun was not averse to feeding the wild tribes or to adding local militia to the few federal troops there in order to "enforce enlightenment." And to implement his program, he organized a territorial militia and appointed Ceran St. Vrain and Kit Carson to command volunteer companies to guard the northern frontier. Other officers were appointed in the south. In 1851 and 1852 the governor succeeded in making treaties with the Apaches east of the Rio Grande, with the Utes at Abiquiu, and with still other Apaches at Jemez west of the river.[28]

Calhoun's success in Indian affairs depended upon three factors: the cooperation of the military commander within the territory, the appropriation of funds in Washington for goods and food, and the existence of a corps of subagents who would carry out his policies.

25. Ibid., p. 150.
26. Abel, *Calhoun*, pp. 53, 78–80.
27. Ibid., p. 55.
28. Bender, *March of Empire*, pp. 154–55.

Unfortunately, none of these necessary items was forthcoming. Despite the most eloquent pleas from Calhoun, there was an almost criminal indifference in Washington to the Indian situation in the Southwest. Calhoun's agents, with some notable exceptions, followed the long-established Indian Bureau tradition of being more interested in lining their own pockets than in Indian welfare and general peace. But Calhoun's greatest problem was the new military commander of New Mexico, Colonel Edwin Vose Sumner.

Sumner was an intelligent but stubborn Vermonter with many years of experience at frontier posts. He had come to New Mexico in 1851 to replace the unpopular Colonel Munroe.[29] A vigorous man dedicated to his profession, he was appalled at the condition of his command and the barrenness of the country and disgusted with the government and inhabitants of New Mexico. In a highly unflattering report to Washington made in 1852 he declared:

> The New Mexicans are thoroughly debased and totally incapable of self-government, and there is no latent quality about them that can ever make them respectable.
>
> They have more Indian blood than Spanish, and in some respects are below the Pueblo Indians, for they are not as honest or as industrious.
>
> . . . No civil Government emanating from the Government of the United States can be maintained here without the aid of a military force; in fact, without its being virtually a military government. . . . All branches of this civil government have equally failed —the executive for want of power, the judiciary from the total incapacity and want of principle in juries; and the legislative from want of knowledge.[30]

From his remarks it was obvious that Sumner felt that he himself was the logical director of Indian relations and the savior of that worthless country. To institute his own program for New Mexico, he

29. Ibid., p. 153.
30. *Congressional Globe*, 32nd Cong., 2nd Sess. (January 10, 1853), Appendix, p. 104.

removed the troops from Santa Fe—where they were fast becoming demoralized in that convivial and permissive city—to Fort Union near Las Vegas. Located on the Santa Fe trail, the Fort would give him "more direct control over all the affairs of the department." The new fort was destined to become the supply and nerve center of a vast perimeter of small forts radiating outward up to a distance of 500 miles. (See Map.) Near Taos, Sumner created Cantonment Burgwin. To contain the Navajo, he built the appropriately named Fort Defiance in the mouth of Canyon Bonito 190 miles west of Albuquerque. To the south he built Fort Craig at the entrance of the *Jornada del Muerto* and Fort Fillmore toward El Paso. Along the Rio Grande itself, new posts were added at Valverde, Socorro, Albuquerque, and near the Santa Rita copper mines.[31] Sumner's successors were to add new ribs to the huge fan of defense, so that by 1860 an impressive Indian control system was in the making. The presidios that Pedro Pino had asked for in 1812 were at last being built.

Sumner was determined that neither Calhoun nor the Indian Bureau, with their treaty-making and gift-giving proclivities, should interfere with his own plans for subduing the wild Indians. Soon the two men were at loggerheads, and an aggressive, correlated Indian policy was the victim of their war of words. As the two men argued, the Indian raids and attacks continued, and the issues inevitably got into politics. With a supply line stretching all the way to the Mississippi River, the cost of New Mexico's defense now averaged more than $3,000,000 a year. Over a thousand civilian workers were employed at Fort Union alone, and Professor Averam Bender has estimated that more than 8 per cent of the money in circulation in New Mexico came through Army expenditures. Sumner himself observed: "the truth is, the only resource of this country is the government money. All classes depend on it, from the professional man and the trader down to the beggar."[32]

Whether he liked it or not, Sumner and his successors in the

---

31. Thomas J. McLaughlin, "History of Fort Union, New Mexico" (Master's thesis, University of New Mexico, 1952), pp. 16 ff. Bender, *March of Empire*, pp. 37–39.

32. Bender, p. 170. *Cong. Globe,* 32nd Cong. 2nd Sess. (January 10, 1853), Appendix, p. 104. See also Chris Emmett, *Fort Union and the Winning of the Southwest* (Norman, Okla., 1965).

military command headed the biggest business in the territory and perforce made the military a stronger power than the civil government. A military decision to economize caused a howl from merchants; the prosecution of an Indian war meant good prices and large sales. But Indian wars also meant that the Indian Bureau officials took a back seat and lost control over Indian patronage. Sumner himself was so convinced that American adventurers were keeping alive the Indian troubles just to fleece the government that he urged a drastic solution to the War Department. "Would it not be better to abandon a country which hardly seems fit for the inhabitations of civilized man," he asked, "by remunerating them for their property, in money or in lands situated in more favorable regions?"[33]

Ironically, the presence of federal troops both guaranteed the continuation of those conditions Sumner so deplored and dictated that the army would play a key role in politics. When the first delegate election occurred in 1851, for example, the Missouri merchants who were supplying the army and the American party of Taos chose one of Sumner's own officers, Captain A. W. Reynolds, as their candidate. This same group demanded Calhoun's removal, spread the rumor that the governor intended taking Pueblo lands away from their owners (in 1851, the Pueblos were still allowed to vote in elections), and cried for an Indian war.[34]

On another occasion, when Calhoun authorized local militia companies to take the field against raiding Navajos, Colonel Sumner thought such an action undercut the whole purpose of Fort Defiance and warned Calhoun that he would use federal troops against militia if necessary to sustain his policy. In anger Calhoun wrote Washington that: "The Civil and Military Authorities of the Territory with but few exceptions are in hostile array and *one* or *both* should be relieved from duty in this territory."[35]

Fortunately federal soldiers did not have to fire on militia men, and before the feud could continue further Calhoun, becoming ill with jaundice and scurvy, realized that he had but a few months to live.

33. *Santa Fe Gazette*, February 19, 1853.
34. Abel, *Calhoun*, pp. 372–75.
35. Ibid., p. 431.

Stoically he ordered his coffin built and, loading it on a wagon, joined a merchant train headed for the States. With luck the Governor thought he might see his beloved Georgia before death should find him. But the disease had advanced too far. Somewhere on the grassy Kansas plains outside Kansas City, he was buried.

Calhoun's successor, another Whig politician, was William Carr Lane, five times the mayor of St. Louis, a physician of some prominence and a relative of the Ewing family, who were active in the Santa Fe trade.[36] Lane was also determined to feed the Indians into submission but to cooperate with Sumner and the military while doing so. For a time his policy worked, but he discovered, as Calhoun had, that Washington could not supply sufficient goods to keep down the raids of starving Indians.

It fell to David Meriwether, a Kentucky Democrat who became governor in 1853, to reap the brunt of Lane's failures. The California gold rush had brought migrants through New Mexico on their way to the Pacific coast, and a few local miners, stimulated by the local discoveries of ore, began to invade the Organ Mountains in southeastern New Mexico. Whether migrant or miner, the Indians chose to attack them. As the number of raids increased, Jicarilla Apaches seized herds grazing near Fort Union itself and attacked the troops at Cantonment Burgwin so successfully that at the end of the fighting some forty men lay dead. In 1854, after a stay with his Mormon troops in California, St. George Cooke was back in New Mexico tracking down the Jicarillas with orders to drive them across the Rio Grande. Indian damages continued to mount, however, and Governor Meriwether reported that $112,000 in property and animals had been lost to the white settlers that year.[37]

By 1855 major action was called for. General John Garland, Sumner's successor, pushed further into enemy territory by constructing Fort Massachusetts in the San Luis Valley (in present-day Colorado) and Fort Stanton on the Rio Bonita in the south near Ruidoso. By that spring Garland had a thousand soldiers in the field chasing Indians. While Colonel Thomas Fauntleroy led troops in the

36. Bieber, Historical Society of New Mexico, *Publications*, 6, 179–181.
37. Ibid., pp. 183–84.

north and Dixon Miles pursued Indians in the south, Governor Meriwether, himself an old Santa Fe trader and experienced frontiersman, permitted six companies of local militia to join in the fray against Utes and Apaches. As soon as peace was secured in the fall of 1855, he forced treaties upon the Indians.

By the Christmas of 1855 conditions in New Mexico seemed more hopeful than they had in many a year. With plenty of rain and a good harvest, Acting Governor Davis told the Assembly that "Prosperity has attended every avenue of business." Perhaps, he suggested, the Bonita country might be opened to settlement soon.[38] The optimistic Davis was a bad prophet, however, for Meriwether's treaties were rejected by the Senate just as 500 Mogollon Apaches in Arizona (then part of New Mexico) went on the rampage. Seeing the ruin of all his efforts, Meriwether left the territory in disgust.

Meriwether's successor was Abraham Rencher, a North Carolinian who had once been a Congressman and who had also served as minister to Portugal. Before he had actually entered upon his duties in 1857, however, he learned that the office of Indian Superintendent had been separated from the governorship and had been turned over to James L. Collins, editor of the Santa Fe *Gazette*.

Though Collins was an intelligent, well-informed Indian expert, this change of jurisdiction appears to have made little difference either to the wild Indians or to the military commanders. From 1857, when Collins assumed office, to the outbreak of the Civil War, in fact, Indian conditions became worse. Comanches now attacked along the Cimarron cutoff of the Santa Fe Trail. Mangas Coloradas and his Apache braves cut a swath of destruction from Tucson to the Rio Grande. The Navajos also became so troublesome that a new campaign was planned against them in the summer of 1858. Before it got started, more than a thousand warriors of this tribe descended on Fort Defiance to take the war to the enemy's doorstep. A smaller band got within ten miles of Santa Fe.[39]

This latest outbreak occurred during the command of Colonel Fauntleroy, who had replaced General Garland. Experienced in Indian

38. Davis, *Message, 1855*, p. 3.
39. Keleher, *Turmoil in New Mexico*, pp. 102 ff.

warfare, Fauntleroy was convinced that he needed a large force to bring about peaceful conditions. As he struggled to bring extra troops all the way from Utah, once again divided councils ruined his campaign, for Superintendent Collins chose this moment to begin a press war against Fauntleroy in the Santa Fe *Gazette*. Governor Rencher also joined Collins in the attack on the military and the old feud of governor versus general blossomed again. To complicate matters, the New Mexican Delegate to Congress, Miguel A. Otero, attacked Rencher at this point, so that the politics of disunity in New Mexico reached a new high. To add to the existing confusion, the Assembly in 1859 and again in 1860 authorized the formation of militia companies, to conduct campaigns independently of Fauntleroy, but both the commander and the governor refused to issue arms to the volunteers.[40]

Faced with constant raids and divided councils, the people of New Mexico began to take matters into their own hands. In August 1860 a convention met in Santa Fe to consider Indian defense. Don Jose Leandro Perea was called to the chair as its president. Backed by James L. Collins and certain merchants and speculators who agreed to furnish arms for a price, the convention proposed to raise 1,000 men to punish the Indians. Acting with a unanimity seldom seen in New Mexico, they established a committee of correspondence for each county, to consult on strategy and to report raids and the like. Much of the old anti-American sentiment crept into their public statements. Breathing fire and brimstone against the federal government for leaving them unprotected, they told the public in sonorous Spanish that "for months the bells of your sacred edifices have tolled the obsequies of your slaughtered citizens." It was no accident that besides Perea, three of the convention members were home rule advocates: Padre Jose Manuel Gallegos, Miguel E. Pino, and Felipe Delgado.[41]

While merchants and speculators seem to have had a mercenary interest in this private militia organization—and in the livestock

40. Ibid., pp. 105–07. See also *Council Journal, New Mexico, 1860–61* (Santa Fe, 1861), pp. 18–19.
41. Address to the People of New Mexico, August 28, 1860, broadside, HEH.

they could capture as spoils of war—that body did raid the Navajo successfully. Their actions, coupled with a new campaign led by Fauntleroy's successor, Colonel E. R. S. Canby, won a three-month truce in 1860. Although the Indians were not cowed, they were beginning to feel the effects of ten years of battle with American troops. Perhaps a turning point would come soon and the Indian problem would exist no more.

At this auspicious juncture outside events again intervened to remind New Mexicans that they were but a colonial appendage to a nation-state. In the fall of 1860 Abraham Lincoln was elected to the Presidency, the Union began to dissolve, and a majority of the federal troops in New Mexico went home to fight in the Civil War. An elaborate defense system ten years in building was abandoned, and Indian relations returned to the unhappy conditions of 1846. The four-year war between the Union and the Confederacy was to give the wild tribes of the Far Southwest an unexpected respite.

Other than the troubles over Indian affairs and the difficulties attending the initiation of American government in New Mexico, the most revealing insight into territorial politics can be gained by observing the role of the delegate in these early years. He was the territory's voice in Washington, its lobbyist for patronage, troops, and appropriations as well as the consultant for Indian affairs and the advocate of annuities.

In the delegate elections all the multitudinous factions that split the Assembly coalesced into two temporary parties. Nothing could be more incorrect, however, than to call the two groups Democrat or Whig. These names had meaning only to the Americans in New Mexico, and even then the labels were often misleading.

Given the fact that the Whigs were in national office when New Mexico became a territory, a large number of the first American politicians in the Southwest declared loyalty to that party. When the Pierce Administration assumed office in 1853, however, many local Whigs conveniently took refuge under the rubric "National Democrat." Those in opposition, for want of a better name, were called "states rights," "Douglas," "Buchanan," or regular Democrats. Rather than parties, New Mexico had cliques, usually led by one man and generally organized for the specific purpose of winning an election or controlling patronage.

The nearest thing to a real issue could be found in the division between the more conservative native forces, advocating home rule and preservation of the status quo and their opponents, who felt that New Mexico must move with the times. Certain Americans, such as Calhoun and Weightman, appreciated and cooperated with home rule forces. But the majority of the merchants and the whole of the military felt that New Mexico must be Americanized and that the best method of achieving this was to put Americans into key offices. It is true that the national issues of free soil, slavery, and the tariff were discussed and debated by politicians and newspaper editors in New Mexico with great ferocity, but this was more for consumption in Missouri and Washington than it was for the local citizens.

The operation of the two parties can be seen in the delegate election of 1851. With Calhoun's backing the native party chose Richard Hanson Weightman as its candidate. Boastful and self-confident, he attacked the Missouri merchants for their domination of the economy, and he dubbed the stiff-necked Colonel Sumner a tyrannical "Roman proconsul." To counteract Weightman, the Missourians and the military led by Joab Houghton—whose dislike of Weightman was so great that the two men had fought a duel in 1849—chose Captain A. W. Reynolds as their candidate. A member of Reynolds' staff in the quartermaster corps somehow found time to bring out a paper in his superior's behalf, and the fight was on. The contending forces considered the stakes so great and tempers grew so hot that William C. Skinner, a Reynolds supporter, was murdered. National issues got into the campaign when Weightman was accused of being a proslavery man.[42]

When the count was in, it looked as if Weightman and the home rule forces had won. But Reynolds, backed by Houghton, William Messervy, and Ceran St. Vrain, contested the election and took the fight to Congress. There the Missouri merchants persuaded Missouri

42. Abel, *Calhoun*, pp. 374–75, mentions those opposed to Calhoun. Hugh N. Smith, St. Vrain, and Joab Houghton are among the signers.

congressmen to declare that Reynolds had been elected. After a
prolonged investigation, however, Weightman won the contest,
although his term was nearly over before he was seated.[43]

Before the next delegate election occurred, still another element
entered the already complicated politics of New Mexico. This was
the presence of a remarkable new religious figure in Sante Fe: Bishop
Jean Baptiste Lamy.[44] In a sense his appearance in the Far Southwest
in 1852 was comparable in effect to that of General Kearny in 1846,
for Bishop Lamy had been sent by Rome to reform the long-
antiquated and often corrupt religious establishment of provincial
New Mexico. After forty years, Pedro Pino's appeal for a bishop was
being answered. Certain liberals, such as Donaciano Vigil, had begged
for reform, and Lamy's coming was preceded by anonymous articles
in various Missouri papers urging a change in church government.[45]
The spare, mild-mannered Lamy, who spoke Spanish with a French
accent that betrayed his national origins, was a superb choice for the
difficult assignment. Willa Cather has portrayed him in *Death Comes
for the Archbishop* as the gentle Father Latour, whose incredible
saintliness finally brought about the religious reformation desired in
New Mexico. Actually, Lamy was a tough fighter, a realistic executive,
and an excellent diplomat. With as much tact as possible he soon
removed the Vicar General, Juan Felipe Ortiz. Then he found Padre
Martinez' life to be so secular and nonconformist that he relieved
the Taos priest of his parish duties. The eye of Rome quickly discovered other Spanish-Mexican priests gravely lacking in spiritual high
standards. Among those unfrocked by Lamy was Padre Jose Manuel
Gallegos.

Lamy did not intend either to ruin Spanish-Mexican culture or
to Americanize or secularize New Mexico. Ironically, he sought on
another level what Padre Martinez had sought twenty years before,
a restoration of the Church in the life and society of New Mexico.
Aided by a corps of devoted French priests and by the Sisters of
Loretto, who established an academy to educate children in Santa

43. *Cong. Globe,* 32nd Cong., 1st Sess. (1851–52), pp. 706, 752–59.
44. "Jean Baptist Lamy" in *DAB.*
45. Caughey, "Early Federal Relations," pp. 62–63.

Fe, he placed the Church on a new footing in the Southwest. Said a Protestant minister with envy: "he will give Catholicism a new life."[46] American conquest had been followed by a religious Counter-Reformation, as it were.

Lamy's program had far-reaching and sometimes unexpected consequences. The good bishop had demoted some of the most trusted leaders and high-born families in New Mexico, and they refused to bear this latest disgrace in silence. What Lamy had done was to split the many political factions still another way by creating pro-Lamy and anti-Lamy wings within the Church—the latter being led by Ortiz, Martinez, Gallegos, and the Pinos. Eventually the ex-Vicar General gave up the unequal fight, but Padre Martinez set up his own chapel in defiance of the bishop. There in his declining years he held services for those of his parishioners who refused to acknowledge the local Lamy priest. Padre Gallegos, released from his vows, married and went into politics.

These religious feuds produced some fascinating episodes for the New Mexicans. In June 1857 rumors reached Sante Fe from Taos that the Martinez family were in rebellion against local authority and that violence was expected. So believable did the account seem that Governor Davis ordered Kit Carson and a local army detachment to quell the disturbance. To his great embarrassment Davis then learned that the dispute was a religious one and that no troops were needed.[47]

The new alignments, partly shaped by Lamy's actions, first showed up in the 1853 delegate election, when Gallegos appeared as the candidate for the home rule and anti-Lamy forces. His opponent in the campaign was Governor William Carr Lane, an able and popular man, even though he was a symbol of the Missouri and American

46. Ernest S. Stapleton, Jr., "The History of the Baptist Missions in New Mexico, 1849–1866" (Master's thesis, University of New Mexico, 1954), p. 63.

47. The feud broke out again when Vicar General Ortiz died in January 1858. His supporters, the Pinos, tried to persuade Lamy to bury Ortiz under the altar. The reform-minded Bishop refused but did grant him a place within the walls of the church. By the day of the funeral one observer reported that "a high state of excitement existed between the two parties." The services were postponed until a consultation between the leading men could be held. Even then "The Bishop carried his point." J. T. Sprague to W. W. H. Davis, January 31, 1858, Davis Letters, YWA.

influence. And in Lane's case his home state played a key role in the election. Thomas Hart Benton, having opposed Lane in Missouri, pressured Missouri Democrats in New Mexico to defeat Lane by backing Gallegos. This curious alliance, Benton and Gallegos, worked together for victory. Lane was shocked that New Mexicans could be so wrong-headed—"You will be amazed at their conceitedness," he wrote his wife.[48]

If the ex-padre was influential in his native territory, he was an unknown in Washington, hampered by a limited understanding of English and unacquainted with the process of American legislation. His disappointing leadership put the 1855 delegate campaign on still another tack. This time the New Mexicans who were less conservative got the upper hand and chose an able Spanish-American merchant from the Rio Abajo, Miguel A. Otero, to run on the Democratic ticket. Educated in the United States and married to an American woman—having served as Governor Lane's private secretary—Otero was better prepared to look after New Mexican interests and those of the merchants as well in Washington. Otero also made some irresistible promises: he would control the arrogant army colonels, restore Indian affairs to civilian direction, and secure a railroad for the territory. Backed by Americans, New Mexicans, and vast family connections, he defeated Gallegos in 1855 and 1857 and was returned to Congress again over Spruce M. Baird in 1859.[49]

Otero's election symbolized the ever-shifting center of power in New Mexico. Where Delegates Weightman and Gallegos had played second fiddle to the governor or depended upon others to help them, Otero was a man of ability and many projects. As a Democrat with Southern connections, he stood ready to forward the course of the South. Fortunately his territory lay athwart the southern route to California, so that during his incumbency the Butterfield Overland Mail—federally subsidized to the tune of some $600,000 a year—ran through southern New Mexico.[50] Like the Secretary of War, Jefferson

---

48. Caughey, "Early Federal Relations," p. 61. Bieber, Historical Society of New Mexico, *Publications, 6,* 198.

49. See U. S. House of Representatives, *Report No. 90,* 34th Cong., 1st Sess., 1855–56 (Washington, 1856), pp. 1–15, for accounts of the contested election between Otero and Gallegos.

50. Caughey, "Early Federal Relations," pp. 70–71.

Davis, and many other Southerners, Otero advocated a transcontinental railroad which would pass through the territory. While he worked with Senator Gwin of California to forward the project, he persuaded a friend, Merrill Ashurst, a Southern lawyer in the New Mexico Assembly to push through a charter for the "Southern Pacific" in 1859.

To please the Southerners even more, Otero persuaded the New Mexico Assembly to pass a slave code in 1859, which officially put the territory in the Southern column in Washington.[51] By 1859 New Mexico had a Southern governor and secretary, Abraham Rencher and Alexander M. Jackson, and Otero's own brother-in-law, William J. Blackwood of South Carolina, was on the territorial supreme court. He was in partial control of the Santa Fe *Gazette,* in alliance with wily Charles Clever and with James L. Collins, Superintendent of Indian Affairs; Otero had a large hand in determining Indian policy for the territory.[52] Otero was actually well on the way to establishing a machine in New Mexico when once again national politics intervened to defer his plans. The election of Lincoln and the Republicans severely limited Otero's influence in Washington, and by 1861 he was out of office. John S. Watts, an ardent Unionist and former territorial judge, took his place as delegate.

One unfortunate result of the complex struggle to win a delegate election was the resorting of each faction or party to fraud and intimidation to win. The Americans, hampered by numerical inferiority, did not hesitate to use methods that would have ruined them politically in the states. In the early years each side vied to corral the support of anyone they could get. Pueblo Indians and Mexican citizens still living in the territory were invited to vote, and the federal soldiers there often voted repeatedly in a single election. The New Mexicans, unused to the American concept of the franchise, were willing to sell this new thing—the vote—for some economic advantage. Governor Lane learned to his amazement in 1853 that while many ballots had been cast in his favor at Taos, not a single one had been

51. *An Act to Provide for the Protection of Property in Slaves in this Territory* (Santa Fe, 1859), broadside, YWA.

52. James L. Collins to Eliza Edgar, June 30, 1857, provides evidence for the Collins-Otero alliance: Ritch (Box 8), HEH.

reported. The canvassers had been "influenced" by the opposition. Then there was the case of the priest of San Juan, who, knowing that right was on his candidate's side in 1855, sat down with the ballot box and carefully removed all the votes unfavorable to his choice.[53] A persistent pattern in elections had been established that was to continue until statehood.

What had ten years of American rule accomplished? A civil government of sorts was operating and was accepted. Whether he cared for Americans or not, the New Mexican never again chose to rebel, as did the Taoseños of 1847. If there was opposition, it was in the honorable tradition of state rights or home rule. Indeed, one of the plotters in the December 1846 uprising, Diego Archuleta, was, by 1857, the United States Indian agent for the Utes and Apaches. During the Civil War he became a brigadier general in the Union militia. *"El antiguo revolutionario,"* as Vigil derisively called him in 1846, was to die at 70 having served fourteen years in the Territorial Assembly.[54] Similarly, Padre Martinez' own opposition was diverted toward his fruitless struggle with the powerful Lamy, while ex-padre Gallegos found a career in the Assembly so much to his liking that he served there for some years.

One of the reasons American rule was accepted with such good grace was that the ten years from 1851 to 1861 were relatively prosperous. Ranching—especially sheep-raising—flourished. Some of the surplus animals were marched all the way to California to be consumed by the voracious argonauts there. The profits were so alluring that ex-mountain men Kit Carson and "Uncle Dick" Wootton began to engage in the less romantic business of mutton.[55]

Like the Romans the nineteenth-century Americans also had a talent for good communications, and the Army's concern for decent roads and the civilian's demand for postal facilities resulted in a better Santa Fe trail, a good road between Taos and Sante Fe, and at least well-marked paths to the many camps and forts in the territory. A visitor to the southern part of New Mexico in 1860 said that the

53. Caughey, "Early Federal Relations," pp. 62–63.
54. Twitchell, *Leading Facts*, 2, 232, 251, 393 n.
55. Caughey, "Early Federal Relations," p. 76.

presence of the Overland Mail was "working wonders in this region, [by] opening the country, and inducing the enterprising to venture from home and to try their fortunes in a new land."[56]

New Mexico also experienced a mild population boom in the decade before the Civil War, when the number of its white inhabitants increased from 60,000 to 90,000. While army personnel, scores of merchants, and hundreds of adventurers came down the Santa Fe trail during these years, the increase was largely due to the birth rate of the local Spanish-American population.

With better roads, a burgeoning population, and an extensive military and Indian establishment, the trading system of New Mexico experienced both change and expansion. A permanent rather than a seasonal market at the army camps and at Santa Fe called for a regular supply of goods from the States and for large freighting firms capable of handling huge army and Indian contracts. The small individual trader began to give way to partnerships and companies. The foundations for the great Southwestern business houses—Otero and Sellar, Brown and Manzanares, Tully and Ochoa—were being laid in this crucial decade.

In the towns and hamlets another and more subtle change was occurring. That wanderer on the face of the earth, the European Jewish merchant-peddler, joined the American trader in New Mexico, where he, too, began to establish regular stores and trading posts. Although the newcomers made up only a tiny percentage of the population, they demonstrated that a resident mercantile group could succeed there. With the coming of the Spiegelbergs, the Ilfelds, and the Seligmans, New Mexico became part of the regular American commercial system. Often as not, one member of the family firm lived in New York as a buyer while the others did the selling and distributing in New Mexico itself.[57]

Although the population was expanding and the economic picture was hopeful, there were grave faults in New Mexico. After fifteen years of conquest it was not yet clear who ruled: the governor, the

56. Ibid., pp. 70–71. J. T. Sprague to W. W. H. Davis, May 13, 1860, Davis Letters, YWA.

57. Parish, *New Mexico Quarterly*, 29 (1959), 321 ff.

commander, or the Indian superintendent. Governor Lane's complaint, made in 1852, was still valid in 1861: "There is a strange state of things, in every Dept. of the Gov't of this Territory—civil, military, and Indian; and so ill-defined is the line of duties, in both the Civil and Indian Depts., that we are compelled to grope in the dark in discharging our duties."[58]

To the civil–military–Indian conflict could be added the battle of the clergy and the sham war—imitative of national politics—over the role of slavery in New Mexico. And now, after ten years, none of the basic issues, such as peonage, public education, or the land-grant question, had been resolved. No court system worthy of the name really existed; no regular party system operated. To the United States, as to Mexico formerly, New Mexico was an obscure border province, easily neglected in the concern over more important matters of state. In 1859 Congressman Phelps of Missouri visited New Mexico and told the inhabitants quite bluntly that the region was important chiefly as part of Missouri's economy.[59] Rather than a visiting politico, he was more the inspector general of an imperial company sent to look over one of the more distant plantations. But this view was not new to the residents of New Mexico. A dozen years before, Major Emory had remarked that only "in a commercial and military aspect [is New Mexico] an all important . . . possession of the United States."[60] It would be a long time before Americans realized that a people lived there—both Indian and white—with an interesting culture, and that the region itself could be a "land of enchantment."

58.　Bieber, Historical Society of New Mexico, *Publications*, 6, 189. Caughey, "Early Federal Relations," p. 54.

59.　*Visit of Hon. John S. Phelps to . . . New Mexico* (Quincy, Ill., 1859), pamphlet in HEH.

60.　Burl Noggle, "Anglo Observers of the Southwest Borderlands, 1825–1890: The Rise of a Concept," *Arizona and the West, 1* (1959), 119.

5

Civil War, 1861–1869

> The Civil War is an important chapter in the history of
> Western America. It involved the struggle between Union and
> Confederate forces for control of the Southwest and a conflict
> between the Indians and the whites. It was a venture in
> territorial development and the welding of pioneers with
> diversified ideals into the sturdy citizenry of the
> Intermountain West.
>
> Ray C. Colton, *The Civil War in the
> Western Territories*

 When the secession-minded states of the South began to leave the Union in the winter of 1860–61, most national observers believed that New Mexico would cast her lot with the Confederacy. Delegate Otero wrote doleful letters from Washington predicting the inevitable collapse of the Union while at the same time building up sentiment in favor of the South. "All is gloom and sadness. You see in the streets long and sad faces, indicating that they are mourning, as it were, over the death of a friend." Two of the three newspapers in the territory ground out pro-Southern editorials. Governor Abraham Rencher, a North Carolinian, seemed to be neutral, but Alexander M. Jackson, the popular territorial secretary, was a secessionist heart and soul. He boasted of the coming new order, claimed to be a close friend of President Jefferson Davis, and campaigned openly to move New Mexico into Southern ranks.[1]

1. M. A. Otero to Charles Clever, June 16, December 10, 29, 1860; Ritch (Box 17), HEH.

These men were only a part of the secessionist corps that operated throughout the Southwest. Officers like Colonel Henry Hopkins Sibley, second in command at Fort Union, and Colonel William Wing Loring, at Fort Marcy in Santa Fe, declared their loyalty to the South. "Nothing is talked of here but secession," wrote one irate northern soldier, "All the officers seemed for it." Many native Spanish-Americans were attracted by the possibility of a states-rights government, which would allow home rule. This sentiment was stronger south of Santa Fe and particularly in the booming town of Mesilla just forty miles above El Paso, where many former Texans now lived and ranched. Ex-governor Manuel Armijo and his brother Raphael saw in the Confederacy a chance to regain political prestige lost in the fateful summer of 1846.[2] By the time of Lincoln's inauguration in the spring of 1861, the Union seemed a lost cause in New Mexico.

Well might the Southerners at Santa Fe and Fort Union expound the new dispensation with confidence, for they knew that behind them stood an interested South. In the ten-year fight for Southern rights between 1850 and 1860, no man had been so conscious of the Southwest in his policies as Jefferson Davis. When the soft-spoken Mississippian became Secretary of War under Franklin Pierce in 1853, the United States Topographical Engineers were ordered to explore nearly every unknown corner of the Southwest. These officers had just completed the Mexican boundary survey, which revealed that the United States still had no adequate southern route to the Coast. To make this possible, Davis persuaded Pierce and Secretary of State Marcy to send James Gadsden, a South Carolina railroad president, to Mexico City to secure the Gila Valley for the United States in 1853. The resulting Gadsden Purchase cost the U.S. $10,000,000. Then Davis got a survey of a southern transcontinental route along the 32nd parallel. Exacting a loyalty and devotion from his army lieutenants seldom seen in Washington, Davis imported camels to see if they could be used in the Southwest and investigated the possibility of growing cotton in southern Utah. When he left the War Department in 1857, he probably knew as much about the far western frontier

2. Henry Hopkins Sibley, "Report on the Operations of the Army in New Mexico," in *Official Reports of Battles* (Richmond, 1862), p. 149, YWA.

as any high ranking Southerner there. Cognizant of the Confederate President's past interest, William Need, an ardent Unionist wrote despairingly from New Mexico that:

> With an eye that never winked and a wing that never tired has Jeff Davis for more than ten years turned his thoughts and desires to the Mexican line for expansion. . . . His military prototypes and proteges, Ewell, Fauntleroy, Steen, Loring, Longstreet, Crittenden, Grayson, Rhett, Reynolds, and others were placed here purposely to second and forward his ulterior designs.[3]

Curiously enough, the most salutary and efficient method of developing the Southwest would have been to solve its wild Indian problem. But because of the divided jurisdictions of the Indian Bureau and the Army, neither the Pierce nor the Buchanan administration ever faced this basic issue. They did, however, exhibit a continued interest in the region by routing the Butterfield Overland Mail through the Southwest. Buchanan also recommended in his annual message of 1859 the establishment of a temporary protectorate over Chihuahua and Sonora. And now that secession was a fact, perhaps the South might secure the Southwest and even Southern California as needed colonies for her new empire. A sea-to-sea South would have been an impressive new country.

The Southern dream of empire coincided not only with the plans of Southerners in Santa Fe and Fort Union, but also with those of three local Southwestern factions scattered from the sweltering mining town of LaPaz, on the muddy Colorado, to El Paso, on the equally muddy Rio Grande. The first of these groups operated in the western part of New Mexico Territory in what is now southern Arizona. Since the early fifties a hardy set of American, Mexican, and German miners had pitted the hills around Tubac and Tucson and in the beautiful Sonoita Valley for silver and lead. Many of the intrepid miners, who worked despite constant attack from the Apaches, were adventurous Southerners, such as Granville H. and William S. Oury of Virginia, who had settled there. Some were ex-army officers like

3. Keleher, *Turmoil*, p. 394.

the irrepressible Sylvester Mowry, owner of the rich Patagonia Mines. Although a Rhode Islander by birth, Mowry openly sympathized with the South.[4]

The anti-Union attitudes of these frontier miners in Arizona may be partly explained by the fact that their problems were ignored in Santa Fe, under whose distant political and military jurisdiction they were. Actually they had been badgering Congress unsuccessfully since 1856 to make their region a separate territory. Mowry himself had twice been elected delegate to Congress by extralegal proceedings. Armed with memorials, petitions, pamphlets, and a quiver of spread eagle speeches about the glories of his Apache-ridden Arizona, Mowry had cut such a swashbuckling figure in Washington that he became the darling of high society there. Try as he might, though, he could not persuade Congress to organize Arizona.

Another reason for anti-Union feelings occurred when federal troops abandoned Forts Breckinridge and Buchanan in Arizona, leaving the unhappy miners completely at the mercy of the Apaches. To Mowry and his friends in Tucson and Tubac the Confederacy offered a new chance to make Arizona a territory and to secure protection from the Indians as well. After the soldiers had left, Granville Oury openly declared for Davis and the South and rounded up enough voters to elect himself delegate to the Confederate Congress.[5]

Some three hundred miles east of Tucson lay the river town of Mesilla in Dona Ana County. Small but growing, the village had prospered as the crossroads of the overland route from San Antonio to Tucson and the trail from Missouri to Chihuahua. There another set of Southerners, many of them ranchers from Texas, joined with several ambitious Spanish-Americans to make Arizona a territory which included the southern half of New Mexico. The Mesillaños were usually in opposition to Santa Fe, where they felt their interests were ignored. Beginning in 1856, they memorialized Congress for a separate territory annually for four years. Finally in 1860 they held a full-scale territorial convention and elected officers of their own.

---

4. "Sylvester Mowry," MS biographical file in APHS.
5. C. C. Smith, "History of the Oury Family," pp. 45–88, APHS.

As of March 1861, the two settlements joined in a convention of the "People of Arizona" and turned to the Confederacy for territorial organization and protection.[6]

Much of the impetus for the Mesilla territorial movement actually came from El Paso, where various Texas leaders—now that secession was a fact—once again intrigued to annex New Mexico to the Lone Star State. It was evident that Texas pride still rankled over the disaster of 1841 and the failure to secure the Rio Grande as a border in 1850. This time the Texans were able to enlist the aid of that adept diplomatist and trader James W. Magoffin, who now lived in feudal splendor at Magoffinsville just outside of El Paso. By exerting influence over leading native New Mexicans in the southern portion of the territory, Magoffin helped create a seccessionist sentiment. Texans, Tucsonians, Mesillaños, and the Confederate government, then, all had plans for New Mexico's dismemberment and occupation.

Plans became action in the spring of 1861 when Colonel John R. Baylor, an ambitious young frontier lawyer, advertised throughout Texas for men to hunt buffalos. Baylor's buffalo hunt was actually to be a filibuster against New Mexico. By mid-July Baylor had assembled some 300 men at "the Pass" and had seized Fort Bliss there. Later that month they fell into marching order along the banks of the Rio Grande and, heading north, occupied the pro-Southern town of Mesilla with little difficulty.[7]

Baylor's easy occupation was overshadowed by the fact that in nearby Fort Fillmore federal troops outnumbering his own men by 300 or so could contest his invasion of New Mexican soil. But luck was with Baylor in this early period. The commandant of Fort Fillmore, Major Isaac Lynde, either by miscalculation of Baylor's strength or sheer panic, hastily abandoned the fort without a fight and plunged his ill-equipped companies into a desert march to Fort Stanton some 150 miles away. His straggling army—half-dead from heat and thirst or drunk from canteens unwisely filled with whiskey

6. Charles S. Walker, "Causes of the Confederate Invasion of New Mexico," *NMHR*, 8 (1933), 92–97.

7. William I. Waldrip, "New Mexico during the Civil War" (Master's thesis, University of New Mexico, 1950), pp. 15–16.

instead of water before the march began—were easily taken by Baylor's forces.[8]

Lynde's surrender sent a chain reaction of fear and confusion through the ill-organized Union forces of New Mexico. Upon hearing of the surrender, Lt. Colonel B. H. Roberts abandoned Fort Stanton and retreated to Santa Fe. The new Union commander there, Colonel E. R. S. Canby, appealed to Fort Leavenworth for more troops and urged the governors of New Mexico and Colorado to organize volunteer militia to complement his own troops, but he expressed little faith in the ability of New Mexican volunteers to fight.[9]

While Canby struggled to restore the morale of his men and to prepare for Confederate invasion, Baylor, riding on a wave of enthusiasm, created the Confederate Territory of Arizona, chose Mesilla for its capital, and modestly appointed himself the military and civilian governor of the new body politic. The Southerners in Tucson echoed his actions by formally declaring for the South and accepting territorial status within the Confederacy. The indefatigable ex-secretary of New Mexico, Alexander M. Jackson, now appeared in the more exalted role of "Chief Justice" of Arizona.[10]

Baylor's easy but nonetheless impressive accomplishments—the first fruits of Southern initiative in the Southwest—brought the region to the attention of both Lincoln and Davis. The former appointed Dr. Henry Connelly as governor of New Mexico. A merchant and land-owner who now maintained an impressive estate at Peralta, Connelly had been a resident of the Southwest since 1824 and had been a key figure in the negotiations which led Armijo to flee in 1846.[11] By word and deed the new governor urged resistance to the invader. With a real understanding of the native New Mexican mind he stressed the word "Texan" rather than "Confederate" in his proclamations and correspondence.[12] What was more impressive was that Connelly and

8. Max L. Heyman, Jr., *Prudent Soldier: A Biography of Major General E. R. S. Canby, 1813–1873* (Glendale, Cal., 1959), pp. 141–52.

9. Ibid., p. 144.

10. Waldrip, "New Mexico," pp. 21–22.

11. Twitchell, *Leading Facts*, 2, 391–92.

12. Connelly to William H. Seward, May 4, 1862, to April 1863, in which the history of the Texan invasion is reported in detail. State Department TP: New Mexico, 1851–72 (microcopy T–17).

the Unionists managed to stir the New Mexican electorate enough
that fall to send Judge John S. Watts to Congress in place of his
opponent, Diego Archuleta, an avid states-righter. That winter the
Union Forces also seated a pro-northern legislature in Santa Fe.[13] It
should be remembered that in all these actions the New Mexicans
maintained a neutral attitude toward the slavery issue and toward
secession. The question for them and for the Americans in Santa Fe
was a more practical one: do we wish to surrender our trade and
political organization to the authority of Texas? The answer, as it
had been in 1841 and 1850, was no. It was not surprising to find
Connelly, who had often been at political odds with the Taos leaders,
now enlisting Ceran St. Vrain and Kit Carson to raise volunteer
regiments.[14]

While Connelly, St. Vrain, and others worked to save the integrity
of New Mexico, Colonel Henry Hopkins Sibley visited Davis in
Richmond. He convinced the Confederate President that he possessed
a workable plan to seize Arizona and New Mexico and to tap or take
the gold regions of California and Colorado. Davis was easily persuaded, for the Southwestern forts held needed Union supplies, the
region bordered on neutral Mexico, and the reputed proslavery
sentiments of New Mexico seemed to make it an easy task. In any
event Sibley proved so persuasive that he left Richmond a brigadier
general with the impressive title "Commander of the Army of New
Mexico." The high rank fitted Sibley, who was a loquacious, oratorical
officer with a penchant for champagne and elegant living. But he was
also a good organizer. By the late fall of 1861 he had assembled what
one participant called the best set of men "as ever threw leg over
horse." Numbering some 3,500, they left Fort Bliss in early February
1862 for the river settlements of New Mexico.[15]

As Kearny had done in 1846, Sibley tried to conquer wherever
possible by pronunciamento. In addresses and broadsides he, too,
promised the New Mexicans that he would respect their religion and
maintain a "strong and lenient government." Sibley also appealed to

13. *Proclamation del Gobernador*, September 9, 1861.
14. Santa Fe *Gazette*, May 11, 1861.
15. "Henry Hopkins Sibley" in *DAB*.

his former soldiers still in Union ranks to join the Confederate forces. Sibley was not to be as fortunate as Kearny, however, for the war of words soon became a shooting affair.

Small though the New Mexican Civil War battles and skirmishes were when compared to the enormous and complicated bloodlettings in Virginia and along the Mississippi and Ohio Rivers, they never lacked for drama, daring, or the kind of surprise which inevitably makes the story of a war romantic. In the first place, the difficulties besetting the Union commander, Colonel E. R. S. Canby, were herculean in miniature. Largely ignored by the federal government, which was preoccupied with the preservation of the Union east of the Mississippi, Canby had to rely on fewer than 2,500 regular troops, who had not been paid for a year. He roundly distrusted the native volunteers, who had been cajoled into a period of service. He also had to deal with the maddening passive neutrality of the New Mexican population and with a crippling scarcity of supplies. Even so, his major problems were pyschological, for not only was the morale of his troops low, but everyone knew that in Colonel Sibley, Canby was fighting an old friend.[16] It was also a fact that the enemy were Texans with a disdain for New Mexicans, which made the former conspicuously self-confident. As Canby placed part of his troops at Fort Craig on the Rio Grande entrance to the *Jornada del Muerto,* he must have been aware, too, that he was taking only a defensive position. Only by consideration of all these factors does the New Mexican Civil War campaign make sense.

By the middle of February 1862 General Sibley's Texans stood defiantly before Fort Craig and taunted Canby to fight it out in an open field battle. Always a cautious general, Canby preferred to meet the Confederates on better ground. A few miles north of Fort Craig could be found a pleasant crossing of the shallow Rio Grande called Valverde. There on February 21, 1862, in the first major encounter between Union and Confederate soldiers in New Mexico, the two armies fought it out in a furious all-day struggle. By late afternoon

16. The Army rolls list Canby as having 3,690 men in November 1861, 4,945 by December 31, and 5,790 in February 1862. Heyman, *Canby,* pp. 142–43 n.

it was clear that the aggressive Southerners had broken the spirit of the New Mexican volunteers commanded by Kit Carson, and despite heavy Confederate losses the Union forces were slowly giving ground. When certain of his officers and men refused to cross the river under Confederate fire, Canby withdrew to Fort Craig, where Governor Connelly anxiously awaited news of the battle's outcome.[17]

After the wounded had been collected and the dead buried, General Sibley and his men could claim that they had been victorious at Valverde; but it was also true that the Texan success was superficial, for the bulk of Canby's men remained intact and Sibley's own supplies were now so short that he had to move on to Albuquerque to avoid starvation rations for his men.

Nevertheless, the ebullient Sibley continued what seemed an easy conquest. At Socorro more volunteers under Colonel Nicholas Pino surrendered without firing a shot; commandeering supplies at Albuquerque and wantonly burning many valuable goods, the Confederates marched on to Santa Fe. By March 10 Sibley had occupied the capital, which Union troops had hastily evacuated for the safer bastion of Fort Union across the mountains. Governor Connelly himself fled to Las Vegas, where he established a government in exile. In Santa Fe ex-Surveyor General Pelham, a loyal Texan, emerged from the guardhouse where he had been a political prisoner to become the Confederate Governor of New Mexico. The flags of Texas and the Confederacy now flew over Fort Marcy and the Palace of the Governors.[18]

Such quick success bred a festive air. Sibley feasted on champagne; and from the comments of observers, one gathers he had done so all the way from El Paso. Southern sympathizers now openly aired their views and hobnobbed with the new rulers. James L. Collins, the Superintendent of Indian Affairs, somehow permitted vast Indian stores to be used by the Confederates.[19] The average Santa Feans,

17. Waldrip, "New Mexico," pp. 27–32.
18. Heyman, *Canby*, pp. 173–75. See also Diary of Charles Emil Wesche for an account of Pino's surrender of Socorro: Ritch (Box 18), HEH. See too Connelly to Seward, March 11, 23, 30, April 6, 11, 13, 1862. State Department TP: New Mexico, 1851–72.
19. Waldrip, "New Mexico," pp. 32–33.

now much more sophisticated about new flags and new loyalties than they had been in 1846, accepted this latest change of authority with an urbane shrug of equinamity.

The celebrants in Santa Fe could not ignore certain unpleasant facts, however. Sibley's losses at Valverde were irreplaceable, and his troops were suffering heavily from pneumonia and smallpox.[20] Fort Craig still stood athwart his attenuated supply line, and Fort Union was still to be taken. It was now obvious what Canby's strategy had been all along—the Confederates should be allowed to overextend themselves. They would have to withdraw eventually of their own accord, Canby argued, for want of food and animals. As if to prove his point, Sibley's men had been forced to forage on the land in such an outrageous manner that Union sentiment kindled in the basically neutral New Mexican population.[21] Finally, it was clear that Sibley's closeness to Colorado had aroused both the federal government and the Coloradans. In the mining towns of that new territory, Governor William Gilpin, the only man in his Missouri county to vote for Lincoln, had formed several companies of volunteers for service against the Confederates. Having cowed the Southern sympathizers in Denver and elsewhere and having chased off several Texas raiding parties, the Colorado volunteers were a far more formidable body than their New Mexican counterparts. Made up of miners and frontiersmen and a sprinkling of former Kansas free-soilers, the companies possessed officers who seemed not to know the meaning of caution or fear.[22]

When news of Sibley's successes reached Colorado, Colonel John P. Slough marched the First Colorado Regiment of Volunteers—or Pike's Peakers as they were called—over Raton Pass to Fort Union. Spurred by the urgency of the situation, the footsore troops had made 400 miles in only thirteen days![23] Unlike the federal officers at Forts Craig and Union, the Pike's Peakers were roaring for a fight. Slough

20. Heyman, *Canby*, p. 165. Sibley, "Official Report," p. 144.
21. Connelly to Seward, March 23, 1862, State Department TP: New Mexico, 1851–72.
22. Ray C. Colton, *The Civil War in the Western Territories* (Norman, 1959), pp. 45–46.
23. Heyman, *Canby*, pp. 174–75. Colton, *The Civil War*, p. 47.

himself, reflecting the aggressive sentiments of his men, ignored the vigorous protests of the commandant of Fort Union, Colonel Gabriel R. Paul, and sent them forward toward Santa Fe to meet the Texans.[24]

For the second time in less than twenty years the fate of New Mexico was to be decided at the pass through the Sangre de Cristo Mountains, through which the Santa Fe trail twisted before coming out onto the tablelands, where the capital city was located. Over Glorieta Pass and into Apache Canyon now marched the Colorado Volunteers. There advance units of the Union under Major John Chivington and Rebel forces under Major Pyron blundered into contact on March 26, 1862. In the lively skirmish that ensued, it appears that the flanking movements of the federal soldiers overcame the Confederate superiority in artillery. The battle at Apache Canyon was fought, however, with the commanders on both sides absent from the field and with the bulk of both armies unused. This skirmish was preliminary to the major engagement, which, after a day of respite to bury the dead and reconnoiter, took place on March 28.

While the Confederates were pushing forward out of Apache Canyon and up across Glorieta Pass toward Pigeon's Ranch, the Union officers had decided on a bold maneuver. Colonel Slough would engage the main body of Texans, and Major Chivington would go over the mountains south of the Pass to attack the enemy in the rear. The plan was less simple than it looked, for Chivington's route was a little used and little known defile, while the region chosen for the major battle was so full of boulders, arroyos, and bush that it was impossible to use cavalry troops. Nevertheless, by 11:00 A.M. on March 28 federal and rebel soldiers were once more engaged. In a complex set of skirmishes and hand-to-hand fighting the two sides contended for the Pass and for New Mexico. After a battle of six hours it became evident that although the Texans claimed victory, neither side had won, nor did either have the strength to continue.[25] Like so many early Civil War encounters in the East, the result was indecisive.

The stalemate at Glorieta Pass was not in vain, however, for Colonel Chivington with 430 men had won the battle in the rear.

24. Colton, pp. 51–56, covers the Battle of Apache Canyon.
25. Ibid., pp. 58–68, covers the Battle of Glorieta Pass.

After crossing the mountains, his force had spotted a large Confederate supply camp with a skeleton guard, some 1,000 feet below at Canyoncito. At the proper moment the Union troops dashed and slid down the heights to the encampment below, yelling like wild Indians.[26] The startled sentries were no match for the Union avalanche of men. Confederate supply wagons were soon in flames, and some 400 horses and mules were put to the sword. Chivington's raid broke the back of Sibley's invasion of New Mexico. The Confederate commander at Glorieta—Sibley was still in Santa Fe—hearing that they were being attacked in the rear, mistakenly assumed that Canby had arrived behind them in force and began to retreat to Santa Fe; there, after commandeering still more supplies, the Confederates initiated what Sibley evasively called a "retrograde movement" toward Albuquerque. A few weeks later, federal troops—now headed by Canby, who had finally emerged from Fort Craig to join forces with Chivington and Slough—began to harass the Confederates. After a cannon duel in Albuquerque the Texans retreated down the Rio Grande. It was not yet a rout, for the Texans feasted and sang as they went. At Peralta once again they invaded Governor Connelly's household and made themselves royally at home. Canby followed at a discrete distance, occasionally engaging in a cautious exchange of artillery. One of these encounters, somewhat grandly called the battle of Peralta, could have been more decisive if Canby had permitted. Indeed, Canby's caution led his subordinates to wonder if he intended fighting at all, and the restless Coloradans, led now by Colonel Chivington, were almost in mutiny.[27]

After more skirmishing and cannonading, the Confederates, now low on supplies and with morale slipping, crossed the Rio Grande at Los Lunas, and the two armies traveled down opposite banks in sight of one another—Sibley on the east bank and Canby on the west. Lacking proper supplies and men, the Confederate situation now became desperate; plans to attack Fort Craig were abandoned, and instead the Confederate army decided to cross the mountains as

26. Ibid., pp. 69–72.
27. Ibid., pp. 83–90 passim. Ovander J. Hollister, *Boldly They Rode* (Denver, 1949), pp. 91–95.

a short route to El Paso. Ill-equipped for such an effort, they suffered incredible hardships before Sibley and his starving, ragged men straggled into Fort Bliss. The Army of New Mexico was back where it had started.

The more unpleasant results of this campaign were no hindrance to General Sibley. In his report to Richmond, which was so misleading in its tone as to be dishonest, he claimed that he had invaded and conquered New Mexico and had returned his army in good condition. But a certain harshness found its way into his orotund missive. The fact was, he admitted, it was impossible to supply an army in New Mexico. Further, it was an area not worth "one quarter of the blood and treasure expended on it." And lastly, the General concluded, his troops had "manifested a dogged, irreconcilable detestation of the country and the people."[28] Whatever he might say about his campaign, New Mexico was now in Union hands; California, Colorado, and Utah remained loyal to the North, and the northern provinces of Mexico remained unconquered.

Sibley's defeats were only one side of the Confederate military debacle. His men had rekindled in the New Mexicans north of Mesilla a new dislike for Texans and the feeling that if they must put up with outside rulers, let it be Unionists. Sibley himself complained that the native *ricos* or capitalists had cast their lot with the Union and had become "absolute followers" of the federal army. Whether he had got to Fort Union or not, Sibley's retreat to El Paso was inevitable; by 1862 the complexion of Colorado loyalty was clearly Unionist, and the settlers there would have rallied against him. But the real reason for his "retrograde movement" came in the rumor from California that General Edwin V. Sumner had ordered Colonel James H. Carleton to raise a set of volunteers in California to retake Arizona and New Mexico. By the summer of 1862 the California column had recaptured Tucson and the other Arizona settlements, had made cocky Sylvester Mowry a prisoner at Fort Yuma, and was cautiously picking its way toward New Mexico. Despite desperate delaying tactics by Captain Sherod Hunter in Arizona, Confederate standards were being furled everywhere in the Far Southwest.

28. Sibley, "Official Report," p. 149.

When Sibley's and Canby's Civil War ended, a new one took its place: the federal war against the wild Indians of New Mexico. Its protagonist was General Carleton, commander of the California column. The Civil War was actually only another turbulent episode in New Mexican history, but General Carleton's campaigns against the Apache and Navajo were a turning point in New Mexican history and the beginning of the end of an Indian-White civil war, then over 250 years old.

As Carleton marched his troops up to Santa Fe in September 1862 and toward Fort Union, it became obvious that he was more than a military man. After some years in the Maine militia, Carleton had entered the regular Army and had been trained under Colonel Sumner at the Pennsylvania Cavalry School. Stationed at Fort Gibson in Indian Territory for some time, he became familiar with the Indian problem. Active in the Mexican War, his accounts of the Battle of Buena Vista were a classic in excellent reporting and suggested something of the orator in the young officer. Carleton's post-Mexican war service was in the Southwest, where he served under his hero, Colonel Sumner.[29] The two men were both in the California Department when the Civil War began.

Carleton not only had the manner and bearing of a superior officer but was a rabid unionist and War Democrat with a genuine dislike for Confederates. To him they were all guilty of treason; and any measure, military, economic, or civil, seemed justifiable as methods to curb them. To these qualities one must add a practical one. His duty in California had touched Carleton with the gold fever. Some of the men of the California column had joined Carleton, in fact, with the expectation of reaching the Arizona mining regions at government expense. And once in Arizona, the actions of Carleton and his adjutant general, Benjamin C. Cutler, in confiscating the mining property of rebels like Sylvester Mowry went far beyond the demands of the situation.[30]

Since he could not seek glory on the eastern front, Carleton,

---

29. Aurora Hunt, *Major General James Henry Carleton, 1814–1873* (Glendale, California, 1958).
30. Colton, pp. 109–10.

instead, assumed the role of deliverer of the Southwest. Upon arrival in New Mexico he saw as his threefold task: the curbing of Confederate activity, the defeat and subjection of the wild Indians, and the opening of the country to prospectors. Although Carleton came to New Mexico too late to participate in the expulsion of Sibley's bedraggled army, the Indians had gone on new rampages while federal troops were preoccupied with Sibley. In a memorial to Lincoln five months after Carleton arrived, the legislature gave a grisly report of sixty-two persons killed, thirty-four wounded, and stock losses of more than $340,000 because of Indian raids.[31]

Undoubtedly Sumner had briefed Carleton on New Mexican conditions, so that he arrived with a solution in mind for the Indian problem. His first move was a shrewd one. Once in Santa Fe he used his eloquence to enlist the cooperation of such figures as Governor Connelly; Chief Justice Kirby Benedict, the powerful boss of the local Republican party; members of the Chavez family; and that veteran Indian fighter, the soft-spoken Kit Carson of Taos. The General's most remarkable conversion, however, was that of James L. Collins, editor of the Santa Fe *Gazette* and Indian Superintendent.[32] Once again New Mexico felt the hand of military rule.

Carleton's Indian program was harsh and simple: to kill or capture wild Indians until they agreed to surrender and live on a single reservation, where they could be taught Christianity and agriculture. At a breathless pace he ordered Kit Carson into the field to round up the Mescelero Apaches, a task that was completed by January 1863. While this was being accomplished, other troops temporarily subdued the Gila Apaches of Arizona in a winter campaign; and under circumstances which were to prove embarrassing later, the impressive Apache chief Mangas Coloradas was captured and killed.[33] Cruel though they were, Carleton's dogged, unceasing campaigns—or "scouts," as he called them—had their effect. Remnants of once proud

31. *Memorial of the Legislative Assembly of New Mexico to . . . Abraham Lincoln,* January 26, 1863, Ritch Coll. (Box 19), HEH. See also *Report of the Commissioner of Indian Affairs for the Year, 1863* (Washington, 1864), p. 110.

32. "General Carleton's Indian Policy," in the Santa Fe *Weekly Gazette,* November 19, December 24, 1864.

33. Colton, pp. 126–30 passim.

tribes trickled in to bid for peace, and the stockades at Fort Sumner on the Pecos—which Carleton had built and named in honor of his superior officer—filled with defeated Indians.

By the summer of 1863 Carleton was being hailed as the deliverer of New Mexico. Santa Fe was at his feet, and the Collins press, in which Carleton now had an interest, had difficulty finding new adjectives to praise the General. At this point Carleton turned to the question of the Navajo raiders. Abandoning the concept that these nomadic Indians lived in inpenetrable canyons and mountain reaches in northwestern New Mexico, the commander established Fort Wingate in the midst of Navajo country and turned the faithful Kit Carson loose on the tribe in July 1863. Scornful of treaties or negotiations, he declared his policy to General West: "Entire subjugation, or destruction of all the men, are the alternatives." As before, Carleton's men ignored the seasons; and in a brilliant set of winter battles, skirmishes, and captures, Kit Carson rounded up several thousand Navajos.[34] It was a war with no quarter; every Navajo cornfield or food cache was destroyed. For every horse captured, the Army paid out twenty dollars; for every Navajo sheep taken, the Quartermaster Department promised a dollar reward.[35]

As the Navajo captives streamed into Fort Wingate, Carleton initiated the second phase of his Indian policy. He would also move them to the reservation at Fort Sumner on the Pecos River. There in a pleasant grove near the fort, called the Bosque Redondo, the General had established his "reformatory" for the Navajo away "from the haunts and hills and hiding places of their country. Here the Navajos would be treated kindly, the children taught to read and write, the old Indians would die off, and the younger ones would take their place."[36]

So far, Carleton's plan had succeeded magnificently. New Mexicans welcomed the return to peace, and the local government supported him so completely that Carleton was virtually the ruler of New Mexico. The legislature tended their thanks by calling him the deliverer of

34. Ibid., pp. 137–45 passim. Keleher, *Turmoil,* p. 295.

35. A MS fragment of a "Diary Kept on Kit Carson's Navajo Campaign, 1863" describes the ruthless campaign vividly; Ritch Coll. (Box 20), HEH.

36. Keleher, *Turmoil,* p. 310.

the territory, and, as usual, the pro-Carleton Santa Fe *Gazette* pulled out all the stops in praise of the new order. Ironically, capturing Indians proved easier than feeding and civilizing them, and his whole program was to be defeated by the federal government's failure to furnish adequate supplies, the hostility of the Indian Bureau and subordinate officials at Santa Fe to army control of Indian affairs, and Carleton's own active and often tyrannical hand in New Mexican politics. Carleton insisted, for example, on martial law in a region now devoid of Confederate troops.

The details of Carleton's difficulties in securing food need not be given here. Suffice it to say that federal supplies did not come up to expectation, and Carleton's own crops, planted by the Indians at the Bosque Redondo, suffered heavily from drought in 1864 and from unpredicted freezing in 1865. Faced with starvation, some 9,000 Indians at the Redondo were soon in a mutinous mood, and this on a reservation where Apache and Navajo—traditional enemies—were crowded together for the first time in history. What had been a brilliant policy now began to seem a fiasco. Lorenzo Labadie, the Indian agent at Fort Sumner, admitted that it was a fatal mistake. Old New Mexicans began to murmur that Apache and Navajo could never live together. At this crucial moment James L. Collins, the opportunistic Superintendent of Indian Affairs and editor of Carleton's *Gazette*, was removed and Dr. Michael Steck became his successor.[37] Honest and well-meaning, with a touch of the reformer in him, Steck was soon at odds with Carleton over his handling of the Indians. As Steck's criticisms spread about the territory, various factions—some anxious to curb Carleton's increasing use of arbitrary power and others desirous of seizing the Bosque Redondo area for ranching purposes—joined in the attack.[38] Still others—Carleton accused—wanted a return to the time of captured Indian servants, and of small wars and raids that were profitable, although they were often paid for in blood. Then there was the old game of partisan politics. New Mexico had now been under martial law for nearly four years, and Carleton's military control by this device

37. Ibid., pp. 376, 410 ff.
38. Ibid., p. 438. See also Miguel Romero y Baca to Dr. Michael Steck, June 23, 1864; Ritch (Box 22), HEH.

rankled federal officials whose acts were, as often as not, counter-manded by the vigorous General. Finally, Carleton's harsh treatment of Confederate sympathizers, particularly the population of Mesilla, left many an angry citizen hankering for the General's hide.

As early as the winter of 1863–64, it was obvious that the whole of New Mexican politics centered around the Carleton Indian and martial law policies and that two parties were forming. When Carleton had first appeared in New Mexico and when Republican supremacy in Washington seemed to be safely established, most Americans and New Mexicans in the territory realistically became Union men and nominally Republicans. This was demonstrated in the delegate election of 1863, when Francisco Perea won on a Union and pro-Carleton ticket. Nevertheless, the basic factionalism of New Mexican politics, divided into family parties and further split between liberal and conservative stands on Lamy's reforms, could not remain submerged for long. To cause still more difficulty, the Americans there were splintered into Republican and Democrat and Northern and Southern sympathizers.

When the national election of 1864 approached, it was evident that the Republicans or Unionists were actually split into three groups: the regulars, consisting of Governor Connelly, Delegate Perea, and Judge Watts, who openly declared for Lincoln; another faction, led by Connelly's own secretary, W. F. M. Arny, who supported Chase and the Radicals; and still a third group, who were actually old-time Democrats and wanted McClellan for President.[39] While many in the latter faction might have been Southern sympathizers, General Carleton complicated the already muddled political picture by letting it be known that he had been a Democrat and was for McClellan.

Of those in opposition to Carleton, the most curious was the faction led by the territorial secretary, William Frederick Milton Arny, and the Indian superintendent, Dr. Steck. Arny had been a free-soiler in Kansas and had been in the body that produced the Wyandotte Constitution. Though a sincere abolitionist, he was also a professional and ambitious politician. During the long intervals of Governor Connelly's absence from office because of travel or illness, Arny was more

39. The Santa Fe *Weekly Gazette* (February 18, 1865) contains a résumé of the election politics of 1864.

often than not acting Governor, and in this capacity he had quietly built up a small cadre of office-holders loyal to himself. Having failed to get the delegateship in 1863, he began to intrigue for the removal of James Collins as Indian superintendent, recommending himself for the post. While this maneuver failed, his friend Dr. Michael Steck did get the position. The two joined forces in their war on Carleton's Indian policies.[40]

The chief point of opposition to Carleton was that he would not permit the Navajos to return to a reservation in their native area. Arny and Steck argued that the Indian would be happier there and that in western New Mexico they could feed themselves. This would save the government many thousands of dollars. At the same time, Arny, as territorial secretary, clashed with Carleton frequently over civil government. When the General levied license fees in Dona Ana County, for example, Arny protested bitterly that this was a function of the civil government and ordered him to stop.[41]

As Arny fished in the troubled political waters of wartime New Mexico, another federal official, Judge Joseph Gillette Knapp, also attacked the General. A cantankerous, outspoken lawyer with a strong feeling for his civil liberties, Knapp chafed under Carleton's martial law regime.[42] He was infuriated that criminal cases often went to military courts and that he could travel about the territory only with a pass from the haughty Carleton. Knapp aptly fitted Burke's remark about the gentleman who could sniff tyranny in every tainted breeze. Fortunately for Knapp, his court district was the southern portion of New Mexico and included Mesilla and Dona Ana County. The citizens there were now heartily sick of being treated as rebels by Carleton's officers. They were even more angry at the property confiscations carried out by Abraham Cutler, who had resigned from the Army to become United States Marshal of New Mexico. Eagerly they joined Knapp in his denunciations of the General. Knapp himself

40. Ferdinand Maxwell to W. F. M. Arny, June 11, 1863. For the Arny-Steck alliance see Steck to Arny, October 20, 1863; Ritch (Box 20), HEH.

41. Arny to Carleton, April 30, 1863, Ritch (Box 20), HEH. Santa Fe *Weekly Gazette,* December 31, 1864.

42. Carleton to Arny, February 26, 1863, Ritch (Box 20), HEH. See also Arie W. Poldervaart, *Black-Robed Justice* (Santa Fe, 1948), pp. 62–63.

bombarded Washington with complaints of Carleton's invasions of judicial and civil rights, and he spoke wherever he could against the military regime. Before the verbal battle was over, Knapp had publicly accused Carleton of having the Apache chief, Mangas Coloradas, murdered in cold blood.[43]

Yet the further one looks into the Mesilla troubles, the more it becomes apparent that Knapp's fight was not just for civil liberties. A new movement to form southern New Mexico into a separate territory called "Montezuma" was under way by 1863, and both Knapp and Arny—as well as several politicians in Albuquerque—were supporting it. Arny, in fact, persuaded a Mesilla convention to elect him delegate to Congress. John Greiner, Receiver at the United States Depository in Santa Fe, indicated the complexity of the intrigue in a letter to Arny in early 1864:

"Gen'l West . . . [who opposed Carleton's policies] is expected daily when we look for a lively time among the military. Knapp is keeping up the fight in Mesilla valiently and is earning the reward of the Victor. The Montezuma matter is working well and they look to you for the organiaztion of the Territory. . . . We hope Dr. Steck will not have left [Washington] for with both of you there you can resist the world the flesh and the devils of the Perea faction."[44]

The wing of the Republican party which supported Lincoln was led by Judge Kirby Benedict, who tried to wield political power: first by cooperating with Carleton and then by attacking him. As part owner of the Santa Fe *New Mexican*, Benedict opposed the Carleton-dominated *Gazette*. But under the restrictions of martial law and in view of the Civil War, Benedict obviously thought it the better part of valor in 1863 and early 1864 to support Carleton. He saw that the General's popularity was declining in the fall of 1864, however, and appreciative of the fact that Arny had recommended federal printing contracts for the *New Mexican*, the Judge launched an attack on Carleton which became increasingy bitter.[45]

43. Edward D. Tittmann, "Exploitation of Treason," *NMHR*, *4* (1929), 128–45.
44. John Greiner to W. F. M. Arny, February 28, 1864, Ritch (Box 21), HEH.
45. Arny to Seward, February 23, 1863, Ritch (Box 19), HEH. Santa Fe *Weekly Gazette*, December 4, 1864.

By 1864 the split over Carleton's policies had permeated every level of New Mexican politics. As the Santa Fe *Gazette* observed that fall: "If a person happens to be a contractor and in favor of the Bosque Reservation he is charged with being so because of the profit he can make out of it, and acting the hypocrit in the most approved style."[46] Its die-hard opponent, the Santa Fe *New Mexican*, retorted that the description fitted the *Gazette* and its friends, who were "generally petted with patronage in some form from the military crib."[47]

The dispute continued into the spring and summer, when a Senate committee to investigate Indian affairs, under the chairmanship of Senator J. R. Doolittle of Wisconsin, journeyed to New Mexico to inspect the Carleton regime. All the famous men of New Mexico, from the aged Padre Martinez to the venerable Kit Carson, turned out to give their opinions.[48] The committee gave the Bosque Redondo an unqualified approval, but this did nothing to quiet the crisis. When the electioneering for the delegateship began that fall, the chief plank of both candidates concerned their position on Carleton. Colonel J. Francisco Chavez, himself a veteran Navajo fighter, ran on a pro-Arny and anti-Bosque ticket, while his cousin Francisco Perea, the incumbent delegate, defended the General. Chavez's election by a majority of 2,000 suggested that Carleton's day would soon be over.[49]

Continuing complaints persuaded Washington to send out a special agent, Julius Graves, in 1866 to test the local reaction to Senator Doolittle's favorable report. Graves wrote that while Indian affairs were still "the all absorbing topic of conversation," the legislature had refused to answer his questions. Just as the Doolittle Committee had done, Graves upheld Carleton's policies, but Congress could no longer ignore territorial feelings. In the winter of 1865–66 the legislature passed a memorial condemning Carleton and asking his removal. The memorial, incidentally, was in Arny's handwriting.[50]

Carleton's opponents finally had their way in September 1866: he was removed, just four years after he had entered the territory in triumph. It took longer, however, to undo his program, for it was

---

46. Santa Fe *Weekly Gazette*, October 22, 1864.
47. The *New Mexican*, quoted in the *Weekly Gazette*, October 22, 1864.
48. Santa Fe *Weekly Gazette*, July 8, 1865. Kelcher, *Turmoil*, pp. 352 ff.
49. Waldrip, "New Mexico," pp. 87–88. Santa Fe *Weekly Gazette*, August 5, 1865.
50. MS "Memorial" (undated), Ritch (Box 23), HEH.

1867 before the government signed a treaty at Fort Sumner allowing the Navajos to return to their beloved hills and canyons.[51] In the summer of 1868 the remnants of the tribe who had survived the rigors of the Bosque Redondo retraced their steps over the paths of the "long walk" five years before. Accoutered in their gayest clothes, smiling, and happy, the returning exiles experienced such overwhelming emotions as they came into view of familiar horizons and the lovely blue mountains that the American soldiers guarding them were affected as well. One Indian became temporarily deranged at the glorious sight; and others, in the natural poetry of an unwritten tongue, cried out: "When we saw the top of the mountain from Albuquerque we wondered if it was our mountain, and we felt like talking to the ground, we loved it so."[52]

General Carleton's Indian policy, a strange paradoxical mixture of the concentration camp and benevolent despotism, was somewhat like Reconstruction in the American South, in that it was considered both radical, and a failure. Carleton had by no means solved the Indian question in New Mexico and Arizona, but henceforward it would center around the problem of controlling specific outbreaks in specific regions. Warfare and anarchy—the natural state of New Mexico since Juan de Oñate—was now to be the exception rather than the rule. After 1868 the Navajos were a broken power, reduced by disease and war to less than half the number they had been in 1863. The whites in New Mexico now clearly outnumbered the Indians; although raids and killings would continue to 1885 and Arizona was to be at the mercy of Apaches until that date, no longer was the Southwest forbidden territory to the settler, the miner, or the rancher. On the very heels of the Navajo retreat from Fort Sumner, ranchers and sheepmen moved in to establish grazing grounds. A small number of miners— many of them wintering in New Mexico to escape the harsher winters of Colorado—penetrated the local mineral frontiers of New Mexico and Arizona. Speculators began to form companies to sell land and mining schemes to New York investors. A negative American attitude

51. Santa Fe *Weekly Gazette,* October 3, 1868.
52. Paul A. Horgan, *Great River: The Rio Grande in North American History* (2 vols. New York, 1954), 2, 333.

toward New Mexico had at last begun to change, and Carleton, aided by men like Kit Carson, had brought about the new age.

Just as Indians and whites were feeling the strong hand of Carleton's "reconstruction,"on their lives, the federal government turned to the problem of Reconstruction in the South. In their concern for the ex-slave, the radical Republicans did not forget that New Mexico had legalized slavery in 1859, that debt and Indian peonage existed in the territory, and that New Mexican use of captured Navajo Indians as domestics was another thinly disguised form of slavery. General Carleton himself brought this peculiar set of Southwestern institutions to the attention of authorities in Washington, with the result that Congress outlawed the ancient systems of peonage and slavery in New Mexico in 1867, and a year later the laws were enforced there.[53] Although little actual change in the relation of servant to master actually occurred, the new laws signified that another old Spanish colonial custom had come to an end. The Union victory over the South had truly far-reaching consequences when it reached into the internal affairs of neutral New Mexico and legally abolished an established caste and economic system. In both dramatic and subtle ways, Carleton and the federal government were slowly making the Southwestern frontier into a part of the United States.

In the history of American frontiers the first stage of an unoccupied or undeveloped region is an international one, in which contending powers maneuver for control of the prize. This period occurred along the borders of northern Mexico from 1821 to 1846. With Kearny's conquest the second, or national, stage began, when the frontier came to depend heavily upon the national government for its defense and development. It is in this stage that a frontier region becomes a true colony of the nation, with its destinies directed from without rather than from within. Sibley's invasion, Canby's eventual victory, Carleton's Indian and martial law policies, and the end of slavery and peonage—all these highlighted an era when the nation rather than the province called the turns. By 1865 the supreme crisis of the Union

53. *An Act to Abolish . . . The System of Peonage, March 2, 1867,* proclaimed in New Mexico, April 14, 1867.

had been resolved, however, and New Mexico entered into a third stage, with an increasingly provincial attitude, during which there was an assertion of local rights, the rise of a working local political system, a calculated use of outside aid for local benefit, and a growing sense of identity with the region as a home. The eventual result of such attitudes is political self-rule in the form of statehood and a certain degree of economic self-sufficiency.

The date of General Carleton's removal marked the beginning of this final period for New Mexico, and it was symbolized by the emergence of political patterns typical of other developing American territories in the nineteenth century. Such patterns may be illustrated by three events occurring in New Mexico between 1865 and 1870. The first of these developments was the ordering of local politics to the point where no single federal appointee or commander could assume the position of exceptional power once held by Governor Calhoun or Generals Sumner and Carleton. By 1868 the governorship had declined to the level where political hacks more often than not held the post. Governor Robert B. Mitchell (1866–69), despite a violent temper and a contempt for the legislature, made little impression on the territory. Governors William A. Pile (1869–71) and Marsh Giddings (1871–75) left even less.

On the county level it was clear by 1865 that the probate judge was the virtual ruler in local politics, for he continued to act as much an alcalde as a judge. On the territorial level, observers commented that by 1868 Assembly members were as adept as any American professionals in the game of politics. As of 1870, territorial judges were still struggling to introduce the jury system and American procedures into their courtrooms.

The second characteristic of the postwar period was the use of the federal government largess for local purposes. Although this had occurred throughout the 1850s, it reached a new level when Indian relations were turned back over to the Indian Bureau. As Carleton prepared to leave the territory, a ring of Santa Fe politicians who had favored the Indian Bureau were waiting to take over. Since Arizona had been organized as a federal territory in 1863, Indian affairs for New Mexico at least seemed a less overwhelming problem. The official correspondence of the superintendent, once full of alarms and the sad statistics of a raid, now was filled with applications for appointments to Indian agencies or contracts for their feeding and supply. In describing the new order, the *Gazette* aptly called it "a paradoxical compound of dishonest speculation and well-meant philanthropy."[54] The profitable nature of peacetime Indian affairs was reflected in the career of ex-Secretary Arny, who had been a candidate for nearly every high office in the territory. Now he happily settled for the post of Indian agent at Abiquiu.

The basically selfish and provincial nature of the Indian policy favored by New Mexican residents was revealed when Ulysses S. Grant became president in 1869 and initiated his famous "peace policy" through the Indian Bureau. Among other things, Grant's program envisaged the control of local agencies by various Christian denominations, who might appoint ministers as agents should they wish. It was New Mexico's fate to be reformed by Indian Commissioner Vincent Colyer, a noble but difficult Quaker humanitarian.[55]

Within a week of his arrival the old Indian debate had revived. The *Gazette*, still loyal to Carleton and the Army, argued that the Indians should remain under War Department control.[56] Arny and the regular Republicans swallowed the ambitious new peace policy for a time, but the utopian qualities of Colyer's program soon proved too much even for them. The whole territory finally revolted against the "silly theories of Quakerism and Puritanism" and began to agitate for the pious Colyer's removal.[57] The episode suggested that while Indian policy was still a basic issue in territorial politics, it was now a question that the local population felt it could deal with more effectively than reformers in Washington. Governor Mitchell, Connelly's successor, reflected this view when he permitted volunteer militia units to form to defend themselves in case of Indian attack from "Colyer's angels."[58] Obviously, the territory now looked upon the Indian ques-

54. "An Indian Policy Wanted," Santa Fe *Weekly Gazette*, August 17, 1867.
55. "Vincent Colyer" in *The National Cyclopaedia of American Biography*, VII (New York, 1897), p. 541.
56. Santa Fe *Weekly Gazette*, March 27, 1869.
57. Ibid., June 19, 1869. See also Las Cruces *Borderer*, September 27, 1873.
58. Santa Fe *Weekly Gazette*, August 7, 1869.

tion as a profitable, everyday business, which investigators and reformers should not disturb.

In this connection it should be remembered that in 1865 much of
New Mexico's economy was still based on the expenditures of the
federal government for army and Indian supplies. The once exotic
and occasional wagon trains that meandered down the familiar rutted
trail had given way to an everyday freighting business of 5,000 teams
a year and an enterprise of national importance.[59] In such a situation
it was impossible to tell where the economic man in New Mexico left
off and the political man began. Twenty years after 1846 Santa Fe was
still as much under a rule of merchants as it was of politicians and
army officers.

The third pattern that reflected an increasingly cynical use of Washington, while exhibiting the traditional factionalism in politics, is
amply illustrated by the history of the delegate's office. In the 1865
delegate election, for example, it was a question whether to declare
for Radical Reconstruction or to support President Johnson's more
moderate program. Chameleon-like in their efforts to reflect national
trends and therefore to ensure the awarding of territorial patronage,
the Republicans of New Mexico also split. One group—actually the
old states-rights and pro-Carleton forces—chose to support the Johnson
delegate, Francisco Perea. The Radicals, led by Judge Kirby Benedict
and Arny, received the support of the anti-Carleton forces and selected
J. Francisco Chavez as their candidate.[60]

To a logical man this election and those of 1867 and 1869 could be
described only as a set of paradoxes, explainable only in terms of
extreme political expediency. Arny and Benedict, ardent Unionists
and abolitionists, backed Chavez, described by his opposition as being
conservative, anti-Mason, an advocate of peonage and slavery, and,
withal, a tool of the so-called anti-American Pino family. Yet the
opposition party making this charge consisted of states-rights Democrats such as John T. Russell (Collins' successor as editor of the
Gazette), Diego Archuleta, and the former anti-American and anti-
Lamy delegate, J. M. Gallegos.[61]

59. G. P. Hammond and T. C. Donnelly, *The Story of New Mexico, Its History
and Its Government* (Albuquerque, 1937), pp. 132–33.
60. Santa Fe *Weekly Gazette*, August 1 to October 21 passim.
61. Ibid., April 6, 27, 1867.

In the confusion of these strange alliances, Chavez secured election in 1865, when he ran against his cousin Francisco Perea, and in 1867, when he ran against Charles Clever. In 1869, however, Don Vicente Romero, running on an anti-Peace Policy plank, carried the day for the conservatives. And two years later ex-Delegate Gallegos won on a similar anti-Peace Policy ticket.[62] In the ever-shifting factions struggling for public office, little could be seen in the way of patterns except that a reaction to an unpopular edict or policy imposed from Washington led to a refuge in localism.

Some thirty years after American conquest, New Mexican local politics were still based more on family alliance, cultural ties, anti-Americanism, church faction, and crass economic interest than on any party principles. The privilege of the vote was still taken so lightly that corruption characterized every election. The mere party labels Republican and Democrat became caricatures in this unique situation. Yet there were new forces and new issues abroad in New Mexico. By sheer persistence and propinquity, American ideas were insinuating themselves into the local customs. More Americans began to appear in the legislature. And down the trail from the states came such an amazing number of lawyers that soon one in every ten Americans in the territory was reputed to be a member of the bar. What was in the air? How could an attorney survive in a community where even federal courts were often dismissed for lack of a docket? The answer lay in the exploitation and amortization of another old Spanish colonial custom. These shrewd and aggressive young lawyers, still stumbling over their Spanish, would build their own political and economic empire out of the tangled heritage of land grants.

62. *Ibid.*, February 27, 1869.

6

The Santa Fe Ring
1865–1885

> Many years ago a few sharp, shrewd Americans came here—
> discovered a number of small Mexican and Spanish Grants—
> purchased them at nominal prices—learned the Spanish
> language—ingratiated themselves into favor with the Mexican
> people, and proceeded to enlarge the Grants they had
> purchased, and to manufacture at will titles to still others,
> and to secure therefore Congressional recognition. . . .
>
> The holders of the Grants were simple Mexicans who never
> would have thought of claiming more than their papers called
> for, but the ring soon taught them a few tricks they had
> never thought of.
>
> Governor Edmund G. Ross, 1887

 After the Civil War many young veterans found the docile life of their home towns so unattractive that they headed West in search of new careers and new excitement. Some, having learned to command men, knew they were destined for bigger things. Others could not shake off acquired habits of violence. The conflict had made still others so psychopathically bitter that they continued to wage a private war against the world long after the surrender at Appomattox. The border state of Missouri, which had already dotted the Far West with mountain men and traders, now seemed to have just such a surplus of restless and ambitious veterans. Out of the counties of southwestern Missouri in the postwar decades rode the Coles, the Youngers, the Jameses, and scores of obscure drifters and

gunmen hunting their destiny in the wide-horizoned West. Their doings made West Texas a land for tough men only; they brought notoriety and death to a score of Kansas cattle towns, and for a time it was literally true that there was "no law West of the Pecos." Always drawn to a region where society was in a developmental stage, such a large number of these men came into Lincoln and Colfax counties in New Mexico that Ralph Twitchell has called that area "catch-basins for the reckless and criminal element." Southeastern New Mexico in the twenty years after the Civil War, wrote Emerson Hough, was "as dangerous a country as ever lay out of doors."[1]

Not all the immigrants were from Missouri, had a gun at their side, or possessed an itchy trigger finger. Members of Carleton's California Column remained in the Southwest, to find a livelihood after their service had ended. Colonel W. L. Rynerson, future political leader of southern New Mexico, was one of those who stayed. Major Lawrence G. Murphy, attracted by cattle ranching and the profitability of stores in army towns, became a trader at Ft. Stanton and a rancher and political boss in Lincoln County as well. Other able young men, in pursuit of one of the professions, continued to drift down the Santa Fe Trail. Among these were two graduates of the University of Missouri who were members of the class of 1860. After they had parted company at graduation, Stephen Benton Elkins, the more openly brilliant and urbane of the two, joined the Union Army, while the other, Thomas Benton Catron, crusty, blunt, energetic, and domineering by nature, sided with the Confederates.

Elkins and Catron made no great reputation in the Civil War and, unlike half their political colleagues in New Mexico, did not assume the title of major or colonel after the fighting was over. By 1864, in fact, Elkins had left the Army for the troubled town of Mesilla, where he became a lawyer. An attractive personality and a quick mastery of Spanish won him a seat in the New Mexican House of Representatives the next year. Later he was advanced from the territorial attorney general's office to become the United States district attorney for New Mexico. Only twenty-six years old, he seemed to be a second Henry

---

1. Twitchell, *Leading Facts*, 2, 418.

Clay in the making, and both his admirers and detractors referred to him as "Smooth Steve" Elkins.[2]

Elkins' meteoric rise persuaded his college chum to join him. The ever-practical Catron loaded two wagons with flour in 1866 and set out for Santa Fe. The sale of the flour would pay the cost of the trip. Undoubtedly warned by Elkins and others that he was coming into a new culture, Catron doggedly memorized a Spanish grammar on the trail and deliberately lived with a Spanish-speaking family for a few months after his arrival, until he was fluent in the language. After studying law with Merrill Ashurst and clerking for Chief Justice Kirby Benedict, the boss of a wing of the Republican Party, Catron was appointed district attorney for the third judicial district in 1867.[3]

Then the intertwining of two famous legal and political careers began. In 1869 when Elkins was United States attorney, Catron was the territorial attorney general. By now they had pooled their resources as the law firm of Elkins and Catron, an office that was to carry the names of half the attorney generals or chief justices to serve in New Mexico. In this firm and its branches in Albuquerque and Las Vegas, much of the political history of territorial New Mexico was to be made. Both partners dreamed of reaching the United States Senate one day, and when Elkins discovered that statehood was not imminent for New Mexico, he moved his fortune and his career to West Virginia. An important figure in national Republican circles, he became Benjamin Harrison's Secretary of War in 1891 and served as senator from West Virginia from 1895 until his death in 1911. Catron, however, once having identified himself with New Mexico, remained there for the rest of his life and became, as William A. Keleher has accurately observed: "the one man, who more than any other, dominated New Mexico's political and business affairs for fifty years."[4]

As Elkins and Catron looked about their adopted territory, it was obvious that aside from Indian affairs, five things preoccupied the

2. Mary Elizabeth Sluga, "The Political Life of Thomas Benton Catron" (Master's thesis, University of New Mexico, 1941), pp. 5–6. "Stephen Benton Elkins" in *DAB*.

3. Vioalle Clark Hefferan, "Thomas Benton Catron" (Master's thesis, University of New Mexico, 1940), pp. 8–10.

4. William A. Keleher, *The Fabulous Frontier* (Santa Fe, 1945), p. 97.

Preoce of early polit minded frontersmen

thoughts of business and politically minded New Mexicans: the land-grant question (details of which Catron learned in Merrill Ashurst's office), statehood, open-range cattle ranching, railroads, and mining. With the possible exception of statehood, all problems were clearly related to land and its control. As attorneys their concern was to associate their careers with these five questions. Their methods and activities helped make the political and economic history of New Mexico for the next three decades.

From the time of the Taos Rebellion until 1854, when Washington finally appointed a surveyor general for New Mexico, the title to all property in the territory had lain in uneasy status. The United States, by the treaty of Guadalupe Hidalgo, had promised to respect New Mexican holdings, but these were enormously complicated by the existence of three kinds of grants: one to a community, usually for grazing purposes; a second to an individual for some outstanding service, such as defense against wild Indians or as a reward for settling a new area; and a third to the various Indian pueblos. As has been demonstrated elsewhere, there were further complications, because such grants had been variously awarded by the King of Spain, the Republic of New Mexico after 1822, and the provincial governor—particularly Manuel Armijo—in the five years before American conquest. There were even more refined distinctions between grazing and irrigated land grants, individual and common grants, and Pueblo and white grants.[5]

When Surveyor General William Pelham arrived in Santa Fe in 1854, he must have been dismayed at the task facing him. Over one thousand claims awaited settlement, of which 197 involved large private grants. Moreover, many of the private holdings overlapped one another. Outside of California and possibly French Louisiana, Americans had never before dealt with such complicated land questions. At the same time, Congress had given Pelham such elaborate and burdensome instructions that he was actually hampered rather than helped by them. One clause, for example, written into the act which created his post, declared: "Until final action of Congress on such claims, all lands

5. Herbert O. Brayer, "The Pueblo Indian Land Grants of the Rio Abajo" (Master's thesis, University of New Mexico, 1937).

covered thereby shall be reserved from sale or other disposal by the government."[6]

This was the equivalent of denying the existence of a public domain in New Mexico, while at the same time it guaranteed that long legal battles climaxed by acts of Congress would characterize the history of the New Mexican land system. A paradise for lawyers and politicians had been created. Commented William A. Keleher: "The claims approved by Congress were generally those with the most persistent influence on the outside and the most powerful political influence on the inside."[7] And as if to clinch the necessity for lawyers in land settlement, the grants in their wording were so extraordinarily vague that a claim could be stretched to include an estate of almost imperial size.

Despite many difficulties, including faulty, hasty, and fraudulent surveys and the refusal of many distrustful Spanish-American grantees to cooperate, a number of grants had been confirmed by 1857. In the process, however, the legal profession of Santa Fe had become involved in securing title for their clients. They were men whom Governor E. G. Ross described as "sharp, shrewd Americans . . . possessed of some local lore and with a large amount of cheek and an unusual quantity of low cunning and astuteness."[8] The first chief justice, Joab Houghton, erstwhile builder of the capitol, was also an attorney for twelve claimants, among them Ceran St. Vrain. Hugh N. Smith, the "delegate" to Congress elected by the extralegal statehood forces of 1849, was concerned with at least ten land grant clients. Later in the fifties Judge John S. Watts told a Congressional committee that he was handling forty-three cases. Other pioneer lawyers such as Merrill Ashurst, Theodore Wheaton, and Spruce M. Baird were also engaged in the land-title business.[9]

6. William W. Morrow, *Spanish and Mexican Private Land Grants*, (San Francisco, 1923), pp. 21–23, pamphlet, HEH.

7. William A. Keleher, *Maxwell Land Grant: A New Mexico Item* (Santa Fe, 1942), pp. 7–8.

8. Edmund G. Ross to John O'Grady, March 26, 1887, Ross Papers, NMSRC.

9. *John S. Watts to the Chairman of the Committee on Private Land Claims* (Washington, 1871), pp. 1–2, HEH. See also volume entitled *Private Land Claims, New Mexico* in the law library of T. B. Catron in HEH for a list of attorneys involved. See finally the manuscript list of New Mexican private land claims in Ritch, HEH.

In the rush to clear title Carlos Beaubien and Guadalupe Miranda, two of the largest claimants, decided to take no chances. They hired three lawyers; Houghton, Wheaton, and Smith. The old Taos merchant's dream of empire seemed to come true when Congress confirmed the grant in 1860. In doing so, however, Congress was guided by the Mexican Colonization Law of 1824, which limited the size of a grant to eleven square leagues for each claimant. Had Congress stuck by this ruling, the solution of the New Mexican land question would have been relatively simple. But there were too many other Spanish and Mexican laws contradicting the 1824 statute. Shrewd lawyers began to stretch their clients holdings on this basis until, as Governor Lionel A. Sheldon later remarked, the grants took on remarkable "India rubber qualities."[10]

The history of the scores of land-grant cases and their role in New Mexican history might be epitomized by a brief account of the most famous and notorious of all tracts, the Beaubien-Miranda claim, which came to be called the Maxwell Land Grant. When Carlos Beaubien died in 1864, his enterprising son-in-law, Lucien Bonaparte Maxwell—husband to Luz Beaubien—bought the grant from his in-laws and purchased Guadalupe Miranda's part as well.[11] Maxwell's was a princely domain. At his house in Cimarron scores of guests and dozens of retainers mingled in an atmosphere of luxurious frontier hospitality. Kind-hearted and affable, he was loved by Indian and white alike. But Maxwell was also a businessman. He had made money selling cattle and grain to Indian agencies and to the Army. Now that title was secure—or so he thought—he saw a chance to sell the grant for a fantastic price. He had been made aware of the possible great value of the grant when gold was discovered on the land in 1867 and prospectors and investors had swarmed onto the grant regardless of his claim to ownership. Maxwell also knew that his neighbor at Mora, the elderly Ceran St. Vrain, was negotiating with Colorado financiers for the sale of the huge Vigil and St. Vrain tracts.[12]

10. Keleher, *Maxwell*, p. 9.
11. Jim Berry Pearson, *The Maxwell Land Grant* (Norman, 1961), pp. 12–15, traces Maxwell's history of acquisition in excellent detail.
12. Dunham, *Government Handout*, pp. 221–22. Pearson, *Maxwell*, pp. 17 ff.

In 1869 Maxwell asked for a new government survey and learned that by the 1824 Colonization Law his claim was 22 leagues or, roughly, 97,000 acres. By now Maxwell's name, already known and liked all over the Southwest, became familiar to frontier businessmen and speculators as well. In Colorado, Jerome B. Chaffee, a wealthy mine owner and future senator, made overtures to Maxwell for the purchase of the grant. At Chaffee's side was George H. Chilcott, former land register for Colorado—who had doubtless gathered details on the New Mexican grants, since parts of several of the large grants had been included in Colorado when it was created a territory in 1861. And in the background was ex-Governor William Gilpin, Colorado owner of the Sangre de Cristo grant, who had been interested in St. Vrain's and Beaubien's land activities for over twenty years.[13] (See Map.)

The importance and the extent of the interest in New Mexico land grants becomes obvious when it is realized that the Colorado contingent was but one of four groups interested in Maxwell's land. In New Mexico itself Stephen B. Elkins, Thomas Catron, Governor William A. Pile, ex-Delegate Watts, and Miguel A. Otera (the wealthy partner of Otero, Sellar and Company) were among the purchasers. And, as always, the current surveyor general was a party to the scheme. After some negotiations, in 1869 Maxwell agreed to give Chaffee and Elkins an option to buy. A year later the purchase was concluded for a paper price of $1,350,000. The buyers called their acquisition The Maxwell Land Grant and Railroad Company. At the same time Elkins, who never did things by halves, bought various Colorado mines on Chaffee's recommendation and persuaded Maxwell to use part of his money to found the first regular bank in New Mexico—the First National of Santa Fe. The bank, in turn, was chiefly interested in handling the Company's securities.[14]

The men who purchased Maxwell's Grant had even larger plans than Beaubien, St. Vrain, or Lucien Maxwell had ever envisaged. Acutely aware of the vagueness of the grant, they hired W. W. Griffin, United States Deputy Surveyor of New Mexico, to survey the grant

13. "Jerome B. Chaffee," in *DAB*. "George M. Chilcott," *Appleton's Cyclopaedia*. "William Gilpin" in *DAB*. Pearson, *Maxwell*, p. 49.

14. Keleher, *Maxwell*, pp. 35–36. Dunham, *Government Handout*, p. 223. Pearson, *Maxwell*, pp. 49 ff.

as a 2,000,000 acre plot—in contrast to the 97,000 acres to which Congress and Secretary of the Interior Cox had limited it in 1869. The results of Griffin's report were filed in Washington; and without waiting for confirmation, Wilson Waddingham, an English rancher connected with the new company, went to London and sold the grant to English purchasers.

The London firm constituted the third group interested in the Maxwell Grant. In a maneuver that looked suspiciously like passing the buck, the English company persuaded a fourth party, Dutch financiers in Amsterdam, to handle the mortgage. Stock was then issued for $5,000,000. The company then elected an Anglophile American Civil War general, William Jackson Palmer, as its president. At the time, Palmer was superintendent of the Kansas Pacific Railroad; Stephen Elkins, the leading lawyer in New Mexico, was to be the resident director and local attorney of the company; while Governor Pile, M. A. Otero, and Judge Watts were to be vice-presidents. Full knowing that its claim to 2,000,000 acres was quite shaky, the ambitious firm eventually got the opinion of a half-dozen leading lawyers—among them William M. Evarts and Judah P. Benjamin—that the enlarged grant size was the valid one.[15]

So far, things had gone remarkably well for these bold American and British speculators. Then in 1871 the new Secretary of the Interior, Columbus Delano, once again ruled that the grant covered only 22 leagues or 97,000 acres. Unless the company, now busily selling $5,000,000 worth of stock on the European market, could suspend this ruling, its fate would be that of other great frontier land schemes like John Law's Mississippi Company or the Scioto Land Company in Ohio.[16]

Too much was at stake to give up now. Already the company was making overtures to Kansas Railroad men to extend their lines into southeastern Colorado. General Palmer had undoubtedly accepted the presidency with the idea that the Kansas Pacific would traverse the northern edge of the grant, and from that point one branch would

15. *The Maxwell Land Grant Company–Prospectus* (1872), William Blackmore Collection, microfilm, CSA.
16. Dunham, *Government Handout*, pp. 223 ff. Pearson, *Maxwell*, p. 62.

run northwest to tap the rich town of Denver, while another branch would follow the Santa Fe trail through New Mexico to the Pacific. To Palmer, Elkins, Chaffee, and their far-flung associates, the Maxwell Grant—and other grants as well—promised to be a modern Bent's Fort through which the riches of Colorado and the Southwest could be filtered, while their railroad would replace the Santa Fe trail. If their plans were to succeed, they could control the economy of Colorado and the entire Southwest, just as Bent, St. Vrain, and company had done thirty years before.

To circumvent the 1824 Colonization Law and hostile Secretaries of the Interior, the Company resorted to court action and Congressional influence. Fortunately for the firm, Chaffee was elected delegate from Colorado in 1870, and two years later "Smooth" Steve Elkins—now president of the Company in Palmer's place—ran for the delegateship from New Mexico on an irresistible ticket: he promised his constituents that he would settle all land claims and at the same time secure statehood for New Mexico.[17]

Elkins' proposals were political strokes of genius. The land issue was a question in which many prominent New Mexicans and every American lawyer was interested. Statehood was what the old states-righters and anti-American conservatives—for the most part Democrats—had wanted since Padre Martinez had first declared for admission in 1849. There had been a new movement for statehood in 1872, in fact, led by the archconservative Tomas Cabeza de Baca and *el antiguo revolutionario*, Diego Archuleta. A constitution was written, and an election held; but while the results were favorable, they were not strong enough to impress Congress.[18] Elkins' platform, then, appealed to frustrated Democrats and ambitious Republicans alike. Aided by promises, money, pressures, and fraud at the polls, he was elected by a majority of 4,000! This was an incredible margin in a territory where nearly every delegate election was so close that it was contested.

As urbane and diplomatic as Delegate Elkins was, his efforts to get Congress to accept his proposals for settling land grants (and that of

17. Dunham, *Government Handout*, p. 225.
18. L. Bradford Prince, *A Concise History of New Mexico* (Cedar Rapids, Iowa, 1912), pp. 227 ff.

Maxwell in particular) were in vain. The company was becoming desperate, and in its distress, several factions appear to have formed. The investors were demanding returns on their money; the Amsterdam financiers were questioning the claim, and local speculators in Colorado and New Mexico were determined not to let go. To keep Elkins in Washington where he was needed, his supporters secured his re-election in 1875, although Elkins himself was in Europe the whole time selling company stock. In an effort to corner more votes, his partner, Catron, reputedly used 600 pending land-case indictments as weapons to get at least that number of votes. The territory was well aware of the stakes, for the *Las Cruces Borderer* said during Elkins' first campaign that it was "the honest people of New Mexico against a foreign company of Monopolists and its attorney."[19]

Despite all that could be done, the company was in bankruptcy by 1875, but the legerdemain practiced by the New Mexicans interested in the company now became more subtle than ever. Having secured a state of bankruptcy from a friendly judge, the company's claim in 1877 was sold to cover a tax debt. It was bought by M. W. Mills, a Colfax county attorney, who sold it a few months later to Thomas Benton Catron, Elkins' old friend and law partner.[20] In reality bankruptcy appears to have been a means by which the company could escape its creditors and at the same time remain under the direction of its original New Mexican promoters, but the Dutch bankers managed to regain control at the last minute.

The question still remained whether the grant was 97,000 or 2,000,000 acres. This time the company took the tack of seeking confirmation of its enlarged survey. Rather than appeal to a new Secretary of the Interior—and especially to a reformer like Carl Schurz—they persuaded Land Commissioner James A. Williamson to establish the precedent that court decisions based on a surveyor's recommendation would henceforth determine the size and validity of a claim, regardless of the 1824 Law. The Maxwell case was reopened and a new survey ordered. Again the company tried to rely on the expanded vision of Surveyor W. W. Griffin, but Secretary Schurz wisely ruled him out as an official

19. Las Cruces *Borderer*, August 16, 1873.
20. Pearson, *Maxwell*, p. 74. Dunham, *Government Handout*, p. 231.

surveyor. The company then gave the contract to two engineering
innocents: R. T. Marmon and J. T. Elkins, the latter a brother of
"Smooth" Steve. After a swift and almost meaningless survey lasting
only twenty-two days, they filed their reports, declaring that the grant
was indeed nearly 2,000,000 acres in size. On May 19, 1879, a ten-year
battle ended because of favorable court decisions and land-office rulings,
and Land Commissioner Williamson issued patents of ownership for
1,714,764,094 acres of land.[21] While many grants remained unsettled
until the 1890s, the Maxwell Company had made old Carlos Beaubien's
dream of empire come true with a vengeance.

The schemes and successes of the Maxwell Company had many important consequences for the political and economic makeup of New
Mexico Territory. It became obvious that to succeed in settling land
questions, Elkins needed a machine to back him, made up of lawyers,
judges, politicians, businessmen, and a friendly press both at home
and in Washington. Out of such a need grew the first so-called Santa
Fe Ring. Many legends surround its purpose and its membership, but
it was essentially a set of lawyers, politicians, and businessmen who
united to run the territory and to make money out of this particular
region. Although located on the frontier, the ring reflected the cor-
porative, monopolistic, and multiple enterprise tendencies of all
American business after the Civil War. Its uniqueness lay in the fact
that, rather than dealing in some manufactured item, they regarded
land as their first medium of currency.

The famous Santa Fe Ring was a logical and sometimes brilliant
combination of able men. Besides Elkins and Catron, both declared
Republicans, Henry L. Waldo, another law partner of Elkins also
belonged. As open, trustworthy, and frank as anyone in the territory,
Waldo was a Democrat who was respected by friend and foe alike.
Other members were the current surveyor general and the wealthy

21. The decision in a crucial Supreme Court Case, *John G. Tameling v. The
United States Freehold and Immigration Company*, in October 1876, cleared the
way for Colorado holders of the Sangre de Cristo Grant and set the precedent for
the larger grant claimed by the Maxwell Company. Court cases, new rulings, and
reversals went on for the Maxwell Company until 1887, when a favorable decision
upheld the company's expanded claims.

New Mexican merchant, A. Staab. The ring also found it useful to ally the county probate judges with the organization. Particularly valuable were the services of Dr. Robert H. Longwill, probate judge of Colfax County, in which a large portion of the Maxwell Grant was located. Among the federal judges, Chief Justice Joseph G. Palen —and, later, Judges Samuel B. Axtell and L. B. Prince—were counted as members of the ring.[22] From the late 1860s until 1885, nearly every governor appears to have been a member, as well as other federal officers.

Further requirements for success were a strong press and contacts in Washington. The ring found the former in a superb team, William Manderfield and T. J. Tucker, who began publishing the Santa Fe *New Mexican* about the time the Beaubien-Miranda grant was purchased from Lucien Maxwell. The paper gave the Maxwell Company and the ring open support, and so able and powerful a paper did it become that it remained the leading newspaper throughout the territorial period.

Elkins, the ring, and even the *New Mexican* would have experienced great difficulty, nevertheless, in maintaining their preeminent positions had not the Republican Party been in power in Washington in the key years from 1865 to 1885. Unbroken patronage flowing from the nation's capital sustained all three. Nor could the ring have survived without excellent Eastern connections. Elkins and Chaffee were well known in New York business circles. Among those interested in New Mexican speculation were Senator Stephen W. Dorsey, who developed a giant ranch in Colfax County, and George M. Pullman, builder of sleeping cars and a friend of Chaffee. Prominent lawyers and public men, such as William Evarts and Senator Thomas F. Bayard, were friends of the company, as were several New York, Philadelphia, and Providence bankers.[23]

Finally, the ring survived because it was realistic enough to accept within its circle any cooperative or useful official, so that every five years the personnel changed somewhat. In a similar way the ring changed its economic interests as the economy of New Mexico altered:

22. Kelcher, *Fabulous Frontier*, p. 104 n. Twitchell, *Leading Facts*, 2, 485–86.
23. Dunham, *Government Handout*, p. 224.

after the heyday of land grants, they were more interested in ranching, mining, and railroads. This sort of flexibility gave them a reputation as monopolists and for having economic and political omniscience.

The last characteristic that made for success was its nonpartisan view of able men. Though it was a Republican ring, it had many Democratic adherents, among them the chairman of the Democratic Party between 1884 and 1889! "A well formed Ring," wrote Governor L. B. Prince, "embraces members of both parties and the New Mexican one is remarkably well formed. They seem to fight when in reality they are pulling together."[24] Governor Edmund Ross also observed that each combination had a Republican and Democratic lawyer "for prudential reasons, so that whichever side might come uppermost, the dominant party was represented, and there was an average of one lawyer to every ten Americans."[25]

In the realm of the remaining land grants the methods and successes of the Maxwell Company triggered other claimants and speculators into action. At the same time that the Maxwell purchase was being made, Colorado speculators were buying the Las Animas (originally Vigil and St. Vrain) grant in southeastern Colorado. The Sangre de Cristo grant (Narciso Beaubien, and Lee) was being sold to William Blackmore, an English investor with extensive holdings in the Southwest. In less than a year the suspect Gervacio Nolan grant went to still another British investor. Once bitten, Blackmore became interested in the Cebolla and Conejos grants and the Canon de Chama claim. And by 1872 negotiations for the purchase of the Beck, Cucilla, San Cristobal, Cinequilla, Mora, and Los Luceros grants were being carried on.[26]

To interest Eastern and European investors, impressive brochures were printed providing a résumé of the documents relating to the grant, its possibilities, and the opinion of some prominent attorney. Typical of these was a pamphlet issued in 1879 which carried General

24. L. B. Prince to W. B. Sloan, n.d., 1884, "Account of the Delegate Election of 1884," MS in the Papers of Thomas Benton Catron, University of New Mexico Library, Albuquerque.

25. Ross to O'Grady, March 26, 1887.

26. LeRoy R. Hafen, "Mexican Land Grants in Colorado," *CM, 4* (1927), 85 ff. Edmond C. Van Diest, "Early History of Costilla," *CM, 6* (1928), 140 ff. Ralph Carr, "Private Land Claims in Colorado," *CM, 25* (1948), 10–30, covers these activities. See also Herbert O. Brayer, *William Blackmore* (Denver, 1949).

Benjamin F. Butler's legal opinion that the Vigil and St. Vrain grants of 1843 were valid. All the owners needed, he cautioned, was to find the "missing document" in which Governor Armijo had been given the power to suspend the eleven-league limitation of 1824. Butler succumbed to his own eloquence and bought up a portion of the Mora grant a year or so later.[27]

In the decade from 1875 to 1885, the remaining unconfirmed grants continued to stretch impressively. When George W. Julian took over the surveyor general's duties in the latter year, he was shocked to find that the Cañada Ancha grant, which had originally been for 130 acres, was now a claim for 375 square miles of territory. Others were even more spectacular: the Canon de Chama grant of 184,000 acres was increased by the claimants and preceding surveyor generals to 472,000 acres; the Tierra Amarilla grant was by then some 932 square miles, while the Mora claim was for a mere 1,400 square miles. Counting the Maxwell grant, some thirty-four claimants alone declared their holdings to be over 100,000 acres each![28] It was patent that here was the territory's largest industry.

Naturally the lawyers of Santa Fe exacted their fees for clearing titles. Being paid in land, they themselves gradually acquired ownership of the largest grants and became, as it were, their own clients. Eventually over 80 per cent of the Spanish grants went to American lawyers and settlers.[29] Most impressive of all were the accumulated holdings of Thomas B. Catron. Never a modest man, on June 23, 1893, he listed his estate as being:

50,000 acres of the Mora Grant
80,000 acres of the Beck Grant
2/3 of the 78,000 acres of the Espiritu Santo Grant
1/2 of the 21,500 acres of the Tecolote Grant
7,600 acres of the Juana Lopez Grant

27. *Grant Rio Las Animas and Huerfano in New Mexico. Opinion of General Benjamin F. Butler as to the Validity of the Same* (N. Y., 1879) , pamphlet, HEH. See also O. D. Barrett, *The Mora Grant of New Mexico* (Washington, 1884) , pamphlet, HEH.
28. George W. Julian, "Land Stealing in New Mexico," *North American Review* (July 1, 1887) , pp. 20–25.
29. Brayer, *Blackmore*, p. 19.

24,000 acres of the Piedra Lumber Grant
11,000 acres of the Gabaldon Grant
15,000 acres of the Baca Grant
a portion of the Tierra Amarilla Grant
8,000 acres in patented homesteads

Not even these told the whole story. A year later the Santa Fe *New Mexican* estimated that he was interested in seventy-five grants, owned nearly 2,000,000 acres, and was part owner or attorney for 4,000,000 more.[30]

Perhaps the most significant consequence of the land-grant speculations and of ring rule was that Elkins and Catron and their colleagues had discovered a method by which New Mexico could be profitably exploited by Americans, whether it was in land, ranching, mining, or railroad development. The country that once seemed worthless to Kearny's soldiers was now an item in the stock exchange and a topic of interest in a dozen investment houses in Europe. Wrote Governor E. G. Ross irately:

From the Land Grant Ring grew others, as the opportunities for speculation and plunder were developed. Cattle Rings, Public Land Stealing Rings, Mining Rings, Treasury Rings, and rings of almost every description, grew up, till the affairs of the Territory came to be run almost exclusively in the interest and for the benefit of combinations organized and headed by a few longheaded, ambitious and unscrupulous Americans.

Ross also observed that each combination had a Republican and Democratic lawyer:

Thus the Santa Fe Bar became to all intents and purposes a close corporation, and the syndicate it represented and controlled, came to be and has for many years been known as the Santa Fe Ring, a great combination which included all the less Rings, and dictated at will the legislation and general conduct of the affairs of the Terri-

30. Hefferan, "Catron," p. 156. Santa Fe *New Mexican*, October 31, 1894.

tory, with branches here and there in the lesser towns, but all sub-
servient to the Central head.[31]

A brilliant frontier technique of exploitation, reminiscent of the
Holland Land Company and of the Ohio Associates, had been revived,
modernized, and given the trappings of the corporation and of the
post-Civil War political ring common to the era of Ulysses S. Grant.
The Santa Fe Ring was a sophisticated combination of the eighteenth-
century speculator and the nineteenth-century businessman.

Of equal significance was the Ring's political power. To succeed, it
had to control the territorial and local governments, and to do that
required some control over the exhausting factionalism that characterized New Mexican politics. After the arrival of Elkins and Catron,
the seesaw rise and fall of delegates and the frequent coming and
going of the governors, surveyor generals, and judges was no real indi-
cation of change. A local bureaucracy, as it were, continued to run
things as they saw fit and made the necessary federal official a part of
their schemes. Thus Governor Pile (1869–71) was a willing member
of the Maxwell Land Grant Company, and as early as 1872 Governor
Giddings (1871–75) was described by the Las Cruces *Borderer* as a
"tool" of Elkins.[32] Governor Lew Wallace (1878–81) sarcastically
remarked that the office of governor had so little power that his only
function was to count sheep and people for the annual report to Washington. Governor Sheldon (1881–85) found that the territory ran itself
and willingly let a member of the ring, Attorney General Breeden,
virtually assume all gubernatorial duties. Governor Ross aptly summarized the ring's role in politics when he remarked: "For years its
rule was imperious and unquestioned. . . . It elected Legislators and
Delegates to Congress. It had the ear of the Administration at Washington, and could build up or pull down men at its pleasure."[33]

The Santa Fe Ring's attempt to control both the economy and government of New Mexico did not come without its full share of excite-

31. Ross to O'Grady, March 27, 1887.
32. Las Cruces *Borderer*, August 16, 1873.
33. Ross to O'Grady, March 27, 1887.

ment, violence, and fraud. And the two "catch-basins" of the reckless element, Colfax and Lincoln Counties, came to be apt illustrations of such activity. The Maxwell Company claims, for example, encroached on the lands of scores of settlers who had innocently settled in the lovely Cimarron country, little knowing that they were trespassers on private property. As early as 1870 great bitterness was evident in the relations between the settlers and company representatives. By 1876 even the Indians residing at the Cimarron Agency were declared trespassers and were forced out.

The issue was complicated by the presence of two other groups. In 1867 gold had been discovered on the grant and a sizable community of miners, estimated at one time to be 10,000 persons, lived at Elizabethtown and in surrounding camps. The saloon element—gamblers, drifters, and robbers—naturally followed the miners there to clip their share of the coin. Simultaneously Texas ranchers, eyeing the fine grasses of Colfax county, pushed their herd across the boundary and established ranches on what they called the public domain. With this latest Texas invasion came the inevitable rustler and cowboy gunman.

To complicate matters even more, two local factions fighting for control of the Maxwell Company appeared on the scene. One of these was headed by a young lawyer named Frank Springer, who opposed Santa Fe control of the company during the early 1870s. The other group was composed of the Santa Fe interests, led by Doctor Robert Longwill, Probate Judge of Colfax County and a member of the ring in good standing.[34] Given so many unstable elements in Colfax County and the company-squatter issue, it was inevitable that violence would result.

Although these factions shifted back and forth in their loyalties, and a general confusion existed as to who stood for what, by 1873 the real lines were eventually drawn between the company and squatters. A squatter club was formed at Cimarron that year to protect settlers' rights, while in nearby Raton two groups, both anti-Grant, organized. One wanted to shoot it out with the company, while the other determined to wage a press campaign against its monolithic enemy. The

34. Keleher, *Maxwell*, pp. 24, 76. Twitchell, *Leading Facts*, 2, 486 n.

anti-Grant groups were encouraged by a new Interior ruling in 1874 which stated the Grant was a part of the public domain.

The first victim of the many-faceted feud, ironically, was a man of God, the Reverend T. J. Tolby, a strong-willed, outspoken Methodist minister. In September 1875, a few days before he was mysteriously killed on the road to Elizabethtown, he had declared to Judge Joseph G. Palen, a member of the ring, that he intended to expose Palen. Suspicion pointed to two New Mexican toughs, Cruz Vega and Manuel Cardenas. When apprehended by a mob, Vega said that Cardenas had committed the murder after having been hired to do so by one Pancho Griego and one Donahue, a mail contractor against whom Tolby also had damaging evidence of fraud.[35] Vegas' statement did not help his own predicament; the mob hanged him just in case he might have been guilty.

Manuel Cardenas then came forward with the story that Dr. Robert Longwill and M. W. Mills, a local attorney for the company—along with Donahue and Griego—had hired Cruz Vega to murder Tolby. In a tortuous sequence of events stretching over two years, Vega was hanged by a mob, Pancho Griego was shot by a Texas gunman and rancher named Clay Allison, Dr. Longwill fled—first to Fort Union and then to Santa Fe—in fear of his life, and Cardenas and Donahue were committed to jail. When Donahue's trial finally opened, excitement was at a high pitch. But before the accused could testify, Cardenas was killed from ambush while going from the jail to the courtroom, and Donahue, out on bail, joined Dr. Longwill in exile at Santa Fe.[36]

Onto this troubled scene came a tragicomic figure, another Methodist minister, the Reverend Oscar P. McMains. A cantankerous fire-eating crusader against the Maxwell Company and at times editor of a local paper, he became the self-appointed sleuth to track down Tolby's murderer. McMains himself was such a violent personality that he was tried in 1877 for leading the mob that killed Cruz Vega. His attorney on this occasion, paradoxically, was Frank Springer, solicitor for the Maxwell Company. Although he was acquitted a year later for lack of evidence, McMains was to carry on his private war throughout the

35. Pearson, *Maxwell*, pp. 68–70.
36. Ibid., p. 69.

coming decade, despite the fact that the Company finally had its patent validated by a Supreme Court decision in 1887.[37]

Obviously the Colfax County troubles and the hopeless confusion in northeastern New Mexico did not take place in a vacuum. They agitated the officials at Santa Fe and particularly the new governor, Samuel B. Axtell, (1875–78) a former California congressman who had also been territorial governor of Utah for a brief time.[38] A man of strong feelings and great dignity, Axtell seemed determined to solve the Colfax troubles. After Cardenas was killed, the Governor declared that Cimarron was in a state of "riot and anarchy" and sent troops from Fort Union. This proved no solution, for many of the soldiers were Negroes, whom the Texans refused to respect. Within two weeks of their arrival two of them lay dead by bullets from Clay Allison's gun.[39]

It was not long, however, before the Santa Fe Ring recognized in Axtell an exceptionally able man and useful official. They persuaded him that it would be unfair to return Dr. Longwill for trial under such hostile conditions and in such a violence-ridden community. To secure a just trial and to bring order to Colfax, Axtell, on January 14, 1876, attached Colfax to Taos County for judicial and administrative purposes.[40] This meant that cases concerning the Cimarron trouble would be held in Taos, where Longwill, Donahue, and others might easily be declared innocent.

Frank Springer, then a leader of the anti-Santa Fe wing of the Maxwell Company, was quick to feel that Axtell was an enemy. In eloquent pleas he and his faction demanded return of their courts, charging that most of the Taos jurors were Penitentes and that the boss of Taos was a member of the Santa Fe set. While this open attack was occurring, the Company also spread the rumor that Axtell was a Mormon bishop, whose secret policy it was to declare the grant public domain and settle Latter Day Saints thereon. At the same time, a contradictory

---

37. Ibid., pp. 89 ff. F. Stanley, "O. P. McMains, Champion of a Lost Cause," *NMHR*, 24 (1949), pp. 1 ff.
38. "Samuel Beach Axtell," MS Autobiography in Ritch (Box 27), HEH.
39. Allison's career is summarized in F. Stanley, *The Grant That Maxwell Bought* (Denver, 1952), pp. 147–57. Pearson, *Maxwell*, pp. 38, 69–70.
40. Pearson, *Maxwell*, p. 66.

rumor spread that ex-Senator Dorsey and Axtell were speculators themselves and were intriguing to buy the Una de Gato Land Grant in the county.[41] Although Longwill was acquitted and local courts were returned to Colfax County, the Cimarron feuds continued into the 1890s with frequent outbreaks of violence.

What is the significance of the Colfax County troubles? Why should violence erupt in a territory now some thirty years under American rule? First of all, it is obvious that Colfax and the Maxwell Grant region represented the coming together of three American frontiers in one place. The mining center of Elizabethtown was a small echo of the California and Colorado mining camps, with their usual boisterous and often criminal society; second, the Texan and local ranchers reflected the booming Great Plains cattle frontier, of which Colfax County was the western edge; and, third, there was the transportation and land speculation frontier, which wanted to develop and exploit northeastern New Mexico and southeastern Colorado as a multifaceted big business enterprise. Here for the first time in New Mexico was an area which resembled other American frontiers. In the fight for the spoils, however, the heritage of large private land grants, the absence of a public domain, and the existence of the Santa Fe Ring immensely complicated the usually easy process of frontier settlement. Colfax County, then, was in essence the scene of a fight between men who held an American or public domain concept of the frontier and an organization which insisted that the region, because of its Spanish-Mexican origins, was private property. Once again the difficulty of governing and settling a region where different land laws and approaches to government existed were dramatically evident. Even so, the Colfax War lost the center of the stage for a time after 1878, for a new war had broken out in Lincoln County.

Charles Goodnight and Oliver Loving were two intrepid Texas ranchers who realized that beeves were needed for the federal soldiers, the Mescalero Apaches, and the Navajo Indians whom General Carleton had gathered at the Bosque Redondo. As soon as the Civil War

41. Charges Preferred against Governor Axtell; Affidavit of Harry Whigham, MSS in Ritch (Boxes 25, 26), HEH.

was over, they braved the dangerous Staked Plains several times to succor Fort Sumner and the Indians there. In so doing they established a trail which bore their name and set in motion the open-range ranching industry on the Pecos River. Their success was noted by a tough, shrewd, old bachelor, John Chisum, who, rather than cross the Staked Plains and hostage his life to Comanches each year, settled his cattle on a ranch near Roswell, New Mexico. In an area where land grants were not a hindrance, he carved out of the public domain a constantly growing empire until, by the 1870s, he had a herd estimated at 75,000 and was called the "Cattle King of America." Naturally, word of Chisum's success spread, and a general movement to feed cattle on the rich grasses of eastern New Mexico began. By 1880 it was being hailed as the "preeminent industry" of the territory, in which nine-tenths of the developed wealth was invested.[42]

As in Kansas, Texas, and Colfax County, this latest ranching frontier attracted saloons, storekeepers, drifters, cowboys and gunmen, fly-by-night ranchers, and on-the-make young attorneys. Here, too, settled some of Thomas Catron's in-laws, the Walz family. Catron himself invested in the Carrizozo Land and Cattle Company near White Oaks. Among the firstcomers to Lincoln was Major Lawrence G. Murphy, a former storekeeper at Fort Stanton, and J. J. Dolan, Murphy's partner and a rancher as well. Even an Englishman, John H. Tunstall, was so attracted by the region that he established a general store and acquired a ranch in the area. In January 1869 this heterogeneous population was organized as Lincoln County; this was the same month that Colfax was created. Lincoln became the seat of government, and local officers were chosen. Among the most important were L. G. Murphy, as probate judge, and William Brady, his friend and supporter, as sheriff. Thus the stage was set for yet another classic from the rich folklore of the American frontier: the enduring popular tragedy called "The Lincoln County War."

The outbreak of violence in Lincoln appears to have been caused by a dispute over a life insurance policy, a business rivalry between

---

42. Ray Willoughby, "The Cattle Range Industry in New Mexico" (Master's thesis, University of New Mexico, 1933), pp. 36, 44, 52–7. See also Cimarron *News and Press*, May 13, 1880.

two firms—*Tunstall and McSween versus Murphy and Dolan*—and cattle stealing. The dispute began when one of Major Murphy's former partners, Colonel Emil Fritz, died leaving a valid $10,000 life insurance policy on a New York company. A. A. McSween, a young Kansas lawyer living in Lincoln, went to New York, successfully cashed the policy, and with a portion of the money paid some of Fritz' debts in Santa Fe. Upon his return to Lincoln, McSween, for some reason, refused to turn the remainder of the money over to the heirs. Since Fritz at the time of his death also owed money to Murphy's friend J. J. Dolan, the latter two sought to collect it from McSween. Upon his refusal, Murphy—who, after all, was probate judge—and Dolan charged McSween with embezzlement. The complicating factor was that McSween was also a partner in the rival store of Murphy's run by Tunstall, who was nicely described as "an Englishman of means."[43]

In an effort to force McSween to deliver, Dolan and Murphy, aided by their friend, Sheriff William Brady, attempted to attach both Tunstall's store and his ranch, since the latter was McSween's partner and therefore legally liable for his obligations. Attachment would also serve the purpose of closing down the opposition to Murphy's store. A trigger-happy posse, riding out to serve papers on Tunstall on February 18, 1878, began the real violence when they shot and killed the Englishman. The incident became a feud when the Deputy United States Marshal at Lincoln, Robert A. Widenmann, chose to side with McSween, refused to let Sheriff Brady attach Tunstall's property, and organized a band of "regulators" to resist Brady's posse.[44]

The next act of the tragedy began when four of Tunstall's men, who had witnessed his death, swore vengeance on the Murphy-Dolan-Brady forces. Within a short time they had killed three members of the party serving papers on Tunstall and had ambushed and killed Brady and a deputy named George Hindman. A proclamation by Governor Axtell ordered all bodies of men in Lincoln County to

43. Willoughby, "Cattle Range Industry," pp. 69–73. Santa Fe *New Mexican*, May 31, 1878. Miguel A. Otero, *The Real Billy the Kid* (New York, 1936), pp. 27–33.
44. Otero, p. 39.

disarm and warned that "those who take the sword shall perish by the sword." His words had little effect, for the feud was now out of hand; each side organized gangs of gunmen for protection, and there were many fatal encounters.

Rustlers and more gunmen now came to Lincoln and took advantage of the lawlessness—as in Civil War Missouri—in the name of one side or the other. Lieutenant Colonel N. A. M. Dudley wrote from Fort Stanton in 1878 that new parties had come into the territory in the past six days and were stealing horses, robbing houses, and even raiding the Mescelero Apache.[45] Men looking for trouble, such as Charles Bowdre, Doc Scurlock, and Frank and George Coe rode about terrorizing the region. With one of the gangs rode a Tunstall and McSween sympathizer—a buck-toothed, left-handed youth, fond of dancing and a marvelous shot. Destined to play the dual role of villain and hero in the piece, he was variously called William H. Antrim alias William Bonney alias Billy the Kid.[46]

Now that Murphy and Dolan had their own armed backers and McSween boasted a following of fifty men, the town of Lincoln became a no-man's land, in which the two factions fought it out. On one occasion the McSween forces conrolled the unhappy village but were driven out in an ambuscade lasting five days and nights. To vent their feelings, his frustrated men robbed a nearby Indian agency. The turning point finally came when a new sheriff, George Peppin, and a posse aided by Colonel Dudley with soldiers from Fort Stanton surrounded McSween's house and after a seven hour battle forced him and his men into the open by successfully firing the house. There, in the lurid blaze of his own home, McSween was killed by the posse as his friend Billy the Kid miraculously dodged every bullet and escaped into the shadows.[47]

McSween's death in a sense ended the war, but not its effects. What had been curious throughout its course was the inability of Santa Fe and of Governor Axtell to act effectively. It gradually became apparent

45. Santa Fe *New Mexican,* August 24, 1878.
46. Ibid., March 23, April 20, 1878. Mesilla Valley *Independent,* April 13, 1878. For recent coverage of the Lincoln County War see Ramon F. Adams, *A Fitting Death for Billy the Kid* (Norman, 1960), and C. L. Sonnichsen and William V. Morrison, *Alias Billy the Kid* (Albuquerque, 1955).
47. Santa Fe *New Mexican,* August 3, 1878.

that Axtell favored the Murphy-Dolan faction, as did United States Attorney Thomas Catron, who was retained by Murphy as a legal adviser. Further, Axtell had appointed a pro-Murphy sheriff to succeed the dead Brady. Until the McSween faction felt it could secure justice, it was not likely to surrender to such partisan authorities. The strange inability of Axtell and the law forces of New Mexico to cope with Lincoln County came to the attention of the Interior, Justice, and War departments, who jointly appointed Frank Warner Angell as a special investigator to look into the difficulties.[48] Then on October 7, 1878, President Hayes declared Lincoln County in a state of insurrection.

What Angell found in the way of fact was not nearly so significant as the attitudes he encountered. The Santa Fe *New Mexican* greeted his coming with great hostility. He also got little cooperation from Axtell, and even less from the United States District Attorney Catron, who had sided with Murphy and Dolan. Indeed, Catron's own brother-in-law, Edgar Walz, worked in the old Murphy-Dolan store. At the height of the troubles Catron also appears to have imported his own set of "cowboys" to participate in the war.[49] Angell listened sympathetically, therefore, to the charges of Montague R. Leverson, editor of the Mesilla Valley *Independent*, who stated both to Angell and to President Hayes that the New Mexican violence was actually being caused by the agitation of United States officials in the area.[50]

Leverson also stated that Tunstall had been murdered by order of the district attorney of the third district (W. L. Rynerson), a member of the Santa Fe ring, by whom "the District Judge (Warren Bristol) is used as a tool." As to Axtell, said Leverson, he had protected the murderers, "influenced more by weakness and want of intellect than by intentional criminality." Finally, he declared that the United States Attorney and the Surveyor General at Santa Fe were plunderers.[51]

48. Ibid., August 10, 1878. Willoughby, "Cattle Range Industry," p. 72.

49. Hefferan, "Catron," p. 27.

50. In *Billy the Kid* Otero, p. 191, states flatly that Murphy was a member of the Santa Fe Ring and journeyed to Santa Fe frequently to consult them during the war.

51. Montague R. Leverson to Rutherford B. Hayes, March 16, 1878, Ritch (Box 26), HEH.

Robert A. Widenmann, the former United States Deputy Marshal, seemed to corroborate Leverson when he stated in print that Tunstall's death had been "a cold-blooded and pre-meditated murder, committed in the interest of the New Mexico ring, and as the ring controls the courts of the territory, it is difficult to bring the murderers to justice. Even our sheriff here is in the ring and refuses to allow the murderers to be arrested."[52] In the mass of conflicting evidence, Widenmann himself was hardly a reliable witness, for along with McSween in 1878 he had been confined at Fort Stanton for complicity in the murder of Sheriff Brady.

Although no member of the Santa Fe Ring was taken to court for his partisanship and meddling in the Lincoln County War, Angell's report did have the effect of removing Axtell from office in 1878 and of securing the hasty resignation of Catron as the United States Attorney.

Axtell's successor in the governor's chair was General Lew Wallace of Indiana. A hero in the Civil War, a politician of sorts, and a writer of historical novels, he was to begin his famous book, *Ben Hur,* while unable to sleep in the airless Governor's Palace at Santa Fe.[53] Since the robberies and rustling continued after he acceded to office, Wallace conducted his own investigation of the war. He soon became convinced that the McSween faction had more justice on its side that its opponents did. Therefore he censured Colonel Dudley for allowing soldiers to participate in the posse that killed McSween. The lines of alliance became clear not only when Dudley defended himself but when H. L. Waldo, the territorial attorney general—and a law partner of Catron's—resigned in order to take Dudley's case. Wallace then discovered how tight a control the ring had on lawyers in the territory, for he was unable to find anyone who would serve as attorney general whom the legislature would accept! Wallace's efforts in behalf of peace have usually been played down; but by offering amnesty to those who had participated in the war and by exhibiting patience and fairness, he finally brought a semblance of peace to Lincoln County. Writing to Carl Schurz, he said the Murphy-Dolan organizations were

52. Santa Fe *New Mexican*, March 23, 1878.
53. "Lew Wallace" in *DAB*. Otero, *Billy the Kid*, p. 54.

"dead," and that "the only disturbing element remaining to be put out of the way is the *confederacy of outlaws and their friends.*"[54]

War with the ring and a recurrence of violence in other counties in 1880–81 left Wallace so disgusted with his job that he resigned in 1881. While waiting for his successor, Lionel A. Sheldon, he wrote a friend: "as soon as he comes, I will take up my sheep skin bed, and chassez down to San Simon and give myself to the development of some mines in that district. No need, you see, for a statistician there." Having acquired some good mining properties, he left Santa Fe for the more exotic position of Ambassador to the Ottoman Empire.[55]

While Wallace was not successful as a political reformer, and other "county wars" continued to break out in New Mexico, the tide was at least turning against the Lincoln County lawbreakers. When Judge Warren Bristol held court at Fort Stanton in 1879, some 200 indictments covering fifty people were returned.[56] The youths and small ranchers who had ridden so boldly up and down Lincoln County were now hiding in the mountains west of Fort Sumner or moving quietly about staying with friends at obscure ranches and camps. With a price on their heads they, too, came to know the meaning of fear. One of the ex-gunmen, Charles Bowdre, sounded the denouement when he wrote:

I have broke up housekeeping and am camping around, first one place and then another on the range, so that no one can say that Yerby's ranch is the stopping place for anyone.

If I don't get clear I intend to leave sometimes this winter for I don't intend to take any hand fighting the territory, for it is a different thing from what the Lincoln County War was. . . .

I saw the two Billies [Antrim? and ?] the other day and they say they are going to leave this country.[57]

54. Lew Wallace to Carl Schurz, June 11, 1879, Interior Department TP: Executive Proceedings, New Mexico, 1851–1914 (microcopy 364), NA.
55. Wallace to Ned ———, March 30, 1881, Papers of Governor Lew Wallace, NMHS.
56. Mesilla Valley *Independent,* May 10, 1879.
57. Charles Bowdre to J. C. Lea, December 15, 1880, Ritch (Box 27), HEH.

Neither Bowdre nor Billy the Kid moved soon enough. Caught between two fires, the former was killed by outlaws with whom he was feuding. Then in 1881 Pat F. Garrett, an old gambling friend of William Bonney, was elected Sheriff of Lincoln County and set out to end the violence and capture the "Kid." Cornering him in a dark room at old Fort Sumner, now the home of Peter Maxwell, son of Lucien Maxwell of land-grant fame, Garrett killed the Kid as Billy excitedly asked his unknown assailant: *"Quien es? Quien es?"*

Success in evading and accounting for their deeds in Lincoln and Colfax left the quasi-organization called the Santa Fe Ring in complete control by 1881. Ex-Governor Axtell, now that the war was over, secured the chief justiceship of New Mexico in 1882. The territorial secretary, William G. Ritch, retained his office for eight years (1876–84) by pursuing a cautious let-sleeping-dogs-lie policy. The ring also found two strong new allies in Governor Lionel A. Sheldon (1881–85), and Colonel William Breeden. Sheldon was a former carpetbag congressman from Louisiana, who turned his gaze westward at the end of Reconstruction. A genial, affable man, the picture of an imposing public figure, he had no great wish to change the status quo in New Mexico. Within a few weeks after his arrival, he was a quiescent member of the ring. His permissive nature and sense of humor allowed him to comment on the situation quite aptly but without doing anything about it.[58]

As an accurate reflection of the legal profession's control of New Mexican politics, the center of political power shifted once Elkins had left the territory to the office of attorney general. To this position Sheldon appointed Colonel William Breeden, who was a law partner of Catron's, chairman of the Republican party in the territory, and a forceful, aggressive, stubborn lawyer. Breeden gradually assumed most of the duties of governor from his lenient superior.[59]

Sheldon and Breeden came to office in a time of prosperity. The Atchison, Topeka, and Santa Fe had now penetrated the territory

---

58. "Lionel Allen Sheldon," MS Autobiography written for H. H. Bancroft, Bancroft Library.

59. Edmund G. Ross to Hon. H. Manning, January 15, 1886, Ross Papers.

and new towns were springing up along its lines.[60] The land business was good and cattlemen now had a territorial organization that met in Santa Fe at the same time the legislature was in session. The Assembly itself was busy in the 1880 session passing general incorporation laws and attracting foreign capital by permitting incorporation on an equal footing with the American investor.[61] The Assembly also set up a bureau of immigration, incorporated gas companies and street railways—and in celebration of the new railroad connection—took a trip on the Santa Fe line all the way to the Missouri river. The mining industry, after some rich discoveries in The Black Range in the hills near Cerillos and in the northeast where the Aztec Mine was being developed, became—with livestock—a major territorial enterprise. The number of American settlers increased appreciably, and it finally looked as if New Mexico was about to be truly Americanized.[62]

In their hour of triumph, the Santa Fe Ring and the Republican Party developed the familiar trouble of victors fighting among themselves over the spoils. The struggle between factions to gain control of the Maxwell Grant was but one aspect of the disagreement. A more fundamental issue existed in the split between members of the ring from southern New Mexico and those from Santa Fe and the Rio Arriba. The southern contingent claimed that Santa Fe had a disproportionate share of land grants, representation in the Assembly, and federal patronage. The politicians from the new mining and ranching counties as well felt that Santa Fe interests were speculative, merchantile, and railroad rather than cattle and mining.

The situation was aggravated by intense personality feuds between such men as Colonel W. L. Rynerson, described by Judge Prince as a member of the ring for twenty years and boss of Dona Ana County, and Colonel William Breeden, the party chairman. Similarly, Colonel J. Francisco Chavez, boss of Valencia County, ex-delegate, and one of the most powerful leaders of the native Spanish-Americans in the

60. Jim F. Heath, "A Study of the Influence of the Atchison, Topeka, and Santa Fe Railroad upon the Economy of New Mexico, 1878 to 1900" (Master's thesis, University of New Mexico, 1955), pp. 48, 72, 87, 106, 117–18.

61. See *Compiled Laws of New Mexico*, 1884, Chap. 1, Secs. 54–104.

62. Twitchell, *Leading Facts*, 2, 490. James I. Culbert, "Distribution of Spanish-American Population in New Mexico," *Economic Geography*, *19* (1943), pp. 171–76.

entire territorial period, found it difficult to play second fiddle to Breeden.[63] The new editor of the Santa Fe *New Mexican*, Colonel Max Frost, was so arrogant and opinionated that he, too, was soon disliked by members of the Republican Party. Finally, there were in the railroad boom towns of Las Vegas, Albuquerque, Deming, and Silver City a rising local pride and evidence of a new business and political acumen, which threatened the traditional supremacy of Santa Fe over the rest of the territory.

The coming split first appeared in the delegate election of 1882 when Colonel Chavez—already three times a delegate—ran against Francisco A. Manzanares, choice of the Democracy. After such brilliant majorities for Elkins, the territory was once more divided almost evenly, and a contested election was the result. Chavez was seated in 1883, but upon investigation in March 1884, Congress eventually declared Manzanares the victor. Although he was a Democrat and much praised by his supporters for having demolished the ring in the territory, Manzanares was a conservative merchant and actually the secret choice of many Republicans, who preferred him to Chavez. Since the chairman of the Democratic Party, C. H. Gildersleeve, was a land-grant speculator and unofficially a member of the ring, Manzanares was hardly free to be a reformer.[64]

By the time of the legislative meeting of February 1884, both Democrats and insurgent Republicans were in rebellious moods. Chavez himself was irritated by lack of full Republican support in his still pending, contested election. A vital controversy appeared when various Republican businessmen and lawyers in Albuquerque began in the name of reform to campaign to move the capital from Santa Fe to Albuquerque. When rival contestants showed up to claim Council seats from Bernalillo and Santa Fe Counties, the Santa Feans, fearful of losing the capital, hastily seated the antiremoval delegates. This was the breaking point. Chavez, already itching for a fight and always a brilliant organizer, set up his own council of insurgent members. After a session of split legislatures and incredible maneuvering, Thomas Catron, leading the antiremoval forces, pushed

63. "Account of the Delegate Election of 1884," Catron Papers.
64. "The Gildersleeve, Springer, Joseph Combination," undated MS, Ross Papers.

through an act that permanently located the capital in Santa Fe. But the price paid was open rupture within the Republican Party.[65]

With a delegate election coming up that fall, both Republican factions began politicking early. In April, Colonel Rynerson, supported by Colonel A. J. Fountain, held a mass meeting at Las Cruces in front of the Montezuma Hotel to excoriate the acts of the late legislature. Phrases like "Capital steal" and "ring rule" were hurled at the Santa Fe opponents.[66] A few weeks later the Valencia County Republican Convention met at Los Lunas and under the careful tutelage of Colonel Chavez picked its delegates and jointly denounced Secretary Ritch, Governor Sheldon, and the whole Santa Fe Ring. By May 3, the date set for the Republican territorial convention, the whole territory stopped to watch the fireworks. As he had done in the legislature, Chavez bolted and with him marched Rynerson, Fountain, and the delegates from the southern and western counties. The remaining Republicans chose a relatively new member of the ring, Judge L. B. Prince, while the Chavez forces picked Colonel Rynerson.[67]

Naturally the Democrats saw in the Republican split an excellent chance to win. New faces and new forces there persuaded the Democrats to pass over the conservative Manzanares to choose Antonio Joseph, a smiling, urbane merchant and land speculator from Taos. Adept at angering no one, "the sleek and apparently unobtrusive Joseph," as the hostile *New Mexican* called him, quietly campaigned with "nice, neat and slick talks," while Rynerson and Chavez fulminated against Prince and ring rule.[68] The national trend in 1884, which elected a Democratic president to office for the first time in twenty-four years, was reflected in New Mexico, where Joseph won over Rynerson and Prince. At the last moment, Chavez, seeing that Rynerson would not win, switched his support to Joseph.

65. Twitchell, *Leading Facts*, 2, 493–94.

66. Albuquerque *Morning Journal*, April 13, 1884. Santa Fe *New Mexican*, September 25, 1884.

67. Albuquerque *Morning Journal*, April 27, May 3, 1884. Weekly *New Mexican*, September 1, 1884.

68. Taos County *Herald*, September 5, 1884. Weekly *New Mexican*, October 16, 1884.

All these complicated maneuvers show that party labels were still worn lightly in New Mexico and that personality, family and cultural ties, and economic influence were more important factors of loyalty. Beneath the surface, too, were other issues that made mincemeat out of party lines. The most important of these were the statehood movement and the public-school question.

When Diego Archuleta and Tomas Cabeza de Baca declared for statehood in 1872, it appears to have been a final conservative effort by native New Mexicans to gain home rule. Their view was bluntly summarized by the president of the Council that year who told a representative of the Atchison, Topeka, and Santa Fe: "We don't want you damned Yankees in the country. We can't compete with you, you will drive us all out, and we shall have no home left us. We won't have you here."[69]

On the other hand, the Americans of the southern counties took up a hue and cry against statehood, claiming that it would result in a nondemocratic state dominated by Spanish-Americans. Let New Mexico wait, they argued, until enough Americans were there to balance the Spanish influence effectively. Such a cry, whether by Democrat or Republican, had its effect in all the statehood movements right down to 1912.[70] Though Elkins allied himself with such prostate forces in 1873, he had in mind a state controlled by the American lawyers and railroad men, with himself as a senator. The later Santa Fe rings generally held the Elkins view. As spokesman for this group, Colonel Max Frost, editor of the *New Mexican,* was preeminent. He argued that until statehood could be achieved, New Mexico could never get out of Congress her share of the national wealth, nor would businessmen and financiers invest in an unstable territory. Statehood was the key to future development in the minds of Elkins and Frost.

Heartened by the friendly manner in which the Colorado statehood movement was being received in Washington, Elkins had introduced a similar bill into Congress in 1873 for New Mexican admission. While it was being considered, Elkins made the mistake of seeming to ally himself with the bloody-shirt element of the Republican

69. Glenn D. Bradley, *The Story of the Santa Fe* (Boston, 1920), p. 148.
70. Las Cruces *Borderer*, May 15, 22, 1872.

Party. Southern congressmen—watching him congratulate a Michigan congressman just after the latter had made an anti-Southern speech—voted down Elkins bill. After this failure, a serious statehood movement did not occur again until the late 1880s.

The school problem in New Mexico not only troubled the people of New Mexico but worried Congress and the Catholic clergy as well. What might have been an early movement toward public education had been deflected by the heroic efforts of Archbishop Lamy to establish parochial schools wherever possible, or if not that, to permit priests to serve as the local schoolmasters. The result was that most teachers in both public and parochial schools were members of the clergy.[71] This arrangement guaranteed that the education would be Catholic in orientation, and that Spanish would remain the language of the pupils. Given these conditions, American officials did not consider these schools to be secular, public, or American. In a belated effort to initiate a regular public-school system before Elkins statehood bill came to a vote to Congress, the Assembly of 1875-76 was given a school bill for passage.

The leading advocate and probable author of the bill was Secretary W. G. Ritch, one of the more enduring federal officials in New Mexico. Whatever his business connections with the Santa Fe Ring may have been, Ritch always remained a vigorous Protestant with a strong distrust of the Catholic religion. He was also obsessed with the idea that free schools were the key to modernizing, secularizing, and Americanizing New Mexico. To gain support for his program, he trotted out ancient Donaciano Vigil to write public letters urging public education. The issue was considered so important that Lamy—. now an Archbishop—called Ritch in for a conference, but no compromise was forthcoming. At the time of the school bill's consideration Ritch was already involved in a press debate with Father Donato M. Gasparri, a Neopolitan Jesuit at Las Vegas who edited the *Revista Catholica*. Father Gasparri's press also published nearly every textbook used in the existing 138 schools and in the thirty-three private schools as well.[72]

71. Frederick G. Bohme, "A History of the Italians in New Mexico" (Ph.D. dissertation, University of New Mexico, 1958), p. 68.

72. Ibid., pp. 63, 66-67. See also Donaciano Vigil to W. G. Ritch, May 10, 1876, Ritch (Box 25), HEH.

Ritch's bill would have prohibited New Mexico from diverting any public monies into parochial institutions and would have forbidden clerics to teach in public schools. Not satisfied with this, Ritch and his followers also introduced bills to prohibit burial within a church or town limits, eliminate burial and dispensation fees, and establish a state definition of marriage requirements as opposed to a religious definition.[73] Angered by such anticlerical bias, Gasparri referred to to the public education bill as a "Cancer which corrodes and consumes the societies of the United States." Gasparri himself journeyed to Santa Fe and joined the speaker of the House on his bench during the debate over the bill. The legislation met defeat.[74]

Ritch's indignation knew no bounds. Furious at the "carpetbagger from Naples," his description of Gasparri, he wrote such violent press attacks that the *New Mexican* wisely declined to print them. The fight broke out in a new form in the next legislature (1878), when Gasparri and the New Mexican Jesuits, who had begun to replace the French clerics originally imported by Archbishop Lamy, tried to incorporate themselves under the territorial laws, ostensibly in order to charter a college. The Jesuit Act, as it was called, passed the legislature only to run into a second vigorous opponent, Governor Axtell, whose hatred of Gasparri exceeded even that of Ritch's. Although Axtell returned the Jesuit law with a resounding veto, the Assembly repassed the Act with the necessary majority, and it became law on January 23, 1878. Gasparri had shown his strength at home and incidentally revealed the Spanish-American distrust of American public schools. Unlike Ritch and Axtell, however, he was without influence in Washington. There the two officials persuaded Delegate Vicente Romero to get Congress to annul the territorial law, and the issue was at an end.[75]

In the legislature of 1884 the public-school advocates again introduced a bill, which finally passed; but like all its predecessors it proved a dead letter law. It is doubtful whether New Mexico realized the unfavorable impression their educational attitudes made on the

73. Bohme, "Italians in New Mexico," pp. 68–69.
74. Ibid., pp. 70–71.
75. Ibid., pp. 69–74, 77–81. Poldevaart, *Black-Robed Justice*, p. 122.

rest of the country. The high percentage of illiteracy—over 42,000 could not read or write in 1880—suggested a backward people and second-class citizens.[76] A cultural conflict that would play a major role in the eventual struggle for statehood between 1901 and 1912 had already begun in the 1880s.

By 1885 New Mexico was no longer an isolated "territorial isle," as Delegate Otero had called it in 1858. The Atchison, Topeka, and Santa Fe connected it with the Mississippi Basin and the East. After 1881 the Southern Pacific ran along the 32nd parallel and connected the territory with the West Coast. Celebrities now stepped from the train in Santa Fe and stayed a few days at the Exchange Hotel. Thus began the long and enduring history of the city as a tourist attraction and as a health resort for tubercular victims. With its ranching frontier in the eastern portion and a mining frontier stretching from the southwestern corner right up to the Aztec mine in Colfax, it showed promise of becoming a second Colorado. New towns sprang up monthly, and a mild boom, of the sort most American frontiers experienced, finally occurred in New Mexico.

A psychological change toward the country and its Spanish-Mexican-Indian culture also took place in 1884, when the writer Charles Lummis began to praise the beauty of the Southwest. Meanwhile, archaeologists, among them Adolph Bandelier, fascinated by Pueblo ruins, began a heroic battle to uncover the territory's remote past.[77] Judge L. B. Prince, conscious of the values of the culture in which he found himself, sternly refused to let his fashion-minded wife remodel their Spanish adobe house in Santa Fe—which had been the former home of the Sena y Baca family—into a Victorian mansion.[78]

On the other hand, New Mexico was still a land of limited industry and monopolies. The Santa Fe Ring controlled its internal economic life, and the Atchison, Topeka, and Santa Fe, though benign in its control, was, nevertheless, a natural monopoly. And although the county commission system, adopted in 1876, had begun to curb the extraordinary powers of the probate judge, Spanish patrons or

76. *Report of the Governor of New Mexico to the Secretary of the Interior, 1885* (Washington, 1885), p. 10.
77. Noggle, "Anglo Observers of the Southwest Borderlands," pp. 121, 129–30.
78. Interview with Dr. Myra E. Jenkins, October 1959, Santa Fe.

American bosses like Longwill and Murphy still ran local counties with a firm hand; family alliances still decided the outcome of political elections, and a man's vote was still a very purchasable item. Although great changes had occurred, New Mexico was still dramatically behind the rest of the country in income, education, population, economic opportunity, and political standards.

What New Mexico needed—or so thought the reformers under Grover Cleveland's administration—was a radical reconstruction of its economy and its politics. Only in that way could the Far Southwest conform to American cultural and economic norms and be admitted to statehood. Appropriately, Cleveland's revolutionary agents were two ex-abolitionists: Edmund G. Ross of Kansas and George Washington Julian of Indiana.

7

New Mexico Comes of Age
1880–1900

People are worth more to the state than steers. . . . For with
people comes capital and the spirit of commercial adventure,
development, prosperity, and greatness.
Governor Edmund G. Ross
July 22, 1885

In the old days one could rule New Mexico by coercion, threats
and bulldozing. That seemed to succeed until the railroad
came. But conditions have changed and modern and American
systems are needed. The native people will not stand what they
did 15 years ago. The new population will not stand it at all.
Governor L. Bradford Prince
April 23, 1892

 In the last twenty years of the nineteenth century
New Mexico experienced fundamental changes,
which modified her economy, affected her native
culture, modernized her government, and laid the
basis for her admission to the Union in 1912. The
first of these changes occurred when the historic
Santa Fe Trail was replaced by the Atchison, Topeka, and Santa Fe
Railroad. When the line entered New Mexico, by following Uncle
Dick Wootten's toll road through Raton Pass in January 1879, it
brought the first cheap system of transportation in New Mexican
history. Before that date, the region's economy was a curious and
outmoded survival from an earlier age, characterized by expensive
goods, an unfavorable balance of trade, and a nonindustrial and even
primitive market, which could absorb only mercantile goods. Given

such conditions, all territorial business came to be dominated by sedentary merchant capitalists who ran large wholesale and retail houses, with branches throughout the Southwest. The famous firm of Chick, Browne, and Company was one such house. Another, which operated during most of the territorial era, was Otero, Sellar, and Company," "engaged in the multiform and very profitable activities of banking, outfitting, wholesaling, and retailing." After 1850 these firms were joined by the German-Jewish family establishments of the Spiegelberg Brothers, the Seligmans, Charles Ilfeld and Company, and a dozen others.[1]

By default these merchant capitalists filled the place of the storekeeper who specialized in one line of goods, and of the non-existent banker as well. Their surplus funds provided most of the money for mining, cattle, land investments and, indeed, every territorial enterprise before the railroad came. By default, too, they were often monopolists, for they had such few competitors they could exact what interest rates or charges they wished. Well-established, able to sell on long-term credit or to bear the high freight costs of shipping by team from the Missouri and Kansas outfitting towns, they and the land-grant lawyer held the key to economic development in New Mexico before 1878.[2]

Under what circumstances did railroads finally come to New Mexico, and how did they affect the territorial economy? While Santa Fe and Albuquerque had been impressively connected, on paper, since the 1850s by the Atlantic and Pacific, the first real impetus for a road came from Kansas. There, in 1859, Cyrus K. Holliday, a vigorous businessman, founded the Atchison, Topeka, and Santa Fe Company. On its original board of directors were Richard H. Weightman, former delegate from New Mexico, and Edmund G. Ross, editor of the *Topeka Record*. By 1863 the Atchison and Topeka had received a land grant from Congress which stretched westward into Colorado. Consisting of alternate sections of land ten sections deep on either

---

1. Parish, "The German Jew," *New Mexico Quarterly, 29,* 307–32. Miguel A. Otero, *My Life on the Frontier* (2 vols. New York, 1935), *1,* 1. See also Parish, *The Charles Ilfeld Company.*
2. Heath, "Influence of the Atchison, Topeka, and Santa Fe," pp. 156–59.

side of the right of way, the grant was to revert to the United States if the road was not completed in ten years.[3]

Although the Kansas legislature subscribed to stock in the company, the shortage of money, the interruption of the Civil War, and the eventual control of the railroad by conservative Boston investors intervened to prevent a fast growth of the firm. Only by the greatest difficulty did the road complete its track to La Junta, Colorado, in time to make the 1873 deadline for the grant. It took two more years to reach Las Animas, the region of Bent's Old Fort, and still another year to reach the prosperous mining center of Pueblo, Colorado.

The turning point in the unimpressive record of the Atchison, Topeka, and Santa Fe came in 1877, when William B. Strong became general manager. With more vision than his Boston directors, Strong was convinced that the line should not be content to tap the mines of southern Colorado but should veer southwestward as well, to carry the freight of the Santa Fe Trail. His decision was undoubtedly influenced by the activities and promises of the Maxwell Land Grant Company to turn northeastern New Mexico into a modern paradise of settlers, miners, and ranchers. Since Miguel A. Otero was both a director of the Maxwell firm and a vice-president of the Atchison, Topeka, and Santa Fe, Strong had a first-hand acquaintance with the Maxwell plans.[4]

Strong made his decision to turn the Santa Fe Trail into a railroad just as the Denver and Rio Grande—chief competitor of the Atchison, Topeka, and Santa Fe in southern Colorado—also decided to move into New Mexico. And from the West came a new threat in the form of the Southern Pacific, which under various guises was slowly building toward New Orleans over the 32nd parallel route that Jefferson Davis had advocated more than thirty years before. When Strong, accompanied by Otero, arrived in Santa Fe in 1878 to get a charter from the legislative Assembly, they found that the Southern Pacific lobby had already pushed a bill through requiring any road coming into the territory to pay 10 per cent of the estimated cost of the road

3. Bradley, *The Santa Fe*, pp. 55–65 passim, 145.
4. Otero, *My Life, 1,* 65–77.

before any building should start. This would have been a severe if not impossible financial strain on the Santa Fe line.[5]

Aided by Otero's great influence, however, and by compromising with the Southern Pacific forces, Strong managed to get a charter under the name of the New Mexico and Southern Pacific railroad. At a breathless pace Strong then rushed to gain control of Raton Pass before the Denver and Rio Grande forces could secure it. Arriving only a few hours ahead of their opponents, they managed to seize the pass, both by threat of shooting Denver and Rio Grande claimants and by purchasing Uncle Dick Wootten's toll road. The first of many hairbreadth battles with the Denver and Rio Grande line had been won.[6]

The Atchison, Topeka, and Santa Fe celebrated its entrance into New Mexico on January 1, 1879, at which time Vice-President Otero drove a golden spike into a tie that lay on the Colorado–New Mexico line. By July 4 the line had reached Las Vegas. There the building stopped until Santa Feans could be persuaded to help the line into the City of the Holy Faith. Virtually an "estates general" of New Mexico met there late in July. At the extraordinary meeting were Archbishop Lamy and Vicar-General Truchard, who represented the Church. Lehman Spiegelberg spoke for the merchants. Territorial Treasurer Antonio Ortiz y Salazar and Secretary William G. Ritch were delegates from the territorial and federal wings of the government. Judge Waldo and C. H. Gildersleeve represented the Democratic Party. William Breeden was there in behalf of the Santa Fe bar, the ring, and the Republican Party. W. H. Manderfield covered the event for the press.

Jefferson Raynolds, owner of the second bank established in New Mexico, presented the town worthies with three choices: they could give money and vote county bonds, build the roadbed, or organize their own local railroad to act as a spur line doing business exclusively with the Santa Fe. Since all agreed that they must have a railroad, after much debate Santa Fe County voted to issue enough bonds to raise the money.[7] The following February 1880 the first train rolled

5. Bradley, *The Santa Fe,* pp. 147–48.
6. Ibid., p. 204. Otero, *My Life, 1,* 129–30.
7. Santa Fe *Sentinel,* July 24, 1879, Ritch, HEH.

into the adobe capital amidst elaborate and almost hysterical ceremonies. The Santa Fe line was then extended to Albuquerque, where
a similar meeting of town dignitaries produced the required funds,
and by 1881 the Santa Fe had joined the Southern Pacific at Deming
to give New Mexico her first transcontinental connection. Ebullient
speeches, prognostications of the new era to come, and much flag-
waving accompanied the event.

Unlike that of many Western lines, the history of the Santa Fe
was not to be one of stock manipulation, ruthless exploitation, trips
to the bankruptcy courts, or frequent changes of ownership. In
contrast to the Union Pacific, its handling of land grants was a model
of decorum.[8] Its presence pleased the Santa Fe Ring, the Maxwell
interests, miners, cattle ranchers, and merchants. Shortly after the
railroad's arrival, Strong became its president, and under him the road
prospered. The Company bought into the Santa Fe *New Mexican*
and wisely retained as its chief solicitor H. L. Waldo, the most
respected lawyer in the territory.[9] With a good press and legal counsel,
it had come to New Mexico to grow up with the country.

The more obvious effects of the road and of the Southern Pacific
—which reached Deming, New Mexico, in 1881—were soon evident.
The rail lines literally created the new towns of Raton and Springer
in the northeast, Las Cruces in the south, Deming and Silver City in
the southwest, and Gallup in the West. They also boomed Albuquerque, Las Vegas, and Santa Fe. The mere presence of the lines caused
property values in the territory to jump from $41,000,000 in 1880 to
$231,000,000 in 1890. The cattle business expanded so dramatically
that for a time beeves accounted for the major item of freight for
the line. Where the number of cattle had been 347,000 in 1880, it was
1,630,000 by 1890. And where two banks had existed before 1878,
more than fifty were chartered in the twenty years that followed.
Santa Fe now boasted a Board of Trade, and the territory established
a vigorous Board of Immigration. As a student of the New Mexican
economy has observed, "the arrival of the Santa Fe heralded the

8. William S. Greever, *Arid Domain: The Santa Fe Railway and Its Western
Land Grant* (Stanford, 1954), p. 158. See also Greever, "A Comparison of Railroad
Land Grant Policies," *Agricultural History*, 25 (1951), 83–90.

9. Otero, *My Life*, 1, 77.

replacement of merchantile capitalism by the industrial capitalism still prevalent today."[10]

The railroad also affected population. While New Mexico had had a slow but natural increase in citizens since American conquest, immigration between 1880 and 1900 brought the population from 119,000 to 195,000 in that period. Now that Americans in sizable numbers were coming to the territory, many of the new towns became truly American in their makeup and institutions. It also meant that population shifts toward Albuquerque and southward into the mining communities of Grant and Socorro Counties would necessitate new political alliances and configurations. The thin line of Spanish settlements along the Rio Grande lifeline was now flanked by Americans to the east and the west. In this uncomfortable transition period it was perhaps appropriate that Edmund G. Ross, one of the founders and promoters of the Atchison, Topeka, and Santa Fe should become governor of New Mexico, for he was one of the most articulate crusaders for New Mexico's coming of age.

In 1868 Edmund C. Ross as the Radical Republican senator from Kansas had stood in the United States Senate Chamber and pronounced the death sentence of his own political career by voting against the impeachment of President Johnson. Cursed by fellow Radicals, censured by the Kansas legislature, threatened with physical violence, the small, frail Ross soon returned to Kansas as an ex-senator. Not content to accept his fate quietly, in 1880 he tested the public attitude toward his course in the Senate once again by running on the Democratic ticket for governor. His resounding defeat suggested that the legislature censure, now some twelve years old, remained in force.[11]

Having fought for free soil in Kansas and as a gallant soldier throughout the Civil War, his energies were too great to be quashed

10. Heath, "Influence of the Atchison, Topeka, and Santa Fe," pp. 5, 46–48, 50 ff., 72, 106.

11. John F. Kennedy, *Profiles in Courage* (New York, 1956) . See also "Edmund G. Ross" in *DAB*. For a detailed account of Ross's administration see Howard R. Lamar, "Edmund G. Ross as Governor of New Mexico Territory: A Reappraisal," *NMHR, 36* (1961) , 177–209.

by public displeasure. Since he had been one of the founders of the
Atchison, Topeka, and Santa Fe, it was only natural that he should
follow the road into New Mexico. His destination was Albuquerque,
then booming as a freighting and supply center for the mining towns
in the Black Range and Cerillos districts.

Ross' move was typical of many small-scale businessmen who now
felt New Mexico had a future. His brother-in-law H. C. Bennett, had
settled in Silver City and was full of praise for the mines of the
region. Two of Ross' former Kansas friends had already located in
Albuquerque. Elias Sleeper Stover, an ex-lieutenant governor of
Kansas, had moved there some years before to found the large
wholesale grovery concern, Stover, Crary, and Company. A former Free
Soiler and a Civil War veteran of fifty-one engagements, Stover was
destined by nature and background to become Ross' friend. It is not
surprising to find that the two men were soon closely allied in
ambitious projects to advance their own and Albuquerque's future.
Having arrived in the "Duke City" before the Atchison, Topeka, and
Santa Fe reached there, Stover, in association with Franz Huning and
William C. Hazledine, had bought up the land between the Barelas
road and the proposed depot and laid out the "new town." In this
way they capitalized handsomely on the coming of the railroad. Stover
was also one of the founders of the First National Bank of Albuquerque.[12]

Ross' other Kansas acquaintance was W. S. Burke, editor of the
Albuquerque *Morning Journal*. A Civil War veteran, he had worked
on papers in Iowa and Kansas before coming to Albuquerque in 1881.
Although the *Journal* was Republican in tone, Burke asked Ross,
who was now a Democrat, to join his staff. Ross appears to have done
much editorial writing for the paper, so that soon he and Burke were
as much of a team as Ross and Stover were. When the Albuquerque,
Copper City, and Colorado Railroad Company was organized in

12. E. G. Ross to Fanny Lathrop Ross, February 6, 1883; Lillian Ross Leis,
"Memoirs of Edmund G. Ross"; "Papers and Documents Relating to Railroads";
MSS in Ross Papers. For some account of the effect of the railroad on Albuquerque
see Bernice Ann Rebord, "A Social History of Albuquerque, 1880–1885" (Master's
thesis, University of New Mexico, 1947), p. 11. Victor Westphall, "History of
Albuquerque, 1870–1880" (Master's thesis, University of New Mexico, 1947), p. 87.

1883, Burke and Ross appeared as two of the directors. Ross was also listed as the vice-president and financial agent of a narrow-gauge company which at one time had no less than five railroad schemes under consideration.[13] His activities vividly illustrate the proliferation of business enterprises after the Santa Fe Railroad entered New Mexico.

It was of equal importance to men like Burke, Stover, and Ross, however, that their new home be American culturally as well as economically. They were concerned that after nearly forty years of American rule the territory still had no real public school system. They were appalled that much of the population still spoke only Spanish. Burke lamented that not one in ten justices of the peace had a territorial code of laws in his office, or that if he did, he could not read them. Revealing their abolitionist backgrounds, they saw the public school and education as the essential instruments necessary to Americanize and democratize New Mexico. Since he saw little chance of a local impulse for school reform, Burke's solution was to take education "out of the hands of the legislature and county officers altogether" and to permit only the federal officers to run the system.[14] His proposals—and others like it—were introduced into Congress but were never passed. They provided a useful insight, nonetheless, into Ross' and Burke's attitudes toward New Mexico. Just as the Radicals had tried to reconstruct the post-Civil War South, they were willing to use federal law to reconstruct New Mexico. When Burke's bill died in committee, he continued the educational struggle by becoming the first superintendent of public instruction in Bernalillo County. Some years later, Ross' other Kansas friend, Elias Stover, was to become the first president of the University of New Mexico.

The goals of the newcomers to Albuquerque did not stop with matters of economic and cultural progress. Surrounding Ross were intelligent and ambitious young lawyers and merchants of both

13. Rebord, "Social History," pp. i–vi, 13. Albuquerque *Morning Journal*, August (n.d.) 1883 (clipping in Ross Papers). *The New Mexico System of Narrow Gauge Railroads* (New York, 1883), pamphlet.

14. Albuquerque *Morning Journal*, July 23, 1883. W. S. Burke to George F. Edmunds, December 21, 1883; W. S. Burke to Ross, January 3, 1884; both in Ross Papers.

parties chafing under the rule of the Santa Fe Ring. It was they who had sent contesting members to the Assembly of 1884 and had tried to get the capital removed from the City of the Holy Faith to Albuquerque. Embittered by the questionable tactics that the Santa Feans had used to retain the seat of government, the fight broadened into a war between ring and anti-ring Republicans in the delegate election of 1884.[15]

Seeing a chance to bring about new political alignments, Ross threw himself into the Democratic campaign of that year with real vigor. For territorial delegate he supported Antonio Joseph. The better Ross came to know his own party members, however, the more disturbed he became. He discovered that both the chairman of the Democratic Central Committee, C. H. Gildersleeve, and Delegate Joseph were allies of the ring.[16] To check such men, Ross himself became a candidate for the governorship upon the news of Cleveland's election in November 1884.[17] Much to the surprise of the New Mexican press and the disgust of Gildersleeve, by May 1885 Ross had received the appointment.

Ross was the first Democratic governor of New Mexico in twenty-four years and the first reformer since Lew Wallace. His administration serves therefore as a useful study both of a crusader trying to modernize New Mexico and of the new reformist attitudes toward the West held by the Cleveland administration.

Hampered at the outset by a hostile press and party chairman as well as his own distrust of the delegate, Ross' first problem was to establish a working bureaucracy out of the remaining officers of the territory. While the new secretary, the United States attorney, and the surveyor general were congenial to Ross, political realities demanded that Joseph and Gildersleeve control most of the patronage. Thus the

15. Twitchell, *Leading Facts,* 2, 493. For an excellent summary of the Republican split in 1884 see The Santa Fe Weekly *New Mexican,* September 1, 1884 (Bancroft Library). See also the Albuquerque *Morning Journal,* May 4, 1884.

16. "The Gildersleeve, Springer, Joseph Combination"; Napoleon B. Laughlin to Ross, April (n.d.), 1886; both in Ross Papers. Archie M. McDowell, "The Opposition to Statehood within the Territory of New Mexico, 1888–1903" (Master's thesis, University of New Mexico, 1939), p. 27.

17. Ross to Grover Cleveland (copy), April 30, 1885; W. S. Burke to Cleveland, May 20, 1885; manuscript "Petition" of Albuquerque citizens, 1885, Ross Papers.

new chief justice, William A. Vincent, soon proved to be such a friend of the Santa Fe Ring that Cleveland was forced to remove him. The new United States marshal, Romulo Martinez, was so deeply involved in a fight over the ownership of the Canon del Agua grant that his worth also seemed questionable to Ross. The new governor cooperated with Judges Elisha V. Long and William F. Henderson, but he roundly mistrusted Reuben A. Reeves, in whose court many of Ross' executive acts were eventually declared invalid.[18]

Within his own evecutive branch Ross faced an equally complicated problem. Ever since New Mexican affairs had stopped centering around military and Indian problems, a local territorial bureaucracy had been developing. Gradually such officers as the territorial treasurer and the territorial attorney general assumed powers previously held by federal appointees. In many territories the locally chosen officials were in conflict with their federal colleagues. The territorial bureaucracy was a useful training ground for future state leaders, but it also vastly complicated and duplicated the work of federal officials. As a Democratic governor, Ross was faced with the problem of dealing with local officials who were Republican. Somehow he had to oust Republican appointees from the important territorial (as opposed to federal) offices before he could put a Democratic administration into gear. A territorial court ruling of 1880 declared, however, that the incumbents of territorial office could hold their positions for two years from time of appointment or until the biennial legislature should again meet and confirm their successors. At the request of the Santa Fe Republicans, Governor Sheldon had shrewdly reappointed all these officials just before leaving office. Since the legislature did not meet again until the winter of 1886–87, Ross would normally have to wait over a year to replace Republican incumbents.

Like the man he had refused to impeach in 1863, Ross himself was now faced with a local "tenure of office act," designed to curb the governor's power. By persuasion he secured two resignations; but his chief stumbling blocks were Colonel William Breeden, the attorney general, and Antonio Ortiz y Salazar, the territorial treasurer. Since

18. "The Gildersleeve, Springer, Joseph Combination." See also Poldervaart, *Black-Robed Justice*, p. 135; and Rio Grande *Republican*, January 25, 1887.

Breeden was also chairman of the Republican party, he obstructed Ross' every move during the latter's first year in office. By November 1885 Ross felt he had enough evidence of misconduct in office to suspend Breeden. Using the trusted medium of the press, he fired that obstreperous official in a broadside proclamation whose language electrified the territory. "As to the 'cause' for your suspension . . . you were suspended for drunkenness, licentiousness, gambling, and misfeasance, malfeasance and nonfeasance in office; crimes which ought not to be tolerated in a public official."[19]

Ross waited until July 1886 to remove Salazar, the territorial treasurer. Again he used the method of public proclamation. Charging Salazar with having speculated in territorial warrants and with mismanagement of funds designed for building the territorial penitentiary, he removed him and appointed Bernard Seligman in his place.[20]

Knowing that the legislature might not confirm his new choices, Ross tried to get Congress to pass a bill reapportioning the gerrymandered legislative New Mexican districts so that a more amenable body might be elected to the 1886–87 session.[21] With opposition from Gildersleeve at home and with lukewarm support from Delegate Joseph in Washington, this plan failed. Ross' interference with the legislative branch naturally embittered his relations with the members of the Twenty-Seventh Assembly. They convened in 1887 ready with mailed fist to do battle with the Kansas interloper. Although the Republicans had only a slight majority in both houses, they were so tightly controlled by a caucus system, set up and run by Colonel Chavez, that Ross could not break the phalanx.[22] And to hamper him still further, in the fall of 1886 the lawyers of New Mexico had formed a bar association with none other than ex-Judge William Vincent as its president. Whenever the legislature considered a bill,

19. Ross to William Breeden, November 13, 1885. See also broadside dated November 24, 1885, Ross Papers.
20. Public Letter of Ross to Salazar, July 28, 1886, Ross Papers. The Las Vegas *Chronicle*, August 18, 1886, contains an account of the Ross-Salazar fight (Bancroft Library).
21. Antonio Joseph to Ross, May 31, 1886; Shelby M. Cullom to Ross, June 3, 1886; Benjamin Harrison to Ross, June 7, 1886, Ross Papers.
22. Ross to L. Q. C. Lamar, January 26, 1887, Ross Papers.

it went to the association for approval first. If no approval was forthcoming, the bill went no further.²³ This was even more the case in 1889, when the association virtually wrote and introduced every act passed. Never had all the elements making up the Santa Fe Ring functioned so cleverly and brilliantly in defeating a governor's program.

The complicated infighting that characterized Ross' relations with the New Mexican legislature, the Santa Fe Ring, and his own party need not be detailed here, for the outcome was that all his proposals for a good school system, fiscal and tax reform, and abolition of corrupt offices were defeated. Nor were most of his major appointees confirmed. In turn, Ross vetoed more bills ground out by the Assembly than any governor in territorial history.

The most significant fight of Ross' administration actually concerned land grants and land policy, for here the beliefs of the governor and the surveyor general, both old abolitionist Free Soilers, collided with those of the Spanish Southwest. To solve the labyrinthine land-grant puzzle, Cleveland had appointed the venerable public figure George W. Julian of Indiana as surveyor general. Like Ross, Julian was known to be a fearless and incorruptible man, and an expert on public lands. Constantly encouraged by letters and notes from Secretary of the Interior Lamar and Land Commissioner Sparks to continue the good work of "reformation and restoration," Ross and Julian struggled to settle the land grants once and for all.²⁴

Unfortunately, Julian took the view that truly Draconian measures must be employed. After casting doubt on all decisions made by his predecessors in office, he announced that 90 per cent of all land entries in the territory were fraudulent.²⁵ While this was probably true, it also struck at every citizen of means and at the livelihood

23. A good analysis of the makeup of the Twenty-Seventh Assembly may be found in the Deming *Headlight*, January 2, 1887.

24. L. Q. C. Lamar to Ross, September 23, 1885; A. J. Sparks to Ross, November 7, 1887; both in Ross Papers. In acknowledging Ross' Annual Report, Sparks wrote: "In the name of the homeseekers I thank you. Let the good work go on. The Land 'grabbing' rascals will die hard, but as sure as God is just we'll beat them" (Ross Papers).

25. Deming *Headlight*, September 19, 1886. See also Rio Grande *Republican*, January 1, 1887.

of the entire legal profession in New Mexico. Much of the intense bitterness over Ross' administration, therefore, was actually caused by Julian's ruthless scrutiny of land records and his scathing reports to Washington.

Julian's findings led to the arrest of former Land Register Max Frost on charges of fraudulent land entry and to his conviction in a trial before Judge Long, although the decision was later reversed.[26] Julian also summarized his investigations in a blunt article for the *North American Review,* in which he fiercely denounced ex-Senator Stephen Dorsey, who now operated a vast ranching enterprise in northeastern New Mexico and was a claimant to many suspect land grants. Enmity to Dorsey called forth the opposition of the Maxwell Company, with whom he was allied. Then Julian, in a clean sweep, denounced C. H. Gildersleeve, chairman of the Democratic Party in New Mexico, as a "politician for revenue only."[27] The hornets' nest had been stirred and the effects soon began to appear. Senator Preston B. Plumb of Kansas warned Ross that letters were pouring into Washington complaining that Julian's methods had brought all business in New Mexico to a standstill, since no one was sure of title to property.[28] In a slap at Julian and the Cleveland administration, the 1886 Democratic territorial convention unanimously adopted a resolution to play down land frauds. Delegate Joseph successfully ran for reelection on a ticket endorsing this view.

This was only part of the difficulty, however, for, good friends though they were, Ross and Julian disagreed over methods of land reform. At first, in his annual report, Ross urged the creation of a federal commission to deal with the question. He persuaded Joseph to introduce a bill to Congress to that effect and asked prominent New Mexicans to go to Washington to lobby in its behalf.[29] Ross encountered the opposition of both Julian and Land Commissioner Sparks,

26. Twitchell, *Leading Facts,* 2, 498 n.
27. Julian, "Land Stealing in New Mexico," pp. 27–30.
28. Preston B. Plumb to Ross, July 9, 1886, Ross Papers. A typical reaction to Julian's charges may be found in the Rio Grande *Republican* for July 16, 1887.
29. *Report of the Governor of New Mexico to the Secretary of the Interior, 1885* (Washington, 1885), pp. 4–5. See also Antonio Joseph to Ross, May 31, July 19, 1886, Ross Papers.

however, so that a year later he declared instead for the creation of a court of private land claims. This was the solution Congress eventually adopted in 1891.

As a former Free Soiler and homestead advocate, Ross inevitably came into conflict with the range cattleman, just when the latter was in his heyday. Although mining provided some $6,000,000 in wealth annually for New Mexico in 1886, the product of the cattle industry that year was estimated at $13,000,000.[30] Moreover, it was Texas cattlemen and ranchers living in eastern and southern New Mexico who comprised an important section of the territorial Democratic Party. Nevertheless, when Ross learned that the Lincoln County Stock Association was harassing sheepmen in that district, his sympathies were immediately on the side of the sheepmen.[31] The more he learned, the less he approved of cattlemen in general. To him the ranching industry implied a sparse population, huge landed estates—which he called "a constant menace to popular government"—and oligarchic rule. It does not seem too far-fetched to suggest that Ross saw in the rancher the same threat to freedom that he saw in the slave-owning planter in Kansas in 1856.

Ross expressed his anticattle bias in his first annual report to the Interior Department by recommending that there be no further disposal of public lands except for homesteading purposes. In subsequent reports he commented that the cattleman's theory of a permanent range was a bad one, for a cattle frontier was by nature temporary.[32] In a speech to the Aztec Club of New Mexico in July 1885 he complimented the cattlemen upon their contribution to the settlement and wealth of the territory, but he warned them that there must be order between them and the sheepmen. That order was needed, he said, so people would migrate to New Mexico. "People are worth more to a state than steers," he exclaimed . . . "for with people comes capital and the spirit of commercial adventure, development,

30. Hammond and Donnelly, *The Story of New Mexico*, p. 137. *The Stock Grower* (Las Vegas), February 11, 1888.

31. ———— to Ross, June 22, 1885; John Y. Hewitt to Ross, June 23, 1885; both in Ross Papers.

32. *Report of the Governor of New Mexico . . . 1885*, pp. 7–8. Ibid., *1887*, pp. 6–8.

prosperity, and greatness." Two years later he bluntly told a crowd at the territorial fair that the "granger was coming and coming to stay."[33]

Naturally, Ross' position caused comment. J. E. Curran, editor of the *Sierra Grande Press,* wrote in the fall of 1885: "I love you for the enemies you have made! The rings and cliques don't like you. The Deming ring don't like you. The Hopewell and Grayson cattle ring are down on you, and the Las Cruces gang would betray you on the first chance."[34] A week later Jesse E. Thompson, superintendent of public schools in Sierra, warned that the "cattle barons" and "land jobbers" were down on Ross and were allied with Breeden and Thornton.[35]

Ross' failure to reform New Mexico internally finally led him to think that the only way to modernize the territory was to secure its admission as a state. But all efforts to persuade Congress to pass a statehood bill failed as well. It would be unfair, nevertheless, to call Ross' career "barren of result," as some historians have done, for Ross and Julian, unlike any other public officials, so dramatized the evils of the New Mexican political and land systems that reforms were not long in coming. Though Ross was unable to turn New Mexico into another free-soil Kansas, his failure was not nearly so significant as his dream.

The Republican Party, the Santa Fe Ring, and many business interests and lawyers heaved a great sigh of relief when President Benjamin Harrison removed Governor Ross in April 1889. After four years of Democratic rule they wanted to make sure that never again could a hostile administration disturb the internal affairs of New Mexico, as Ross and Surveyor General Julian had. To achieve this

33. *Governor Ross' Banquet Speech to the Aztec Club of Albuquerque* (July 22, 1885), pamphlet. See also Albuquerque *Morning Journal,* July 23, 1885; Albuquerque *Morning Democrat,* September 21, 1887; Deming *Headlight,* September 23, 1887; and Willoughby, "The Cattle Range Industry," p. 89.

34. J. E. Curren to Ross, November 29, 1885, Ross Papers.

35. Jesse E. Thompson to Ross, December 8, 1885, Ross Papers. "Thornton" was William F. Thornton, a law partner of Thomas B. Catron's and a Democrat who opposed Ross' appointment. Thornton served as governor of New Mexico during Cleveland's second term in office.

end they began a movement for statehood in the winter of 1888–89, when it was learned that Harrison and the Republicans had won the national election.

Harrison's choice for governor was L. Bradford Prince, a former territorial judge, a willing member of the ring, and an ambitious, suave, affable, politician. An amateur historian, and a lay leader in the Episcopal Church, he was also a man with many business connections in New York City, where he maintained an office.[36] Like Ross, Prince had been a resident of New Mexico for some years, and he could see that it was time for a change. As a member of the existing Republican hierarchy, however, he was interested not in Ross' type of reform but rather in consolidating Republican rule of New Mexico through modernization, statehood, and settlement of the problems hindering capitalistic development. On this last point Prince was particularly sensitive: he was involved in at least a dozen mining enterprises and land grant speculations, which never seemed to succeed.[37]

When Prince assumed office, the legislature had already issued a call for a constitutional convention to meet in September 1889. With a favorable administration in Washington and with the precedent of the admission of the Dakotas, Wyoming, and Washington in 1889, the time seemed right for New Mexican entry. The Santa Fe leaders also realized that Stephen Elkins' influential position in national Republican circles would undoubtedly work for admission. Feeling that the moment of success was upon them, the statehood forces, in their great haste to achieve their goal, rode roughshod over the opposition, made embarrassing compromises, and acted so selfishly that they generally defeated their own aims and laid bare once again all the old cultural, economic, and political issues that had plagued New Mexico for forty years.

The first difficulty for statehood men occurred in the legislature itself, where it was evident that the Spanish-American members, having grown used to the territorial system, displayed no great interest

36. Prince, *Concise History*, p. 208.
37. This conclusion is indicated by the voluminous correspondence relating to mines and lands in the Papers of Governor L. Bradford Prince, NMSRC.

in admission to the Union. This lack of enthusiasm turned into hostility when Russel A. Kistler of Las Vegas introduced a bill that would have laid a solid foundation for a public school system in New Mexico. Everyone knew that Congress would look dimly upon any territory applying for statehood which could not boast a functioning school system. Ross himself brought out the damning facts that of 109,505 persons in New Mexico some 57,156 were illiterates, and that out of 44,000 children of school age only 12,000 attended any school at all.[38] The statehood men were caught in a dilemma. If they voted for schools, the Spanish-Americans would not vote to call a constitutional convention. If they did not establish schools, Congress would not admit them.

Faced with this choice, Thomas Catron, who was leading the statehood movement in the legislature, joined forces with Pedro Perea, the wealthiest sheep rancher in New Mexico and probably the most powerful Spanish-American leader in the Republican Party. In a cynical and complicated set of parliamentary moves, the school bill was deliberately amended to death. Meanwhile the call for a constitutional convention passed. The Republicans had prevented a rupture with the Spanish-Americans who made up the bulk of their party, but they had angered many Americans in the territory. Retiring Governor Ross was indignant enough to write a public letter denouncing the killers of the school bill. "They have denied us our most cherished right," said he. Only the general government can destroy "the influence of these dangerous men." Newspapers and citizens from every party and every section of the territory joined Ross in the denunciation.[39]

As the election drew near, the Republicans, uncertain of Democratic support because of a disagreement over proportional representation, exhibited so little faith in the popularity of the statehood cause that they resorted to foul means as well as fair to make sure that their men were elected. The suspect election became further suspect when

38. E. G. Ross, *Public Schools and Statehood for New Mexico* (March 31, 1890), pamphlet. See also McDowell, "Opposition to Statehood," p. 21.

39. Lordsburg *Western Liberal*, March 8, 1889. New Mexico *Interpreter* (White Oaks), May 8, 1889.

Colonel Chavez, as chairman of the canvassing board, blandly declared a majority of Republicans elected. So spurious did the whole movement seem that only fifty-one out of seventy-three possible delegates turned up to write a constitution in Santa Fe that September.[40]

Actually, the delegates who came were a good cross section of the business, cultural, and political interests of New Mexico and were, by and large, men of ability. But once again the dominant Republican forces decided on bulldozing methods. It could hardly have been otherwise, when fourteen of the leading delegates turned out to be the owners and attorneys for 9,000,000 acres of land grants. There sat Catron, and F. W. Clancy, his law partner. Frank Springer of the Maxwell Company was a delegate, and Colonel Rynerson represented Dona Ana County. Catron's friend Pedro Perea was also a delegate, along with his brother-in-law M. S. Otero, as was the wily maverick Colonel J. Francisco Chavez, who just now was cooperating with the Catron forces.[41]

These men wrote a conservative constitution protected themselves by declaring that taxes on property were never to exceed one per cent, while mines and industries might be more heavily dutied. Once statehood was achieved, they promised to pay full value for territorial militia warrants, now selling for 25 to 40 per cent below par and largely owned by A. A. Staab, one of the charter members of the Santa Fe Ring. In districting the seats for the state legislature, the Democratic counties were gerrymandered out of full representation.[42] All these measures naturally made for trouble when the constitution was made public.

The school dilemma also persisted, for the delegates dared not ignore demands of Congress and the American residents for public

40. L. Bradford Prince to M. S. Otero, June 28, 1889; Prince to Benjamin Harrison, July 13, 1889; Prince to J. Francisco Chavez, April 27, 1889, Prince Papers. See also Springer *Banner*, July 11, 1889.

41. The membership is reported in the Rio Grande *Republican*, September 7, 1889.

42. *Western Liberal*, September 13, November 1, 15, 1889. New Mexico *Interpreter*, February 28, 1890. The history of the statehood movement of 1888–90 is well covered in McDowell, "Opposition to Statehood," and is summarized in Marion Dargan, "New Mexico's Fight for Statehood, 1895–1912," *NMHR, 14* (1939), 1–33, 121 ff.

schools. At the same time, Archbishop J. B. Salpointe, Lamy's successor, warned the delegates by public letter that they must support parochial schools. Nonsectarian education, he observed, was "in reality either sectarian, non-religious, godless, or agnostic."[43] The convention, nonetheless, refused to go along with the Archbishop and adopted a clause providing for state aid to schools in the poorer counties, where local taxes could not support public education.

The delegates seemed fated to arouse hostility, whatever course they took. In a combination of idealism and selfishness, they adopted William G. Ritch's proposal that no one could vote or serve on a jury in the future state who did not understand the English language without the aid of an interpreter. This baldly guaranteed that the new government would be dominated by Anglo-Americans.

From the first moment the constitution received its full share of public criticism. While both parties nominally endorsed it, and Max Frost turned the Santa Fe *New Mexican* into an organ wholly devoted to achieving statehood, the general public and large segments of the local press did not. It was a Catron-inspired document, shouted one paper, and should be called the "Tom-Cat constitution." The *Black Range* called it a device by which the "political bosses and land grabbers" could continue to run the territory. The Springer *Banner* rang the changes of criticism on the mining tax clauses and gave an "economic interpretation" of the constitution by printing the land holdings of the convention members.[44]

The statehood advocates waited until the spring of 1890 to step up their campaign. Their first move was to send a delegation of fifty-four men to Washington to persuade Harrison and Congress to give them statehood. When the committee arrived in the capital, the members were somewhat dismayed to learn that Delegate Joseph was lukewarm toward statehood, as was Congressman Springer of Illinois, chairman of the House Territorial Committee.

These factors were but a portent of things to come, for in May 1890 Chairman Gildersleeve announced that the Democratic party in New Mexico could not support the constitution as it was written. Gilder-

43. Rio Grande *Republican*, September 7, 1889.
44. Springer *Banner*, October 2, 1890.

sleeve said that the apportionment of representation to the legislature, the canvassing methods thus far employed, and the selfishness of the Republicans were the reasons for the decision.[45]

These were but the public excuses. Throughout the territory ran a strong feeling that New Mexico was not ready for statehood. Most Democrats and many Republicans privately admitted that they feared a state government would be a Spanish-American government; they were also convinced that Spanish-Americans were not yet Americanized enough to run a state in any democratic way. Ironically, many Spanish-American leaders feared that statehood meant Anglo-American rule, taxes, public schools, anti-Church policies, and the acquisition of their remaining lands. As the voting time drew near, it became clear that the opposition conformed less to party lines than to prejudice and culture. Thomas Catron wrote Senator Stewart of Nevada that "the Democrats and Catholic Church are opposing Statehood." "Many of the priests of the Catholic Church have been delivering political sermons against it [the Constitution] on account of the school clause which is made irrevocable."[46]

The debate over the constitution did much to reveal the makeup of the Republican and Democratic parties in New Mexico in 1890. Catron himself estimated that the Republicans in New Mexico were one-third Anglo-American and two-thirds Spanish-American while the Democrats were three-fourths Anglo-American and one-fourth Spanish. He might also have added that the Democrats came from the American counties of Eddy, Grant, Lincoln, Colfax, Mora, and San Juan. Their most promising leaders furthermore, were Southerners from Texas, Kentucky, Tennessee, and Alabama. Thus the Democrats in many ways reflected anew that old division between the Rio Arriba and Rio Abajo, which existed in the days of Martinez and Armijo and which had been replaced by a Yankee-Southern division represented by Mesilla and Santa Fe during the Civil War period. It now became a multileveled fight between the old guard at Santa Fe and the new population in the burgeoning cities of Albuquerque and Las Vegas, as well as a struggle between Santa Fe, the

45. Las Vegas *Optic,* June 27, 1890.
46. T. B. Catron, quoted in McDowell, "Opposition to Statehood," p. 54.

mining southwest and northeast, and the ranching southeast. And as if to revive the ghost of Montezuma Territory, the southern counties of New Mexico and the counties in southwest Texas began a movement in the late eighties to organize themselves into the "Territory of Sierra."[47] The movement did not get very far, but it exhibited discontent with the Santa Fe rule and a dislike of sharing the government with Spanish-Americans.

Given all these factors, plus the lack of enthusiasm, and the mutual suspicions between factions and parties, the results of the ratification vote cast in October 7, 1890, were anticlimatic. As expected, some 16,000 voted against the document and statehood, and only 7,493 declared for it. The Democrats claimed they had voted against the document but not against statehood; the likelihood was that they had secretly opposed both.

The defeat of the Tom-Cat Constitution left Governor Prince more convinced than ever that New Mexico must solve its internal problems or statehood would never be forthcoming. When the legislature met in December 1890, he presented that body with a stinging recital of New Mexican faults. The system for confirming land titles through a surveyor general and Congress "has been a miserable failure," he observed. The existing school law was a "flagrant example of . . . utter failure." "Not a public school has been open for a single day in the capital county of Santa Fe," he reported. On a county level he found that excessive fees made the offices of tax assessor and collector so economically important that in the "active work of elections everything is subordinated to them." Of the territorial code of laws, he bitingly concluded that "there was no country in the world, Christian or Pagan, in which the court practice was so antiquated, cumbersome and complicated as in New Mexico."[48] Under such vigorous prodding a reluctant legislature passed its first effective school bill. Nearly forty years after Calhoun had recommended such legislation, a basic American institution had at last been accepted by New Mexico.

47. *Western Liberal*, May 3, 1889, and October 7, 1890.
48. *Message of Governor L. B. Prince to the Legislative Assembly . . . 1890* (Santa Fe, 1890).

The land-grant problem was less easy to settle. Although Ross had persuaded various congressmen to introduce bills establishing a Court of Private Land Claims in 1889, a change of administration and modifications of the bill prevented enactment until 1891. But that July five judges finally sat down in Denver, Colorado, to untangle the greatest land imbroglio in American history. It was to take the justices until June 30, 1904, to complete their labors. During those years interested parties sometimes managed to get friendly judges appointed to the court, and although the court itself frequently ruled in favor of the large claimants, a great stumbling block to the development of the Far Southwest was in progress of removal by 1892 when the court held its second session in Santa Fe.[49] The questionable heritage of Beaubien, St. Vrain, Vigil, and Maxwell was finally being probated and executed.

As these two problems were at least in passage toward solution, Prince never lost sight of statehood as a goal. The problem after 1890 was to get the various factions of the Republican Party to cooperate. Prince himself was still strongly disliked by party members from the southern counties. Colonel W. L. Rynerson carried on a running war against the Governor from within the party. E. S. Stover and the Albuquerque reformers detested the local ring in their city, run by the powerful Hubbell family. In Las Vegas the Oteros and Jefferson Reynolds made up still another maverick faction, and in Santa Fe itself Catron and Prince grappled for party control. Politically New Mexico was a frontier in flux, where immigration, sectionalism, divergent cultures, and a changing economy kept the factions in constant turmoil. This was only the American side of the squabble, for traditional feuds between family parties periodically broke out between the Oteros, the Pereas, the Lunas, and Colonel Chavez. "It is the curse of this country that political prejudices run so high," lamented Prince in 1892.[50] Hydra-headed as it was, the party needed strong measures to keep the factions in line during an election.

49. Twitchell, *Leading Facts*, 2, 463–68.
50. L. B. Prince to Victor L. Ochoa, July 22, 1892, Prince Papers.

The economy was now too diverse for the old Santa Fe Ring to exercise its monolithic power, so in its place sprang up several rings. In the severe struggle for political place, New Mexican politics naturally developed a seamy side. Political murders, beginning with the Provencher assassination in 1889, were followed by others. Assemblyman J. A. Ancheta was seriously wounded in 1891 while sitting in the law offices of Catron, Knaebel, and Clancy. In 1892 the territorial capital was burned mysteriously, and still other killings occurred.

This aspect of New Mexican politics was laid bare in the delegate election of 1892, which began with a complicated set of intrigues followed by murder. The intrigue commenced when Governor Prince tried to prevent Thomas Catron from becoming the delegate candidate for that year and from controlling New Mexico's delegation to the national Republican convention of 1892. Both possibilities seemed disastrous to Prince, for not only was Catron an anti-Harrison man, but his association with the repudiated constitution and his lack of tact would hurt chances for statehood.[51] Matters were in a particularly delicate state just then; Delegate Joseph had just pushed an enabling act for New Mexico statehood through the House. Prince himself was already applying pressure to every senator he knew to secure a favorable reception of the bill in the upper house.

Catron, on the other hand, was equally convinced that his own presence in Washington and his friendship with Steve Elkins, now Harrison's Secretary of War, would achieve statehood. Putting his powerful following into motion, he won the first battle and went off to Minneapolis to the national convention as a delegate. While he was there, he learned by telegram that a gang of assassins, later identified as the "Alliance League," had ambushed and killed Francisco Chavez, former sheriff of Santa Fe County. A promising Democratic politician, Chavez had made enemies, nevertheless, by being a tough and—so the rumor ran—brutal official. The Chavez murder itself would have caused a minor sensation, but his violent death had been preceded by the killing of his close friend Sylvestre

51. L. B. Prince to John W. Noble, April 23, 1892: "Mr. C. is the most arbitrary and dictatorial of men. Those who are not his 'peons' he considers his enemies."

Gallegos, the police chief of Santa Fe. Other murders had followed that of Gallegos.[52]

All these acts had political overtones, since it was thought that the gang which killed Chavez specialized in doing professional dirty work for politicians. In this instance rumor mongers hinted that a faction of the Republican Party had been behind the assassination.[53] Inevitably the Chavez murder became a political issue; when Catron returned to run for delegate that fall, the air was full of insinuation and suspicion—a situation made worse because neither Governor Prince nor his Republican appointee to the dead sheriff's office could find the assassins. In the course of the campaign that fall the Democrats resorted to "dirty little circulars" about Catron. The Republicans responded in kind with innuendos about the sordid side of Joseph's career. Throughout the electioneering Catron was on the defensive and tried to counter the gloomy prospect of defeat by spending money with a free hand, but to no avail.[54] Once again the bland and imperturbable Joseph returned to Congress as delegate.

The 1892 campaign had revealed that New Mexico was full of gangs and secret societies. Throughout the territorial period religious groups like the Penitentes had occasionally exhibited a junta-like influence in elections in the Rio Arriba, but the new groups were bent on robbery, vengeance, terror, and political control as well. Vicente Silva, for example, periodically terrorized Las Vegas with his forty bandits, three of whom were on the Las Vegas police force. The Alliance League in Santa Fe boasted an ex-chief of police and his brother as members. Secret vigilante groups called "White Caps" —sometimes claiming to belong to Eugene Debs' American Railroad Union—operated in Colfax and Mora counties to organize the vote, cut fences, harass the railroad, or drive out homesteaders.[55]

By 1893 criminal conditions in the territory were so bad that when

52. Twitchell, *Leading Facts*, 2, 510–13.

53. Ibid., pp. 511–12 n.

54. "The democratic committee is getting ready to use dirty little circulars and I presume we must fight them the same way. In every town we must have them distributed." Max Frost to Judge A. A. Morrison, September 26, 1892, Catron Papers.

55. O. D. Barnett to Benjamin Butler, January 26, 1890, Interior Department TP: New Mexico, 1851–1914 (microcopy, 364).

Grover Cleveland returned to the White House he appointed William T. Thornton as Governor. A good lawyer, reputed to be honest and fearless, Thornton's job was more that of district attorney than chief executive, for his sole task seemed to be to root out the gangs and political terrorists in the territory.[56] During his administration members of the Alliance League were arrested; and although one was killed in the process, five others were eventually tried for the murder of Gallegos and, by implication, for the death of Sheriff Chavez. Since two of the five were the Borrego brothers, the sensational proceedings came to be known as the Borrego cases.

By a curious twist of fate, Governor Thornton, a law partner of Thomas Catron, was in essence the prosecutor, while Catron, whose very career was at stake, chose to defend the Borregos. Since the case did not come up until 1895, Catron had managed to unite enough Republicans to win the delegateship in 1894, but he was now having to prove his innocence to his party. In a fiercely contested, almost violent, trial lasting thirty-eight days, Catron lost the case when the jury, on the third anniversary of Chavez's death (May 29, 1895), brought in a verdict of guilty. Motions for retrial and appeals to Cleveland, McKinley, and the Supreme Court failed; and the five prisoners were executed in 1897.[57]

The Borrego cases stood as both a symptom and an example of what was wrong with New Mexican government and politics. On another level, they suggested that in a severe test the American jury and court system had functioned as an accepted method of justice. The case also marked the passing of an era in that it marked the climax of Catron's popularity. After his rough and ready performance before the court, which so angered the judge that Catron was cited for contempt and temporarily disbarred, he was a trifle too battle-scarred to be a delegate or to dominate Republican politics without

56. William T. Thornton to Hoke Smith, October 1894, Interior Dept. TP (microcopy 364).

57. In response to a pardon appeal Governor Thornton grimly replied on February 19, 1897: "It is time that the criminal classes of this Territory should learn that when they deliberately defy the law, deliberately plan and commit a crime, that they must expect to the law to be meted out to them to its fullest extent." He did grant a reprieve until March 23, 1897. Interior Dept. TP (microcopy 364).

a strong challenge.[58] The old Santa Fe Ring was giving way to new patterns in politics.

The criminal problem in New Mexico, coupled with that of party factionalism, naturally hurt chances at statehood. After 1890 still another factor had to be considered by the crusaders for admission. The new American immigrants into the territory had brought with them an interest in national affairs, not a characteristic of native New Mexican residents. As early as 1889, for example, a Farmer's Alliance had been formed in Colfax county, and a year later a statewide organization existed under the presidency of J. N. Coe. Several territorial newspapers also supported the local movement and covered the activities of the National Alliance in full.[59]

The growing interest in free silver and currency reform also attracted the attention of the silver-mining communities in New Mexico, and by 1894 Populism had a following there. The decline of the open-range cattle industry after 1889 allowed New Mexico's traditional sheep-raising industry to boom. Naturally the local wool growers became keenly concerned with the tariff question.

Since Washington was now less than a week away by train, both the national parties and the federal government could easily watch territorial activities. The world now sat on New Mexico's doorstep. Governor Prince sounded the new attitude when he wrote Secretary of the Interior Noble that the old way was "rule by coercion, threats and 'bulldozing'. That seemed to succeed until the railroad came. But conditions have changed and modern and American systems are needed. The native people will not stand what they did 15 years ago. The new population will not stand it at all."[60] Henceforth national politics and issues would play an intimate part in New Mexican affairs.

That influence was not long in coming, for in 1896 the whole of New Mexican politics revolved around the silver controversy. As early as 1890 the Democratic Party in the territory had endorsed free

58. Heffernan, "Catron," pp. 32–34.

59. Springer *Banner*, October 17, November 7, December 19, 1889, January 23, 30, 1890. New Mexico *Interpreter*, September 12, October 17, 1890. Raton *Daily Independent*, February 28, 1889.

60. L. B. Prince to John W. Noble, April 23, 1892, Prince Papers.

coinage of silver. Two years later the mining counties followed the proceedings of a silver convention in El Paso with intense interest; and by 1894 a Populist party existed in New Mexico. The new group declared for free silver—appropriately at Silver City—reaffirmed the Omaha platform, and selected T. B. Mills to be their candidate.[61] While they did not prevent Catron's election—indeed by splitting the Democratic Party they may have guaranteed his victory—it was certain that a sizable segment of the American electorate was interested in the Populist cause.

The effects of the free-silver issue were not strongly felt in New Mexican politics, however, until the national and delegate elections of 1896. More cautious than usual, Catron urged his party to ignore the silver issue and concentrate on statehood and tariff.[62] But factional and personal feelings ran too high. Governor Prince, W. H. H. Llewellyn, and many other Republicans with mining interests joined the free-silver standard; while two of the most promising Democrats in the territory, W. B. Childers and N. B. Field, declared for the gold standard. Childers left the Democratic Party never to return. On the other hand, his law partner, Harvey Fergusson, a brilliant orator from Albuquerque, became a free-silver Democrat and advocated many of the Populist reform planks.[63] In general it was the merchant versus the miner and the rancher versus the farmer, but the issue cut across party lines. Amidst confusion, great hope for the future, and the deep excitement of change, Harvey Fergusson won the delegateship. The first reformer ever to do so, he was a fitting symbol of New Mexico's first serious identification with national problems. The two party system had at last become a meaningful institution in the territory.

In the seesaw of politics it was expected that William McKinley would restore the gold-standard Republican old guard to power in

61. *Western Liberal,* October 12, 1894.

62. See "Political Letters, 1896," MSS in Catron Papers. "The American towns were pre-occupied against you because of the Silver craze, and a thousand other things. Some money was raised by the enemy, given to a few prominent natives who influenced the Mexican people a great deal against you, although I can tell you that the Mexican people were more inclined to support you than the Americans." M. W. Mills to Catron, November 6, 1896.

63. Robert W. Larson, "Statehood for New Mexico, 1888–1912," *NMHR,* 37 (1962), 176.

New Mexico in 1897. Tom Catron rushed to Washington to urge Pedro Perea's appointment as governor, while seeking the position of United States district attorney for himself.[64] As the usual Republican factions maneuvered for place, Jefferson Raynolds, founder of a chain of banks in New Mexico and one of its most responsible citizens, also journeyed to Washington to see McKinley. The new President happened to be his boyhood playmate and cousin. Acquainting McKinley with the political situation in New Mexico, Raynolds urged a change from the old guard and the appointment of a native Spanish-American resident as governor. McKinley agreed, and at Raynolds' bidding, he selected young Miguel A. Otero to replace Governor Thornton. Otero had actually befriended McKinley in 1892 and had come to Washington with hopes of becoming United States marshal for New Mexico. When he learned of his appointment as governor, his surprise was nearly as great as that of the Catron and Prince factions.[65]

Without realizing it, McKinley had worked a minor revolution in New Mexican politics. Otero was the first native governor of American New Mexico. He was also the representative of a new generation of Spanish-Americans who felt equally at home in both cultures. Born in St. Louis in 1857, raised on the frontier, and educated in Missouri and New York, he was the son of a leading New Mexican family. His father had twice been delegate, had founded Otero, Sellar, and Company, and had helped bring the Atchison, Topeka, and Santa Fe to New Mexico. Ross had been the transition figure for the economic change following the appearance of the railroad; Prince represented the effort to standardize schools and the land system and to develop it economically; but Otero represented the fusion of two cultures and two ways of life.

The "little governor," as the diminutive Otero was soon to be called, quickly demonstrated that he was, indeed, a combination of the old and the new. Moving with an air of vigor, sensitive to the right publicity, and adept at supporting popular measures, he soon had an efficient political machine of his own in operation, which ignored both

---

64. For the details of the appointment see Miguel A. Otero, *My Nine Years as Governor of the Territory of New Mexico* (Albuquerque, 1940), pp. 1–3.
65. Ibid.

the Prince and Catron factions. He demanded control of certain federal appointments and built his following out of territorial justices, a friendly United States marshal, and a friendly United States attorney general. While Otero did not get along with Delegate Pedro Perea, through Colonel Chavez and Solomon Luna he soon organized a Spanish-American grass-roots support for his administration which no other territorial governor had ever known. Overnight the governorship became an important post in New Mexican politics.

Given his double heritage, Otero somewhat revived old pre-conquest roles of the governor as the supreme arbiter in local disputes and pardoner of criminals. "The monarchial system has been introduced here," Prince complained, "for every holiday is used as an excuse for the pardon of some murderer or robber and for the overthrow of the acts of the Courts."[66] The Democratic delegate, Harvey Fergusson, also felt the power of the governor. He remarked to a job-seeker that his own patronage power was nil, but that "Governor Otero will be very valuable to you in this matter."[67] Spending money with a lavish hand, Otero made the Palace of Governors once more into the social and political center of New Mexican affairs. But if Otero's appeal was to tradition, his methods were modern. His political machine was efficient; his press was well controlled; he played a large role in picking delegates; and he ran the government like a growing business. It was no wonder that, unlike any other gubernatorial appointee, he remained in office for nine years (1897–1906).

A rigorous test of New Mexico's new attitude and participation in national affairs came quickly after Otero's appointment. The outbreak of the Spanish-American War meant that the United States was fighting the spiritual and cultural mother country of native New Mexicans. This proved no problem at all. In response to a call for volunteers, Spanish-Americans as well as Americans flocked to the colors with such enthusiasm that the New Mexican companies were oversubscribed. And when the promising son of the Luna family lost his life in the war, the whole territory gave him a hero's funeral.[68]

66. "Otero Pardon Policy," MSS in Prince Papers.
67. H. B. Fergusson to A. C. Emery, May 7, 1898. Official Files of the Governor of the Territory of New Mexico, Otero Administration. NMSRC.
68. Twitchell, *Leading Facts*, 2, 541–42 n.

Otero himself seemed happy under the territorial system and appears to have joined Colonel Chavez in secretly opposing a new statehood movement that blossomed in 1901. However, the majority of the population—both Spanish and Anglo-American—were converted to home rule through statehood by the turn of the century.[69] Even ex-Delegate Joseph, that barometer of native opinion, declared for admission after 1895. The more subtle impact of the nation upon the province also became increasingly obvious. New Mexicans now fretted over the tariff and free silver; they worried about the burgeoning conservation movement, which threatened their free use of New Mexico's woodlands; they agitated for a change in land laws; like good Americans they began to lobby for reducing the size of Indian reservations, or debate over whether public or private interests should build dams in their region.

While these debates went on, the New Mexican economy became tied to that of the nation; specialists in business set up shop; homesteaders, small ranchers, and farmers took up the remaining land or bought chunks of the fabled land grants. As Jim Heath has noted, the railroad had activated two economic laws in New Mexico. First, from its own original investment others had followed with a "multiplier effect, so that both the level of the economy and the number of investments went up together"; and second, "that as a region progresses from an underdeveloped status to a more developed one, the inequality of income diminishes." Thus property values rose 372.5 per cent in twenty years, with no population explosion to accompany the increase.[70]

As New Mexicans readied themselves for admission to the Union, they could also note the survival of the Spanish-Mexican culture. In surrendering politically, the Spanish-American had not yet abandoned the concept of the trusted native leader or patron in politics, nor had family political parties, or a certain economic caste system, been abolished. In accepting public schools, they had relinquished neither their Catholic heritage—which under Lamy, Salpointe, and Gasparri had actually experienced a healthy renaissance—nor their beautiful

69. McDowell, "Opposition to Statehood," p. 87.
70. Heath, "Influence of the Atchison, Topeka and Santa Fe," pp. 5, 168.

and somewhat archaic Spanish language.[71] In the picturesque mountain villages a simple folk culture and subsistence economy stubbornly persisted in the face of the great drive toward Americanization. Nearby, in their unique storied apartment communities, those grand masters of cultural isolation, the Pueblo Indians, exercised their own arts of living as if the white man did not exist at all. The Penitentes still thrived; the moradas and fiestas went on in Chimayo, Taos, and Arroyo Hondo; the priest remained a political as well as spiritual leader in Spanish-American lives. In the brown adobe villages, whether set amidst the azured hills or straggling along the muddy Rio Grande, time still moved imperceptibly.

Without surrendering her traditions, nonetheless, Spanish-American New Mexico had come to accept—in the fifty-four years since American occupation—certain institutions and to identify herself with the national image. While a distinct people and a charmingly different region remained, the conquest begun so cockily by Kearny in 1846 now began to have a deeper meaning, for an invisible frontier of misunderstanding had at last begun to disappear.

71. In assessing the role of the Italian Jesuits who came to New Mexico, Frederick G. Bohme has said: "They came to the Territory during its formative period and encountered both the traditional "native" culture with its values, and the incoming "Anglos" who had a different way of life. The Jesuit contribution lies in their ambivalence: as Italians they could understand and adapt to both cultures and thus provide a bridge between the two." "Italians in New Mexico," p. 145.

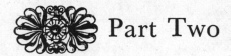 Part Two

8   Gold and Popular Sovereignty: Jefferson Territory, 1858–1861

There are many incidents in the history of statehood movements in which settlement has rushed forward more rapidly than legal institutions, with results in the erection of illegitimate provisional governments. But none of these illegitimate governments has been erected more deliberately or conducted with more propriety than this territory of Jefferson.

Frederick Logan Paxson, 1906

Shall it be government of the knife and revolver or . . . a new and independent state?

Call for State Convention, 1859

With a large amount of capital invested in improvements and a circulating medium, we have already become a Commercial people—Hence the great necessity of some rule of law regulating our affairs in this respect.

Governor R. W. Steele
To the Jefferson General
Assembly, 1860

 The first major gold rush in the United States occurred in the wooded southern Appalachians, where the mountains rise as smoky blue ranges in eastern Tennessee and northern Georgia. There, at the beginning of the nineteenth century, gold deposits were discovered, and cotton planters, small farmers, Cherokee Indians, and assorted adventurers congregated to produce ore in such quantities that the federal government optimistically located a mint in northern Georgia. On this modest mining frontier new towns were founded with mellifluous names like Auraria and Dahlonega.

The Georgia and Tennessee gold diggings were almost forgotten in the subsequent craze for lead mining in Illinois and Iowa during the 1820s, and in the national preoccupation after 1848 with the fabulous discoveries in California. It was but logical that among the California argonauts would be a Cherokee half-breed named John Beck and a Georgian named William Green Russell, both of whom had been miners in Georgia. On their trek across the continent in 1850 their experienced eyes had spotted traces of the yellow metal on the south fork of the sprawling Platte River. This tantalizing evidence was not strong enough to hold them back from California, but eight years later Beck and Russell—apparently none the richer for their sojourn on the Coast—remembered the traces of gold on the eastern slope of the Rockies and returned to the Platte region to prospect.[1] Appropriately, veterans of the two known gold regions in the United States began the famous Pike's Peak gold rush of 1859.[2]

Ironically, the sixty men forming the joint Beck-Russell party in 1858 found only small amounts of gold in the region where Denver, Boulder, and Central City, Colorado, are now located. Nor did another exploring party from Lawrence, Kansas, which was busily combing the Rockies south of the Platte, find much pay dirt that same summer. But when the Georgians and Kansans met by accident on the borders of Cherry Creek, they both resorted to a second get-rich-quick scheme, which had been the rage in Iowa, Kansas, Nebraska, and along the Upper Mississippi River for nearly ten years: this was land speculation in the form of townsite booming. The Kansans staked out St. Charles and a paper city called Montana. That fall members of the Russell group, who had not gone home for the winter, laid out the town of Auraria (obviously named for the Georgia town). Later in 1858 General William Larimer, merchant, engineer, and experienced land speculator, brought a party to the same spot on Cherry Creek, seized the partially abandoned St. Charles townsite, and renamed it Denver City in honor of Governor James Denver of Kansas Territory.[3] Whether gold was in the eastern Rockies or not, townsite boomers were in the mountains in force by 1858.

1. LeRoy R. Hafen, ed., *Colorado Gold Rush: Contemporary Letters and Reports, 1858–1859* (Glendale, Cal., 1941), pp. 249–50.
2. Ray A. Billington, *Far Western Frontier, 1830–1860* (New York, 1956), pp. 259–66; and Rodman W. Paul, *Mining Frontiers of the Far West, 1848–1880* (New York, 1963), pp. 109–34, have excellent recent summaries of the Colorado mineral frontier.
3. A. J. Fynn, "Creating a Commonwealth," *CM, 1* (1924), 204–13. Frank M. Cobb, "The Lawrence Party of Pike's Peakers (1858) and the Founding of St. Charles," *CM, 10* (1933), 194–97.

The Georgians, Kansans, and Cherokees were not alone that summer. A party from Missouri also roamed the creek edges. Though all these prospectors were pioneers, they were in territory that constituted the northern boundaries of Bent's fur-trade empire. Near the new diggings, in fact, was old Fort St. Vrain, once run by Marcellin, the wild younger brother of Ceran. There were also three other trading posts in the area—Forts Lupton, Vasquez, and Lookout—which New Mexican Indian traders still frequented. Indeed, trading paths were so well established that a recognizable one led up from Bent's Fort and the Santa Fe Trail to old Fort St. Vrain and the other posts.[4] Among the men frequenting the trail, whether miners or Indian traders, rumors spread about the extent of the new gold finds. These word-of-mouth reports became further enlarged as they filtered back to the Mississippi and Missouri valleys. Russell and Beck had made only modest strikes, but after the California experience Americans were prepared to believe anything. Overnight the national cry became "Pike's Peak, a new Eldorado." Pike's Peak also sounded like economic salvation as well, for the entire country was still deep in the grips of the Panic of 1857. Whatever the reasons, an overwhelming gold rush was in the making.

How could men stay at home when one paper reported that gold lumps weighing four pounds were discovered, and another asserted that a man could average between ten and twenty dollars a day by mere panning. What youth was not restless after reading the optimistic headline:

> California and Frazer River "no whar!"
> Cherry Creek and Pike's Peak ahead!!!
> Great Excitement!! The Atlantic Cable
> Not Thought Of!!![5]

Could one resist going when a guidebook soberly remarked: "The gold region is unlike that of California. In the latter a few men would make their piles by striking a good lead; but in the Kansas Gold

---

4. LeRoy R. Hafen, *Colorado: The Story of a Western Commonwealth* (Denver, 1933), pp. 80–86.
5. Hafen, *Gold Rush*, p. 42.

Mines every man can find gold and make wages."[6] To many the report that more than forty Frenchmen had been hired by William Bent to take supplies to the mines seemed adequate proof of a strike.[7]

Naturally Missouri, Kansas, and Nebraska merchants, who were feeling the pinch of depression, fanned the Pike's Peak rush into a large-scale operation with an eye to increasing sales. They were abetted by optimistic spread-eagle journalism in the form of newspaper accounts and dishonest guidebooks. Every railroad in Illinois and Missouri advertised itself as the shortest and quicket route to the gold fields.[8] Every store in St. Louis, Kansas City, Omaha, Fort Leavenworth, and a dozen other towns declared that they were an outfitting center for the Pike's Peak region. The propaganda and huckstering element in this gold rush was illustrated by the citizens of Wyandotte, Kansas, who called a public meeting "for the purpose of taking measures to inform the world of the nearness of Wyandotte to the Kansas gold mines."[9] While relatively little gold trickled in from Pike's Peak, few voices of skepticism were heard in the summer or fall of 1858, so thousands of argonauts set out for the Rockies. Kansas City was described as in a "perfect furore" while Leavenworth was in a "perfect mania." And the Wyandotte merchants blissfully reported being "over-run with customers outfitting for the mines." As Omaha prepared to become an outfitting center, the word came in that so were a dozen small Iowa towns.[10] The extent and degree of the gold fever could be seen in Fort Leavenworth, where an amazed newcomer remarked that he had found " 'Pike's Peak Hotel,' 'Pike's Peak Ranch,' 'Pike's Peak Lunch,' 'Pike's Peak Outfits' . . . and Pike's Peak almost everything greets you upon either hand."[11] Meanwhile, the excitement at Fort Laramie had reached such a pitch that the "quartermaster

6. John W. Oliver, *Guide to the Gold Regions of Western Kansas and Nebraska* (New York, 1859), p. 6, YWA.

7. Hafen, *Gold Rush*, pp. 41, 43.

8. *Pacific Railroad of Missouri* (Chicago, 1859); *North Missouri Railroad Company* (St. Louis, 1859); pamphlets, YWA.

9. Hafen, *Gold Rush*, p. 69.

10. Ibid., pp. 61–62.

11. Libeus Barney, "Early Letters from Auraria" (Bennington, Vt., 1859–60), YWA.

was compelled to withhold the pay due the hands in the government employ in order to retain them."[12]

In the lull that necessarily attended even a gold rush during the winter of 1858-59, many thousand would-be miners of all ages laid plans for a spring assault upon the Rockies. As they perused the guidebooks pouring off the presses in Chicago, Cincinnati, and St. Louis, the great debate centered around two questions: what was the quickest and cheapest method of transportation, and which was the best route? The Pike's Peakers found a plethora of answers. Most guides were at least honest enough to advise against walking, but they succeeded in making the six-hundred-mile trip west of the settlements seem so easy that some men actually set out pushing handcarts. Others tried a "wind wagon" to be wafted westward by sails, and at least one goldseeker got himself a dog team as his means of locomotion. Generally, however, the guides recommended a team of mules or oxen and listed the supplies needed.[13]

On the question of the best route there was downright dishonesty. Three major trails were available. The first was the much traveled Santa Fe Trail to Bent's Old Fort, whence the goldseeker could journey northwestward past the motley Mexican-American settlements of Pueblo and Fort Hardscrabble to Pike's Peak, Cherry Creek, and the diggings. Since this trail led from Kansas City, that community rang all the changes on its preferred desirability. To the north, Iowans and Nebraskans were equally complimentary about the Platte River route to the gold fields.

In successful competition with these two, however, was the more direct "air line" route, as it was ingenuously termed, via Fort Leavenworth and the Smokey Hill River. It was perhaps a hundred miles shorter than the other trails, but the disadvantage was that it was devoid of way stations and water for long stretches and headed directly into hostile Indian country. But speed and haste were the cry when

12. Hafen, *Gold Rush*, p. 67.
13. For typical guidebooks see William B. Parsons, *The New Gold Mines of Kansas and Nebraska* (Cincinnati, 1859); O. B. Gunn, *New Map and Hand-Book of Kansas and the Gold Mines* (Pittsburgh, 1859); Pratt and Hunt, *A Guide to the Gold Mines of Kansas* (Chicago, 1859); Luke D. Tierney, *History of the Gold Discoveries on the South Platte River* (Pacific City, Iowa, 1859); all in YWA.

the new rush of emigrants set out in the spring and summer of 1859. What followed was comic and tragic, absurd and serious, and, withal, fantastic.

It has been estimated that 100,000 people started for Pike's Peak by the three routes mentioned. Although William H. Russell, of Russell, Majors, and Waddell fame, established the Leavenworth and Pike's Peak Express, and Horace Greeley's bumpy ride made the determined drivers for the line notorious for speed at any cost, most goldseekers could not afford to go by stage. Nor did all choose to go by the safer Arkansas or Platte River routes. Instead they set out in caravans or went singly, or as families, or in companies of every size. Most were ill-prepared both for the rigors of the trail and for the trials of gold mining.

The contrast of experiences is well illustrated by the treks of George Willing, Libeus Barney, and Daniel Blue. Willing was a St. Louis physician with political ambitions, who went to Pike's Peak with dreams of political office as well as gold. He chose the Santa Fe Trail, which he negotiated without difficulty in a buggy, though he wrote that it was "plain, plain, plain all the way. I am _so_ tired of the plains." While Willing jogged along clearly bored to death, Libeus Barney on the Smokey Hill Trail encountered snow and rain and saw destitute and starving immigrants. Some with insufficient supplies had been reduced to eating prickly pears or feasting off decaying, dead oxen found on the trail. Others like Daniel Blue of Illinois had set out with a party that included his three brothers. Through a series of bad decisions the four brothers had become separated from their group; and after wandering in circles through heavy storms, Daniel watched in horror as each brother died of starvation. He was still more horrified to find himself eating their remains. An Arapahoe found Daniel delirious and fainting beside the partly consumed corpse of the last brother. He was delivered to a station house of the Pike's Peak Express, broken and half-crazed by the knowledge of his cannibalism.[14]

14. Ralph P. Bieber, ed., "Diary of a Journey to the Pike's Peak Gold Mines in 1859," _MVHR, 14_ (1927), 360–78. Barney, "Letters." Daniel Blue, _Thrilling Narrative of the Adventures, Sufferings, and Starvation of Pike's Peak Gold Seekers_ (Chicago, 1860), YWA.

Inevitably a reaction to so much unexpected hardship and suffering set in. Perhaps 50,000 of the would-be argonauts, disillusioned by the difficulties and exhausted by the trail, turned back before reaching the Rockies. Still others, upon reaching the diggings, found little or no gold, high prices, and such primitive conditions that they were repulsed. After one day's panning, young Sam Curtis, son of an Iowa congressman, wrote: "It is very hard work, and after I had washed one pan full, I concluded that it was here, but that I was not adapted to digging it."[15] Libeus Barney, an articulate and skeptical New Englander, wrote satirically that Pike's Peak was a "country of premature fame and undeserved celebrity." "Five cabins, three women, seven men, a cat, dog, pig, and two or three children constitute a city in this most ambitious country." Many were ill-equipped to mine or pan gold once they arrived. Barney reported during the summer of 1859 that "hundreds leave daily for their homes; hundreds turn back before they arrive here, and none have any confidence in the "diggins." In the words of a New York *Tribune* correspondent, the gold fields threatened to become "the most prodigious humbug of this or any other age."[16]

The firstcomers of 1859 had been bitterly disappointed at the small amounts of ore to be found in the Cherry Creek, Denver, and Auraria region. But just as they were turning back and placing signs "Pike's Peak be Damned" and "We Want to Go H-O-M-E" on their wagons, a red-headed Georgian, John H. Gregory, digging on the banks of Clear Creek near the present town of Blackhawk, panned dirt that netted him $900 in four days. The news leaked out, and within a few days all of Denver seemed to have moved to Gregory Gulch. This strike and another one by George A. Jackson on Chicago Creek were the turning point. The previously suspect and ephemeral nature of the Pike's Peak gold rush now vanished before the solid appearance of genuine nuggets and real dust in respectable quantities. Further discoveries at Gold Hill near Boulder made the mineral area appear to be a large one.

15. Samuel S. Curtis to Henry Z. Curtis, November 15, 1858, MS in Samuel Ryan Curtis Letters, YWA.
16. Barney, "Letters," p. 13.

The timely arrival of Horace Greeley, Henry Villard, and A. D. Richardson a month after Gregory's strike to inspect the diggings meant that Pike's Peak would now have even more publicity. In a public letter sent to Beverley D. Williams, agent for the Pike's Peak Express, they jointly testified that the gold rush was justified. Despite Greeley's caution that the population should not rush to the Rockies ill-prepared, by summer of 1859 his favorable words had helped bring out a second wave of gold seekers.

By early autumn the familiar elements of the California gold camps of 1849 were in evidence. Experienced miners, hundreds of greenhorns, the saloon keeper, the gambler, and the prostitute all appeared in Denver and Central City. Missouri badmen, many leaving behind a record of trouble in Kansas, also came out to drink and fight over their cut of the gold. Uncle Dick Wootton and Edmond St. Vrain, nephew of Ceran, freighted in supplies and built an imposing warehouse and store. As early as March 1859 General Larimer wrote that "heavily loaded teams with 50 Mexicans has come in with flour, bacon, potatoes, onions, etc." So dominant were the New Mexican merchants—of whom St. Vrain, Wootton, and Vasquez were the most important—that Blake and Williams of Council Bluffs, Iowa, were described as the only "eastern" outfitting firm with a regular store in Denver.[17] In Denver and in the diggings two worlds met when the Santa Fe trader found his market among California mining veterans.

All the ambitious, gregarious, and restless young men who joined the rush of 1859 did not come to Colorado to seek fame by digging gold. Many an incipient politician was prepared to lay down his shovel and run for office at the first opportunity. The first news of gold in the fall of 1858 led Governor Denver to assert Kansan jurisdiction over the new Eldorado by creating Arapahoe County around Denver and Auraria and by sending out county officers. H. P. A. Smith was to be probate judge, Edward Wynkoop, sheriff, William Larimer, treasurer, and Hickory Rogers, chairman of the county commissioners.

17. Hafen, *Gold Rush*, pp. 248–49. "Col. C. St. Vrain's train of twenty-six wagons freighted with eleven hundred sacks of flour, one hundred sacks of corn and other supplies for his Denver house, arrived yesterday from Taos, N. Mex." *Rocky Mountain News*, October 13, 1859.

From their subsequent history each of these men appears to have been politically ambitious. Few people took them seriously, however, and the population held its own local election in November; with the result that H. J. Graham, a townsite boomer from Pacific City, Iowa, was sent to Congress to beg for territorial organization, while one A. J. Smith rode east to sit in the Kansas legislature.[18]

From the very first it was clear that a majority of the Pike's Peakers envisaged themselves as making up a territory separate from Kansas or Nebraska. By January 1859 Graham was already in Washington petitioning Senator James S. Green, chairman of the Senate Committee on Territories, for an organic act. The slavery crisis was too far gone and bleeding Kansas was still too vivid a memory at that time for Congress to attempt to organize another territory and disrupt the Union still again. Thus Graham's pleas failed to move either Green or Alexander H. Stephens, who was on the House Territorial Committee.[19]

The pioneers who came to Denver City and its environs had little need of Congress at this point, for they were as well-versed in self-government as any people in the world. A majority of the population were from the Mississippi Valley border states of Kansas, Nebraska, Iowa, and Missouri. During the turbulent fifties they had learned much about local self-government, town founding, and territorial organization. Whether they were Northern or Southern in their proclivities, by 1859 they were all sophisticated practitioners of popular sovereignty. As the *Lawrence Republican* observed: "The miners are resolved upon carrying out the doctrine of squatter sovereignty to the utmost extent." In March of 1859 they held a local election under Kansas laws, and a month later called for an election of delegates to a constitutional convention to call into being the new "State of Jefferson." The delegates were duly elected in May, met in

18. Fynn, "Creating a Commonwealth," pp. 205–08. H. H. Bancroft, *History of Nevada, Colorado, and Wyoming* (San Francisco, 1890), pp. 401–03.

19. The history of Jefferson is covered in three overlapping articles by Frederick Logan Paxson in "The Territory of Jefferson: A Spontaneous Commonwealth," University of Colorado *Studies, 3* (1905), pp. 15 ff.; "The Territory of Colorado," ibid., *4, 63–76;* "The Territory of Colorado," *American Historical Review, 12* (1906), 53–65.

imp of politics + speed + force w/ which it evolved

June, farmed out work to committees, and scheduled themselves to reconvene on August 1 to adopt a state constitution.

When the voters were called upon to ratify the constitution of the State of Jefferson in September 1859, however, experienced miners and wiser leaders remembered that statehood was a financial burden as well as a political privilege. Therefore they rejected the document by a three to one vote, arguing that it would be better to have a territory, since its basic expenses could then be underwritten by the federal government.[20]

Despite the defeat of "statehood" and the general obsession with new strikes around Central City and at Boulder, and regardless of rumors of more gold in California Gulch and in South Park at the Tarryall diggings, politics would not be downed. In October 1859 the miners turned out again, to elect to Congress, as a squatter delegate, Beverley D. Williams, the expansive and loquacious Pike's Peak Express agent. The popularity of the position was suggested by the fact that Williams had six aspirants running against him. Shrewdly, the voters also sent Richard Sopris as a representative to the Kansas legislature. Not content with this healthy display of popular sovereignty, the more ambitious politicians met a few days later to write an organic act for the "Territory of Jefferson." On October 24 the miners, diverted from their occupation by an early winter, voted in the provisional government of the Territory of Jefferson and elected R. W. Steele, a member of the Nebraska legislature, as governor.[21]

The whirlwind pace continued when a full-fledged legislature convened in November to write a civil and criminal code for the new

20. Paxson, *American Historical Review, 12,* 53–65.
21. The Jefferson government was made up of the following officers:

Governor: R. W. Steele	*Chief Justice:* A. J. Allison
Secretary: L. W. Bliss	*Associate Justices:* J. M. Odell and E.
Auditor: C. R. Bissell	Fitzgerald
Treasurer: G. W. Cook	*Marshal:* John S. Merwick
Attorney General: Samuel McLean	*Superintendent of Public Instruction:*
	H. H. McAfee

See *Rocky Mountain News,* October 20, 27, November 3, 10, 1859; and Fynn, "Creating A Commonwealth," pp. 210–12.

Rocky Mountain body politic. After the legislature had established twelve counties, it provided Jefferson with justice courts in precincts, district courts, a territorial supreme court, and a county probate court. Where necessary they also accepted the more informal miners courts, which had sprung up in the various district camps. After recognizing miners' laws, petitioning Congress for territorial organization, and providing for a census, the frontier solons adjourned with what seemed a real popular sovereignty government in control.[22]

The provisional government was only one aspect of Pike's Peak political activity. It should be remembered that probably three out of every ten miners in the gold region were veterans of the California mines. These men were already well acquainted with the local problems of law and order and set out, as in California, to create mining districts complete with a president, a judge, a recorder, and sheriff. They also quickly established a miner's court to try civil cases and a people's court, with jury, to consider criminal cases.

Typical of these laws was the Code of the Eureka District, adopted in the spring of 1860. Meeting at H. G. Otis' store at seven in the evening, the miners ruled that on gulch claims a lead would be limited to 100 feet by 50, while a placer would be 100 feet square. Then they proceeded to define the limits of tunneling and the size of a quartz mill claim and to regulate ditch and water claims. The code went so far as to specify that all farming or ranch claims must be purchased and restricted to a 160 acre plot, while building lot claims must be only 40 feet by 100 feet.[23]

Smoothly written and clearly expressed, there is even evidence that the local code was written by professional code writers who went from camp to camp suggesting their form and scope. The California experience meant that the miners knew exactly how to go about organizing and that they could avoid a great deal of the lawlessness and confusion so characteristic of early California.

22. See *Provisional Laws and Joint Resolutions Passed at the First and Called Session of the General Assembly of Jefferson Territory* (Omaha, N.T., 1860). A nice summary of the legislation enacted may be found in *The Western Mountaineer*, December 14, 1859, copy in CSHS.

23. *Laws of the Eureka District, May 9, 1860* (Denver, 1860), pp. 1–8, YWA.

Even so, there were the usual crime waves, acts of violence, and resulting vigilante committees. In Denver and Auraria—soon to become one town—the Auraria toughs made things so hot that extra-legal action was necessary. In one instance a mass stealing of turkeys led to a "Turkey War," when the good citizens tried to drive out the thieves of such desirable edibles. And the code of honor came into tragic operation when P. M. McClure and Richard E. Whitsett fought a duel that resulted in McClure's death. William Byers, the doughty editor of the fledgling *Rocky Mountain News,* found his life threatened by a mob of ruffians because of an editorial he had written. Unafraid, he and his friends faced the attackers and carried the day. Naturally men began to pack revolvers, and soon young Samuel S. Curtis could write his family that: "What with claim jumping in Denver, and turkey stealing and the attendant circumstances in Auraria, all law abiding citizens had had enough to do without counting their own private business."[24]

Obviously such a confident do-it-yourself bunch of pioneers were not really prepared to submit to the authorities they themselves had created in the provisional government. The legislature's attempt to levy a poll tax was challenged by many miners almost immediately. Another group continued to refuse to accept territorial status and declared for immediate statehood. A minority still argued that Kansas had jurisdiction over them, and still another insisted that north of Denver the region belonged to Nebraska. To compound the confusion, in September 1859 Denver elected a people's government that was independent of the provisional government. Similarly, the South Platte Mining District, acting on its own, sent T. C. Wetmore to Congress, while the Mount Vernon District pompously declared itself independent of everything and everybody but the Congress of the United States.[25]

The basically law-abiding nature of the miners appears to have prevailed, nonetheless, for in October 1860 a second election was held, keeping Governor Steele in office and returning B. D. Williams as delegate.

By the summer and fall of 1860, new mines were being opened

24. Samuel S. Curtis to ———— Curtis, February 8, 1859, Curtis Letters, YWA.
25. "Chronology of Jefferson Territory," CSHS.

in South Park and near the headwaters of the Arkansas, and the
need for government became even greater. Yet the provisional
government was becoming impotent. Men elected to serve without
pay took only a casual interest in their job. The miners themselves
took oaths not to pay the one dollar poll tax levied by the legislature.
Further, statehood advocates held a convention in Golden in October
1860, and still another convention met at Central City to send its
own delegate, C. L. Morgan, to Congress and representatives to Kansas
and Nebraska. Then they renamed the region "Idaho Territory," and
called for the organization of judicial districts in which a judge would
handle all governmental business until Congress acted.[26] Side by side
sat the Idaho "central judicial" officers, the provisional government
of Jefferson, the Kansas county officials, the Denver people's government, scores of miners' courts, and local governments and vigilante
committees. Never had frontier democracy blossomed so vigorously.
With popular sovereignty in the saddle, the northern part of Bent's
old empire was already a far cry from the tradition-bound and caste-
conscious territory of New Mexico. A new kind of democratic, middle-
class, commercial-minded frontier had arrived on the borders of the
Spanish Southwest.

Although Pike's Peak had its ardent advocates in Congress, the
latter did not get around to considering Colorado until May 1860,
when Congressman Galusha A. Grow reported a bill to organize
"Idaho" territory. He ran into a storm of opposition and counter-
proposals, indicating that the controversy over the slavery issue, the
transcontinental railroad route, and the still-debated popular sovereignty concept would ruin any chances of passage. Clark of Missouri,
for example, demanded that a clause protecting slavery be left in the
organic act. Grow insisted that it be omitted. The controversial Eli
Thayer of Massachusetts, a Republican committed to his own version
of popular sovereignty, urged the House to throw out the Idaho bill,
organize Pike's Peak as the Jefferson Land District, appoint a surveyor
general, and let the people elect their own government.[27] Thayer's

26. *Rocky Mountain News*, October 17, 24, 31, November 7, 1860.
27. "Territory of Idaho," *Cong. Globe*, 36th Cong., 1st Sess. (May 10, 1860),
pp. 2047–49. The Congressional debate over the organization of Colorado, Dakota,
and Nevada during 1860–61 is summarized in Lamar, *Dakota Territory*, pp. 60–65.

proposal lost by only ten votes—a suggestion of the degree to which popular sovereignty ideas had infiltrated even a Republican House.

The next day Grow reported bills for the territories of Chippewa, Idaho, Nevada, Arizona, and Dakota, and explained that they were shaped so that southern, central, and northern transcontinental rail routes all could be developed with equal ease. The opposition was so great, however, that the bills were tabled. On May 12 Grow tried once again, but Thayer and Kellogg of Illinois demanded popular election of officers instead of federal appointees, and the bill failed.[28]

Between May and the following February, when the Colorado question came up again, the national triumph of the Republican Party, the withdrawal of Southerners from Congress, and the prospect of disunion and war suddenly placed the Western problem in a new focus. Unless the West was put under federal control, it might drift away. Strategically, communication with California was all-important; politically, new territories and lands were needed—especially along the Upper Missouri—to make the promised homestead bill a reality. Anxious Union men, whether Republicans or Democrats, also agreed that the territories might now be used as a political peace-offering to show the mildness and tolerance of the incoming administration. If they could be organized without reference to slavery, the South might return. Senator Green of Missouri, who represented the border-state point of view, and Ben Wade of Ohio, who represented the Republicans, therefore agreed on compromise bills for Colorado, Dakota, and Nevada which would omit any reference to slavery. In the House, Galusha Grow, David Wilmot's law partner, was also party to the arrangement. James G. Blaine has called these compromises "the conspiracy of silence."[29]

The results of the agreement appeared when Senator Green produced a bill to organize Colorado on February 2, 1861, with the explanation that though the boundary had been changed slightly—and Delegate B. W. Williams had insisted on the name Colorado in

28. *Cong. Globe*, 36th Cong. 1st Sess. (May 12, 1860), pp. 2079–81. See also "Letter from B. D. Williams" in *Rocky Mountain News*, June 6, 1860.

29. David M. Potter, *Lincoln and His Party in the Secession Crisis* (New Haven, 1942 and 1962), p. 278. See also James G. Blaine, *Twenty Years of Congress* (2 vols. Norwich, Conn., 1884), *1*, 269–71.

place of Idaho—it was the same familiar bill they had considered before. No debate ensuing, the bill—and similar ones for Dakota and Nevada—quickly passed both the Senate and House. Four days before his term ended, President Buchanan signed the Organic Act and left the territorial appointments to his successor.[30]

The so-called conspiracy of silence was not to succeed without comment from the father of popular sovereignty, however. The Colorado bill had passed the Senate while Senator Stephen A. Douglas was ill and absent from the floor. When he returned on February 6 to find passage a fait accompli, he urged reconsideration. Wade and Green begged him to desist. Douglas then suggested that intrigue had surrounded the writing of the bill. He noted particularly that the bill provided that the territory could not pass any law "destructive of the rights of private property." And he wondered if this did not prevent the building of highways, or forbid the right of eminent domain to the new government? After objecting to this, he questioned why the boundaries had been changed so that parts of New Mexico were included in the new territory, for it is true that the boundary had been pushed southward from the Arkansas river to the 37th parallel. "Is the effect of this bill to abolish slavery in that part of the territory thus cut off [slavery was legal in New Mexico in 1861] and make it free territory? Is that the compromise that has been made?" To this Green hurriedly retorted that the new boundary "does not cut off five inhabitants and not a single nigger," and as to slavery, the Colorado organic act was "a perfect carte blanche, without expression on the subject either way." Green angrily closed his remarks with the statement that it was an "unexceptionable bill concocted by honorable gentlemen." To support Green, Ben Wade rose to add: "It happened that neither of us could organize the Territory upon the principles we hold; and yet it was essential, as it was proved to us, that there should be a territorial government for the people of Pike's Peak."[31]

---

30. *Cong. Globe*, 36th Cong. 2nd Sess. (February 4, 1861), pp. 728–29. Ibid. (March 1, 1861), pp. 1330–35.

31. Ibid. (February 6, 1861), pp. 763–65. Frank Hall, *History of the State of Colorado* (4 vols. Chicago, 1889), *1*, 245–63.

[handwritten marginalia: personal interests poss, short compro—, shaped Colo's, mise]

Did Wade and Green tell the whole story? Douglas himself hinted at some of the implications when he asked if the land laws and problems of the New Mexican strip were not incompatible with those of Colorado. Could not the prohibition of the right to pass laws destructive of private property be equally used to protect slaves or to prevent a transcontinental road from being pushed across Colorado? And most curious of all, was it accidental that the area taken from New Mexico included parts of the Nolan, Sangre de Cristo, and Vigil and St. Vrain land grants, and part of the Beaubien and Miranda tract? Was it an accident that the last three had been confirmed in June 1860? Could it be that New Mexican lobbyists had decided to remove at least part of their claims into a new and friendlier jurisdiction and were to be protected from becoming public domain by a provision that no laws destructive of private property be passed? Green himself had remarked that New Mexican friends had urged the change.[32] Although only circumstantial evidence exists, it appears that the Colorado bill was far more than a mere compromise over slavery.

The Colorado boundaries themselves, which form a proper rectangle, had interesting implications. Significantly, the border did not reach northward enough to include Fort Laramie and the Wyoming region, which because of its nearness to South Pass would undoubtedly be the route of a transcontinental line. This left the way clear for Chicago interests. If a pass through the central Rockies could be found, however, Missouri, Kansas, and Colorado had a chance to develop another railroad. To the West the boundary cut still further into the arid domain of Mormon Utah, as did the creation of Nevada, and the two virtually cut off the Mormons from any probable control over gold fields within their own borders. To the abolitionists the southern boundary meant that a slice of slave territory was now a part of a nonslave region by an act of Congress. At the same time, it pleased certain speculative interests from Santa Fe. Finally, it meant that by Congressional fiat, part of Colorado's population was to be Spanish-Mexican and a segment of its lands kept from public domain

32. *Cong. Globe*, 36th Cong. 2nd Sess. (February 4, 1861), pp. 728–29.

in such a way as to relate Colorado's problems to those of the Far Southwest for the next few years. The "honorable gentlemen" in Congress had concocted what was, indeed, a most interesting "unexceptionable" organic act.

The state of the Union was already so perilous when Lincoln took office that many of the time-consuming formalities that usually accompanied the appointment of federal officials were curtailed. In such a crisis the criterion was loyalty, the appointment was hasty, and often official directions were verbal. This was precisely the manner in which Lincoln chose Colonel William Gilpin to be governor of Colorado. Gilpin was one of the hundred men who had formed a personal bodyguard to accompany the President-Elect to Washington in 1861. He had also been the only citizen in Jackson County, Missouri, to vote for Lincoln in 1860.

Outside of William Clark, Andrew Jackson, and Brigham Young, Gilpin is possibly the most remarkable man ever to be appointed territorial governor. Colorado's first chief executive was born into a distinguished family living at the site of the Battle of Brandywine. He had been educated by private tutors in England and was used to polite Philadelphia society. But he was also a restless romantic with a love of the West. Andrew Jackson, a friend of the Gilpin family, secured young William a post at West Point; and although William did not stay to graduate, he was so attracted to military life that within a few years he returned to the Army and served as an officer in the Seminole War.[33]

Naturally such a free-roaming soul was fascinated by the center of Western enterprise: Missouri. In 1838 he went to St. Louis—undoubtedly armed with introductions from Andrew Jackson to T. H. Benton—and made himself known to Old Bullion. Almost immediately he went to work as an editor of the Missouri *Argus,* a paper that sought the reelection of Benton and Arthur Linn to Congress. This

33. See H. H. Bancroft, *History of the Life of William Gilpin* (San Francisco, 1889). Henry Nash Smith, *Virgin Land: The American West as Symbol and Myth* (Cambridge, Mass., 1950), pp. 35-43. "Gilpin File" and "Gilpin Miscellany," MSS and newspaper clippings in CSHS.

tall, spare, young Pennsylvanian, possessed of an impressive head, a distinct military bearing, and cultivated French gestures, actually had much in common with Benton, for like the Missouri Senator he was pompous, oratorical, and visionary. He also shared Old Bullion's expansionist spirit, and found the optimistic atmosphere of prosperous Missouri so much to his liking that he settled there and is supposed to have fallen in love with Jessie Benton, the Senator's delightful and intelligent daughter.

Missouri was but the outfitting center for Gilpin's restless mind. In 1843 his intense interest in the Pacific Northwest led him westward to Oregon. On the trail he fell in with John C. Fremont, whose expedition Gilpin joined. During his *wanderjahr* in the Northwest, Gilpin claims to have laid out the city of Portland, Oregon, and to have been at the Oregon convention of Americans who petitioned Congress in 1844 to annex the Oregon country. Gilpin himself carried the petition to Washington, when he rode east that year.[34]

The young adventurer's return trip was via Fort St. Vrain and Bent's Fort, where he learned of the fabulous land grants just awarded Beaubien and St. Vrain. Either then or later he purchased an interest in the Sangre de Cristo grant. Gilpin also invested in Kansas City sometime during the 1840s. By the time Gilpin had presented the Oregon petition to Benton and to incoming President Polk, however, the country was being swept away with cries of Manifest Destiny, and phrase-maker Gilpin was soon in the forefront, expounding the mystical right of the United States to Texas and Oregon.[35]

When General Zachary Taylor marched across the Nueces and war came in 1846, it was no surprise to learn that Gilpin was one of the first to volunteer to fight. Given the rank of Major in Doniphan's First Missouri Volunteers, Gilpin jogged with Kearny down the Santa Fe Trail to occupy New Mexico. Once conquest was effected, he was sent on an expedition to Taos and later into Navajo country

34. Smith, *Virgin Land,* p. 36.

35. "They laughed at me when I came back from Oregon and I just sat down on the brink of the plains and made my home near Kansas City, Missouri from 1841 to 1861, and began to travel, write, fight, and lecture and work up the Western feeling, assisting to make the Mexican War." Gilpin to a reporter, Denver *Daily Tribune,* May 25, 1879.

to overawe portions of that tribe. He completed his service by acting as military guard on the Santa Fe Trail in 1847–48.

On these expeditions Gilpin saw first hand the lands of the San Luis Valley and was impressed by the good prospects for ranching there. His romantic spirit was exhilarated by the splendor of the Rockies. He alone of his men showed genuine enthusiasm for the region, so much so that one of his officers later remarked on Gilpin's endless monologues about "the great grazing region," "the land of beef and wool," "the unbounded pastoral domain of the continent."[36]

Retaining his interest in the West throughout the troubled 1850s, Gilpin was so inspired by reports of gold in the Pike's Peak area that he published an ambitious book, *The Central Gold Region*, in 1860, in which he claimed that this was to be the new center of America. On a more practical level it was also to be the path of a central rail line leading from Missouri across the continent. Gilpin's theorizing was to go even further and lead him to assert that the last world civilization would be harbored in the enormous bowl formed by the region between the Appalachians and the Rockies.[37] In the words of one historian, Gilpin was the "John the Baptist of the West."

Far from appointing a political hack, Lincoln had chosen the spiritual heir of Thomas H. Benton to govern the Pike's Peakers. After receiving verbal orders from Lincoln—reputedly in the White House vestibule—to keep Colorado in the Union at all costs, the new Governor made his trip westward. On May 27 his coach pulled up before the Tremont House in Denver, where he was welcomed by the miners and merchants. Later he was given a formal reception, and Provisional Governor Steele graciously proclaimed that Jefferson Territory was no more.[38]

Despite rumors of secessionist sentiment in Colorado and several Union-Confederate incidents preceding Gilpin's arrival, the new

36. R. S. Elliott, "Notes Taken in Sixty Years" (1883), p. 224. Gilpin File, CSHS.

37. William Gilpin, *The Central Gold Region, The Grain, Pastoral and Gold Region of North America* (Philadelphia and St. Louis, 1860). See also Gilpin's *Mission of the North American People, Geographical, Social and Political* (Philadelphia, 1874).

38. Hafen, *Colorado*, p. 156.

Governor and the other federal officers were well received. The young territorial secretary, Lewis Ledyard Weld, was a Coloradan whose energy and fierce sense of patriotism pleased Gilpin. Of the three judges, B. F. Hall, S. N. Pettis, and C. L. Armour, only the popular Hall was considered capable. The new marshal, Copeland Townsend, was a popular local appointment. Although the appointed attorney general never showed up, an acceptable substitute, James E. Dalliba, soon filled that slot.[39]

With characteristic energy Gilpin set out on a tour of the mining districts, where he acquainted one and all with his capacity for long speeches. He also directed the Marshal to take a census, which brought to light the disappointing information that only 25,331 persons resided in Colorado. After districting the territory, he called for the election of a territorial legislature and a delegate to Congress. The wheels of government, after three years of popular sovereignty, had at last been properly set in motion.

Gilpin himself was terribly excited by the prospects of his Rocky Mountain empire. As a pupil of Benton's, he held the old views that gold, control of trade routes, and a flourishing commerce were the sources of true wealth and imperial greatness. In his mind's eye the new territory sat squarely athwart the route to and from India; the region could also produce gold, beef, and wool. The search was ended; Gilpin had found the land of his dreams. His continuing enthusiasm was demonstrated years later when he approached a young Philadelphian on the Denver streets and asked: "Harry have you got a horse?" "No, sir." "Have any of your friends got a horse?" "Yes, sir." "Well get a horse and go there," said Gilpin, pointing his finger to California Gulch. "That is the center of the territory, and the center of the United States, and the center of the Universe. Go there, my boy, and stay."[40]

Governor Gilpin's enthusiasm might have reached still greater heights had he considered the significant developments in American

39. The background and appointment of the federal officials is treated briefly in Hall, *Colorado, 1,* 263–68.
40. Reminiscences of H. G. Elder in Thomas F. Dawson's Scrapbook, Vol. 62, CSHS.

frontier history which the Pike's Peak region symbolized. Here four distinct frontiers had met: the fur-trapping and Indian-trading element were represented by Bent and St. Vrain, who had been in economic control since 1830; the Spanish-Mexican settlement frontier was well-established in southern Colorado by 1858; from the West came the California pioneers with their ten years of experience in mining techniques and self-government; and from Kansas and Nebraska came the midwestern agricultural ideas of family farming, townsite booming, and middle-class commercial views—all of which had been reinvigorated by popular sovereignty and free soil concepts.

Most significant of all was the coincidence of three basically non-rural patterns of settlement. In southern Colorado tiny adobe villages like San Luis, Guadalupe, and Conejos, or others on the Costilla and Culebra Rivers were built around the traditional plaza. There Spanish-Americans lived a tight, tradition-directed community life. In the remainder of the territory the mining town, ambitiously calling itself a "city," blended with a third, the midwestern town plat.[41] Here, as Robert G. Athearn has so acutely observed, the usual frontier pattern was inverted: an urban frontier of sorts came before a rural and farming frontier. And the commercial frontier preceded, with the exception of the Spanish-Americans, the subsistence frontier. Colorado was a region in which both settlement and exploitative techniques perfected elsewhere were to be used with signal success.

Unlike New Mexico, Colorado was no terra incognita; it possessed no large native population, and it seemed wealthy rather than poor. The pioneers of Jefferson Territory came dazzled with the memory of California gold and the vision of an easily realized American commonwealth. Although the conditions they encountered were frontier, their psychological state could be described as optimistic and entrepreneurial. The key to early Colorado history lay in the juxtaposition of this condition and this attitude.

41. Athearn, *High Country Empire*, p. 77.

9

Colorado Territory: Politics and War, 1861–1868

There is no peace for any United States officer here unless
he will endorse all the horrible atrocities of Sand Creek and
utterly ignore the famous frauds in the Quartermaster
Department by which the government was swindled out of
millions of dollars under pretence of suppressing
Indian hostilities.

Governor Alexander Cummings, 1866

This damn stinking Indian business!

James B. Thompson, Indian Agent

 The seeming unanimity and good will characterizing
Governor Gilpin's reception in May 1861 was soon to
be shattered by the demands of the Civil War, debilitating Indian hostilities, and a controversial statehood movement. These problems and issues added
new dimensions to the already lively game of local
politics in frontier Colorado.

Shortly before Gilpin reached the territory, a Southern sympathizer
raised a Confederate flag over Wallingford and Murphy's store in
Denver. This act sent rumors and alarms flying through the town
until a bold citizen pulled down the rebel banner to the noise of
hearty cheers for the Union. Although it was said that many mining
camps preferred the gray over the blue and that southern Colorado

was supposed to be a hotbed of Confederates—whether miners in camp, soldiers at Fort Garland, or settlers at Fountain City—it was clear from the first news of Fort Sumter that a majority of Coloradans would back Lincoln.

At the same time, three factors made the war seem unusually pertinent to the miners and dangerous to the territory. The first was that Colorado bordered on slave-holding New Mexico. The latter could become a base from which a Southern invasion of Colorado might be launched. The relative nearness of Confederate Texas and Indian Territory—where the Cherokees were rumored to be pro-Southern—actually persuaded local Colorado secessionists to organize bands and buy up guns, powder, and provisions. Two such bands, those of A. B. Miller and Captain Joel McKee, were already making considerable trouble by the summer of 1861.[1]

The second factor was the population itself. Many of the Colorado miners hailed from the border states, and while they were Unionist, they were not particularly Republican or abolitionist. Their watch-and-wait attitude infuriated the territorial officials and radical Republicans, who mistook disinterest for secession sentiment. Judge Benjamin F. Hall reflected such views when he wrote Seward:

> There is not much difference in effect here between malcontent office seekers whom Gov. Gilpin cannot appoint to office and the Secessionists or open rebels. They seem to have no idea of loyalty either to the General or Territorial Government. If one of them gets an order or contract for rations, the rest turn in and fight him and the Governor. They number some 5000 of the border ruffians of Kansas and the destroying Angels of Brigham Young—I presume they are the worst people on the face of the earth to govern.[2]

Given such attitudes, the Civil War inevitably became a whipping

1. Benjamin F. Hall to William H. Seward, October 30, 1861, State Department TP: Colorado, 1859–74, NA. William Gilpin to Indian Commissioner W. P. Dole, October 8, 1861, Interior Department, OIA, Colorado, NA. Gilpin wrote that "companies of malignant white men [had] formed into atrocious guerilla parties," and that "Cherokees and Texans in rebellion tamper with and agitate the warriors."

2. Hall to Seward, October 30, 1861.

boy for local political factions. Epithets like "Secesh," "Copperhead," and "traitor" were thrown about with absurd abandon, real feeling, and a great deal of deliberate exaggeration—the latter often for the purpose of impressing Republican authorities in Washington.

In the camp of the ardent Unionists was William N. Byers, pioneer editor of the already powerful *Rocky Mountain News*. Byers was one of the most energetic, aggressive, and capable newspaper men ever to come West. Born in Ohio, the future editor developed a real case of wanderlust in his youth. He went to Iowa in 1850 as a surveyor, but after a year's stay he hit the Oregon trail. For a time he helped run the boundary line between Oregon and Washington, then, unable to resist the siren call of golden California, he sojourned in the mining camps of that new state until he returned to the Midwest via Panama to grow up with the booming territory of Nebraska. He was busy platting the town of Omaha when news of Pike's Peak reached him.

Byers knew enough about the nature of a frontier to realize that businessmen and not miners usually made money in the gold fields. So he went to Colorado with a printing press, qualified as a surveyor, and prepared to dig gold as well.[3] As Byers had guessed, gold in his case lay in the printed word. Early in Colorado history he made the *Rocky Mountain News* the official organ of the Republican Party, and he never hesitated to boost a friend or attack an enemy. Armed with the pithy phrase and the bold editorial, he set out to save Colorado for the Union and for the Party.

Although Byers crusaded for the Union, Governor Gilpin and Secretary Weld could be called Unionists with abolitionist inclinations. They were backed by free-soil men from Kansas like Richard Sopris, Jacob Downing, and Edward Wynkoop. Gilpin did not care for Byers, and Byers viewed the Governor as an alarmist and a crackpot theorist, but they all agreed on strong measures where rebels were concerned. Gilpin had moved in the nightmare of panic and fear that had gripped Washington in the early days of the new administration, and he was now convinced that a similar situation of

3. Hall, *Colorado, 4,* 368–69.

emergency and danger existed in Colorado. He wrote a friend that "the struggle with treason [here] is a perpetual death struggle."[4]

To meet the threat of Confederate raids and possible seizure of Colorado, Gilpin, who had seen military service in two wars, put the territory on a war footing as soon as he arrived. He could see that, strategically speaking, Colorado was poorly defended. The closest outposts were Forts Riley, Larned, and Leavenworth in Kansas, Fort Lyon in southeastern Colorado near Bent's New Fort, and Fort Garland in the San Luis Valley. None of these was within a hundred miles of Denver. To the north, Fort Laramie was not close enough to be of much value. Being neither on the Santa Fe nor on the Oregon trail, the actual gold regions of Colorado had been ignored so far as military posts were concerned.

Excited and challenged by Colorado's dangerous plight, Gilpin decided on strong measures. After organizing a military staff, he began buying arms from citizens and appealing to the authorities at Laramie for still more weapons. His vigor prompted others to act. Patriotic Coloradans overtook A. B. Miller's Confederate train of guns and supplies heading for Indian country and captured it. Soldiers at Fort Wise (now renamed Fort Lyon) also seized McKee's men and turned them over to Marshal Townsend, presumably to be tried as traitors. These actions prompted the pessimistic Judge Hall to admit to Seward that "We make some progress. . . . We have apparently suppressed the rebellion here."[5]

Gilpin was so certain Lincoln would approve of his course that he also recruited men for a regiment of volunteers without troubling to secure permission from Washington. He moved in haste, because many of the more patriotic Unionists were leaving Colorado to join the Army in the East. To keep these needed men in the territory, the grandiloquent Governor made such extravagant promises that his recruits came to be known as "Gilpin's Pet Lambs."[6] By October 1861 his vigorous measures were paying off. Camp Weld, named in

---

4. *Rocky Mountain News,* December 21, 1861, Gilpin File, CSHS.
5. Hall to Seward, October 30, 1861.
6. Frederick J. Stanton, "History of the First Regiment of Colorado Volunteers, 1861: Gilpin's . . . Pet Lambs," *Trail, 1,* (1909), 5 ff.

honor of the territorial secretary, was erected just south of Denver, and soon enough men had been mustered to round out a skeleton organization of ten volunteer companies. A Denver lawyer-politician, John P. Slough, was made colonel, while Samuel F. Tappan became lieutenant colonel. An extraordinary Methodist minister, John M. Chivington, some six feet five in height and possessed of a booming voice, laid aside his church duties to become the regimental major. The remaining officers included many a former Kansas free-soiler whose fighting spirit was equaled by his antislavery convictions.[7]

The difficulty attending all these impressive preparations was that when payment was demanded for the enormous amounts of supplies, food, and buildings for the volunteers—Camp Weld alone cost $40,000 —Gilpin was forced to reimburse the merchants and contractors with drafts on the United States Treasury. By Christmas 1861 the word had spread that the drafts were unauthorized and would not be honored. Just then Colorado was suffering a depression, since no new gold discoveries had been made and segments of the disheartened mining population were slipping away. Thus the mobilization expenditures, which at first seemed such a godsend to local businessmen, now seemed a major debacle.

As shouts of fraud, humbug, and tyrant rose, Gilpin himself hastened to Washington in December to explain his actions and to secure payment of the drafts. But close on his heels was Byers of the *News,* who saw in Gilpin's embarrassment a chance to engineer the Missourian's removal. The *News* had always favored General William Larimer for governor; and since Gilpin had forced Byers to share government printing patronage with a competitor, a second reason for the editor's enmity was not hard to find.[8]

By the early spring of 1862 Gilpin was so unpopular that his replacement seemed imminent, although the government did acknowledge his drafts and a military officer was sent to Colorado to adjust the debts. Eventually some $300,000 was paid out to cover Gilpin's war costs.[9] Ironically, just as Gilpin's reputation reached its nadir, news reached Denver on February 10, 1862, that the Confederates

7. Ibid.

8. *Rocky Mountain News,* December 26, 1861, January 11, February 15, 1862.

9.` Ibid., March 21, 22, 1862. Colorado *Republican* and *Rocky Mountain Herald,* both May 1, 1861.

under Sibley had invaded New Mexico and were on their way to Fort Union—the best stocked federal arsenal in the Southwest. Suddenly the months of barracks life, the low morale, and the heavy drinking that had come to characterize life at Camp Weld were forgotten in the frantic bustle to get reinforcements under way.[10] The real Civil War had come to Colorado at last.

Once again armies marched across the old Bent and St. Vrain empire, past the infant village of Colorado Springs, through the still-Mexican town of Pueblo, and by Bent's Old Fort—now abandoned and crumbling—to fight a war. Once again the Santa Fe Trail became a military highway. This was an expedition not for expansion and occupation but for meeting an aggressive enemy, and the reports of Major Lynde's capitulation at Fort Fillmore and Sibley's successes along the Rio Grande made for solemn reading. The Colorado Volunteers learned of the disastrous defeat at Valverde while in Pueblo. Hastening forward through cold and snowy weather, the Weld men joined three companies of volunteers who had been stationed at Fort Lyon and marched to Raton Pass to meet their uncertain destiny.

Just as they reached the summit of that historic gateway to the Spanish Southwest, more disquieting news greeted Slough and his men: Sibley was already in Santa Fe, and Fort Union appeared to be the next Confederate objective. Colonel Gabriel R. Paul, the harassed and fearful commander at Union, urged all possible speed on the volunteers. By an impressive forced march the doughty Coloradans traversed the remaining distance and reached Union on March 10. They had traveled 400 miles in thirteen days. After a short rest the volunteers, having come this far, were ready to move again. Slough ordered his eager and now well-equipped men onto the historic trail to meet the enemy. In the ensuing battles of Apache Canyon and Glorieta Pass, the Confederates were turned back from Union and Colorado and eventually from New Mexican soil.[11]

The Union victory at Glorieta Pass had important consequences

10. Colton, *Civil War in the Territories*, pp. 45–46.
11. See above, pp. 118–20. The achievements of the First and Second Regiments of the Colorado Volunteers in New Mexico are ably summarized in Colton, pp. 29–30, 43–74, 86–89. The classic account is by Hollister, *A History of the First Colorado Regiment*. Originally published in 1863, it was reprinted under the more dramatic title *Boldly They Rode* (Lakewood, Colo., 1949).

for Colorado far beyond the fact that the latter was now safely a federal territory. It created miltiary reputations, making public heroes out of men like Colonel John M. Chivington, whose capture of the Confederate wagon train determined the uncertain outcome of the Glorieta fighting. It made Colonel Slough the possible successor of Gilpin in the governor's chair, and it eventually secured him a federal judgeship in New Mexico. It elevated officers—Tappan, Wynkoop, Downing, and others in the public eye. Such leaders, backed by a devoted following of soldiers, now felt that they could handle the defense of Colorado, solve a troublesome Indian problem, and play politics as well. Inadvertently, Gilpin had created still another frontier power center in the land of popular sovereignty, and the actions of its leaders both made and complicated Colorado history for the next five years.

While Gilpin sought to save Colorado for the Union, he also had to organize and run a territorial government. After districting the territory, he set August 1861 as the time for the first election. Quickly the numerous amorphous political cliques and factions that had characterized the Jefferson period coalesced into the Union and People's parties.

The Union group met in lively convention on July 1 and chose Hiram P. Bennet as its nominee for delegate.[12] Bennet's choice indicated both the professionalism of the Colorado political frontier and the middle-class and middle-western backgrounds of many of the Denverites. Born in Maine, Bennet had lived in Ohio and had taught school in northwestern Missouri. After that he had practiced law in Iowa and had been a candidate for delegate in Nebraska Territory in 1854, all before he was thirty years old. He failed to secure the Nebraska delegateship, but he did become a member of the Nebraska Council in 1856 and was speaker of the house in 1858. By the time he got to Denver, Bennet was an old hand at territorial politics. It was characteristic of him—and of many of his constituents—that he

12. "Hiram P. Bennet" in *Biographical Directory of the American Congress.* Hall, *Colorado, 4,* 366–67.

had been both a Douglas Democrat and a Free Soiler, but now he was shrewd enough to run on a vague "Union" ticket.[13]

Bennet's opponent, the choice of the People's Party, was Beverley D. Williams, a pioneer merchant and stage-line manager in Denver. Boasting a Kentucky upbringing, Williams was one of those expansive, gregarious frontier politicians who delighted in public office and public notice. Already familiar with Washington as the squatter delegate and lobbyist from Jefferson, he undoubtedly felt that after having labored for territorial organization for two years and having saved Colorado from such names as Colona, Osage, Idaho, and Tehosa, he was entitled to reelection. An ardent popular sovereignty advocate, he had urged Colorado to go it alone when the Union seemed to be dissolving. Though he was probably a Douglas Democrat, his main support appears to have come from Missourians and the settlers in the Arkansas and San Luis valleys, many of whom were old Santa Fe traders or in business with Ceran St. Vrain. Finally, many Southern miners saw in the former Kentuckian a spirit more kindred than Bennet's.[14]

Thus the first delegate election, quite apart from personality, rested on the loyalties of the voter to the North or to the South and indirectly upon whether one was oriented toward Missouri and the Santa Fe trail or toward Nebraska and the South Platte route. In a curious way it was a Nebraska versus Missouri contest, and, as expected, Nebraskan Byers turned his editorial guns on Williams, while Nebraskan Bennet spread the rumor that Williams was supported by the secessionists in southern Colorado. Such charges infuriated old frontiersmen like Colonel Albert G. Boone, son of the great Daniel, who wrote a fellow Democrat that this was how the Black Republicans besmirched Union Democrats.[15] Nevertheless, Bennet's tactics were successful, and he won the Colorado delegate election in 1861.

Bennet's victory symbolized among other things the fact that Col-

---

13. Hall. Bancroft, *Colorado*, p. 429 n.

14. *The Western Mountaineer*, August 2, 1860. Bernard O. J. Linnevold, "A Study of the Attitudes on Public Questions of Colorado's Territorial Delegates, 1861–1876" (Master's thesis, University of Colorado, 1931, pp. 8–13.

15. A. G. Boone to Francisco, Denver, July 13, 1861, John M. Francisco Papers, CSA.

orado was anxious to get beyond the frontier stage, for in Washington Bennet demonstrated the qualities of a typical delegate. Ever the ardent localist, he spent his two terms working for the reduction of Indian reserves, the establishment of a local land office with a resident surveyor general in Denver, a railroad land grant, and the usual appropriations for post and military roads. He also voiced the familiar frontier plea for lower postal rates. To please his mining constituency, he opposed the war tax on territories, lobbied successfully for a branch mint to be located at Denver, and urged that miners be allowed access to the public domain. Naturally he introduced bills in Congress to legalize miners' court decisions.[16]

Even Bennet's vigorous efforts could not quiet the frontier factionalism that was so much a part of Colorado politics. When he ran for reelection in 1862, he was opposed by ex-Governor Gilpin, who felt that Bennet was not a true Republican. Gilpin also wanted some popular vindication of his own tempestuous course while governor, for he had been removed from office in May 1862 on charges of extravagance and exceeding his authority.[17] A second opponent that year was John M. Francisco, a former Virginian and an old Santa Fe trader, who took over Beverley Williams' following. Francisco represented the Spanish-speaking portion of the terrtiory as well as the vast St. Vrain trading firm, which still furnished Colorado with many of its supplies. A Breckenridge Democrat, Francisco epitomized the frontier desire to be let alone, for he was neither interested in the war effort nor happy with radical Republicans.[18] Both he and Gilpin fought losing battles, however, for Bennet, aided by Byers, was reelected.

On the local scene the first and second Colorado assemblies appear to have been dominated by men wearing a Unionist label. They also seemed much more professional than most frontier lawmakers. Speaker of the House Charles F. Holly was a Boulder miner and lawyer who was also interested in Colorado's Mexican land grants.[19]

16. Hall, *Colorado*, 2, 251–53. Linnevold, "Delegate Attitudes," pp. 18–38. See also *Rocky Mountain News*, September 11, 1862.

17. See "Petition" for Gilpin's removal, January 23, 1862, in State Department Appointment Papers, TP: Colorado, NA. Among those signing the petition was Delegate Bennet.

18. Hall, *Colorado*, 2 251–53.

19. *Rocky Mountain News*, September 18, 1861.

One of his colleagues was the extremely capable businessman, miner, and stamp-mill owner Jerome B. Chaffee, who was to dominate Colorado politics after 1865. Chaffee, like Delegate Bennet, had been born in the East and had lived in Michigan and Missouri before becoming a townsite boomer in Kansas. Shrewder than most businessmen and with some experience in banking, he realized at the outset of the Colorado gold rush that quartz mining would be more profitable and enduring than placer efforts. He formed a partnership with a Californian veteran, Eben Smith, who possessed the technical knowledge to run a stamp mill. Loading their heavy machinery onto wagons, they came to Pike's Peak to extract and refine gold in a professional way. From the very first his ventures were enough of a success to make him one of the wealthiest men in the territory. Anyone as successful and popular as Chaffee was bound to become politically prominent.[20]

An associate of Chaffee's, both in and out of the House, was George M. Chilcott, a Pennsylvanian who had come West by way of Iowa and Nebraska. In the latter territory he had served in the House of Representatives, while H. P. Bennet was on the Nebraska Council and William Byers was platting the future city of Omaha. Like Chaffee, Chilcott was a flexible businessman who also dabbled in lands and mines and was to serve both as land register for southern Colorado—where he learned the details about Mexican land grants—and as delegate to the 40th Congress. Once Colorado statehood was achieved in 1876, the popular Chilcott was to become a United States senator.[21]

Still another pioneer member of the legislature was Daniel Witter, brother-in-law to Senator Schuyler Colfax of Indiana. Witter came West as a land lawyer and was soon one of the largest property owners in Colorado. Eventually he engaged in banking and ranching and became a large stockholder in railroads. Like many of his colleagues he often served as the middleman who persuaded Eastern businessmen to invest in Colorado development schemes.[22]

If one turns to the early councils, similar entrepreneurial figures

20. Hall, *Colorado, 1,* 362–63. New York *Tribune,* March 10, 1886.
21. Hall, *Colorado, 4,* 402–04. Bancroft, *Colorado,* p. 435.
22. Hall, *Colorado, 4,* 616–17.

and professional politicians may be found. Hiram J. Graham, the squatter delegate and Auraria townsite boomer, was there for a term. Amos Steck, a well-educated veteran of the California gold fields, was there, having come to Denver as the postal agent of the Overland Express. Many other names could be added to Steck's, which would suggest that this frontier body was a far cry from the coonskin and bowie knife frontier politicians usually to be found in a pioneer legislature.[23]

Perhaps closer to the latter type were the People's Party members of the Assembly, of whom Colonel Francisco—future delegate candidate, business partner of Ceran St. Vrain, and former sutler at Forts Massachusetts and Garland—was a chief representative. Obviously sympathetic to the South while loyal to the Union, Francisco saw his duty as protecting his region from the "Negro thieves" and "Black Republicans," terms his friends used consistently to identify his opponents.[24]

In sharp and often amusing contrast to the ambitious, huckstering, American members of the early assemblies were its Spanish-Mexican representatives from Pueblo and the San Luis Valley. Their first representatives were Victor Garcia and Jesus Barela, who came to Denver to the initial Assembly in 1861. They were so completely baffled by the strange ways of lawmaking that they hesitated to take their seats. After a plea from the governor brought them into the House, they sat not understanding a word until an interpreter was provided.

Spanish-Americans sat in every Colorado Assembly, but they were not well represented until 1867, when the charming and inimitable Casimiro Barela invaded politics. Barela had been educated at Mora, New Mexico, by no less a tutor than Archbishop Salpointe, Lamy's dedicated assistant and successor. Barela then migrated north of Raton Pass, only to find himself in Colorado after 1861. Gracious and

---

23. The members are listed in *House Journal of the First Legislative Assembly of the Territory of Colorado* (Denver, 1861), pp. 3–4. For Amos Steck's biography see William N. Byers, *Encyclopaedia Biography of Colorado* (Chicago, 1901), *I*, 232–84.

24. See A. Thomas to J. M. Francisco, June 7, 1861; and A. G. Boone to Francisco, Denver, July 13, 1861, Francisco Papers.

popular, but lordly, once he entered politics he was returned to the legislature for forty years. At each session Barela moved up to Denver in grand style. "It was like a picture of mission days," wrote one observer, "to see the Barela entourage arrive in Denver for the biennial gathering at the State house. It was a gala day for the Barela retainers." Aided by various compatriots, Barela saw to it that the legislature provided them with a translator, that the laws were printed in Spanish, and that Las Animas, Costilla, and Conejos counties did not get swallowed up in ambitious American schemes. His whole career, in fact, was dedicated to the preservation of his people, his language, and his culture.[25]

After hearing a moving and florid but surprisingly brief speech from Gilpin urging the founding fathers to establish military defense and legal and educational systems fitted to the geography of the Rockies and the background of Colorado's people, the Assembly got down to work. Gilpin, incidentally, appears to have envisaged a Jeffersonian government for Colorado, leaving much power in local districts and precincts, for, as he declared, "It is in these complete little republics where the sovereign power is always in exercise, where self-government has a perpetual vitality, and independent freedom is practiced and enjoyed."[26]

The Assembly nevertheless proceeded to adopt the Illinois code of laws in toto—again revealing their midwestern backgrounds—and to pass the usual laws necessary to establish a territorial government. So similar were these to Nebraska, Kansas, and Dakota that they need no comment here.

As in all other new regions, the permanent location of the capital was a subject of great debate. The southern county men, led by Chilcott and Jesus Barela, urged Pueblo on the Assembly, while Chaffee and others sang the praises of Denver. In a compromise the two factions agreed on Colorado City for the 1862 session. After holding a four-day session in that still-to-be-built city and having suffered from bad accommodations, the solons of 1862 removed to Denver in

25. *House Journal . . . Colorado, 1861*, pp. 30–35. Denver *News,* December 21, 1920. *Rocky Mountain News,* December 19, 1920. Byers, *Encyclopaedia, I,* 331.
26. *Gov. Gilpin's Message to the First Territory Assembly of Colorado* (Denver, September 10, 1861), State Department, TP: Colorado.

search of the comforts of a real town. In 1864 ambitious politicians maneuvered the capital to Golden, where it remained until 1867. After that year, however, Denver became the permanent seat of government.[27]

There appears to have been less horseplay than was usual in frontier assemblies, but this did not mean that the Coloradans had lost their sense of humor. Tiring of the solemnity of their duties, they passed a mock-serious resolution urging the sergeant-at-arms to "a better observance of the ninth commandment." That august official had been caught stealing wood from neighborhood piles in order to warm the Assembly rooms. The legislature also passed an act allowing James Lee Longbottom to change his name. And in late October the House recorded a charming note of resignation from its page, Master Willie Shaw, who explained that he resigned "in order that I may start for the States in the morning to attend school this winter."[28]

More significant were the acts passed by the various early assemblies which were variations from regular American legislation. Of first importance was the formulation of a working code of mining law and the corresponding need to establish the right of the miner to the gold lands. Legally speaking, the minerals being extracted still belonged to the federal government. Until such questions were settled, the Colorado mining industry would never be efficiently developed. The Assembly provdied a temporary solution to the first problem by legalizing the district miners' court decisions and by petitioning Congress to do the same. While this was quickly accomplished, the question of ownership of the mineral lands dragged on for another ten years, for Eastern and Western congressmen held opposing views. In brief, the miners, and particularly Governor John Evans—Gilpin's successor in 1862—demanded that the American agricultural land system be applied to mineral lands, i.e. that they be sold outright to buyers or claimants at a nominal charge. They also wanted the principle embodied in the Pre-Emption Law of 1841 (claimants who preceded the land surveys had first choice to the

---

27. Bancroft, *Colorado*, p. 417.
28. *House Journal . . . Colorado, 1861*, pp. 50–51, 154–55, 299.

lands they had preempted) applied to unsurveyed mineral lands.[29] The stakes involved here went far beyond Colorado's need, for both California and Nevada were still waiting for Congress to settle the mineral rights question within their own borders.

In the absence of any decision, Delegate Bennet offered a solution bearing some resemblance to British policy in the Fraser River gold region. Bennet proposed a seigniorage act that would permit access to mineral lands on a lease and fee basis, by which the miner would pay some twenty dollars a year for the privilege of extracting ore from a claim.[30] The Seigniorage Bill was controversial, some arguing that it helped prospectors, others that it favored only large mining industry. The lease system also smacked of federal control and interference to the popular sovereignty miner who had been raised on fee-simple concepts of ownership.

The first major Eastern proposal came from George W. Julian of Indiana, who introduced a bill in Congress in 1865 calling for subdivision of the mineral lands and their sale to the highest bidder. By hard lobbying on the part of Senator William M. Stewart of Nevada and the Colorado delegate, the Julian bill was defeated. The administration itself appears to have favored some lease and tax system similar to what had been attempted in the Galena lead-mining area, but the mining regions would have none of it. What finally emerged was the United States Minerals Act of 1866, which gave the miners the right to acquire full title to mineral bearing lands at a nominal price.[31] As with its agricultural lands, the United States had more or less adopted the policy of giving its minerals to its citizens.

The preoccupation with mining in Colorado led to still other legislative variations. The territory eventually refused to accept English common law where water rights were concerned. Cognizant that the region practiced irrigation as well as hydraulic mining, they enacted codes more fitted to the Colorado situation. The mining industry even affected school revenue—in theory at least, for Governor Evans

29. Hall, *Colorado, I,* 319.

30. Ibid., p. 317.

31. Ibid., pp. 320–21. For a brief discussion of Congressional mining laws see Paul, *Mining Frontiers,* pp. 172–73, and Percy S. Fritz, *Colorado, the Centennial State* (New York, 1941), pp. 148–50.

and the Assembly proposed that claim number three on each new lode discovery should be set aside for school use.³² When probate courts came to consider estates and cases involving mining claims, they discovered that the value of such claims usually so exceeded the courts' jurisdiction that Congress was persuaded to modify the restrictions.³³

Finally, the Colorado Assembly was faced with the problem of passing laws that took into consideration the customs of the local Spanish-Americans. All laws had to be translated into Spanish; and since Congress refused to pay for such a task, the cost fell on the territory.

The territorial legislatures of the first decade tackled all these difficulties with great confidence and sureness. Generally intelligent and forward looking, they acted with a supreme faith in Colorado's future. They undoubtedly felt they had carried out Gilpin's dramatic challenge to exhibit the "wisdom, moderation, and energy to set the foundations of a commonwealth which shall beat back the shocks of time, and stand as firm as the loftiest mountain."³⁴

Gilpin's successor was Dr. John Evans of Illinois. The new Governor was appointed to the position in reward for faithful service to the Republican Party. A former Ohioan, Evans had been trained as a physician and had taught as a part-time professor at Rush Medical College in Chicago. But he had a wide-ranging mind, tremendous energy, and a great talent for business organization. Increasingly, he had moved away from medicine into railroads. By the 1850s he was builder and part owner of the Chicago and Fort Wayne Railroad. His local prominence is suggested by the fact that Evanston, Illinois, was named in his honor. At the same time, he was an active lay leader in the Methodist Church. Through this connection he was to be a future benefactor of Northwestern University. Acutely aware of the public movements and moral issues of his time, Evans became an

---

32. "Governor's Message" in *Council Journal . . . Colorado, 1862* (Denver, 1862), p. 18. See also Henry A. Dubbs, "The Unfolding of Law in the Mountain Region," *CM*, *3* (1926), 131.
33. *Council Journal . . . 1862*, pp. 17–18. Fritz, *Colorado*, pp. 143–50.
34. *House Journal . . . 1861*, p. 12.

abolitionist some time during the 1850s, and this conversion in turn channeled his political inclinations toward new Republicanism.[35] Capable, articulate, and confident, he had watched his friend Abraham Lincoln rise to national political prominence and was himself soon swept into politics as a candidate for Congress in 1860 on the Illinois Republican ticket. Since he did not win the election, he was a logical choice for an appointive position in the new Republican administration.

Evans came to Colorado bringing his railroad interests and many ambitions with him. The new Governor was immediately at home with such energetic men as William Byers, whose friend and business partner he soon became.[36] He understood the plans for Colorado development thought out by Jerome B. Chaffee and the extraordinary businessman David L. Moffat, Jr. Perhaps between them they could get the transcontinental railroad to go through Denver. This was a project close to Evans' heart, since he was on the board of directors of the Union Pacific. Or they might secure Colorado's admission as a state. Or, better still, one of them might sit in the United States Senate one day. Before Evans' plans and dreams could come true, however, he had to solve a pressing Indian problem in Colorado, which proved to be the major task of his public career and the eventual cause of his retirement from public life.

In a superficial sense the Indian-white situation in Colorado resembled that of New Mexico, for the American settlements ran roughly in a north–south line from Fort Collins and Boulder, thickened in width around Denver, Blackhawk, and Central City, and then concentrated around Pueblo and the Arkansas and Upper Rio Grande valleys. And as in New Mexico, the wild tribes were on all sides. In the parks and valleys of the eastern Rockies ranged the various Ute bands. To the east on the High Plains were Arapahoe and Cheyenne tribes, occasional bands of Kiowa and Comanche appeared from Texas, and a few Sioux tribes lived just north of the Platte. The situa-

---

35. Denver *Illustrated Weekly*, October 10, 1900. Wilbur F. Stone, *History of Colorado* (4 vols. Chicago, 1918), *2*, 52–55. Edgar McMechan, *Life of Governor Evans* (Denver, 1924), pp. 79 ff.
36. The Diaries of William N. Byers indicate this business association; MSS in the Western History Department, Denver Public Library.

tion also resembled that of New Mexico in that the number of Indians probably equaled the number of whites in Colorado during the early '60s.[37]

But here the similarity ended. The Utes, for example, were not actively hostile. Used to trading in Taos or at Bent's Fort for more than a generation, and having been in treaty relations with the United States since the late 1840s, they were rapidly becoming annuity Indians more venal than fierce, more petty raiders than warriors. They knew the way to Abiquiu, where Kit Carson had served as their agent; they dealt with Agent Lafayette Head at Conejos; and they had come to respect American troops stationed in the heart of southern Ute country at Forts Massachusetts and Garland. At least one of their chiefs, Ouray, was beginning to see the futility of fighting the whites and consistently worked for peaceful relations. By and large they were more interested in raiding their traditional enemies, the Cheyenne and Arapahoe, than in attacking whites.[38]

The Cheyenne and Arapahoe tribes on the other hand were more vigorous and hostile than the Utes and also occupied a more strategic position. Roaming on the High Plains and in the Platte and Arkansas River valleys, they could be a mobile, tough, and able enemy to find along the Santa Fe and Oregon trails. But they, too, were used to trading with the whites and had signed treaties of friendship. Generally speaking, they also respected the white man's right to travel unmolested over the Platte and Arkansas routes. When the Pike's Peakers rushed westward between 1859–60, however, it was obvious that new treaties would have to be drawn to avoid conflict, for the new Smoky Hill route cut directly across their hunting lands. In 1860 the government instructed Agent Greenwood on the Upper Arkansas to persuade the tribes to withdraw to a reservation above Fort Lyon near Sand Creek. Greenwood experienced difficulty in finding all the chiefs and in the end left the task to Colonel Albert G. Boone, who lived at Booneville below Pueblo. The resulting Treaty of Fort Lyon,

37. George B. Grinnell, *The Fighting Cheyennes* (New York, 1915), pp. 118 ff. In a report on the Indian tribes in Colorado, Gilpin estimated that there were 25,000 Indians under his jurisdiction. See Gilpin to Commissioner W. P. Dole, June 19, 1861, Interior Department, OIA, Colorado.

38. McMechan, *Evans*, pp. 113–26.

which only a few chiefs signed in February 1861, was actually a dead letter before the ink was dry, for the area where the Indians were confined was too small to carry on a hunting life.[39] The young braves were particularly vehement about the treaty and immediately repudiated it.

Indian discontent was heightened by wanton white killing of the buffalo herd, resentment at the use of the Smoky Hill route, and general bad treatment from the individual white migrants. With the perspective of time, an Indian-white war in Colorado appears to have been preventable, but between 1861 and 1863 it seemed inevitable. General Carleton at this time was fighting Apache and Navajo in New Mexico. The Sioux outbreak of 1862 had just taken a heavy toll in Minnesota and Dakota; and there were constant rumors that the Texans were seeking Indian alliances with the Five Civilized Tribes with an eye to plundering Colorado and Kansas. What really made the Indian menace seem so threatening, though, was that the hostiles stood athwart all Colorado lines of communication with the East. Had the region been agriculturally self-sufficient, this would not have mattered greatly, but the nonappearance of a wagon train could skyrocket prices and produce severe shortages in all Colorado. At the height of the Indian troubles, in fact, the price of flour in Denver climbed to $25 for a hundred pounds, and the Assembly had to appoint a flour inspector to bring some order into the wildly speculative situation.[40]

Locally, white isolation was sometimes responsible for Indian trouble. Individual families, acting in the great American frontier tradition, had already begun to strike out from the Colorado settlements to ranch and farm in 1861. Such isolated persons and their herds were fair game for hungry Indian raiders. In a similar situation were the lonely stage stations and freighting stops on the Platte and Arkansas trails. Naturally, Indian raiders concentrated upon such ranches and stations and upon the slow-moving, under-manned freighting trains, with the double effect that the Indians not only

39. Lavender, *Bent's Fort,* p. 346. The background for the Sand Creek Massacre is covered in William E. Unrau, "A Prelude to War," *CM, 41* (1964), 299–313.
40. Hall, *Colorado, 1,* 359. *House Journal . . . Colorado,* 1865, p. 56.

brought privation to the settlements but built up their own capacity
for further war by use of captured guns, food, and supplies. Colorado's plight seemed even more grim because the desperate need of
troops for the Civil War had drained all frontier outposts of men. By
1863 only 215 soldiers guarded the heavily traveled Platte route,
while fewer than one hundred were stationed on the Arkansas road.
With Colorado volunteers stationed either in New Mexico or in Kansas,
the citizens of Denver and the mining camps stood a good chance
of being cut off.[41]

Governor Evans was in no mood to let the savages hold back the
development of Colorado or permit its citizens to suffer. When Indians
were reported attacking ranches along the South Platte in the summer of 1862, Evans appeared in force with a company of volunteers
and successfully ordered them off to their hunting grounds on the
Republican.[42] In 1863, however, hungry Indians, including some Ute
bands, had become bold or desperate enough to step up their raids.[43]
From February until midsummer disheartening reports trickled into
Denver that various overland stations and outlying ranches on the
Platte had been sacked. When Evans sought to make a treaty with
northern bands of Arapahoe and Cheyenne who had not signed the
1861 Treaty of Fort Lyon, they flatly refused. Later that fall Evans
joined Lafayette Head, the knowledgeable agent of the Southern Utes,
in a parley and persuaded the Tabeguache Utes to move into the
Gunnison River Valley.[44] By this arrangement at least one side of the
rectangle of settlements was protected.

Even so, the Governor's faith in a peaceful solution to the Indian
problem appears to have diminished late in 1863. That November he
received a report from a renegade white, Robert North, that a war
by Comanches, Apaches, Kiowas, Northern Arapahoes, Cheyenne, and
Sioux was in the making. The news appears to have converted Evans
to a policy of active military campaigning against Indians. Late in
1863 he begged Secretary of War Stanton to allow no more troop

41. Colton, *Civil War in the Territories,* pp. 151 ff.
42. Ibid.
43. Grinnell, *Fighting Cheyennes,* pp. 140, 143–58.
44. *Annual Message of Governor Evans . . . February 3, 1864* (Denver, 1864),
pp. 3–4.

withdrawals from Colorado, to arm the territorial cavalry with carbines (instead of sabres and revolvers), and to station regular troops along the Platte and Arkansas. He also wanted Stanton to give the commander of the Colorado District—Colonel Chivington, the hero of Glorieta—the power to call out the militia for Indian service.[45] While Evans did attempt to feed all friendly tribes in 1863–64 who appeared at Fort Lyon or at Camp Collins, and though he urged a similar policy on the commanders at Forts Laramie and Larned, this practice was but a temporary solution in his eyes.

In such a crisis Evans was not a man to act alone as Gilpin had done. By 1864 the able Governor was backed by Byers and the *News;* by the territorial secretary, Samuel H. Elbert, who was to become Evans' son-in-law in 1864; and by Colonel Chivington, the district commander. Evans' friend and future business associate, David H. Moffat, Jr., was adjutant general of the territory and a member of the Assembly. Seldom had there been such cooperation between the civil and the military authorities on the frontier. The question remained: when and where could a showdown with the hostiles be brought about?

The Indians themselves provided the answer by stepping up raids in the spring of 1864. On April 9 the Cheyennes stole 175 cattle from a freighting firm. Young Lieutenant George Eayre was sent out to chastise the thieves and recover the cattle. Though his force attacked an Indian camp, it may not have been the one containing the guilty parties. On April 12 there was another skirmish with Cheyennes on the South Platte. The following May at least one of these skirmishes turned into a real battle when Major Jacob Downing attacked a Cheyenne camp and killed some twenty-six hostiles. Lieutenant Eayre accomplished a similar feat a short time later.[46] Both sides were becoming used to a ruthless catch-and-kill policy.

At this point the demands of the Civil War intervened to cast the lot for tragedy. In 1864 General Samuel Ryan Curtis ordered all available Colorado troops to Fort Lyon, in expectation of a Con-

45. Evans to William F. Stanton, 1863. The John H. Evans Collection, CSA. Grinnell, *Fighting Cheyennes*, pp. 128–29.
46. Colton, *Civil War in the Territories*, pp. 152 ff.

federate raid on Arkansas and Colorado. This order had the effect of removing troops from the Platte River road, over which most of Colorado's supplies now came, at the very time Indian raids were increasing in tempo. Evans, having just asked Curtis for hundreds of reinforcements along both routes, was now worse off than ever. Under such conditions the Indians were bound to push the Colorado settlers to a breaking point. It came when Cheyenne raiders attacked a ranch within ten miles of Denver and scalped, killed, and mutilated the Hunsgate family, consisting of the parents and two children. Another adult was also killed.[47] This news coincided with a report that the Sioux had attacked whites further east, and a general Indian war involving thousands of warriors seemed imminent.

The horror at the tragic news became outrage when the Hunsgate dead were carted to Denver on wagons and put on public view. Governor Evans ordered a curfew in the town, and panic-stricken citizens huddled for a few nights at the mint and other stout buildings, expecting an attack on Denver itself. Then Evans sent circulars to the Indians ordering them to go to Fort Lyon or face extermination. As the raiding continued, he authorized parties of citizens to protect themselves by killing all hostiles. The break was now complete. The Indians, far from obeying, so increased raiding on the the Platte trail that they closed the highway for a month.[48]

The next Indian move caught the whites off guard. In late August the bands of Arapahoe and Cheyenne who were following Chief Black Kettle decided to heed Governor Evans' circular and proceed to Fort Lyon. Black Kettle's logic was simple and practical: it was the end of the season, and he preferred to winter in peace. Then came the first of a series of rebuffs—all of them understandable, given the state of the white settlers' minds. When the Indians arrived at Lyon, Major Wynkoop explained that he had no authority to end the war; instead, the Indian leaders must visit Evans in Denver. Evans gave them the same answer, while warning them that the Civil War was about to end and the federal soldiers could be turned loose on the Indians. Watching this fateful interview was the brooding giant Colo-

47. Ibid., p. 153.
48. Ibid.

nel Chivington, who also warned Black Kettle that "his" rule for fighting white men or Indians was to fight them until they lay down their arms and submit.[49]

Somewhat mystified by the refusal to treat with them, the Indians returned to Fort Lyon, where, for a short time, Wynkoop fed them and promised protection from hostile whites. Indeed, rumors spread that Wynkoop had signed a peace treaty, a report that angered civilian and military leaders alike. Chivington was furious; General Curtis, who headed the Department, forbade peace without severe punishment unless he permitted it. Evans himself agreed and remarked in a letter to General Patrick E. Connor, who was to assume command of the Colorado area that winter, that he hoped the General would "pursue, kill and destroy them."[50]

Before Connor arrived, the Indian war reached a climax when Evans secured permission to raise a regiment of hundred-day volunteers to chastise the Indians. These volunteers, only one-third of whom had seen service, were a rambunctious crew, anxious to act but frustrated by false alarms and failure to stop Indian raids. Their mood is suggested by a notation in John L. Dailey's diary. Dailey, a member of the Third Colorado Cavalry in 1864, recorded laconcially that while marching to Colorado Springs in September, they had taken some Indian prisoners, all of whom had been shot by their guard.[51]

The hundred-day men were spoiling for a fight and Chivington, their commander, sympathized. Their zeal had been kept alive by news that General Blunt's troops had been attacked while marching from Fort Riley to Larned, and their anger was kept alive by rumors of Wynkoop's treaty-making. To forestall the latter possibility, on November 2 Chivington relieved Wynkoop of his command and re-

---

49. Major Edward W. Wynkoop, "Wynkoop's Unfinished Colorado History," MSS in CSHS. See also Grinnell, *Fighting Cheyennes*, p. 154. Raymond G. Carey in "The Puzzle of Sand Creek," *CM*, *41* (1964), 293, suggests that Chivington was anxious to imitate General Connor's successes against the Indians in Utah while at the same time forestalling Connor's chance to achieve a similar victory in Colorado.

50. Evans to Connor, October 24, 1864, Evans Collection.

51. Journal of John L. Dailey, MS in the Western History Department, Denver Public Library. The "hundred day" men actually constituted the Third Regiment of the Colorado Volunteers.

placed him with Major Scott Anthony.[52] The new officer appeared friendly to the Indians, but the great number of the tribes camped near Fort Lyon made Anthony nervous. He was also in secret agreement with Chivington's no quarter policy. Pointing out that he lacked food to feed the Indians, Anthony ordered Black Kettle to move up to Sand Creek—one day distant from Lyon—until further developments.[53]

To force a showdown, Chivington marched his excited volunteers through mid-November snow and cold to Fort Lyon. There was much drinking among the soldiers, and fights broke out. Near Pueblo still more trouble occurred when Spanish-Americans there were insulted by the troops. Later in the march Chivington stopped briefly at William Bent's ranch to post a guard, so that news of his movements could not be sent to the Indians by the man who had traded with them so long.[54] Even Colonel Boone was arrested. After reaching Lyon, Chivington took his troops through a freezing night to the Indian camp located on the dry bed of Sand Creek—a tributary of the Arkansas. Sometime between daybreak and sunrise the troops fell upon the sleeping Indian camp; the cavalry rode along the embankment shooting, while Chivington's footsoldiers advanced steadily up the creek bed. Despite Black Kettle's frantic display of an American and a white flag, the shooting and killing went on. The result was a massacre. After some four hours of fighting an estimated 450 corpses lay on the ground, two-thirds of them women and children. In their frenzy of hate, built up over three years of trouble and frustration, the Colorado troops spared no one. Running tots were shot down like game, Chivington's famous excuse being that "nits make lice." Several turned their guns on already wounded or dying Indians to have a final go. The genitals of women and men were cut out, and the chiefs who fell were mutilated beyond recognition. At least a hundred scalps were later exhibited as an entre-act attraction at a Denver theatre.[55]

52. "Wynkoop's History," an unfinished account of some forty manuscript pages, traces the Sand Creek story in detail; CSHS.
53. Ibid., pp. 34–35. Grinnell, *Fighting Cheyennes,* pp. 160–61.
54. Dailey Journal, entry for November 17, 1864.
55. The most recent accounts of the Sand Creek affair are Stan Hoig, *The Sand Creek Massacre* (Norman, 1961); Michael Straight, *A Very Small Remnant* (New York, 1963); and Janet LeCompte, "Sand Creek," *CM, 41* (1964), 315–35.

As the men gathered plunder from the lodges and coralled ponies, Chivington was in his glory. His report to Curtis brought congratulations; his reception and that of his troops when they returned to Denver was the sort of public accolade reserved for conquering heroes. Moreover, it was peculiarly Chivington's show, for Governor Evans had left for Washington before the Sand Creek battle. After three years it was now clear that at least some of Gilpin's pet lambs were in need of a new nickname.

The celebration of Sand Creek was short-lived. The nation, sick to death of fighting and killing after four years of Civil War, reacted unfavorably to news of the massacre. When Agent S. G. Colley, undoubtedly furious at army interference in Indian affairs, sent the circumstances of Sand Creek to the Missouri *Intelligencer,* calls for an investigation began to pour into Congress.[56] In Washington the Radical Republicans responded by creating a series of commissions to investigate Indian affairs all over the West. A committee headed by Senator J. R. Doolittle came to Colorado and New Mexico, both to look at Carleton's Bosque Redondo project and to question officers about Sand Creek. After weighing the testimony taken at Fort Lyon, the committee eventually condemned Chivington for his acts, and General Curtis somewhat lamely attempted to courtmartial the aggressive ex-minister. But Chivington, having already resigned from the Army, was beyond the military pale.

This was but one consequence of Sand Creek. When the remaining Indian tribes learned from Black Kettle and other survivors what had occurred, they took to the warpath in earnest. In the first two months of 1865 Indians attacked the stage and freighting town of Julesburg, killing nearly forty men and ruining seventy-five miles of road. The situation was so bad that Colonel Thomas Moonlight declared martial law in Colorado until the Assembly provided militia to supplement his exhausted and inadequate troops.[57] After these larger attacks, the war settled down to guerilla tactics in the spring.

Throughout the whole conflict William Bent, who was still living on the Arkansas and ranching on the Purgatory River, had watched Indian-white hostilities with growing dismay. Since the gold rush had

56. Grinnell, *Fighting Cheyennes,* p. 169.
57. Hall, *Colorado, 1,* 360.

first begun, he had worked to make equitable arrangements between Indian and white, first as an Indian agent and later in a private capacity. In his testimony before the Doolittle Committee in August 1865 he had exclaimed that, given a free hand, he could bring peace in three months.[58] Through his efforts a treaty was signed with the Arapahoe and Cheyenne in October 1865; and while its severity displeased Bent, it removed the Indians from the lines of communication. Actual hostilities did not end, however, until ambitious George A. Custer charged a camp of southern Cheyennes on the Washita in 1868. In the following slaughter Black Kettle, symbol to the Coloradans of all their Indian troubles, was finally killed.[59]

It was a multiple irony, as David Lavender has written, that William Bent should be the agent of peace, since his half-breed son, Robert Bent, had been forced to lead Chivington to Sand Creek. More ironic still, two of William's other sons, George and Charlie, were in Black Kettle's camp in 1864, where they were saved by New Mexican troops who recognized them. Both sons, outraged at white behavior on that occasion, became fighters for their mother's people and for the Confederacy until Charlie died in 1869 and the return of peace took George from the warpath.[60]

What the young Bents saw at Sand Creek on November 29 was not just the slaughter of a tribe but the end of an era when whites could mingle, trade, and live—however uneasily—in some sort of frontier modus vivendi. The economic and cultural bases upon which the Bent empire had been built—and the assumptions it had implied by its very existence—had now been destroyed. This suggested in turn that the centuries-old Spanish method based on limited war and trade with the Indian was now at an end. Chivington and Carleton would agree that there was to be no stalemate between races: no slow blending of peoples and cultures as in New Mexico. Kit Carson and William Bent had come to the end of a trail: Bent's Fort and

---

58. Grinnell, *Fighting Cheyennes*, p. 236. LeCompte, "Sand Creek," pp. 330–35, traces in detail the investigation which followed the battle.

59. The fighting between 1864 and 1869 is traced in Hall, *Colorado*, *1*, 360 ff.; in Lavender, *Bent's Fort*, pp. 361 ff.; and in Grinnell, *The Fighting Cheyennes*, pp. 174–298.

60. Lavender, *Bent's Fort*, pp. 347–48, 358–68.

Taos were now to be replaced by Denver and Central City, while the American businessman, miner, and rancher replaced the Santa Fe trader. Chivington, for all of his critics, was but a part of the juggernaut of civilization, a believer in progress, in cities, and in towns, even if the concepts got mixed up in his case with a large dose of Old Testament justice. As Governor Cummings remarked to the Colorado Assembly in 1866, the Indian question had to be settled, for "civilization must rule this continent." Sand Creek was but a major step in the Americanization of Colorado. What history would never condone was Chivington's method of taking that step.

Ind + Am cud not coexist in Colo.

10

The Politics of
Admission and Development
1864–1871

Old Tom Benton was the only man who understood it
[the West]. Benton introduced into this country a new internal
central plateau policy, which has added civilization and wealth,
without discord, to the nation.
William Gilpin, 1879

Colorado without railroads is comparatively worthless.
John Evans, 1870

 The mettle, vigor, and impatient ambition of the
Colorado settlers during the troubled 1860s is amply
revealed by the fact that at the very height of the
Indian troubles, a serious movement for statehood
was going on. While Governor Evans struggled with
hostile Indians and tried to get adequate mining
legislation, he was also in the forefront of the statehood forces.

The great haste to be a state in 1864 was explicable in a number of
ways. Most important, businessmen and political leaders in Colorado
were convinced that their enterprises were slowly atrophying, for no
major gold discoveries had been made in three years. The effort to
extract and refine what gold there was had proved so expensive as
to narrow the margin of profit. To be developed, Colorado needed

Statehood meant transport: 6 cap: development
Rep. votes

large-scale Eastern capital, which was not forthcoming unless cheap transportation were available. In turn, the transportation problem could not be solved unless Colorado could become a state and could lobby in Congress for railroad land grants. As a state Colorado might even persuade Congress to reroute the still-to-be-built transcontinental Union Pacific through its borders. The railroad, wrote the new territorial secretary, Frank Hall, would end the Indian problem, give the region an adequate food supply, and promote the development of the region. "It is impossible to achieve great results without it," he said, "even though our mountains were paved with gold."[1]

Such house-that-Jack-built logic only partly explains the fervor of the 1864 statehood movement. Colorado's politicians acted with considerable outside promoting from the national leaders of the Republican Party. Should the territory be admitted in time, its electors might cast the necessary votes to return the party to power for four more years. All these considerations, combined with the ambitions of certain Coloradans to hold state and federal offices, led Delegate Bennet to introduce a statehood bill as early as January 1863. The movement did not really get under way, nevertheless, until Congressman James M. Ashley of Ohio and Senator George W. Lane of Kansas introduced enabling acts for Colorado, Nebraska, and Nevada in February 1864. The reasons for Lane's support were not hard to find, for the proposed Kansas Pacific Railroad as well as the Atchison, Topeka, and Santa Fe were Kansas projects to tap Colorado gold fields. The role the Western territories were expected to play in the coming national election became apparent when Lincoln quickly signed the acts. Some weeks later bluff Ben Wade pushed through an amendment that permitted the territories to become states in September.[3] Obviously this would have allowed their citizens to vote in the national election in November.

A word to the wise was sufficient. In Colorado a statehood party quickly formed, and the *Rocky Mountain News* took up the cudgels in favor of admission. Byers struck heavily at every possible argument

(William, editor)

1. Frank Hall to Emma Hall Law, May 15, 1866, MS Letters of Frank Hall to his Mother, Western History Department, Denver Public Library.
2. Black Hawk *Mining Journal*, February 13, 1864.
3. *The Commonwealth*, June 15, 1864.

raised against admission. Statehood, he asserted somewhat mysteriously, would be a blow at the Copperhead movement; statehood would get Colorado federal appropriations which would not come to a territory, and statehood would force the nation to respect their railroad needs; statehood would defeat Delegate Bennet's seigniorage act and guarantee fee simple ownership of the mines. And again, somewhat illogically, he argued that a vote for admission would uphold "the immortal principle of Douglas." As to the increased expenses of statehood, the new creation would cost only $16,000 more than territorial expenses, a sum that could be paid by a mere two-dollar poll tax.[4] Throughout the summer and early fall of 1864 Byers was everywhere meeting objections and fostering favorable opinions.

Apart from Byers, who were the statehood men and how did they promote their cause? By and large they were Republicans and Unionists living in and around Denver. A definite sectional divergence could be seen, for few if any state men hailed from Pueblo, Colorado Springs, South Park, or the San Luis Valley. The Spanish-Americans to a man "opposed any change which would leave them under a local government in which they were a minority." Another way of discerning the leaders was to look at the territorial officials and the Colorado Volunteers in 1864, for they generally supported Governor Evans, Secretary Samuel H. Elbert, and Colonel Chivington, all of whom wanted statehood. A friendly Assembly meeting in May 1864 also passed a joint resolution asking for admission.[5]

Prodded by Republicans in Washington, the statehood forces proceeded at a rapid pace. In June 1864 the territory elected delegates to a constitutional convention that met in July. The statehood forces, anxious to unite all Republican factions, chose a prominent merchant from Golden to be convention chairman. This was a peace offering to the "Golden Crowd," who were vigorous economic competitors and political opponents of the "Denver Crowd." The convention itself ground out a standard American state constitution.

With their eyes on the November elections, the statehood men set the ratification date for early September and provided for the elec-

4. *Rocky Mountain News,* July 20, August 3, 10, 17, 31, October 5, 1864.
5. Elmer Ellis, "Colorado's First Fight for Statehood, 1865–1868," *CM, 8* (1931), 25.

tion of state officers at the same time. Such all or nothing propositions, produced at the height of Indian troubles and in the midst of the formation of the hundred-day volunteers, proved to be very unwise. Not only was part of the public skeptical of Evans' harsh Indian policy, but many citizens honestly felt that Colorado could not afford the added cost of statehood. One authority has estimated, in fact, that by August 1864 half of Denver was opposed to statehood. Certainly the southern counties were against statehood, and the important town of Pueblo was reported to be unanimously against the movement.[6]

In a frontier community with a small population the objections were based as much on personality as on principle. The Union party meeting at Denver on August 2 had nominated D. T. Towne for Governor, Colonel John Chivington for Congress, and Evans and Henry M. Teller for the Senate. In an effort to gain the support of a promising young lawyer and former Iowa judge who had migrated to Colorado, the convention chose Allan A. Bradford for a position on the state supreme court.[7]

These choices and the statehood movement itself released a political storm in Colorado, which was undoubtedly intensified by the high feeling over the Indian policy. Evans bore the brunt of the attack; he was accused of instigating the Indian war "for the express purpose of demonstrating the necessity for direct representation in Congress." He was also charged with mobilizing the third regiment of Colorado Volunteers to "further the proceedings."[8] So acrimonious did the attack become that the Governor published a circular stating that he would not seek office if the constitution was ratified.[9]

More difficulties appeared when Allan A. Bradford turned on the statehood group, refused their supreme court nomination, and ran instead for delegate to Congress on an antistate ticket. This and other defections, plus the opposition of the Spanish-Americans and Democrats, resulted in a decisive defeat for statehood in September.

6. LeRoy R. Hafen, "Steps to Statehood," *CM, 3* (1926), 97–107.
7. Ellis, "Statehood Fight," p. 25.
8. Ibid.
9. Ibid., p. 26.

When the votes were counted, 4,672 were cast against statehood, and 1,520 only were in favor of admission.[10]

A taste of gall was added to the cup of defeat when Allan A. Bradford easily won the delegate election in the autumn of 1864. It is worth noting that when Colonel Chivington marched off to Sand Creek two months later, he carried with him the memory of a major political defeat. Like General George Custer on his way to meet the Sioux in 1876, presumably the politically ambitious Chivington did not intend to come back from Sand Creek except as a hero.

The unfavorable reaction to the statehood movement had an unexpected and sometimes amusing side result. Almost unconsciously the voters had elected an Assembly that fall, dominated by antistate and Democratic members. When the legislature met that winter, almost all the members were new men. Such an able representative as D. H. Moffat, Jr., had his seat contested, and the whole bearing and level of this Assembly smacked of the amateur. The uncertainty of their course became evident when the House spent five days balloting for a speaker. At the same time the Assembly declined to organize a militia or to remodel their now unworkable local defense system until Colonel Moonlight called their bluff by declaring martial law.[11] The members fought over the public printing contracts and refused to award them to Byers. Then they attacked the incumbent territorial school superintendent and librarian, branding them incompetent. They even threw out the Assembly chaplain and appointed a new one. It was they who established the office of flour inspector, when the price rose to $25 per hundred pounds. Although the legislature did support Lincoln and the national war effort and strongly approved of General Patrick E. Connor's winter campaigns against the Indians, they climaxed their opposition by resolving against statehood.[12]

As the Union Administration Party glumly sat around conducting a postmortem on their stillborn state, certain facts stared them coldly in the face. The first was that the so-called Republicans of Colorado

10. Ibid.
11. *House Journal . . . Colorado, 1862*, pp. 4 ff., 31–31, 67–70.
12. Ibid., pp. 51–56, 61, 193.

were split into two wings—the already mentoined Golden Crowd and the Denver Crowd. The former had within its ranks W. A. H. Loveland and the serious minded, harsh-speaking, young lawyer Henry M. Teller of Central City.[13] In the Denver group could be found Governor Evans, Jerome B. Chaffee, George Chilcott, Colonel Chivington, and others. Until these two wings could be made to cooperate, it was not likely that statehood could be achieved. Part of the trouble was simply that of a rivalry between two ambitious towns vying for the seat of government. Each also dreamed of becoming the distribution and wholesale market center for the mining towns of Colorado. But these larger issues came to be centered in a conflict of personality between the passionate and tempermental Chaffee and the stubborn Teller.

Just when the political situation seemed blackest, however, the leaders of the former antistate faction came forward to suggest a new movement, which they would support if given a proper share of the resulting honors and office. Within a few weeks after the September defeat the political skies brightened, and a new statehood movement arose out of the ashes of the old. The new combination decided to resubmit the constitution for ratification in September 1865. This time the statehood men were certain they had victory within grasp; they had chosen William Gilpin as their gubernatorial candidate, with the expectation that he would carry the Spanish-American vote, since he had large interests in the southern counties. For a similar reason they picked the ever-popular George Chilcott of Pueblo to run for Congress. The senatorial aspirants were Teller, Chaffee, and Evans.[14]

This time the voters of Colorado endorsed the constitution and statehood, but by a majority of less than 200 votes (3,025 to 2,870). They also voted down a proposal for Negro suffrage, 4,192 to 476.[15] None of these statistics was likely to please the Republicans in Washington. The narrow victory was further impugned when, as a result of the Congressional investigation of the Sand Creek massacre, Seward asked Governor Evans to resign the governorship. This oc-

---

13. Ellis, "Statehood Fight," pp. 26–28.
14. Ibid.
15. Henry J. Hershey, "The Colorado Constitution," *CM*, *3* (1926), 67.

curred in July 1865 just two months before the state election. Evans' removal revived the whole fight over Indian policy and led to a "Sand Creek Vindication" movement headed by one Stephen Decatur.[16] Thus three sets of nominees, Union, Sand Creek, and Democratic went to the polls to elect a state government that fall. Although the Union Party elected a majority of its candidates, and Congress seemed favorable to admission, President Johnson declined to proclaim the area a state, since Colorado proceedings had differed from those methods of admission specified in the Enabling Act of 1864.[17] Johnson's refusal to admit Colorado had many unexpected repercussions. Johnson himself was obviously hostile to Evans and the statehood men, so the latter turned to the Radicals in Congress for support. Yet Colorado was still a territory, and Johnson had the power to appoint its federal officials. Congress, on the other hand, could hold up approval of these appointments. Thus a local statehood crusade became entangled in national Reconstruction politics.

The statehood movement suffered a further setback when Evans' successor, Governor A. A. Cummings (1865–67), arrived in Denver early in the fall of 1865. Cummings has not received a good press either from his contemporaries or from historians, for he was by almost any standard a hack politician, a spoilsman, and somewhat corrupt in handling government funds. Appropriately, Cummings had been a protégé of Secretary of War Simon Cameron, for whom he had been an army contractor. Indeed, it appears that news of Cummings' speculations persuaded Lincoln to remove Cameron from office. Frank Hall, who succeeded Elbert as territorial secretary in 1866, has described the Governor as a stiff-necked, willful, crafty person, "an Aaron Burr in fertility of resource, but lacking his diplomacy, educated, scholarly, a clear and forcible writer and speaker, but pigheaded and dictatorial to the last degree." The *Rocky Mountain News* took such an aversion to Governor Cummings that it was soon calling him "Old Hod-Nose."[18]

16. *Rocky Mountain News,* December 20, 1865. Stephen Decatur to Evans, November 2, 1865, Evans Collection.

17. Hafen, "Steps to Statehood," p. 107.

18. Hall, *Colorado, 1,* 369–70. S. T. Sopris, "Denver's First Railroad," *Trail, 1* (July 1908), 5.

Cummings

Here was a politician of the genus carpetbagger come to fleece and reconstruct Colorado to his own liking, as so many others were now doing in the South. Yet much of the animus against Cummings was caused by his successful attempts to kill the Colorado statehood movement of 1865–66 and to seize control of the territorial patronage. In his public addresses Cummings was eloquent and intelligent, and in his politics he was both bold and crafty. Even so, much of Cummings' power came from the secret support of Henry M. Teller and former United States Marshal Alexander C. Hunt.[19]

From the outset it was clear that Cummings reflected the views of Andrew Johnson when he opposed statehood for Colorado. This stand naturally led Cummings into immediate conflict with Secretary Samuel H. Elbert, who was both a statehood man and a son-in-law of Evans. A showdown came when the so-called "state" legislature convened in December 1865 to hear a ringing message from Governor Gilpin and to choose Evans and Chaffee as senators. Elbert felt that since the "state" legislature was now the official law-making body of Colorado, there was little need for the territorial Assembly to convene in January 1866. Cummings, on the other hand, insisted on calling the territorial Assembly into session. Then he made such war on Elbert that by June 1866 the latter had resigned and Frank Hall had taken his place.[20]

Cummings, an ex-reporter and an artful manipulator of newspaper copy, next turned on the statehood movement itself. Statehood was but the conception of a small party in control of three local newspapers seeking political aggrandizement, the new governor announced to the world. He pointed out that when the 1865 constitutional convention met, only eleven of Colorado's seventeen counties were represented. He used these statistics to prove that the movement was not popular; as a good Radical, Cummings noted that Colorado's was a white supremacy constitution, which denied the Negro the

19. "Henry M. Teller" in *DAB*. Elmer Ellis, *Henry Moore Teller, Defender of the West* (Caldwell, Idaho, 1941), pp. 74–77. Donald Wayne Hensel, "A History of the Colorado Constitution in the Nineteenth Century" (Ph.D. dissertation, University of Colorado, 1957), pp. 70 ff.

20. Hall, *Colorado, 1*, 376–77.

vote.[21] Cummings was aided in his fight by still another maverick legislature, whose lower house contained only three members who had been in the preceding legislature.

The obstreperous Cummings was only one headache for the state men. When Evans, Chaffee, and Chilcott appeared in Washington in 1866 to claim seats as congressmen from the "State of Colorado," they ran further afoul of the war between President Johnson and the Radicals. The statehood forces had generally taken the side of the Radicals, but if they continued to do so, Johnson would veto the enabling act; if they supported Johnson, the Radicals would not pass an enabling act. In trying to steer between congressional and presidential shoals, Chaffee and Evans assured Johnson's secretary, Edward Cooper, that they had not sold out to the Radicals. Johnson did not seem cooperative, so the two—thinking Johnson's star was on the wane—began to work with Ben Wade in the Senate. They managed to push a new enabling act through the House and Senate that spring, but a new veto by Johnson killed all chances of admission in 1866.[22]

Before Congress met again Evans, Chaffee, and Chilcott had to rush home to mend political fences. A new delegate election was in the offing, and they wanted a man in Washington who was sympathetic to admission. Thus the Union Party chose their would-be congressman, Chilcott, as their candidate. In their absence, however, Cummings had established a rapport with the opposition wing of the Republican Party and had entered into political cooperatoin with ex-Marshal Alexander C. Hunt, a promising and energetic businessman. The Cummings Republicans ran Hunt for the delegateship. The resulting vote was so close that the election was contested. While it appears that Chilcott did have a slight margin of votes over Hunt,

21. Ibid., 376. ———— to Ben Wade and John Evans, December 13, 1866 (telegram), Evans Collection. See also *Message of Gov. Cummings to the Territorial Assembly* (Golden City, 1866), p. 8.

22. *The Rocky Mountain News*, August 24, 1866, stated that Johnson sent for Evans and Chaffee and asked them to sign an endorsement of his policies. When they refused he vetoed the enabling bill. See also Hafen, "Steps to Statehood," p. 107. Johnson was fairly well informed about Colorado politics. On May 10, 1866, George T. Clark gave the President's secretary a full account of conditions there. See State Department TP: Colorado, Vol. 1; also Chaffee to Hon. Edward Cooper, May 12, 1860, ibid.

Cummings was not one to worry about such details. Dramatically he presented Hunt with the certificate of election, despite the protests of Secretary Frank Hall, the leading newspapers, and all the state men.[23] Cummings was not to be dissuaded, nonetheless; wearily, Evans, Chaffee, and Chilcott packed their bags for still another trip to Washington. This time they had to fight both Hunt's election and Johnson's antistate intransigence.

During 1866–67 bills for the admission of Colorado and Nebraska came up in Congress, and after the Radical Republicans forced the Coloradans to strike out the word "white" in their constitution, an enabling act finally passed both houses of Congress.[24] But another familiar scene was reenacted; Johnson vetoed the Colorado bill on the bases that the territory still had too small a population to become a state and that the constitution had not handled the suffrage questoin correctly.[25] This time the Coloradans would not take no for an answer. The statehood leaders persuaded Chief Justice Moses Hallett, one of the most respected members of the federal bench ever to serve in the territories, to support their cause. D. H. Moffat, Jr., by 1866 one of the leading businessmen in Colorado, also came to Washington to lobby. Even Delegate Bradford came to the aid of Chaffee, Evans, and Chilcott. Early in 1867 the statehood lobby persuaded Congress to entertain a motion to override the veto. The outlook for success seemed extremely favorable. When the Senate teller announced the result, however, Colorado had missed statehood by three votes. Curiously, the defeat had little to do with Reconstruction or national politics. In a bitter analysis of those voting no, the *Rocky Mountain News* found that Senator Grimes of Iowa had cast his negative vote out of fear that Colorado, once in the Union, could reroute the Union Pacific below Iowa. For other reasons involving the railroad question, McDougal of California had voted no. Lastly, Senator Edmunds of Vermont, convinced that no white man had a right to live west of the Mississippi, cast his vote against the further invasion of the red man's domain.[26]

The paper could also have added that Republican Henry M. Teller

23. S. E. Browne to W. H. Seward, September 14, 1866, ibid.
24. McMechan, *Evans*, pp. 149 ff.
25. *Rocky Mountain News*, January 30, 1867.
26. Ibid., March 6, 1867.

1866-7 movmnt also unsuccessful (barely)
- due to Golden Crd. in part.

262   *The Far Southwest, 1864–1871*

and his brother Willard had gone to Washington to lobby against
statehood. Once again the Golden Crowd had blocked the ambitions
of the Denver Crowd. The Golden *City Transcript,* which had always
opposed statehood, wrote an epitaph for the 1866–67 movement with
the remark: "Messrs. Evans and Chaffee can come back to their
mountain homes wiser if not better men, and can expatiate upon the
'two long and bloody wars' they have gone through. Still they may
by some sly turn of the wrist try to land on their legs again."[27]

Among the most lukewarm of statehood advocates in 1864 had
been Jerome B. Chaffee, the wealthy owner of the Bob-tail and other
paying mines. His own business partner, Eben Smith, had actually
opposed the movement.[28] Chaffee's own popularity and influence
was so great that, inevitably, contending factions bade for his support
and forced him to take a side. Chaffee himself was always fascinated
by the impossible. He delighted in intrigue and in a manipulation of
human beings. High-spirited and outspoken, he was a natural fighter
for a cause, especially when that cause meant a possible seat in the
United States Senate for himself. By the time the statehood forces
had experienced their second defeat in 1866, Chaffee was more than
an advocate of statehood—the cause became an obsession of sorts—
but the desire for statehood largely determined his political maneuvers from that year until Colorado entered the Union in 1876. The
cause, and Chaffee's own considerable political talents, combined to
make him the virtual boss of the territory from 1870 to 1876.

To make sure that Colorado would not fail again, Chaffee began
to explore every possibility of increasing the chances for success. He
considered changing the northern boundary of Colorado to include
the Union Pacific and Fort Laramie.[29] By this act Colorado would
experience a significant gain in population, a large source of future
taxes (the railroad), and cheap transportation over a route favored
by powerful Chicago interests. Although Chaffee's ambitious project
never came to pass, he did succeed in bettering statehood chances by
a second and even more sophisticated maneuver. He proposed to

27. Ellis, "Statehood Fight," p. 28. Golden City *Transcript,* March 6, 1867.
28. *Rocky Mountain News,* July 21, 1865.
29. John Q. Charles to Evans, February 4, 1867, Evans Collection.

steal the ablest man from the local opposition by making him governor. This was Alexander Cameron Hunt, supposedly Cummings' mentor and the erstwhile contestant for Delegate Chilcott's seat. By so doing Chaffee would unite the warring factions of the Republican Party in Colorado under one banner. "Keep our State friends in the background," wrote Chaffee to Evans, "enough to secure the cooperation of Hunt's friends as much as possible. We are working to admit this state and when dealing with such men it is policy not to dictate too much."[30]

To succeed in this latter scheme, Chaffee and his backers had to remove Cummings. John Q. Charles, Elbert's law partner, had ferreted out the interesting information that the Governor's daughter, May, and son, Boyd, were on the government payroll as Indian clerks. The Chaffee forces also discovered that the Governor, in partnership with certain freighters and contractors, was charging exorbitant prices for carrying Indian goods to Middle Park in Colorado. Armed with these facts, the anti-Cummings party sent a removal petition bearing hundreds of names off to Johnson. Cummings, they declared, had "sought in all things, to retard our growth." Delegate Bradford also asked Johnson to remove Cummings on the basis of misappropriation of Indian funds. Even Gilpin and Evans, once political enemies, now joined in testimony against their successor.[31]

Most of the charges leveled against Cummings were explained away; but it was also apparent that the old friend of Simon Cameron had once again lined his pockets, so that he was eventually removed in 1867. As Chaffee had planned it, an amazed territory soon learned that Johnson had appointed Alexander C. Hunt (1867-69) as governor.[32] Many of the more cliquish Republicans could not understand Chaffee's logic and declared they would punish him. Replied Chaffee in anger: "They can do as they please." He explained he had done this for statehood and to defeat the Democrats, for "I know that the opposition headed by Hunt has beat us so far." Impatient with the simple-minded jealousy his critics exhibited, he wrote Evans:

30. J. B. Chaffee to Evans, November 27, 1867, ibid.
31. Charles to Evans, February 4, 1867, ibid. Petition, State Department TP: Colorado, Vol. 1.
32. Chaffee to Evans, December 10, 1867, Evans Collection.

"I have little disposition to work any longer for the interest of such a set of d—nd hedgehogs."[33] The failure to achieve unity, Teller's continued opposition, and a decline of Congressional interest in state-making so vitiated Chaffee's elaborate plans that a third attempt at statehood failed in the spring of 1868. On that occasion Teller actually challenged Evans and Chaffee to hold a new referendum on statehood. Fearing the results of a plebiscite, the two senators-elect resigned from their unrecognized offices, and the statehood movement was laid on the shelf for five years.[34]

The whole effort to gain admission had revealed that Colorado was still not organized along regular two-party lines. The potpourri of Spanish-Americans and Southern Democrats in the lower half of the territory and the factions clustered in Central City, Golden, and Denver were more cliques than parties. One observer wrote that it was impossible to call the statehood group a party—they were simply Unionists as opposed to Copperheads. This was well illustrated in the 1865 election, when Chilcott ran on a Union ticket, Chivington ran on a Sand Creek Vindication plank, and Hunt ran on an Independent Party ticket. The Colorado population was still too amorphous and its resources too underdeveloped to make parties and statehood feasible. They had first seen statehood as the means to quick economic development. What they now realized was that economic development—and particularly railroad communication—seemed a necessary prerequisite to political maturity and independence.

The Colorado entrepreneur's first task was to make the mines profitable enough to attract the railroads; but the local mines produced refractory ores that were difficult to smelt. As Professor Rodman Paul has noted, the pioneer businessmen of Colorado used a scientific, logical, and big business approach to the problem. A group of Central City capitalists, for example, imported Nathaniel W. Hill, professor of chemistry at Brown University, to analyze and solve their refining problems. Obviously his employers had no mere extract-and-leave approach to a profitable frontier resource. After securing

33. Ibid.
34. Ellis, "Statehood Fight," p. 29.

samples of the ores in 1864, Hill took them all the way to Swansea, Wales, where experienced refiners worked on the Colorado refining problem.[35]

By 1868 with the aid of Richard Pearce, an English expert in smelting whom he found living in Freiburg, Hill gained the technical knowledge to make Colorado mining profitable. Hill brought over German-trained engineers to work in Colorado, and he himself took the transition from classroom to industry with extraordinary ease. His practical success soon resulted in his becoming mayor of Black Hawk in 1871. A year later he was in the territorial legislature, and three years after Colorado became a state, he was a United States senator. Hill's business acumen also persuaded him to locate his main smelter near a trunk railroad, so that his plant could handle the ores of Utah, New Mexico, and the remainder of Colorado; thus he moved his works to Argo near Denver.[36]

The success of Hill's methods coincided with the first use of power drills, in 1869, to tunnel into the veins found in the new silver districts around Nederland and in Boulder County. Three years later, in 1872, rich tellurides of gold and silver were also found, guaranteeing Colorado's mining future once and for all.[37] The uneasy residents of Central City and Black Hawk, Georgetown, and a dozen other towns could now count on some permanence.

Unlike previous American frontiers, however, Colorado's future depended upon technological advances. In his way Hill was the harbinger of the scientific exploitation of the last American frontier. After the Civil War agriculturalists set out to master the techniques of dry farming and to develop a strain of hardy winter wheat, which could survive Great Plains winters. This same scientific attitude led to fencing with barbed wire and the use of windmills for drawing water. By taking a similar approach to her own problems, Colorado appeared as a community in step with her times.

The mining and smelting methods employed also suggested that Colorado mining was too expensive and precise for the amateur.

35. Hall, *Colorado*, *4*, 462. Stone, *Colorado*, *3*, 302–03. Paul, *Mining Frontiers*, pp. 123–24.
36. Hall, *Colorado*, *4*, 462.
37. Fritz, *Colorado*, p. 228

Colo. mining required lg investment / E cap

Thus companies (rather than individuals) and professional miners—
many of them Welshmen—were to become characteristic of the Colorado mining industry. This meant, in turn, that Colorado was to become a logical region for Eastern investment and that, rather early,
a sense of division between labor and capital would develop. Given
these conditions, the region would inevitably take on certain attri-
butes of the national economy.

The development of profitable mining techniques was not the only
device used by the Colorado entrepreneurs. The older frontier businesses of land speculation and colonization were also employed.
Nearly twenty years before Hill came to Colorado, in fact, William
Gilpin had become aware of land speculation possibilities in the San
Luis and Arkansas valleys. As has been mentioned before, he learned
of the Beaubien-Miranda, Sangre de Cristo, and Vigil and St. Vrain
grants while visiting Bent's Fort on his return from Oregon in 1844. He
had again visited the areas involved while on army service in 1847–48.
Actually Gilpin had been interested in land speculation for a long
time. In 1844 he wrote his brothers in a perfect frenzy of excitement
about a Congressional grant of 500,000 acres to Missouri, which was
to be sold to pay for various internal improvements. He urged them
to come out and profit on the sales.[38]

Undoubtedly Gilpin had a similar scheme in mind for the Colorado
grants when he accepted the governorship. His unexpected removal
from office in 1862 left him free to pursue just such a project. He
knew that the Sangre de Cristo grant, once the property of the ill-
fated Narciso Beaubien and Sheriff Luis Lee, had been confirmed
and that Carlos Beaubien, now breaking in health and fearful of
taxes, wished to sell it. In December 1862 Gilpin bought one-sixth of
the grant and managed to buy all but a remaining sixth in March
1863.[39]

38. Gilpin to Richard and Henry Gilpin, December 1, 1844, Gilpin Miscellany,
CSHS.

39. It is very probable that Gilpin had already invested in New Mexican grants
before he became governor of Colorado in 1861. His own account of his land
activities in Bancroft, *Gilpin*, pp. 48 ff., is confusing as to time of purchase and
name of grant. Gilpin's friendship with Martin Coates Fisher during the 1850s
suggests that Gilpin's land schemes were under way even before gold was found
in Colorado. See Hall, *Colorado*, *1*, 216, and Van Diest, "History of Costilla
County," *CM*, 6, 140.

This magnificent tract situated in the San Luis Valley, through which flowed the Upper Rio Grande, was surrounded by some of the most splendid peaks of the Rockies—mountains which the bombastic Gilpin always called the "snowy Cordilleras." Here was a property equal in size to Gilpin's lofty way of thinking and acting. As an early geopolitician he already saw Colorado as the center of the country with Denver as its metropolis. The San Luis region would be, in his racing imagination, a new colony stimulated to industry by the pure air and genial climate. It promised to be a source of wool, cattle, timber, and food for Colorado and Eastern markets.

There was always a practical side to Gilpin's fantasies, however. He knew he could not pay taxes on such property, nor could he develop it alone. Consequently Gilpin tried to sell his holdings for a profit, while retaining an interest in them. Armed with optimistic reports furnished him by willing surveyors, engineers, and scientists, Gilpin first turned to Philadelphia, where his prominent family had many banking connections. Despite his own enthusiasm and a trip by Pennsylvania investors to the Valley—where local Spanish-Americans gave them a *baile*—the cautious investors concluded that San Luis, a little like Gilpin, was "too far out of the world."[40]

After three years of failure Gilpin's associate in the land business, Martin Coates Fisher, a former merchant-trader in New Mexico, made the acquaintance of William Blackmore, an English promoter and solicitor, who agreed to handle the sale of the Sangre de Cristo grant in Europe.[41] To facilitate the handling of so much property, Blackmore divided the grant into the Trinchera Estate, which was eventually to be developed by the Colorado Freehold Land and Emigration Company, and the Costilla Estate which was to be promoted by a similar firm, the United States Freehold Land and Emigration Company.[42]

Without funds himself, Blackmore had to look to Dutch bankers in Amsterdam for the money to carry through the sale. European investors had been burned enough times by American land booms, repudiated state bonds, and stocks in defaulting railroads to be ex-

40. Brayer, *Blackmore*, *1*, 67 ff.
41. Ibid., p. 68 n.
42. Ibid., pp. 76–86.

ceedingly cautious. Thus the firm of Wertheim and Gompertz demanded that certain conditions be met before buying the Costilla Estate. As Professor Herbert Brayer has noted, these conditions were: that the title be clear, and that the company organized to manage and develop the property be chartered by no less a body than Congress. Finally Wertheim and Gompertz wanted expert proof that the Costilla Estate contained real agricultural and mineral possibilities.[43]

These demands sent Gilpin and his colleagues back into politics and to Washington, where they lobbied for chartering the United States Freehold Land and Emigration Company. After many reverses, Congress, roused to action by several members interested in the company, incorporated the firm in 1870. Wertheim and Gompertz then agreed to buy a million dollars worth of stock and made Gilpin the manager of the estate. In 1876 Gilpin also secured a significant Supreme Court decision in *U. S. v. Tameling,* by which his and other land grants were validated.[44]

Blackmore, Wertheim, and Gompertz, and even Gilpin, formulated elaborate plans to colonize Costilla with Dutch settlers, connect the San Luis Valley with the nation via a railroad, and farm its lands.[45] But neither the Costilla nor the Trinchera Estate lived up to the exaggerated promotional literature ground out by its managers and owners. Nevertheless, Gilpin's dealings were important, since they showed a pattern of Colorado frontier land exploitation and speculation used to develop part of the state. The negotiations and first sale of the Sangre de Cristo tract were repeated in the sale of the Maxwell Grant to Wertheim, Gompertz, and other Dutch bankers.[46] Similar promotion and sale characterized the Vigil and St. Vrain or Las Animas grant, which was all the more valuable since it was on the Santa Fe trail. After being maneuvered through Congressional confirmation by former Judge and Delegate Watts of New Mexico, it was purchased from St. Vrain by James A. Archer of Denver (described as a minor business associate of Gilpin's), Spruce M. Baird of New Mexico, Blackmore, and others. Its history from the sale was one of

43. Ibid., pp. 76–86.
44. Ibid., pp. 90–95.
45. Ibid., pp. 81–89.
46. Pearson, *Maxwell Grant,* pp. 72 ff.

tangled litigation and misunderstanding, but eventually the bulk of the property was sold to new holders, among whom was the famous P. T. Barnum.[47] A decade later Celedon Valdez and others—who had petitioned for a community grant in the Conejos Valley when St. Vrain and Beaubien were acquiring their vast holdings during the 1840s—sold their own lands through Blackmore.

The last major Mexican grant in Colorado was that of Gervacio Nolan, a Taos mountain man. This was a wedge-shaped piece of property which ran south of Pueblo and had been acquired by Mrs. Annie Blake, Charles Goodnight, and Peter and Jacob Dotson. The grant eventually found its way into the hands of General William Jackson Palmer, builder of the Denver and Rio Grande railroad, and his associates, Dr. William A. Bell and Governor Alexander C. Hunt. Behind them stood the usual English promoters and Dutch bankers. As had been the case for the other grants, the purchasers formed a firm—the Central Colorado Improvement Company—actually a creation of the Denver and Rio Grande railroad—to exploit the agricultural and coal resources of the Arkansas Valley.[48]

Scores of businessmen-speculators in Denver and Santa Fe worked with bankers, investors, and promoters in New York, Philadelphia, Providence, London, and Amsterdam as well as with key political figures in Washington to sell throughout the world nine million privately claimed acres in southern Colorado. Their activities, like those of the Santa Fe Ring, smacked of high finance, intricate legal arrangements, and the latest techniques of investment and exploitation. They did not hesitate to use newspaper publicity, print expensive brochures, and employ high-pressure salesmanship. Like earlier large-scale American land speculations of the eighteenth and early nineteenth century, however, the rewards were disappointing. Water was not available to permit a population density that would make individual sales of small plots profitable. Water scarcity also dictated that many of the holdings be limited to ranching or irrigated farming.

47. Hafen, *Colorado*, pp. 96–97. Brayer, *Blackmore*, pp. 136–38, 142–45.
48. Hafen, *Colorado*, pp. 96–97. The history of the Mexican land grants in Colorado is traced in Hafen, "Mexican Land Grants in Colorado"; Carr, "Private Land Claims"; Van Diest, "History of Costilla County"; and Dunham, "Coloradans and the Maxwell Grant."

Much of colo Land by derives d space + massive Land dealing of men like Gilpin, Blackmore, etc, But, Limitations of environment kept these attempts from being fairly successful.

370   *The Far Southwest, 1864-1871*

Here man could not bend nature to his wish, as Hill and Pearce were attempting to do in Black Hawk and Argo. As one noted authority has concluded, men such as Blackmore and the Dutch bankers—and even Gilpin—failed in their Western enterprises because they did not "realize the basic immutability of the country itself."[49] The important fact was that private Mexican land grants had affected the economic, railroad, and political history of territorial Colorado.

While the dreams of empire and profits swirled in the heads of Blackmore, Gilpin, and Dutchmen, an older way of life in southern Colorado went quietly on. William Bent, once the feudal lord of Colorado, traded and ranched near Fort Lyon until his death in 1869. Ailing Kit Carson, the perennial public servant, still served in the army in the region. Colonel A. G. Boone and Thomas Boggs ranched and traded near Pueblo. Colonel Francisco, the sutler-politician, still fulminated against Black Republicans; and the smiling assemblyman, Casimiro Barela, remained a patron and a hidalgo to his people. Every citizen in southern Colorado knew the rancher and trader Ferd Meyer, who fought a lifelong battle against the outsider land-grant kings.[50]

No one was more typical of this breed of men than Major Lafayette Head, who had marched to New Mexico with Sterling Price's column in 1846. There he pursued a checkered career of clerking, Indian trading at Abiquiu, and service as a deputy marshal for northern New Mexico. Head's marriage to Martina Martinez—part claimant to a land grant—and his own popularity led to his choice as a special agent to the Jicarilla Apaches and Capote Utes during the 1850s. Later the fun-loving and genial Head was elected to a seat in the New Mexican legislature for three terms. In 1857 he also held the office of sheriff of Rio Arriba County.[51]

Successful as he was, Head had the same kind of land fever that had persuaded so many frontier Missourians to set up their own empires in the wilderness. In 1854 the Major had gathered fifty families from New Mexico and had settled them in the San Luis

49. Brayer, *Blackmore, 1,* 26.
50. Ibid., p. 108.
51. Hall, *Colorado, 4,* 91–94.

Valley, where, as the local patron, he ruled for more than twenty years. His nearness to the Utes persuaded the government to make him agent to the Tabequache Tribe, a position he held for ten years. When his section of New Mexico was attached to Colorado in 1861, Head did not find Denver and the Colorado pioneers to his liking; his easy ways and his condoning of frauds in Indian supplies led men like Governor Evans to denounce him as a crook. But Head stayed in federal office longer than the chief executive.[52] Immensely popular with his wife's people, he was elected to the Colorado legislature from Costilla and Conejos counties and sometimes acted as interpreter for Mexican assemblymen. The climax of his career came in 1876, when he was elected lieutenant governor in the first state election in Colorado.

Head was a friend of Kit Carson's and a chum of Albert Henry Pfeiffer of Del Norte, whose career in the Southwest almost paralleled his.[53] All three men dabbled in the land-grant business, bought part-interests, and watched the confirmations and court decisions. In the meantime, they ran general stores or mills and grubstaked local gold prospectors. In their letters they exchanged news of the Jaramillo family, the Chatos, and the Lopezes; and occasionally Head urged Pfeiffer to come to Conejos for a visit so that Father Kolley could challenge him to chess.[54] Head, Boone, Pfeiffer, Boggs, and Barela were the second generation of an order born of the Santa Fe trade and the Mexican War. They were the transition figures between the generation of Bent, St. Vrain, and Beaubien and the new generation of Gilpin, Palmer, Chaffee—and in New Mexico—of Stephen Elkins and Thomas B. Catron. While the former group lived, southern Colorado would remain a cultural and economic borderland of the Spanish Southwest, and the echoes of a wilder, more dangerous, and exciting way of life would sound down the splendid valleys between the snow-capped Spanish Peaks.

52. Ibid. Petition of Citizens of San Luis Valley for the Removal of Agent Head, January 18, 1864, Interior Department, OIA, Colorado, NA.
53. See the Papers of Albert Henry Pfeiffer, 1822–1881, MSS in CSA.
54. Head to Pfeiffer, April 1, 1868, and February 4, 1869, Pfeiffer Papers, CSA.

11   The Centennial State
1876

The Centennial State was on the last frontier. It was a mining
state, a farming state, a cattle and sheep ranching state, but
more than all of these it was an industrial state. . . . An
industrial state on the frontier seems paradoxical. But
Leadville was almost as near the White River Agency where
Meeker died as it was to the bustling and brawling metropolis
of Denver. Before the Utes had been moved out to the Uintah
reservation in Utah, Governor Pitkin had . . . to declare
martial law in Leadville, not because of any Indian menace,
but because of a miners' strike for higher wages and
shorter hours.

> Dudley Taylor Cornish in
> *Colorado Magazine*, 1943

 One of the most significant periods in the political
development of a frontier region comes when a
territory tries to enter the Union as a state. At this
time the desire for self-government is at its highest,
and the awareness of the differences between the
local community and the nation is most pronounced.
This sense of difference has often been provoked by outside events,
which at first seem to have little bearing on the problem of admission.
Colorado's statehood movement occurred, for example, in a time of
economic depression brought on by the Panic of 1873. It also coincided
with the age of the Robber Barons, a national preoccupation with
railroads, and a rising tide of agrarian unrest. Thus economic factors,
public issues, and even the partisan attitudes of Eastern congressmen

 Illustrations

By trading throughout the Mexican borderlands, William Bent (left) and Ceran St. Vrain (right) helped open the Far Southwest to Americans.

Carlos Beaubien (left), Taos merchant, and Governor Manuel Armijo (right) cooperated to lay claim to vast land grants in Northern New Mexico. Their actions significantly affected the political and economic history of territorial New Mexico and Colorado.

General Stephen W. Kearny's (left) occupation of New Mexico allowed Americans to further their plans for the development of the Far Southwest. One of the officers in his Army already interested in Spanish-Mexican land grants in 1846 was William Gilpin (right), who became governor of Colorado in 1861.

President Brigham Young (left) sought to create a Mormon state which would embrace the whole of the mountain Southwest and used the Mormon Battalion in Kearney's army as a reconnaissance party to explore the Southwest. General William Jackson Palmer (right), both as an official of the Kansas Pacific and as the founder of the Denver and Rio Grande Railroad, succeeded in developing a modern regional economy for the Bent's Fort area of the Far Southwest.

Father Jose Antonio Martinez
(upper left) spent most of his later
career resisting the changes brought
to New Mexico by Americans such
as Governor Charles Bent
(upper right).

Governor Henry Connelly of
New Mexico (lower left), while
very much the American merchant
who had adjusted to Spanish-
Mexican society, defended the
territory for the Union and tried to
develop its economy.

Archbishop John B. Lamy (lower
right) dreamed of clerical reforms in
New Mexico while preserving the
Catholic heritage of the region.
Through his efforts an invigorated
Church spread its influence over
most of the Far Southwest.

Perhaps more than any other section of the
country, the Four Corners territories experienced
Army rule and sought military solutions for
its Indian problem. General Edwin V. Sumner
(above) began constructing a web of defense
out of forts and roads which helped bring the
New Mexican tribes under stricter control
during the 1850s. Sumner's friend
General James H. Carleton (top) used the
reservation–concentration camp system to
pacify the Navajo in the Civil War period.
One of Carleton's chief agents in rounding up the
Navajo was the famous scout General Christopher
Carson (right).

In Colorado, General John M. Chivington, Union hero at Glorieta, pursued an extermination policy at Sand Creek as his solution to the Indian problem.

General Patrick E. Connor (left) saw himself as both an Indian fighter who kept the central overland trail to California open and as the military ruler of Mormon Utah. By using Indian allies and a no quarter policy, General George Crook (above) finally subdued the Arizona Apache in the 1870s, so that the territory could at last be settled by whites.

Delegate Thomas B. Catron
of New Mexico

With the exception of Utah, a small group of able political figures usually allied to the Republican party ran the southwestern territories. Variously called the Santa Fe Ring, the Federal Ring (Arizona), and the Denver and Golden Crowd, they played a major role in the political and economic development of their respective territories.

Delegate Stephen B. Elkins

Governor John Evans of Colorado

Governor Richard C. McCormick
of Arizona

Governor A. P. K. Safford of Arizona

Delegate Jerome B. Chaffee of Colorado

Opponents and Proponents of Change in Utah

Alfred Cumming (upper left), Brigham Young's successor as governor of Utah, was a symbol of change, but he and his immediate successor did little to curb Young's power. As successors to Brigham Young, Presidents John Taylor (upper right) and Wilford Woodruff (lower left) had to contend with the federal government's crusade to end polygamy and the one-party system in Utah. Among the leading advocates for compromise and adjustment to government and Gentile demands was Delegate John T. Caine (lower right).

Senator George F. Edmunds of Vermont (upper left) spent nearly a decade securing legislation to outlaw polygamy and to curb Mormon political power. Judges Jacob Boreman (upper right) and Charles S. Zane (lower left) tried to make federal laws effective in Utah. Governor Edmund G. Ross (lower right) attempted to reform the land, economic, and educational systems of New Mexico between 1885 and 1889 with little success.

The Agents of Cultural Compromise and Americanization

Apache Indian Agent John P. Clum

Governor George W. P. Hunt of Arizona

Mark A. Smith, Delegate and
Senator from Arizona

Governor Miguel A. Otero of New Mexico

were as important in the history of state-making as were the beliefs
and activities of local political leaders. All of these factors operated
vigorously in the Colorado admission fight between 1872 and 1876.

To understand the history of the last years of territorial politics,
new reference must be made to four able Denver entrepreneur-
politicians, who were friends and often business partners. The first *divers!*
was William Byers, the outspoken editor of the *Rocky Mountain business-*
News. Having succeeded in the publishing business, Byers and his *man.*
associate, John Dailey, were soon in partnership with Governor Evans
as a firm interested in buying up promising mining claims. A typical
entry in his diary for March 1, 1864, stated: "Very fair day—Recorded
101 claims for B. E. and D., and perfected records on Dean and Casto
Leads." Nearly a year later, Byers recorded that he had loaned
A. W. Barnard one hundred dollars for three months at 3 per cent,
and had taken a mortage on 600 feet of water power in Downieville.
In 1866 he was also running an assay office with Fred Schirmer. In a
single war year he had made enough money to pay $336 in income
tax.[1]

When Bela M. Hughes, president of the Central Overland California
and Pike's Peak Express, joined Governor Evans and David Moffat,
Jr., in forming the Denver Pacific Railway and Telegraph Company
in 1868, Byers turned his surveyor's talent to the building of the
telegraph line.[2] Like so many other businessmen he also turned his
interests southward and built a telegraph line to Santa Fe. In so
doing he visited Maxwell's ranch, St. Vrain's home at Mora, Fort
Union, and Santa Fe. In his negotiations for a right of way for the line
he dealt with Stephen Elkins, Judge Watts, and others of the Santa
Fe Ring. It was not long before the keen-eyed Byers was jotting down
notes about lands for sale. By the 1870s he was listed as land agent
for at least two land companies. Byers' diary also suggests a similar
affiliation with the Maxwell Company, for in 1871 he charged them
for his railroad fares and meals to and from Trinidad.[3] Later in his

1. Diaries of William N. Byers, entries from March 1, 1864, to July 1866, MSS
in the Western History Department, Denver Public Library.
2. Stone, *Colorado, 3,* 499–503. Entry for November 12, 1868, Byers.
3. Entries for December 1867 to November 1868, and July 15–23, 1871, Byers.

career he invested in the Indian supply business and also became a promoter of Pagosa Hot Springs in the San Juan Valley. These were only a few of the many enterprises he engaged in before he settled down to become postmaster of Denver.[4]

The multifarious activities of the editor often paralleled those of his friend and partner, Governor John Evans. Already experienced as a railroad builder in Illinois, Evans came to Colorado with a certain amount of capital and with great plans for a new railroad career. Evans was such a born executive, his critics humorously remarked, that he never appeared at a public affair without organizing it for some purpose. Flanked by his devoted son-in-law S. H. Elbert, Byers of the *News*, and John Q. Charles, Elbert's law partner, Evans worked with a truly impressive team.[5]

Having failed to secure statehood for Colorado and a senatorship for himself, between 1864 and 1868 Evans turned to railroading. With Bela Hughes he founded the Denver Pacific and built the tracks as far as Cheyenne, where they connected with the Union Pacific tracks running east. In June 1870 the long-awaited steam engine puffed into the Denver freight yards.[6] Evans appears to have been unhappy with these arrangements. He persuaded the Kansas Pacific to abandon its plans to build to California along the 35th parallel, to come to Denver instead and tap the Colorado gold fields.[7] After this rail connection became a reality later in 1870, Evans turned his attention to the mining towns themselves: he ran the Denver, South Park, and Pacific up the South Platte into South Park. His eventual success with these local spurs led him to organize a line to run from Denver to New Orleans, but this latter company never materialized.[8] Besides his railroad and mining interests, Evans owned a newspaper and dabbled in many other enterprises.

It would be misleading to suggest that Evans possessed the necessary

4. Entries for April–June 1873, Byers. See also Byers, Letterbooks, 1879–1883, MSS in Denver Public Library.

5. The affection and respect Elbert had for Evans is seen in Judge Samuel H. Elbert, "Public Men and Measures," MSS in CSHS.

6. Sopris, "Denver's First Railroad," *Trail*, *1* (July 1908), 5–11. Evans' railroad activities are mentioned in *CM*, *2*, 42; *5*, 175–76.

7. Elbert, "Public Men."

8. Ibid.

capital to do all these things alone. His financial techniques resembled those of Gilpin's land schemes and of other railroad builders. After mobilizing the local wealth of D. H. Moffat, Jr., Walter Cheesman, and others in Denver, Evans was forced to turn to Dutch and English bankers to finance the Denver Pacific and to friendly congressmen for a needed land grant. Finally, he resorted to the classic *Credit Mobilier* pattern, when he and his colleagues organized their own construction company in order to experience a profit long before the road did.

Among the vigorous businessmen of Denver none was more ambitious than the slim youth David H. Moffat, Jr. One evening at a dinner party in Denver, Moffat admitted that he had come to Colorado to make $75,000, after which he would return to New York to live in comfort and peace.[9] The acquisitive process proved much too fascinating to Moffat, who had in him that genius for organization and detail which made John D. Rockefeller an industrial giant. Beginning as a messenger boy in a New York exchange bank, he went west to work as a teller in Iowa and Omaha banks. Like nearly all his colleagues he arrived in Denver with a business other than gold-panning in mind. Moffat originally established a stationery and book store, but soon he was buying bullion to ship east. Clark and Company, Denver's first bankers, recognized Moffat's talents and employed him in their own firm. Later, when Chaffee organized the First National Bank of Denver, Moffat was first a partner and, in 1867, cashier. From that date on, the First National prospered.[10]

The bank was but the springboard to other activities. Moffat became interested in mines: he speculated heavily in the private land grants of southern Colorado and participated in every local railroad scheme. After helping Evans complete the Denver Pacific, he built the Boulder Valley line on his own. He was to die while trying to realize an old ambition to build his own transcontinental line by tunneling through the Rockies.[11] Always the shrewd, cautious, thorough jack-of-

9. Alice Polk Hill, *Colorado Pioneers in Picture and Story* (Denver, 1915), pp. 293 ff.

10. Stone, *Colorado*, 2, 49–50. Hall, *Colorado*, 3, 169–75. Byers, *Encyclopaedia*, 1, 193–95. Smiley, *Denver*, 1, 508, 520.

11. Smiley, 2, 457–58.

all-trade, Moffat eventually became a millionaire. He was a key, if retiring, figure in every business undertaking in the territory. Even his reticence did not prevent him from serving in the Assembly, however, or from acting as Evans' adjutant general, or from holding the post of territorial treasurer for four years. As a stalwart Republican, he played a major role in the history of the local party.

The most colorful of the early Denver entrepreneurs was Jerome B. Chaffee, builder of the first stamp mill and owner of the Bob-tail, the Pittsburgh, and nearly a hundred other gold and silver claims. By 1864 the restless Chaffee was already seeking means of amassing capital in fields other than mining. Undoubtedly he had watched Clark, Gruber, and Company prosper as bankers and as a minting firm. He had seen Warren Hussey make impressive profits as gold purchasing agent in Denver and Central City—so much that in 1865 Hussey was able to open a branch firm in Salt Lake City. Still more imposing was the success of the remarkable Kountze brothers, with a long and enviable record as frontier bankers. The four—Augustus, Herman, Luther, and Charles—had begun banking operations in Iowa and Omaha. The solid strike of 1860–61 persuaded Luther to open a bank in the corner of Walter S. Cheesman's drug store in Denver. By 1864 Charles had joined him, and the two organized the Colorado National at Denver and the Rocky Mountain National at Central City. After establishing still another branch in the booming Union Pacific railroad town of Cheyenne in 1867, the Kountze brothers set up a branch on Wall Street a year later, and the impressive skeleton of their family banking empire was complete.[12]

Disgruntled at the refractory ores his mines were producing in 1864, Chaffee bought out Clark, Gruber, and Company and a year later transformed the firm into the First National Bank of Denver. Since no bank existed in New Mexico, Chaffee was soon handling the monies of that territory's businessmen. This enterprise undoubtedly acquainted him further with the Maxwell Land Grant, which in turn led to his organization of a company to sell to investors. As a man

12. Hall, *3*, 180–84, 188–89. Harry H. Lake, "History of the First National Bank of Central City and Joseph A. Thatcher," MS in Western History Department. Denver Public Library.

whose income averaged $50,000 a year, Chaffee was soon a figure in nearly every major mining, railroad, and land venture in the territory. With Bela M. Hughes and Moffat he is reputed to have started George M. Pullman on his way to fame and fortune.[13] Naturally the wealthy Chaffee was a welcome figure in local and national Republican Party circles.

Chaffee's career, almost more than any other, suggests the curious ability of the frontier entrepreneur to put a limited amount of money to extraordinary use, as well as to force the region itself to provide the collateral with which to develop itself. His stamp-mill profits led to successful mining ventures, which led to banking, which led to land speculation. Then the money from Maxwell Land Grant shares held by Chaffee's friend, the English promoter Wilson Waddingham, turned out to be the necessary capital with which General William J. Palmer was able to start the Denver and Rio Grande Railroad Company. Colorado was indeed a house built by able jacks of all trades.

By engaging in "phase capitalism," i.e. a method of making a profit on the actual process of Colorado's development, these men were soon the wealthy leaders of their community. Later they were called upon to invest in still more businesses—street railways, gas and water companies, and smaller industries—with the result that they had a strong voice in an extraordinary number of enterprises. Together they formed an impressive and highly successful frontier oligarchy, and all of them would have agreed with Calvin Coolidge that "the business of government is business."

Along the dangerous Smoky Hill route, where so many Pike's Peak argonauts came to grief between 1859 and 1861, the Kansas Pacific tracks inched their way westward in 1869. Forced to abandon the goal of a transcontinental system, its directors decided instead to tap the Colorado settlements. The line reached Denver in August 1870. The manager of the Kansas Pacific's construction work was William Jackson Palmer, a cultivated, imaginative, ambitious, briga-

13. Hall, *1*, 363–65. See also "Interview with Mrs. Fletcher Jordan" (n.d.), typescript in CSHS.

dier general from Delaware. Like Nathaniel P. Hill, Palmer was no rough and ready frontiersman. He was more in the tradition of the empire builder who made so much of the world's map British pink in the nineteenth century. Cecil Rhodes was more to Palmer's liking than Ceran St. Vrain or William Bent. At the same time, Palmer was also very much a general, a wielder of men, a captain of business, and a thorough planner.[14]

Palmer was only in his early forties when he came to Colorado, but he already had a fairly distinguished career behind him. In 1855, as a young railroad man in Pennsylvania, he had been sent to England to study railways and mines and to master the technical difficulties of coal-consuming locomotives. Upon his return Palmer put his knowledge of locomotives to use by forming the Westmoreland Coal Company. Palmer also served as the confidential secretary to J. Edgar Thomson, president of the Pennsylvania Railroad. After a Civil War career that resulted in his rise to the rank of a brigadier general, he became interested in the Eastern division of the Union Pacific Railroad. This interest was soon channeled into an ambitious project to build the Kansas Pacific—as it came to be called—along the 35th parallel via Raton, Albuquerque, and then due west. In 1867–68 Palmer actually conducted a survey for his line to California and in so doing became well acquainted with the Spanish Southwest. Palmer's papers suggest that early in his association with Western railroading he became interested in exploiting Spanish-Mexican land grants.[15] When the Kansas Pacific went to Denver instead, Palmer began to formulate his own railroad plans.

General Palmer shared with William Gilpin a sense of the striking physical beauty of Colorado. He, too, saw the region as unique, one that could be developed along certain distinct lines. Like Gilpin, Palmer was something of an amateur geopolitical scientist, for he was tremendously impressed by a 400-mile belt of semiaridity between the

14. "William Jackson Palmer" in *DAB*. See also George LaVerne Anderson, *General William J. Palmer: A Decade of Colorado Railroad Building, 1870–1880* (Colorado Springs, 1936); and John S. Fisher, *Builder of the West: The Life of General William Jackson Palmer* (Caldwell, Idaho, 1939).

15. Stone, 3, 5–7. Robert G. Athearn, *Rebel of the Rockies: A History of the Denver and Rio Grande* (New Haven and London, 1962), pp. 3–21.

farming communities of eastern Kansas and the Rocky Mountain settlements. To Palmer this meant that Colorado must exist as a separate economic region and achieve a certain amount of self-sufficiency. Thus Palmer fully expected that Colorado would have to grow its own food, service its local rail lines with its own coal, and run a large number of local industries. Here was an opportunity to adapt a railroad to the distinct needs of a regional community.

Palmer's truly regional concept has been somewhat obscured by the historian's fascination with his daring vision of a north–south railroad running from Denver to Mexico City—a line that would presumably tap the trade of the Santa Fe Trail, provide a Gulf outlet for Colorado (through a Texas branch line), and cross the several east–west railroads then in the process of completion. As impressive as this scheme was, it should be remembered that Palmer's interests were equally centered on the establishment of a local empire in Colorado which would reflect his social and cultural wishes as well as satisfy his railroad-building and money-making urges.

Even before Palmer formally organized the famous, narrow-gauge line called the Denver and Rio Grande, he had begun to buy up property around Pike's Peak. No less a personage than ex-Governor Alexander C. Hunt acted as his agent in these transactions. The property itself was destined to become Palmer's company town of Colorado Springs.[16] Nor was it long before Palmer had conceived a master plan that revealed both his ambitions and his love of ordered society. Confiding to a friend, he wrote:

I thought how fine it would be to have a little railroad a few hundred miles in length, all under one's own control with one's friends. . . . The workers would form a happy if somewhat large family which he would provide with schools, bathhouses, libraries, and lectures. Living in perfect understanding there would be no strikes or class strife. . . . My dream was not a new mode of making money, but of a large model way of conjoining that with usefulness on a large scale solving a good many vexed social problems.[17]

16. Athearn, pp. 13, 21, 36. See also Brayer, *William Blackmore*, 2, 17, 21.
17. Brayer, 2, 18–19.

Palmer's "little railroad" was first incorporated on February 1, 1870, under the name of the Rio Grande Railroad and Telegraph Company. Significantly, its incorporation notice was filed in New Mexico not Colorado, where that restless seconder of grand schemes, Governor William A. Pile, was joined by Judge Joseph Palen, Stephen B. Elkins, Thomas B. Catron, and U. S. Marshal John Pratt as investors. To represent the usual and highly necessary Eastern investors, Thomas Scott, S. M. Felton, and J. Edgar Thomson of the Pennsylvania Railroad were joined by Cyrus Field of New York and still others.[18] Obviously, since Palmer was a heavy investor in the Maxwell Land Grant Company and was its president in 1872, this early Rio Grande company was designed to develop the Grant and tap the Santa Fe trade.

Palmer soon had in mind, however, a plan for a line running along the eastern slope of the Rockies to Mexico City. For the time being, though, his activities were confined to purchasing—again through A. C. Hunt—the attractive right-of-way between Denver and Pueblo.[19] Palmer and Hunt moved none too soon, for the idea of tapping New Mexico and the Santa Fe trade and funneling it through Denver had become almost a fad for local railroad men. Governor E. M. McCook (1869–73), Hunt's successor in office, was busy trying to wheedle a land grant out of Congress for a "Colorado and New Mexico Railroad," a line to follow the Pecos Valley and then veer towards El Paso.[20]

McCook's failure to secure a grant left Palmer alone in the race. Rounding up locally wealthy men including (it is said) Gilpin and Wilson Waddingham, Palmer founded the Denver and Rio Grande Company with plans to build three roads: (1) from Denver to Pueblo; (2) a line to tap the mining regions of South Park; and (3) a spur to exploit and develop western Colorado. That same spring Palmer organized a fourth project by joining Miguel A. Otero and others in organizing a line that would run from the main trunk of the Kansas Pacific at Kit Carson, Colorado, to Fort Lyon and Pueblo. This road

18. Athearn, pp. 10 ff.
19. Brayer, 2, 26.
20. Ibid., p. 22.

would give him both an Eastern connection and the chance to replace the freighting and outfitting center of Kit Carson with his own end-of-track town on the Santa Fe trail.[21] This time, however, at least two other paper companies had the same scheme in mind. In Denver still another railroad combination had formed a north–south Denver and New Mexico Company.

The time had come for Palmer to build or lose the chance to create his own empire. On October 27, 1870, the Denver and Rio Grande incorporation papers were filed with the terriorial secretary of Colorado. The new company stated that it intended building to Pueblo. It would then cross into the San Luis Valley, where it would continue down the banks of the Rio Grande. Before building, nonetheless, Palmer went to England to study narrow-gauge railroads, since they were cheaper to build and maintain and seemed best fitted for the narrow mountain valleys common to Colorado. Palmer also needed English funds for the line. At the same time he and A. C. Hunt were avidly studying the land-development and colonizing projects of other rail lines.[22]

With these items mastered, Palmer and his associates, among whom was William Blackmore—promoter of the Costilla and Trinchera estates—Dr. William A. Bell, and many others, put into operation still another classical example of nineteenth-century railroad building. In imitation of the Union Pacific, Palmer created his own construction firms; first the North and South Construction Company and later the Union Contract Company. To develop land along the right of way, he created the National Land and Improvement Association. Still another subsidiary, the Colorado Springs Company, was used to develop the town as a resort; and when the railroad began to come near Pueblo, Palmer and his associates purchased the famous Nolan Grant, to be developed and exploited by the Denver and Rio Grande.[23]

Palmer also used the familiar threat and bribe technique employed by many lines who had much gall and little cash, i.e. he refused to build into a town unless the local county voted bonds to finance the

21. Athearn, pp. 15 ff. Brayer, 2, 29.
22. Athearn, p. 15.
23. Ibid., pp. 15–16, 23–25.

line. Thus the citizens of Pueblo were forced to issue bonds for the use of the Denver and Rio Grande only to discover that the company went straight past Pueblo to their own townsite of South Pueblo on the Nolan Grant. Later Palmer held up the citizens of Canon City and in 1876, the town of Trinidad in the same way.[24] The panic of 1873 left the Denver and Rio Grande in such severe financial straits that the road's second great expansion came after statehood, when it battled with the Atchison, Topeka, and Santa Fe for control of Raton Pass and later engaged in a local war for the right of way in the Royal Gorge in southern Colorado.

Palmer's methods, like those of so many nineteenth-century railway builders, often exhibited ruthless and cynical qualities. Nevertheless, he was influenced by a regional concept of a self-contained railroad empire, so that by the time Colorado became a state the Denver and Rio Grande dominated the southern counties. What was most impressive, though, was Palmer's technical knowledge of his domain. As a coal expert, he soon turned one of his development firms into the Colorado Coal and Iron Company; as a narrow gauge expert, he mastered the problem of getting railroads up the deep gulches to the remote mining towns; and since his road ran through sparsely populated ranching and arid lands, he did not count on passenger income. Finally, Palmer built his line without a Congressional grant of land; rather, he used the existing Mexican grants to organize his own land and colonization companies in the Arkansas Valley. Just as N. P. Hill was grappling with refractory ores, a scientific railroad captain had come to grips with the physiographical exigencies of the High Plains and Rockies.

Not all of Colorado's railroad enterprises were cast on a grand scale. In contrast to Palmer's design for empire—symbolized by his handsome, wide-streeted town of Colorado Springs and his impressive estate at Glen Eyrie—were the local politics of business surrounding the building of the Colorado Central Railroad. This line first ran from Denver to Golden, then to Black Hawk, and eventually to Central

24. Ibid., pp. 25-29.

City. Later it found an eastern connection by joining the Union Pacific at Cheyenne Junction, and stretched further into the mountains by climbing the steep canyons to tap the silver boom at Georgetown.[25]

Who were the builders of the Colorado Central, and what role did they play in the politics of business? From the beginning days of the territory, political factions in Golden and Central City had vied to bypass Denver, striving to make their own community the political capital as well as the outfitting center of Colorado. Headed by W. A. H. Loveland of Golden, the Golden Crowd contained men of real talent.[26] Most of the time the independent Alexander C. Hunt was in their camp; there, too, could be found the stern and impressive territorial Chief Justice Moses Hallett, who served on the court for ten years (1866–76).[27] In nearby Central City the Golden Crowd boasted the loyalty of Henry M. Teller, a lawyer and businessman from New York, who successfully fought the Evans-Chaffee statehood movement throughout the 1860s.[28]

The Golden-Denver feud took on added economic meaning in 1865, when Teller laid plans for a railroad from Denver to Golden and eventually to Central City. This line promised to make both towns supply centers for the extraordinary triangle of mining districts found in Clear Creek and Gilpin counties. So stubborn were the founders of the Colorado Central that when their line was built they declined to connect it with the Denver Pacific; even when the Union Pacific, which now owned the Denver Pacific, stepped in to make peace, the Central directors ignored the colossus.[29]

Meanwhile, Teller, as president of the Central, laid plans to build from Golden eastward to Julesburg, where he could connect to the Union Pacific. This accomplishment, had it been realized, would

25. See *Report of the Board of Directors of the Colorado Central Railroad* (Golden, 1873), pamphlet, YWA.

26. Hall, *4*, 496. Stone, *4*, 749–50.

27. "Moses Hallett" in *DAB*. Stone, *3*, 29–30. Byers, *Encyclopaedia, 1*, 199–200.

28. Ellis, *Teller*, pp. 80–85, gives the details of the railroad intrigues. See also *Rocky Mountain News*, October 2, 1862, and Central City *Register*, May 12, June 25, 1871. See also Thomas F. Dawson Scrapbooks in CSHS. Dawson was Teller's private secretary.

29. Ellis, *Teller*, pp. 80–85.

have hurt the Denver Pacific and would have bypassed Denver. Other plans called for a connection between the Denver and Rio Grande and the Colorado Central so that Denver would have been bypassed a second time![30] The Panic of 1873 called a halt to such spiteful competition, but it continued to affect local politics. The irony of it was that each of the companies involved eventually wound up in the hands of Eastern railroad magnates, who either abused the roads or used them as pawns in national games of high finance and speculation.

Connected with the East and a national market, however, Colorado boomed. Its population, aided by the attraction of new mineral discoveries in 1872 and the fabulous Leadville silver strike of 1877, increased so that by 1880 some 194,327 people lived there. Native production in sheep, cattle, wheat, gold, and silver generally increased six to eight times in value between 1870 and 1880.[31] Pueblo, once a minor Bent's Fort, was now a manufacturing town. Colorado Springs was a sophisticated resort, which Palmer hoped would be settled by the "better class" of people. Denver was, indeed, the vaunted emporium of the West; and on Central City and Georgetown streets the soft Welsh accents of imported miners rose and fell amidst the twang of American Yankees. The frontier was still there: saloons like the Golden Goose still thrived; soiled doves like wealthy Ruby Lee still plied their questionable trade; shootings still occurred; and the last Indian outbreak—the so-called Meeker Massacre of 1879—was still to come.

Yet every visitor after 1870 commented that Colorado was tame—so tame that one writer described Black Hawk as positively proper. Even in the smaller towns brick blocks were going up, and painted houses with lace curtains could be seen perched above the maze of cabins, pits, tunnel openings, and water ditches which crosshatched every gold- and silver-bearing canyon. The mining towns of Colorado were American in character and spirit. They prided themselves on their opera houses, their schools, their newspapers, their churches, and their devotion to fire prevention. They forced the observance of

30. *Report of Colorado Central*, 1873. See also McMechan, *Evans*, pp. 145 ff.
31. Brayer, 2, 263–65.

Sunday closing for businesses and very soon sent the saloon men below the social salt. Said one visitor:

> The Clear Creek towns were known throughout the mountains for their relative sobriety and want of violence. Society here early acquired "tone" as mine managers, doctors, lawyers, merchants and others of substance brought their families, their crystal and china, their fine linens and furniture to establish homes in Black Hawk and Central City.[32]

Psychologically, Central City, Denver, and all of northern Colorado had been in the Union and part of the nation ever since blue-coated General Larimer had first called a railroad meeting to order in Denver City in 1859.

Through local political and military action, scientific and engineering feats, and clever manipulation of borrowed monies, Coloradans had partly solved their basic transportation problem, were tackling their mining difficulties, and were now pushing into the agricultural and ranching industries. All this had been done by 1870. Still many problems and issues remained before statehood could become a certainty.

Among the continuing difficulties was the Indian question, since various bands of Plains Indians continued to raid stage stations and outlying ranches. The treaties signed in 1865 and 1867 with these Indians were not observed, and in 1867 the attacks became so severe on the Platte and Smoky Hill routes that Governor Hunt wired General William T. Sherman for immediate help. Regular troops under General Hancock, augmented by local volunteers, overawed the Indians, but only temporarily, for they renewed the raids in 1868. That fall, warriors under Roman Nose actually held a group of army men and scouts at bay for nine days until rescue forces saved the survivors, on what has come to be known as Beecher's Island. The last Indian battle in eastern Colorado did not take place until 1869,

32. Oliver Henkel, "Central City," MS seminar paper, Yale University, 1957.

when Tall Bull and fifty followers were killed in a pitched encounter.[33]

Since sporadic Indian outbreaks were still occurring all over the West in the late 1860s, it is not surprising to learn that the Coloradans feared that a coordinated effort on the part of the Utes and Plains tribes might wipe out white settlements. Such a rumor led Governor Hunt to end half of the threat at least, by persuading all the Utes in Colorado to sign a treaty in 1868 that put them west of the Continental Divide.[34] For this accomplishment the territory was properly grateful. Hunt's very success in Indian affairs led to his downfall, however. The treaty he made provided for the payment of considerable amounts of goods and monies to the ceding bands. Here was an attractive business to the patronage-minded politician. Almost immediately after Grant's inauguration in 1869, General Edward M. McCook, one of four brothers who became famous during the Civil War as the Fighting McCooks, appeared in Denver as the new governor. Before long it was evident that McCook was interested not so much in governing as in Indian contracts for annuity goods.

McCook was no newcomer to Colorado; he had been a pioneer in the Pike's Peak Rush and had been elected to the Kansas legislature in 1860 by frontier miners. Undoubtedly he already knew the political situation in Colorado and appears to have cooperated with Teller and members of the Golden clique.[35] McCook's success at garnering Indian beef contracts angered former Delegate George M. Chilcott and the Denver postmaster, Hiram P. Bennet, who were also in the beef supply business and who had usually obtained the government orders. The evidence strongly suggests that McCook—who was an old friend of Grant's Secretary of War, Belknap—had his own Indian ring in operation. Friendly contractors, interpreters, and agents worked with the Governor. McCook's own brother-in-law, James B. Thompson—who was also his private secretary and a special agent to the Utes—handled the details of the business.[36] McCook himself

33. Grinnell, *Fighting Cheyennes,* pp. 254–98.
34. Denver *Post,* May 7, 1920.
35. Hall, *1,* 467–68; *2,* 155–57.
36. See the colorful and pithy correspondence of Thompson in Letters of James B. Thompson, 1871–1874, MSS in Western History Department, Denver Public Library.

had herds in southern Colorado, speculated in lands there, and tried to get into the Maxwell Land Grant organization. He had a finger in railroad projects that threatened both the Denver Pacific and the Rio Grande lines. The whole McCook approach was aptly summed up in a letter from Agent Thompson to his younger brother, Sam, back East, in which the latter was promised a post under a friendly Indian agent. "If you make yourself useful to him," said the elder Thompson, "you can feather your nest."[37] Sam was soon at work in his new post.

The Chaffee forces were at first hampered in their opposition to McCook's regime by the fact that the Colorado delegate in 1869-71 was Allan A. Bradford, who had been an antistate leader in 1865 and who had never cooperated closely with the Evans-Chaffee set. In 1870, however, Chaffee himself was elected delegate, so that the anti-McCook forces at last had a strong voice in Washington. Through detective work carried out by Samuel Elbert and David Moffat, Jr., it was revealed that McCook had bought cattle at $7.50 a head and had sold them to the government at $35 or $40 a head. On one occasion the Governor had made a net profit of $23,000.[38] Such facts, plus Chaffee's high standing in national Republican circles, finally persuaded Grant to replace McCook in 1873 with Evans' son-in-law, Samuel H. Elbert (1873-74). At last the road seemed clear for the Denver Crowd to achieve statehood on their own terms.

Two could play at the game of accusation and charges of corrupt practices, however. In retaliation, McCook informed Grant that Elbert's appointment had placed a Colorado land-stealing ring in power. It appears that Elbert, Chaffee, and Moffat together had seized certain public lands in southern Colorado, and they had recorded their claims in a midnight session with the Bent County clerk, much to the consternation of Mexicans and others living on the property.[39] McCook went on to tell the President that these activities were all part of an effort to grab land ahead of a soon-to-be-built railroad. Aided by reports of federal investigators who did find evidence of irregularity, McCook was able to convince Grant that the accusation

37. James B. Thompson to Sam Thompson, May 21, 1872, Thompson Letters.
38. Hall, 2, 164-68.
39. Ibid., 4, 160-63.

was true. Angered at what he considered misrepresentation and deception, Grant summarily removed Elbert on January 27, 1874, after he had been in office less than a year. To replace Elbert the President reappointed the unpopular McCook (1874–75).

This act cause "consternation in the royal household," as McCook's secretary sarcastically described Delegate Chaffee's reception of the news.[40] Walter Cheesman and David Moffat, Jr., who were sworn enemies of McCook, immediately boarded a train for Washington to protest, while Chaffee, absolutely furious at Elbert's removal, declared he would defeat McCook's confirmation in Congress. The struggle that followed had some of the elements of opera bouffe. Here was a mere delegate, without so much as a vote in Congress, making war upon Grant—a delegate who at the same time wanted statehood and who aspired to be a senator! It must be admitted that Chaffee made a heroic fight. He used all his Eastern connections, and he organized the other Southwestern delegates, Elkins of New Mexico and McCormick of Arizona, into a battle team. Although he lost the war, he had the pleasure of knowing that McCook was reconfirmed by a margin of only one vote.[41]

This was only the first act of the comedy, for Elbert, Moffat, and others renewed their efforts to ferret out more information about McCook's Indian contracts. They were joined by H. P. Bennet, the Denver postmaster whose position the McCook forces wanted. Suddenly the Governor began having trouble with his mail. All kinds of strange items appeared in his box. Wrote McCook's secretary irately: "It has become a bore to me to take out of our Box, and return to the general receptacle letters and papers addressed to Dr. McCormick, R. R. Mc——, Ed McClintock; John S. McCool, and David C. Cook."[42] Thompson's and McCook's ire was kept at fever heat by attacks in the *Rocky Mountain News,* the *Times,* and the *Register,* papers owned respectively by Byers, Elbert, and Hall.[43]

The controversy over McCook was heightened by the delegate election of 1874. In a many-cornered fight the Republicans split: one

40. James Thompson to McCook, February 2, 1874, Thompson Letters.
41. Chaffee to Elbert, January 7, 1874 (telegram), CSHS.
42. Thompson to McCook, January 26, 1873, Thompson Letters.
43. Thompson to McCook, April 13, 1874, Thompson Letters.

wing renominated Chaffee while the other chose a former Illinois congressman, H. P. H. Bromwell. The Democrats, seeing a chance to break the Republican stranglehold on Colorado, bypassed the older battle-scarred members to select Thomas M. Patterson, an eloquent Irish-born lawyer for their candidate. At the same time, the older Democrats—many of them with Southern backgrounds—so disliked the seizure by Northern leaders of their party that they persuaded Colonel A. G. Boone of Booneville to run on an independent party ticket. Bitter indeed was the campaign that resulted in the defeat of Colorado's master politician, Chaffee, and the election of Patterson.

Regardless of the outcome of the delegate election it was soon clear that McCook simply would not be accepted as governor. Grant, finally seeing the futility of fighting the wishes of Coloradans, declared a plague on both political wings of the Republicans and appointed John L. Routt, a plain-spoken, square-built Civil War veteran. The new Governor had been a sheriff and a United States marshal before becoming second assistant postmaster general in 1872.[44] He left this position in February 1875 to become the last territorial governor of Colorado. Keenly aware of the schisms and controversies, paralyzing the Republican party in Colorado, Routt set out to unite the ranks and to lobby with Chaffee and others for statehood. His intelligent efforts were rewarded by his election as the first governor of the new state of Colorado in 1876.

The last statehood movement really began when Jerome B. Chaffee was elected delegate in 1870; but little progress was made until 1872. In December of that year he had pleaded Colorado's cause before the House Committee on Territories; and although the Committee's reaction that year was unfavorable, Chaffee persisted.[45] Meanwhile, local newspaper sentiment was being organized to make admission seem popular. In 1873 Grant himself was wined and dined in Colorado; and when in Central City, he walked over a silver brick sidewalk from his carriage to the Teller House. The bricks must have had their desired effect, for in January 1874 he recommended that the territory

44. Hall, *4*, 547.
45. John M. Buchanan, "The History of a Ghost Town, Caribou," *CM*, *21* (1944), 204.

be made a state. By June the House had passed an enabling act, but the Senate tabled it along with a New Mexican statehood bill for which Delegate Elkins, Chaffee's New Mexican business and political crony, had worked so hard. The failure to secure admission in 1874 was seconded by Chaffee's defeat in the delegate election that fall, but before his retirement from office he introduced another enabling act in early 1875. Through various adroit maneuvers, he was able to push it through both houses, and Grant signed it in March 1875.[46]

Back in Colorado, the statehood advocates moved forward much more cautiously and in broader manner than they had previously. They knew that the United States Senate was hostile and that Chaffee's enabling act had passed the upper house only after Senator Edmunds of Vermont had postponed the time for ratification until 1876. Another Vermonter, Congressman Morrill of the House, had evinced a similar hostility to admission.

Sobered by such opposition, the *Boulder News* urged the territory to elect nonpartisan delegates to the constitutional convention slated to meet in the fall of 1875. The Denver *Daily Tribune* also called for a "Constitutional Association" to make sure Coloradans would have a good organic act.[47] Nevertheless, when the voters went to the polls they chose their men on a party basis. The Republicans claimed 24 of the 39 seats, and the Democrats controlled the remainder.[48]

The delegates themselves hardly resembled frontiersmen; and if their origins suggested certain attitudes, then this was an extraordinary assemblage indeed. No less than fifteen of the delegates were from Pennsylvania, and the majority of the rest were from New York or the Midwest. Two were from Germany, two from England, and one was from Canada. Their occupations were varied: fifteen were lawyers, and among the rest were a scattering of bankers, merchants, ranchers, and farmers. Most of them had good educational backgrounds, and at least one was a temperance advocate. Several listed their religion

46. Hafen, "Steps to Statehood," p. 109. The Enabling Act is reprinted in *Proceedings of the Constitutional Convention . . . to Frame a Constitution for the State of Colorado* (Denver, 1907), pp. 9–13.
47. Denver *Daily Tribune*, February 17, 1875.
48. Hershey, "Colorado Constitution," p. 70.

merely as "liberal," which, it was later revealed, meant that they were anticlerical.[49]

A certain flavor of the old and the new permeated the Odd Fellows Hall in Chaffee's First National Bank Building—the convention meeting place. Side by side with Lafayette Head, the former Indian agent, and John S. Hough—a California pioneer and frontier forwarding merchant who had traded over the Santa Fe Trail—sat H. P. H. Bromwell, the scholarly and learned former Illinois congressman. The legislators respectfully dubbed Bromwell the Orthodox Blackstone of the convention. There inevitably could be found the defenders of the Spanish-Americans, Casimiro Barela, J. M. Garcia, and Agapito Vigil. The delegation was also interesting for the number of Republican leaders who were missing. Not Evans, Chaffee, Chilcott, Teller, Loveland, Bradford, or a single ex-delegate or governor was in the convention. With the exception of Judge Wilbur F. Stone, Henry C. Thatcher, Barela, and Head, it tended to be a new generation of local political figures. One Denver paper explained that it was the "new crowd" as opposed to the "old crowd."

The delegates convened in Mr. Chaffee's building amidst depressing conditions. The Panic of 1873 had halted a new surge of expansion in railroads and mining, and its effects were now being felt by everyone in Colorado.[50] A mercantile firm caught the tenor of the times by its ad:

> Hard Times! Of Course! And the prices of everthing seem affected, and yet trade is brisk at the O.K. Store, why? Because A. Jacobs & Co. knowing that the people have not much money to spend, have since the holidays marked their goods down.

The territory had also suffered a severe locust plague, and as a result of hard times and seemingly high prices—especially in freight rates—echoes of the Granger movement could be heard in the convention, where several recent emigrants from Illinois—then a center of Granger agitation—sat as delegates.

49. Biographies of each delegate were printed in the *Daily Tribune*, February 14, 1876.
50. Hershey, "Colorado Constitution," pp. 69–70.

Finally, the convention was troubled occasionally by memories of the Civil War. Two former Confederates, one from Georgia and one from Kentucky, who were described as very much "Southern gentlemen," unhappily found themselves the colleagues of two bitter Union veterans who had suffered confinement in Libby Prison.[51] Such were the national, local, and emotional factors that went into the creation of a constitution for Colorado.

The many difficulties facing the convention in the fall and winter of 1875–76 led its members—who were independent and frequently liberal-minded—to move cautiously. The first major issue to face them was cultural and religious: a petition from a group of citizens requesting that churches and all ecclesiastical property be taxed, that no chaplains in prison be paid out of public monies, and that there be neither public appropriation for sectarian charity nor any official recognition of religious festivals and feasts. The petitioners also demanded that the Bible not be used in schools, even as literature. Finally, the petition asked an end to Sabbath closing laws and the passage of acts on the basis of "natural" rather than Christian morality.[52] This bombshell provoked a wide discussion in the papers and led both the Protestant and Catholic clergy of Denver to protest.

Yet a surprising number of delegates appear to have approved the petition, so that the issue was not a sham one. Lafayette Head, in reporting an early version of the preamble, left out all reference to God. The real focus of the anticlerical attack, however, seems to have been the Catholic Church and parochial schools, for the issue soon centered around a debate over whether or not church schools should be supported by public funds. When Bishop Joseph P. Machebeuf, Lamy's former Vicar General in Santa Fe, appealed to the convention for such support, the reaction was so severely unfavorable that Machebeuf himself retreated to requesting merely that the constitution allow future assemblies the power to allocate public funds for private schools. Even so, the convention adopted a firm separation of Church and State clause in its reference to school funds. In summarizing

51. *Daily Tribune,* February 14, 1876. Colin B. Goodykoontz, "Some Controversial Questions before the Colorado Constitutional Convention of 1876," *CM, 17* (1940), 4.
52. *Colorado Proceedings,* pp. 83–85.

Colo convention issues- art'cler.
people vs development

these fights, Donald Hensel has written: "The educational and religious disputes . . . revealed that the main social cleavage in Colorado cut between the English-speaking residents of the North, and
the Spanish-speaking citizens of the South. The division was aggravated because the former were mostly Protestant while the latter
were preponderantly Catholic."[53]

The next major issue faced by the Colorado founding fathers was
the most basic of the entire convention: reconciling a desire to promote and encourage "an immediate expansion in economic activity"
by writing a document on the one hand pleasing to business and
capital, and, on the other, with an equally ardent endeavor to protect
the public from robber barons, corporate fleecings and the like.[54]
Colorado wrote its organic law at a watershed in economic history.
The gilded age of big business and railroads was coming into its
own in such a brawling rambunctious way that the acts of the new
titans had already prompted economic and political protests and
calls for reform. Colorado rested on the horns of a dilemma, for the
infant state was still in need of railroads and capital; and yet it
wanted to curb abuses and lash out at the high freight rates, plaguing
its citizens.

The leader of the so-called Granger element in the convention was
H. P. H. Bromwell, who had been a member of the Illinois Constitutional Convention of 1870. Already familiar with Granger legislation,
Bromwell wanted the new state to give its supreme court original
jurisdiction over railroad controversies and to have the right to order
and decree just and reasonable rates.[55] While such measures met
with popular reception, they greatly alarmed the established entrepreneurs of Colorado. Byers, Evans, Moffat, and a delegation of
some fifty businessmen petitioned the convention not to frighten
capital, with the result that Bromwell's proposals were lost in a vote
of the committee of the whole.[56]

When the economic debates were over, Coloradans found that

53. Ibid., pp. 102–08, 112–13, 235–36, 329, 687. Goodykoontz, "Controversial
Questions," p. 4. Hensel, "Colorado Constitution," p. 215.
54. Ibid., pp. 1–5.
55. Hershey, "Colorado Constitution," p. 70. Goodykoontz, "Controversial Questions," pp. 10–12.
56. Goodykoontz, p. 12.

their constitution-makers had chosen a middle way so typical of the region itself. No corporation was to be created by special law; all railroads were to be public highways; the railroad companies were to be common carriers; all persons and corporations were to have equal rights in dealing with railroads; and the legislature was to have the power to revoke any law injurious to the new state. In general, however, Colorado incorporation and business laws were favorable to capital. Mines were not to be taxed for a certain number of years, and state aid for scientific investigation and development of the mining industry was stipulated.[57]

The convention also pursued the same cautious course with the explosive subject of woman's suffrage. Governor Routt, usually a man of few words and conservative tastes, turned out to be a strong advocate of female suffrage. Nor would outside groups allow the delegates to deliberate in peace. Massachusetts and Missouri female suffrage associations called upon them to be the first to give woman her rightful place. Eloquent arguments were presented after posing the loaded question: "Would not the ballot be safer in the hands of intelligent, cultivated and refined women than in the possession of ignorant male imbeciles, brutal drunkards, and degraded saloon bums and lunch fiends."[58]

With a small but noisy set of lobbyists and agitators crusading for the housewife, the convention could not escape taking a position. After much debate they agreed that women might vote in school elections and even hold school offices, but would do nothing further except to permit the General Assembly to allow women to vote at any future time.

One other question, basically Eastern in character, cropped up to bother the lawgivers. A forest culture clause was proposed, which would have protected the forests of Colorado from exploitation and would have, in effect, initiated a local conservation system. Although it was seriously considered, the proposal was lost.

The more regional issues centered around irrigation and mining. Delegate Byron M. Carr pled that the ownership of waters in all

57. Ibid., p. 13.
58. Ibid., pp. 13–16.

natural streams be allowed to remain in state hands and be subject to control of the legislature, which could redistribute their disposal from time to time. The final result, however, was a relatively weak irrigation law.[59] At least some system was devised, nonetheless, for domestic users of water were allowed prior right, and agricultural demands were placed above those of manufacturers where water was concerned.

The convention looked both ways at mining. Aware of the need to stimulate that industry, the delegates gave it a temporary tax exemption. At the same time, they were aware of the large-scale industry coming to the state, so they created the position of a mining commissioner with vague regulatory powers. He was to enforce proper ventilation standards and to see that mines did not employ child labor under twelve years of age. Finally, they provided for a school of mines under the patronage of the state.[60]

In structuring the state government, the delegates were again compelled by considerations of the hour. Vivid memories of Governor Cummings' arrogance and of McCook's cynical peculations led the convention to reduce the powers of the executive impressively. One authority has observed, that the chief executive was "denied the initiative and freedom essential to vigorous leadership."[61] It is interesting to note that virtually every new state that had undergone the territorial experience had reacted in a similar way by clipping gubernatorial wings.

The most impressive thing about the Colorado document was its imitation and acceptance of existing American political ideas and forms. Donald Hensel has commented that "except for the promulgation of irrigation law, the legal and constitutional declarations were slightly altered clauses conveyed from well-settled areas. The pioneers of Colorado felt no compulsion to chisel new law from mountain granite."[62] Pleased with their labors and excited by their future, the constitution-makers got the public to ratify their document in July 1876, by a vote of some 15,000 to 4,000. On August 24, 1876,

59. Ibid., pp. 16–17. *Colorado Proceedings,* p. 700.
60. *Colorado Proceedings,* p. 700.
61. Hensel, "Colorado Constitution," p. 133.
62. Ibid., pp. 1–5.

Acting Secretary of State John Cadwalader verified the fact that all requirements had been met. After sixteen hectic years as a territory, William Bent's former fur trade empire was in the Union.

It remained for Colorado to organize a state government and elect senators and congressmen. The Republicans chose the safe and sane John Routt to be governor, while the pioneer Indian agent Lafayette Head was nominated for the lieutenant governorship. Chaffee was unanimously conceded a Senate seat. In a bitter fight Teller won the other Senate seat, despite the determined opposition of Nathaniel P. Hill and Henry R. Wolcott.[63] For congressman the Republicans chose colorful James B. Belford, nicknamed the Red-headed Rooster of the Rockies because of his crowing speeches. Heartened by the election of Thomas Patterson as delegate in 1874, the Democrats now put him up for Congress, while nominating Bela M. Hughes, the pioneer director of the Overland Stage, for governor. Even given the popularity of the local Democrats and the strong showing of that party in the national elections in 1876, the outcome in Colorado was largely a Republican victory.

The Republican success in achieving statehood and office at the same time coincided with a victory of another kind. In 1876 prospectors working high in the Rockies finally realized that the heavy blue sand that had so hampered their mining of gold in California Gulch was actually silver carbonate. Overnight a new rush began, and by 1877 Leadville was one of the most fabulous mining towns in the West.[64] With that boom railroads began expanding again, and new industries started up.

As one heard opera in Central City, found millionaires strolling in Leadville, listened to the noise of factories in Pueblo, or watched gold, silver, coal, and iron ore being extracted, the frontier seemed a dozen years away. Yet Colorado's citizens were to learn that the region was not yet self-sufficient and that the state was still economically at the beck and call of Eastern financiers. Already Colorado railroads were coming under the control of Jay Gould and other

63. Hall, *Colorado*, 2, chaps. 15–16.
64. Paul, *Mining Frontiers*, pp. 127–313.

Robber Barons, and its silver miners would one day turn Populist in protest.

Thus it was that a strange paradox of the old and new existed in Colorado in 1876. The mining, ranching, farming, and industrial frontier stages were roled into one and functioned simultaneously. It was a commentary on Colorado's fast rise to statehood—which was in turn a commentary upon the nature of its settlers—that before the Indian problem had been solved, Governor Pitkin was forced to declare martial law in Leadville, "not because of any Indian menace, but because of a miners' strike for higher wages and shorter hours."[65]

Utes, Spanish-Americans, Santa Fe traders, border-state Southerners, Welsh miners, and Union veterans now all lived under a constitution borrowed from Pennsylvania and Illinois. The region they inhabited was crisscrossed by railroads that had been promoted by English brokers, and financed by Dutch bankers. Meanwhile, Texans like Charles Goodnight and German-Americans like Colonel Pfeiffer ranched on Mexican land grants in the southern counties, while whole colonies of settlers from New York, Chicago, and St. Louis settled at Longmont and Greeley. Colorado was indeed a frontier melting pot.

The Colorado territorial experience from 1861 to 1876 was typical in a number of ways. The early gold rush itself resembled that of California. "All the conditions of a newly occupied *gold country,* as in California, re-occur here," wrote Gilpin in 1861. In creating local government the Colorado argonauts borrowed precedents both from the California mining camps and districts, and from squatter sovereignty practices common in the Mississippi Valley during the 1850s.

Familiar methods were also employed in Indian-white relations. Gilpin warned the authorities in Washington in 1861 that existing laws regulating Indian tribes were inapplicable to the mobile Indians of the Great Plains and the Rocky Mountains.[66] Nevertheless, in the

---

65. Dudley Taylor Cornish, "The First Five Years of Colorado's Statehood, 1878–1881," *CM,* 25 (1948), 183.

66. William Gilpin to the Indian Commissioner, June 19, 1861, Interior Department, OIA, Colorado.

end the government pursued two alternating policies: either feeding them until they became dependent or fighting them until the tribes were reduced in strength and had to go onto small reserves. Like most Americans the migrants to Colorado chose to see the Indian question as temporary, and they believed that the chastisement given the Indians at Sand Creek in 1864 was necessary. They also believed in, and insisted on, Indian removal.

Colorado territorial government itself exhibited patterns of development that could be found in many other territories. By and large the federal appointees were far more able men than those normally sent to the territories. But all the Colorado officials were as much businessmen as politicians and consequently used the powers of government to develop the territory—and their own fortunes—in every way. Of the eight men who served as governor, at least four were major land speculators, and Governor McCook was rumored to be the largest landowner in Colorado. All the officials were keenly interested in railroads and mining. Seen as a group, the careers of the federal officers were so similar that the men themselves formed a local oligarchy of entrepreneur politicians.[67]

The origins of the seven governors, six secretaries, fourteen judges, and five delegates of Colorado reveal an even more strikingly uniform pattern. Except for a single delegate, all thirty-two men appear to have been native born, and more than 80 per cent were from the Midwest, New York, or Pennsylvania. A majority of them had also gained experience on other frontiers before coming to Colorado. Five out of the six governors had either lived in Nebraska, Illinois, Missouri, or Kansas, as had four of the delegates and six of the secretaries. They followed, therefore, the classical frontier pattern of migrating westward one state at a time. Both politically and culturally they appear to have been a homogeneous group.

Political party growth in Colorado also exhibited some traditional frontier traits. Given the prospect of federal patronage, aid to railroads, and helpful mining laws, a majority of the pioneers soon declared their loyalty to the party in control of the national government. Since the Republican Party was dominant in Washington from 1861

67. The major territorial officers are listed in Pomeroy, *Territories*, pp. 124–25.

to 1876, Colorado's political complexion also became Republican during those years.

With a majority of citizens claiming to be in one party, political strife naturally took the form of intraparty struggles and revolved around fights over desirable offices, conflicts of personality and economic interest, and control of patronage. Often the fight was merely geographic i.e. members from a southern section of the territory demanded that the northern section share political and economic spoils. In pursuing the politics of economic development it was all important to a section to obtain a railroad, government-built roads, post offices, and the like. Thus the territorial political contests, wrote Governor Elbert, took place among the officials and legislators rather than between them and the public.[68]

Republican dominance between 1861 and 1876 meant that the Colorado Democratic Party had rough sledding. That party was sustained by shrewd Democrats working through Republican officers, by migrants to Colorado who brought with them their Democratic Party loyalty, or by a major political opportunity presented them when the Republicans occasionally split into two warring factions. Yet in the fifteen years that Colorado was a territory, the Democrats elected only one delegate. Many of the Democrats were from Missouri, Kentucky, and the South and had to carry the brand of Copperhead through most of the territorial period. A majority of them lived in southern Colorado, and so localist were they in their views that they not only fought the Denver-Republican oligarchy, but often opposed Democrats from northern Colorado.

Ever since Andrew Jackson became president in 1828, historians have made much of the rise of "a western man" who held unique political views, reflecting the influence of his frontier origins. In a study of the attitudes of Colorado delegates toward public questions, Bernard O. J. Linnevold has found that only Delegate Hiram Bennet had truly Western views. On the other hand, he found that all the Colorado delegates were ardent localists and that all of the legislation they sought from Congress was to aid territorial development. Provincial economic needs, rather than political principle, guided

68. Elbert, "Public Men."

their actions. Indeed, their actions were so inconsistent, Linnevold has noted, that "one is forced to conclude they desired to use Congress as a football to be kicked about as their interests required."[69]

Colorado's judicial system, unlike New Mexico's, was generally competent and professional. This had to be the case where the disposition of such valuable claims and properties was concerned. Thus wild decisions and civil and criminal vigilante action were not so common in the future Centennial State. Judge Benjamin F. Hall (1861–64), for example, successfully persuaded the miners that they must respect decisions made when Colorado was still under Kansas and Nebraska law. By this tack the court established continuity and precedent covering nearly all phases of the gold rush.

Later, Chief Justice Moses Hallett (1866–76) boldly faced the question of adjusting traditional American laws to the needs of a mining society and to the Western environment. He did so with such competence that he played a large part in shaping early mining law for the entire West.[70] Hallett and his colleagues also restricted the jurisdiction of English common law and modified the doctrine of riparian rights. Nevertheless, these changes and those in mining law did not constitute a legal and institutional revolution. Similarly, no major revolutionary change occurred in the operation of local government in Colorado, although county courts replaced probate courts when the 1876 constitution was adopted.[71]

Still it would be wrong to say that Colorado was a typical Western territory in every way. Questions such as the separation of Church, and State and the maintenance of a public school system—as opposed to state-supported parochial schools—produced a real crisis in the constitutional convention of 1875 and among Spanish-American citizens. The issues reminded Coloradans that they were on the borderlands of another culture and shared problems with neighboring New Mexico. Territorial politics and party structure were complicated, too, by the presence of this cultural minority. Even the most pro-

69. Linnevold, "Delegate Attitudes," p. 127.
70. "Moses Hallett" in *DAB*. Stone, *Colorado, 3*, 29–30.
71. Dubbs, "Unfolding of Law," *CM, 3* (1926), 118–32. See also Fritz, *Colorado,* 245–67.

gressive Anglo-American leaders could not resist dabbling in Spanish-Mexican land claims.

In their attempts to exploit these land claims and related railroad, mining, and ranching projects, Colorado public and business leaders actually joined in a regional effort with New Mexican leaders to realize a profit. Men like Gilpin, Palmer, Evans, Chaffee, and Moffat went even further to conceive of a rgeional empire, a regional economy, and ways they could tap both the Spanish Southwest right down to Mexico City and the intermountain West right through Utah. During the territorial period, then, the destinies of Colorado and New Mexico often seemed intertwined. It was not mere coincidence that Chaffee and Elkins, both of the Maxwell Land Grant Company, should become territorial delegates at the same time and seek statehood for their constituencies in the same years. Nor was it accident that General Palmer should be president of the Maxwell Company and founder of the Denver and Rio Grande Railroad, while his partner, A. C. Hunt, served as governor of Colorado. Finally, it was not caprice on the part of Washington that once the Court of Private Land Claims was organized, it met not in Santa Fe but in Denver. The activities of all these men not only gave new meaning to the "internal, central plateau policy" about which Thomas Benton had talked in the 1840s, but turned a part of the Great American Desert into the Centennial State.

Part Three

Deseret and Utah
1847–1858

And I will bring you in unto the land, concerning which I did swear to give it to Abraham, to Isaac, and Jacob; and I will give it to you for an heritage.

Exodus 6:4, 8

For Deseret is emphatically a New Country; new in its own characteristic features, newer still in its bringing together the most inconsistent peculiarities of other countries.

Thomas Leiper Kane
"Discourse on the Mormons," 1850

 On a threatening cloudy day in late June 1844 a swirling mob of men with blackened faces surrounded the stone jailhouse in Carthage, Illinois. In a single charge they overpowered the jailer and burst into an upper floor cell, where they killed one prisoner, wounded another, and fatally shot a third as he leaped from a window. Amidst curses and cries of "Kill him! Kill him!" Joseph Smith, the third man, died in a heap before the murderous mob of Illinois militiamen.[1]

Although a shaft of sunlight broke through glowering skies to fall upon Joseph Smith's dead body—overawing some of the more super-

1. Fawn M. Brodie, *No Man Knows My History: The Life of Joseph Smith* (New York, 1945), pp. 389–97.

stitious in the crowd around the jail—most of the participants went home that evening thinking they had rid Illinois of a religious imposter, a political demagogue, a person of libidinous tastes, and a utopian with socialist inclinations. Yet by killing Joseph Smith, the Vermont farmer's son who founded the Church of Jesus Christ of the Latter Day Saints, the mob inadvertently provided the young sect with two martyrs—for Joseph's brother Hyrum had also died at Carthage. Their deaths engendered a strong sense of group persecution in a loosely allied religious body. The feeling of persecution eventually gave the organization a closed-rank unity. Equally important, their martyrdom permitted the Latter Day Saints to select a new and more practical leader than Smith. Unknowingly, the mob had set in motion a chain of events that would result in the occupation and settlement of the northernmost barren lands of the Old Spanish Empire: the Great Basin Frontier.

What had the popular, blue-eyed Joseph Smith, leader of some 30,000 believers in 1844, done to merit such a grim end? If one looked to Smith's religious teachings, the answer was only partly visible. Although he claimed to be the latest of the Biblical prophets and brought an extraordinary set of messages and revelations to his believers, on the surface his teachings were neither revolutionary nor violent. Briefly, Joseph as a young man living in western New York claimed to have had a series of visions and revelations, beginning in 1823. In these visitations God—through the agency of the Angel Moroni—led Joseph to discover the true history of the Church of Christ. According to Smith, the history had been inscribed on a set of golden plates, buried near Palmyra, New York, until the correct time for their revelation should come. Claiming to be the divine instrument of the restored Church, Smith said that he not only had found the plates but had been empowered to translate them, by means of a set of magical lenses or peepstones, from the reformed Egyptian in which they were written. The eventual result of a slow verbal translation called out over a screen to Oliver Cowdery, a New England school master and convert, was the famous *Book of Mormon* published in 1830.[2]

2. Ibid., pp. 53 ff.

The Book of Mormon itself was but one foundation stone in the ideological edifice of Joseph Smith's new church. It was supplemented by further revelations—well over a hundred in number—to Joseph in his capacity as a Prophet and Seer. In turn these were supplemented by collected teachings and doctrines published under the titles *The Book of Doctrines and Covenants* and the *Pearl of Great Price*. The three works, coupled with a continuing reverence and acceptance of the *Old* and *New Testaments*, formed the theological basis for the Church of the Latter Day Saints of Jesus Christ.

The rather extraordinary origins of the new sect, with its revelations, visions, and golden plates, persuaded most men to remain skeptical, and many proclaimed Mormonism altogether absurd. Nevertheless, there was little in Smith's religion to offend a public which throughout the 1830s was indulging in mysticism, setting up socialist utopias at New Harmony, Indiana, and engaging in mass religious revivals featuring trances and visions. Joseph Smith's appearance as a religious leader coincided roughly with the rise of Shakerism, the flourishing of the Rappites, and the practice of communal experiments by the Campbellites. More generally, the acceptance of emotional evangelistic preaching, stemming from the Kentucky revivals and prompting the rise of a whole body of uneducated ministers, placed Joseph Smith in a context that made him seem far less extraordinary than he might appear today.

If one turned from the origins of Mormonism to its known beliefs and general philosophy, it was equally hard to discern the cause of Joseph Smith's death. Smith, for example, held that man was by nature a good person, whom God would one day reward by sending Christ to reign on earth. In this belief Smith embraced both an acceptable American doctrine of progress and the recurring surge of millennial hopes—hopes that were to reach a high point in 1844, the year William Miller and his followers predicted that the world would end.

Smith's religion also offered answers to questions that troubled many an American. In the *Book of Mormon* and later revelations he suggested the origin of the Indians, gave reasons why the American continent was not mentioned in the *Bible*, and explained the fate of the lost tribes of Israel. He also dwelt at length on the nature of heaven, the ultimate allegiance in the next life of a widow who remarries in this one, and a host of other such questions. Moreover, Smith in his writings salvaged much of the familar Apocrypha which scholars were then excising from official versions of the Bible. Many Americans agreed with Smith in thinking that the Apocrypha contained great truths, which must not be ignored.[3]

The Prophet was in the vanguard of the theological trend to elevate man in God's eyes—a movement that would eventually break forth in the opposite forms of rational Unitarianism and the emotional revivalism of James Finney and others. Though they were poles apart, Smith would have agreed with both Emerson and William Ellery Channing that every true believer had access to a personal knowledge of God and was, once saved, sure to live a good life both in this world and the next. "If there is anything virtuous, lovely, or of good report or praiseworthy," Smith wrote, "we seek after these things."[4] Generally speaking, then, Joseph Smith's new religion was not at war with the optimistic, perfectionist, comfort-seeking society of Jacksonian America. And ever-patriotic, he saw the United States as the gathering place for the Mormon faithful, the future center of the reign of Christ on earth, and a nucleus from which the true gospel would emanate.

Smith exhibited still another Jacksonian trait in his belief that Mormonism was, like America, an expanding phenomenon, destined to sweep the earth. Quite naturally he looked to the West as a new Garden of Eden where his religion might flourish. Smith was aware of the frontier, but he also realized that success lay not in exclusiveness but in great numbers. Thus he organized a complex and vigorous missionary system to spread the gospel of the Latter Day Saints. Rather than sectarian, his view was catholic; and somewhat after the fashion of Fourier he envisioned key Mormon cities stretching at intervals from a central point, which would first engulf Amer-

3. Mario S. DePillis, "The Development of Mormon Communitarianism, 1826–1846" (Ph.D. dissertation, Yale University, New Haven, 1960), p. 102.
4. Joseph Smith in "The Wentworth Letter," March 1, 1842, reproduced in William Mulder and A. Russell Mortensen, eds., *Among the Mormons: Historic Accounts by Contemporary Observers* (New York, 1958), pp. 10–17.

ica and then the world, so that all mankind would be subject to conversion and salvation.[5]

Joseph Smith did not stop with an imperial missionary effort, a doctrine, and a Church. Again in step with his times, he wanted to perfect man's society as well as his soul. But Smith, unlike Robert Dale Owen at New Harmony, had no well-constructed theory of an earthly utopia. Rather, he borrowed from a half-dozen other thinkers and social planners as he learned of their ideas. As a syncretist who used and absorbed what he found around him, Smith and his key disciples studied the Shakers, investigated the Rappites, lived near and recruited among the Campbellites at Kirtland, Ohio, listened to the Baptist ideas of his eloquent follower Sidney Rigdon, and considered the Methodist ideas of vigorous, outspoken Brigham Young. Certainly he knew of Owen's experiment at New Harmony. Undoubtedly he borrowed some of his church organization from the Methodists, while the role of the Mormon bishop and the territorial divisions of the Church clearly resembled those of the Shakers.[6]

From such sources Smith evolved a variety of societal precepts. One of these was a communal approach to daily living. This view, in turn, led to a developing theory of Church ownership involving control of both real property and business enterprise. This communitarian aspect of the early Mormon Church naturally set Smith's followers apart and created the impression that theirs was a distinct economic—as well as religious—community.

Not only did Smith borrow other men's ideas and mix them with his own, but often he discarded his own older concepts for some new and better system. This meant that Mormon beliefs, whether religious, economic, or societal, were constantly evolving and even experimental. They often seemed—and were—self-contradictory. Thus Smith, who was at first attracted to the communal life practiced by the Campbellites at Kirtland, Ohio, eventually rejected it for a theory of stewardship of property. This was later modified still further by an attraction to the entrepreneurial and speculative attitudes so charac-

5. Lowry Nelson, *The Mormon Village. A Pattern and Technique of Land Settlement* (Salt Lake City, 1952), pp. 25–53 passim. Brodie, *Smith*, p. ix.

6. DePillis, "Communitarianism," pp. 18–35, 73 ff., 177. E. E. Ericksen, *The Psychological and Ethical Aspects of Mormon Group Life* (Chicago, 1922), p. 17.

teristic of the Jacksonian era. In short, Smith hovered between the two diametrically opposed economic theories of a communal society and a capitalistic-private property one. The result was an ever-shifting pot-pourri of both.

These economic views involved Smith and his followers in many economic and legal difficulties both among themselves and with outsiders. When Smith left his home near Palmyra, New York, and settled at Kirtland, Ohio, he was well on the way to establishing a communal society. Once in Ohio, however, he became interested in the opportunities offered by rising land prices and a booming economy. He founded a cooperative banking institution that was swept away by the Panic of 1837. This disaster and rising dislike by nonbelievers forced him to flee to Missouri, where a group of Mormons had already settled. There more temporizing with the principles of communal enterprise led him to allow Church members to consecrate their property in whole or in part to the Church. The owners were to remain stewards of that portion deeded to the Church. Before this system was clearly established, however, angry Missouri mobs drove the Mormons to Illinois, where they settled in the compact but individually owned community of Nauvoo. There Smith himself displayed a healthy interest in small private enterprise, even to the point of turning part of his home into a profitable hotel for the scores of curious travelers visiting the Mormon capital.[7]

It is obvious that Joseph Smith, unlike the leaders of other sects and utopian communities, was neither a purist nor an exclusivist but an eclectic, whose temporal as well as spiritual teachings developed or changed with the tide of the times. This approach—as bewildering as it might seem—actually saved Mormonism from oblivion, for it allowed a flexible religion and way of life. It was more permissive than narrow, and it could rationalize disaster and change its course. Most important of all, as a multifaceted theology it attracted followers on a broad scale and not simply because of a single and often self-destructive precept such as the Shaker belief in celibacy.

7. This summary is drawn from three detailed accounts of the early economic activities of the Latter Day Saints: DePillis, "Communitarianism"; Leonard J. Arrington, *Great Basin Kingdom: An Economic History of the Latter Day Saints, 1830–1900* (Cambridge, Mass., 1958), pp. 5–35; and Ericksen, *Group Life.* See also Brodie, *Smith,* pp. 106 ff., 332–33.

Besides its flexible approach, Smith gave Mormonism still another necessary quality that other religious and utopian movements lacked. This was authority. In Smith's case this authority stemmed partly from his own personality, for he was an attractive, even mesmeric person. One of his most devoted followers, the learned and scholarly Dr. John M. Bernhisel of Pennsylvania, always stood when Smith entered the room, claiming that he did so instinctively since he was in the presence of the Lord. Tall and muscular with deep-set hypnotic blue eyes, Smith could be warm, informal, and charming. These qualities naturally enhanced his claim to still more authority by virtue of the fact that he was a Seer, Prophet, and Revelator. Here was no mere spell-binding sectarian minister, but a holy man claiming to be possessed of mystic vision and a world view.[8] Last of all, the mystical authority was buttressed by a complex yet workable religious hierarchy—perhaps the most elaborate system outside of the Roman Church to develop in America.

Superficially, the hierarchy seemed a most undemocratic system, with Smith at the top as Prophet and Seer. On the next level Smith and two other officials formed what was called the First Presidency. After that came the Quorum of the Twelve Apostles, the Council of the Seventies, and a score of other bodies and dignitaries ranging down to the local level of ward bishop.[9] Yet for all the ranks every man was considered a priest of either the Melchisedek or Aaronic order, and so many Saints had titles and duties of a spiritual and temporal nature that all had a deep sense of belonging and participation. Through his Church hierarchy Smith had created such a united body of followers that he was automatically clothed with a personal temporal power perhaps unequaled in America since the Puritan magistrates controlled colonial Massachusetts.

He also understood and manipulated the frontier urge to acquire and develop landed property. Thus he was recognizable as a Jacksonian businessman. It is this extraordinary and often contradictory

8. Brodie, *Smith*, pp. 21–25, 99, 117–18, 294–95.
9. Every book that treats Mormon history contains a summary of Church organization. For a voluminous official history see Brigham H. Roberts, *A Comprehensive History of the Church of Jesus Christ of Latter-Day Saints* (6 vols. Salt Lake City, 1930). A concise summary of doctrine and organization may be found in Seligman and Johnson, *Encyclopaedia of the Social Sciences* (15 vols. New York, 1930), *11*, 14–17.

combination of qualities which led to his death and which forced the Mormons into the Great Basin frontier. Smith's claim, for example, to be gifted with divine revelation soon led unbelievers to denounce him as a charlatan and imposter. His failure as a banker in Kirtland, coupled with his flight to Missouri with the sheriff at his heels, it is said, persuaded others that he was a defaulter and a bankrupt. After his followers had turned the frontier county of Jackson, Missouri, into a booming, prosperous set of settlements, envious Gentiles began to fear Mormon political influence within the state, for the latter were rumored to be abolitionists and, moreover, boasted of their coming power in Missouri. In such an atmosphere it took little persuasion to convince frontier Missourians that the Mormons were Yankee cranks. A rising hostility between 1833 and 1838 led to barn burnings, beatings, secret reprisals by Mormon toughs, and finally the brutal massacre of nineteen Mormons at Haun's Mill, Missouri, in October 1838. The disgraceful refusal of Governor Lilburn Boggs to protect the Mormons and the failure of the courts to function on their behalf during these troubles resulted in the flight into Clay and Caldwell counties. And in the winter of 1838–39 Mormons began to leave Missouri itself. Their losses in property alone amounted to more than three million dollars.[10]

Smith now sought a third refuge in Illinois, for there a favor-currying Democratic legislature, anxious for votes to outnumber the evenly-matched Whig Party, granted the Prophet a tract of land and an unusually broad set of charter rights for the "City of Nauvoo," Smith's name for his new colony. Mormons who had been scattered and ill-organized in Jackson, Clay, and Caldwell counties now clustered together at the new capital, where Smith was determined to make them into a separate society well protected by charter rights. In a short time Nauvoo grew from a few cabins on a deserted marshy promontory on the east bank of the Mississippi into a city of 20,000 persons, the largest in Illinois. Not only did it have its own militia, the Nauvoo Legion, which constituted a formidable local army, but its population was great enough to hold the balance of power between

10. The Missouri troubles are epitomized in a fine selection of contemporary documents in Mulder and Mortensen, *Mormons*, pp. 96–112.

the Whigs and the Democrats in Illinois. Nauvoo's prosperity was such that the Mormons were soon able to begin building a marble temple atop a lush green hill overlooking the Mississippi.[11]

In such a situation Joseph Smith inevitably became a political, religious, and economic figure of note. Courted by both parties, he soon came to be feared by non-Mormons, whether Whig or Democrat, as a disturbing influence. This new political role coincided with four events occurring between 1839 and 1844 which brought about his death. The first of these concerned the militia, the Nauvoo Legion. Not only did it drill and parade separately from the regular state militia, but Smith himself began to assume military titles and affect elegant uniforms. Non-Mormons also came to believe that within the Legion's ranks existed a secret military group employed by the Church, who were called "Destroying Angels" or "Danites." Whatever their real purpose it was rumored that they existed to punish offenders against the Mormons.[12] They appear to have taken part in some of the Missouri troubles and to have exercised a disciplinary role within the Church itself. What seems to have made the "Danites" such a threat, however, was the news that an attempt had been made on Governor Boggs' life. The finger of suspicion pointed to certain of Smith's bodyguards who were thought to be Danites, and thus indirectly to Smith himself. Missouri authorities actually tried to arrest him in 1843 and return him to that state for trial, but the Illinois governor, seeking Smith's political support, refused to grant extradition. Nevertheless, Smith's name was henceforth inevitably connected with secret acts of violence and political assassination—a belief heightened by the fact that Smith was to be involved in at least forty arrests and court litigations during his lifetime.[13]

As stories about Avenging Angels worked their way into the Gentile

11. Thomas Leiper Kane described Nauvoo as "half-encircled by a bend in the river; its bright new dwellings set in cool, green gardens, ranging up around a stately dome-shaped hill, which was crowned by a noble marble edifice, whose high tapering spire was radiant with white and gold." *The Mormons: A Discourse Delivered before the Historical Society of Pennsylvania* (Philadelphia, 1850), p. 3.

12. Brodie, *Smith*, pp. 314–24.

13. Brigham Young stated in a public address that Smith had been arrested 46 to 48 times: *Deseret News*, September 14, 1856. Milton R. Hunter in *Brigham Young the Colonizer* (Independence, Mo., 1945), p. 6, says that it was 38 times.

legends about Mormonism, Smith brought disaster nearer in 1843 by revealing to certain of his Church leaders that he had been ordered to "restore" the doctrine of plural marriage—a doctrine he already practiced. This latest revelation shocked and split the few followers who learned of it and gave rise to an anti-Smith faction in Nauvoo itself.[14]

Just as this dissent was coming to the surface, the election of 1844 occurred. Smith, in a series of political maneuvers too lengthy to be detailed, unwisely made promises to both Whig and Democratic leaders in local elections. A sudden change of mind led him to break his promise to the Whigs, and a further change persuaded him to run for president himself. Illinois political leaders were furious over these betrayals and were also fearful of burgeoning Nauvoo, which seemed well on the way to becoming an independent republic with its own army. Soon the whole of Illinois became alarmed at Smith's activities and political pretensions.[15]

At this crucial moment in the life of the young Mormon sect leaders of the anti-Smith faction in Nauvoo published an exposé of polygamy in the *Nauvoo Expositer*. Aided by his trusty military followers, Smith broke up the press and suppressed the paper. Already guilty of maintaining a private army, of violating the institution of monogamous marriage, and of political betrayal, Smith now added an attack upon the freedom of the press. On this occasion the Prophet realized he had gone too far, for he accepted the advice of Governor Ford of Illinois to submit himself and his brother Hyrum to arrest, after having been promised protection and a fair trial. Thus it was that Joseph and Hyrum Smith were in the Carthage jail when a mob, fed on a dozen ugly rumors, sent them to their deaths.

It was easy to see that out of the events of Smith's life suspicious Americans could abstract characteristics of Mormonism which could be heartily condemned: union of Church and State, extralegal justice, censorship of the press, a standing army, polygamous marriage, secret societies, economic communism, and foreign converts. To secular, democratic, legal-minded, monogamous, nativist Americans such a set

14. Mulder and Mortensen, *Mormons*, pp. 126–27. Brodie, *Smith*, pp. 343 ff.
15. Ibid., p. 354.

of values seemed terribly wrong, and indeed, set at naught American ideals. Whether correct or not, the image of Mormonism set by Smith and continued by Brigham Young, his successor, determined the relation of Mormon to Gentile for the next fifty years and shaped in large part the territorial history of Utah.

After the death of Joseph Smith it seemed as if the elaborate Mormon society at Nauvoo would disintegrate. For a time the believers were leaderless, as Smith's disciples—Sidney Rigdon, the Smith family, and Brigham Young—quarreled over the choice of a successor. By the time the vigorous ex-Methodist and former painter and glazier Brigham Young had established himself as the new president, the Church itself had become racked both internal factions and by persecution on the part of Illinois Gentiles. Emma Smith, Joseph's faithful, grieving widow, bitter at the turn of events and refusing to believe that her husband had ever countenanced polygamy, broke off from the main group to establish the Reformed Church of Jesus Christ of the Latter Day Saints. Still another faction, under James J. Strang, broke away to form another sect.[16]

By September 1846 Gentile hostility had driven most of the Saints from Nauvoo into winter quarters on Indian lands across the Missouri River near Council Bluffs, Iowa. There, scurvy, sickness, and near starvation took a heavy toll. Reports that the Mormons were squatting illegally on Indian reserves roused the Secretary of the Interior to question their right to be there. Even appeals by Colonel Thomas Leiper Kane, a Philadelphia Quaker who chose to befriend the unfortunate Saints during their time of troubles, did not get a favorable hearing in Washington.[17]

After these experiences it was but natural that the Mormons would seek a haven in the West. Shortly before he was killed, Smith him-

16. Mulder and Mortensen, *Mormons*, pp. 152–55. For an account of the Strangites see Milo M. Quaife, *The Kingdom of St. James* (New Haven, 1930).

17. "Account of the Inhuman Behaviour of Anti-Mormons in Illinois in 1846," in The Letters, Documents, and Petitions to and by Col. Thomas L. Kane, YWA. See also T. H. Harvey, "Description of the Mormon Encampment near Council Bluffs, Dec. 3, 1846," and "Report to the Commissioner of Indian Affairs on the Status of the Mormons Encamped on the Omaha Lands . . . April 21, 1847," MSS, YWA.

self had been considering a move—to Oregon, to West Texas, or into the Pecos Valley of eastern New Mexico.[18] After Young succeeded to the presidency, he contemplated moving the Mormons to Vancouver Island and sought the mail contracts for Oregon as a method of financing and establishing way stations for the migrants. Before such a plan could be effected, however, the United States found itself at war with Mexico. Ever the practical strategist, Young saw in the conflict an opportunity to better the Mormon position in a number of ways. First, he offered the government a battalion of some 500 young Mormon soldiers—a gesture obviously designed to ingratiate himself with both President Polk and the Democratic Party. Second, he saw to it that they were attached to General Stephen W. Kearny's Army of the West, which was destined to march across the Southwest to California. These troops, whose immediate commander was Colonel William Doniphan of Missouri, could serve as a reconnaissance party for the Church in the Southwest and as a nucleus of settlement in California—a province Young was also seriously considering as a new refuge.[19] As this part of Young's plan was being carried out, some 200 Mormon families actually sailed to San Francisco, where, under the guidance of Elder Sam Brannan, they settled for a time.[20]

Despite the attractions of California, by the fall of 1846 Young had decided that the Church could not survive unless it was removed from contact with the world. Young had read the reports of John C. Fremont's 1843 expedition into the Great Basin region; and after consulting with mountain men, he was persuaded by the famous pathmarker's praiseful description to think that the Salt Lake Valley might be the perfect mountain-ringed retreat for his flock.[21]

The Church leaders approved the decision, and in April 1847 Brigham Young and a party of 148, including three women and two children, struck out on the Oregon Trail. At South Pass they inter-

18. Brodie, *Smith*, p. 360.

19. Mulder and Mortensen, *Mormons*, pp. 163–65. Hunter, *Young*, p. 10. For a reliable account of the Mormon Battalion see Daniel Tyler, *A Concise History of the Mormon Battalion in the Mexican War* (Salt Lake City, 1881).

20. Hunter, *Young*, pp. 184–92. For a description of the *Brooklyn's* arrival, see Lamar, ed., *Joseph Downey, Cruise of the Portsmouth: A Sailor's View of the Naval Conquest of California, 1845–1847* (New Haven, 1958 and 1963), pp. 136–37.

21. Arrington, *Great Basin*, pp. 39–42. Hunter, *Young*, pp. 10–11.

viewed two mountain men, Major Harris and Jim Bridger, about the little-known country to the south. Both men were pessimistic, and Bridger is supposed to have wagered that not an ear of corn could be found in a 500-mile area. To Young, nevertheless, the country possessed the requisite barrenness to provide a refuge for the Saints. Turning south, he and his party wandered in canyons and up and down mountains, until the advance scouts, Orson Pratt and John Brown, struggled up a peak on July 19 and beheld the Great Salt Lake. Two days later Pratt and Erastus Snow, following the future famous path of empire through Emigration Canyon, pushed into the Salt Lake Valley itself. On July 22 and 23 Pratt, George A. Smith, and seven other pioneers camped and explored the area. Then they reported finding both the lake and suitable lands. As the main party of Saints emerged from Emigration Canyon on July 24 onto the benchland east of the lake, Young, who was lying in an ambulance ill from fever, sat up to exclaim: "This is the place. Drive on." The new resting place of Zion's annointed had been chosen.[22]

After staking out a settlement east of Great Salt Lake, Young and a party left the remaining pioneers to plant crops while they hurried back to bring the rest of the Mormons over the trail to the Great Basin. At this point Young's pronounced talent for practical organization came into focus. Before he left, the Salt Lake camp possessed a semimilitary set of officers; duties were carefully delegated, and— most important of all—the Mormons learned to dam up streams and irrigate the hard alkaline Utah soil for crops, a farming technique they had anticipated in their discussions about the Great Basin back in winter quarters.[23] Two vital methods of conquest and survival in the desert—group cooperation and irrigated farming—had been brilliantly hit upon and adopted.

While the pioneers were planting crops, Young was back in winter quarters organizing the first migration. Caravans were formed on a semimilitary basis with a "captain of ten" operating under a "captain of fifty," who in turn functioned under an officer of a hundred. Every man had a job, and such a strict routine was maintained that

22. Ibid., pp. 29–32.
23. Ibid., p. 10.

most migrants arrived in Salt Lake Valley that fall without mishap.[24] Forced to share and to suffer together in two previous migrations, experienced in cooperative if not communal living, the Mormons who reached the Great Basin were now a disciplined mobile unit. They were psychologically ready and equipped for survival on the most hostile of frontiers. With Young and high Church officers acting as an absolute directorate, the new arrivals brought timber from the canyons and built cabins. Using a town plan drawn up by Joseph Smith, they laid out 120-foot-wide streets for their future capital. Meanwhile the Saints dug irrigation ditches and began to construct an adobe wall around their inner settlements for Indian defense. With remarkably little suffering a corporate body of settlers—in essence a theocracy—initiated the first major white settlement in the Great Basin region.

When Young and the Mormons arrived in the Great Basin, it was still a portion of Mexico, but no Spanish-Mexicans lived in this barren region. It had been partially explored in 1776–77 by two redoubtable Spanish fathers from Santa Fe, Silvestre Valez de Escalante and Francisco Dominguez, who were hunting for a shorter route from Mexico to the newly settled province of California.[25] The so-called Spanish Trail, leading from New Mexico to California, crossed along the lower rim of the Great Basin, but at most the region could be called a wild and occasional hinterland market for a few of the bolder New Mexican Indian traders, who periodically came into southern Utah to bargain goods with Utes and Navajos. In return for goods they got Indian children who became slaves to their Mexican owners.

By the Treaty of Guadalupe Hidalgo, signed in 1848, however, the area became part of the United States, and once more the Mormons found themselves under American jurisdiction. To anticipate and even forestall the imposition of American rule, Young and the Church leaders decided to create their own body politic, almost in the form of an independent nation, and as rapidly as possible to settle its

24. Kane, "Discourse," p. 34.
25. For a description of Escalante's trip see Philip Harry, "The Journeyings of Father Escalante, 1776," in J. H. Simpson, *Explorations across the Great Basin of Utah in 1859* (Washington, 1876).

habitable parts with the Mormon faithful. The result of the political effort was the highly informal but nevertheless significant and revealing State of Deseret, which functioned until Utah Territory was created in 1850. It was to contine as a paper government until 1872.

It is difficult to say just when the State of Deseret began, for there is evidence that it functioned as an informal government before a constitution was drafted. Even before the Mormons came to Utah, Young was in the habit of calling a Council of Fifty to make major civic and economic decisions.[26] But after a Church council, which met in Heber C. Kimball's home early in 1849, the Mormons were informed that a convention was to be held on March 5, to consider "the propriety of organizing a Territorial or State government." On that date Daniel Spencer called the delegates together; and with that unique political efficiency later to infuriate suspicious Americans, a Committe of Ten reported a complete state constitution within three days![27]

Physically, the new creation, Deseret, was impressive. It revealed much about Young's colonization plans. Extending north to the 33rd parallel and east to 180° of longitude, it dipped southward to the Gila River in Arizona and then ran along the northern border of Lower California to the Pacific. After including San Diego and Los Angeles—where members of the Mormon battalion had settled—the western boundary line veered inland along the Sierra Nevadas to the mountains forming the Columbia watershed.[28] (See map.) In one swoop the Saints had claimed much of the northern borderlands of Spain and most of the region that Manifest Destiny had added to the United States. Nor was it accident that the southern and western boundaries of Deseret coincided with the marching path of the Mormon battalion, when it went from southern New Mexico to California in 1846.

Deseret claimed an extraordinary amount of territory, but its form of government seemed only conventional. The Constitution of 1847 provided for a bicameral legislature, a governor and lieutenant gov-

26. Arrington, *Great Basin,* pp. 32, 39, 40, 50–51.
27. *Constitution of the State of Deseret with the Journal of the Convention Which Formed It* (Kanesville, 1849) , pp. 1–3, YWA.
28. Ibid., p. 4.

ernor, minor state officials, and the usual three-man supreme court. Elections, a militia, and a bill of rights were all provided for. More striking was the language and brevity of the document, for it was phrased in nonlegal language and ran to less than six pages. Proceeding with a swift pace, the convention adopted the constitution on March 10, ratified it in May, and convened the legislature elected at that time on July 2.[29]

It was then that the real nature of the Deseret government became apparent, for Brigham Young was governor, Willard Richards was secretary of state, and the supreme court judges were Heber C. Kimball, Newell K. Whitney, and John Taylor. All of these men were either members of the First Presidency or Apostles. Similarly, every member of the legislature was a high church official or the bishop of a ward. The Mormons, as Dale Morgan has so aptly put it, "simply elaborated their ecclesiastical machinery into a government."[30]

The sheer informality of the Deseret government suggested its echo personality, for it merely rubber-stamped what had been decided in the Council of Fifty or in other church meetings. Its casualness naturally led to some inconsistencies. The state officers had already been chosen, for example, before the constitution was written in March. When the second session of the Deseret legislature was called in December 1849, Hosea Stout noted in his diary: "On Tuesday evening I received a notification to meet in the House of Representatives on Saturday next, I being a member of that Body. By what process I became a Representative, I know not."[31]

While drafting a memorial to Congress for admission as a state, the legislature also elected a territorial delegate. In the memorial they pointed out that Congress could make them a state and save itself great expense. At the same time, they voiced a strong belief in popular sovereignty. The actual inhabitants of all newly settled areas, they asserted, were the best judges of the kinds of government and laws necessary for their growth and prosperity. Finally, they took oaths of loyalty to the United States but declared theirs a free and

29. Ibid., pp. 11–12.

30. Dale Morgan et al., "The State of Deseret," *UHQ, 8* (April, July, October 1940) , 83–87.

31. Hosea Stout, "Diary," entries for December 3, 4, 1849, original MS in USHS (copy in HEH) .

independent government. All these actions seemed very much in the American frontier tradition, but what was missing was a single voice of dissent, an opposition, an evidence of popular elections. The explanation was put best by Franklin D. Richards, who said, "Theoretically, Church and State are one. If there were no gentile and no other government there would be no Civil Law."[32] Although the Deseret Assembly officially adjourned until a second meeting in December 1849, it actually met whenever Young needed it, and continued to do so until April 1851.

The problems of forming a body politic were overshadowed by the equally important ones of exploring the desert domain of the Great Basin, establishing efficient communication with the outside world, creating an adequate defense system and Indian policy, and realizing successful settlement of the habitable parts of Utah. In each of these fields Young and the Mormons were to prove remarkable improvisers, strategists, and colonizers.

Even before the State of Deseret was formally organized, Young hastened to explore and found colonies. Wilford Woodruff recalled that as early as 1847 Young had declared that he "intended to have every hole and corner from the Bay of San Francisco known to us." And he might well have added, "and occupied by us, if humanly possible."[33] The President listened avidly to early reports on the Cache and Utah valleys in 1847. He thoroughly questioned the Mormon soldiers, who came overland from California, about the nature of the northern route. After Captain James Brown briefed Young on that trail to California, he sent another ex-soldier, Captain Jefferson Hunt, on a difficult trip back to Southern California in 1847–48 by way of the Old Spanish Trail. Hunt had orders to explore the route and to bring back cattle and supplies from the Williams Santa Ana del Chino Ranch.[34] Trying and hazardous though Hunt's 750-mile trek proved to be, his report apparently convinced the Mormons that the southern route represented the most feasible path over which immigrants and supplies could come from the outside world.

Young concentrated, therefore, on making the route a Mormon

32. Morgan, "Deseret," pp. 84–85.
33. Quoted in Hunter, *Young,* p. 32.
34. Ibid., pp. 35–36.

'corridor to the sea." In 1849 the Southern Exploring Company, under Parley P. Pratt, was created to find colony sites and report on soil and minerals along the way. Provo and Parowan were founded, both as colonies and as way stations, on the trail. Later, Young encouraged no fewer than 1,500 colonists to settle in San Bernadino, California, which he hoped would become a Mormon center second only to Salt Lake City. The result was that by the spring of 1855 twenty communities were established in a direct line from Salt Lake to Cedar City, a distance of 265 miles. They were connected by a good wagon road, and the road itself was being extended on to the Pacific Coast.[35]

Intimately related to the desire of the Mormons for good communications was their fear that the trails might also become avenues of invasion used by hostile Gentiles. A superb strategist, Young could see that the Saints must control certain key points as an outer shell of defense. Concomitant with his policy of planting closely grouped inner-core colonies near Salt Lake City, he also tried, in 1849–55, to hold more distant key spots. In addition to developing San Bernadino, California, he eventually seized Fort Bridger from Jim Bridger at South Pass. He also placed a colony in Carson Valley, Nevada and sent Saints down into southeastern Utah to Moab and up into the Salmon River region of Utah. Others were ordered to explore the possibility of navigating the Colorado River.[36] More grandiose, ambitious, and elaborately thought out than most frontier defense arrangements, Young's vast perimeter of protection vaguely resembled that which Colonel Sumner established in New Mexico in 1852.

Young's tactics were not aimed exclusively at non-Mormon Americans. Church leaders were very aware that they were ringed about with backward and starving Indian tribes, eager to lay hands on Mormon supplies, food, and cattle. The Saints were forced to build protective walls and cattle stockades in nearly every new colony and to send out expeditions periodically to chastise thieving or murdering bands. Mormon theology dictated, however, that the Indian deserved civilizing and saving. So after undertaking two expeditions against

35. Ibid., pp. 38–47.
36. These activities are traced in detail in Hunter.

the Timpanogos and Shoshone Indians in 1850, which adequately demonstrated Mormon prowess, the government began a policy of feeding, teaching, and converting Indians rather than fighting them— a policy that would eventually lead the Indians of the Great Basin to distinguish between Mormons and Americans in their contacts and dealings. "It has been our habit," boasted Franklin D. Richards, "to shoot Indians with tobacco and bread biscuits rather than with powder and lead, and we are most successful with them."[37]

Young's Indian policy was much more than a policy of buying peace. In fact, the variety and scope of the Indian missions in Utah has never really been appreciated. Patiently the Mormons mastered the dialects of the Bannocks, Utes, Navajo, and Hopi; taught them to be ranchers and farmers; and discouraged the selling of children to the New Mexican traders. The Deseret policy produced frontier diplomats of great talent, who negotiated delicate day-by-day unwritten treaties of coexistence. Jacob Hamblin, a soft-spoken, Ohio-born convert who had joined the Church in 1842, was so successful with the difficult Indians of Tooele Valley that he was soon appointed missionary to the equally difficult ones in southern Utah. There he not only brought a peace that permitted white settlement but tried to bring Hopi tribes living south of the Colorado River under his jurisdiction. Later he even attempted to establish friendly relations with the hostile Navajo.[38] For their quiet and patient labors, Hamblin and his colleagues deserve comparison with Fathers Kino and Serra in their successful relations with the Indians of the Southwest.

In colonizing, as in Indian relations, Deseret authorities attempted to settle the Great Basin with remarkable order and foresight. Young insisted that the inner core settlements be as nearly contiguous as possible. Thus the Mormon village was, with the exception of missions and way stations, never far from another village. As Wallace Stegner has observed, the Mormons soon discovered what the Cliff Dwellers had done centuries before: that the "only way to be a farmer in the

37. Leland H. Creer, "The Activities of Jacob Hamblin in the Region of the Colorado," University of Utah, *Anthropological Papers, 33* (1958), 3.

38. Ibid., p. 23. See also Hunter, *Young,* pp. 290–322. Hostile accounts of Young's Indian policy are contained in Garland Hurt's charges, which are summarized in Norman F. Furniss, *The Mormon Conflict* (New Haven, 1960), pp. 45–46, 50–51.

Great Basin and on the desert plateaus of the Colorado watershed was to be a group farmer."[39] When new settlements were staked out, they were not isolated farms but true villages chosen with a view to Indian defense, the existence of water for irrigation, and the presence of arable land. The land itself was awarded by the local bishop according to family need and ability. Trained leaders were always sent out to guide the new community, and technicians or artisans were also provided to balance its economy and to provide the necessities of life, so that the new colony would be as self-sufficient as possible.

Under Young's all-seeing guidance the Saints soon explored the western side of the Wasatch Mountains all the way from Weber and Cache valleys in the north to the future border of Arizona Territory in the south. A string of settlements followed, which by the midfifties was 450 miles in length. The degree of Mormon success is indicated by the fact that they had settled a stretch of barren land in five years which was nearly equal in size to that which New Mexicans had taken over two centuries to occupy.

Since the village rather than the individual farm was the standard unit, and since superficially the bishop was the local equivalent of a New Mexican *patron* and *padre* combined, a resemblance to New Mexican life existed. Mormons used adobe houses, depended on irrigated lands, and cooperated in an economy that was more subsistence than commercial. These apparent similarities to other portions of the Far Southwest were balanced, however, by an equal number of vivid contrasts. The Mormon village possessed a spirit of unity and cooperation, a sense of order and participation, and a moral rectitude that was unique. Although it operated under the aegis of a Church hierarchy, it was a surprisingly democratic community whose leaders were picked for talent and not by their heredity. They were not on an unchanging plateau of life but were building for a new world. A curious combination of an arid region environment, village group settlement, a dynamic new religion, and American frontier habits were well on the way toward creating a distinct American subculture.

39. Quoted in Leland H. Creer, "Mormon Towns in the Region of the Colorado," University of Utah, *Anthropological Papers, 32,* (1958), 31–32. See also Wallace Stegner, *Beyond the Hundredth Meridian* (Cambridge, Mass., 1954), pp. 227–28.

To complete his grand scheme of occupation and colonization, the greatest since Stephen Austin's in Texas, Young's final requisite was to convert colonists, for if Deseret was to remain Mormon it had to be peopled with believers. Long before the Mormons arrived in Utah, leading Saints were sent on missions throughout the world to gather converts. Since the majority of those who joined the Church came from the poorer classes in England and Scandinavia, the major problem was to pay their way to Utah. This was the reason Young took such an interest in the Mormon Corridor, for if immigrants could make it to San Diego or San Pedro by sea, the final overland trip would be relatively short and easy in contrast to the weary trek from distant ports like New York or New Orleans. Actually most colonists chose to come overland, so that by 1849 Young and the Church hit upon the device of a Perpetual Emigrating Fund to finance these poor. The income for passage money was to be raised by taxes on ferries, bridges, and toll roads in Utah, and the money itself was to be made available in the form of a loan to the migrant, who would pay it back later. Naturally, the Assembly unanimously chartered the emigration company, and Young became its president.[40]

With a government, a system of defense, a technique of ordered settlement, a source of population, and a transportation system, the skeleton of a complete and developing independent society had been constructed in the Great Basin. It now remained for Congress to give it the manly sinews of statehood or the adolescent flesh of a territory. To secure these ends Young first turned to the Mormons' great defender in the East, Colonel Thomas Leiper Kane of Philadelphia.[41] Kane's family was influential both in the halls of Congress and at the White House. Ever the champion of a minority cause, Kane gladly lent his support to the Mormon petition for statehood and pulled strings wherever he could. To aid Kane a free wheeling, high-living rather atypical Mormon, Almon W. Babbitt, also appeared in Washington, on Young's orders. But Babbitt's behavior was so brash that Young virtually replaced him by dispatching Wilford

40. *Deseret News,* September 21, 1850. Arrington, *Great Basin,* pp. 97 ff.
41. "Thomas Leiper Kane" in *DAB.* Morgan, "Deseret," pp. 113–19.

Woodruff and Dr. John M. Bernhisel to Washington in May 1849 to ask Congress to admit Deseret as a territory.[42]

Upon their arrival Kane warned them to demand statehood instead. Territorial status meant outside appointees and inevitable conflict. "You do not want corrupt political men from Washington strutting about you," he said prophetically.[43] Despite the efforts of Bernhisel, Woodruff, and Kane, Mormon wishes played little or no part in the final Congressional decision to make Utah a territory. That decision, in fact, was only a minor part of the vast political settlement known as the Compromise of 1850. After September 1850 the frontier state of Deseret was no more, but generations would pass before the Saints abandoned the dream of a self-contained, virtually autonomous "nation within a nation."

42. Morgan, ibid. Robert H. Sylvester, "Dr. John Milton Bernhisel, Utah's First Delegate to Congress" (Master's thesis, University of Utah, 1947), pp. 22–29, 36–37. See also Bernhisel to Young, March 21, 1850, in the John M. Bernhisel Scrapbook, USHS.

43. Kane, quoted in Nels Anderson, *Desert Saints: The Mormon Frontier in Utah* (Chicago, 1942), p. 10.

13   Politics, Religion, and War
1851–1861

President Brigham Young in his sermon declared that the
thred [sic] was cut between us and the U. S. and that the
Almighty recognized us as a free and independent people, and
that no officer apointed [sic] by government should come and
rule over us from this time forth.
> Hosea Stout
> September 6, 1857

Please to let us know what you want of us before you prepare
your halters to hang . . . do you wish us to deny our God
and renounce our religion?
> Memorial of Utah Assembly
> To James Buchanan, December 1857

 When Utah was organized in September 1850, the
Church authorities hoped that President Fillmore
would appoint only Saints to territorial office, so that
the Deseret officials would continue to be in effect
the true government. Through the hard work and
courteous diplomacy of Dr. Bernhisel in Washington,
Young was made governor, and two Mormons, Joseph L. Heywood
and Seth M. Blair, became United States marshal and district attorney
respectively. The Mormons were also happy to learn that a figure
friendly to the Saints, and allied to them by marriage, had been
appointed associate justice of Utah. This was Zerubbabel Snow of
Ohio. Orson Hyde, upon learning of the new officials, was so pleased
he declared it was "God working through the Whigs."[1]

1. Sylvester, "Bernhisel," p. 40. Andrew Jensen, *Latter Day Saints Biographical
Encyclopaedia* (Salt Lake City, 1901) *4*, 691.

These popular appointments were more than matched by a number of bad ones. Had Fillmore searched the length and breadth of the land, he scarcely could have found men less suited to deal with the Saints than the two non-Mormon judges: Chief Justice Lemuel G. Brandebury and Associate Justice Perry G. Brocchus. The same was true of the territorial secretary, Broughton D. Harris, and the Indian agent, Henry R. Day. All were political hacks who came to Utah expecting to handle court, executive, and Indian office patronage. Brocchus, in fact, accepted his post in hopes of returning to Washington as Utah's delegate.[2] The stage was set for the first of many bitter battles between Mormon and federal appointees for control of Utah's government.

To forestall the division and disunity he knew outsiders would bring to his kingdom, Young quickly accepted office in February 1851, some months before the remaining appointees arrived in Salt Lake City. Then he convened the legislature in March 1851, called for a delegate election, and ordered a census taken by August 1.[3] The latter task was usually the function of the territorial secretary, but since Harris did not reach Salt Lake until late August, he was faced with a fait accompli. Similarly, the justices arrived to find probate judges had been chosen by an all-Mormon legislature and that these courts were already handling the cases usually handled by federal courts. Agent Day found that Young, as ex-officio Superintendent of Indian Affairs, was in full control of all Indian business down to the last patronage penny. Mystified, frustrated, and quickly enraged, these opportunistic frontier extroverts were soon sniping away at the Church and penning letters to Washington accusing Young of tyranny.

The real break came when Governor Young invited Judge Brocchus to speak before the semi-annual conference of the Church—a sort of mass meeting of officers—on the anniversary of the organization of Utah Territory. Brocchus replied to some pithy remarks Young had

2. Letters in Brocchus' appointment file suggest that he preferred to be a judge in either Minnesota or Oregon Territory. See U. S. Dept. of State, Appointments Division, Letters of Application and Recommendation, Utah, NA. Brocchus' desire to be delegate is suggested in W. W. Phelps to T. L. Kane, June 25, 1852, Kane Papers, YWA.

3. *Deseret News*, July 12, 1851.

recently made about the late Zachary Taylor and the national government while speaking at the great Mormon celebration in Emigration Canyon on July 24. Warming to his subject, the arrogant and pugnacious Brocchus condemned Young for rejoicing that Taylor was "roasting in hell" and proceeded to attack Mormonism itself. Plunging head on, he made thinly disguised references to polygamy and climaxed his series of insults by asking if the audience was fit or patriotic enough to contribute a stone to the building of the Washington Monument.[4] By the time he had finished, the conference was in an uproar, and threats and denunciations from all sides made the foolish judge fear for his life.

A few days later, a new crisis came when Secretary Harris declared Young's August delegate election invalid. In company with Brandebury, Brocchus, and Day, Harris left Salt Lake City on September 28. The officials took with them the territorial seal, public books and papers, and some $24,000 in cash earmarked for legislative expenses. Once safely back in Washington, Judge Brocchus charged that federal laws were resisted in Utah to such an extent that an army was needed to restore federal rule. Fortunately for the Mormons the sleazy reputations and the low caliber of the runaway officials—or the "flying officers," as Brocchus and the rest were soon dubbed—were such that their protests created little real stir. In June 1852 Secretary of State Daniel Webster told the runaways to return to their posts or resign.[5] By August 31 they had taken the latter course as the better part of valor.

At the precise moment that Brocchus and Harris were admitting defeat, Brigham Young and the leaders of the Church were announcing to the world that Mormons believed in—and practiced—the doctrine of plural wives. In explaining the doctrine to the Saints, Orson Pratt couched it in stern theological terms, relating plural marriage to the Mormon conception of the nature of the soul and the need to replenish the earth with the seed of Saints.[6] But to the

4. See Jedediah Grant's description of the event in a letter to James Gordon Bennett of the New York *Herald*, March 9, 1852, in Mulder and Mortensen, *Mormons*, pp. 253–61.

5. Bernhisel to Kane, Washington (n.d.), 1852, Kane Papers.

6. *Deseret News Extra*, September 14, 1852, YWA.

general public it signified that the Mormons had established some vast immoral system of concubinage in the Great Basin. All the old issues that had led to Joseph Smith's death were revived, and the American public saw the Mormons once more as a misled minority terribly out of step with the times.

Curiously, the reaction to Young's startling announcement was delayed for several years. It came too late to be used as a debating point in the national election of 1852. Moreover, the triumph of Pierce and the southern Democrats guaranteed that the administration would proceed cautiously in interfering with a domestic institution—a category including both slavery and polygamous marriage. A similar attitude appears to have been shared by the men sent to replace Brocchus and the other federal officers. Associate Justices Lazarus H. Read and Leonidas Shaver proved to be disinterested in the legality of polygamy. The new secretary, Benjamin Ferris, was soon so enamoured of golden California that he abandoned the office to a Mormon, Almon W. Babbitt. Judge Read's successor in 1853, John F. Kinney, was a Gentile, but one who proved cooperative.[7] Thus from September 1851 to the arrival of Governor Alfred W. Cumming in 1858, Brigham Young was the absolute ruler of Utah. W. W. Phelps wrote Kane in 1852: "We enjoy our government and everything else like a little nation, far from the *Beau mundi, eclat, sin* and *war*, sickness and misery."[8]

The legislature continued to consist exclusively of Mormons. No opposition party developed, and the Saints themselves pushed outward from Salt Lake to occupy new fertile valleys. Each year several thousand immigrants poured into Utah, to be greeted by singing and dancing at the mouth of Emigration Canyon. There, as the weary parties came onto the benchland in view of Salt Lake, housewives served out fresh cakes and melons while the Nauvoo band played and President Young blessed the new arrivals.[9] By 1860 over 30,000 Mormon faithful had gathered in the Great Basin region.

Mormon Utah, as remote as it was, could neither remain in a

7. Scattered correspondence relating to Read, Shaver, Kinney and Babbitt may be found in State Department Appointments Division, Utah, NA.

8. Phelps to Kane, Salt Lake City, June 25, 1852, Kane Papers.

9. *Deseret News Extra*, September 14, 1852, p. 47.

political vacuum unnoticed by Washington nor—its people growing in number and full of expectation—be kept at a sustained pitch of faith and optimism. In Washington the introduction of the Kansas-Nebraska bills by Stephen A. Douglas once more brought the whole territorial question into national prominence and dragged Utah into the withering crossfire of debate. Unfortunately, national scrutiny was turned toward Utah at the very moment the Saints themselves were undergoing a frenzied religious revival or reformation. The coincidence of the two crises shook both Utah and the nation and presented Young and the Latter Day Saints with the largest set of challenges they had ever faced: an invasion of Utah by 2,500 troops of the United States Army, the appearance of another 2,500 non-Mormon hangers-on, and the imposition of a new and largely non-Mormon territorial government on the Saints.

The breakdown of Young's personal rule began when Judge W. W. Drummond of Illinois succeeded Leonidus Shaver in 1855 as associate justice of Utah. Although married, the thirty-five-year-old Drummond arrived in Salt Lake City that fall accompanied by his mistress, Ada Carroll. Rather than content himself with a clandestine relationship, Drummond flaunted the shocking Ada in the faces of the Saints and permitted her to sit on the bench with him during court sessions.[10] Within a few months of Drummond's appearance, the friendly Judge Zerubbabel Snow was replaced by George P. Stiles. The latter was a Mormon who had actually been a legal counselor to Joseph Smith in Nauvoo, but the Saints did not trust him. Nor were they completely happy with Chief Justice John F. Kinney, who was busily playing the double game of cooperating with the Mormons on the local level while bombarding Washington with secret strictures against Young.[11]

Given the new judges, it was not long before a new court struggle was in the making. The difficulty this time was similar to the one

10. Furniss, *The Mormon Conflict* (New Haven, 1960), pp. 38, 54–56; See also "Address" (n.d.) in State Department, Letter Books, 1853–1859, TP, Utah, which refers to Ada and Drummond.

11. Stout, "Diary," May 26, 1855. T. L. Kane to Benjamin Pierce, August 23, 1855, State Department Appointments Division, Utah. Brigham Young to Kane, January 31, and June 29, 1857, Kane Papers.

faced by Brandebury and Brocchus: the new judges had nothing to do. In 1851 and 1852 the Utah Assembly had taken advantage of a vague clause in the Organic Act to give probate courts "original jurisdiction both in civil and criminal cases." The Assembly then created a territorial attorney general, a marshal, and district attorneys and permitted the Assembly to appoint the probate judges. Since the Assembly usually appointed a bishop to the probate position, this meant that every crime and judgment in Utah was really handled by Church authorities. At Brigham Young's suggestion the Assembly also allowed any person to act as his own lawyer, permitted the persons involved to refuse payment to a lawyer, and provided that cases could be settled out of court at any stage in a trial.[12] In this homespun but brilliant way the Saints made the legal profession a hazardous and extremely unattractive calling at best and virtually guaranteed the absence of lawyers in Salt Lake. Their success in negating the duties of the federal courts was vividly illustrated in January 1856, when the *Deseret News* stated that only one case had appeared on the Supreme Court docket that term.[13]

Determined to change the order of things, Judge Drummond declared in November 1855 that the Utah Judiciary Act was unconstitutional. He ordered the probate courts to relinquish their jurisdiction over civil and criminal cases. The irate judge even called for an indictment of the probate judges who refused to do so. As a result, Drummond's name was denounced throughout Utah.[14] Judge Stiles was also increasingly restive in his incompatible roles as both Mormon and federal officer.

At this point nature and the economy of Utah intervened to give the two judges a chance to make their moribund courts effective. The winter of 1855–56 in Utah was unusually severe. The usual Mormon precautions, in terms of both food and fuel resources, proved

12. For an excellent summary of the role of probate judge in Utah see W. N. Davis, "Western Justice: The Court at Fort Bridger, Utah," *UHQ,* 23 (1955), 99–125; see also Pomeroy, *Territories,* pp. 58–60. For Young's recommendations concerning probate courts see his *Annual Message, December 13, 1853* (Salt Lake City, 1852). YWA.

13. *Deseret News,* January 23, 1856.

14. Stout, "Diary," November 12, 1855.

inadequate for the booming population. Editorials commenting upon the hard times began to appear weekly in the *Deseret News,* the official newspaper for the Church. Money was also extremely scarce, since it had been drained from the territory to pay for expensive machinery, supplies, and imports. The Indians, feeling the pinch of hunger, began to raid Mormon herds in Utah and Cedar valleys. The depredations became so frequent that Young ordered the militia to be ready to march at a moment's notice.[15]

The drought coincided with the failure of heroic Mormon attempts to start manufacturing iron in Cedar City and lead in Carson Valley. Efforts to spin wool, refine sugar, and make leather goods had also been unsuccessful. All these projects had consumed enormous amounts of scarce Church capital. The attempt to manufacture sugar, for example, had cost over $100,000.[16] Immigration costs, e.g. wagons, teams, and supplies, drained off still more precious specie. And in the fall of 1855 the founders of a Ute Indian mission at Moab had to retreat in the face of warlike Indians.

In this harsh winter of discontent and discomfort scores of Mormons, some of them bishops and high officials, began to accept jury duty at the federal courts, or volunteered to be witnesses. Doing anything seemed worth while if it earned money for food. Faced with the prospect of a revived set of federal courts, Brigham Young's fury was not long restrained. At the Tabernacle on February 24, 1856, he attacked lawyers and Mormon court witnesses. "Grayheaded men running after them [lawyers] and asking 'can you call me up as a witness, or put me on the jury?' in order that they may get a dollar or two. . . . I am ashamed of you." Cursing "men who love corruption, contention, broils," Young prayed that "God would rout them out from the society of the Saints." He warned the faithful:

Keep away from courthouses. . . . I wish such persons to go to California if they wish to. I counsel you to keep away from courts. We have got the names of those who attended that court room,

15. *Deseret News,* January 16, 30, February 13, 27, 1856.
16. Arrington, *Great Basin,* pp. 112–30.

and we will send those characters on long missions, for we want to get rid of them, and we do not care whether they apostacize or not.[17]

Young's magnificent diatribe triggered a chain reaction. Seeing that his words had produced an effect, on March 2 he took up the theme in a more general way. What the Saints needed was to "have it rain pitch forks, tines downwards, from this pulpit Sunday after Sunday. . . . You should have sermons like peals of thunder and then we can get the scales from our eyes." He declared that he cared not for half or quarter rations, "I would rather that this people should starve to death in the mountains than to have the Lord Almighty hand us over to a cursed, infernal mob."[18]

Young's remarks struck a responsive cord in Jedediah M. Grant, a new member of the First Presidency and the first mayor of Salt Lake City. In Grant's hands the anticourt protest became a general call for a reformation to weed out the weak among the Mormons.[19] The spirit of revivalism, a form of preaching that had been obnoxious to Smith, now seized the Mormons. Since hard times continued and drought damaged crops in the spring and summer of 1856, the Saints soon came to see nature as an instrument of punishment for wickedness and weakness among their own number. As Young ordered farmers to let the starving destitute glean their fields, the revival turned into a search for the sinful.[20] Erring Saints were urged to confess, and church commissions visited the frontier communities to inquire into the most initimate details of men's lives. Above it all sounded the thrilling, vibrant voice of Jedediah Grant, who was now urging not just repentence but blood atonement. The guilty, he cried in a famous discourse, should not only confess their sins but appoint a place where the faithful might shed the sinner's blood even to the taking of life.[21] Only in this Old Testament way could the Church be purified.

17. *Deseret News,* March 5, 1856.
18. Ibid., March 12, 1856.
19. See Gustive O. Larson, "The Mormon Reformation," *UHQ, 26* (1958), pp. 45–63.
20. *Deseret News,* January 25, 1856.
21. Ray B. West, Jr., *Kingdom of the Saints: The Story of Brigham Young and the Mormons* (New York, 1957), pp. 218–22.

Soon the reformation had permeated every aspect of Mormon life. The Assembly itself, upon convening in 1856, met in a committee of the whole "on the state of the Reformation and passed a unanimous Resolution to repent and forsake of our sins and be re-baptized for their remission and in conformity therewith." In commenting upon the zeal exhibited in the legislature, Hosea Stout exclaimed, "It was truly a Pentecost."[22]

The fierce religious, emotional, and economic crises were punctuated by news in the fall of 1856 that hundreds of emigrants had been caught by early snows while traveling across the Plains and had perished. Most of the victims were members of the so-called handcart expeditions organized by Young in the spring of 1856 to save the enormous expense of animals and wagons. Two expeditions of handcarters—pushing what was often a 300-pound load on clumsy, two-wheeled vehicles—had made the laborious journey safely. But the remaining migrants, already exhausted by a trek of several hundred miles, were unprepared to reckon with a Plains blizzard. Some two hundred had died. The handcart disaster was yet another warning and humiliation for the Saints. An even earlier immigrant party, which had arrived safely in Utah, now experienced a smallpox epidemic. It seemed as if the trials of Providence would prove unbearable.[23]

The spirit of the reformation naturally affected relations between the Saints and the federal officials. At the beginning of the revival Judge Stiles had been tried for adultery by the Seventies, found guilty, and "cut off from the Church root and branch." Hosea Stout, caught up in the fervor, declared in his diary: "Amen to the damnation of that wicked and corrupt judge."[24] Stiles in turn became extremely hostile toward Mormons in his court. In revenge some unidentified youths broke into his office and removed court records, papers, and the library of a Gentile lawyer, T. S. Williams. At least some of the contents of the office were thrown into a privy and there burned. The vendetta continued a few weeks later when an outburst between

22. Stout, "Diary," December 24, 1856.
23. "It is presumable that every man, woman and child in Utah over four years of age, is fully aware that almost the entire population has been on short rations for many months." *Deseret News*, July 23, 1856. See also ibid., August 13, 1856.
24. Stout, "Diary," December 23, 1856.

Stiles and Mormon lawyers disrupted his courtroom. "Feelings ran so high," wrote Hosea Stout, "that several laid off their coats while two Gentiles, not willing to take a hand, left the court."[25] After one participant was kicked out of court for wearing pistols, Stiles disbarred several Mormon attorneys.

The bitter impasse in judicial affairs was reflected in other areas. David H. Burr, the first surveyor general, and Dr. Garland Hurt, an Indian agent, found their work so hampered by Mormon hostility that they, too, reported Utah was in a state of rebellion.[26] Gentile merchants and lawyers, and even recently arrived Mormon converts, unprepared for the revival, began to fear for their lives. A series of murders at Springville led to the rumor that the Danites were actually exacting blood atonement. The floodgates of horrid supposition released, stories now began to circulate that Captain John W. Gunnison and his party of U. S. Topographical Engineers, all of whom had been killed by Indians while exploring along the 38th parallel in 1853, had actually been massacred by Mormons. Others suddenly remembered that Mormon authorities had not helped Colonel Edward J. Steptoe find the culprits in 1854–55 and that Indians supposedly responsible for the killings had been let off with easy sentences.[27] Whispering gossips noted that Judge Shaver had died under strange circumstances, and the news that the brash, free-living Almon W. Babbitt, who had been no friend to the reformation, had died on the Plains while traveling east led to still other accusations. At the same time verifiable stories of beatings, thrashings, and whippings gave credence to the more desperate rumors.[28]

Although Utah finally had a good harvest in the fall of 1856, and the blood and thunder preaching of Jedediah Grant was silenced by

25. Ibid., February 13, 14, 1857.
26. Furniss, *Mormon Conflict,* pp. 45–51. The material on the Mormon War is voluminous but often very biased. For the most accurate summary coverage see LeRoy R. and Ann W. Hafen, eds., *The Utah Expedition, 1857–1859: A Documentary Account* (Glendale, 1958); Leland Creer, *Utah and the Nation* (Seattle, 1929); and Furniss' excellent *Mormon Conflict.* See also a good unpublished history: Everett Cooley, "The Utah War," (Master's thesis, University of Utah, 1947).
27. Furniss, p. 41.
28. Ibid., pp. 56–57.

his unexpected death in December, the reformation was still spoken of as a current affair in March 1857. Moreover, the April *Deseret News* began to carry reports of militia reorganization and the mustering of new members.[29] In this situation fearful persons did flee Utah, and among their number were Judges Drummond and Stiles, Surveyor General Burr, and, later, Agent Garland Hurt. Rather than view these departures with alarm, Young declared at the Bowery on June 7: "The spirit of the reformation has taken hold on the people; it has kindled the fire of the Almighty in Mount Zion to burn out many of the ungodly that could not stand it and they had fled."[30]

At the beginning of the reformation the Mormons had been in conflict with still another federal function—that of the postal service. The mail contracts for Utah had been awarded to a hard-drinking, free-speaking Marylander named W. M. F. Magraw.[31] To carry the mails, Magraw, in turn, had hired a shouting, swearing, set of men who rode into Salt Lake coloring the air with their remarks. The townspeople felt so strongly about the mail carriers that on one occasion the roughnecks were put under guard and escorted to the city's edge before being allowed to cut loose verbally.

By assiduous complaints and maneuverings in Washington, the Saints secured Magraw's removal, and a Mormon, Hiram Kimball, received the mail contract in his place. Kimball had neither the equipment nor the money to transport the mails, and his contract was quickly absorbed into a larger firm, the Brigham Young Express and Carrying Company.[32] It represented yet another understandable effort of the Saints to control the economy and communications system of Utah.

Magraw's removal made him a vindictive enemy of the Mormons. As a friend of the incoming President Buchanan, whom he had known since 1853, Magraw's was yet another voice in Washington equating reformation zeal with rebellion.[33] Other events, not necessarily related

29. *Deseret News,* April 1, 25, 1857.
30. Ibid., June 17, 1857. Furniss, pp. 48–49, 59.
31. Furniss, pp. 51 ff.
32. Ibid., p. 52.
33. William P. MacKinnon, "W. M. F. Magraw and the Utah Expedition" (typescript shown author, 1963), p. 11.

to the reformation, were also seen as part of a pattern of rebellion. To
the north, for example, Mormons had virtually pushed Jim Bridger
from his South Pass fort and had established their own jurisdiction
in the Weber Valley.[34] From the Mormon view, all these events—
placed in the context of wretched federal appointees, a drought, hard
times, bad mail service, and a fierce religious revival—made sense.
But a federal court had been disrupted, official records had been
seized and burned, and public officials could honestly report that
they had been unable to perform their duties. Every single function
the federal government was responsible for in a territory, outside of
tax collection and defense, had been defied. It was no wonder non-
Mormons tended to report that a full-scale rebellion existed in Utah.

The combination of patronage pressures for territorial appointments
and the accumulation of charges against Young, made it impossible
for James Buchanan to follow Pierce's policy of ignoring Utah
problems.

Pierce himself had been anxious to replace Young with Colonel
Steptoe of the Topographical Engineers. Steptoe not only declined
but suggested that Young be retained. The Colonel did advise the
President, however, that a military force, or some symbol of the
power of the federal government, be established in Utah to remind
the Mormans they were under American rule.[35] Obviously Buchanan's
primary concern upon assuming the presidency was not to make Utah
loyal but to solve the question of Bleeding Kansas and to stabilize
the increasingly dangerous slavery issue. But he also realized that the
difficulties in Utah were related to these more basic issues, since
Democratic doctrines of popular sovereignty and states rights implied
tolerance of polygamy as a domestic institution. The new Republican
Party had already made the connection in their 1856 platform by
promising to abolish the "twin relics of barbarism: slavery and
polygamy."

34. Furniss, p. 37.
35. Colonel E. J. Steptoe to Colonel S. Cooper, Salt Lake City, October 11, 1855,
in Records of the War Department, Office of the Adjutant General, 1855. NA
(copy in USHS).

The first Buchanan move that was to affect Utah actually started as a part of his Kansas policy. Having appointed Robert Walker of Mississippi to be governor of Kansas, he also recalled General W. S. Harney from Florida and ordered him to station and command 2,500 troops at Fort Leavenworth, Kansas. Buchanan clearly expected to back his Kansas government with a show of force. But the strong and vociferous Republican minority in Congress, fearing that federal troops would inevitably take a pro-Southern stand in any crisis, wanted them stationed elsewhere. At the same time, the American press was demanding an expedition to suppress the Mormon "rebellion." Buchanan also had in his possession—or at least the State Department had on file—a letter from Magraw which stated: "There is no disguising the fact that there is no vestige of law and order, no protection for life or property; the civil laws of the territory are overshadowed and neutralized by a so-styled ecclesiastical organization as despotic, dangerous and damnable as has ever been known to exist in any country."[36] Turning to specific items, Magraw mentioned the midnight vigilantes or Danites, the expected bloodshed, and the preeminence of the Mormon-controlled probate courts. Undoubtedly Buchanan did not act on this single piece of evidence. He must have known of the previous complaints by Colonel Steptoe in 1855 and have heard of the flight of Drummond, Stiles, and Burr.

It was also the case that Magraw knew Buchanan personally. At this time, Magraw's brother, Robert, was actually courting Miss Harriet Lane, Buchanan's niece and official hostess.[37] Given the task of stamping out Mormon polygamy and rebellion, Buchanan also saw

---

36. Hafen, *Utah Expedition*, pp. 361–63. See also MacKinnon, "Magraw," pp. 3–6. The most impressive and telling indictment actually came in a letter from Garland Hurt to Governor Cumming, December 17, 1857, in which he maintained that Church leaders artificially fostered anti-American feeling by harangues, and that the reformation was a desperate effort to scare the mass of Mormons into new loyalty and submission. "When this reformation commenced, there was not a distillery, brewery, grogshop, gambling saloon, or house of ill fame in the Territory. . . . No rowdyism, incendiarism, prostitution, homicides, suicides, infanticides, forgeries or murders. . . . What then . . . is the condition of the people that they require reform?" Hurt then detailed accounts of court troubles, beatings, and house burnings, all of which came *after* the reformation. State Department, Letter Books, 1853–1859, TP, Utah.

37. Mackinnon, "Magraw," p. 11.

a way out of his Kansas difficulties by ordering Harney's troops to
Utah. This act would please the Republicans and demonstrate that
to believe in popular sovereignty was not to condone polygamy. The
Utah crisis could divert the whole nation from its preoccupation with
slavery.[38] The sight of the United States reasserting jurisdiction over
a region practically claiming independence would also give pause to
Southern secessionists and delimit the more extreme demands uttered
in the name of states rights. It is easy to see why the President felt
justified in dispatching one-sixth of the United States Army to Utah
in 1857.

To the Saints, Buchanan's acts were those of a good man misled by
"lying office seekers." Young himself compared Buchanan to Pontius
Pilate and declared nostalgically that if Hickory Jackson were president "he would kick some of the rotten-hearted sneaks out."[39] Yet
Stephen A. Douglas, undoubtedly the Congressional spokesman for
the Democrats, said that popular sovereignty and polygamy were
incompatible. He told an Illinois audience that if Young and his
followers were guilty of rebellion, they must be replaced by bold and
able men, backed by a powerful army, so the nation could "cut out
the loathsome, disgusting ulcer" Utah had become.[40]

Buchanan's Mormon policy went into effect on May 28, 1857, when
General Winfield Scott ordered General W. S. Harney to move 2,500
troops from Leavenworth—soon to be an outfitting center for Pike's
Peak—toward Salt Lake. Kansas troubles and a shrewd reluctance to
become involved in the Utah affair kept Harney behind, and the
expedition was first commanded by an Army bureaucrat, Colonel
Edmund Alexander. Meanwhile, Buchanan appointed the affable,
portly Alfred W. Cumming of Georgia to be the new governor of
Utah.[41] Cumming and a whole new roster of federal appointees were
sent West in July to join the army expedition. Among them was
the new United States Attorney General for Utah, J. M. Hockaday,

38. Ibid., pp. 1 ff.
39. *Deseret News*, August 12, 19, 1857.
40. Quoted in William P. MacKinnon, "President Buchanan and the Utah
Expedition" (Honors paper, Yale University, 1959), p. 99.
41. Cumming had previously been an Indian official on the upper Missouri and
was used to frontier life. See "Alfred E. Cumming" in *DAB*.

who was also a former mail contract partner of W. M. F. Magraw. Magraw himself was on the Utah expedition as the superintendent of a wagon road crew, holding a Department of the Interior contract to build a portion of the Pacific Wagon Road.[42]

Many technical and practical problems remained to be solved before Buchanan's policy could become a reality. Although the Utah expedition had been ordered within three months of Buchanan's accession to office, General Scott and others warned the Chief Executive that it was too late to move troops to Utah without the likelihood of their spending a winter on the Plains. Both Buchanan and his anti-Mormon Secretary of War, John B. Floyd, ignored the warning. Maintaining that he could buy time with money, Floyd literally forced Russell, Majors, and Waddell, the famous freighting firm, to accept huge contracts to supply the Utah expedition. Since public opinion and most newspapers were in a thoroughly anti-Mormon and antipolygamy mood, Floyd and Buchanan felt they were free to do as they pleased in solving the Utah question.

One of the least explicable and justifiable aspects of Buchanan's Utah policy was his failure to investigate the situation in Utah itself before mounting a military invasion and risking war. The President even neglected to inform Young that he had been removed as governor, an oversight the Church leader used later in his own defense. Nevertheless, in September 1857, long before troops reached the borders of Utah, Captain Stewart Van Vliet rode into Salt Lake City to arrange forage and food for the expedition. He also had orders to find a suitable place for a military camp, but these duties hardly disguised the fact that he was on a reconnaissance trip.[43]

Van Vliet was a wise choice for this delicate task, for he had known and befriended Mormons in their winter quarters station at Florence, Nebraska. Courteous and noncommittal, he let the Saints do most of

---

42. In his article "The Buchanan Spoils System and the Utah Expedition," *UHQ, 31* (1963), 127–50, MacKinnon challenges Furniss' contention that Buchanan did not know of Magraw's complaints until after the Utah Expedition was under way. See Furniss, pp. 62–64.

43. Furniss, pp. 105–06. *Deseret News,* August 16, 1857. Stout, "Diary," September 6, 1857. For documents relating to Van Vliet's mission see Hafen, *Utah Expedition,* pp. 35–55.

the talking. After being greeted with a curious mixture of hospitality and hostility, he, Young, and various church leaders talked and dined together for nearly a fortnight. On one occasion, Van Vliet found himself strolling with the Lion of the Lord up and down the rows of an orchard, munching ripe peaches. On Sunday, Van Vliet went to Mormon services. In that delightfully informal and rambling way so characteristic of his discourses, Young asked how many Saints in attendance were not citizens, in order to refute a popular Eastern assertion that the Mormons were all foreigners. Only a fourth of the audience raised hands.[44]

In his conversations with Van Vliet, Young had done his job almost too well: he had so impressed the Army officer with the Mormon spirit of intransigence that Van Vliet reported the Saints might well resist by force and that no food or forage was available.[45] At one point Young threatened to close the California trail by saying, "I shall not hold the Indians by the wrist any longer." Doubtless Van Vliet had read of Young's sermon of September 6, 1857, in which he declared that "the thread was cut between us and the United States and that the Almighty recognized us as a free and independent people and that no officer appointed by government should come and rule over us from this time forth."[46] Van Vliet also warned that the occupation of Utah might prove extremely difficult, since the Mormon militia already controlled all passes into the territory.[47]

The Van Vliet report undoubtedly strengthened Buchanan's and Floyd's argument for an aggressive stand in Utah. Where the resistance had previously been of a political nature, it now seemed to be military as well. Fortunately, at this point Colonel Albert Sidney Johnston replaced Colonel Alexander as commander of the Utah expedition. A brilliant if stiff and formal officer, a martinet in discipline, fearless and doggedly determined, Johnston took quite literally Floyd's instructions that a rebellion existed in Utah, and he went west with the clear intention of fighting a war.[48]

44. *Deseret News,* August 16, 1857.
45. Furniss, pp. 106–07. H. H. Bancroft, *History of Utah, 1540–1886* (San Francisco, 1889), pp. 543 ff. Hafen, *Utah Expedition,* pp. 50–55.
46. Stout, "Diary," September 6, 1857.
47. Furniss, pp. 98–101, 112–13.
48. Ibid., pp. 98–101, 112–13. William Preston Johnston, *The Life of General Albert Sidney Johnston* (New York, 1878), pp. 195–231.

In Utah, Young had already launched his own campaign of resistance. In the first stage, as Norman Furniss has observed, he was full
of fight, arguing that since the U. S. Army had no legal right to be
there, it could be rightfully resisted. His confident air was seconded
by a strong Nauvoo Legion, which had been under process of reorganization and expansion since February. Young's defiance was
buttressed by the conviction that the whole affair was an office-seekers'
political scheme for getting money out of the United States Treasury.
Finally, he maintained that such a travesty of the Mormons' political
rights gave them the excuse to be independent of the United States.
In connection with these arguments, Young issued a proclamation in
September 1857, which declared "we are now invaded by a hostile
force," and placed the territory under martial law.[49] Again Young
played into the hands of Buchanan and Floyd, for as Johnston
remarked upon hearing of the proclamation: it proved the "necessity
of a conquest of these traitorous people."[50]

Young's strategy of defense was dictated by many factors, something
Johnston did not appreciate. The first factor was Young's vivid
memory that his beloved Joseph Smith had died at the hands of an
unrestrained Illinois militia. To Young, armies—federal or state—
were roaring, looting, irresponsible mobs. The presence of Colonel
Steptoe's rambunctious troops in Utah in 1855 had caused riots in
Salt Lake City. Such groups he would never allow again in Utah.
Thus he ordered the Nauvoo Legion to hold and fortify Echo Canyon
and to keep watch on all passes into Utah. Meanwhile, a frantic
search for food and ammunition began. Lead mines were sought out.
Saints from California and Nevada were called home, and the militia
was further enlarged in size.

Another factor that persuaded Young to keep the Army out of
Utah in 1857 was the Mountain Meadows Massacre. While Young
and Van Vliet had talked in Salt Lake City that September, a bizarre
tragedy occurred some three hundred miles to the south. A party of
Missourians and Arkansans migrating to California had chosen to
take the southern route, which led them through the attenuated chain
of settlements known as the Mormon Corridor. Local Mormons, with

49. *Deseret News*, September 1857. Stout, "Diary," September 14, 1857.
50. Furniss, pp. 112–115.

bitter recollections of their treatment in Missouri, were still excited
by the reformation and were angry at the news of the recent assassination of their beloved missionary Parley P. Pratt in Arkansas. The
trouble began when the Gentile migrants tried to trade with the
Mormons. When the latter refused to sell supplies, the Missourians
appear to have appropriated goods and cattle here and there.
Unafraid, some of them had named their oxen Brigham and had
shouted obscene anti-Mormon remarks as they passed through the
settlements.[51]

The arrival of the Missouri-Arkansas party in southern Utah
coincided with a whirlwind tour by George A. Smith of the First
Presidency, who gave the settlers an emotional and militaristic set of
discourses somewhat after the fashion of Jedediah M. Grant. Smith
also brought vague orders from Young which seemed to say that the
Mormons should not restrain Indians from attacking non-Mormon
settlers.[52] The upshot was that on September 7, 1857, the Gentile
train was attacked by several hundred Indians at a creek in Mountain
Meadows. Outnumbered, short of water, and with quite a few
wounded, the members of the train seemed doomed until a Saint
named John D. Lee appeared under a truce to say that the Indians
would spare them if they loaded the women and children in a wagon.
The men were to give up their arms and then walk single file toward
a safer spot. The offer was accepted and was being carried out when
the Indians and Mormons, at a pre-arranged signal, killed some 120
adults and children of speaking age.

The question remained: who had actually ordered the massacre?
Was it Colonel Dame, who was in charge of the local Mormon troops?
Was it Colonel Isaac Haight? Or was it John D. Lee, who negotiated
the fake truce? Did the authorities at Salt Lake City order the attack,
or did the Indians—who were clearly furious at their own high losses
—force the final slaughter? Or was it the inevitable effect of reformation zeal? These questions have never been fully answered, but the
Mountain Meadows Massacre affected Mormon strategy. Young

51. Bancroft, *Utah*, pp. 546 ff.
52. Ibid. Juanita Brooks, *The Mountain Meadows Massacre* (Norman, 1962),
pp. 35 ff.

appears to have learned of it in September and immediately saw that it could be the excuse for the U. S. Army to fall upon the Saints in revenge. The whole affair was hushed up or referred to as an Indian ambush. The surviving infant children were quietly adopted into southern Utah homes or kept at Jacob Hamblin's ranch.[53]

By October, Mormon forces were ready for action. Lacking cannon or proper arms and acutely aware that they must not be guilty of starting a shooting war, they resorted instead to economic attrition. On October 3 Major Lot Smith destroyed three wagon trains, ran off stock, and burned thousands of acres of needed grazing grounds along the Army's route. Having already seized Fort Bridger and constructed their own Fort Supply near South Pass, the Saints now burned these outposts. Not the least of their tactics was to keep the weary soldiers and teamsters awake at night by fake raids and feints.

No one was killed in the practice of this "scorched earth" policy, but the Mormons succeeded in convincing the Army that the occupation of Utah would be a harrowing, thankless, and incredibly expensive task. They also prevented the Army from reaching its destination that fall, thus giving Young and the Church a breathing spell in which to lay further plans.

As Young and the Mormons congratulated one another on their successes and began a spirited, exciting, and even pleasant winter in Utah, Johnston's troops and the federal officers arrived at Ham's Fork on the Green River. Since Alexander had wasted much time moving the Army back and forth over terrible terrain, Johnston found it necessary to settle at Bridger's Old Fort, where he established Camp Scott. There the Army and the civil officials dug in to survive a harsh mountain winter.[54]

The slowness with which the Utah rebellion was being put down, and the enormous expenses incurred by an expedition whose supply lines stretched nearly a thousand miles, were not lost on Congress

---

53. Brooks, pp. 171–73. Bancroft, pp. 552–56.
54. Governor Cumming's wife, Elizabeth, wrote graphic accounts of the cold, and of the lack of food and fuel in Camp Scott. See esp. Elizabeth Cumming to Anne Cumming, November 27, 1857, in Alfred E. Cumming Papers, 1857–1858, USHS (microfilm).

when that body convened in December 1857. The following January, the House asked Buchanan to furnish information which gave rise to the expedition and to throw light "upon the question as to how far said Brigham Young and his followers are in a state of rebellion or resistance to the government, of the United States."[55]

To this inquiry Buchanan replied with *ex post facto* evidence. His main case rested on the accusing letter of W. M. F. Magraw of October 3, 1856. The remainder of Buchanan's 215-page justification, however, contained the familiar charges of Drummond, Stiles, Hurt, and others. Drummond's charges made strong reading, for he declared that the federal officers, the national government, and its chief executives, both living and dead, had been publicly abused and insulted by the Saints. In his defiance of law, said Drummond, Young had freed convicted murderers and dictated grand-jury decisions. He had also ordered the massacre of the Gunnison party of 1853 and had engineered the deaths of Judge Shaver and Secretary Almon W. Babbitt. Altogether the combined documents produced an impressive indictment of the Saints, but the fact remained that many of them were not written when Buchanan ordered the expedition.

At the same time, Young was using equally spurious methods to justify the charge that it was a contractor's war. It was true that the Utah conflict was proving to be one of the most expensive in peacetime history—so much so that the national debt jumped from $25,000,000 to $65,000,000 in Buchanan's four years, and the war itself cost an estimated $15,000,000.[56] In 1858 alone, Russell, Majors, and Waddell handled $3,361,340 in Utah contracts. The cost eventually produced such a drain on the War Department budget that Secretary John Floyd resorted to illegal means to pay his bills—an act which later resulted in his indictment for malfeasance in office.[57] The shortage of cash also left Russell, Majors, and Waddell in serious trouble. Although Young was wrong in saying that contractors had caused the war, he was correct in believing that once the war had started, it

55. See *Utah Expedition*, 35th Cong., 1st Sess., 1857–1858, House Exec. Doc. 71 (Washington, 1857). Furniss, pp. 56–57.

56. MacKinnon, "Buchanan and the Utah Expedition," p. 143.

57. "John B. Floyd" in *DAB*.

became a contractors' paradise. There is even evidence to suggest that the administration itself used the new Utah contracts of 1858 as bait to influence the Congressional vote on the LeCompton bill in March of that year.[58]

By 1858, it was also clear to Buchanan that he must bring the Utah troubles to a conclusion. Most historians traditionally picture a desperate President, anxious to extricate himself from a nightmare situation. But as a recent scholar of the Mormon War has pointed out, Buchanan's desire to end the war stemmed not from chagrin or a sense of disaster but from the very practical fact that Congress—although still hostile to the Saints—had refused new appropriations for the expedition.[59] Neither Buchanan nor Floyd had changed their views about the necessity of suppressing rebellion.

By nature James Buchanan was a compromiser, so he listened to the pleas of the faithful Mormon defender, Colonel Kane, who volunteered to go to Utah and mediate the dispute soon after the Army began its march west. The "Little Friend," as Young always called the diminutive Philadelphian, struck out on a heroic journey to Panama. There he crossed the Isthmus on the newly built railroad, sailed on to San Francisco, and traveled over the mountains to Salt Lake City, which he reached on February 25, 1858. Homesick, exhausted, and at times even hysterical, he conferred with Mormon leaders about a peace settlement and pushed on to Johnston's camp. At Camp Scott, Kane encountered the extreme hostility of Colonel Johnston and of his soldiers, who thought he was a Mormon spy. Several of the civilian officials, notably Chief Justice Delana R. Eckels, felt Kane was a Quaker meddler in an affair destined to be settled by military force.[60]

Kane's self-appointed task grew more onerous after he naïvely

58. MacKinnon, "Buchanan and the Utah Expedition," pp. 168–71.

59. Buchanan's annual message contained a fierce denunciation of the Mormons as rebels. See James D. Richardson, *Messages and Papers of the Presidents, 1789–1897* (10 vols. Washington, 1897), 5, 454–57. Note also the tone of the Amnesty Proclamation of April 6, 1858, ibid., pp. 493–95. Furniss, p. 171.

60. Kane was horrified at Eckels' intransigent attitude and expressed wonder that the Mormons had not shot him. See Elizabeth Cumming to ———, May 28, 1858, Cumming Papers; and O. O. Winther, ed., *The Private Papers and Diary of T. L. Kane, a Friend of the Mormons* (San Francisco, 1947), pp. 10–32.

delivered an offer of food from Young in return for withdrawal of troops. Johnston sternly rejected such an idea. But just as Kane began to despair of making peace, he discovered that Camp Scott was a hornet's nest of buzzing dislikes and conflicting ambitions and aims. Johnston had come to Utah to fight a war and direct a military occupation. Governor Cumming, on the other hand, was anxious not to be overshadowed by the Army. Justice Eckels was jealous of both, for he sought to make the federal courts the true weapons of reform and justice in Utah. Hockaday and Magraw were fast becoming drunkards.[61] Almost unconsciously Kane began playing a game of divide and conquer. Concentrating upon Cumming, within a few weeks he had considerably softened the new Governor's attitude toward the Mormons. Cumming himself then became a man with an obsession: he would end the war singlehandedly. On April 3, 1858, he agreed to go to Salt Lake and negotiate with the Saints.[62]

Cumming's decision came none too soon: while he and Kane were talking, the administration had ordered reinforcements for Johnston's army, had contracted for more freight, and had even created a military department for Utah.[63] General Scott, undoubtedly remembering his own campaign in Mexico, sent Johnston advice "as to the best strategy to 'force the passes to Salt Lake.' "[64] Miracle of miracles, food was on the way from Laramie. And after experiencing incredible hardships, Captain Randolph B. Marcy was traveling northward along the eastern Rockies with animals and mounts, secured in New Mexico, for the cavalry. If all went according to plan, a well-victualed and equipped army would sweep down on Utah in late June 1858.

The changing situation had impressed Young as early as November 1857. Rather than stop the federal government, he had strengthened its determination. He could also see that the Saints simply did not

61. MacKinnon, "Magraw," p. 11, finds that Magraw was fired from his position as superintendent of a stretch of the Pacific Wagon Road in the fall of 1857, while Hockaday resigned as Utah's federal district attorney to be a mail contractor again.

62. Cumming's official instructions, dated July 11, 1857, described the Army as being there "for the performance of the ordinary military duties of security and protection upon our frontiers, and also if necessary, to aid in the enforcement of the law." State Department, Letter Books, 1853–1859, TP, Utah.

63. Furniss, *Conflict*, pp. 171–75.

64. Ibid., p. 172.

have the firepower to maintain a long war. Subtly the tone of his remarks altered. In January 1858 both the legislature and mass meetings in the Tabernacle drafted petitions explaining the Mormon views to Buchanan while defending Young. Young himself began to speak as an extreme states-righter rather than a ruler of an independent country.[65] Utah was now so short of cash that the tax laws were repealed, and Young organized the Bank of Deseret to handle locally printed currency. Standing armies were to be fed by the "wards and counties from whom they are raised." So desperate was the lead and powder situation that Mormon officers talked seriously of resorting to bows and arrows.[66]

The turning point for the Mormons came on March 18, when the Council of the First Presiding Twelve and the officers of the Nauvoo Legion decided to attack the enemy "while they are yet distant" and when they came near, but only in "unavoidable self-defense." This stand was modified when the leaders agreed to burn their homes and flee to the mountains. "Burn up and flee," was the new policy, wrote Hosea Stout, for this would make "the folly, and the meanness of the President [Buchanan] . . . the more apparent."[67] More specifically, the Mormons planned to evacuate the northern part of Utah. "Move South" became the cry of the day, and though many families seemed loath to do so, official teams came to load up goods and people. Another exodus for the Saints had begun. Where they would eventually go was not certain, for Young's scouts could find no rich oasis toward the southern rim of the Great Basin. It might well be a wandering in the wilderness like the people of Israel.

As records and papers were bundled into wagons and the *Deseret News* started up in Fillmore, the Saints in Salt Lake witnessed a remarkable sight. On April 12 the rotund Governor Cumming was seen in the capital, having come alone and unarmed with only a Mormon escort. Pompous and vain though Cumming was, his bravery made a profound impression. Young, was so completely antagonistic,

65. See Young's annual message to the Utah Assembly in *Deseret News*, December 23, 1857, and the Assembly's eloquent "Petition" in *Cong. Globe*, 35th Cong., 1st Sess., 1857–1858, Part II (Washington, 1858), pp. 1151–52.

66. Furniss, pp. 133–35.

67. Stout, "Diary," March 18, 1858.

however, that when he saw the new official he could only think of him as a "besom of destruction." Cumming himself traveled on to Provo, where he labored among the rank and file of Saints to return to their homes, but to no avail. Yet two weeks after his arrival, the Governor, seemingly undaunted, met still more Mormons in the Tabernacle. Sarcasm, hissing, and cries greeted him, but he took it well and explained that the purpose of the officials and the Army was simply to bring law and order to Utah.[68]

Cumming had planted a reasonable doubt in the Mormon mind and was making progress, but before he could capitalize on his labors, Buchanan interfered. While Cumming was negotiating, Colonel Kane had returned to Washington to assert that peace was restored. The President, after quizzing the Philadelphian ruthlessly, finally agreed to send two peace commissioners to Utah to settle questions and to offer amnesty to those formerly in rebellion. The olive branch was held in a clenched fist, however, for Buchanan insisted on Army occupation of Utah.

When the two commissioners, Lazarus Powell and Benjamin McCulloch, appeared in Camp Scott on the eve of the Army's departure for Salt Lake, Johnston greeted them with even less enthusiasm than he had Kane. But they had precedence over Johnston, and, taking up where Cumming had left off, they demanded army entry into Utah, while offering terms of amnesty. Young procrastinated as much as he dared, but he finally came to terms. On June 12, 1858, Commissioner Powell somewhat optimistically informed a public meeting that all difficulties were settled.[69]

The denouement was painfully slow, for the Saints returned reluctantly and suspiciously to their homes in Salt Lake City and to the north. Some had stayed away for over four months. The peace almost failed when Johnston, unaware of the final negotiations, began to march southward before he was supposed to. Once these details were ironed out, the United States Army marched through the still deserted Salt Lake City to a new camp in Cedar Valley. Disciplined to the

68. Ibid., April 25, 1858. Cumming to Cass, Great Salt Lake City, May 2, 1858, State Department, Letter Books, 1858–1859, TP, Utah.

69. Hafen, *Utah Expedition*, pp. 342–43.

hilt but anxious to show their pent-up feelings, the soldiers were delighted to hear the band play the obscene "One-Eyed Riley," while passing the Lion and Bee Houses of Brigham Young. In this innocuous way a frustrated army of nearly 3,000 men expressed their defiance of the Mormon president. To one officer, however, the scene was poignant, even tragic. Philip St. George Cooke, who had commanded the Mormon Battalion in the Mexican War, now rode as one of their conquerors. In memory of a happier time the emotional Cooke journeyed uncapped, his hand over his heart, through the empty desert capital.[70]

70. Furniss, p. 201.

My office is a mere sinecure. By the artful legislation of the
dominant power, a most miserable skeleton of it merely
remained. . . . In the midst of this fair Republic is established
a theocracy, and for twenty years [Young] has carried it on in
insolent defiance of the authority of the United States, and
in the face of our Republican institutions.

Governor J. Wilson Shaffer, 1869

 On June 14, 1858, Colonel Johnston declared that
federal law in Utah was no longer being defied, and
by July 7 Governor Alfred Cumming had published
and put into operation Buchanan's proclamation of
amnesty. The Mormon War was officially at an end.[1]
In the twenty years that followed the conflict,
however, a quieter but equally determined struggle continued
between the federal officers and the Church of the Latter Day Saints.
From 1859 until the start of the Civil War, long-standing, basic disputes
over the local court system of Utah were continued by Young and the
new federal judges. On the heels of this disagreement a bitter fight
followed between Young and General Patrick E. Connor, commander

1. Hafen, *Utah Expedition*, pp. 333–37, 345–46.

of the federal troops stationed in Utah during the Civil War. A third
struggle over the powers of the governor flared periodically into a
major crisis, and Congress itself in these years occasionally passed laws,
designed either to strengthen the federal officers in Utah or to abolish
polygamy. Not until the 1880s came the massive attack on Church
leaders, on the civil rights of the rank and file, and on the institution
of polygamy. But only the defeated Southern states could point to a
similar history of federal interference in the local life of a community
and to the deliberate political and social reconstruction of an entire
territory over so long a time.

Shortly after Johnston established Camp Floyd in Cedar Valley,
Utah, and the civil officers began their duties, the first of many court
crises arose to embitter Mormon-Gentile relations. The new chief
justice of the territory, Delana R. Eckels, was determined to assert
federal authority at all costs. He was partciularly anxious to curb
the probate courts. Convinced that Governor Cumming was both a
compromiser and a dupe of Young's, Eckels wrote his old friend,
Lewis Cass: "Brigham Young is *de facto* Governor of Utah whatever
Cumming may do *de jure*. His reign is one of terror." Seeking to
"combat terror with terror," a policy suggested by the anti-Mormon
Indian Agent, Garland Hurt, Eckels advocated the use of the army
as a civil posse and the stationing of troops within Salt Lake City.
We must "govern them *come what may* . . . [for] a peace with
traitors begun by concession, must end in disgrace."[2] The Judge
himself must have been regarded with some of the terror of which
he so often spoke: in the fall of 1859 he reported to Cass that he had
experienced great difficulty in holding a court at Nephi, since two-
thirds of the male population had fled at his approach.[3] Some feared
jury duty, while others feared conviction. Such acts gave Eckels the
excuse to use numerous teamsters from Camp Floyd and nearby
Frogtown for jurors.

Associate Justices John Cradlebaugh and Charles E. Sinclair were
equally busy at making their courts effective. When Cradlebaugh

2. Eckels to Cass (n.d.), and Garland Hurt to Eckels (n.d.), State Department
Letter Books, 1853–1859, TP, Utah.

3. Eckels to Cass, Camp Floyd, September 27, 1859, same source as above.

opened his term at Provo in March 1859, he made a strong charge
to the grand jury in which he commented on the Mountain Meadows
Massacre and the Potter-Parrish killings at Springville.[4] He demanded
that the guilty parties be brought to trial. In order to guard prisoners
—the town had no jail—the Judge persuaded Johnston to station
800 troops in Provo. Every Saint saw the move as a military threat
to force juries to convict those being tried, and Cradlebaugh's use
of the Army as a civil posse thus provoked the greatest furor since
the war itself. The citizens of Provo, headed by their mayor, protested
the presence of troops, while the Mormon papers began a press war
against the action. The efforts of United States Marshal Peter K.
Dotson to make arrests sent scores of Saints into hiding, among them
John D. Lee. General Daniel Wells alerted the Nauvoo Legion for
action, and Brigham Young began to talk of a new exodus.[5] The
crisis finally passed when Dotson's failure to find prisoners rendered
federal court proceedings useless. In obvious disgust, Cradlebaugh
resigned and went to Nevada, where he was elected delegate to
Congress on a Mormon-hating ticket, when that area became a
separate territory.[6]

Cradlebaugh's course was pursued at a more petty level by Judge
Sinclair, who stretched his court sessions to sixty sitting days as
opposed to sixty calendar days. This was done, the Mormons
explained, only to impress the federal government with the court's
vigor and to pad the payroll of the clerks and the marshal. But as
John Taylor noted: "Notwithstanding the 'terrible things in the
land of Ham, and wonderful things by the red sea [sic],' they have
as yet convicted no one."[7] Even an effort by the Judge to disbar
James Ferguson for disrupting Judge Stiles' court in 1856 failed.
Governor Cumming explained to Lewis Cass that when a judge stated
publicly that the "entire community had forefeited their right to

4. These killings had taken place during the reformation. Garland described
Potter and Parrish as dissenters from the Church. See Garland Hurt to Cumming,
December 17, 1857, same source.
5. Cumming to Johnston, April (n.d.) 1859, same source. *Deseret News*, March
30, 1859.
6. See "John Cradlebaugh" in *Biographical Directory of the American Congress*.
7. John Taylor to George Q. Cannon, January 12, 1859, Kane Papers.

self-government" and should be subject to martial law, no citizen in his right mind would trust the courts.[8] Had Eckels, Cradlebaugh, and Sinclair proceeded with more moderation, they might have broken Mormon unity in 1858. Instead, they were reprimanded by Jeremiah S. Black, Buchanan's attorney general, for using troops and exceeding their authority.

The never-ending court war also had its comic aspects. After the new judges had ended their federal term and began to sit as a territorial court, they discovered that the legislature had failed to provide appropriations for such courts or for the pay of its juries, clerks, and marshals. Cried the *Valley Tan,* an anti-Mormon paper subsidized by Camp Floyd, this was a studied omission. The Church also sent stenographers to the federal courts to copy down every word to make sure that justice was done. When Judge Sinclair remarked that there were omissions and discrepancies in the territorial laws of Utah, Daniel H. Wells, President of the Council, immediately demanded a report from Sinclair on such omissions. Sinclair, seeing the trap of commenting on laws out of court, declined amidst much bluster.[9] A pattern that would continue throughout the territorial period had been established: every real or imagined encroachment and every sign of persecution would be so quickly aired and so vigorously protested that the Mormons would usually get their way.

The elaborate interplay of pressure and counterpressure was also evident in the assemblies which met during Cumming's term of office. In 1858 the legislature forbade anyone to vote who had not been a resident or a property-holding taxpayer for a year. The law was clearly designed to prohibit soldiers and teamsters from participating in Utah elections. Other acts strengthened the probate courts and tried to prevent Utah lands from being declared public domain.[10] At its next session in December 1859, the Assembly ignored Cumming's pleas to settle the probate court issue; to clarify land, water, and grazing laws; and either to divert the extraordinary appropriations

8. Cumming to Cass, February 2, 1860, State Department Letter Books, 1860–1872, TP, Utah. See also *Deseret News,* June 29, 1859.
9. Young to George Q. Cannon, December 24, 1858, Kane Papers.
10. *Deseret News,* January 26, February 2, 1859.

for the militia into a school fund or to institute a tax on tithing for school support.[11] In this way Cumming struck at tithing (seen by Gentiles as one of the mainstays of the Church), Mormon controlled schools, and the huge size of the Nauvoo Legion. The legislature listened politely but declined to do more than pass an ineffectual school bill.

Nowhere was the difference between Mormon and American attitudes more dramatic than on the question of land policy. In contrast to the urgent demands of most territories for land offices and a surveyor general, Young wrote Delegate Hooper in March 1860 to "omit using any effort for the establishment of a land office in Utah during this session, and, if necessary, even operate to counteract a movement of that kind." Later Young explored the possibility of using land warrants, which many veterans of the Mormon battalion still held, to get Utah land "previous to such land coming into market."[12] At all costs the speculative and often corrupt character of the American public land system was to be kept out of Utah.

In January 1861 the Assembly once again tried to counter federal rule by appealing to Congress to admit Deseret as a state. Young knew that the appeal was hopeless, for Congress was preoccupied with saving the Union. He admitted privately, "we are very thankful that Congress had not admitted us into the Union as a State. However, we shall continue to tease them on that point so long as they even pretend to legislate for the past Union."[13] Despite Buchanan, Cumming, federal judges, and the United States Army, Brigham Young still ruled Utah and was conducting a brilliant, coordinated, unceasing, passive resistance movement unique in American history.

Brigham Young wrote sarcastically to Delegate Hooper soon after Army occupation of Utah, "You may observe [that] courtesy is the order of the day." He was referring to the stiff but polite demands that he and Governor Cumming frequently made upon one another.

11. Ibid., December 14, 1859.
12. Young to W. H. Hooper, March 8, April 12, May 24, 1860, in MS Letters of Young to Hooper, 1853–1859, YWA. See also George W. Rollins, "Land Policies of the United States as Applied to Utah, to 1910," *UHQ,* 20 (1952), 239–51.
13. Young to Hooper, February 7, 1861, YWA.

This was the more genteel aspect of occupation, for the teamsters, saloon keepers, army contractors, and Missouri Gentiles and soldiers who had accompanied Johnston's army were not so diplomatic. Soon clubs, gaming houses, and saloons had sprung up on East Temple Street in Salt Lake City. They became a center for soldiers and a resort for Mormon haters. George A. Smith, a member of the First Presidency, called it the "headquarters of Rowdyism" and noted that the mayor's court had such a full docket of shootings and brawls it "resembles those of our more refined cities in the east." "Hell has boiled over," wrote John Taylor in dismay, "and the scum has floated among us."[14] Such environs attracted the new territorial secretary John P. Hartnett, Dr. Garland Hurt, and other anti-Mormon officials who constituted Utah's first "Gentile Ring."

The non-Mormons soon had a public voice as well, for in November 1858 Kirk Anderson, a former Missouri newspaper man, began to publish the *Valley Tan*. This Gentile paper represented the first significant press opposition to the *Deseret News*. It is likely that nothing exercised Young as much as the remarks in this paper, for he was convinced that Anderson wanted to "provoke a collision" between troops and Saints, so that soldiers would be stationed in Utah permanently. John Taylor remarked to George Q. Cannon, "The merchants and sutlery had been foremost in creating these difficulties . . . for such is their greed of gold."[15] But Young and his advisers did their raging in private or through the columns of the *Deseret News,* for violence was generally avoided.

The uneasy peace was maintained not by self-restraint alone, but by the device of a large police force in Salt Lake City. When the soldiers arrived, the city fathers met in Brigham Young's barn and passed an ordinance creating the "City Watch." The force was not to exceed forty men unless "the exigencies of the time should require it," but Mayor Smoot soon enlisted more than 150 men "armed with clubs and pistols [and] bearing the insignia of Stars." Perhaps 300 more were on duty as "ward police."[16] The *Valley Tan* screamed

14. John Taylor to George Q. Cannon, January 12, 1859, Kane Papers.
15. Ibid.
16. *Valley Tan*, November 26, 1858.

that this was not a police force but an "ecclesiastical patrol." Whatever it was, the city watch kept order, enforced a virtual curfew, and handled the drunks and rowdies with such bone crushing vigor that even the denizens of East Temple behaved on the streets. Salt Lake City "is as quiet as a New England Village," wrote Elizabeth Cumming, the Governor's wife.[17]

Before the *Valley Tan* could provoke some tragic incident, the approach of the Civil War led to the abandonment of Camp Floyd, the withdrawal of troops from Utah, and a virtual hiatus of federal rule for nearly two years. The Mormons viewed the Civil War almost as an act of Providence, for the abandonment of Camp Floyd allowed them to purchase hundreds of wagons and animals at rock-bottom prices from the departing quartermaster. With the troops also went Governor Cumming, Secretary Hartnett, and nearly all the troublesome federal officials. Many observers felt that in the crucial days of 1860–61 Young would take Utah out of the Union, using as his excuse the states-rights and secession doctrines of the Southern states. But in contrast to some of his public declarations, the Mormon President adopted a policy of watch and wait. During December 1860 he wrote Delegate Hooper that he thought secession was foolish and "peaceable secession was laughable." After Lincoln's inauguration in March 1861, he told Hooper: "We like Mr. Lincoln's address very well and wish you to call his attention to that portion in which he claims to be the President of the whole people." Young then asked Lincoln to continue no one in office in Utah except Judge Kinney and to appoint only Mormons to all other posts.[18]

Young's initial tolerance of the Lincoln administration was to be severely tried, however, by the presence of General Patrick E. Connor in Utah, the appointment of Governors John Dawson and Stephen S. Harding, and the efforts of radical congressmen to outlaw polygamy during the 1860s. Of these, perhaps the greatest irritant was the red-headed, Irish-born officer from California who marched into Salt Lake City in October 1862 with 750 California Volunteers.

The initial reason for Connor's presence in Utah concerned Indians.

17. Elizabeth Cumming to ———, September 24, 1858, Cumming Papers.
18. Young to Hooper, December 20, 1860, March 28, 1861, YWA.

One of the new federal officials Buchanan had sent to Utah was Dr. Jacob Forney, Superintendent of Indian Affairs. Unlike most of his federal colleagues, Forney appears to have worked well with the Mormons. But Forney naturally relied on federal troops when Indian troubles developed. This meant that Johnston's army had played an increasingly active role in Indian control after 1858. When the soldiers left in 1861, however, Indian conditions quickly deteriorated. The California trail was now such a major highway that it became a natural target for Indian raids. At the same time, the Civil War and the discovery of gold in Nevada in 1859 made the central overland route seem even more vital than ever. Meanwhile, the Mormons themselves were discommoding the primitive Utah tribes by pushing settlements into Cache and San Pete valleys.[19] To the east, the Pike's Peak rush had agitated not only the Plains Indians but the mountain Utes on the borders of Utah and Colorado. Thus the hasty withdrawal of troops was a signal for Indians to step up raids and rob the overland stations in Utah and Nevada. By late 1861 the closing of the central overland route—the only life line to California—was a growing possibility.

To forestall the closing and reopen the southern overland route across Confederate Arizona, Lincoln called upon the Californians themselves to keep the trail open and recapture Arizona. As General James E. Carleton marched toward Tucson with his California Volunteers, a similar body under General Patrick E. Connor marched toward Utah, with the threefold purpose of ending Indian depredations, opening the trail, and keeping the Mormons loyal. Connor and his men also cherished the hope that they would eventually be called east to participate in the war for the Union.

Connor's first task—of curbing Indian raids—was accomplished by 1863. In a series of ruthless winter campaigns, he tracked down marauding bands and so effectively defeated them that within a year of his arrival the Shoshone Utes sued for peace. By January 1865 some 8,650 Great Basin Indians had been brought under treaty relations. Forney's successor, James Duane Doty, worked closely with

19. Ibid., April 19, 1860, YWA.

Connor to restore peace and reopen the trail to California. He also secured treaties in 1863 which opened lands in southern Utah for settlement. Much of the credit, however, went to Connor, who, like Carleton in New Mexico and Chivington in Colorado, was being hailed as a great hero and Indian fighter.[20]

His first two missions accomplished, Connor now saw his main assignment as one of keeping Utah loyal. He himself wrote: "I intend to quietly intrench my position [near Salt Lake City] and then say to the Saints of Utah, enough of your treason."[21] Connor was as good as his word. Ignoring deserted Camp Floyd, he marched his troops up to the benchland east of the Utah capital and laid out Camp Douglas. Directly below it stretched the orderly wide streets of the city. The proximity of soldiers and Saints naturally alarmed Young and prompted him to write mournfully that the new commander was not so cooperative as the previous one. Nor was the struggle between Church and Army long in coming. To prevent speculation, war profiteering, and consequent hardship for poor Mormons, Young persuaded the legislature to standardize all prices. Connor retaliated by making all merchants who sold to the Army take an oath of allegiance.[22]

Naturally a vigorous press war also began between the *Deseret News* and the *Union Vedette*. The latter paper was owned and operated by Connor and some fellow officers. Infuriated by its constant editorial barbs, Young exclaimed: "Every day does this foul stream of slander and abuses roll forth. . . . blackening and defaming every prominent citizen in the Territory."[23] He was soon urging Delegate Hooper to use every influence to secure Connor's removal. Later he warned friends that in most communities persons suffering such unjustified calumny would have resorted to lynch law. "Were we what they represent us to be," said Young, commenting on the

20. See "Patrick E. Connor" and "James Duane Doty" in *DAB*. Doty's life has been covered in Alice E. Smith, *James Duane Doty, Frontier Promoter* (Madison, Wisc., 1954) ; see esp. pp. 365–75.

21. Quoted in Fred B. Rogers, *Soldiers of the Overland, Being Some Account of the Services of General Patrick Edward Connor and His Volunteers in the Old West* (San Francisco, 1938) , p. 24.

22. Ibid., p. 78.

23. Young to Hooper, December 26, 1865, YWA.

Vedette's charge that Mormons were lawless and violent, "they would not have been spared."[24] So bitter were the passions on one occasion that the *Vedette* offices were mobbed and the staff whipped.

Fortune seemed even more on Connor's side when he and his men in the fall of 1863 found silver-bearing galena in Bingham Canyon, Utah. Quickly organizing the area as the Wasatch Mining District, he virtually ordered his soldiers to prospect for still more finds. In February 1864 the General incorporated the Jordan Silver Mining Company under California law, while miners organized the Mountain Lake and Rush Valley mining districts. For Connor the mineral discoveries offered more than riches. In his own florid words it would solve the Mormon problem by inviting hither "a large Gentile and loyal population sufficient by peaceful means and through the ballot box to overwhelm the Mormon by mere force of numbers, and thus wrest from the Church—disloyal and traitorous to the core— the absolute and tyrannical control of temporal and civil affairs, or at least a population numerous enough to put a check on Mormon affairs."[25] To realize these aims, Connor himself broadcast the news of the Utah ore discoveries, using public circulars and the *Union Vedette.* He promised incoming miners full protection.

The Saints did not take Connor's actions lying down. The Utah Assembly of 1864 passed an extraordinary mining act, which created the office of superintendent of mines. This official had the power to supervise "all mining claims, to locate the same, to determine the extent of each mining district, and to establish the bound of each lot and mining claim—and assess the value of such claim for taxation." The law also provided for a 20 per cent tax per year on the assessed value of each claim. In his veto Acting Governor Amos Reed aptly commented that the act was the surest way of preventing the mining industry from developing in Utah that could have been devised.[26]

This act defeated, Connor himself eventually wrote a mining law for Utah based on California precedents. By 1866 Connor had also

24. Ibid., February 13, 1866, YWA.
25. Connor to Lieut. Col. R. C. Drum, Camp Douglas, July 21, 1864, MS in Bancroft Library.
26. *Union Vedette,* January 21, 22, 1864.

founded the mining town of Stockton, had laid plans for the building of a silver and lead smelter there, and had begun to agitate for the coming of the transcontinental railroad to Utah; for in all of these developments he saw the means of toppling the Church. As he journeyed eastward toward Colorado in the fall of 1865 to accept the command of the troops in that beleaguered region, he must have smiled at the title non-Mormons had given him—"The Liberator of Utah."[27]

Mormon relations with the various governors sent to Utah by the Lincoln and Johnson administrations were nearly as crisis-ridden as were those with the United States Army. After John W. Dawson (1861–62) appeared to claim the office of governor in 1861, he was soon in serious trouble: almost immediately he vetoed a legislative call for a convention to write a state constitution; and he made improper advances to a Mormon wife.[28] The ire of the Saints forced Dawson to flee the territory, but not before he was pursued and severely beaten. In a fervent, almost hysterical letter written from Fort Bridger, Dawson harped on the familiar themes of Mormon disloyalty and lawlessness, the primacy of probate courts, polygamy, and the like.[29] His letter undoubtedly helped to kill any chances for statehood for Utah in 1862.

Dawson's successor, Stephen S. Harding (1862–63) of Indiana, was a free-soil abolitionist who counted Salmon P. Chase and George W. Julian as friends. Harding had known Joseph Smith as a young man and had followed his unusual career with inquisitiveness and even sympathy. Yet Harding's term was in some ways more harrowing than Dawson's. Soon after his arrival in 1862, he confided to Seward that he was convinced that no mail went east without first passing through Brigham Young's headquarters. Young was a disloyal tyrant,

27. Bernice Gibbs Anderson, "The Gentile City of Corinne," *UHQ, 9* (1941), 141–54. See also Connor "Obituary" in Salt Lake Daily *Tribune,* December 18, 1891.
28. Cumming apparently left Salt Lake City in April 1861 and was succeeded by the territorial secretary, Francis H. Wooton, who served as acting governor until Dawson's arrival in 1861. See John W. Dawson to Abraham Lincoln, January 13, 1862, Dawson Letters, 1861–1862, USHS.
29. Ibid. See also Dawson to Hon. W. P. Dole, February 27, 1862.

he said, who planned to use Indians to wipe out the Gentile whites in Utah. The Governor begged for a military force—Connor was still on the way—to make "treason dumb."[30]

Once Connor had arrived, Harding sent the Assembly an annual message boldly discussing the court system, requesting the power to commission and remove officers in the Nauvoo Legion, and asking for the abolition of polygamy. Since Harding's proposals struck at the entire political system in Utah, the Assembly soon replied in a series of moves that revealed great planning. The two new federal judges, Thomas J. Drake (1862–68) and Charles B. Waite (1862–64), who had helped Harding draft his message, were deliberately assigned to the wrong court districts. Then the Assembly conveniently lost Harding's message, only to have it show up weeks later at a mass meeting in the Tabernacle, where it was read aloud to an indignant audience. Of Harding himself one speaker remarked: "we know of no person who has not shrunk from his presence, as if from a nuisance. His language and his actions have been in perpetual hostility." After the band played "Hail Columbia" and "The Star Spangled Banner," other speakers followed suit. Said Albert Carrington, "There was one deep feeling of contempt" for the Governor. To cries of "Hear! hear!" John Taylor denounced Harding's veto of some fourteen legislative bills. Resolutions to Congress were drafted which accused Harding of attempted military dictatorship through control of the militia. The congregation then appointed a committee to ask Harding, Drake, and Waite to resign. As the band somewhat ominously played the "Marseillaise," some 2,100 persons lined up to sign the petition.[31]

Harding grew even more pessimistic about the fate of Utah when he learned of Judge Kinney's mock arrest of Brigham Young for polygamy in 1861. Naturally the Mormon grand jury refused to indict Young—for under territorial law, polygamy was declared not a crime. This set a precedent for legal protection of polygamy, and Young himself remarked that the judge had fined him sixpence and had held him in prison for an hour, and "who would not stand that for a

---

30. Harding to W. H. Seward, August 30, 1862, State Department, Letter Books, 1860–1872, TP, Utah.

31. Ibid., February 3, 1863. *Deseret News*, March 4, 1863.

handsome young girl." Similar incidents persuaded Harding that Utah must have more soldiers, or rebellion would break out again. "We are resting upon a volcano of human passions thinly crusted over by the hypocritical cant of a Love and Respect for the Constitution," wrote Harding. "This is the picture this Brawling Brat of a Territory now presents for contemplation—*mirabile visu-mirabile dictu.*"[32]

Before Harding's fears could disturb him further, he was removed and succeeded by James Duane Doty (1863–65), who had been Superintendent of Indian Affairs for Utah since 1861. In the territory's fifth governor the Mormons happily found another tolerant and seemingly goodnatured official. An exceptionally able man, Doty had spent his early life on the Wisconsin frontier, where he had served both as delegate and as governor during the territorial stage. After Wisconsin became a state, he seemed well on the way to national prominance as a congressman when his career was cut short by accusations of land fraud in 1852.[33] Now in his sixties, Doty was starting afresh on the Great Basin frontier.

Doty had high hopes Utah would soon become a state and that he might return to Washington as a senator. Thus he worked closely with his friend General Connor in Utah and with Senator James Doolittle in Washington to remove the Indians from the central overland route and to bring peace to Utah. He was also a lobbyist for a transcontinental rail line, and when the first Pacific Railroad bill passed Congress in 1862, Doty journeyed to San Francisco to visit Leland Stanford, it is thought, in order to lay plans for the road. At the same time Doty was certain he could never be a senator without the friendship of the Mormons. His own attitude was summed up in his remark: "There are three powers governing this country; the Mormon Church; the military, and the Civil. It is difficult to prevent collisions, but they are to be avoided if possible."[34]

Doty's own ambitions were cut short by death in 1865, but his policies were continued by Charles Durkee (1865–69), also of Wisconsin, who had been a United States senator from 1855 to 1861.

32. Harding to Seward, March 17, 1863, State Department Letter Books, 1860–1872, TP, Utah.

33. "James Duane Doty" in *DAB*.

34. Doty to Isaac Newton, December 20, 1864, State Department Letter Books, 1860–1872, TP, Utah.

Accepting the wisdom of Doty's approach, Durkee was soon in Young's good graces, since he had "refrained from assuming the character of a missionary and a zealot."[35] Even Durkee could not remain completely silent about certain public issues, however. He was disturbed by the incompatibility of an annual surplus in the territorial treasury and the lack of a real school system in Utah. He was also upset that public land surveys and the operation of the Homestead Act had not really come to Utah. But though he occasionally vetoed Mormon laws, Durkee was generally quiescent. "I was sent out to do nothing," he remarked to a friend, and as H. H. Bancroft has concluded, "his instructions were faithfully executed."[36]

From time to time either a governor or a judge revived the debates over the probate courts, the Nauvoo Legion as a militia independent of the governor's control, the lack of public schools, and the absence of a regular land policy. The issue of polygamy also remained to irritate Mormon-Gentile relations. Generally speaking, however, the Lincoln and Johnson administrations both appear to have accepted the status quo in Utah. On the other hand, the Radical Republicans in Congress did not. Once they had gained control of the national legislature in 1864, the Saints began to hear of antipolygamy and anti-Mormon bills and land surveys, and had to reckon with the coming of the Union Pacific to Utah. A new stage in Mormon-federal relations was in the offing.

One of the great ironies of Mormon history is that Vermont, the state of Joseph Smith's birth, should have furnished so many public figures to lead the attack on Mormonism in Utah. The first of these was the father of the land-grant colleges, Justin R. Morrill. While the Mormons were undergoing their reformation in 1856, they learned that Congressman Morrill had introduced a bill to suppress polygamy in Utah. Young tried to counter the possibility of its passage by holding a statehood convention that same year. Morrill's bill failed, but in 1860 the Vermonter introduced a new antipolygamy measure. At the same time, Congressman John A. Logan of Indiana filed a measure

35. Young to Hooper, May 14, 1866, YWA.
36. "Charles Durkee" in *Biographical Directory of the American Congress.* Bancroft, *Utah,* p. 622.

which would turn over all court business in Utah to the district courts. Still another bill appeared, proposing to vest the legislative power in "the governor and thirteen of the most fit and discreet persons of the Territory, to be called the legislative council." They were to be appointed biennally by the President of the United States by and with the advice and consent of the Senate. After many delays, the Morrill Act to suppress polygamy became law on July 7, 1862.[37] The Mormons' dislike of Governor Harding is partly explained by their conviction that he had inspired the Morrill Act. It subjected polygamous persons to a $500 fine and a possible five-year term of imprisonment. The law proved to be ineffective, for the local probate courts and juries refused to use it to try and convict offenders.

In 1863 Congressman Orville H. Browning of Illinois introduced a bill providing for the popular election of probate judges in Utah to remedy this defect, but this proposal failed, as did a bill submitted by George W. Julian of Indiana, which would have discouraged polygamy by granting the right of suffrage to women. On July 12, 1866, Senator Wade of Ohio proposed legislation that would permit the governor to appoint probate judges, allow U. S. marshals to choose jurors, and give Congress the power to tax Church property in Utah valued in excess of $20,000.[38] A variation of Wade's bill, introduced by Senator Andrew Cragin of New Hampshire in 1867, would have permitted nonjury trials for polygamists.[39] Other minor bills of a similar nature, along with some designed to create new land districts in Utah, were also introduced. In 1869 Congressman James M. Ashley of Ohio proposed legislation that would have virtually dismembered Utah and given most of it to other territories.[40] This was followed by the Cullom Bill, which gave federal authorities extraordinary powers and disqualified polygamists for jury duty and public office.[41]

37. *United States Statutes at Large, 12,* 501. Debate on the Morrill Act can be found in *Cong. Globe,* 36th Cong., 1st Sess., 1859–1860, pp. 1150, 1411, 1492, 1515, 1520, 1546, 1557.

38. *Cong. Globe,* 39th Cong., 1st Sess., 1865–1866 (July 12, 1866), p. 3750.

39. Roberts, *Comprehensive History of the Church, 5,* 227.

40. *Cong. Globe,* 40th Cong., 3rd Sess., 1868–1869 (esp. January 14, 1869), pp. 363 ff. *Deseret News,* February 3, 1869.

41. *Cong. Globe,* 41st Cong., 2nd Sess., 1869–1870 (esp. December 1869–February 1870), pp. 2142–53, 2178–81, 3571–82.

The failure of all these measures greatly encouraged the Saints. Rather than passively submit to Congress, however, they used a familiar series of tactics to counter the bills. When the Morrill Act became law in 1862, the Mormons launched a drive for statehood, with the obvious idea that a state had the power to legislate for its own peculiar domestic institutions. When the Cullom jury bill was pending, the able, urbane delegate from Utah, W. H. Hooper, lobbied so vigorously against it that the irate Illinois Congressman dubbed Hooper "the Mormon Richelieu."[42]

The attempts to pass most of these anti-Mormon bills took place while Congress was preoccupied with reconstructing the South. And it was Utah's fate to feel the effects of a remote national problem of no concern to her citizens. In seeking or claiming the constitutional authority to force the South to be loyal, Radical Republicans concerned with polygamy and court reform felt that they also had the power to use extraordinary measures to reconstruct Utah. Thus nearly all legislation designed to curb polygamy actually came to be based on four theories of reconstruction. The first suggested that Congress had the right to outlaw polygamy, just as it had the power to end slavery. Next, Congress asserted the right to suspend voting privileges for those refusing to conform. Third, the Republicans assumed they had the power to exact oaths of loyalty—in this case a pledge not to be polygamous. Finally, the radicals felt they could overhaul or oversee local government in Utah, just as they had in the South, either by giving extraordinary powers to the governor or by appointing federal commissioners to see that Utah was properly run.[43]

That "reconstruction techniques" were being applied to Utah was particularly apparent in the Cragin bill. Innocently entitled "a bill to regulate the selection of juries in Utah," it was actually a mammoth catch-all act. It stated that United States marshals should be allowed to pick juries and that the governor be empowered to appoint all probate judges for four years, and to name militia officers as well. It

42. Stanford Orson Cazier, "The Life of William Henry Hooper, Merchant-Statesman" (Master's thesis, University of Utah, 1956), p. 101.

43. See Lamar, "Political Patterns in New Mexico and Utah," *UHQ,* 28 (1960), 363–87.

gave Utah the secret ballot and declared that the Mormon Church was a corporation subject to taxation. The measure attacked polygamy by outlawing plural marriage and by requiring that all marriages in Utah be the result of a civil ceremony. Children of a polygamous union were to be declared illegitimate, and all females who consented to "spiritual marriage" were subject to two years' imprisonment. The *Deseret News,* in a series of furious editorials, called the Cragin bill more despotic than rule by Judge Jefferies.[44] Delegate Hooper again attempted to counter the Cragin measure by introducing a statehood bill for Utah.

Although the Cragin bill was defeated in 1868, Congressman Shelby M. Cullom of Illinois submitted still another bill in 1870, and the original Cragin bill was revived. This time the Mormons organized mass meetings all over Utah to protest the passage of either proposal. Even the ladies of Salt Lake held an indignation meeting to deny that they hated polygamy. Assemblies convened at the Tabernacle to register protests, and Delegate Hooper lectured Congress on the principle of religious toleration.[45] The Cullom and Cragin bills may well have been as ineffective as the Morrill Act had been; but while they were still being considered in 1869 and 1870, Ulysses S. Grant appointed a set of territorial officials who seemed as anti-Mormon as Cullom himself. The first of these was Governor J. Wilson Shaffer (1869–70), a military man and a personal friend of Cullom, who vowed he would cleanse the "Augean Stable" Utah had become.[46]

Shaffer's position was strengthened by the presence of an energetic anti-Mormon Chief Justice, James Bedell McKean. Although born in Vermont, he had been a New York congressman when the Morrill Act passed. Rather more able than his predecessors, McKean was to succeed in bringing test cases to the federal courts which focused

44. *Deseret Evening News,* December 14, 16, 30, 1867, January 2, 4, 1868. See also *Cong. Globe,* 41st Cong., 2nd Sess., 1869–1870, pp. 1367, 1373, 2145, 2178, 3571–76.

45. *Deseret News Weekly,* January 19, February 2, April 6, 1870. R. N. Baskin, a Gentile lawyer in Utah, claims that he drafted Cullom's bill for him. See his *Reminiscences of Early Utah* (Salt Lake City, 1914), pp. 28–31.

46. Bancroft, *Utah,* p. 658. Shaffer to Shelby M. Cullom, April 27, 1870, State Department Letter Books, 1860–1872, TP, Utah.

the conflict over polygamy and federal rule and gave Congress a chance to legislate more effectively.[47] In October 1871 Young himself was arrested on sixteen charges of "lascivious cohabitation," but upon Supreme Court review of other cases involving polygamy, it was found that a lower court had exceeded its jurisdiction. As a result, Young and other prominent Mormons on trial were released.

The Mormon countermoves to Shaffer and Cullom were almost Machiavellian in their cleverness. When Shaffer attempted to issue commissions for probate judges, limiting their acts to chancery and probate duties, the Mormon incumbents refused them. When an influx of Gentile miners threatened to change voting patterns, the Saints gave their wives the vote, permitted probate judges to choose the polling places, and even passed a law giving the latter jurisdiction in counties in which they were not even resident.[48]

Luck was on the Mormon side: the Congressional bills met defeat, and Governor Shaffer died suddenly in November while futilely conducting a struggle with General Daniel H. Wells over the control of the Nauvoo Legion. Shaffer's successor, George L. Woods (1871–75), was a blustering Oregon politician with little ability, although he continued to dramatize the fact that the Nauvoo Legion was not under gubernatorial control.[49]

By 1873 the polygamy issue had stirred up so much national sentiment that Congress began to make still newer attempts to end the institution. The New York *Herald*, already the self-appointed crusader against polygamy, urged Congress to appoint a commissioner to rule Utah. Delegates Claggett of Montana and Merritt of Idaho introduced anti-Mormon bills. John A. Logan, now an Indiana senator, also produced an act to "promote public justice in the several territories." Senator Frederick T. Frelinghuysen submitted yet another. President Grant himself was reported to be so hostile to Utah, the *Deseret News* suggested, that Justice McKean's anti-Mormon court decisions were actually being written in the White House. The anti-

47. Bancroft, *Utah*, p. 663.
48. Shaffer to Hamilton Fish, July 22, 1870, State Department Letter Books, 1860–1872, TP, Utah.
49. Bancroft, *Utah*, pp. 658–63.

Mormons in Washington used as grist a memorial from twenty-six Salt Lake lawyers which declared that Utah legislators were "inimical to and subversive of federal authority."[50]

Throughout the early 1870s a series of test cases concerning probate jurisdiction, the powers of United States marshals, and the right of habeas corpus were appealed either to the territorial or to the Supreme Court. It was evident that the fight to end polygamy in Utah had taken the form of a struggle to control the territorial judicial system. In his annual message in December 1873, President Grant urged legislation which would end overlapping jurisdiction, while Governor Woods urged the Utah legislature to do the same locally. The climax came in 1874, when Senator Luke Potter Poland of Vermont introduced a bill in Congress to reform the Utah court system. Poland was an expert on judicial problems and was keenly aware of the constitutional limits of power within which Congress had to operate. His bill soon edged all others aside, and by the summer of 1874 it had become law. Although the *Deseret News* dismissed it as "more ornamental than useful" and withal "a pompous fraud," it proved to be the first law that effectively limited the probate courts of Utah. It also provided that juries in Utah were to be half-Gentile and half-Mormon, and it increased the responsibilities and powers of the United States marshal.[51] When the Supreme Court upheld the Poland Act in December 1874, it was clear that the outer walls of the elaborate Mormon defense of polygamy and self-rule in Utah had been breached.

The agitation surrounding the question of federal authority in Utah cannot be understood without a brief reference to the small clique of territorial appointees and lawyers who lived there. United by their dislike of the Church, they seized every opportunity to provoke a crisis or engage in litigation. Mormon dominance in the Great Basin denied them a full chance to participate in the economic development of the territory. Granted only a minimum of territorial patronage, and despairing of a career in territorial politics, their two

50. *Deseret News Weekly,* February 12, 26, 1873.
51. *United States Statutes at Large, 18,* 253–56. The Poland Act was upheld in *Ferris v. Higby* [20 Wall. 375].

remaining sources of livelihood were federal patronage and litigation. Ironically Brigham Young had constructed a local court system to protect the Church, preserve polygamy, and defeat conniving lawyers. Now he found himself in a fight with the most able constitutional experts in Congress. More ironic still, the questionable legality of plural wives lured scores of lawyers to Utah during the 1870s, to argue for and against polygamy. With relatively few trained lawyers of their own, the Saints and the entire Church were soon to be the prey of the legal profession. The frontier lawyer, who had found his niche in New Mexico in land-grant troubles and in Colorado mining disputes, now could draw a livelihood in Utah from the complicated war over home rule and polygamy.

The Church had to face an even more basic threat in the coming of the Union Pacific to Utah, for it was bringing secular diversions from the outside world into the Great Basin kingdom. From California, General Connor wrote General Dodge, the Union Pacific construction engineer, "I intend to go back to Utah as soon as your railroad gets within a day or two's ride of Salt Lake. If God spares me I propose to fight it out on that line with Brigham."[52] Others were equally certain that a railroad would undermine Church authority and unity: the *Chicago Republican* entitled an editorial on the railroad's arrival in Utah: "Mormonism Doomed."

Such commentators never seemed to realize that Young's entire public career had consisted of countering non-Mormon influences and of controlling communications with the outside world. When the telegraph was extended to Utah in 1861, for example, he profited materially by taking contracts for post holes and accepting a position on the Board of Directors of Western Union. But he also proceeded to build and control his own spur lines to remote parts of Utah. So absolute was Young's reputed influence over the local companies that Governor Woods complained he dared not send policy messages or secret information to Washington via telegraph.[53]

52. Connor to Dodge, June 30, 1867, Dodge-Connor Letters, in Historical, Memorial, and Art Department of Iowa (Des Moines).
53. Woods to Hamilton Fish, June 29, 1871, State Department Letter Books, 1860–1872, TP, Utah.

In the case of the railroad, Young's chief concern was the inevitable invasion of non-Mormon merchants which the Union Pacific would bring in its wake, for he knew the power of the purse could affect the rule of Utah as much as lawyers. During the first two decades of Utah history, Mormon hostility had driven many merchants away, but the discovery of new mineral deposits in the Great Basin almost guaranteed the permanent return of an increasingly large mercantile group. As Leonard Arrington has observed, Young met the latest threat with intelligence and careful strategy. In 1867 a School of the Prophets was set up—in reality an economic planning committee— which worked out an eight-point protectionist policy for Utah. First, the Church tried to prevent the influx of a floating population of railroad workers, by taking the contracts for construction of the line themselves. Next, a number of Mormon-supported stores and small manufacturing firms were started, to reduce outside dependence on expensive finished products. At the same time, wages were cut to make the more costly manufactured Mormon goods cheap enough to export. Land policies were also initiated to prevent the Union Pacific from dominating whole areas through its control of sections of the public domain granted by Congress. Austerity campaigns were launched, to cut out luxuries such as tea and coffee. These savings would go to the Perpetual Emigrating Fund, so that more of the faithful could come to Utah. As a parallel distaff agency to the School of the Prophets, a Women's Relief Society was organized, to encourage home manufactures and to boycott Gentile merchants.[54]

By far the most important item in the eight-point program, and the one which made the others work, was the plan to keep all phases of merchandizing and sales in Mormon hands by setting up cooperative stores. This could not have been achieved without the help of several excellent merchants who were Mormon converts. Among them was William H. Hooper, who had at various times been a bank clerk, a merchant in Illinois, and a steamboat captain on the Mississippi River. By the time he was elected as Utah's delegate in Congress he was a wealthy man.[55] Even closer to Young than Hooper was Hiram

54. Arrington, *Great Basin*, pp. 245–56.
55. See Cazier, "Hooper."

B. Clawson, a merchant who was in charge of the President's private business. Clawson was also in partnership with another merchant, Horace S. Eldredge, a former New Yorker who had served as territorial assessor and collector of taxes. The firm of Clawson and Eldredge was one of the most successful in territorial Utah.[56]

To this capable trio could be added William Jennings, an English butcher who arrived in Utah in 1852. After receiving a contract to supply grain for the Overland Mail in 1861, Jennings made a small fortune. In 1864 he built the Eagle Emporium and came to be respected as one of Utah's leading businessmen.[57] Together these men —and others such as the Walker Brothers and Godbe and Mitchell— formed an oligarchy in Salt Lake City, which handled the economic affairs of Utah and the Church.[58] All stood to lose if the railroad and the influx of new merchants could not somehow be controlled.

At the same time, both Mormon and non-Mormon merchants did not hesitate to build up sentiment for the railroad. On June 11, 1868, Warren Hussey called a mass meeting to order in Salt Lake City, which endorsed the line. The audience heard enthusiastic speeches from two Church leaders, George A. Smith and George Q. Cannon. Almost at the very moment that Salt Lake citizens were celebrating the new railroad age, however, the *Deseret News* printed an editorial on "Cooperation and its Benefits."[59] Beginning in early September 1868, a series of editorials appeared in the *News* which centered on the necessity of adjusting business to the railroad. On October 3 the paper reported that "coops" were spreading throughout the territory and asserted that "There should be, also, a wholesale house in this city, on the same principle, that all who desired might buy goods here at fair jobbing rates." In swift succession there followed an annual conference of the Church and the announcement on October 10, 1868, that a "cooperative wholesale store" had been founded in Salt Lake and that all the wards were to be told about it. The campaign continued when Young discoursed on the will to be

56. Jensen, *Latter Day Saints, 1,* 196–97, 629–30.
57. Ibid., 2, 500–04; and "Obituary" in *Deseret News,* January 20, 1886.
58. Bancroft, *Utah,* pp. 647–51. Arrington, *Great Basin,* pp. 306–07. Arrington, "Taxable Income in Utah, 1862–1872," *UHQ, 24* (1956), 21 ff.
59. *Deseret Evening News,* May 26, 29, June 9, 10, 11, 12, 1868.

self-sustaining at the Tabernacle. Still another editorial appeared on the "Results of Cooperation."[60] The chief Mormon countermeasure to the deleterious economic effects of the railroad had been found.

The eventual result of the campaign for cooperation was the Zion's Commercial Mercantile Institution, or ZCMI, as it soon came to be called. What ZCMI amounted to was a huge general department store formed from an amalgamation of the firms of individual merchants like Hooper, Clawson, Eldredge, and others. The new organization was to buy goods cheaply in mass quantity and sell them directly to the public through its Salt Lake store and provincial outlets.[61] If all Mormons were to trade exclusively at ZCMI, the Gentile firms would, it was reasoned, wither away. At the same time, new firms would never be able to get started in Utah. In short, Young created a monolithic commercial firm to work with a theocratic state and an overwhelming Church.

Although non-Mormon merchants railed against this latest Church experiment, and merchants like the Walker Brothers and William Godbe preferred to apostatize rather than give up their extremely profitable individual businesses, ZCMI succeeded admirably. Soon it was not only handling purchases but trading grain, hay, produce and the like. The investors themselves prospered and branched out into other enterprises; for as in New Mexico and Colorado, the merchants of Utah were the first pioneers with surplus capital sufficient to found other businesses. Typical of the Utah entrepreneur was William H. Hooper, the tall, dark Marylander, who played a leading role in the organization of ZCMI and who had become its superintendent in 1873, its president in 1877. While performing these duties, he, Horace S. Eldredge, and Lewis S. Hills began a bank in 1869, which was incorporated as the Bank of Deseret in 1870. Further success led to its reorganization as a national bank in 1872. From that date he served as its president until his death in 1882. As bankers, Hooper and his associates were able, in turn, to invest in Utah mines.

Similar careers could be recorded for Jennings, Clawson, and others. A frontier pattern of commercial and industrial evolution common to the entire Southwest had at last begun to develop in Utah. The diff-

60. *Ibid.*, September 9, October 3, 10, 16, 20, 1868.
61. See Arrington, *Great Basin,* chap. 10.

erence was that economic growth and change were regulated to fit the needs and wishes of the Church. With Church planning and backing, for example, Jennings helped organize the Utah Central and Southern railways in 1869 and 1871 respectively, in an effort to protect local roads from outside control. Here again were evidences of a planned cooperative society instead of the free-wheeling, competitive and often wasteful economic development so characteristic of other frontiers. One unique result was that Utah was able to retain control over its own economy much longer than had other frontier territories.[62]

Perhaps the most difficult economic adjustment Young had to make in the new railroad age was to the burgeoning mining industry of Utah. Ever since the California gold rush, he had regarded search for precious minerals with extreme distrust. Gold in California in 1849 had threatened to lure Saints from Utah. Then the discovery of silver in Utah in 1863 threatened to overwhelm them with non-Mormon miners at home. Rumors of gold discoveries on the Sweetwater River in 1867 led the *Deseret News* to caution that the gold diggings were no place for a man professing to be a Latter Day Saint. "We can think of no labor that is not positively dishonorable, the effects of which are more degrading than gold digging."[63]

The Mormon desire to avoid the bad side effects of mining were eventually modified by several factors. The first was the realization that the presence of coal beds in Utah meant a source of power for future industry and domestic heat in a timber-scarce country.[64] Second, Mormon business simply could not pass up a chance for quick capital, which mining of any sort promised. Finally, it was apparent by 1877 that unless the Saints took action, Utah's mineral wealth would fall by default into the hands of outsiders. Foreign investors had already given Utah mines a bad reputation by their cynical speculations in the Emma Mine.[65]

62. Ibid., chap. 9.

63. *Deseret News*, March 21, 1868.

64. Arrington, *Great Basin*, pp. 275–76.

65. William T. Jackson, "The Infamous Emma Mine: A British Interest in the Little Cottonwood District, Utah Territory," *UHQ*, 23 (1955), 339–62. See also Clark Spence, *British Investments and the American Mining Frontier, 1860–1901* (Ithaca, 1958), pp. 139–82.

While certain Mormons ventured into mining, Young himself turned to an even more basic scheme of cooperation: that of communal living within a village or town unit. Some of the revelations of the Prophet Joseph Smith, which Young had never forgotten, concerned the creation of "the United Order of Enoch." The inspiration for the Order appears to have had three sources: the pattern of an idealistic communal society mentioned in the Old Testament, Shaker and Campbellite doctrines, and Smith's own visions. While the Prophet had talked of this ideal economic society, he had never been able to put it into practice. Beginning in 1874, however, Young and the Church leaders tried to revive the Order by talking Utah communities into property and work-sharing arrangements, but they failed to convince a majority of the Mormon population to accept the communal idea. They did succeed in persuading such isolated towns as Georgetown, Parowan, and Orderville to try the United Order, however, so that in those villages varying degrees of communal living were practiced for a number of years. These extreme attempts to realize cooperation proved too much even for the Saints, and within a few years after Young's death, his successor, John Taylor, quietly let the experiments come to an end.[66]

As Young and the Church leaders struggled by exhortation and pleading to launch the Order of Enoch, it was obvious to those closest to the President that age was beginning to take its toll. Always a large man, Young was now corpulent and subject to frequent illness. The enforced hidings during the polygamy arrests of 1871–75, the trial of John D. Lee for the Mountain Meadows Massacre, and various "custodial arrests" had taken some of the vigor and spirit from his voice and role. He began to abandon his habit of taking the air in his carriage and of traveling to every corner of Utah so that he could be intimately acquainted with the problems of his people.[67]

Even in this afterglow of power, the presence of Young was still great enough to produce awe. He was a legend in his own time, and when he died at the Lion House on August 29, 1877, everyone knew

66. Arrington, *Great Basin*, chap. 11. Anderson, *Desert Saints*, pp. 14 ff., 297–300, 375–83.

67. Morris R. Werner, *Brigham Young* (New York, 1925), pp. 451 ff.

that it was more than the passing of an era. He had been one of the strongest personalities ever to attempt to impose his will on the desert West.[68] Anxious to catch a last glimpse of the Lion of the Lord, more than 25,000 Saints gathered in the Tabernacle on September 1 to pay their respects. After a mammoth funeral, Young was laid to rest in sight of the ring of pale mountains surrounding the Mormon capital.

There is no doubt that Young had carried a new and fledgling religion far beyond the mere demands of survival; in the process he had created not just a Church but a unique society, a governmental system, and a distinct economy. The miracle was that he had managed to do it in the desert and virtually without capital. Young, then, may be called a frontiersman, not merely because he led a people to a new and forbidding land but because he also was a pioneer in the same sense as Sir Thomas Dale and John Rolfe, who came to grips with the realities of colonial Jamestown and the problems of establishing an unfamiliar economy in a new environment. He had also sustained a community of Saints and a total society, much as John Bradford of Plymouth and John Winthrop of Massachusetts had done. He had made the desert bloom, and had guaranteed, perhaps for all time, that Utah would be predominantly Mormon in population.

By his resistance to the fundamental American beliefs in secular courts, the two-party system, public schools, a weak militia, separation of Church and State, and monogamous marriage, and his defense of the community concept of property, Young must be held responsible for many of the Saints' difficulties in their relations with Washington and the Gentiles. However he is judged, he was certainly one of the most successful rebels against accepted American religious, social, and political traditions in the nineteenth century. With Archbishop Lamy he stands as one of the few great and complex men to play a cultural role in the American occupation of the Far Southwest. Partly because of these two men, two religiously oriented Southwestern subcultures exist today within the borders of a standardized and secularized America.

68. Herbert E. Bolton, "The Mormons in the Opening of the Great West," *Utah Genealogical and Historical Magazine, 44* (1926), 64.

15

Government, Polygamy, and Statehood 1870–1896

> Mormonism embraces the economic and political as well as the religious life of its adherents. Its ideals are temporal as well as spiritual.
>
> E. E. Ericksen, 1922

> From 1847 to 1896 a single issue, Church vs. Anti-Church, dominated the political arena.
>
> Frank Herman Jonas, 1940

During a Utah election campaign George A. Smith once declared: "What we do we should do as one man. Our system should be Theo-Democracy—the voice of the people consenting to the voice of God."[1] In his remark Smith touched upon the one item outside of polygamy which most angered non-Mormons: a Church-dominated, one-party system of government in Utah. Since the Saints used local government to buttress their doctrine of polygamy, the two issues were irrevocably joined. Gentile politicians, whether in Utah or in Washington, were as outraged by the closed system of politics as by plural marriage. The Saints, in turn, were certain that Gentiles were not really interested in suppressing polyg-

1. "Journal History, July 12, 1865," quoted in Cazier, "Hooper," p. 72.

amy but only in despoiling Utah as a patronage colony. Much of the
political history of Utah from 1870 to 1896 centers around the two
issues, and the coming of a two-party system to Utah after 1890 was
in many ways as significant as the abolition of polygamy.

The first political effort to break the Church monopoly on Utah's
elective offices came in August 1858, when the followers of Colonel
Johnston and Governor Cumming put up candidates for the Assembly
and nominated Dr. Garland Hurt for the delegateship. Not a single
Gentile candidate achieved office, and William H. Hooper was elected
to Congress that year. In 1860 the Saints ran the faithful Dr. Bernhisel
again, and he was elected unanimously. After the Civil War began,
Young tried a new tack in dealing with the Lincoln administration by
hand-picking Judge John F. Kinney as delegate in 1862. Kinney had
been the chief justice of Utah from 1854 to 1857 and had been reappointed, after a lapse of three years, to succeed Judge Eckels. Although Kinney was a Gentile, Young apparently felt he would have
more influence in Congress than a Mormon. He also hoped Kinney
might get Utah into the Union as a state.

Kinney was the only non-Mormon delegate ever elected from
Utah. His success in dealing with Young and the Saints suggests what
kind of political figure they liked. Kinney appears to have been a
lifelong Democrat and a practical, efficient businessman, who asked
no questions about polygamy. His state of birth was New York, but
by the time he was twenty-one he had begun to move west in stages,
first to Ohio and then to Iowa. In the latter state he dabbled in
politics and managed to secure a judgeship on the Iowa supreme
bench. He left this office to become Chief Justice of Utah in 1854.[2]

Kinney's career is important only in that it demonstrates a fundamental characteristic of the American territorial system. As a pro-
Mormon delegate, he found himself in opposition to Governor Harding on the one hand, and opposed to General Connor on the other.
Meanwhile, Frank Fuller, the territorial secretary (1861–64), was also
allied with Mormon interests rather than with his fellow federal ap-

2. "John Fitch Kinney" in *Biog. Dir. of Am. Cong. Union Vedette*, January 14,
1864. See also Harding to Seward, April 15, 29, 1863, State Dept. Letter Books,
1860–1872, TP, Utah.

pointees. James Doty, the Superintendent of Indian Affairs during these years, appears not to have cooperated with any of the civilian officials but to have allied himself with General Connor. Any chance that the federal bureaucracy of Utah could present a united front toward the Mormons vanished in the face of these chaotic and divisive alliances. A pattern had been established which was to operate in Utah through most of the territorial period.

When the statehood efforts of 1862 and 1864 failed, Young bypassed Kinney to choose Hooper again. He was returned to office in 1866 and 1868. In the latter year a bold if obscure optimist, William McGroarty, ran against Hooper, and though he received only 105 votes, he contested the incumbent's right to the post. The federal officials who backed McGroarty saw in the farce a good chance to air election procedures in Utah and to call attention to its one-party system.[3]

No real turning point in Utah electoral politics came until 1870–72. In the first of these years the Mormons themselves decided to abandon their ghost state of Deseret. The government of this ephemeral state had met once a year since 1850 to ratify the acts of the Utah Assembly. In 1870 the Saints also voted to retire the Deseret Constitution, which they had proposed as their state constitution in 1862 and again in 1864. They explained that the latter now had "the odor of defeat about it."[4] In 1872 the Church again called a serious statehood convention and wrote a constitution that used Nevada as a model. Far from proceeding in an exclusivist manner, they invited Young's arch foe, General Connor, to sit as a delegate, but the intractable Irishman declined. That year the Saints also resorted to outside help in their statehood efforts by enlisting the aid of Thomas Fitch, the able but notorious Nevada lawyer, and of Frank Fuller, the former territorial secretary. In a classic plea for statehood they resorted to the familiar frontier charges that territorial government was "inherently oppressive and inherently anti-Republican."[5]

During 1865–78 another change developed when miners, merchants, federal officials, and Mormon apostates finally managed to form an

3. *Deseret Evening News*, February 10, May 20, 1868.
4. Morgan, "Deseret," p. 149.
5. Ibid., p. 152.

opposition party, which the Mormons christened the Gentile Ring. In their few but noisy ranks was General Connor, who now lived in the mining and freighting town of Corinne. Another prominent figure was William Godbe, a merchant and publisher whose business had been ruined by the formation of ZCMI in 1868. Irate at the Church's interference with his pocketbook, the spirited Godbe had broken with the Saints and now led an outspoken faction of apostates called the "Godbeites." Among other opposition leaders were a future diehard apostate, Henry W. Lawrence and a thin, humorless, hardbitten Gentile mining lawyer, Robert N. Baskin.[6]

In 1869 and 1870 these men and various incumbent federal officials formed the Liberal Party of Utah. Since most of their early followers were either connected to the Union Pacific or in mining, one of their strongholds was Corinne, a Union Pacific way station and freighting depot for the Idaho mines. There, as if in a foreign compound, clustered enough non-Mormon Americans to make Corinne a typical rip-roaring frontier town. A Union Pacific land agent, J. A. Williamson, was its mayor and, as one might expect, the city council outlawed polygamy within the town limits.[7] To sustain their morale and spread their own gospel, the Liberals ran a paper in Corinne and founded the *Tribune* in Salt Lake City.

The first Liberal Party candidate was General George R. Maxwell, a convivial and hard-drinking politician who had served variously as the Surveyor General and as the United States Marshal for Utah. Running on what was to be a classic anti-Mormon platform, Maxwell came out against the political union of Church and State, Mormon economic policy, and polygamy. With his Gentile supporters in mind he also declared for any legislation that would help the mining industry. Although Maxwell was roundly defeated by Delegate Hooper in 1870 and by George Quayle Cannon in 1872, the redoubtable General contested Cannon's election.[8]

With the passage of the Poland Act in 1874, however, the Liberals took new heart and nominated the cantankerous Robert Baskin as

6. Bancroft, *Utah,* pp. 647–51. Baskin, *Reminiscences,* pp. 80–81.
7. Anderson, "Corinne," pp. 142–54.
8. *Deseret News Weekly,* May 6, 1874.

their delegate candidate. A lawyer of some ability, he had helped draft the Cullom bill of 1869, which in turn had been a basis for the Poland Act and for all later anti-Mormon legislation. Baskin conducted such a noisy campaign in 1874 that the *Deseret News* took great pains to refute his many charges and to warn readers that the "ring-streaked" Liberals' real purpose was to get at the public till, increase taxes, and, of course, cause litigation.[9]

On election day, 1874, the aggressive Liberals fully lived up to their reputation. They challenged voters, questioned results, and with the aid of the federal marshal intimidated the Salt Lake police who were guarding polling places. While Delegate Cannon was easily returned to Congress by a vote of 23,000, Baskin did garner 4,523 ballots. Even so, Baskin claimed to be the victor by arguing that Cannon, born in England, was an alien and a polygamist as well. By December the whole case had been referred to Congress, where, after a prolonged set of hearings, the House voted to seat Cannon.[10]

The first crack in the one-party system appeared even larger when one Lawrence A. Brown of Tooele County defeated the Mormon probate incumbant, Judge John Rowberry, who was bishop of the county. When Rowberry refused to give up the office and its records, he was hauled into federal court. Just then all the federal judges, led by Chief Justice McKean, were so anti-Mormon that the Saints knew the outcome before the verdict was rendered.[11] So far did the Mormons come around to traditional practices in delegate elections because of Liberal pressure that by 1876 they had formed their own "People's Party." For the first time in their history the Saints named a central committee and began to engage in political speech-making. Three years later the *Deseret News* admitted there was now a party committee in each county and a central committee for the whole territory. Commenting on the new era the *News* reminisced that:

For many years of our sojourn in these valleys there was no need for any particular political organization. The citizens would come

9. Ibid., August 5, 1874.
10. Ibid., August 12, September 16, 1874.
11. Ibid., September 16, 1874.

together in mass meetings, make their nominations in peace, sustain them with uplifted hands, and on the day appointed go to the polls and vote without noise, excitement, or ill feeling of any kind.[12]

The editorial concluded by saying that the bipartisan way, with all its sound and fury, "is barbarous to us." Although the Liberals never won a delegate election, they did succeed in bringing the Utah electoral process to Congress' attention throughout the next decade by cries of fraud and by contesting elections.[13]

What was the role of the Utah delegate in Congress? Most of them were prominent wealthy merchants or physicians in Utah and affable, urbane men of the world. All were conservative in their views and habits. Unlike most frontier politicians they were seldom lawyers. In their effort to minimize Mormon federal differences, these delegates willingly identified with a national party while in Washington, although to their constituents this was of no consequence. Always in harmony with the Assembly and the Church authorities, they tended to be judged upon their merits. Most of them were reelected at least three times. In short, Utah had a shrewd diplomatic minister who advocated a nineteenth-century policy of mutual coexistence by constantly persuading Congress either to leave Utah alone or to give her home rule through statehood. While most territorial delegates were busy scrounging for appropriations, the Utah representative was busy defeating antipolygamy bills or holding off the American land laws. As a result, Utah got a minimum of federal funds throughout the territorial period.[14]

The slow chipping away at the granite of Utah's single-party government was in contrast to the increased acceleration of court activity in Utah after the passage of the Poland Act in 1874. A few months

12. Ibid., July 13, 1881.
13. In the delegate election of 1880, for example, the Liberals once again contested Cannon's eligibility for the office by claiming that the Saint was not a citizen. Ibid., July 6, 1881.
14. Ibid., October 14, 1874.

after the act became law, Judge McKean managed to empanel a petit jury—the first in four years. When the Supreme Court upheld the Poland Law in December and mixed Mormon-Gentile juries were called, a new era began for the federal judiciary.

The increasing power of the federal courts was further demonstrated in 1875, when John D. Lee was brought to trial for the Mountain Meadows Massacre of 1857. That tragic affair, in which some 120 people lost their lives and some eighteen children were orphaned, had troubled the consciences of the white participants, the Church authorities, and the American government for nearly two decades. Now at last the specter was to be laid. According to Juanita Brooks, whose study of the Mountain Meadows affair appears to be exhaustive, the Church agreed that someone must be punished.[15] Although the responsibility for the massacre could be laid at many doors, John Lee—who admired the President slavishly—had negotiated the false truce that lured the victims out of their wagon barricade to their grisly deaths. Somehow it was he who had to pay the penalty.

Lee had been living in the solitude of a southern Utah canyon and had been apprehended while hiding in a hogpen. He was brought before Judge Jacob S. Boreman, who was presiding over the Beaver City district court in 1875. In Lee's first trial the mixed Mormon-Gentile jury could not reach an agreement. But in a second trial the court, with a jury of twelve Mormons, found the unhappy Lee guilty and sentenced him to die at the scene of his crime. An appeal to the territorial supreme court having been denied, on March 27, 1877, the law was carried into grim execution on barren, windswept Mountain Meadows. Before his death Lee requested the firing squad to "aim at my breast boys and don't maim my limbs." Then Lee calmly asserted his innocence, since he had merely obeyed orders. After declaring his faith in God, he took Young to task for having made mistakes—so much so, Lee explained, that he no longer followed the Lion of the Lord personally. This dramatic valedictory, which was delivered by the prisoner standing before his coffin, convinced anti-

15. Juanita Brooks, *The Mountain Meadows Massacre*, (Norman, 1962), pp. 184–200 passim.

Mormons anew that the Saints had often been a lawless and mis-
guided sect.[16]

Having laid the ghost of the 1857 massacre, the federal government was soon hammering away at other longstanding issues. Beginning in 1870, every Utah governor thereafter made a sustained effort
either to abolish the Nauvoo Legion or to bring it under control as a
territorial militia. Governors Shaffer and Woods claimed to have abolished the Legion, but it was 1884 before the legislature voted it out
of existence.

Another secondary Mormon problem that plagued all Utah governors after 1857 was peculiar territorial legislation. Common law did
not apply to Utah, for example, nor did standard marriage, estate,
surrogate, or incorporation laws exist there. It was also true that
taxes on ferries and bridges went to a Church firm, the Perpetual
Emigrating Fund, while school taxes went to sectarian schools.

Chief Justice McKean aired still more discrepancies between Utah
and national customs in a famous charge to a Mormon grand jury
in 1874. He reminded them that the national government had a primary right to dispose of the public domain, a right the Assembly had
ignored in granting lands to Church members. The Assembly, he noted,
had also passed laws disguised as resolutions pertaining to land and
other matters, so that the governor could not veto these acts. He then
questioned the provision by which the property of intestate deceased
persons could go to the Perpetual Emigrating Fund, and he wondered how a law had ever passed which stated that the physician
must lecture his patients on the nature of the medicine he was
prescribing. McKean asked of such acts, "what shall be said? Legislation to exclude from Utah the authority of Coke, Blackstone, Mans-
field, Kent, Story, and Marshall; to defraud the lawyer of his just
compensation. Language fails properly to characterize such legislation."[17]

Another Utah custom that upset the federal officers was a practice of
permitting one man to hold several public offices. Governor George
I. Woods, who succeeded General Shaffer in 1871, found a striking

16. Ibid., pp. 208–10.
17. *Deseret News Weekly*, October 14, 1874.

example of this practice in the 1874 Assembly. Among its members were seven probate judges, three county clerks, two city mayors, and the territorial warden of the penitentiary! "It is a principle in a government, too well understood to require argument," he dryly observed, "that the several departments should be kept separate and distinct from one another."[18] Yet the same problem had faced the governors of New Mexico when they analyzed the membership of the early legislators sitting in Santa Fe.

Among the other annoying secondary Mormon problems was the refusal to establish a true public school system. While Young was willing to found the University of Deseret and many ward schools, he had a genuine fear of Gentiles teaching Mormon children. He also appears to have believed only in a basic practical education consisting of the three R's, instruction in the arts of husbandry, commerce, and bookkeeping, and church directed sessions on the nature of religion.

The effects of a limited amount of schooling soon began to show in Utah. Mormon youths grew up like frontiersmen, living an outdoor life of riding, shooting, and rough sport. Gangs of them, wearing Spanish sombreros fastooned with fox tails and leather chaps, would wheel and dash their horses through Salt Lake City terrorizing pedestrians.[19] With the influx of miners and Gentiles, the discrepancy between Mormon education and that of the outside world became even more obvious. Judge Jacob S. Boreman reminisced that he had found an ignorant population almost devoid of lawyers when he arrived in Salt Lake City in 1873. William Jennings later admitted that the railroad had arrested a dangerous backsliding into ruffian ignorance.[20] Yet a vote on the question of initiating public schools in Salt Lake City in 1874 was defeated four to one. Reasoning that "schools supported by general taxes cannot be conducted on a religious basis," Young declared they must be prohibited.[21] Despite laws passed in 1854, 1866, and 1876, no real progress was made until

18. "Special Message of Governor Woods to the Legislature, January 21, 1874," ibid., January 28, 1874.

19. William Jennings in "Material Progress of Utah," *UHQ, 3,* (1930), 89–90.

20. Ibid. Jacob S. Boreman, in "Reminiscences of My Life in Utah," pp. 6 ff., MS, HEH, stated that he "found the bar of Salt Lake to be composed almost wholly of non-Mormons."

21. Stanley S. Ivins, "Free Schools Come to Utah," *UHQ, 21* (1954), 321–23, 336, 341–42.

a new education bill became law in 1880, and the Collett bill of 1890 was passed.

With the exception of a brief Ute outbreak in 1894, Utah remained remarkably free of the usual frontier phenomenon of Indian troubles, once the difficulties of the 1860s had been resolved. On the other hand, the problem of public land disposal bothered both federal officials and Mormons throughout the territorial period. Since regular surveys of the public domain in Utah did not really begin until 1869, the Mormons had been forced to develop their own land system in the twenty-two years between 1847 and 1869. Yet to Congress they were still squatters in the eyes of the law.

The land system of Mormon Utah represented the most remarkable nonprofit and social approaches to the ownership and use of real property, since the Puritans had introduced a similar policy into seventeenth-century Massachusetts. Beginning in 1849, the Saints passed legislative acts giving key ranch lands, timber grants, and water rights to prominent members of the Church, who were to hold them in trust. The herd grounds of Cache Valley, for example, were granted to Brigham Young as "Trustee in trust." Another device employed by the Assembly was to incorporate a municipality with exceptionally large town or city boundaries.[22] Within the community or village itself lands and water were awarded by the bishop according to need and circumstance, so that the more able man or the person with a large family usually got a larger share.

When the American land laws finally came to Utah, they seemed unrealistic in a desert climate where irrigation was necessary for farming. Consequently the Church made the most out of an awkward situation by directing the local bishops to ask one man to apply for 160 acres under the Homestead Law. Then, the valuable, irrigated acreage was divided up among the many families already living on it. Through this use of the Homestead Act, the practice of preemption, and the technique of stretching townsite plats over large areas, the Mormons eventually reacquired their lands.[23]

One of the points at issue between Mormons and Gentiles, where

22. Boreman, "Curiosities of Early Utah Legislation," MS, HEH.
23. George W. Rollins, "Land Policies of the United States as Applied to Utah to 1910," *UHQ*, 20 (1952), 242–45.

land was concerned, was the refusal of the Saints to speculate in lands or to make a frontier industry out of the disposal of the public domain. This sense of difference was echoed in their practice of co-operative irrigation—instead of commercial irrigation. The former was the dominant pattern until 1872, and it worked well. By such practices, Utah was spared the long feuds over acequias, which punctuated and embittered community relations in New Mexico, and the frenzied commercial efforts to build dams and impound waters for profitable sale at monopoly prices, which existed in Arizona, Colorado, and California. Rather than borrow Eastern capital for the development of Utah, the Saints constructed their community water ditches with tithing labor under the direction of local bishops. The results were magnificent, as village after village blossomed forth in the desert. By 1870 familiar trees and fruits thrived to remind thousands of the orchards of their homeland. Unlike the pioneers in the Great Plains, the Utah settlers had conquered land without capital, and with little hope of farming commercially until the railroad came. Somehow their patient conquest seemed far more impressive than the dramatic invasion of Kansas and Nebraska by commercial one-crop farmers, using borrowed capital and labor saving machines.

By far the greatest issue that embittered Mormon-federal relations was polygamy. As has been mentioned earlier, federal legislation to suppress this institution in the 1860s and 1870s had proven ineffectual. Outsiders, feeling that time was on their side, expected Mormonism to disintegrate after the death of Brigham Young in 1877, but three factors prevented this. The first was the superb, almost self-functioning complex bureaucracy which Young had created to run the Church. Everyone called this mysterious organization the Hierarchy. The second factor was the success of the Mormon cooperative endeavors in the manufacturing, mercantile, railroading, and agricultural fields. These efforts, as Leonard Arrington has demonstrated, held up the impact of the national economy on Utah for two decades. The third factor was the personality of President John Taylor, who succeeded Young as the head of the Church.

In Taylor, the Saints found another true defender of the faith in the most literal sense of the word. A member of the Church since 1836, he had been in the Missouri exodus and had been wounded in the Carthage jail when Joseph Smith was killed. But he had escaped death to continue as one of the Apostles of the Church. Taylor's career in Utah was also closely tied to political affairs, for he was speaker of the House from 1857 to 1876. By 1877, the thin lipped, gray-eyed Saint was sixty-nine and ill-disposed, after a whole life of bitter struggle, to change Church dogma or to compromise with the enemy. "Be quiet," he counseled his followers, "but do not surrender."[24]

Taylor's accession to the presidency in 1877 coincided with an ever-widening public attack on polygamy. In the East, James Gorden Bennett, editor of the *New York Sun,* carried on a running editorial war against plural wives. These sentiments were echoed by Missouri newspapers, and locally by the Salt Lake *Tribune.* At the same time, the outspoken Methodist chaplain of the United States Senate, Dr. John P. Newman, turned his pulpit into an anti-Mormon sounding board. Kate Field, the popular lecturer, carried on a public-speaking war against the Saints. In June 1881 the *Deseret News* complained that Episcopalians, Methodists, Baptists, Presbyterians, and Congregationalists had all launched a "Sectarian Crusade" against Mormonism. Not content with word wars, four of these denominations donated money to found free schools in Utah; and by 1889 some 7,000 children were enrolled therein. Throughout the 1880s missionaries and ministers made places like Ogden, Logan, and Mount Pleasant, Utah, local centers of Protestant influence.[25]

In addition to the press and sectarian campaigns, Senator George Franklin Edmunds, another Vermonter acting in the traditions of Morrill and Poland, began a new anti-Mormon drive in Congress.[26] Edmunds had entered the Senate as a Radical in 1865, in the time to cast the necessary vote for the passage of the Civil Rights bill. Later he helped to push through the Tenure of Office Act, and he served on the committee which tried President Johnson for impeachment.

24. "John Taylor" in *DAB.*
25. *Deseret News Weekly,* June 29, July 27, 1881.
26. "George Franklin Edmunds" in *DAB.*

Like his fellow Vermonter, Poland, Edmunds was an expert in judicial affairs and, understandably, served as chairman of the Senate Judiciary Committee from 1872 to 1891. In that capacity he helped pass the Ku Klux Act and the second Civil Rights Act of 1875. He was probably the true father of the Sherman Anti-Trust Act of 1890. With his Illinois colleague in the Senate, Shelby M. Cullom, Edmunds was also a vigorous supporter of any reform measure that curbed railroad abuses and advanced the Civil Service system. Given his radical and abolitionist heritage, it was but natural that Edmunds would think that polygamy was somehow a form of tyranny. Possessed of a waspish tongue, brilliant in repartee, and devastating in attack, this dour New Englander was so unapproachable that he was called "the iceberg of the Senate." Backed by Morrill of Vermont, Cragin of New Hampshire, Hoar of Massachusetts, and a set of midwesterners— among whom were Cullom of Illinois, Boreman of West Virginia, and a number of Ohio and Indiana congressmen—Edmunds was in a powerful position to attack polygamy through federal law.[27]

Revived congressional interest in Utah came about partly as a result of Delegate Cannon's reelection in 1880. At that time, the Liberals accused the Church of using marked ballots, of running an alien polygamist, and of generally controlling all electoral processes. Up to this time the Liberals had not had the cooperation of Governor Woods' successor, George B. Emery (1875–80), a Tennesseean who saw no reason to create difficulties in Utah. The impetus for the anti-Mormon crusade during these years stemmed largely from the federal judges and from the Liberals.[28]

The new Governor of Utah, Eli H. Murray (1880–86), was of a very different breed. He became an ally of the Liberals; and after the 1880 delegate election, he ignored the fact that Cannon had received the largest number of votes and, instead, gave the certificate of election to Arthur G. Campbell, the Liberal candidate.[29] This sent the whole affair to Washington, where the House Committee on Elections investigated the contest for nearly a year.

27. Lamar, "Political Patterns in New Mexico and Utah," *UHQ*, *28* (1960), 384–85.

28. Bancroft, *Utah*, p. 661–67.

29. *Deseret News Weekly*, January 18, 1882.

When Congress met in the winter of 1881–82, rumors began to fly that a commission to govern Utah would soon be created. So certain did it seem that stringent legislation was in the making that the Utah Assembly accepted the fact that Cannon was not yet a citizen and declared the post of delegate vacant. In his place they elected a nonpolygamist, John T. Caine. Then the Assembly itself memorialized Congress for a commission to investigate Utah before passing any laws. In truly moving language they explained that Utah now used a secret ballot and that most of the charges against the Church where elections were concerned were untrue.[30] Unimpressed with these arguments, Senator Edmunds introduced a bill designed both to break the one-party system and to outlaw polygamy.

After much debate the Edmunds bill became law on March 22, 1882. Briefly, it provided a $500 fine for those found guilty of polygamy and made them liable to imprisonment for not more than five years. To prevent even cohabitation, the government imposed a $300 fine and a prison sentence of six months on those who were only nominally polygamists. As further punishment, belief in plural marriage could be used as a jury challenge, and children born of polygamous marriages after 1883 were to be illegitimate in the eyes of the law. A section similar to the second and third Reconstruction acts denied polygamists both the franchise and the right to hold public office, just as Confederate officials had been barred from these privileges after the Civil War.[31] To carry out the Edmunds Act, Congress created a five-man "Utah Commission" to take over the registration of voters and to handle territorial elections. After holding organization meetings in Chicago and Omaha, the Utah Commission was ready to go into action by September 1882.[32]

The first Mormon rejoinder to the Edmunds Act was an almost classic one by now. In May 1882 they called a convention to write a state constitution and to press for admission to the Union. That June a committee under the chairmanship of Daniel H. Wells, the veteran

---

30. Ibid., March 8, 1882. See *Memorial to Congress by the Legislative Assembly . . . of Utah* (1882), YWA.

31. *United States Statutes at Large*, 22, 30–32. *First Report of the Utah Commission* (Salt Lake City, 1883), pp. 1–5.

32. *The Reports of the Utah Commission* (1883–96) may be found in the Utah State Archives.

commander of the Nauvoo Legion and many times president of the Assembly Council, climbed on the train to Washington to present the case for Utah statehood. Congress and President Arthur turned a deaf ear on statehood appeals; Utah had to prepare for the visitation of the Commission and await the effects of the Edmunds law.[33]

By the Edmunds Act, only citizens registered by the Commission could vote. But in August 1882, the traditional time for Utah elections, the new commissioners had not had time to register any voters, so no elections were held. The prospect that many local offices would soon be vacant led Congress to propose that Governor Murray fill the vacancies until a new election could be held in November. The possibility that Murray, whom the Mormons roundly hated, would acquire new appointive powers provoked a new crisis. At the last moment, a territorial law was discovered which would permit the incumbents to remain in office in the event of no election.[34] Nevertheless, from this time until his removal in 1886, Murray did make appointments to scores of offices which the Assembly had traditionally filled, and the Mormons, in turn, contested the appointments in court.

As the Saints awaited the invasion of the Utah Commission, the local press thoroughly probed the careers of its five members, Alexander Ramsey, Algernon S. Paddock, F. F. Godfrey, A. B. Carleton, and James R. Pettigrew. Since the first three were Republicans, the *Deseret News* direfully predicted that all Democrats would be disfranchised and Utah admitted to the Union as a Republican state. President Taylor, flanked by George Q. Cannon and Joseph S. Smith, issued a policy guide for the Mormons in late August. Do not give in, said Taylor: take the non-polygamy oath if you can, but under protest. Complete unity, he warned, was necessary to "maintain and sustain our political status." Taylor then urged aliens to go to a district court and be naturalized as soon as possible. He also cautioned young people to register to vote.[35] Taylor knew that if democratic

33. *The Deseret News* bitterly assailed the Edmunds law but initially welcomed the idea of a commission. See April 5, 12, 1882. For the constitutional convention see the April, May, and June 1882 issues of the *News*. A copy of the 1882 constitution is in YWA.

34. Ibid., August 23, 1882.

35. Ibid., September 6, 1882.

procedure was followed, the Church need not worry about its political power; for by the Census of 1880 the Mormons in Utah numbered some 120,000, while the total of Gentiles and Apostates came to only 23,000.[36]

The lines were drawn, and that fall Utah was the scene of the most furious election activity in its history. Daily crises occurred, as registrars throughout the territory challenged the right of certain Mormons to enlist as voters. Many questions were raised about the right of women to vote. The *Deseret News* added to the heat by accusing the Liberal Party of raising funds simply to hire lawyers to bring test cases against Saints.[37]

Determined to impress the Commission with their open political methods, the Saints held a People's Party convention with great fanfare and publicity. They wrote a Declaration of Thirteen Principles as a party platform, and put forward three candidates for nomination as delegate. Franklin S. Richards, a young Ogden lawyer, and the former delegate, W. H. Hooper, lost to John T. Caine, the popular incumbent. The "new approach" continued, as Caine traveled about Utah attending ratification meetings to endorse both his own candidacy and the party platform. On the night before election it was hard to tell Utah from any other American state in the throes of a campaign, for the newspapers reported a traditional election eve rally complete with bonfires, roman candles, and fireballs.[38] But as everyone had predicted, John T. Caine was elected the next day.

The denouement for the anti-Mormons was disappointing. In a sober, fair, first report, submitted in December 1882, the five commissioners told Secretary of the Interior Teller that even after excluding 12,000 men and women on grounds of polygamy, some 33,266 voters had been registered. Of these 23,000 had clearly voted for Caine, while Philip T. Van Zile, the Liberal candidate, had received only 4,884 ballots. The commissioners also observed that their own presence had agitated the public in Utah "to a remarkable degree." With this fact in mind they recommended that no more radical legislation be passed for Utah. Finally, the commissioners pointed

36. Ibid.
37. Ibid., September 20–November 20, 1882.
38. Ibid., November 15, 1882.

out that the Gentiles of Utah were in banking, mining, and mercantile pursuits; and though in the minority, they were generally well off and were not being economically persecuted.[39]

Neither the Liberals nor certain congressmen accepted the first report of the Utah Commission as trustworthy. Nevertheless, in 1883 the fight settled down to a series of word duels and court suits designed to test the Edmunds Act. The presidential election of 1884 brought local politics to a new boiling point, however, when some of the members of the Liberal party and a few members of the People's Party broke ranks to form Democratic party clubs in support of Grover Cleveland. Many Mormons who had always inclined towards the Democratic party in national politics were attracted by vaguely worded remarks about polygamy and religious beliefs in the 1884 Democratic platform. Fearing for the future of the People's party, the *News* warned that "one solid impregnable party is the best political policy for Utah today."[40]

To observers there were also other signs of progress in Utah politics: in 1885 the Commission noted that no polygamist's name now appeared on the voting lists and that the solid front had been broken by the election of an entire non-Mormon slate of officers in Summit County. They also reported that the Assembly no longer had a single polygamist in its ranks. On the other hand, a Gentile had been elected to that body. Nevertheless the Commission, partly for partisan reasons, was not satisfied. They used the fact that only 23,000 out of 40,000 eligible voters had exercised their right of franchise in 1884 to suggest that this was "stay-at-home" passive resistance. Given these subtler evidences of rebellion, the Commission recommended that appointment powers enjoyed by Governor Murray be transferred to them.[41]

From the Mormon point of view, in 1885 the world seemed ready

39. *First Report of the Utah Commission.* See also *Deseret News Weekly,* December 13, 1882.

40. Ibid., June 18, December 3, 1884.

41. *Report of the Utah Commission for 1884,* p. 7. Other recommendations called for increased powers for federal courts, omission of the statute of limitations where cases of polygamy were concerned, and extension of the power of subpoena (in matters relating to polygamy cases) to all states; ibid., p. 8.

to close in for the kill. To the north the Idaho legislature had already passed an act disfranchising any citizen who subscribed to the doctrine of polygamy, while to the south cases against Mormon polygamists were now a common feature of Arizona federal courts. Between 1880 and 1885 Presidents Hayes, Garfield, Arthur, and Cleveland had all condemned polygamy and had urged strong measures for Utah. Grover Cleveland informed Congress, in fact, that he would attack the Mormons from yet another angle by preventing the immigration of that "servile class" of Europeans from which Mormons supposedly recruited their converts.[42] All hopes that the Utah Commission would prove to be unconstitutional were dashed when the Supreme Court upheld the Edmunds Act. For the Mormons the final nightmare of persecution was at hand.

As the Utah Commission laboriously interviewed thousands of voters between 1882 and 1886, the federal courts continued their own attack on polygamy under the remaining provisions of the Edmunds law. To understand the nature of the judicial assault, however, one must first consider the judges and attorneys involved.

One of the most important figures in the entire history of the Mormon-federal fight over polygamy was Charles Shuster Zane, a member of Senator Shelby M. Cullom's law firm back in Illinois and a former law partner of Lincoln's friend, William Hearndon. Like Shaffer and Cullom, Zane was one of those midwestern public men whose lives and careers had been shaped by the antislavery crusade and the trauma of the Civil War.[43] All of these men had emerged from the War with a fiery love of the Union and of freedom, which bordered on zeal. Also forged in the same crucible of war and antislavery was Jacob S. Boreman, a scholarly, stern, mustachioed lawyer from West Virginia. Boreman was born in Virginia, but he and his brother, Kemer Boreman, raised a company to fight for the Union during the Civil War. Kemer then became the first governor of

---

42. William Mulder, *Homeward to Zion: The Mormon Migration from Scandinavia* (St. Paul, Minnesota, 1957), pp. 289–90.
43. "Charles Shuster Zane" in *DAB*.

Unionist West Virginia and later served as a senator from that state. Jacob himself moved to Missouri, where, as a judge in Jackson County, he undoubtedly learned much about the troubled Mormon sojourn there.[44] Similarly, Zane, who had sat as a judge on the Illinois bench for eleven years, must have learned much about the Mormons at Nauvoo.

These men represented a new type of Republican with whom Mormons had to deal after 1880. By and large they were neither venal nor vindictive; they did not form a ring for patronage purposes; and they stayed in office for long periods of time. Professional in their attitude toward the law and determined to achieve justice, their position was summed up admirably by Judge Boreman when he remarked that the only way to settle the Mormon problem was "simply to enforce the laws. . . . A rigid but just enforcement of the laws is the most terrible process to which the priestly criminals who rule this territory can be subjected. They dread it more than anything else."[45] By their incorruptibility and fairness, they eventually won the grudging respect of the Mormons. Under their ceaseless prodding, and with the aid of new Congressional legislation, the Church finally conformed on the key issues of political democracy and polygamy.

The Mormons had seen Judge Boreman preside over both trials of John D. Lee during the 1870s. In 1880 he was reappointed, and Zane joined him on the Utah bench. But the first break in the Church's united stand on polygamy did not come until October 1884, when Rudger Clawson, a Saint who had been convicted of polygamy, agreed to sign an oath foregoing that marital status in return for his freedom. Since Clawson was a prominent Mormon from a still more prominent family, his decision was a serious blow to the Church.[46]

Early in 1885 President Angus M. Cannon, one of the most beloved of the Saints, was arrested by federal officers. When his case came to trial in May, the government attorneys, contrary to previous practice,

44. Boreman, "Reminiscences"; and his obituary in the Ogden *Standard*, October 10, 1913, the Salt Lake City *Herald-Republican*, October 8, 1913, and the Salt Lake city *Tribune*, October 8, 1913.

45. Boreman to Rutherford B. Hayes, September 3, 1880, MS in Boreman Papers.

46. *Deseret News Weekly*, October 15, 29, 1884.

did not attempt to prove polygamy by testimony of sexual inter-
course with more than one wife but merely asked for evidence of
"cohabitation" under the same roof. In a desperate editorial the
Deseret News pleaded with Judge Zane, who was hearing the case,
not to give in to this broader definition of polygamy. But the new
definition stood, with the result that the number of arrests increased
greatly.[47]

That September, Bishop John Sharp, an able businessman and a
political mentor of the Saints, found himself on trial. A month later
the *Deseret News* reported that its own editorial writer, John Nicol-
son, was off to jail. In late Ocotber 1885 the Utah Commission recorded that 83 indictments and 23 convictions had taken place and
that 43 cases were awaiting trial. In February 1886 George Q. Cannon,
past delegate and a member of the First Presidency, was arrested in
Nevada and brought home to trial by United States Marshal E. A.
Ireland. Mormon feeling ran so high over this arrest that two of
Cannon's sons assaulted United States Attorney William A. Dickson,
at the Continental Hotel soon after the trial began.[48]

On every front and at every level, the story appeared the same.
Each time the legislature met, Governor Murray and its members
were soon at loggerheads over the question of their respective powers. The courts were now supporting Murray's right to appoint probate
judges and other territorial officials. Rumors were also spread that
Congress would no longer pay the costs of the Assembly unless it
were more cooperative. As the *News* had noted earlier in the year,
"The flow of the tide has set in against the Saints. It looks as if no
popular movement was favoring them. The executive, legislative,
judicial, and religious influences are against them."[49]

When Congress convened in the winter of 1885–86, Senator Edmunds introduced still another bill, more radical than the 1882 version, to abolish polygamy for all time. When this proposal reached
the House, it was modified by John Randolph Tucker of Virginia, a

47. *Report of the Utah Commission for 1884*, pp. 5 ff.
48. *Deseret News Weekly*, January 28, May 6, September 10, October 21, 1885;
February (24, 1886).
49. Ibid., May 6, 1885.

former professor of law at Washington and Lee, who appears to have felt that some of Edmunds' provisos were unconstitutional. Even so, the resulting Edmunds-Tucker Act of 1887 was one of the most far-reaching pieces of federal legislation ever passed in peacetime history. By it the original Poland Act was so strengthened that probate courts were now clearly limited to jurisdiction over estates and guardianship, while the probate judges themselves were now to be appointed by the President of the United States. The act gave federal marshals the powers of sheriffs and constables with great latitude to decide who was an offender of the law. The Utah Commission was continued in existence and was now empowered to administer a qualifying oath to would-be voters. The Edmunds-Tucker Act then took three new tacks: it dissolved the Perpetual Emigrating Company, abolished the Nauvoo Legion, and dissolved the Church of Jesus Christ of the Latter Day Saints as an incorporated body, placing its assets in the hands of a receiver.[50]

To carry out its many provisions, hundreds of federal officers and men were eventually employed to deal with Utah. There followed new arrests and trials, along with a corresponding increase in the number of Mormons taking an oath of amnesty. Hounded by United States marshals, polygamists everywhere either went into hiding or fled the country to Mexico or Europe. Those who were caught went off to prison to live for months in filthy, crowded conditions. Yet when Cleveland's new governor, Caleb W. West (1886–89), arrived in Utah, and tried to ameliorate things by visiting the penitentiary and offering fifty "cohabs" "conditional amnesty," not a single polygamist came forward to sign an oath.[51] Mormon-federal relations had once again reached an unbearable state. Somehow a way out of the nightmare had to be found, or the Latter Day Saints of Utah might perish at the hands of their enemies, as did their spiritual ancestors at the ancient battle of Cumorah.

The year 1887 was one that no one in the Mountain West would ever forget. Freak weather of subzero cold, piling snow, and biting

50. *United States Statutes at Large, 24,* 635–41.
51. *Deseret News Weekly,* June 2, 1886. John Taylor and George Q. Cannon to John T. Caine, Salt Lake, May 18, 1886, MS in Caine Letters, USHS.

winds, which blanketed the region from Montana to New Mexico. The toll of cattle was so great it ruined the openrange cattle industry and turned a young Dakota rancher, Theodore Roosevelt, back eastward and into politics. Railroad trains were halted, and many persons caught in isolated areas lost their lives. For the Saints these natural disasters were more than complemented by two man-made ones: the passage of the Edmunds-Tucker Act, and the refusal of Congress for the sixth time to grant Utah statehood. To these were added the personal loss of the third president of the Church of the Latter Day Saints, John Taylor, who died on July 25, 1887, some forty years and one day after the Mormons arrived in the Great Basin.[52]

Taylor's death was the signal for a crisis within as well as without Church circles. Enough nonpolygamous Mormons had felt the effects of persecution to begin to doubt the wisdom of further resistance for a principle which had now almost ceased to be practiced. Moreover, two new generations, not just one, were waiting to take their places in Church and Utah affairs, for Mormondom, once ruled by a physically powerful and fairly youthful set of leaders, now depended on patriarchal wisdom rather than vigor. Wilford Woodruff, the senior Apostle and the heir designate to Taylor, was turning eighty.[53] Still waiting in the wings was George Q. Cannon, the perennially energetic member of the First Presidency and often the expeditor of church policy.[54] He was a full twenty years younger than Woodruff. In Cannon's generation could be found John Sharp, W. W. Ritter, and the Utah delegate, John T. Caine, an active, effervescent official who loved amateur acting.[55] As close as they were to Taylor and Woodruff, they were men of a railroad age, familiar with big business, and aware of the national scene. Still a generation behind these men were two promising young lawyers, Franklin S. Richards and Joseph L. Rawlins, and a journalist, Frank J. Cannon, the son of George Q. Cannon.[56] All of them

52. See late July and early August editions of the *Deseret News*, 1887.
53. "Wilford Woodruff" in *DAB*.
54. "George Q. Cannon" in *DAB*. Jensen, *Saints, 1,* 42. Cannon in *Biographical Directory of the American Congress.*
55. Jensen, *Saints, 1,* 726–38.
56. Ibid., *4,* 55. "Joseph LaFayette Rawlins" in *Biographical Directory of the American Congress.*

were under forty and were specialists with a profession rather than able frontier jacks-of-all-trades.

The antipolygamy laws themselves created much difficulty by forcing many Church leaders into hiding. As a result of their enforced absence, and because 289 more were in jail and 541 had been indicted and were awaiting trial, Church business could not be conducted efficiently. This situation was amply illustrated by the fact that it took two years to go through the ritual of choosing Woodruff as the new president of the Church. As a polygamist, Woodruff himself was often in hiding and was forced to write his letters under pseudonyms and carry on Church affairs under all kinds of subterfuges.[57] George Q. Cannon, after being arrested under the 1882 Edmunds Act, had fled and was in hiding until September 1888, when he surrendered to the courts. Then he spent five months in prison.

Court trials and the threat of prison also meant legal expenses for the Saints. These soared as the Church retained famous men to defend their cause before the Supreme Court. To protect the beloved Lorenzo Snow, on trial for polygamy in 1886, no less a person than George Ticknor Curtis took the case. Senators James O. Broadhead and Joseph E. McDonald, lawyers in their own right, also appeared for other defendants. Wrote President Woodruff acidly from a sick bed in 1887: "Sat up some of the time until midnight talking to lawyers and I can hardly find two of them who agree on our case."[58]

The real drain on Church resources came in 1887 when the Church was taxed under the Edmunds-Tucker law to the limit of its capacity, so that in November it went into receivership. United States Marshal Dyer was appointed Receiver, and Woodruff noted the event by remarking: "Well Lightning has just struck. Dyer and the Marshal came yesterday, took possession of all our offices—the President's office—We left just in time." Unfortunately for the Mormons, Dyer and some of the United States attorneys were soon draining the painfully amassed capital of the Church by charging high prices for their services. The Mormons in turn hauled Dyer into court. "Our law suit is becoming

57. The conditions are dramatically revealed in the Letters of Wilford Woodruff, 1885–1894, MSS in USHS.
58. Woodruff to William Atkin, November 24, 1887, Woodruff Letters.

quite salty," observed Woodruff, for "they are determined to get all the Church property they can."[59] So outrageous were the acts of these men, Judge Zane himself descended from the bench to prosecute Dyer. Zane, aided by veteran Liberal R. N. Baskin, soon halted Dyer's game, and he was removed as Receiver.

Such was the internal state of the Church when Woodruff formally assumed the presidency in 1889. Now over eighty and in frail health, this former Connecticut Yankee was an unusual person with which to deal. Kindly, frank, and sometimes querulous, he combined age with stubbornness and a fierce belief in the Church doctrines of revelation and polygamy. Wearied by hiding from federal authorities, he had written in 1885 that he might leave the country, for "I have got too old to go to prison or hide in the mountains." Whatever his course, he was not a man to surrender. When Church lawyers suggested backing down on polygamy he declared he "would see the whole nation d——d first." A year later his mystical apocalyptic faith in the ultimate victory of Mormonism was exhibited when he declared that if Utah could be a state, then "in the event of the disruption of the general government [we would] be independent of all earthly power and clothed with legal as well as divine authority to assume the position in the earth God has designed or may design to fill in such an event."[60] This then was the official with whom both Church and Gentile leaders had to deal in bringing the "Mormon problem" to a final solution.

On the Mormon side the initiative for a settlement appears to have come from John T. Caine, who had served as delegate since 1882. Ambitious, articulate, popular, and anxious to please, he began rather early to argue for Mormon obedience to federal law where plural marriage was concerned. Though many Mormon leaders now traveled to Washington, dealt with lawyers, and appealed their cases to the Supreme Court, it is likely that Caine, more than the rest, sensed the absolute determination of Congress to solve the Utah question.[61]

59. Ibid., February 13, 1888.
60. Ibid., December 28, 1885, November 2, 1888, and March 18, 1889.
61. The addresses of Caine to Congress, 1887–88, suggest this attitude. See "Congressional Addresses," folder, Caine Letters.

Caine's first chance came in 1887 when Utah replied to the Edmunds-Tucker Act by calling a constitutional convention that year. When the delegates assembled, Caine was elected president. With the aid of other liberal Mormons he wrote a prohibition of bigamy and polygamy into the generally straightforward if conservative document. The convention also revised an extremely evasive public school clause that had been in the 1882 constitution, so that public education now seemed a certainty in Utah. Finally, the delegates of 1887 limited the franchise to males and provided for a secret ballot. The makeup of the convention itself suggested a new order in politics, for only nineteen members of the 1882 convention were there, and none of the 1887 delegates were polygamists.[62]

Naturally, Congress proved hostile to the idea of statehood for Utah in 1887, but the door was kept open for a future settlement when the Assembly of 1888 pushed through a bill forbidding polygamy. The new position was reinforced when George Q. Cannon appeared from prison to endorse the territorial law. By 1890 Caine's crusade was also producing an effect in Washington. In a famous speech he rose in Congress to denounce polygamy as a dead issue.[63] No new cases had been reported, he said, and none would be, for the Church had quit solemnizing plural marriage, and polygamous families no longer ruled Utah politics.

On the Gentile side equally important psychological changes were occurring. Stern though Cleveland might be about Mormon immigration, he had sent to Utah a thoughtful, intelligent governor in 1886, who was anxious to conciliate. This was Caleb W. West, a Kentucky lawyer and former United States Treasury agent. West never seems to have been a popular appointee, but he soon identified himself with Utah. As governor he was intimately concerned with its affairs from 1886 to 1889, and again from 1893 to 1896, when he was reappointed during Cleveland's second term.[64]

62. *Deseret News Weekly,* October 19, 1887. See *Constitution of the State of Utah, 1887* (Salt Lake City, 1887), YWA.

63. John T. Caine, *Polygamy in Utah—A Dead Issue* (Washington, 1888), pamphlet, USHS.

64. Robert Joseph Dwyer, *The Gentile Comes to Utah* (Washington, 1941), pp. 228–30, 244.

It was also evident that a whole new political atmosphere was forming in Utah, for when the Assembly met in January 1888, the People's Party held a caucus before the first session in recognition that four Liberals now sat in that body. More remarkable still, a month later the People's Party and the Liberal Party of Salt Lake City met together and picked a fusion slate of municipal officers. Governor West so approved of this move that when a group of diehards, led by Judge Roseborough and H. W. Lawrence, refused to go along, he chastized them as "cowards and cravens." Speaking as no Gentile official had ever done before, West accused the antifusionists of making a living off the Mormons by court fees and litigation. They were, he thundered, men who had breakfasted, dined, and supped on a Mormon and had a Mormon for "a nightmare." Naturally the governor's remarks were designed to ruin the Liberals—who were actually Republicans—and to foster the Democratic Party as much as they represented an effort to be fair to the Saints. His words caused a near riot. Amidst the shouting and booing, General Connor himself had to appeal for order when the chairman of the meeting failed to do so.[65] The more tolerant attitude even affected the Utah Commission in 1888, for a minority report urged that no more special anti-Mormon legislation be enacted.[66]

The progress toward a rapprochement halted, however, when Benjamin Harrison succeeded Cleveland as President in 1889 and appointed Arthur L. Thomas (1889–93) as the new territorial governor. Thomas had served as territorial secretary from 1879 to 1887, and he knew Utah well, but he was an embittered and suspicious Liberal Party man, who agreed with R. N. Baskin that more stringent legislation was needed to subdue the Saints. He was, complained the *Deseret News*, a true "dis-franchisement missionary."[67]

Thomas' appointment coincided with a new spate of anti-Mormon bills in Congress. Senators Dolph of Oregon and Cullom of Illinois and Representatives Springer of Illinois and Culberson of Texas all introduced new legislation against polygamy. These bills, detailed

65. *Deseret News Weekly*, January–March 1888.
66. See *Report of the Utah Commission for 1888.*
67. *Deseret News*, June 21, 1890.

in themselves, were supplemented by an even more minute measure proposed by Senator Paddock of Nebraska, a former member of the Utah Commission. His measure sought to redistrict Salt Lake City so that the Liberals could win elections. In the Fifty-First Congress other bills by Cullom, Congressman Struble of Iowa, and Delegate DuBois of Idaho were presented which would have turned the government of Utah over to its governor and a twelve-man commission. The news of Harrison's victory in 1888 had led Woodruff to note that "the ring [Utah Liberals] and Republicans now expect to take the Kingdom."[68]

Out of this plethora of Republican measures came the Cullom-Struble bill, which proposed further disfranchisement of the Saints. Backed by the Utah Liberals and the Senate Territorial Committee, it was about to be favorably reported when a desperate delegation made up of George Q. Cannon, Bishop Clawson, Colonel Issac Trumbo, and Frank J. Cannon called on Cullom. They promised that if the bill were "delayed for a reasonable time, the practice of polygamy would be prohibited by the Mormon Church."[69] Typically, Edmunds refused to deal with the delegation, but they appear to have influenced both Cullom and Senator James G. Blaine with their appeal.

Young Frank Cannon now rushed back to Utah to tell Woodruff to act in the face of the impending disaster. Woodruff, though sorely troubled, did not yet feel free to act. Said he sadly, "I had hoped we wouldn't have to meet this trouble this way. You know what it means to our people. Did your father tell you that I had been seeking the mind of the Lord?"[70]

Then suddenly it was over. On September 28, 1890, the news came that the Church now forbade plural marriage, and on October 4 the Church called a general conference and confirmed the historic decision. By prayer and revelation, said Woodruff, the Church had been guided to take the following stand: it did not believe in blood atonement, the murder of apostates, or the power of bishop's courts over civil courts. Further, the Church would no longer dictate the ballot, engage in the practice of endowment, or condone any union of

68. Woodruff to Atkin, November 23, 1888, Woodruff Letters.
69. Baskin claimed that he drafted the Cullom-Struble measure. See his *Reminiscences*, pp. 183–85.
70. Ibid., p. 185.

Church and State. These declarations when added to the specific prohibition of polygamy, did meet all the barriers to citizenship and peace, said Judge Zane. The way was open for settlement.[71]

To make good his dramatic "Manifesto" of 1890, Woodruff himself marched down into Salt Lake City with a set of carpenters and began to raze the Endowment House—symbol to many of Mormon wealth and control and the place where marriages were solemnized. As the rafters fell and the dust of plaster and brick swelled into the still bright air of Great Salt Lake Basin, the world knew that a forty-year war over the rule of Utah had come to an end. Meanwhile, in Washington the Cullom-Struble bill died a quiet death, for the ex-Radicals of New England and the midwest knew they had now fulfilled the ancient party pledge of 1856: they had abolished the "twin barbarisms" of slavery and polygamy.

In a lesser sense the Utah legislature also surrendered in 1890, for when that body had tried to keep its tax-supported Church schools in 1889, Governor Thomas promptly wrote an education bill for Utah, which Senator Edmunds introduced to Congress. The threat was enough. Hastily the Assembly pushed through a satisfactory educational act known as the Collett bill. Dramatic indeed were the results: where school attendance had accounted for only 36 per cent of the eligible children in 1889, by 1892 some 59 per cent were enrolled and teachers' salaries were doubled. Free, tax supported, elementary education now existed in Utah—the first, wrote one authority, "in a series of [Mormon] concessions to the world."[72]

The next year the Church also made good its pledge to end the People's Party. Committees went throughout the territory telling voters they must now vote either Democrat or Republican; and the story is told that in the village of Panguitch, where four voters lived, the Church instructed two to vote Democratic and two to vote Republican.[73] Again the results were almost breathtaking. At the general territorial election in August 1891, Salt Lake City voted in the

71. *Deseret News*, October 4, 1890. "Zane" in *DAB*. *Report of the Governor of Utah for 1891*, pp. 43–48.

72. Ivins, "Free Schools," p. 342. Utah Territory, Executive Record, *4*, pp. 43 ff., MSS in Utah State Archives.

73. Frank Herman Jonas, "Utah: Sagebrush Democracy," in T. C. Connelly, ed., *Rocky Mountain Politics* (Albuquerque, 1940), p. 14.

Gentile party and increased its voting lists from 5,494 to 10,273. Similar changes in Ogden prompted the Utah Commission to report that the "great business centers of Utah have been liberated from the Old Regime." In the territorial elections 14,157 voted as Democrats, 7,404 as Liberals, and 6,339 as Republicans. In the Assembly the Democrats captured twenty-four out of thirty-six seats.[74] In the delegate election of 1892 Frank J. Cannon appeared as the Republican candidate, while Joseph L. Rawlins was the Democratic contender. Since a hard core of the Liberals were not yet convinced of the new order, C. E. Allen ran on their ticket.

The rapid breakup of old political patterns in Utah led both Mormon and Gentile to dream of statehood. The formation of political parties on national lines and a corresponding realignment of newspapers paved the way. In February 1891 the *Ogden Daily Standard* announced that henceforth it would be a Republican paper, a sentiment echoed by the *Salt Lake Evening News*. Meanwhile the Democrats secured the allegiance of the *Salt Lake Herald*. Commented President Woodruff in 1893:

We are having some curious times here of late. About the time our State Bill passed the House, the Clergymen of Utah met, and when Mr. McNiece made a motion . . . to oppose . . . two-thirds of those present voted against him, saying thay had had war enough and now wanted a State Government. At the same time the Liberals met, dug a grave and buried all their Liberal sentiments . . . [and] both parties sent strong telegrams to Washington for a State Government.[75]

When Rawlins, who was a Democrat, was elected at the same time that Cleveland and a Democratic administration were returned to Washington, the chances for statehood seemed just around the corner. The Salt Lake *Tribune,* long a Gentile paper, announced that it would

---

74. *Report of the Utah Commission for 1891,* pp. 5–6.
75. Woodruff to Atkin, December 26, 1893, Woodruff Letters. See also *Report of the Governor of Utah for 1891.*

support a statehood fight. A year later Congress itself passed an Enabling Act for Utah, and in November 1893 the voters of Utah elected their seventh and last constitutional convention. The following spring still more evidence of the changes in Utah politics came when it was found that of the fifty-nine Republicans and forty-eight Democrats who had been elected delegates, twenty-eight were non-Mormons. Utah's fast-developing economy was also reflected in the membership of the constitutional convention, for while twenty-eight were farmers and ranchers, fifteen were lawyers, thirteen were merchants, and eight were miners. The usual scattering of educators, journalists, churchmen, and bankers accounted for the remainder.

The delegates themselves who came together in Salt Lake City on March 4, 1895, were a curious lot of former opponents. In the hall was Charles S. Varian for United States Attorney, who, with his partner William Dickson, had prosecuted many polygamists under Judges Zane and Boreman. From Ogden, which in Mormon eyes had always been a rebellious railroad town overpopulated with Methodists, was David Evans and the brilliant young lawyer Franklin S. Richards. There, too, sat a former Liberal delegate candidate, C. C. Goodwin. Samuel Thurman, the leader of a prominent faction in the Assembly, was there from Provo, while George Q. Cannon represented the Hierarchy. Moving easily among the members was the popular Brigham Roberts, a former polygamist who was soon to be Congressman from Utah. W. F. James of the Democratic Party, C. H. Hart, and Dennis Eichnor made up the remaining leaders.[76]

As in most constitutional conventions, the lawyers did most of the talking. The issues they debated were a curious blend of the political fads of the hour and basic constitutional fundamentals. Several sessions were spent arguing over female suffrage, which had already been tried in Utah. But since the Utah Gentiles saw female suffrage as a Church device to outnumber non-Mormon voters, it was prohibited. The convention also discussed the questions of permitting state aid to private business, prohibition, and the maintenance of free schools. The resulting document was a typically cautious one, trying

---

76. Stanley S. Ivins, "A Constitution for Utah," *UHQ*, 25 (1957), 113.

to avoid the lure of Populist ideas while assuaging a suspicious Congress. It was anything but radical.[77]

When the voters went to the polls in November 1895 to ratify the document, the outcome was no surprise. They voted 31,305 "Yes" and 7,687 "No," with the major portion of the nays coming from non-Mormon communities. It is significant that the sense of cultural divergence between racial or religious groups in New Mexico, Colorado, and Utah was so strong that in each case the minority voted against statehood, looking to the federal government and not to local democratic action for protection.

The news that Cleveland had signed the Utah statehood act came on January 4, 1896, at 8:03 A.M. Salt Lake City and Ogden gave way to celebration: whistles were blown, flags and bunting appeared, and all business was generally suspended. Two days later the first Utah state government was inaugurated. A United States Army regiment from Fort Douglas joined the Utah National Guard, organized in 1894, to parade down the main street of Salt Lake City. As the sun glistened on swords and bridle ornaments, local bands blared forth martial music in competition with a performance by the Sixteenth Infantry Band.

Since Utah had never really had a capitol building, the inauguration ceremonies took place at the Mormon Tabernacle. There in the Temple grounds some 30,000 people strained and struggled to see the dignitaries, and of these some 15,000 were soon packed into the building itself. Appropriately, an invocation by President Wilford Woodruff was read by Republican George Q. Cannon, and Democrat Joseph L. Rawlins read the "Proclamation of Admission." In a medley of the old order and the new, Judge Zane gave Governor Heber M. Wells the oath of office, after which the Reverend T. C. Iliff of the Methodist Church gave the benediction. The ceremonies, the noise of bands, and the sea of smiling faces so deeply moved retiring Governor Caleb West that he called the scene "profoundly impressive."[78] John T. Caine had once advised that a state be erected "on the grave of the unhappy territory . . . of which you will all be

77. *Ibid.*, pp. 101 ff.
78. *Report of the Governor of Utah for 1896*, p. 3.

proud. A state which will be second to none in loyalty, in patriotism, in morality, in integrity, and in the broadest and best Americanism." This had now been achieved. Yet, as in New Mexico and even Colorado, nature and differing customs had so modified American values and traditions that, for a long time to come, a sense of uniqueness would exist among the thrifty, independent, and religious-minded people who lived "in the tops of the mountains a long ways towards sundown."

Good ↓

The Utah experience was perhaps the most turbulent and unusual one to occur in the history of the American territorial system, for nowhere else had the federal government ever faced the problem of turning a desert frontier theocracy into a standard democratic American state. The crisis in Utah between 1850 and 1890 involved the question not just of who should rule at home, but of what form home rule and local institutions should be. By rejecting parts of the common law, public schools, a secular, two-party system, federal land policy, and the primacy of civil courts, Utah had violated even the permissive and passive territorial system so fundamentally that Congress felt compelled to act. Between 1857 and 1890, therefore, the President and interested congressmen framed a specific policy for Utah which would make the territory loyal and which would reconstruct its political and social institutions. To the outside world the practice of polygamy came to be the symbol of the so-called Mormon rebellion, and it was naïvely thought that if this institution could be abolished, all other things would right themselves.

This simplistic view ignored the fact that during their decades of isolation in the Great Basin, the Saints had created a distinct religious society and economy. The frictions that made headlines were caused by a conflict of social orders and of cultures and not by a conflict over polygamy alone. Significantly, the Utah governors and judges always complained of lawlessness, by which they meant an absence of the familiar political, legal, and economic customs normally to be found in a developing frontier community.

In an age dominated by the memory of sectional rebellion and a war to preserve democracy and the Union, Congress could hardly be expected to sympathize with another extreme form of states rights and another unacceptable peculiar domestic institution. Unfortunately for the Mormons, the Republicans in Congress never forgot the parallel between an independent Mormon Utah, which condoned the practice of polygamy, and the Confederacy, with its defense of slavery.

During the long period of difficulties between the Mormons and Congress, several significant patterns emerged, once again throwing revealing light on the relation of nation to frontier and region. Congress, for example, used methods learned in the Civil War and Reconstruction eras to force conformity in Utah. General Connor's presence in Utah was military occupation thinly disguised. The scores of antipolygamy and anti-Mormon bills depended heavily on Reconstruction measures as precedents. Disfranchisement, loyalty oaths, confiscation of property, and threat of imprisonment were phrases as familiar to Mormons as they were to high ranking Confederates. Once again the passions and concerns of the hour shaped policy in Washington and affected events in Utah.

The Utah territorial period also demonstrated the plethora of checks and balances inherent in the territorial system. Not only did the Saints use the office of delegate and the powers of the Assembly to defend themselves, they also took advantage of the fact that before 1882—and the passage of the Edmunds law—their Gentile opponents were never united. Throughout his later life Young himself played a brilliant game of divide and conquer, by setting one federal official against another. He befriended Governor Cumming in 1858 and used him to oppose Colonel Johnston and Chief Justice Eckels. Later, Governor Harding found himself powerless when Chief Justice Kinney decided to cooperate with Young. Between 1863 and 1880 nearly a score of major federal officials were persuaded to be pro-Mormon. It is not surprising, therefore, that Congress eventually had to resort to extraordinary measures to force conformity.

As unique as the Utah story was, it also echoed some familiar patterns in American history. Throughout the nineteenth century each section of the United States was developing at different rates of speed. A frontier area, particularly, had interests and attitudes different from those of a settled region, and even the "mature" sections had begun to develop specific regional habits and customs. The great

problem of the nation and of the federal government was to reconcile
and adjust these differences peaceably. But crisis after crisis, cul-
minating in the slavery issue, finally led to Civil War. This sense of
sectional difference continued after 1865 and was complicated by the
uneven speed with which city, farm, agriculture, and industry were
growing. The resulting Alliance and Populist movements of the 1890s
marked a second breakdown of faith between sections.

In this evolving, continually expanding nation, one part always
seemed to be out of step with the others—a condition that has helped
to give American politics a permanent geographic or regional orientation. It was the fate of the Mormons, however, not only to be out of
touch with all the major economic and social trends between 1830
and 1890, but to have developed their own society while isolated in
an extraordinary environment. Almost more than any other indigenous group of American pioneers, then, the history of the Mormon
sect offers the student of the American frontier a chance to test the
roles of environment and cultural heritage in shaping society. After
looking at the history of the Saints in the Great Basin, one could
seriously question Frederick Jackson Turner's assertion that democracy came out of the frontier, but one could never doubt his belief
that factors of isolation and environment affected society and institutions.

The Mormon Manifesto of 1890, which abolished polygamy and
accepted a secular political system, came in the very year the Census
Bureau reported that no more continuous areas of free land existed.
Six years later the nation itself voted to abandon its Jeffersonian-
agrarian-states' rights heritage for an increasingly centralized industrial future. During the turbulent nineties all Americans experienced
the shock and awkwardness of living with one another in a harsh
new industrial and imperial world. With considerable apprehension
Utah itself threw off its own past Democratic inclinations after 1896
to vote for big business and Republicanism. After fifty years the
Mormons had entered the mainstream of American life once
again, but the sense of painful alienation and persecution which accompanied the process of reentry remains a group experience unique
in American history.

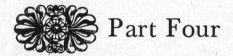 Part Four

16

Arizona: No Man's Land
1846–1863

The territory we have selected for our home is unlike any
other portion of the United States. . . .
Attached as we now are nominally to the Territory of
New Mexico, and situated many hundred miles from its seat
of government, the western portion of Arizona is a region
without the shadow of anything that claims to be law. . . .
So far as we know, no judge or justice, either Federal or
Territorial, has ever visited this portion of the country.

> Edward E. Cross in
> The *Weekly Arizonian* (Tubac)
> March 3, 1859

Arizona . . . [is] just like hell, all it lacks is water
and good society.

> Senator Benjamin Wade, 1863

 Major Philip St. George Cooke, who had played a
key role in the secret negotiations toward the peaceful conquest of New Mexico, was already on his
way to California in the fall of 1846 when his superior, General Kearny, suddenly gave him new orders.
Cooke was to return to Santa Fe and assume com-
mand of the so-called "Mormon Battalion," which had just reached
that city from Fort Leavenworth. He and his Saints were to mark
the way for a wagon road from the Rio Grande to the Pacific Coast.
Although Cooke could not know it at the time, his task, once accomplished, had a profound effect on the history of the Far Southwest. His report on the region bordering the 32nd parallel, coupled
with a lengthy one made by Major William H. Emory of the U. S.

Topographical Engineers, pulled back the blanket of obscurity from western New Mexico. Together they introduced the government and the country to a new, hitherto unknown province, which, by 1856, was to be called Arizona.[1]

Once Cooke's wagon road had been marked, as many as 50,000 argonauts used it to reach the California gold fields in 1849 and 1850.[2] Quite apart from its proven worth as a trail to California, the Polk, Pierce, and Buchanan administrations as well as every Southern, Texas, and California political leader in Congress were convinced that the road would be ideal for a transcontinental rail line. Cooke and Emory had both informed Polk in 1847 that it would be excellent for this purpose. The difficulty was that Cooke's road occasionally veered south of the Mexican-American boundary specified in the Treaty of Guadalupe-Hidalgo of 1848. Despite feverish negotiations between the Mexican and American boundary commissioners from 1850 to 1852, the subsequent boundary agreement—made in the latter year—left part of the Cooke road on Mexican soil. The necessity of securing an all-American route to California was a major factor in prompting the Pierce Administration make the Gadsden Purchase in 1853.[3]

Even before the Gadsden Purchase was secured, the prospects of running transcontinental rail lines along either the 32nd or the 35th parallels persuaded the national government to use the Topographical Engineers to conduct dozens of exploring expeditions into the Far Southwest. By the time of the Civil War they had searched out nearly every corner of New Mexico, Utah, and Arizona. Their lengthy reports on trails, railroads routes, the fantastic Grand Canyon of the Colorado River, Southwestern Indian life, and the flora and fauna of the entire West acquainted the whole of America with the mysterious and romantic Far Southwest. So vigorous was this grand reconnais-

1. See *Report from the Sec. of War, Communicating . . . a copy of the Official Journal of Lieutenant-Colonel Philip St. George Cooke from Santa Fe to San Diego . . .* 30th Cong., Spec. Sess., Sen. Exec. Doc. 2 (1849). See also Goetzmann, *Army Exploration*, pp. 127–44.

2. Rufus K. Wyllys, *Arizona; The History of a Frontier State* (Phoenix, 1950), p. 125.

3. For the standard account of the Gadsden Purchase see Paul Neff Garber, *The Gadsden Treaty* (Philadelphia, 1923).

sance that in a short fifteen years the United States had been able
to compile as much information about the region as the Spanish
padres and explorers had accumulated in over two centuries.[4] By
1858 the Butterfield Overland Mail, heavily subsidized by Congress,
ran over Cooke's route twice a week, and a large part of the American army was stretched out on the 32nd parallel from Texas to
California to protect the line.

Given the prospects that two transcontinental railroads could be
built through the region, private parties and interests were soon as
busy as the Topographical Engineers investigating the Far Southwest.
Often the two efforts became indistinguishable; for the Engineers
themselves were the most avid promoters of the Gadsden Purchase,
and—once the area had been acquired—they were equally interested
in exploiting it for personal as well as public benefit. Andrew B. Gray
of the Engineers had made a private railroad survey in the area in
1852 and had rushed East to help Robert J. Walker, a master politician
in the Democratic Party and a former Secretary of the Treasury, organize a railroad company to build along the route.[5] On the other
hand, many Americans remained skeptical about the value of the
Mexican Cession, and they were particularly dubious about the
worth of the Gadsden Purchase, which had been described as a
desert so barren that even a wolf could not survive there.

Both public and private promoters soon countered this criticism
with the rumor that rich mineral deposits existed in the Gadsden
area. Attracted by the possibility that the purchase might be the
center of a second California gold strike, and led on by the knowledge that neighboring Sonora was full of silver mines, the first American prospectors and settlers marched into this last Southwestern
frontier in the middle fifties.[6]

In contrast to the great American tradition of settlement through

4. The best summary treatment of the early history of the Arizona region is to
be found in Wyllys, *Arizona*, pp. 43–98.

5. "Robert J. Walker" in *DAB*. James P. Shenton, *Robert J. Walker, A Politician
from Jackson to Lincoln* (New York and London, 1961), pp. 129 ff. See also
Robert R. Russel, *Improvement of Communication with the Pacific Coast as an
Issue in American Politics, 1783–1864* (Cedar Rapids, Iowa, 1948), pp. 96–97.

6. H. H. Bancroft, *History of Arizona and New Mexico, 1530–1888* (San Francisco, 1889), p. 497.

"westering," many Arizona pioneers came from California eastward. Most of the first comers were often motivated by passions more akin to the desire to filibuster and to gain riches by quick exploitation than to satisfy a land hunger. Many of them were restless schemers in and out of pocket in San Francisco, who thought that the Gadsden Purchase was just the prelude to an American seizure of all of Sonora. But quite a few were genuine miners and shrewd, hardheaded merchants. The latter knew that there was always a market where miners and army outposts were located.

One of the most ambitious of the Arizona mining pioneers was the brilliant but often erratic Charles DeBrille Poston.[7] Born in Kentucky, Poston migrated to Tennessee as a young man, where he served as clerk of the state supreme court until he joined the rush to California in 1850. There he secured a job in the San Francisco Customs House. Poston was a sharp but entertaining and gregarious man with a head full of plans. He soon befriended his superior, Thomas Butler King, a Georgia politician who was both the collector of customs and a vice-president of Walker's "Atlantic and Pacific Railroad."[8] King and Poston were fascinated by new mining ventures, so that when Poston lost his customs house sinecure to another patronage seeker, it was not surprising to learn that King—who also lost his job in 1852—had sent his ex-clerk on a reconnaissance tour of Sonora while the Gadsden Purchase was still being negotiated.

Since the famous filibusterer William Walker happened to be leading a set of San Francisco toughs on an expedition to take Sonora when Poston arrived, he nearly lost his life in the hostilities between Walker and the Sonorans. Nevertheless, Poston and a Freiburg-trained German miner, Herman Ehrenberg, finally reached the Santa Cruz Valley in 1854. In the hills around the feeble presidio towns of Tucson and Tubac and to the West at Ajo, they ascertained that gold, silver, and copper did exist in the Gadsden Purchase area in paying quantities. The finds at Ajo, in fact, led Poston to found a copper-mining

7. See Poston File, APHS. See also B. Sacks, *Be It Enacted: The Creation of the Territory of Arizona* (Phoenix, 1964), pp. 6–9.
8. "Thomas Butler King" in Hayden File on Charles D. Poston, APHS.

company once he had returned to San Francisco.[9] On his way back to civilization, he and Ehrenberg also engaged in that classical frontier pastime of townsite grabbing. They laid out a paper village, which they named Colorado City, at the crossing on the Colorado River where Fort Yuma was located. While they may never have profited from the venture, their choice was a shrewd one, for it was to be the site of the present city of Yuma.[10]

An ex-customs clerk was not likely to be a financier, so Poston had to go to New York in search of needed capital for his mining activities. There he talked with Robert J. Walker, who now headed the famous "Hundred Million" railroad company, which proposed to build a transcontinental line if Congress would supply land grants, funds, and other means of support. Undoubtedly, Poston carried a letter of introduction from King, his former employer at the Customs House who had returned East and was now vice president of the "Hundred Million" company. Walker himself was not only acquainted with the Southwest but, with Senators Thomas J. Rusk of Texas and William M. Gwin of California, had been an ardent lobbyist for the Gadsden Purchase. Indeed, Walker's own brother-in-law, Major William H. Emory of the Topographical Engineers, was at that very moment running the boundary between the Purchase and Mexico.

Poston's talks with Walker and a group of Ohio capitalists interested in mining were obviously successful, for he returned to the Southwest as an official in the "Sonora Exploring and Mining Company." Throughout the fifties he made other trips east to secure the technical assistance of German mining engineers, to lobby for a port of supply on the Gulf of California, and to raise more capital. In May 1856 Poston also joined Dr. Michael Steck, the Superintendent of Indian Affairs in New Mexico, to make a treaty with the Apaches living near the Santa Rita copper mines east of Tubac, so that a Cincinnati firm affiliated with his Sonora Company could exploit that property in peace.[11]

9. Wyllys, *Arizona*, p. 112. Ehrenberg's career was summarized by Poston in the Arizona *Weekly Star*, February 26, 1880.

10. Sacks, *Be It Enacted*, p. 9.

11. Wyllys, *Arizona*, p. 133. "Joseph Fish Manuscript History of Arizona," pp. 251–57, typescript in APHS. See also Poston File, APHS.

By 1857 Poston had sent a mule load of ore to San Francisco to "show the world" what the Gadsden area could do. At the same time, he persuaded Santiago Hubbell of New Mexico to haul in supplies and, on his return trip, to take 24,000 pounds of ore all the way to St. Louis to be refined.[12] Bright indeed seemed the future of the Gadsden tract pioneer entrepreneurs, backed as they were by a benevolent national administration, Texas railroad men, and assorted speculators and financiers from both coasts and Europe.

Poston's activities in the Santa Cruz Valley were paralleled, and even outshone for a time, by more profitable mining ventures along the Colorado and Gila rivers. In 1858 Colonel Jacob Snively, who had tried to make his fortune in 1843 by intercepting and robbing Santa Fe caravans, now appeared with some of his men to mine gold and silver on the Gila River. Quite in harmony with his own violent nature, a wild gold rush town, Gila City, grew up twenty miles above Fort Yuma with everything "but a church and a jail." There hard-drinking miners eventually extracted nearly $2,000,000 from the soil before the ore played out.[13]

Much in the tradition of Snively's earlier career, one Henry A. Crabb organized a filibustering expedition in 1857, under the guise of the "Gadsden Colonization Company," to take Sonora. Many of Poston's own miners joined the party, only to be ambushed by Mexican soldiers and routed. Snively's and Crabb's brief careers in the Far Southwest illustrated both a common exploit-and-get-out attitude towards the region and a lawlessness all too characteristic of the free-booters who preyed on the border provinces of Mexico in the name of Manifest Destiny.[14]

Besides the legal mining companies and the illegal filibusterers, the inevitable frontier merchants and army sutlers were soon in evidence in Arizona. When the presidio town of Tucson was occupied by American troops in 1856, enough American miners and settlers followed in their wake to elect an American merchant, Mark Aldrich, as

12. Ibid., pp. 278–79.
13. Billington, *Far Western Frontier,* p. 249.
14. Wyllys, *Arizona,* p. 112.

mayor or alcalde of that still Spanish-American town.[15] From that point on, the pattern of political evolution was both familiar and inevitable. To run a successful business, to mine profitably, or even to build a railroad, one needed law and order. In turn, that meant local political organization. In Cincinnati, New York, Philadelphia, and Washington the backers of Arizona projects also knew that their ventures could not succeed unless favorable conditions existed in the region. Almost unconsciously, a sentiment for territorial organization for Arizona had developed by 1856. Undoubtedly, the American pioneers of Tucson had all these considerations in mind when they held a convention in August 1856 and memorialized Congress for a territorial organization. They also elected Nathan P. Cook, a mining company official, as delegate.[16]

The pleas of the men who petitioned Congress in 1856 were not nearly so interesting as the convention members themselves. Besides Mayor Aldrich, who chaired the convention, James Douglas of Sopori, an experienced miner from Mexico and a former member of the Mexican army, was in attendance.[17] Herman Ehrenberg, Poston's German friend, was there. Ignacio Ortiz and Jose M. Martinez signed the memorial for their Mexican countrymen who made up a majority of the white population in the Gadsden Purchase. Granville H. Oury, a Virginia-born frontiersman—and the very epitome of a Southern colonel, was at the convention.[18] One of the most typical signers was Hiram S. Stevens who had been stationed in New Mexico after the Mexican War. Upon his discharge he had become an army contractor and, in that capacity, had followed the first detachment of soldiers to Tucson in 1856. Stevens' future partner, Samuel Hughes, was also at the convention.[19] He, too, had come to Tucson as a merchant and mining speculator. Perhaps the most rugged of the memorialists was Peter Kitchen, a tough frontier rancher from Nogales.[20] At least one

15. Frank C. Lockwood, *Life in Old Tucson. 1854–1864, as Remembered by the Little Maid Atanacia Santa Cruz* (Los Angeles, 1943), pp. 16–23.

16. Sacks, *Be It Enacted*, p. 12.

17. Annie M. Cox, "History of Bisbee, 1877 to 1937" (Master's thesis, University of Arizona, 1938), pp. 35–36.

18. See C. C. Smith, "Manuscript History of the Oury Family," typescript, APHS.

19. Lockwood, *Old Tucson*, pp. 169–74, 200–20.

20. Ibid., pp. 24–39; Sacks, *Be it Enacted*, on the other hand, finds no evidence that Kitchen was there.

of the signers, Peter R. Brady, had come to Arizona as a member of the boundary commission and had stayed on to serve in Andrew B. Gray's private railroad surveying party.[21]

Great expectations did not dwell solely in the hearts of American pioneers in Tucson that summer. Further east the American citizens of Mesilla, New Mexico, had already protested to Congress earlier that year that the territorial officials in Santa Fe ignored their local needs. To remedy this defect they requested a territory of their own, which they proposed to name "Arizona."[22] As in Tucson, the Mesillaños did not act in a vacuum: their requests were also supported by Texan expansionists and by railroad and mining promoters in Washington and the East.

When Congress met in December 1856, the House refused to seat "Delegate" Cook or to organize a new territory. Congress also turned down a bill that Senator Rusk of Texas had introduced earlier that year, calling for the settlement of land questions in the Gadsden Purchase area.[23] Cook did not return to Arizona completely empty-handed, however. Rusk, who had an obsession about establishing adequate communications between the Pacific Coast and Texas and who had been proposing legislation to facilitate construction of a transcontinental railroad since 1852, succeeded in pushing a wagon road bill through both houses which provided $200,000 for the construction of a road from El Paso to Fort Yuma. Once the contract was awarded, Cook became the assistant engineer for the project.

Until 1857 the agitation for a territory had centered in Tucson and Mesilla. Now, two army officers from Fort Yuma entered the lists. The first was Major Samuel Peter Heintzelman, a West Point graduate who had been in the Mexican War and had followed the flag to California.[24] When the gold rush began, Heintzelman had been detailed to establish a military post, Fort Yuma, on the Colorado River where the argonauts crossed into California. As a man of ability with an eye for detail and order, Heintzelman was soon part and parcel

21. Ibid., pp. 79–84.
22. Sacks, *Be It Enacted*, p. 10.
23. Ibid., pp. 12–15.
24. Goetzmann, *Army Exploration*, pp. 259–60. Poston summarized Heintzelman's career in the Arizona *Weekly Star*, May 13. 1880.

of the public and private plans to develop Arizona, for his post lay athwart the proposed 32nd parallel railroad route and the Colorado River, which every person interested in the Southwest hoped would prove navigable. Heintzelman also personally participated in the first American exploration of the lower Colorado in 1850–51. When he learned of the mineral wealth of the Gadsden Purchase from Poston and Ehrenberg in 1854, he became a member of their Sonora Exploring and Mining Company, and by 1857 Heintzelman himself had become president of the firm. The major—who was one day to be a Civil War general—was a valuable man to know, for he had influential friends in Ohio and in Congress, and he used them time and again to promote Arizona interests.[25]

After the Gadsden Purchase had been ratified in July 1854, mining schemes became the rage among Heintzelman's fellow officers, and no one of them was more excited by the mineral promise of Arizona than Lieutenant Sylvester Mowry. Of the many daring young pioneers who came to frontier Arizona, the temperamental, red-headed Mowry was perhaps the most comical, colorful, and tragic. Although Mowry came from a wealthy cultivated Rhode Island family, he chose West Point and the Army for a career. Immediately after his graduation he was assigned to the northernmost Pacific road surveys, but by 1854 he was in Utah as the head of a unit of dragoons under Colonel Steptoe's command. There Mowry's overly ardent nature soon involved him in an affair with a young Mormon wife, and he was quickly transferred to an Army supply depot in California. Two years later he was sent to Fort Yuma to command the Third Cavalry unit there.[26]

The dashing lieutenant did as much as any man at Fort Yuma to enliven the dull routine at that ugly, steaming post. He kept one or more Yuma Indian girls as mistresses and wrote of his conquests in a

25. Sacks, *Be It Enacted*, pp. 89–91. The *Weekly Arizonian* reported in its first issue, March 3, 1859, that the Heintzelman mines were producing fabulous ores. It is significant that the Sonora Company survived the crash of 1857 and that no less a personage than Colonel Samuel Colt, inventor of the revolver, consented to be the company president in 1859. See *Sonora Exploring and Mining Company*, Report of Frederick Brunkow (Cincinnati, 1859), YWA.

26. George W. Cullum, *Biographical Register of the Officers and Graduates of the U. S. Military Academy* (6 vols. Boston, 1891–1900), 2, 483. "Sylvester Mowry" in Hayden File, APHS.

series of extraordinarily frank letters. He drank so heavily that he endangered his health, and he swore and boasted his way through every scorching day.[27] Yet Mowry was both ambitious and something of a businessman, and he, too, was soon involved in schemes to develop Arizona mining. He discussed the commercial future of the Colorado River with his superior, Major Heintzelman, and after he had been given the convenient task of reporting on the Indian tribes contained within the Gadsden Purchase area, he and his fellow officers returned to Yuma greatly impressed by the mineral deposits there. By 1858 Mowry, in partnership with Captain R. S. Ewell and Elias Brevoort, had gone into mining.[28]

Later Mowry himself purchased the Patagonia Mine from Ewell and set out to become the biggest operator in the Purchase. Mowry's mines were located in the beautiful Sonoita Valley. There Sonoran workers brought ore to German mining experts who reduced it to crude ingots. These were then shipped overland to the port of Guaymas, Mexico, and from the Mexican port the ingots went to Swansea, Wales, for refining. Since the mine was in Apache country, Mowry hired American guards to protect his operation from Indian raiders.[29]

From the very first, the problems involved in establishing a mining company on an isolated frontier led Mowry and a dozen other mine owners into politics. The lack of enough soldiers to control the wild Indians of Arizona greatly hampered their mining operations. The large expense of freighting in supplies under heavy guard also made mining costs prohibitive. Mowry therefore became a lobbyist for improved transportation facilities—whether this meant a railroad for Tucson or an adequate port on the Colorado. Thus it was that a year after "Delegate" Cook had been sent to Congress, a motley set of miners, settlers, merchants, and soldiers came together in the small village of Tubac, in September 1857, to elect Sylvester Mowry as "delegate" from "Arizona." The Tucsonians, who obviously saw no

27. Letters in the Mowry Papers, YWA, describe his amorous exploits.
28. *Arizona Enterprise,* March 3, 1892.
29. *Weekly Arizona Star,* June 26, 1879. See also Sylvester Mowry, *Arizona and Sonora* (New York, 1864).

harm in having two lobbyists in Washington, also endorsed Mowry as their amateur delegate. Mowry himself was not even in Arizona at the time, for he had already gone to Washington to work for a territorial organization.[30]

Mowry arrived in Washington with as much support as any extra-legal delegate elect probably ever had. Major Heintzelman, now stationed in Kentucky, came to Washington to persuade doubting senators that the Arizona mines were extremely valuable. Mowry himself had the support of Rhode Island financiers, Senator Rusk of Texas, a number of Southern congressmen, Delegate Otero of New Mexico, and Senator William M. Gwin of California. To Northern congressmen, however, Mowry's supporters spoke with a Southern accent: when Senator Gwin introduced a bill in December 1857 to organize Arizona, the vote was sectional and the bill failed to pass. Both Mowry and Heintzelman now returned to Arizona to look after their respective mining interests.[31]

Neither Mowry nor the territorialists in the Gadsden Purchase were ready to give up. The young lieutenant was now so committed to Arizona that he resigned his commission, and in September 1858 was reelected delegate. A year later, in July 1859, Mowry was endorsed still again by the local voters. By this time Mowry almost had semiofficial status, for the Department of the Interior had appointed him special agent to supervise a survey of Pima and Maricopa tribal lands and to distribute $10,000 in gifts to them.[32] Such a sum was a powerful vote-getter in a frontier community of merchants and contractors.

By 1859 the support for Mowry had broadened beyond the Santa Cruz Valley to Arizona City in the west and to Mesilla in the east. The latter community had become so alienated from the authorities in

30. Sacks, *Be It Enacted*, p. 17.

31. Ibid., pp. 31–32.

32. San Francisco *Herald*, November 13, 1858, in the Ida Reid Leonard Collection, APHS. Mowry was also on the board of directors of the Sopori Land and Mining Company, whose president in 1859 was yet another Topographical Engineer, John Russell Bartlett, who had been on the United States-Mexican Boundary Commission of 1852. Bartlett, Samuel Colt, James Douglas, and Mowry apparently had in mind exploiting the lands of the huge 160,000 acre Sopori Grant as well as its minerals. See *Charter and By-Laws of the Sopori Land and Mining Company* (Providence, 1859), YWA.

Santa Fe that they resolved not to participate in New Mexican elections. With the vision of a lengthy east–west territory running along the 32nd parallel in mind, they again demanded their own territory and agreed to support Mowry as delegate.[33]

It was inevitable that Mowry would make spread-eagle speeches and claim great things for Arizona and that sooner or later they would be challenged. In the spring of 1859 Edward E. Cross, editor of the *Weekly Arizonian* at Tubac, became convinced that Mowry's remarks were terribly misleading and actually harmful to Arizona. Cross himself had been hired by a Cincinnati firm to promote its own interests in the area. All that was needed for Arizona, said Cross, was a government surveyor's office and an adequate law-enforcement and court system. A duel of words ensued between Cross and Mowry, which reached a climax when it was learned that a territorial organization bill introduced by Senator Gwin had been defeated in February 1859. Cross did not regret the defeat. "Better a limited amount of legal rights and privileges than none at all," he said. "We *can* get a U. S. Judicial District, a Branch of the Surveyor General's Office, Justices of the Peace, constables, and deputy sheriffs, which would answer all our need for the present."[34] Mowry took such exception to these and other remarks that he challenged the editor to a duel in July 1859. After shooting at each other with rifles—and missing—the two firebrands settled their quarrel amicably, while the whole of Tubac flooded into cantinas and bars for drinks. Two weeks later the pro-Mowry interests purchased Cross' paper and the fight for territorial government went on.[35]

It was now nearly four years since the Americans in Tucson and Mesilla had first demanded a territorial government. Impatient with Congress and increasingly harassed by Indians, the Mesilla citizens deposed local New Mexican appointees by March 1860, naming their own officials. The pioneers of Tucson met in April 1860, to hold their fifth convention. This time the thirty-one delegates proposed to "or-

33. *Weekly Arizonian* (Tubac), June 19, July 14, 1859. See also San Francisco *Herald*, May 18, September 14, 1859.
34. *Weekly Arizonian*, June 30, 1859.
35. Ibid., July 14, 1859.

dain and establish" a provisional government of their own. Working in conjunction with Mesilla citizens, they chose Dr. Lewis S. Owings as governor, J. A. Lucas as secretary of state, and Granville H. Oury, S. H. Cozzens, and Edward McGowan as justices. Ignacio Orantia of Mesilla, who represented the Spanish-American population, was made lieutenant governor. In recognition of the overwhelming hostile Indian problem Arizona faced, the convention named two frontier fighters, W. C. Wordsworth and Palatine Robinson, to head a territorial militia. After providing for a legislature and for county organization, the delegates adopted the laws and codes of New Mexico territory.[36] Since Mowry resigned the delegateship in the summer of 1860 to assist in running the eastern boundary of California, the voters of Arizona met again in November to elect Judge Edward McGowan in his place.[37] The roster for an Arizona territorial government was at last complete.

Arizona was not alone in resorting to extralegal government that year, for squatter governments were already operating in Colorado, Nevada, and Dakota. Representatives of all four were badgering congressmen to give them official recognition at the very moment the Union was dissolving. The major stumbling block in Arizona's case was that the 1860 convention in Tucson, like all the previous ones, was ardently Democratic and Southern in its outlook. Delegate McGowan was instructed to take his appeal for admission to a Southern congress should the Union split.[38] Lincoln's election in November 1860 virtually guaranteed that all Democratic legislation for the region would be shelved. Senator Rusk was now dead, and Senator Gwin, a Southern sympathizer, was soon to flee to Europe to escape imprisonment. Ten years of Democratic benevolence in the Far Southwest had come to an end. With the outbreak of the Civil War, federal army units at Forts Buchanan and Breckinridge quickly withdrew, the Overland Mail stopped running, and once again Eusebio Kino's "Pimeria Alta" seemed destined to become a no man's land.

At the beginning of the war, wrote H. H. Bancroft, "Public senti-

36. San Francisco *Herald,* March 9, April 16, May 21, August 16, September 6, 1860.
37. Ibid., November 20, 1860.
38. Ibid., December 4, 1860.

ment in Arizona . . . was almost unanimously southern and disunion."[39] Yet, as had been mentioned elsewhere, the Southerners
there were so independent of one another that they produced a two-
headed political infant. In February 1861 the citizens of Mesilla,
prodded by Texan secessionists, called for a convention in March,
where the delegates declared their loyalty to the Confederacy. A
similar convention at Tucson echoed the sentiments of the Mesillaños.[40]

After that point, however, the interests of Mesilla and Tucson began
to diverge. When Colonel John Baylor occupied Mesilla with Texas
troops in early August 1861, he made himself military governor and
appointed territorial officers. The Tucson citizens joined in the creation of the new government by electing Granville H. Oury as delegate
to the Confederate Congress. But Baylor and his fellow officers had
their own plans for the position, so that when Oury reached the
Confederate capital he discovered that Baylor's attorney general, Basil
H. MacWillie, also claimed to be the duly elected Arizona delegate,
and in the end Oury was not seated.[41]

Although the Davis government finally organized the Confederate
Territory of Arizona in January 1862, the Tucsonians were not very
happy with its officers. Mowry himself complained in a letter
that Colonel Baylor had fallen in with the wrong set "who may
do the Territory . . . infinite harm." Oury called Baylor's appointees "a dirty clique of greedy comorants" who were gorging
themselves on the Confederate treasury.[42] Nevertheless, his protests
fell on deaf ears, and Oury himself soon resigned his unrecognized
seat to raise troops and fight in the war.

The fate of the Arizona enterprises of the fifties and of the Confederate attempt to hold Arizona were epitomized in the later career
of Oury's close friend and supporter, Sylvester Mowry. The young
lieutenant's interest in politics had begun when he realized that his
mining ventures could not succeed without government help and

39. Bancroft, *Arizona,* p. 511.
40. San Francisco *Herald,* February 6, March 11, April 1, 15, 24, May 4, 1861.
41. Ibid., July 27, December 4, 1861. Sacks, *Be It Enacted,* pp. 62–63.
42. Handbill, May 21, 1862, in Oury File, APHS.; also Mowry to Davis, December 11, 1861, in Mowry File APHS.

protection. When federal troops withdrew from Arizona in 1861, Mowry was desperate. He had always been pro-Southern, and when Sherod Hunter, a bold Confederate officer, occupied Tucson, Mowry decided to cast his lot with the South. He furnished the ambitious captain with ammunition and supplies, began to speak warmly of the Confederacy, and even boasted that he would soon be appointed governor.[43]

Once again Mowry's hopes were to be dashed, for when Colonel James H. Carleton appeared at Fort Yuma in early 1862 in command of nearly 2,500 Unionist California Volunteers, the days of Confederate Arizona were numbered. Despite brilliant delaying tactics by Hunter and other Confederate officers, the Union army occupied Arizona after only one skirmish at Pichacho Pass. By June, Carleton was in Tucson. Now a Brigadier General, he proclaimed that Arizona was now a federal territory. He named himself military governor, declared martial law, arrested political prisoners, and made all remaining citizens take an oath of allegiance.

Carleton's official acts leave the real story untold. Many a California Volunteer had joined Carleton's command to get a free trip to the Arizona mineral fields. Two of Carleton's officers, Lieutenant Colonel Joseph R. West and his Adjutant General, Benjamin Cutler, appear to have had such an idea in mind, and Carleton himself was seriously interested in mining. Once they reached Tucson, an interesting set of events took place, for Carleton immediately ordered the arrest of Mowry as a Southern sympathizer. Two of Mowry's disgruntled employees, it appears, had reported his friendship with Sherod Hunter to the Colonel. The outraged ex lieutenant was then paraded through Tucson in chains, but ever the showman, Mowry was accompanied by his mistress and a private secretary. Later he was tried before a military board of inquiry, which decided that he must remain a prisoner at Fort Yuma.[44] Mowry's misfortunes were not to stop with arrest. General Cutler, using the authority of the Confiscation Act of

---

43. *Alta California*, July 23, December 2, 1862.
44. Bancroft, *Arizona*, pp. 515, 516 n. Journal of Alexander Bowman, 1861–65, MS in University of Arizona Library, Tucson; see entry for June 15, 1862. Mowry File (Hayden) APHS.

1862, took over Mowry's mines as legitimate war spoil, and they were sold at public auction in 1864. Mowry himself was soon released from custody, and while he managed to retrieve some of his property, never again was he to be the Grand Señor of Arizona.

Mowry's mines showed such a profit after 1865 that he was able to sell the Patagonia for $40,000, but in all other respects bad luck dogged him. In subsequent years he was jilted by a San Francisco beauty and denied his consuming ambition to be the United States minister to Mexico. Meanwhile, Mowry, who was still in his thirties, fell victim to Bright's disease. Desperately seeking to restore his health, he went to London to consult Dr. Bright himself, only to learn upon arrival that the famous physician had just died. Disillusioned and lonely, the young Arizona pioneer died in a London hotel, attended only by his friend Charles Poston.[45]

From 1848 to 1860 the history of Arizona—or more properly that of southern New Mexico—might best be described as the evolution of a great public project run by the Democratic Party for the purpose of assuaging the growing insecurity of the South. The project itself cost an extraordinary amount of money. Besides the $10,000,000 expended for the Gadsden Purchase, several hundred thousand were spent on the various boundary commissions and several hundred thousand more on the 32nd and 35th parallel Railroad Surveys. Senator Rusk of Texas also secured $100,000 to dig artesian wells in the Staked Plains and $200,000 to build a wagon road from El Paso to Fort Yuma. There were the further expenses of the official exploration of the Colorado River during the 1850s and the many Army detachments stationed along Cooke's wagon road route. Beginning in 1858, the federal government awarded a subsidy of some $600,000 a year to the Overland Mail Company. Later Poston was to estimate that at least one private mining company had spent $50,000 to develop local mines.

It is only fair to say that little of the vast treasure found its way into Arizona. Given this policy of hothouse development it is also not surprising that Arizona's few pioneers were Topographical Engi-

45. Lockwood, *Old Tucson,* pp. 123–27. Mowry File (Hayden), APHS.

neers, Army officers, mining and railroad promoters, filibusterers, merchants, and sectional politicians. Except for the Mexicans already there, the bona fide settler was conspicuously absent. Yet while it was a frontier artificially created by public policy and sectional interest, the Arizona story cannot be understood without also remembering that Americans were so overwhelmed by the California gold rush experience that they constantly dreamed of repeating that saga in other mineral rich areas. The devotees of Manifest Destiny firmly believed that this investment of the public treasure would be repaid tenfold. From 1848 to 1860, then, Arizona was a no man's land, into which the golden hopes, the expansionist dreams, and the sectional fears of the United States were projected with extraordinary vigor.

17

Arizona: Beleaguered Territory
1861–1874

It is hard to see a people wasting away by Indian ravages who
are ready and willing to take the field if they had only
something to subsist upon while so engaged.
Weekly Arizonian
October 16, 1869

Hostilities in Arizona are kept up with a view of protecting the
inhabitants, most of whom are supported by the hostilities.
General E. O. C. Ord
January 22, 1870

 One of the many disheartening pieces of intelligence
to reach Washington in the early fall of 1861 was
the news that Rebel forces under Colonel John Baylor had occupied southern and western New Mexico
and had organized the region as the Confederate
Territory of Arizona. As a countermeasure, Delegate
John S. Watts of New Mexico introduced a bill in Congress that
December to organize the federal territory of Arizona. The Watts bill
was subsequently incorporated into another bill proposed by Congressman James M. Ashley of Ohio, who was chairman of the House
Committee on Territories.[1] The Ashley measure was destined to become the Organic Act of Arizona Territory.

1. The details of Congressional organization are carefully covered in Sacks, *Be
It Enacted*, pp. 69–86. A contemporary account may be found in the *Journal of
the First Legislative Assembly of the Territory of Arizona*, 1864 (Prescott, 1865),
pp. 10–12.

Apart from the obvious military and strategic necessity of curbing Confederate claims to the Far Southwest, what were the arguments for the creation of a new territory at this time? The Congressional debates strongly suggest that the new body politic was a product of wartime Republican politics. Congressman William A. Wheeler of New York observed in the early debates on the Ashley Bill that the House had received no petition for organization from the inhabitants of Arizona. Wheeler himself doubted that there were any inhabitants there, in fact.[2]

In answer to Wheeler's allegations, Delegate Watts was able to cite census returns which showed that nearly 5,000 persons lived in the proposed territory. But later Watts shied away from the population theme to discuss the mineral resources of Arizona instead. To press home his argument, he held up a large specimen of rich silver ore taken from the Heintzelman mines for the members to see. When he had finished, Watts had left the strong impression that Arizona might be another California.[3]

Ashley himself seconded Watts' remarks, and he was followed by John A. Gurley, another House member from Ohio, who also spoke in behalf of territorial organization. As Dr. Sacks has pointed out in his recent study of the origins of Arizona Territory, the fact that the chief Congressional sponsors of Arizona happened to be from Ohio was no accident. Two of the four largest firms engaged in Arizona mining had been chartered in Ohio. The directors of these firms, among them John and William Wrightson, were influential men. Both General Heintzelman and Charles Poston, who were affiliated with the firms, were also in Washington in 1861–62, busily lobbying for a federal Arizona.[4] When the House finally passed the Arizona organic act on May 8, 1862, it did so as much to protect property and to

2. Sacks, *Be It Enacted,* p. 71.
3. Ibid., p. 72.
4. Ibid., pp. 73–76. James M. Ashley, *Protection and Freedom in Arizona* (Washington, 1862), pp. 1–8, pamphlet, YWA. Poston later described Ashley as his "political guardian" during the debates over the Arizona bill: *Arizona Enterprise* (Florence), September 26, 1891, Poston File, APHS. Granville Oury recalled that as early as 1858 the Santa Rita Mining Company—a Wrightson firm—and its local paper, the *Weekly Arizonian,* were "black republican." See *Arizona Daily Star,* November 29, 1879.

promote mining interests, as it did so to bring its few citizens the blessings of government.

Once the Ashley Bill reached the Senate, it ran into the same arguments about the lack of population. Senator Lyman Trumbull of Illinois, who had recently secured the governorship of Dakota Territory for his own brother-in-law, somewhat inconsistently criticized the Arizona bill as a device to create new public offices for patronage purposes. Despite pleas by Benjamin F. Wade, the chairman of the Senate Committee on Territories, for immediate passage of the bill, it was tabled until the next session of Congress.[5]

Before Congress reconvened in December 1862, a midterm election occurred. Many new men were elected to Congress, and a number of Republicans lost their seats. And during the summer of 1862, Generals Canby and Carleton had driven the last of the Confederate forces from New Mexico and Arizona. At least Congress now *had* a territory to organize. A combination of patronage pressures, the influence of assiduous lobbyists like Heintzelman and Poston—who came to Washington again in the winter of 1862–63—and the exigencies of wartime strategy, persuaded the Senate to pass the Arizona Organic Act on February 20, 1863.[6] Lincoln approved the bill four days later.

The creators of federal Arizona shrewdly arranged the boundaries of the new territory. Secessionist Mesilla was left in New Mexico, but the mining regions along the Colorado River (gold had just been discovered at La Paz) were placed within Arizona bounds. Two proposed railroad routes along the 32nd and 35th parallels were also included within the territory. In an earlier version of the bill Tucson had been designated as the territorial capital, but on second thought the solons gave the governor and the legislature the right to locate the seat of government. The geographic foundations were laid for an Arizona that would be quite different from the one proposed throughout the 1850s.

When the Organic Act had passed, the lobbyists in its behalf held a celebration to honor the birth of the new territory and to divide the spoils. Charles Poston and General Heintzelman appear to have

5. Sacks, *Be It Enacted,* pp. 76–80.
6. Ibid., pp. 80 ff.

been the hosts at this convivial oyster and champagne supper, to which all interested congressmen and Republican strategists had been invited.[7] In an aura of cigar smoke and drinks, the founding fathers agreed that John A. Gurley, now a defeated Ohio congressman, should be the new governor. Richard C. McCormick of New York, a defeated candidate for Congress, was to be the territorial secretary, and William F. Turner of Iowa, William T. Howell of Michigan, and Joseph P. Allyn of Connecticut were to be federal judges.

In the midst of their pleasant deliberations Poston suddenly exclaimed: "But, gentlemen, what is to become of me?"[8] The genial congressmen, after scanning the remaining vacancies, named him superintendent of Indian affairs. The roster was completed when Almon Gage of New York was made attorney general, Milton Duffield of California was appointed United States marshal, and Levi Bashford of Wisconsin became Arizona's first surveyor general. Historians have made much of the fact that it was a government of lame ducks, but other considerations governed the choices as well, for four of the nine men were from mining states and had business reasons for going to Arizona. Congress then confirmed the appointments of the new officials. When Governor Gurley died unexpectedly in 1863, he was replaced by another former congressman, John N. Goodwin of Maine.[9]

In the late fall of 1863 the new officials gathered at Fort Leavenworth, where they picked up a military escort to guide them as far as Fort Union, New Mexico. As they rode across the plains, it became obvious that Lincoln had appointed a set of political opportunists, for they argued the whole way about which one of them was best fitted to return to Washington as the first territorial delegate.[10]

When these ambitious officials reached Fort Union, General Carleton took them under his wing and soon convinced them that Tucson

7. Poston in *Arizona Enterprise*, September 26, 1891.

8. Lockwood, *Old Tucson*, pp. 73–74.

9. Sacks, *Be It Enacted*, pp. 87–89. Robert L. Swor, "The Development of Prescott" (Master's thesis, Arizona State College, Tempt, 1952), copy in Arizona State Archives, Phoenix.

10. This is Poston's allegation, although he did not travel with the officials. See *Arizona Enterprise*, September 26, 1891. It is true that Goodwin, McCormick, and Judge Allyn wanted to be delegate and that Judge Turner hoped to be governor. See William F. Turner file in Department of State Appointments Division, TP, Arizona.

was full of secessionists and was not worthy of becoming the territorial capital. Carleton then pointed out that the veteran mountain
man and explorer Joseph Reddeford Walker had found gold in Lynx
Creek spring in 1863, and that Henry Wickenberg had
just located more excellent veins of gold and silver near the Walker
diggings.[11] Since these new camps were in dangerous Indian country, Carleton had already sent a detachment of soldiers to ascertain a
route to the new mines and to estimate the extent of the mineral discoveries. The reports had been so favorable that in the fall of 1863 he
had stationed Major E. B. Willis in the region with orders to construct
a fort there. Carleton then urged Governor Goodwin to locate the
new capital at Fort Whipple—the name of the new outpost.[12]

Carleton's suggestion had a dramatic effect. Jonathan Richmond, a
traveler in Governor Goodwin's party, wrote that "every one in the
party are gold struck—the fever is raging furiously. Mules and Mexican ponys in Santa Fe bring $200. Gov. had letter here from responsi-
ble men stating that fortunes are daily made etc., etc."[13] Goodwin
accepted Carleton's proposal with alacrity. Now guarded by a detachment under Colonel J. Francisco Chavez, the officials turned west
at Albuquerque; and on December 27, 1863, they reached Navajo
Springs, just inside the Arizona border. There, two days later, Goodwin proclaimed the organization of Arizona territory. Drinks were
passed around, and Secretary McCormick made a speech.

After a winter's sojourn at Fort Whipple, both the civilians and the
military personnel there decided to move the infant settlement to a
better location nearby. The new settlement was given the name
Prescott, to honor William Hickling Prescott, the historian, whose
works Secretary McCormick had read and admired.[14]

In a sense the government had arrived before the people in
Arizona, for after Marshal Duffield had taken a census in the spring

---

11. Jonathan Richmond to ——— Richmond, Fort Union, New Mexico, November 9, 1863, in Letters from Arizona, October 13, 1863, to May 31, 1865, ASA.
12. Ibid. Bancroft, *Arizona*, p. 522.
13. Richmond to Richmond, November 9, 1863, Letters from Arizona.
14. E. E. Williams, "The Territorial Governors of Arizona," *AHR*, 7 (1935),
50–51.

of 1864, he reported that only 4,187 white persons lived in the huge territory. Of these a clear majority were Spanish-Americans who had pushed into the region from Sonora. The new government also faced the awkward fact that the Anglo-Americans in Arizona were largely from the Southern states and were Democratic in their politics, if not secessionist in their loyalties. Furthermore, most of the settlers were concentrated in three widely separated areas: the pleasant Santa Cruz Valley, where Tucson and Tubac were located; along the hot, lower reaches of the Gila and Colorado rivers, where Gila City, La Paz, and Fort Yuma could be found; and at Prescott, Wickenburg, and Fort Whipple, which were situated in an attractive, cool, tree-covered mountain area in north central Arizona.[15]

The isolation of the white settlers from one another was particularly dangerous, for an estimated 30,000 Indians lived in Arizona, who had never been subdued by either Spain or Mexico. In 1863 they still outnumbered the whites by at least six to one. Although Carleton and Kit Carson were successfully reducing the Navajo on the eastern border, and the Moqui villages in northern Arizona represented no real threat, southeastern and southern Arizona were awash with Apache raiders. The various bands in the Apache corridor had been understandably upset by the invasion of American soldiers and miners during the 1850s. But despite a continuing number of small ambushes and raids, it looked for a time as if the United States would be able to achieve a modus vivendi with some of the Apache groups. The government had actually signed a treaty with the Coyoteros in 1852 and had established a reservation for the Mimbrenos tribe in 1853, near Fort Webster, New Mexico, where Agent Michael Steck succeeded in keeping peace for three years (1854–57). Steck also secured agreements with the Chiricahua chief, Cochise, which permitted the Overland Mail to go through and allowed miners to come into parts of Apache country.[16] White privileges were given military

15. "Report of Arizona Census, 1864" in Dept. of State, TP, Arizona.
16. American relations with the Apache tribes have been recently summarized in Spicer, *Cycles of Conquest*, pp. 241–60. For special studies see Frank C. Lockwood, *The Apache Indians*, (New York, 1948); Ralph H. Ogle, *Federal Control of the Western Apaches, 1848–1886* (Albuquerque, 1940); and Sonia Bleeker, *The Apache Indians, Raiders of the Southwest* (New York, 1951).

backing in 1857, when Colonel Benjamin L. E. Bonneville decisively chastised a number of Apaches in southern Arizona.

With the coming of the Civil War, Apache-white relations deteriorated almost overnight. An army attempt to arrest Cochise in 1861, followed by the treacherous murder of several Apache chiefs by soldiers and the killing of Mangas Coloradas in 1863, sent the tribes on the warpath permanently. They increased their raids against Sonorans, the Pima and Papago Indians, and against the Americans. By the time the federal officials reached Fort Whipple, in fact, Apache warfare had been extended into central Arizona with such force that the whites there were in grave danger of being driven out.[17]

As the constant victims of Apache raiders, the agricultural Pima, Papago, and Maricopa Indians living in the Gadsden Purchase area welcomed the Americans as allies. While the Yumas were initially hostile to the Americans, by 1861 they were being brought under control. The more primitive tribes stretching along the Colorado from the Gila to the Moqui country—the Mohave, Yavapai, Walapai, and others—had been partially subdued during the 1850s, but it was still necessary to maintain troops at Fort Mohave near Hardyville to ensure peace in northwestern Arizona. Even then, a white-Yavapai war broke out in 1863.[18]

Such grim conditions did not prevent the machinery of government and politics from operating in this beleaguered territory. After a month's tour of Arizona, Governor Goodwin created voting districts and called for the election of a delegate and legislative assembly in July 1864. Charles Poston willingly gave up his post as Indian superintendent to run for the nearly expended term of delegate (upon election he would take office immediately and serve until December 1865). Poston was probably a Democrat, but he diplomatically identified himself as a representative of the Union party. He found that he was opposed by W. D. Bradshaw and one Charles Leib, who, with equal diplomacy, called themselves Independents. In a fast, spread-eagle campaign worthy of Davy Crockett, the contenders slammed, banged, and orated their way to election day. Backed by Indian Bureau

17. Spicer, p. 248.
18. Ibid., p. 270.

patronage and the local Republican officials, Poston easily won the election.[19]

When the first territorial legislature convened in Prescott early that fall, the disparate origins of the Arizona settlers became more apparent than ever. Ex-Governor Coles Bashford of Wisconsin, who was the brother of Surveyor Levi Bashford, had been in Arizona less than a year, but now he appeared as the president of the Council.[20] One of Bashford's fellow members in the upper house was Mark Aldrich, the pioneer mayor of Tucson who had been a Confederate sympathizer. King S. Woolsey, an Alabama-born rancher, sat beside Henry A. Bigelow, a former citizen of Massachusetts. The remaining members were a combination of veteran and newly arrived miners. Two members of the Council, Francisco S. Leon and Jose M. Redondo, were leaders of the Spanish-American population. Three of the councilmen were born in New York and two in New England, and the remainder hailed from Alabama, Kentucky, Arizona, and Mexico.[21]

In the House of Representatives the diverse origins of the members were equally striking. Of the eighteen men there, twelve were from the American Northeast, two were from Missouri, and the remainder listed South Carolina, California, Germany, and Arizona as their birthplaces. Yet the predominately northern House elected W. Claude Jones, formerly of Mesilla, to be its speaker. Like nearly all frontier political bodies, the pioneer solons of Arizona were a relatively youthful lot. Five in the first House of Representatives were in their twenties, nine were in their thirties, and only four were over forty. While the average age of the Council was forty-two, Mark Aldrich was the only man there over forty-seven.[22]

Despite their diverse origins, all were convinced that Arizona was to be a mineral empire and that the major task of government was to aid in its development by passing favorable mining laws, by solving

19. Poston File, APHS. Arizona *Miner,* June 22, 1864 et seq. "Proclamation, August 20, 1864," Department of State, TP, Arizona.
20. Bashford's political career in Wisconsin had been ruined by railroad scandals. He apparently came to Arizona to make a fresh start. See Coles Bashford File, APHS.
21. See *Journal of the First . . . Assembly of . . . Arizona, 1864,* pp. 1–9.
22. Ibid.

the Indian question, and by bringing a cheap mode of transportation to the territory. Until these goals could be realized, they could not really afford the luxury of partisan politics.

The legislators listened with sympathy to Governor Goodwin's first annual message, for he urged them to pass laws to protect the placer miners and prevent monopoly. They also must have liked Goodwin's attack on the seigniorage bill of Delegate Bennet of Colorado, which Congress was then considering. It would result in monopolistic owner-ship of mineral lands, he charged, and would "drive from the frontier, the prospector and the pioneer." After recommending that the mining law of Mexico be the basis for the Arizona code, he asked that the laws be "speedy in litigation" and that water monopolies be avoided where possible. What Goodwin wanted, in essence, was the adoption of California mining law for Arizona.[23]

The other major topic of Goodwin's message, and that of all subse-quent annual messages by the Arizona chief executives, concerned Indian affairs. After praising the Pimas, Papagoes, and Maricopas as "our well tried and faithful allies," he leveled a blast at the Apache as a "murderer by hereditary descent—a thief by prescription." Goodwin set the policy for the legislature and for all succeeding governors when he called for a war to compel absolute submission. He praised General Carleton's single reservation policy for the Navajo and hoped it could be applied to tribes in Arizona. He also approved of a recent expedition, organized by local volunteers, to punish hostile Indians. As in New Mexico and Colorado, the Arizona pioneer believed that local militia could best handle the Indian problem. In a good Manifest Destiny peroration Goodwin declared that the Indian and the ante-lope must disappear together before the Anglo-Saxon race, for "the tide of our civilization has no refluent wave, but rolls steadily over ocean and continent."[24]

The legislature itself turned immediately to the question of trans-portation. They incorporated six toll roads, five of which would con-nect the capital at Prescott to the other regions of Arizona, while the

23. Ibid., pp. 35–51.
24. Ibid., pp. 42–45.

sixth proposed to run between Tucson and Libertad, Sonora.[25] Two railroad companies were also chartered. One of these, the Arizona Railroad Company, revived memories of the large railroad schemes of the 1850s, for it was to run from New Mexico to the Colorado River and to operate a second branch, running from La Paz to Tucson and then to Guaymas, Mexico. Since it was by far the most attractive and ambitious of the new paper companies, it is not surprising to find that Governor Goodwin and Secretary McCormick were on its board of directors.[26] Many of the legislators themselves were either the founders or directly interested in the remaining road and railroad companies.

The Assembly then turned to the classic task of requesting aid from Congress. From its territorial beginnings, the settlers had been oriented toward California rather than New Mexico. Thus they asked that the region be placed under the military jurisdiction of the California department rather than that of New Mexico. They also directed Delegate Poston to secure guns, rifles, and adequate mail service from Congress, and they themselves petitioned that body for a grant of $50,000 to place all Indians on a Colorado River reservation. In the next breath they calmly requested $250,000 to mount a war against the Apaches and $50,000 to improve the navigation of the Colorado River.[27]

In its second session the Assembly turned to the question of local government. It created four counties and named a three-man board of supervisors for each. The supervisors were to handle elections, act as a board of canvassers, and act as a tax board of equalization. Making full use of the few people available for public office, the probate judge was to be the board's auditor and the county recorder its clerk. Unlike Utah or New Mexico, however, Arizona's probate judges never had extraordinary powers. In 1865 even their jurisdiction over mining cases was transferred to the district territorial courts.[28]

---

25. *Acts, Resolutions, and Memorials Adopted in the First Legislative Assembly of the Territory of Arizona* (Prescott, 1865), pp. 21, 24, 27, 30, 53–57.

26. Ibid., pp. 25, 51.

27. *Journal of the First . . . Assembly of . . . Arizona, 1864*, pp. 166, 244. *Acts, Resolutions, Memorials . . .* (1865), pp. 76 ff.

28. *Laws of Arizona Territory . . . for . . . 1865* (Prescott, 1866), pp. 24–26, 44–45.

Generally speaking, the Arizona legislators used California county government as a precedent and eventually created a local system noticeably different from those of Utah and New Mexico.

While the basic pattern of local government was American from the start, Governor Goodwin was so impressed with the essentially Spanish cultural heritage of Arizona that by 1865 he had assumed the right to appoint many local officials. He named alcaldes and constables for Mohave City and Hardyville, selected William S. Oury as mayor of Tucson, and appointed probate judges, county recorders, treasurers, sheriffs, and coroners. He and his successors dealt so frequently with Spanish-American leaders or with Spanish-speaking Indians in Arizona that they either had to learn Spanish or keep an interpreter on hand.[29] The question of securing funds to print the laws in Spanish also worried both governor and legislator during most of the territorial period.

Although in 1864 Arizona could hardly be called a community of settlers and farmers, the legislature voted to aid four public schools in Prescott, La Paz, Fort Mojave, and Tucson and agreed to support the Catholic mission school at San Xavier del Bac.[30] The support was merely an expression of attitude and intent, for a real public school system was not established for more than a decade.

As in Colorado, the pioneer lawgivers of Arizona were flexible rather than original. This approach was reflected in the first code of laws, which were prepared by Judge Howell of the territorial supreme court. Howell himself was from the mining state of Michigan, but the mining laws he compiled were a combination of Mexican and California legislation mixed with parts of the New York code. Egalitarian in spirit and democratic in approach, the Howell Code was an intelligent attempt to reconcile local conditions with the national heritage.[31]

By 1865 the vague political lines in Arizona were becoming more clearly focused. The end of the Civil War had permitted local South-

29. Richard C. McCormick to Andrew Johnson, December 31, 1865, Dept. of State, TP, Arizona.

30. *Acts, Resolutions, Memorials . . . 1864*, p. 41.

31. Bancroft, *Arizona*, p. 522.

erners to return to politics. Once again the Oury brothers, Granville and William, appeared in Tucson to reclaim their confiscated property and take up new public careers. King S. Woolsey, who had left the Rebel side early in the fighting to become an Arizona rancher, proved to be such a natural leader that he was elected to the first two assemblies and was appointed by Governor Goodwin to head the territorial militia.[32]

Here was a curious situation: the Southern Democrats and the Spanish-Americans had the vote, but the federal appointees had the power. Unlike the appointees in most territories, however, the Arizona federal officials soon learned to work together. Rather early this constantly changing, odd assortment of Unionists formed what Delegate Poston called the "federal ring." While most of them were from the Northeast, they could hardly be called abolitionists or Radical Republicans.

The first organizer of the ring appears to have been Governor Goodwin himself, who used his own good nature and his patronage and appointive powers to build up enough of a following to elect himself as delegate. He achieved his goal in the fall of 1865, when he defeated Poston in a hotly contested election. Goodwin could not have won, however, without the help of Secretary McCormick, whose newspaper, the *Arizona Miner,* molded public opinion in the territory. McCormick's reason for aiding Goodwin was an obvious one: he wished to succeed the Governor in office. As he had hoped, Johnson tendered him the governorship in 1866; and from that moment until his retirement from public office in 1875, McCormick was the dominant federal figure in Arizona affairs.

Governor Goodwin had been essentially a mining speculator who had used his office as a stepping stone to wealth. But McCormick, like Gilpin of Colorado, was a complicated combination of the educated, romantic dreamer and the speculator-businessman. Strongly possessed of a sense of history, he had helped to found the Arizona Pioneer Society, which was to preserve local history, for "posterity

32. See Judge William F. Turner to Hon. James Harlan (Secretary of the Interior), January 26, 1866, Dept. of State, TP, Arizona.

delights in details," explained McCormick, quoting John Quincy Adams.[33]

Throughout his public career McCormick pounded home the theme that the American pioneer—the trapper and the individual explorer—was the true agent of empire. He praised Jedediah Smith, Kit Carson, Lucien Maxwell, and Bill Williams and made fun of John C. Fremont. McCormick also frequently sounded a second theme, which anticipated the writings of Frederick Jackson Turner, when he argued that "the life of the American mining pioneer is of a kind peculiar to itself. The circumstances which have produced it have existed nowhere else." Let the government take heed, he exclaimed, and give the prospector free reign and forget taxes or confining pro-capitalist laws. True America was "out of doors," said McCormick. It was a place of plain good food, and its true inhabitants were broad-minded, impulsive, and often hard-drinking men. But, he added, they never imbibed for "sordid reasons."[34] McCormick's egalitarian manner and his almost mystical faith in the benefits of public education meant that Arizona's political institutions would be cast in a standard American mold as long as he was in power.

McCormick's noble dreams for Arizona were somewhat belied by his career as a politician. His adeptness at political intrigue led enemy and friend alike to call him "~~Slippery Dick~~." Judge Turner complained in 1866 that McCormick had compromised with the Southerners by appointing Copperheads to office and had won over "the lowest class" by constantly putting "the bottle to his neighbor's mouth." McCormick had laid aside his Eastern habits and notions, said Turner in horror, to become an Arizonian.[35]

Flexible and tolerant, McCormick willingly let the legislature move the capital to Democratic Tucson in 1867. But when it was realized that this was an unpopular choice, he ran for delegate on a ticket in 1868 which called for its return to Prescott. The ability of the Mc-

33. Williams, "Territorial Governors," *AHR*, pp. 50–60. "Oration . . . before the Arizona Pioneer Society, July 4, 1866" (Prescott, 1866), pamphlet in Dept. of State, TP, Arizona.

34. Ibid.

35. Turner to Harlan, January 26, 1866, Dept. of State, TP, Arizona. *Arizona Democrat* (Prescott), October 15, 1880.

Cormick federal clique to perpetuate itself was further demonstrated when one of its charter members, Coles Bashford—now a prominent merchant—won the delegate race in 1866 by running as an Independent. This innocuous title was chosen so he could get the Copperhead votes in southern Arizona. When his two-year term as delegate ended, Bashford then became the territorial secretary, and in his stead McCormick was elected to the delegateship. The Arizona voters appear to have accepted this interlocking political directorate with equanimity, for the ring was very good at securing federal grants, and the officials themselves were as devoted to the development of mining as were their constituents.[36]

McCormick's election as delegate in 1868 led to the appointment of one of Arizona's most able governors, Anson Peacely-Killen Safford (1869–77). A Vermonter who had spent some years in Illinois, Safford had joined the gold rush to California. After running a business in San Francisco, he had then migrated to Nevada in 1862. He was already familiar with the game of politics, for he had been a representative in the California and Nevada legislatures, recorder of Humboldt County, Nevada, and was surveyor general of Nevada when Grant made him governor of Arizona in 1869.[37]

The new Governor was a small, nervous man whom the Arizonians soon dubbed "The Little Governor." It was an affectionate title, however, for Safford shared with McCormick an extraordinary capacity to make friends and effect policies. Safford found at least one outlet for his restless nature by roaming the territory, either on horseback or by buggy, and talking with everyone he met. Not only did he find Delegate McCormick to be a kindred soul, but it is probable that the two were already involved in Arizona mining and other business ventures. So strong was their alliance that McCormick ran for reelection without difficulty in 1870 and was again reelected with virtually no opposition whatever in 1872.[38]

36. Bashford and McCormick in *Biog. Dir. of Am. Cong.* Bashford and McCormick files, APHS. *Weekly Arizonian*, September 17, 1870.

37. A. P. K. Safford File, APHS. Williams, "Territorial Governors," *AHR*, 7 (1936), 69–84.

38. *AHR*, 7 (1936), 80. *Weekly Arizonian*, September 17, 24, October 4, November 12, 1870.

To succeed in Arizona, the McCormick-Safford regime had to grapple effectively with the hostile Indian problem, bring an adequate transportation system to the territory, and expand mining and ranching, which were the obvious native industries of Arizona. Of these, the Indian question was by far the most exasperating one.

When McCormick became governor in 1866, General Carleton had already begun an assault on the Apache nation by building a series of forts which ran in an arc from Fort Webster in southwestern New Mexico to Fort Whipple at Prescott. Between these two more distant posts were Camp Bowie, placed in the heart of the Chiricahua lands; Camp Goodwin, near the headwaters of the Gila; and Fort McDowell, near the Salt River.[39] (See Map.) While these posts made travel safer, they seemed to have had little effect on the Apaches themselves, and the killing of whites and peaceful Indians went on unabated. In 1865 the Papagoes had been so hard hit by these raiders that they agreed to maintain a standing army of 150 mounted rangers to help the whites. That same year General John S. Mason, commander of the district of Arizona, reported: "The town of Tubac was entirely deserted, and the town of Tucson had but about two hundred souls. North of the Gila the roads were completely blockaded; the ranches, with one or two exceptions, abandoned, and most of the settlements were threatened with either abandonment or annihilation."[40]

While the Indian question seemed overwhelming, there was no lack of talk about the best way to solve it. Generally, it was the Army's policy throughout the 1860s to fight the warring Indians and to leave the others alone. It had no ultimate solution in mind. The *Weekly Arizonian,* in reminiscing about the Army's policy between 1866 and 1869, said it was not a war, but a "species of transactions quite indefinite—half remonstrative and half authoritative." General McDowell, the paper concluded, had alternately fed and fought a couple of thousand Indians for three years.[41]

The Indian Bureau naturally advocated reservations, feeding, formal

39. Ray Brandes, "A Guide to the History of U. S. Army Installations in Arizona, 1849–1886," *Arizona and the West, 1* (1959), pp. 42–65.
40. Wyllys, *Arizona,* p. 189.
41. *Weekly Arizonian,* March 21, 1879.

treaty relations, and, increasingly, a peace policy. The local Arizona view was simply that they must be controlled or exterminated and that volunteer militia could best do the job. Given the fact of constant warfare, much of the political history of Arizona during the McCormick-Safford period came to center around these incompatible plans of action.

In his first annual message to the Assembly on October 8, 1866, McCormick stated his own views— which were those of the territory— in fighting words:

> I am confirmed in the opinion that it is idle to talk to the Apache of reservations while he feels any security for life or property outside of them. He must be persistently followed and fought until he sued for peace, and then placed upon a reservation remote from his old haunts, and from which escape is impossible. To welcome him at one fort and drive him from another; to feed him today and refuse him tomorrow; to make spasmodic rather than systematic campaigns against him; to fight him with troops ignorant of his country, and who will have no heart in the work, however good the intent, is but to put the government to great expense for no adequate return.[42]

After declaring a pox on both the Army and the Indian Bureau, McCormick asked for a native volunteer force. The Governor then urged the abolition of the treaty system and the transfer of the Indian Bureau to the War Department. Although more troops were sent to Arizona, the Governor reiterated his main theme a year later in his second message. Faced with the fact that the federal government would probably never turn Indian affairs over to local authorities, McCormick recommended that Arizona be made a separate military department, so that the commanders could make quick, on-the-spot decisions.[43]

42. *Message of Governor R. C. McCormick to the Third . . . Assembly of . . . Arizona, 1866* (Prescott, 1866), pp. 6–7.
43. *Message of Governor R. C. McCormick to the Fourth . . . Assembly of . . . Arizona, 1867* (Prescott, 1867), pp. 1–3.

The Army itself hardly felt that territorial criticisms were justified and agreed with outside observers when they referred to Arizona as "a vortex into which the greater portion of the available military material on the Pacific Coast disappears."[44] By 1869 the Army had no less than thirteen forts in the territory and had established many temporary ones. Meanwhile, General Edward O. C. Ord had assumed command in Arizona in 1868 and taken his troops into the field to chastise the Indians. The raids continued, nevertheless, and between the end of his campaign and 1870 at least one hundred more white men had been shot by the Indians.

When new campaigns under General George W. Thomas failed to produce satisfactory results, Governor Safford and the *Weekly Arizonian* became extremely bitter about the government's Indian policy. "It is hard to see a people wasting away by Indian ravages who are ready and willing to take the field if they had only something to subsist upon while so engaged," wrote the *Arizonian,* in a plea for local militia action. "We have an energetic Governor, willing to risk his life at any time in making war against the Indians; we have a people ready and willing to respond and follow him if they are enabled."[45]

In 1869 these bitter complaints became outrage when Arizonans learned that the Grant peace policy would be tried in the territory. General Ord's successor, General George Stoneman, actually had orders to reduce the number of military posts in the region and to prepare to place the Indians on large reservations. Although Stoneman was merely following instructions, his actions led to the accusation that he was an incompetent officer and an Indian lover.[46] Nevertheless, Stoneman continued to shift from a subjugation policy to an adequate defense policy. He also began to gather and feed as many hostile Indians as he could, before they were placed on reservations.

Faced with what he considered to be an unrealistic military policy toward the Apaches, and the advent of an even more unrealistic peace policy which the Grant administration had inaugurated in 1869,

44. Ibid., p. 2.
45. *Weekly Arizonian,* October 16, 1869.
46. Ibid., January 28, 1871.

Governor Safford went to Washington to secure Stoneman's removal and to counter the Indian lovers. He also got permission to form three volunteer militia companies. Despite the fact that most Apaches were at least attached to a reservation by 1871, the raids went on.[47] The citizens of Tucson became so convinced that a group of Arivaipa Apaches now located at Camp Grant were guilty of recent atrocities that on April 30 a band of Americans, Mexicans, and Papagoes crept out of the city, marched to the camp, and killed 115 men, women, and children in a dawn attack. Two of the most prominent citizens of Tucson, William S. Oury and Jesus M. Elias, had led the attack. Eastern outrage forced a trial of the aggressors, but a Tucson jury, fully reflecting the sentiments of the region, quickly acquitted the 104 participants.[48]

Fortunately for all parties concerned, in June 1871 the government appointed General George Crook to head the Department of Arizona. He was a superb Indian fighter, and the territory was relieved to hear that he planned an energetic campaign in the field.[49] Before Crook could carry out his program, however, Vincent Colyer, member of the Board of Indian Commissioners and an ardent peace-policy advocate, arrived in Arizona to create a new Apache reservation system and institute measures to promote peace and civilization among them. In a whirlwind of activity Colyer established four Apache reserves, of which three were in Arizona. While the whole territory watched in indignation, 4,000 Apaches were located, put under the charge of army officers, fed and clothed, and given instruction in farming.[50]

The enmity to Colyer's policy was so great that the government program was bound to fail. When Indian depredations continued, the peace policy was abandoned; and in December 1871 the entire territory was delighted to learn that General Crook was once more in command. A new get-tough policy was instituted on the reservations, where there was to be a roll call a day for the adult male Indians.

47. Spicer, *Cycles of Conquest*, pp. 251 ff.
48. James R. Hastings, "The Tragedy at Camp Grant in 1871," *Arizona and the West*, 2 (1959), 146–60.
49. Spicer, *Cycles of Conquest*, p. 250.
50. Ibid.

Once again, though, Crook's field campaign was delayed by the appearance of Major General O. O. Howard, a one-armed veteran who had been President Grant's secretary during the Civil War. Unlike Colyer, Howard carefully cultivated the white leaders of Arizona and moved so cautiously that he managed to concentrate the peaceful Apaches into the San Carlos and White Mountain reservations. In 1872 Howard, with the aid of Thomas J. Jeffords, also secured a treaty with Cochise, the formidable and by now ancient chieftain of the Chiricahua tribe. Although Cochise did not consent to move to one of the three Apache reserves—San Carlos, Fort Apache, and Camp Verde—he at least had been taken off the warpath. Crook and Safford heartily disliked Howard's policy, but Eastern indignation over the Camp Grant massacre was so great that they dared not oppose the "Christian General" directly. "At present they have the advantage of us," wrote Crook, "and if we do anything to stir the matter, it may injure General Grant's interests in which case it will react on us." Crook even suggested that Safford get California newspapers to attack Howard, since local newspapers would be suspect if they did so.[51]

Howard's accomplishments, as impressive as they were, coincided with a general breakdown of the peace policy all over the West. The result in Arizona was a renewal of fighting against the remaining hostile Apache bands. The new campaigns in Arizona, however, were directed by General Crook, and the outcome there was successful. After warning all Indians that if they were not on their reservations by 1872 they would be pursued and killed, Crook resorted to the classic divide and conquer technique used by American frontiersmen against Indians since the founding of Jamestown: he employed Indian scouts to find the hostiles; he enlisted Indian allies—even friendly Apaches; and he put his own soldiers on horseback and took the war into the remote mountain strongholds of the remaining Apache hostiles. By 1873 Crook had broken the strength of the more dangerous bands and was being hailed as the savior of Arizona.[52] In summing

51. General George C. Crook to Safford, June 4 and July 12, 1872, MS in Territorial Papers (uncatalogued) , Arizona State Archives.
52. John G. Bourke, *On the Border with Crook* (New York, 1891) , pp. 220–21.

Prob w/ Subduing Inds is that war is that war is good business

up the events of that year, the *Arizona Citizen* noted that the territory could now offer "Safety to person and property, with comparatively insignificant exceptions. Never before since its legal creation, has such a degree of security prevailed in Arizona."[53]

The successes of Howard and Crook also began to end a vicious aspect of the Arizona economy. General Ord explained it best when he concluded at the end of his tour of duty that "hostilities in Arizona are kept up with a view of protecting the inhabitants, most of whom are supported by the hostilities." General Thomas also pointed out in a devastating report that six years of warfare against the Apache had cost the nation $5,000,000, a sum which had virtually sustained the economy of the territory. Even the *Weekly Arizonian* admitted in 1870 that many saw "the presence of the military in Arizona" as the "only inducement held out to immigration."[54]

Arizona merchants and politicians would continue to make money on the supplies sent to Indian reservations, and another ten years would pass before the Apache business—as the Arizonians sometimes called the hostilities—was settled, but in 1874 a turning point had been reached. Symbolic of the new order of things, a small dapper New Yorker named John P. Clum became the Apache agent at San Carlos. For three years he controlled the Indians without the aid of military force, and he gave them a sense of participation in reservation life.[55] After three centuries, white and Apache had stopped fighting long enough to begin to discover one another as people and as individuals.

A key factor affecting both Indian policy and Arizona development—and therefore Arizona politics—was the problem of transportation. Goods freighted overland via the Santa Fe trail or sent from a Texas port via El Paso and Mesilla were extremely costly. Supplies from California were similarly expensive, whether they were taken overland or brought from the coast up to the mouth of the Colorado. As in New Mexico and Utah, prohibitive prices and long-term invest-

53. *Arizona Citizen*, December 27, 1873.
54. *Weekly Arizonian*, December 25, 1869, January 23, 29, 1870.
55. John Philip Clum File, APHS.

new. ↑g Big merch - interests

ments prevented small freighting firms from developing. Since the
small specialized merchant could not exist in a sparely settled, relatively dangerous region, the result was, as in New Mexico, the rise of
an influential set of merchants and freighting concerns, who often
dominated Arizona's political and economic affairs.

In the first years after the Mexican War, Arizona goods came from
Mesilla over an extension of the Santa Fe trail. Even then the first
regular train of goods did not begin to flow until Pinkney Randolph
Tully brought ten wagons to Tucson to stock Solomon Warner's store
there. By the time Arizona had become a territory, Tully had combined forces with Estevan Ochoa of Mesilla to operate a stage and
freight line from Yuma to Santa Fe. Although the Tully and Ochoa
wagons were under constant attack from Apache raiders and operated under the harshest conditions, the firm was the most extensive
in Arizona and southern New Mexico for nearly twenty years. "Prior
to the advent of the railroad," wrote the *Arizona Citizen,* "the wagon
trains of this firm wound like great serpents over every road and to
every town, post, and camp where humanity had found habitation."[56]

Naturally Tully and Ochoa were soon noted public figures. Because
of his business acumen, Tully was made territorial treasurer of Arizona in 1875 and 1876. Later he served as treasurer of Tucson and
then as its mayor. Like so many other frontier freighting merchants,
he converted his holdings into cash and founded a local bank, which,
in turn, became the First National Bank of Tucson. Tully was also a
heavy investor in local mines and ranches. Once the railroad reached
Arizona, he became a stockholder in several companies. He also helped
to found the Arizona *Weekly Star.*[57]

Tully's partner, Estevan Ochoa, had come from a Mexican family
who sent him to Kansas City as a youth to be trained in the mercantile forwarding houses there. His own firm had been located in
Mesilla; but once identified with the fortunes of Arizona, he became
the spokesman of the Spanish Mexicans there and performed the
valuable task of bridging the gap between two cultures and two
peoples. Both McCormick and Safford quickly recognized Ochoa's tal-

56. Arizona *Daily Citizen* (Tucson), October 29, 1888.
57. Pinckney Randolph Tully File, APHS.

ents and continually sought his advice and support in political matters.[58]

While Tully and Ochoa had looked eastward for their supplies, Sylvester Mowry, his brother Charles, and other merchants and freighters were attracted to a route leading from the head of the Santa Cruz Valley directly southward to Arizpe, Mexico, and from there to the Port of Guaymas. Mowry had used this route in the 1850s, and after the Civil War the United States government used it on occasion to furnish its Arizona army posts.[59]

The most romantic of the trade routes, if the hottest, was via the Colorado River. Seagoing vessels would edge as far as they dared to the mouth of the muddy stream, where river steamers pulling freight barges met them. After a burning, tedious, and tortuous trip on the river, goods were unloaded at Yuma or carried even further up the river to La Paz or Ehrenberg and Hardyville. During the 1860s Prescott was furnished by the La Paz route. As in the overland freighting business, however, river transportation soon became a long-term monopoly, owned and run by a single firm, until purchased by the Southern Pacific in 1877.[60]

The relation of the trails and these firms to politics was all too obvious. In 1870, when the government decided to abandon the Guaymas route for its army supplies, it struck at certain interests in Tucson. To counter the blow, the town fathers attempted to elect vigorous Peter R. Brady to Congress to secure reversal of the Army's decision. In response, the recipients of the new Army contract—Hooper, Whiting, and Company—declared that they would spend large sums on McCormick's reelection to keep their business. McCormick won, and army goods began to flow over the Yuma route, in Hooper and Whiting wagons.[61]

The most dramatic example of the freighting firm's power in a frontier community is illustrated by the history of Lord and Williams. As a bright and engaging young man, Dr. Charles H. Lord had come

58. Esteban Ochoa File, APHS. See also obituary in Arizona *Daily Citizen*, October 29, 1888.
59. *Weekly Arizonian*, June 25 and July 16, 1870.
60. Samuel Hughes File, APHS.
61. *Weekly Arizonian*, June 25, October 1, 22, 1870.

to Arizona in 1866 to be a surgeon for the Cerro Colorado Mining Company. He joined forces with W. W. Williams, a local storekeeper, to found a wholesale and retail general merchandising company. By the time Lord was thirty-seven, these enterprises had made him a wealthy man. He operated a bank in Tucson and held the appointment of United States depositor for Arizona. After a brief stint as territorial auditor, he cooperated with McCormick and Safford to corner fat Army and Indian contracts, of which all of them took a share. The original Lord and Williams firm then branched out to invest in sheep ranches, insurance, and a lumber mill. Meanwhile, Williams himself took on the job of postmaster of Tucson. Backed by California and, no doubt, New York investors, the firm was so powerful during the early 1870s that one newspaper declared it "dictated to civil and military authorities as to the management of territorial affairs."[62]

Following in the wake of these larger firms were a dozen or so entrepreneur-politicians who also wielded much local influence. Coles Bashford, the methodical, scientific, former territorial secretary and delegate, set up a wholesale and retail store with his brother Levi, which netted each a $100,000 estate at their deaths. So complete was their stock of goods, one observer commented, that their warehouses contained "everything from carbine needles to pulpits." They, too, put their surplus cash into mines, ranches, flour mills, and eventually railroads.[63] Two Tucson pioneers, Hiram S. Stevens and Sam Hughes, had a similarly successful career in merchandising, ranching, and mining. At the same time, a half-dozen Spanish-American merchant traders, among them M. G. Samaniego, were equally successful.[64]

Perhaps the most impressive success story belonged to the pioneer German and Polish merchant traders, who came from New York, San Francisco, and St. Louis firms to supply miners and Indians all over the Southwest. In part, these in Arizona were an extension of the German mercantile houses already operating in Santa Fe and Taos.

---

62. Charles H. Lord File, APHS. See esp. the *Arizona Champion* (Flagstaff), August 8, 1885.
63. Coles and Levi Bashford files, APHS.
64. Mariano G. Samaniego File, APHS.

Others, however, represented San Francisco firms. Michael Goldwater, a Polish-born merchant, came by way of San Francisco to Fort Yuma and La Paz. The gold strike at La Paz in 1862 increased his business, and he was able to found branch firms in other Arizona towns. Similar careers awaited William, Louis, and Aaron Zeckendorf, who earned such great amounts of capital in Arizona that they had the funds to finance local railroad schemes and large industrial mining ventures.[65] As in New Mexico, Utah, and Colorado, the frontier merchant princes existed side by side with the miner, the settler, and the speculator; and there as elsewhere the former were a major factor in the economic and political development of the Far Southwest.

Arizona's early political parties can best be described as aggregations of many factions owing loyalty to some local leader. Apart from debates over Indian policy, communications, and economic development, they divided annually over issues of geography, cultural background, and personality. Yet as sharply divided as politics often were from 1863 to 1874, the territory was so dependent on the national government for defense and for a livelihood that its citizens usually went along with the Republican federal ring. When it looked as if parties would spring up in 1870 over the issue of freighting routes, the *Weekly Arizonian* said the movement was "premature," for Arizona "must stand united in these crucial years."[66]

In 1874, however, McCormick declined to run again for delegate, and in 1877 Safford resigned the governorship because of ill health. In the delegate election of 1874, four "Independents" appeared to run, although two were actually well-known Republicans and one was a staunch Democrat. The tremendous pressure of a hostile environment and a primitive economy had now lessened enough to allow a Democrat, Hiram S. Stevens of Tucson, to become delegate. This new independence was symbolized in the next three delegate campaigns, when two more Democrats, John G. Campbell and Granville H. Oury, were elected to that office.

Up to this time the Arizona economy continued to be so incom-

65. Zeckendorf File, APHS.
66. *Weekly Arizonian*, September 17, 1870.

plete that the only true agriculturalists in the territory were the Pimas, Papagoes, and Maricopas, the isolated Hopi tribes, and the Spanish-Mexican farmers. But as early as 1865 Governor McCormick had reported that farming people "chiefly from Utah" were beginning to settle near the Virgin River. Towns like Callville, St. Thomas, and Littlefield brought Mormon village life and culture to Arizona. Because of boundary changes, most of these early pioneer Saints eventually found themselves under Nevada jurisdiction. Yet even before Jacob Hamblin had founded a mission at Moenkopi in 1871, other Mormons had moved south from Kanab to build Fredonia. Within a dozen years, still more were using Lee's Crossing to start the villages of St. Johns, Sunset, and Snowflake.[67] By 1880 even more Saints had begun to move southward into the Salt River area near Casa Grande and Mesa. Eventually they penetrated southern Arizona and established other towns. Before the migration from Utah had ceased, one-fifth of the Arizona population would be Mormon. In Apache County, once a Navajo and Pueblo stronghold with a scattering of Spanish-Americans, the new population was soon great enough to send Saints to the territorial legislature.

In these same years Jack W. Swilling and other Arizonians, noting the ruins of ancient canals and acequias on the Salt River, collected enough capital to initiate ambitious commercial irrigation projects there. It was generally known that the land in the Salt River vicinity was excellent, for frontier farmers had raised grain and hay there for Army outposts and for the town of Wickenburg. The prospect of successful farming set the stage for the colonization of the central part of the territory and for the founding of the small town of Phoenix. Organized in 1868, it was a county seat by 1871 and soon thereafter it became a center for ranching and farming. The presence of agricultural settlers, whether subsistence Mormons or commercial Gentiles, meant that the basis had been laid in Arizona for a balanced and permanent economy which could sustain a population. It remained

---

67. *Journal of the Second . . . Assembly of . . . Arizona*, 1865, p. 44. David King Udall and Pearl Udall Nelson, *David King Udall: Arizona Pioneer Mormon* (Tucson, 1959) , pp. 68–74. "The Coming of the Mormons to the Salt River Valley . . . ," unsigned typescript, Arizona State Archives.

for the long-awaited railroad and a burgeoning mining industry to make the economy prosperous and commercial. With the coming of the Saints and the farmers, all the distinctive Indian and white cultures, economics, and religions that were characteristic of the Far Southwest, had come together in Arizona by 1874. Yet the very fact that the Mormons and Spanish Americans were destined to be minority rather than majority groups in Arizona meant that the territory's political development would differ from that of the others. Once again the accident of arbitrary political boundaries had worked to shape the history and institutions of the frontier area.

> Unless we educate the rising generation we shall raise up a
> population no more capable of self government than the
> Apaches themselves.
>
>   Governor A. P. K. Safford

> I was never in a place or business before where there was so
> much chenanniging carried on.
>
>   George Whitwell Parsons
>   in Tombstone
>   March, 1880

When A. P. K. Safford resigned from the governorship of Arizona in 1877, he could look back on an
unusual set of political achievements. He had sustained and fortified the Republican Party begun
by Goodwin and McCormick, and together they
had created a federal ring, which controlled much
of the territory politically and economically. His machine ran two
of the three major newspapers in Arizona and exacted the cooperation
of such usually independent figures as the territorial secretary, the
surveyor general, and the delegate.[1] Safford himself was a silent

1. Williams, "Territorial Governors," *AHR,* 7 (1936), 69–84. Roscoe G. Wilson,
"The Little Governor Does Well by Arizona," *Arizona Days and Ways Magazine*
(March 30, 1958), pp. 40–41. John Wasson, who was surveyor general of Arizona
for twelve years (1870–82), was a member of the Safford-McCormick ring and ran

partner in a dozen enterprises, which included mining, ranching, railroads, banking, and freighting.[2] He was a public supporter of General Crook and the military in Arizona, a friend of key Democrats, and popular among the Spanish-American citizens. But it would be a mistake to think that Safford's success was a party achievement, for the "Republicans" in Arizona never called themselves by that name until the delegate election of 1880. Instead, Safford's machine consisted of a coalition of frontier leaders from Prescott and Tucson, who formed a flexible and openended frontier oligarchy. However great their respective differences and attitudes may have been, the fact remains that the Santa Fe Ring in New Mexico, the Evans-Chaffee machine in Colorado, the Mormon hierarchy in Utah, and the Safford-McCormick federal ring of Arizona all played economic and political roles which were strikingly similar.

The modus vivendi that the politician, the miner, the entrepreneur, and the military arrived at in Arizona might lead one to despair of finding real democracy in the Southwest. But, as in the other territories, Safford's bossism was thought to be beneficial to the territory, since good relations with Washington were necessary for defense and survival, and any method of attracting capital to Arizona seemed desirable. This permissiveness also allowed Safford to do things that fully developed communities would not permit.

An example of the latter can be seen in the early history of the Arizona school system. Beginning in 1865, the legislature voted funds to sustain schools in the principal towns and at the mission school of San Xavier del Bac. While McCormick had strongly advocated public education during his term as governor, the federal census of 1870 indicated that 1,900 children of school age lived in the territory but that not a single public school was in operation.[3] Safford was determined to change this order of things, for the "Little Governor" not

---

the Arizona *Citizen* (Tucson) in behalf of the group; see Joseph Fish, "Manuscript History of Arizona," p. 456, typescript, APHS. Delegate McCormick's *The Arizona Miner* was, naturally, an administration paper. By 1872 it was being run by John H. Marion, who was deep in the councils of the ring. See Marion to Safford, September 1, 1872, uncatalogued MS, Arizona Territorial Papers, ASA.

2. Williams, "Territorial Governors," pp. 81–82.

3. Wyllys, *Arizona*, p. 177.

only was certain that schools were the glory and mainstay of democracy, but also was convinced that education would change the whole nature of the Spanish-Americans in Arizona and turn them into forward-looking citizens.[4] Thus in New Mexico, Colorado, Utah, and Arizona proponents of public education saw schools as a technique by which the local population, whether Mormon or Spanish-American, could be Americanized.

To realize his educational goals, Safford maneuvered bills through the Assembly in 1871 and 1873 which would make the governor ex-officio superintendent of public instruction, while probate judges were to be county superintendents. Since policy was directed by the governor, it was to be a highly centralized system. The new law also forbade aid to parochial schools, and here Safford ran into the opposition of the local Catholic priests and of Bishop Salpointe, Lamy's successor. But by playing up church influence as an evil and by enlisting the help of Estevan Ochoa, who was the spokesman for the Spanish-Americans living in southern Arizona, the Governor had gotten his way by 1875.[5] These rules were later modified so that parochial schools continued to carry a large part of Arizona's educational burden, but interest in public schools did not lag. In 1879 Moses H. Sherman succeeded the Governor as the regular superintendent of public instruction, and a year later the territory could boast that 101 schools were in operation within its borders. By 1885 Arizona had also opened a Normal School at Tempe for training teachers. Even the highly critical Senator Albert Beveridge, who visited Arizona in 1902 to see if the territory was ready for admission to the Union, concluded that it had a good school system.[6]

Governor Safford's efforts to bring railroads to Arizona also demonstrated an unusual use of the governor's powers. It is very probable that Safford was actually appointed to the Arizona governor's chair at the request of certain powerful railroad promoters in California, Nevada, and the East to see that Arizona railroad projects did not hurt their own. Senators William Stewart and James Warren Nye and Congressman Thomas Fitch—all of Nevada—had urged his

4. Williams, p. 78.
5. Ibid., pp. 78–80.
6. Wyllys, pp. 177–79.

appointment in 1869.[7] A year before he came to Arizona, in fact, Safford himself was made an incorporator of the Atlantic and Pacific Railroad, which had received a forty-mile-wide land grant across Arizona and New Mexico from Congress in 1866. The grant ran along the famous 35th parallel line, which Captain A. W. Whipple had recommended as a transcontinental rail route in the 1850s and over which Lieutenant Edward F. Beale had established a wagon road. Since Safford was the surveyor general of Nevada at the time the tracks of the Central Pacific were being laid across that state, he had dealt with the officials of the latter company and had come to know them.[8] Safford, therefore, was hardly naïve about the immense opportunities for railroad speculation and economic development which Arizona now offered.

Among the men who had urged Safford's appointment on President Grant was Coles Bashford, who was also an incorporator of the Atlantic and Pacific. Bashford and his brother Levi, the surveyor general of Arizona from 1863 to 1865, had been deep in railroad promotion in Wisconsin and Illinois prior to their coming west. Obviously they did not forget this previous interest in railroads, once they reached Arizona.[9] The prospects of a line along the 35th parallel also attracted other political and economic figures associated with the Southwest. John C. Fremont of California, William Gilpin, Edward F. Beale, Henry Connelly, Francisco Perea, and King S. Woolsey were also incorporators of the Atlantic and Pacific. While all of these men were public figures, each of them stood to gain personally from the construction of the railroad.[10]

7. Safford's appointment papers indicate that in addition to the Nevada contingent, the Governor had the support of Senator A. A. Sargent of California and of the California congressmen. Delegate McCormick and Coles Bashford also backed him. See Safford File in Dept. of State, Appointments Division, TP, Arizona. A revealing letter from McCormick to Safford suggests that prior to the appointment many arrangements had been made. After expressing the hope that the Southern Pacific would go through Tucson, he added: "Stewart, Nye and Fitch had a clear understanding with me regarding your appointment and we are sincerely anxious that we should pull together." McCormick to Safford, August 4, 1869, MS in Arizona Territorial Papers, ASA.

8. Safford was at the famous gold spike ceremony at Promontory Point, Utah in 1869: ibid.

9. Bashford files, APIIS.

10. See "Atlantic and Pacific Railroad, Act of Congress Granting Lands" (Washington, 1866), YWA.

Since nearly all public figures were given at least honorary positions in new railroad companies, it is not surprising to find that Safford became a commissioner for the Texas and Pacific railroad in 1871 and appears to have been an agent for Collis P. Huntington's Southern Pacific line. Quite naturally, he was interested in local firms which proposed to build short lines within the territory itself. The tactics used by Safford to promote railroads—and the personal motives which often accompanied these tactics—should not obscure the fact that Arizona businessmen, like their counterparts in New Mexico and Colorado, were desperate for a cheap mode of transportation; for without it the territories of the Southwest could not break out of the merchantile–small mining economy and the unfavorable balance of trade system—which characterized the region—to become prosperous, industrial states.

Despite all of Safford's efforts, nevertheless, railroads did not rush into Arizona until Indian difficulties were under control and new mining discoveries made the territory a more attractive place. It looked as if a turning point in Arizona fortunes had come when silver and copper were found in the eastern part of the territory at the Silver King mine in 1872, at Planet near Clifton in 1873, and at the Stonewall Jackson mine in 1874. The discoveries also coincided with Crook's defeat of the Apaches.

The real change came in 1877, however, when a doggedly persistent prospector, Edward Schieffelin, discovered fantastic silver lodes in Pima County near the future town of Tombstone.[11] Miners from California and elsewhere began to trickle into southeastern Arizona, and speculators, now recovering from the Panic of 1873, arrived there by the hundreds. The importance of the strike was suggested by the fact that Safford himself acted as Schieffelin's agent to sell the claims. While the grizzled prospector received over $600,000 for his finds, the Governor is said to have emerged from the transaction some $140,000 the richer.[12]

In 1863 Henry Wickenberg located the famous Vulture Mine, and subsequent discoveries of minerals in the central part of

11. Paul, *Mining Frontiers,* p. 159.
12. Willson, "Little Governor," pp. 40–41.

Arizona led to the founding of the mining towns of Globe, Jerome, Florence, and many others.[13] The Arizona discoveries occurred at the very time that a gold rush to the Black Hills was in progress and the rich silver carbonates at Leadville, Colorado were being located. New mines were also being developed in Montana and Idaho. The mineral promise of the Rocky Mountain West had suddenly become extremely attractive.

The new interest in Arizona was vividly illustrated by the activities surrounding the coming of two transcontinental railroads to the territory. The Southern Pacific had reached Yuma in 1877, just as the Tombstone rush was beginning. Naturally the line planned to build eastward along the famous 32nd parallel route in time, but the silver strike and the fear that the Texas Pacific would rush westward to occupy the right of way, instead, forced Huntington's hand. In classic robber baron fashion the Southern Pacific tried to monopolize the only feasible right of way across the lower Colorado by buying up George A. Johnson's ferry monopoly at Yuma and by seizing the other available crossing further up the river near Needles, California.[14]

To secure a liberal charter and a clear right of way in Arizona itself, the Southern Pacific then began to lobby in the territorial Assembly during its 1878 session. Apparently the company bribed both the legislators and Safford himself—who was out of office by this time—for in 1889 it was revealed that Huntington had sent Safford a large sum to use among the Assemblymen. The efficient Safford was able to turn the tide with only part of the money, and later he returned the rest to Huntington with the laconic explanation that Arizonians were not as expensive as the railroad executive had anticipated.[15]

Meanwhile the Texas Pacific had not been idle. This firm suddenly

13. Paul, p. 157.

14. Robert E. Riegel, *The Story of Western Railroads* (New York, 1926), pp. 179 ff.

15. Collis P. Huntington wrote to David D. Colton on September 27, 1875, and asked: "Can you have Safford call the legislature together and grant such charters as we want at a cost of $25,000?" See the "Huntington-Colton Letters" in *Report of the United States Pacific Railway Commission*, 50th Cong., 1st Sess., Exec. Doc. 51, Part 8, p. 3724.

got permission from General McDowell to run a line across the Yuma Indian Reservation on the Colorado. This had the effect of blocking the Southern Pacific. Refusing to be stopped, the latter road illegally bulldozed its way through the reservation, and Jay Gould, who now controlled the Texas and Pacific, was forced to compromise and join forces with the Southern Pacific.[16] The result of all these maneuvers was that after twenty-four years of waiting Tucson finally became a railroad town in March, 1880—an event it celebrated with a horse race. Three years later the Southern met the Texas Pacific at Sierra Blanca east of El Paso. The "snow free" route once advocated by Jefferson Davis had now become a reality. Since the Southern Pacific also joined the Atchison, Topeka, and Santa Fe at Deming in 1881, Arizona now had access to two trunk lines leading eastward. Sylvester Mowry's dream of a road to Guaymas began to come true a year later when the Sonoran railroad projected a line from that port to Benson on the Southern Pacific.[17]

The Southern Pacific's invasion of the last frontier was but half the railroad story. The Atlantic and Pacific railroad, which Congress had chartered in 1866, was slated to run across northern Arizona, but it had remained a paper railroad up to this time. The more vigorous Atchison, Topeka, and Santa Fe acquired a 50 per cent interest in the company and laid plans to build to the West Coast within the next few years.[18] But before this could happen, the Southern Pacific extended its own line to Needles and blocked the only remaining entrance to California. The Santa Fe admitted temporary defeat by joining the tracks of its rival there in 1884.

Since the Santa Fe ran some fifty miles north of Prescott and the Southern Pacific ran nearly a hundred miles south of the new mining centers of Globe and Florence, plans were soon afoot throughout the decade of the 1880s to connect all these towns to at least one of the main roads by feeder lines. The Arizona Copper Company, for example, built a narrow-gauge line from Lordsburg to the smelter town of Clifton. Other spur lines were added despite many difficulties

16. Riegel, pp. 179 ff.
17. Bancroft, *Arizona and New Mexico,* pp. 603 ff.
18. Riegel, p. 189.

and changes in plans, and with the completion of the Santa Fe, Prescott, and Phoenix Railroad in 1895 the central skeleton of Arizona's rail transportation had been established.[19]

The coming of railroads and the new boom in silver and copper mining, had a truly dramatic effect on the nature of the territory. The silver rush to Tombstone, for example, created a new town out of nowhere, called into being the surrounding villages of Richmond, Charleston, and Contention City, and necessitated the organization of Cochise County in 1881.[20] The location of Tombstone gave Tucson a new lease on life as a supply depot, and it inspired W. W. Williams of Lord and Williams, William Zeckendorf, the merchant prince, and ex-Congressman Thomas Fitch of Nevada to lay plans to build the Southern Arizona Railroad to the diggings.[21]

Ex-Governor Safford rushed to the area to form at least two mining companies and to establish a branch of Safford-Hudson and Company, a banking firm in which he was a major partner. The cantankerous Wyatt Earp, trailed by two of his sullen brothers, arrived from Dodge City, Kansas, to become a noted citizen of Tombstone and to protect Wells Fargo bullion shipments.[22] Nevada businessmen, among them Thomas Fitch, were there speculating, and John P. Clum, the former Apache Indian Agent at San Carlos, arrived to found the *Tombstone Epitaph*. Bands of criminal outlaws drifted in to make trouble. These men robbed and killed miners, rustled cattle from the newly established ranches in southeastern Arizona, and periodically raided towns in Sonora. Mining companies from the East sent engineers and investors; and ambitious young lawyers and politician-businessmen came to Tombstone to get a start in public life. Among the able new political leaders in the town were Ben Hereford, Thomas Farish, and Marcus Aurelius Smith, a future delegate and senator.[23] Smith began his political career there.

19. Swor, "Development of Prescott," pp. 63–67.
20. T. R. Sorin, *Handbook of Tucson and Surroundings* (Tombstone? n.d.), pp. 12 ff., YWA.
21. *Arizona Citizen*, April 7, 1880.
22. Wyllys, pp. 220, 249.
23. "The Private Journal of George Whitwell Parsons," Arizona Statewide Archival and Records Project, WPA (Phoenix, 1936), pp. 102, 163. Sorin, *Handbook*, pp. 12 ff.

By the mid-eighties some 15,000 people lived in Tombstone—which was probably the most hardbitten, sophisticatedly tough boom town in the West. Although its citizens quickly elected a mayor, they found in 1880 that he had deeded the city to a single firm Clark, Gray, and Company in a private deal. This called for a Citizen's League and a new election in which John P. Clum was the victor.[24] Then, after the county voters had elected a sheriff, John Behan, they learned that he was allied to various outlaw cowboy outfits who had drifted into town. Weekly brawls and frequent killings became standard fare until a feud between the sheriff and the Earp brothers led to more killings and a final, great fight near the O.K. Corral.[25]

These were, indeed, exciting and unforgettable days. George White-well Parsons, a former clerk from California who came to Tombstone, began to fill his journal with accounts of fatal saloon brawls, waylaid miners found robbed and dead, and posses riding after highwaymen. Parsons, though a peaceful man was soon wearing pistols—because everyone else wore them. He was even more amazed to realize that he had pulled down the shack of a claim jumper, had stopped a bank run on Safford-Hudson and Company, and had been a heroic fire fighter during two serious fires in Tombstone.[26]

The rush to Tombstone coincided with the rise of less glamorous mining communities at Globe, Miami, Florence, Jerome, and Bisbee. Since engineers and chemists were at last learning to extract Arizona's oldest known mineral—copper—in a more efficient and scientific way, large copper firms came into being in Arizona. Such enterprises as the Copper Queen Mining Company, backed by California capital and Louis Zeckendorf, began operations around Bisbee in 1880.[27] The need for copper for telegraph and electrical wire led Eastern capital to follow suit: during the 1880s the Phelps-Dodge Company acquired major mines there and became one of the territory's largest busi-

24. *Tombstone Epitaph*, November 9, 12, 25, December 9, 1880.

25. For detailed accounts of this famous encounter see Stuart Lake, *Wyatt Earp: Frontier Marshal* (New York, 1931); John M. Myers, *The Last Chance* (New York, 1950); Lloyd and Rose Hamill, *Tombstone Picture Gallery* (Glendale, Cal., 1951).

26. Parsons, "Journal," pp. 203, 206, 236.

27. Annie M. Cox, "History of Bisbee, 1877–1937" (Master's thesis, University of Arizona, 1938), pp. 13–37.

nesses.[28] Side by side the old-fashioned individualistic silver miner and the scientific copper corporation worked to exploit Arizona after 1880.

Significantly, all these developments occurred in a period when industry had become large-scale in the United States, which meant that most capital had to come from outside the territory. The discoveries also occurred at a time when engineering and technology had become an integral part of most production processes. Arizona mineral enterprises took on all these characteristics; and long before the territorial period had ended, the region suffered from absentee ownership. Its citizens came to know all too well the meaning of "company towns"—where workers were paid in scrip—and of debilitating local conflicts between labor and capital.[29] The stage was set for the permanent inhabitants of Arizona to begin feeling that they were a colonial appendage to Eastern and California interests and that their own needs were being ignored.

The new population of Arizona could now feel this way, because by their very numbers they had established a more balanced society and economy. The presence of thousands of miners created an enormous demand for foodstuffs. Cattle were marched in, and soon local ranching enterprises large and small—which had gotten a start by feeding army installations and Indian reserves—expanded to supply the beef for mineral towns.[30] Since lumber was also needed for the mines and choice timberlands existed in northern Arizona, it was inevitable that the lumbering industry would invade that region.[31] Meanwhile, Mormon and Gentile farmers were stimulated to raise more foodstuffs, while promoters in Phoenix began to build a grand canal there to irrigate lands for cultivation.[32]

The sense of exciting change and material development that Arizona experienced between 1877 and the Panic of 1893 naturally

28. Ibid., pp. 37 ff.
29. Ibid., pp. 139–41. Wyllys, p. 290.
30. Wyllys, Ibid., pp. 239–54 passim. Bert Haskett, "Early History of the Cattle Industry in Arizona," *AHR,* 6 (1935), 3–42.
31. Wyllys, pp. 287–88.
32. Ibid., pp. 257–59. Thomas E. Farish, *History of Arizona* (8 vols. Phoenix, 1918) *6,* 137–59.

affected politics. The familiar political rivalry between Democratic Tucson and Republican Prescott gave way to new political alliances in which Tombstone, Globe, Bisbee, and other towns played an important part. New counties broke down the previous political alignment of the legislature, made Indian affairs seem less important, and turned men's concerns away from defense, federal aid, and the like. The two railroads were also politically influential, particularly since the Santa Fe was allied with the Republican Party and the Southern Pacific cooperated with the Democrats.[33]

The most obvious office to be affected by the new changes in Arizona was that of the governor. When Safford resigned in 1877, his successor was John Philo Hoyt. Hoyt appears to have been a competent executive, but he was suddenly the governor of a promising territory.[34] Before he had served for two years, he was replaced by none other than the famous "pathmarker," John Charles Fremont (1878–81). Ostensibly the former explorer was in dire financial straits and needed a steady income. His old friend Senator Zachariah Chandler knew of Fremont's plight and tendered him the Arizona post as a reward for the General's help in the 1876 presidential campaign.[35] Fremont's own reasons for accepting the position, however, appear to have been neither humble nor desperate. He had been a participant in great speculative schemes now for thirty years, and nearly all the enterprises had involved mining and railroads. Ten years before, he had been president of the Atlantic and Pacific, and now this road—under the aegis of the Santa Fe—was about to become a reality. Arizona only represented the newest investment frontier toward which the Great Pathmarker was attracted.

By the time the new Governor reached Arizona, in fact, he had conceived of a giant project to flood the desert Salton Sink with

33. T. W. Spear, *Uncle Billy Reminisces: The Story of a Newspaper* (Phoenix, 1940), p. 10.

34. Hoyt had been territorial secretary in 1876–77; after his short period as governor of Arizona he became governor of Idaho Territory (1878). He then secured a federal judgeship in Washington Territory (1879–87). Pomeroy, *Territories*, p. 131.

35. Allan Nevins, *Fremont, Pathmarker of the West* (New York, 1939), p. 603. See also Fremont to Chandler, May 3, 1878, microfilm, Bancroft Library.

Fremont's schemes

Colorado waters so that it could be turned into a vast southwestern oasis.[36] While this project was not to be undertaken for many years, a dozen other schemes were awaiting Fremont's inspection and cooperation, for several entrepreneur-politicians saw in the new Governor the perfect liaison man to use to secure Eastern capital. One of these was the entrepreneur-politician Judge Charles Silent, a Californian who had been appointed to the Arizona supreme court in 1878.[37] His real interest appears to have been not justice but mining speculation. Thomas Fitch, the Nevada politician who was called "the silver-tongued orator of the Pacific," also suddenly appeared in Arizona as a representative to the territorial Assembly from Yavapai County. He, too, was soon at Fremont's elbow to give advice and to persuade the governor to promote various mining ventures. Arizona was the third territory in which Fitch had pursued a political career. After he had served as a congressman from Nevada, he became Brigham Young's legal counsel in Utah in 1870. During the Utah statehood movement of 1872, Young had actually chosen Fitch to be one of the Utah "senators."[38] Still a third assistant to Fremont was Henry A. Bigelow, an Arizona miner and politician who had been in the First Assembly. Bigelow was now a major voice in the Arizona Republican Party.[39]

It was not long before Fremont and his three lieutenants were demonstrating to what uses a famous name could be put. The Governor, having approved of a territorial lottery to aid in the building of a capitol and to finance schools, went East to sell tickets, and Arizona railroad and mining stock as well. The *Arizona Citizen* reported that Fremont had made "bar'ls of money" by "placing Arizona mines at the East" and added that Judge Silent's success at

36. Nevins, p. 604.
37. Thus far Judge Silent remains a mysterious figure in Arizona history; there appear to be few written accounts about his activities there.
38. Although Fitch was a well-known public figure, his exact role in Arizona history remains ill defined. Bancroft, *Arizona and New Mexico*, p. 189.
39. Bigelow's public career may be followed in the *Journals of the Arizona Assembly* for the years he was a member of that body. See also John H. Marion to A. P. K. Safford, September 1, 1872, Arizona TP, ASA, which suggests that Bigelow was an important member of the Safford-McCormick ring as well.

the same task made him act "as if he was rich enough to tell the Department of Justice to pull down its vest."[40]

The cynical use of Arizona by outsiders to promote huge schemes made Fremont extremely unpopular. The underlying resentment against "federal carpetbaggers," which McCormick and Safford had always been able to control, now burst forth in the delegate election of 1880. The Democrats meeting in Phoenix in June cast caution and compromise to the winds and chose Granville H. Oury, an ex-Confederate, as their delegate candidate. Despite all his faults, at least he was an old settler who could be trusted. When the Republicans met a month and a half later in their first territorial convention, they chose as their candidate M. W. Stewart, a former Colorado politician.[41]

The campaign that followed suggested the many ways in which Arizona was changing. For the first time in history the traditionally Democratic control of Pima County was challenged, since the boom town of Tombstone was still within its jurisdiction. The Republicans, in their effort to win, resorted to waving the bloody shirt. Meanwhile, Oury promised to try to get all Indians removed to Indian territory and to get rid of the soldiers in Arizona! Clearly the day when Tucson merchants lived on Indian and military contracts was over. It must have been hard to remember that Arizona was still a frontier, for torchlight parades were organized on behalf of the candidates wherever they went. When candidate Stewart left for Tip-Top, the *Tombstone Epitaph* reported that he was "accompanied by the Glee Club of Prescott and twenty citizens."[42] In a furious effort to preserve themselves against the new outsiders, the local Arizonians elected Oury to Congress; and soon thereafter the Assembly placed rambunctious Tombstone in its own county. Politics based on local pride, real issues, principles, and the regional backgrounds of the voters had at last come to Arizona.

By 1881 territorial resentment was mounting against Fremont for being an absentee official and for allowing, if not persuading, the

40. *Arizona Sentinel*, quoted in *Arizona Citizen*, June 10, 1879.
41. *Tombstone Epitaph*, June 30, August 24, 25, 1880.
42. *Arizona Citizen*, September 20, October 14, 18, to November 4, 1880. *Epitaph*, October 22, 1880.

Assembly to pass a wide-open railroad incorporation act. That summer the *Tombstone Epitaph,* which was a Republican paper, printed editorials entitled: "Give Arizona a Governor," "Fremont's Pet Railroad Bill," and "Fremont Must Go." When the Governor did resign that October, the *Epitaph* expressed the hope that President Arthur would not "send us another eleemosynary barnacle to be fed from the public crib."[43]

The outside exploitation of Arizona associated with Fremont represented only one of many complex "get-rich" schemes now in operation on the last frontier. Undoubtedly the most daring one was the Reavis land case. Arizona businessmen and California railroad interests, hoping to speculate in Spanish land grants around which so much of New Mexico's economy and politics still centered, had submitted enlarged land claims to ten or twelve vague grants in the San Pedro Valley and in the Gadsden Purchase area. Beginning in the early 1880s, nearly every surveyor general of Arizona voiced his suspicion about the validity of these grants, but each tended to allow modified claims to stand. The El Sopori Tract, which Sylvester Mowry had tried to sell to Rhode Island businessmen in 1859, was one of these fraudulent grants. Arizonians tolerantly felt that this minor land grab might be settled by the Land Office and that survey and settlement could go ahead.

Just as things seemed in process of solution, an imaginative Missouri trolley conductor named James Addison Reavis appeared in Arizona with Spanish documents that purported to be deeds to lands in the Gila and Salt River valleys amounting to over 17,000 square miles! Not only was Reavis the claimant, but his Mexican wife was thought to be none other than a descendant of the original grantee, Miguel Peralta de Cordoba, "Baron of the Colorados."[44] Reavis' claim, while always suspect in the eyes of the United States Land Office, seemed so believable that he and his supporters managed to secure tribute from settlers on the "Peralta Grant" and to make the Southern Pacific pay a right-of-way fee for a number of years. Governor Zulick warned

43. *Epitaph,* March 23, June 16, 18, 21, 23, August 6, October 18, 1881.
44. For a full coverage of the Reavis fraud see William A. Dupuy, *Baron of the Colorados* (San Antonio, 1940).

Washington that the claims were really backed by "certain persons of abundant capital" and a "great railroad corporation," and Surveyor General John Hise said it was another "giant California speculation scheme."[45] But only a thorough investigation by the Private Land Claims Court of 1891 proved that it was a fraud from beginning to end. Ironically, Reavis wound up in prison at Santa Fe, the home of successful land-grant speculators.

The successor to Fremont was Frederick A. Tritle, (1882–85) a miner and merchant who had once run for governor of Nevada. An able politician and an avid mining man, he made Arizona his home, helped build the Central Arizona Railroad, of which he was president, and played a key role in the development of the copper-mining industry.[46] His popularity undoubtedly aided the election of Curtis C. Bean as delegate in 1884, the first Republican to hold that office in ten years.[47]

Before Tritle could establish a firm control over the territory, Grover Cleveland became President and filled the Arizona federal positions with the first Democratic incumbents ever to hold office there. Cleveland's gubernatorial appointee, Conrad M. Zulick (1885–89), was so anxious to build up a machine, however, that he pursued controversial policies that divided rather than united the local Democracy.[48] Zulick himself provoked the first crisis by pardoning a number of Mormon polygamists serving terms at the territorial prison in Yuma. Governor Tritle had opposed the Mormons and had cooperated with the federal authorities to enforce the Edmunds Act of 1882. Zulick's counteraction now made both the question of polygamy and Mormon voting allegiance red-hot political issues.[49]

Zulick's next crisis came when bands of renegade Apaches, among whom was Geronimo, left the San Carlos Agency in 1885 and began to terrorize the inhabitants of southeastern Arizona. In many ways

45. *Annual Report of the Governor of Arizona to the Secretary of the Interior, 1884* (Washington, 1884), p. 527. Ibid., *1887*, pp. 108–606.
46. Wyllys, p. 180.
47. "Curtis C. Bean" in *Biographical Directory of the American Congress.*
48. C. Meyer Zulick File, APHS.
49. Ibid.

the new Apache outbreak was justified, for after 1875 the government had placed all kinds of Indians together at the San Carlos Agency. Then in 1879 a decentralization policy was adopted, and certain bands were place at Fort Apache. Meanwhile a series of crooked agents stole from the Indians, and Congress itself occasionally failed to provide sufficient rations for the Indians. These internal conditions naturally produced discontent, but the real difficulties began after coal and copper were discovered on the San Carlos Reservation. Squatters and miners swarmed in to take up lands and claims. On the east, Clifton and Morenci threatened reservation borders, while on the western side white pioneers of Globe and Miami invaded Apache lands. At the same time, persistent Mormon farmers took up lands at Fort Apache.[50]

Feelings became so strong that the Indians began to seek release in a religious revival. Alarm over the Indian problem undoubtedly helped elect Granville Oury in 1880 and 1882, for he was in favor of removing them to Indian territory. The federal government tried to restore peace by sending General Crook back to Arizona, but it was too late. Crook tried to better conditions, but he was hindered by the fact that he shared jurisdiction over the Apaches with the Indian Office, and the two could not agree on policy. The break came when Geronimo and 143 Chiricahuas left the reservation.[51]

Upon his arrival in the territory, Zulick had told a gathering of citizens at Tombstone that he was no Eastern sentimentalist and would not mind seeing all Apaches killed. He now seized this opportunity to demand their complete subjugation, a policy that soon turned into an attack on General Crook, who was known for his friendship with past Republican administrations. He had also come to practice a kind of "live and let live policy" toward the Apaches, which was perhaps more tolerant than most Arizona citizens cared for.

Crook's failure to bring in the raiders of 1885 and 1886 caused a public panic, which in turn prompted a vigilant press war against the Indians and the General. Citizens began to appeal for arms, and many Arizonians urged Zulick to permit them to raise a company of rangers.

50. Spicer, *Cycles of Conquest*, pp. 253–55.
51. Wyllys, pp. 206–08.

So great was the cry that Secretary of the Interior Lamar wired Zulick to stop the senseless newspaper provocation of a useless Indian war.[52] Cleveland assured Delegate Bean that the government would "give the people of Arizona peace if it takes the whole army."[53] Long before the hue and cry died down, however, Cleveland had removed Crook and had appointed a Democratic general, Nelson A. Miles, to track down Geronimo and his band. This task was accomplished in 1886, and the Indians were carted off to prison—first in Florida and later at Fort Sill, Oklahoma. Nevertheless, the Indian question continued to be an issue, for Miles' accomplishment, which was actually carried out by Lieutenant Charles B. Gatewood, was used to promote the Democratic administration in Washington and in Arizona. Miles' own subsequent Indian policy also resembled Crook's so closely that debate over it split both Republicans and Democrats into Miles and Crook factions.[54] Still, the fact that Indian policy could now be debated was a sign of some progress in Arizona Indian affairs.

Zulick's next crisis was similar to the one that Governor Ross was experiencing in New Mexico. He discovered that his predecssor in office had named a full slate of Republicans to territorial offices just before resigning. By law these appointees were entitled to hold office for two years. Thus Zulick found himself hindered at every step by Republican underlings and by the fact that the legislature was evenly divided by party affiliation. When he tried to replace them with Democrats, Arizona found itself with two sets of territorial officials until the issue was settled in court.[55]

The most controversial event of Zulick's career involved the removal of the capitol from Prescott, where it had been since 1877, to the more centrally located town of Phoenix. Convinced that neither Prescott nor Tucson was destined to become a great center, he persuaded the Fifteenth Assembly to put it in Phoenix in 1889.

52. L. Q. C. Lamar to Zulick, November 25, 1885, telegram in Arizona Territorial Papers, ASA.

53. Bean to Zulick, January 10, 1886; Fred G. Hughes to Zulick, May 26, 1886; Mass Petition of Citizens, 1885; ibid.

54. Katherine Shepard, "The Miles-Crook Controversy" (Master's thesis, University of New Mexico, 1936), pp. 1–55.

55. James M. Barney, "Territorial Governor C. Meyer Zulick's Opinion of Polygamy," *The Sheriff, 11* (September 1953), 71.

Although cries of "steal" and "fix" resounded for years afterward and hurt Zulick's own career, the decision stuck.[56]

The relocation of the capital was but another sign that Arizona was growing. Zulick himself noted in his annual report of 1887 that the population had jumped from 40,000 in 1880 to 90,000 in 1887. For the first time in territorial history, the Anglo-American citizens outnumbered the Spanish-American inhabitants. The value of the territory's taxable property was now twenty-six million dollars, and of this, six million represented the increase for the single fiscal year of 1886–87.[57] By 1890 the territory had a thousand miles of railroad and 700 miles of canals. A year later, Arizona reached a peak in the production of cattle, wool, timber, copper, and silver; and Salt River Valley fruits were beginning to be shipped out over railroads to the world.[58] The beleaguered frontier had at last become a part of the American industrial economy. Instead of Indian defense, its voters were now troubled by national reform issues centering around prohibition, free coinage of silver, trust-busting, and freighting rates; and even the seeds of Populism were to be found in Arizona.

In this transition period the Republicans as well as the Democrats became more factional than ever. When Benjamin Harrison named Lewis Wolfley (1889–90) to succeed Zulick in 1889, Arizonians were quick to find he was more interested in forwarding the Gila Bend Canal scheme than with the public welfare.[59] Since Wolfley was related to Senators James G. Blaine and John Sherman and to the Ewing family of Ohio, which had large holdings in Arizona mines, he was thought to be the epitome of a speculating, nonresident spoils appointee. Undiplomatic in his manner and strongly anti-Mormon in his policies, Wolfley lasted only a year and a half in office. His successor, John N. Irwin, (1890–92) a former governor of Idaho Territory, also resigned within two years, and still a third appointee,

---

56. Wyllys, p. 180.
57. *Annual Report of the Governor of Arizona to the Secretary of the Interior, 1887*, pp. 153–755.
58. Ibid., *1890*, pp. 463–64.
59. Lewis Wolfley File, APHS. Wolfley had also been a Civil War comrade of John W. Noble, the incumbent Secretary of the Interior at the time Wolfley was appointed governor.

Nathan O. Murphy, the incumbent territorial secretary, was named by Harrison in May 1892.[60]

Happily, Murphy (1892–94) was both a resident of Arizona and one of its most popular public men. He had helped complete the Santa Fe, Prescott, and Phoenix Railroad and had served as its president. His appointment represented the triumph of a local Republican machine over the patronage wishes of a national administration. After his first term in the governor's office, he was elected delegate in 1894. McKinley reappointed him to the governorship in 1898 for four more years. Murphy became a prime example of the locally oriented leader—safe, conservative, and trustworthy—whom many Arizonians wanted.[61] His own constant crusade for statehood and for Apache removal and his willingness to compromise with the Democrats made mincemeat out of party lines. As in Safford's time it was still clear that the party label was forgotten when a strong leader appeared.

The roster of Arizona governors from 1869 to 1900 demonstrates once again that the real function of government on the frontier was business development. Safford, Fremont, and Tritle were railroad and mining promoters. Tritle and Murphy were railroad builders; Wolfley and Murphy were irrigation promoters; Hughes was a land speculator.

The most extraordinary figure in Arizona politics after 1886 was not Murphy, however, but Marcus Aurelius Smith, a slight, keen-eyed, young Kentuckian who had come to Tombstone in 1881 to hang out his shingle as a lawyer.[62] Possessed of a Southern accent, an unlimited fund of humorous stories, and an indomitable will, he was one of the shrewdest judges of men ever to come to Arizona. After graduation from Transylvania College and the University of Kentucky Law School, Smith had taught school in his home state before trying his luck as a lawyer in California. When the silver finds at Tombstone proved to be extensive, Smith moved to Arizona. Within months of his arrival he was a noted figure in that wide-open

60. Wyllys, pp. 180–81.

61. "N. O. Murphy," in *Portrait and Biographical Record* (Chicago, 1900), pp. 21–22. See also Spear, *Uncle Billy*, p. 10.

62. Marcus A. Smith File, APHS. *Biographical Directory of the American Congress.* La Moine Langston, "Arizona's Fight for Statehood in the Fifty Seventh Congress" (Master's thesis, University of New Mexico, 1939), p. 11.

town and in Tucson as well. Outspoken, acid in debate, and absolutely fearless, he had become prosecuting attorney of Cochise County by 1882, and by 1886 he had been elected delegate to Congress. Between 1888 and 1912 he was returned to that office for seven more terms. As an almost legendary political boss, he was to serve as one of Arizona's first senators when the territory finally became a state in 1912. Whether in or out of office, Smith's career and attitudes symbolized the wishes and attitudes of most Arizonians in their transition stage to maturity and statehood: his life was in many ways a minuscule political history of the territory.

At the outset, Smith made it clear that he would work within the political and economic framework that he found in Arizona. His Kentucky background made him carefully respect the habits and views of the territory's Southern population. He knew and understood pioneer types like Granville Oury and Peter R. Brady, and he joined them in their rabid hate for the Indian. But he also knew that Arizona's future lay in large-scale mining, cheap transportation, and irrigation, so that, while pleasing the older merchant-small miner oligarchy centered in Tucson, Prescott, and Yuma, he also cultivated the copper executives of Bisbee and the officers of the Santa Fe and Southern Pacific railroads. At various times he was the legal counsel for all these groups.

To the silver miner on the other hand, he stood as a stalwart defender of free coinage and bimetallism. Yet Smith, who advocated the eight-hour day for labor, had, on occasion, worked to secure Mexican contract labor for the copper companies. Smith's paradoxical stands extended to land policy.[63] He pleased the settler and corporation by opposing any recognition of Spanish land grants, and he fought furiously against the establishment of the Court of Private Land Claims in 1891. Still, Smith's own subsequent course in Congress leaves little doubt that he was interested in land speculation schemes involving the public domain.[64]

Smith also seems to have cooperated with the saloon element that

63. See "The Official Record of Mark A. Smith" (6 vols. 1887–1907), deposited in ASA; note esp. *4*, 531.

64. Ibid., *3*, 2–21, 31, 60, 204–06, 265.

now dominated a wing of the Democratic Party and was led by ex-Governor Zulick, and he did not object to Mormons. Last, but far from least, Smith was a politically attractive figure to many Republicans, and like Murphy he, too, made mincemeat out of party lines.

Peace, prosperity, a burgeoning population, and the presence of trusted political and economic leaders who took pride in the territory inevitably meant that Arizona was psychologically ready for statehood. A major reason for Delegate Smith's enduring popularity, in fact, was his identification with the crusade to make Arizona a state. Admission became an important issue in politics in 1889, when the first "Omnibus Bill"—which eventually admitted the Dakotas, Wyoming, and Washington into the Union—originally included Arizona. The success of these territories and the neighboring attempts of Utah and New Mexico to gain admission during 1890 and 1891 whetted the appetites of Arizona politicians. That New Mexico was Republican and Arizona was Democratic suggested to them that Congress might admit both, since this arrangement would not disturb party balance in the Senate.[65] So anxious was Arizona to join in the rush to statehood that in 1891 twenty-one of her leading men, among them Mark Smith, met informally in Phoenix to write a constitution and ask for admission. The convention was Democratic in makeup, but it had the cooperation of territorial secretary N. O. Murphy and of former Governor Tritle.[66]

As constitutions went, the Phoenix document of 1891 was Jeffersonian in philosophy, but it did attempt to deal with current issues. The extravagance of territorial assemblies, for example, led the writers to create a weak legislature and to reduce both the number and salaries of public officials. At the same time, the rising national sentiment against vested interests and monopolies was reflected in clauses that not only prevented wild-cat corporation schemes but wiped out all dormant and exclusive charters.[67]

The writers also engaged in some interesting ambiguities. Loftily

65. Langston, "Arizona's Statehood Fight," pp. 5–6.

66. "Journals of the Constitutional Convention for the State of Arizona," (Phoenix, 1891), ASA.

67. *Constitution for the State of Arizona As Adopted by the Constitutional Convention, October 2, 1891* . . . (Phoenix, 1891), pp. 3–4.

they called upon Congress to survey the Atlantic and Pacific land grants so they could be taxed, and they asked for public school and other federal lands to be awarded upon achievement of statehood. On the one hand, this seemed a way to secure monies to run a state, but on the other, it was a threat to make the Atlantic and Pacific—which held these lands—cooperate with the statehood forces. It also implied that some of the delegates had in mind a big land speculation scheme.[68] Similarly, their promise to revoke the charters of abusing corporations provided a possible loophole whereby Pima and Yavapai counties, which had defaulted on some bonds, could get out of their obligations.[69]

The founding fathers of 1891 faced up to one major issue by declaring for free, nonsectarian schools and preservation of the school lands, but they evaded the issue of female suffrage by allowing women to vote in school elections only. They did state, however, that the full right to vote could come as a result of popular referendum.[70] Woman's suffrage was far from an academic issue, for Governor Murphy, Louis C. Hughes (editor of the Tucson *Star*), and Arizona Mormons all approved of giving the vote to women. What made the issue crucial was that most leaders of the temperance movement—a crusade also backed by the *Star*—were women.[71] To the saloon element, therefore, female suffrage meant prohibition.

Finally, the Phoenix constitution, while seeming to voice Populist and anti-big-business feeling as well as a love of free silver, included a water-rights clause that allowed corporations prior access over the individual owners of lands. Critics were quick to spot these weaknesses and evasions, and they frequently called it a "water and land grab constitution." But the popular desire for statehood and the attractive free-silver stand expressed by the convention persuaded the voters to swallow their objections, and the constitution was ratified in 1891 with an overwhelmingly favorable vote.[72]

The prospect that two silver-producing territories wanted to come in-

68. Ibid., pp. 6 ff.
69. Ibid., p. 4.
70. Ibid., p. 4.
71. Louis C. Hughes "Scrapbooks," 3 vols., clippings, etc., in the University of Arizona Library, Tucson; see esp. Vol. 2.
72. Langston, "Arizona's Statehood Fight," p. 5.

to the Union was not lost in Congress. Although an Arizona Enabling Act passed the House in 1892, the conservative Senate rejected it "on the grounds that it seemed to repudiate certain contracts and set up a double monetary standard." President Harrison explained the real reason to Delegate Smith in more direct language when he said the Republicans were "opposed to the free coinage of western senators."[73]

Congressional rebuffs only temporarily dampened Arizona's enthusiasm for statehood. Cleveland's election in 1892 made the Democrats so optimistic that no fewer than five bills were introduced the following year. Once again Smith's bill passed the House but failed to win Senate approval. The statehood forces themselves met in Phoenix at the Opera House to petition Congress anew, to organize a permanent statehood committee in each county, and to send a bipartisan delegation—headed by N. O. Murphy—to Washington to lobby for admission. The difficulty now was that Smith and standpat Arizona Democrats had voted for Hill over Cleveland at the national Democratic convention in 1892, and the President was in no mood to cooperate with his former opponents. Indeed, he took revenge on Smith by appointing the temperance editor, Louis C. Hughes (1893–96), of the Tucson *Star,* as territorial governor in 1893.[74]

Unfortunately for the statehood advocates, Hughes' appointment highlighted a party split between Smith and the more liberal elements in the Democratic ranks and coincided with the rise of a territorial Populist Party. The effects of the Panic of 1893 also shelved most admission efforts until 1900, although seven more statehood bills were introduced during those years. The intraparty fight among the Democrats in these years was so complex that it is difficult to tell who was protagonist and who was defender. When Governor Hughes, backed by church and temperance groups, came into office and promised certain changes, ex-Governor Zulick and the "wets" were so antagonistic that they turned Hughes' administration into a nightmare of accusations and charges of mismanagement. Marcus Smith, now punningly called "Octopus Smith" by his enemies because of his

73. *Proceedings of the Arizona Convention for Statehood* (Phoenix, 1893), p. 11, pamphlet, ASA.
74. Ibid., p. 17.

far-reaching control, joined in the war on "Pin-head" Hughes.[75] The fact that territorial printing went to Hughes' paper, the Tucson *Star*, led to cries of corruption. Hughes' own decision to cooperate with N. O. Murphy, the leader of the Republicans, who had become delegate in 1895, led to still more. He also angered Smith by supporting the Court of Private Land Claims. Finally, Hughes got into serious trouble by pursuing a land policy that amounted to speculation in Indian lands. The cries of malfeasance by Zulick and Smith were so loud that Cleveland was forced to remove Hughes from office in 1896.[76]

The war with Hughes cost the Democrats the delegateship in 1894, for that year Populist sentiment, particularly in northern Arizona, had grown to such a point that the People's Party chose William "Bucky" O'Neill, an extraordinarily popular rancher and editor of the *Arizona Miner*, to run for delegate.[77] O'Neill had endeared himself to the voters while he was a local tax assessor by billing the Atlantic and Pacific Railroad for $800,000 in taxes. The Populist choice frightened both regular parties into selecting their strongest candidates, however, so that N. O. Murphy ran against Marcus Smith. In a three-cornered election the liberal and prohibitionist Democrats appear to have deserted Smith to vote for O'Neill. As a result Murphy carried the day. In the meantime, Cleveland veered toward the conservative Democrats again when he removed Hughes and appointed as governor a "pure type of the old time Southern politician," Benjamin J. Franklin (1896–97) of Phoenix.[78]

As if committed to some party theory of checks and balances, Arizona went to the polls in 1896 and elected John F. Wilson, a Democrat, over O'Neill, the Republican candidate, and two prohibitionists, while the country itself went Republican. Yet for Arizona, Wilson's election seemed a wise choice, for he was also a silverite; and the national Democratic platform now included a silver plank and other clauses liberal enough to unite party factions. After the Populist fervor was over, Smith himself was reelected in 1898. By

75. The above is really a summary of the voluminous clippings in the Hughes "Scrapbook."
76. *Arizona Citizen*, April 19, 1893. New York *Times*, April 1, 1896.
77. W. O. O'Neill File, APHS.
78. Benjamin J. Franklin File, APHS.

then he had so consolidated his Democratic machine that with one two-year exception the territory returned either himself or his party colleague, John F. Wilson, as delegate for the next twelve years. Smith's task, both as delegate and as conservative, was made easier when McKinley reappointed Murphy to the governor's chair in 1898. With two ardent statehood advocates in office again, it was time to renew the crusade for admission.

Wilson's election in 1896 and the popularity of N. O. Murphy go a long way to support the contention of historians that Western silverites were neither good radicals nor good populists. In Arizona free silver was a practical bread-and-butter issue. Wilson's election was buttressed by the nineteenth Arizona Assembly, which has been described as the most conservative in territorial history.[79] Three-fourths of the councilmen and seven-eights of the representatives were Democrats, and all were successful miners, ranchers, and merchants. Arizona still practiced a politics of development, but increasingly the belief was that local self-development and home rule were the best ways to realize Arizona's full economic promise.

Delegate Smith himself ran for reelection on a statehood platform in 1898, and informal conventions endorsed the movement. Unknown to Smith and the Arizonians, a strange combination of anti-Western attitudes in Congress, the Spanish-American War, the rise of the muckrakers and the progressives, and the simultaneous admission efforts of New Mexico and Oklahoma were to complicate and frustrate the Arizona statehood cause for a dozen years. In the words of Claude G. Bowers, it was to become "one of the most stubborn and historic contests over the conversion of Territories into States in the history of the Union."[80] The final "Americanization" of Arizona and New Mexico was to be a saga that the Southwest would never forget.

In reviewing the evolution of politics and political institutions in Arizona, it is remarkable to see how similar the overall process was to that found in other territories. During its first fifteen years of

79. James H. McClintock, *Nineteenth Legislature of Arizona, 1897* (Phoenix, 1897), p. 6, pamphlet.
80. Claude G. Bowers, *Beveridge and the Progressive Era* (Cambridge, Mass., 1932), p. 182.

existence Arizona was ruled by a combination of federal appointees and a merchant and/or miner oligarchy, variations of which could be found in New Mexico, Colorado, Dakota, and early Montana and Idaho. It must be concluded that a set of frontier conditions operated in territories west of the Mississippi which forced a fusion of political and economic affairs. Because of the Indian menace, the fusion was particularly strong in Arizona. But after conditions were sufficiently peaceful to allow the territorial economy to develop, the local leaders always chose the delegate from their own ranks and came to view the federal appointees as outsiders. This rising provincialism inevitably led to a demand that local men be appointed to federal office and to a firm belief in home rule through statehood.

Arizona had no real parties until the region was sufficiently developed to afford them, and even then the issues continued to be familiar frontier ones concerning Indian defense and policy, federal aid, transportation and railroads, and general economic development. This pattern, too, was common to all territories. The fact that local areas within a territory struggled with other local areas for the chance to be a political capital or a railroad center, or to carry off some other economic prize, was so overriding a characteristic of all American frontiers that states rights and sectionalism were almost inevitably by-products of the frontier condition. The politics of development practiced in the territories would also seem to imply that both a sectional and an "economic interpretation" of frontier history should prove far more rewarding than the view that the West was nationalistic in its views and uniquely democratic in its philosophy.

Yet it would be incorrect to say that a Beardian interpretation best explains frontier or Southwestern history. If daily politics centered around the problems of material progress and development, the institutions themselves were not only traditional but tended to come from the more fully developed neighboring states as well. What was familiar continued to be used until it did not work—unless, as in the case of Utah the population deliberately chose to be different, or, as in the case of New Mexico the cultural heritage was different. For Arizona the two pacesetters were California and Nevada. Not only did county government, mining customs and law, and many political attitudes come from these states, but many of the political figures also came to Arizona via the coast. Of the thirty-six members of the 1897 Assembly, for example, at least twelve had migrated to Arizona only after a sojourn in California. Two of its governors were Nevada politicians, and a third was from California. As a major metropolitan business center, San Francisco was in many ways the economic capital of the territory. Nor could anyone ignore the powerful influence of the Southern Pacific in the territory. The power of California was matched in some areas—particularly in the copper regions—with the power of Eastern corporations, so that Arizona became an economic colony of outside interests just as so many other Western states and territories did between 1865 and 1900.

The majority of Arizona's settlers, whether from California, the Northeast, the Midwest, or the South, were not really at war with American institutions. They accepted the common law, a court system, public education, a standard county and territorial government, American land law, and adapted themselves to new water laws. While there were shades of difference between northern Arizona—which had many settlers with Northeastern and Midwestern backgrounds—and southern Arizona, which boasted a large population of Southerners and Westerners, the two actually worked together to force the local cultural minorities to accept American ways. Indeed the Arizonians were made more conscious of their heritage by its very contrast with Spanish-American customs and the distinct social qualities of the Mormon minority there. The way in which the majority used the minority, either as political whipping boys or as allies, was so familiar that the process needs no further explanation.

While Arizona was safely "American" in 1900, and its expanding population numbered more than 120,000 that year, its people were not yet a whole. Arizona is still a "mining camp," wrote Senator Albert Beveridge disdainfully when he visited the territory in 1902. The makeup of only eight communities during the period from 1880 to 1900 suggests that while it was more than a mining camp, social disorganization did exist there. The Hopi pueblos found themselves enclaved in the midst of a Navajo reserve. Flagstaff was a lumbering town with a population that often hailed from other lumbering regions as far east as Maine. Prescott was a Midwestern town in appearance and population, while Tucson was Southern and "Mexican." Tombstone could have been a California or Nevada mineral rush town. Tempe was Mormon, and Bisbee was a company town half-filled with Sonoran workers. Phoenix, with its mixture of big schemers and small fruit farmers, was beginning to look like a southern California agricultural center or a smaller Los Angeles. And scattered both north and south were huge ranches resembling those found in Texas, Colorado, and New Mexico.

In 1900 Arizona may still have been a frontier physically speaking, and it was not yet a single society, yet its very disparateness was such an American quality that these conditions never prevented a general faith in progress and change. Governor Zulick struck the keynote in 1887 when he said that the territory was being "peopled by a sturdy, liberal, and progressive body of citizens," who were "making social as well as industrial progress."

The Admission of Arizona and New Mexico to the Union 1900–1912

We had rather be a Territory for the balance of time than to
be joined to that Republican unproductive gang.
Delegate Marcus Smith to
Senator John Sharpe Williams,
November 21, 1905

There is no power on earth that will move Beveridge
except the President.
Delegate W. F. Andrews to
Governor George Curry
December 31, 1907

 The final struggle to gain statehood for Arizona and
New Mexico lasted from 1901 to 1912 and was the
longest sustained admission fight in American territorial history.[1] It also took place under conditions
that no other territories had ever experienced, for
the movement became entangled in three great na-
tional debates. The first of these concerned the continuing argument
growing out of the Spanish-American War: whether America should
be an imperial nation with colonies or should accept the new pos-

1. The Arizona statehood fight is treated briefly in Lockwood, *Pioneer Days in
Arizona*, pp. 368–78; that of New Mexico more thoroughly in Marion Dargan, "New
Mexico's Fight for Statehood, 1895–1912," *NMHR, 14* (1939), 1–33, 121 ff.; *15*,
133 ff.; *16*, 70–103, 379–400. See also Claude G. Bowers, *Beveridge and the Progressive Era* (New York, 1932), pp. 182 ff.

sessions of Puerto Rico and the Philippines as an eventual part of the American Union. When Theodore Roosevelt became president after McKinley's assassination in 1901, the imperial approach to backward or underdeveloped areas now had, as it were, administration approval. More important for the Southwest was the fact that the war had been with Spain. Thus the backward and underdeveloped colonies that the United States had acquired possessed a Spanish colonial culture, possessed also by Arizona and New Mexico in varying proportions. This rather tenuous connection between American territories and overseas possessions would not have been important had not Roosevelt himself appointed a number of his Rough Riders to office in the territories. Two of them, Alexander O. Brodie (1902–05) and George Curry (1907–10), were to serve as governors of Arizona and New Mexico.[2]

The second debate concerned the use and disposition of national resources in the Far Southwest. Roosevelt's accession also meant that the conservation movement, now over ten years old, would take on new strength. The appointment of Gifford Pinchot to head the Forestry Service, for example, vitally affected the Southwest, for many of the remaining public lands—now that the Court of Private Land Claims was winding up its work—were in Arizona and New Mexico. Between 1901 and 1912 millions of acres were withdrawn from the public domain in these two states. The eventual result was that 15 per cent of the lands in Arizona and 12 per cent of those in New Mexico were set aside as national forests.[3] Since nearly every prominent rancher in New Mexico was hit by these measures, the resentment and political agitation that resulted kept the territory in a turmoil for ten years. Governor Otero's hostility to Roosevelt, and the fact that education lands granted by Congress to New Mexico in 1898 had been turned into a large speculation scheme undoubtedly prompted the "Little Governor" not to seek reappointment in 1905. A major part of Governor Hagerman's administration (1906–07) was also concerned with land affairs, before he was removed from office for selling certain public lands without proper authority. Two federal attorneys, Ormsby

2. Wyllys, *Arizona*, p. 181.
3. Perrigo, *Our Spanish Southwest*, pp. 336–41.

McHarg and Edward P. Holcombe, who actually appear to have been agents for Pinchot, found evidence of land frauds that implicated the territorial secretary, James W. Raynolds, Attorney General George Prichard, and the representative of a Pennsylvania land company, Willard S. Hopewell. Similarly George Curry's term as governor was filled with protests over withdrawal of lands from the public domain for forest reserves or for land reclamation purposes.[4]

These vigorous measures on behalf of the national welfare brought in their train a host of new government regulations. After 1906 cattlemen and sheepherders needed a license to graze their herds on public lands. Lumbermen had to obey cutting and conservation measures— if, indeed, they were allowed to use the timber at all. The Spanish-Americans who had traditionally grazed their sheep where they wished and had gone to the mountains to cut trees when they needed wood were now forbidden to do these things. From the very beginning, therefore, the Southwest was opposed to the Roosevelt-Pinchot forestry and conservation policies.[5]

An integral part of the conservation program involved the reclamation of arid lands and the preservation of local water supplies. Here the shoe was often on the other foot, for the territories generally badgered the government for aid in developing these resources. But whatever attitudes the territorial leaders held on such questions, the conflict over conservation affected the fortunes of the statehood struggle.[6]

Finally, the Republican Party and the entire country were caught up in the ferment of Progressivism. In Congress the growing split between conservative and insurgent Republicans greatly hindered the

4. These facts are brought out in the voluminous correspondence found in the Official Papers and Letterbooks of Governors M. A. Otero, H. J. Hagerman, and George Curry, located in NMSRC, Santa Fe.

5. See B. S. Rodey to Hon. L. O. Fullen, September 4, 1910; Otero to Rodey, May 4, 1904, protesting the creation of a forest reserve in the Black Mountains, ibid. See also H. J. Hagerman to William F. Andrews, April 30, 1906; Hagerman to W. P. Mudgett (N.D., 1907) ; Hagerman to W. P. Sanders, January 28, 1907; and Hagerman to Theodore Roosevelt, February 4, 1907, in Official Papers and Letterbooks of Governor H. J. Hagerman.

6. Hagerman to Governor Jesse F. McDonald of Colorado, January 2, 1907, Hagerman Papers. Perrigo, *Our Spanish Southwest*, pp. 336–37.

statehood cause. At first, Congressional liberals saw statehood as a conservative plot and therefore opposed admission; after 1908, however, the conservative Taft felt that the Arizona statehood movement was an insurgent plot and opposed admission for that reason. Within the two states themselves progressive ideals threatened to disrupt the unity of both parties. To gain admission, therefore, the statehood politicians had to thread their way past the heritage of the Spanish-American War, the conservation crusade, and the Progressive movement, before they could claim victory. Not since the slavery issue had complicated the admission of new states between 1820 and 1860 had there been so many issues to hamper the cause of statehood.

After 1900 the efforts of Marcus Smith, N. O. Murphy, and the statehood forces in Arizona were paralleled in New Mexico by the activities of Bernard S. Rodey, an exuberant, enthusiastic, Irish-born politician who had come to New Mexico in 1881 as secretary to the general manager of the Atlantic and Pacific Railroad. Rodey had settled in the boom town of Albuquerque, where he was admitted to the bar. He quickly allied himself to Frank A. Hubbell's Republican machine there, and by 1900 he had collected enough of a following to run for the delegateship on a statehood platform.[7] Rodey's witty nature and his ability to fire an audience for a cause soon earned him the nickname "Statehood Rodey." He was elected without difficulty that year.

Once in office Rodey very shrewdly associated statehood with the burning local issues of the day. In 1901 the Spanish-Americans in the territory became concerned that an international dam—the Elephant Butte project—was to be built across the Rio Grande in such a way that it would cut off water necessary for irrigated farming below Hot Springs, New Mexico. Rodey not only promised that statehood could defeat the dam but cleverly built up the idea that the dam itself was a scheme of nonresident Texas "birds of passage."[8]

Shortly after his election Rodey turned the annual territorial fair at Albuquerque into an informal statehood convention. There he and the proponents of admission associated the statehood movement with the possible defeat of a proposed federal lease law that promised to ex-

7. Bernard S. Rodey in *Biographical Directory of the American Congress.*
8. McDowell, "Opposition to Statehood," pp. 76, 82 ff., 88 ff.

clude cattlemen and herders from public lands and forested areas. After securing approval of the statehood crusaders, Rodey marched off to Washington to take his seat in the Fifty-Seventh Congress.[9]

Rodey had considerable cause for optimism that fall, for Delegate Marcus Smith of Arizona and Delegate Dennis T. Flynn of Oklahoma Territory agreed to join Rodey and to fight for the simultaneous admission of all three states. Flynn wrote Smith: "I am going to make a straight out fight for Oklahoma, and if I can be of any assistance to you I will do so."[10] It was also true that the national press now seemed favorable to admission. A majority of Democratic congressmen approved of statehood, and by 1901 Smith and Rodey had persuaded Senators Matt Quay of Pennsylvania, Henry M. Teller of Colorado, Stephen Elkins of West Virginia, and William Clark of Montana to support the cause as well.[11]

After much preliminary work on an omnibus bill to admit all three territories, the measure passed the House on May 9, 1902. While Marcus Smith was in wretched health during these months and was unable to run for reelection in 1902, another Democrat, Colonel John F. Wilson, was chosen delegate in his stead. Wilson joined Rodey and Flynn to carry the fight, until Smith returned to office again in 1904.[12]

Thus far the omnibus bill had experienced no great opposition, but when it reached the Senate, it was referred to the Committee on Territories, whose chairman was Senator Albert J. Beveridge of Indiana. Beveridge was an elegant and eloquent public figure. He was the author of a distinguished biography of John Marshall, and after his retirement from the Senate he was to write a fine study of the early life of Lincoln. He was both an ardent nationalist and a good Progressive. Quite paradoxically, he was also a nativist and an imperialist. What the three delegates did not know was that the Senator had formed a highly unfavorable view of colonial Spanish-Americans during the war with Spain in 1898. Yet all the while he had supported his friends Henry Cabot Lodge and Theodore Roosevelt in their de-

9. Rodey to Otero, August 20, 28, 1901, Otero Papers.
10. D. T. Flynn to Rodey, August 31, 1901, Otero Papers.
11. See Beatrice A. Cottrell, "Senate Action on the Omnibus Bill of 1902" (Master's thesis, University of New Mexico), for coverage of Smith's activities.
12. Langston, "Arizona's Statehood Fight," p. 30.

mands for the acquisition of overseas possessions! These initial views were further entrenched when he made a flying trip to the Philippines after the war, where he had been appalled by the low standards of living and the backwardness of the people there.[13]

When in the early fall of 1902, Beveridge and his committee took up the question of admission, he and a subcommittee made a whirlwind tour of the three Western territories. From the questions he asked it was clear that he liked "American" Oklahoma but that he was acutely hostile to the idea of statehood for "frontier" Arizona and "Mexican" New Mexico.[14] The reasons were not hard to find. As a Progressive and as a friend of many muckraker journalists, Beveridge soon became convinced that the statehood movements in Arizona and New Mexico were part of a massive scheme by large mining and railroad interests to seize political control of the region. He found, for example, that Senator William Clark of Montana owned the United Verde Mine in Arizona and that Senator Boies Penrose of Pennsylvania and his brother had mining properties there as well. In New Mexico, Matthew Quay and Congressman William F. "Bull" Andrews were anxious to launch certain questionable railroad projects there that needed state aid.[15]

Yet it appears that Beveridge's real reasons were not economic or reformist but cultural. He returned to Washington believing that the Spanish-speaking residents of the Southwest were at best second-class citizens—passive, pliant, and uneducated. Beveridge and his supporters were to argue for the next eight years that the Spanish-Americans were not at home with United States law, its court and school systems, or even with the English language. To Beveridge, in fact, the refusal to learn English was tantamount to a mild form of treason.[16] Beveridge's condescending views were not confined to Spanish-Americans, for he and other senators spoke of the Mormon minority in Arizona in disparaging terms throughout the period of the statehood movement.

13. Bowers, *Beveridge,* pp. 182 ff.
14. Charles Edgar Maddox, "The Statehood Policy of Albert J. Beveridge, 1901–1911" (Master's thesis, University of New Mexico, 1938), p. 42.
15. Ibid., pp. 41–43, 57–58.
16. Ibid., pp. 46, 60, 72. Langston, pp. 38–47.

This belief in ethnic and cultural incompatibility was further rein-forced by the impression that the Southwest was some sort of modern-day "Great American Desert," which lacked enough water, good soil, adequate population, and the general wherewithal to support civilized man. Ironically, the Westerners themselves had contributed to this belief by their constant demands for new land and water laws and by their appeals for government aid to develop irrigation.[17]

When Beveridge reported the omnibus bill out of committee in January 1903, he urged statehood for Oklahoma, but he omitted all reference to the other two territories. Beveridge's reasons for the omis-sion probably surprised his hearers, for while he touched on the role of big business in the statehood movement, his real argument was that:

The people must be sufficient in number; they must be on an equal-ity with the remainder of the people of the nation in all that consti-tutes effective citizenship; they must have developed the resources of the land they occupy; and finally have further resources suscep-tible of like development to bring their proposed new state up to the average of the remainder of the nation.

Future senators, Beveridge concluded, "should stand for a quantity of people and not a quantity of land." To the Senator the Far South-west was still a backward and underdeveloped colonial area.

Long before Beveridge had actually made his report, however, the statehood advocates had learned of his hostility. Local leaders from Arizona and New Mexico rushed to Washington to give his subcom-mittee favorable statistics, but to little avail. Speaking of Beveridge's swift visit to the Southwest, Smith complained that he had "met the committee but could never catch up with it," and concluded the whole thing was "a star-chamber proceeding from first to last."[18] By the time Congress convened in December 1902, it was also obvious that Beveridge had lined up a formidable array of statehood oppon-ents, including Senators Thomas R. Bard, Nelson Aldrich, Knute Nel-

17. Maddox, p. 83.
18. Quoted in Langston, p. 49.

son, Chauncey Depew, Henry Cabot Lodge, and even Mark Hanna. President Roosevelt was also impressed with Beveridge's antiadmission arguments and silently upheld him for the next six years.[19] In cooperation with Albert Shaw, editor of the *Review of Reviews,* Beveridge even enlisted the aid of magazine and newspaper writers to question the wisdom of admission, and he called on technical experts and scholars to testify against statehood.[20]

Despite this adverse report on admission, the pro-statehood forces were not worried. Senators Matt Quay of Pennsylvania and William Bates of Tennessee submitted separate reports in favor of the omnibus bill of 1902, while Senator W. R. Hearst and the Democrats also turned in pro-statehood recommendations. Nevertheless Beveridge was not to be defeated. After mobilizing many other senators and using filibuster techniques, he resorted to an unexpected device. For reasons of courtesy no vote could take place without his presence as chairman of the Territorial Committee. At the crucial moment he hid on the third floor of Gifford Pinchot's home for a week.[21] The time passed when a territorial bill could be considered in 1903, and no vote took place in the Fifty Seventh Congress.

Beveridge's attitude, while hostile, was not totally negative. A year and a half later he himself advocated a bill to admit Arizona and New Mexico jointly as a single state. But while "jointure"—as the 1904–05 proposal soon came to be called—seemed reasonable to the East and fitted Beveridge's own rules for admission, it caused a storm of disapproval in the Southwest. Marcus Smith said acidly of Beveridge's one state bill that "he proceeds from his own argument on the principle that one rotten egg is bad, but two rotten ones would make a fine omelet."[22]

Smith himself argued against jointure by declaring that Arizona business connections were with California, while those of New Mexico were Eastern. The opposition was not merely political and economic, for the Spanish-Americans in New Mexico did not care to become a

19. Maddox, pp. 106–07.
20. Ibid., pp. 10–11, 46. Langston, p. 33.
21. Maddox, p. 85.
22. *The Statehood Bill: Speech of Hon. M. A. Smith* (Washington, 1902), p. 11, pamphlet.

minority in a giant state when they could be a majority in a smaller one. Using the same reasoning, the Anglo-American citizens of Arizona were opposed to an increase in the proportion of their own Spanish-American minority. Yet when a committee from the two territories called at the White House to protest jointure, Governor Otero reported that "our talk did not seem to impress President Roosevelt in the slightest degree."[23]

In April 1904 a joint statehood bill passed the House of Representatives, and although the bill failed to pass the Senate that year—an outcome which the citizens of Tucson celebrated—the administration forces had a second jointure measure before Congress by 1905. This bill had the express approval of Roosevelt, who, in turn, applied pressure on his governors in Arizona and New Mexico to accept it. The subsequent local developments beautifully illustrated the basically different reactions and political conditions in Arizona and New Mexico. In Arizona, Governor Brodie's successor, Joseph K. Kibbey (1905–10), refused to support jointure even though virtually ordered to by Roosevelt. An antijointure convention met in Phoenix to back up Kibbey, while Mark Smith was returned to Washington to run the antijointure campaign in Congress. So irate was the Phoenix city council at the President's pressure that it changed the name of Roosevelt Street to that of Cleveland.[24]

In New Mexico, on the other hand, a game of political intrigue ensued which would have been worthy of the most adept members of the old Santa Fe Ring. When he came up for reelection in 1904, "Statehood Rodey," who was by now probably the most popular political figure in the territory, found himself caught in the crossfire of a political feud between his Albuquerque sponsor, Frank A. Hubbell, and Governor Otero. When Rodey refused to abandon Hubbell, Otero persuaded the Republican Party to pass over Rodey for delegate and to nominate, instead, a newcomer: former Congressman "Bull" Andrews of Pennsylvania. Justifiably angry at Otero's action, Rodey ran

23. Mary J. Masters, "New Mexico's Struggle for Statehood, 1903–1907" (Master's thesis, University of New Mexico, 1942), p. 20.

24. Waldemar Westergaard, "Senator Thomas R. Bard and the Arizona-New Mexico Controversy," Historical Society of Southern California, *Annual Publications* (Los Angeles, 1919), p. 16.

on a jointure ticket with the backing of Senator Beveridge, but the Andrews forces, with the backing of Thomas B. Catron, carried the day in a close and questionable election. Clearly a new Santa Fe Ring was in operation.[25]

The election of two single state delegates apparently did not worry either Beveridge or Roosevelt. Matt Quay, the chief defender of the single-state plan, had died in 1904. The jointure plan itself seemed well on the way to realization when Uncle Joe Cannon crushed an insurgent separate-state movement in the House in January 1906 and pushed through Congressman Edward L. Hamilton's jointure bill.[26] Four days later a receptive Beveridge reported it to the Senate. This time, however, it was Marcus Smith's turn to maneuver. First, the Arizona Delegate persuaded Senator Joseph R. Foraker of Ohio to propose an amendment (drafted by Smith) that would allow the two territories to hold a referendum on jointure. A combination of Foraker's old-fashioned eloquence and the Progressive love of referendum got the amendment adopted by a vote of 42 to 29. This was followed by a second vote to delete the name of Arizona and New Mexico from the Hamilton bill. Now only the name of Oklahoma was left in the measure. The act was then passed, and while Oklahomans were overjoyed at the prospect of admission, the citizens of Arizona once again celebrated their temporary escape from jointure with a parade.[27]

It still remained for the two territories to approve or denounce jointure by referendum. The outcome in Arizona was anticipated by Mark Smith when he explained to Senator John Sharpe Williams that "we had rather be a Territory for the balance of time than to be joined to that Republican unproductive gang."[28] True to his words, Arizona overwhelmingly rejected the idea of jointure.

In New Mexico the referendum had a very different history. Ex-Governor Otero, Thomas Catron, and Judge N. B. Laughlin were such outright single-staters that they refused to cooperate with Beveridge or Roosevelt. Roosevelt's young gubernatorial appointee, H. J. Hag-

25. Masters, pp. 39–40.
26. Maddox, pp. 86–92.
27. Langston, pp. 65 ff.
28. Smith to Williams, November 21, 1905, in Private Letter Books of M. A. Smith, University of Arizona Library, Tucson.

erman, agreed to jointure, but his own reformist administration was at loggerheads with the territorial Republican Party machine, which was now headed by a master politician, Holm O. Bursum. The machine disliked jointure as much as the Arizonans did, but its leaders apparently agreed to support it if Roosevelt would remove the unpopular Hagerman and let the conservative Republicans of New Mexico continue undisturbed in power. Just what arrangements were made is not known, but Hagerman was soon replaced by a former Rough Rider and Philippine police commissioner, George Curry, while "Bull" Andrews was reelected delegate on a projointure ticket in 1906! The campaign itself was accompanied by much obvious press propaganda for jointure, and when the vote was counted there was also clear evidence of fraud. But jointure was approved in New Mexico, and Delegate Andrews squeaked in with less than a majority of 400 votes.[29]

Ironically, the whole jointure campaign had helped defeat a reform governor in New Mexico and had reelected "Bull" Andrews, who was in Beveridge's eyes both a speculator and a former ally of Matt Quay. It had also put a new Santa Fe Ring into power, with Holm Bursum as its leader. In Arizona jointure had reelected Mark Smith, Beveridge's sworn enemy. A recent scholar has shown that Bursum himself secretly hoped that by approving jointure while Arizona disapproved it, New Mexico would be rewarded by being admitted as a single state![30] Had Beveridge and Roosevelt deliberately set out to defeat their own program of reform and admission, they could not have been more successful.

During the long drawn-out struggle over jointure, Roosevelt finally appears to have changed his mind, for in 1908 in his last annual message to Congress he advocated the admission of Arizona and New Mexico as two separate states. That previous summer the Republican Party had also endorsed separate admission. Undoubtedly Roosevelt's own warm friendship for Governor George Curry of New Mexico and the fact that Arizona had diplomatically elected a Republican delegate

29. Donald B. Leopard, "Joint Statehood, 1906" (Master's thesis, University of New Mexico, 1958), pp. 11–33 passim.

30. Ibid., p. 62.

in 1908 increased his receptiveness, but whatever the reasons for Roosevelt's change of heart, Beveridge's opposition now seemed less powerful.

Meanwhile, Beveridge's own arguments against admission became increasingly political. By September 1909 he was urging Taft to avoid all statehood legislation, since it would result in sending two Democrats to the Senate from Arizona and would send two nonreform Republicans (Curry and Andrews) from New Mexico. Beveridge also feared that both new states would elect Democratic congressmen.[31]

Taft himself was not particularly favorable to admission, but he refused to agitate to keep the territories out of the Union. The new President actually appears to have appointed Richard E. Sloan (1910–12) and T. B. Mills (1910–12), former judges, as governors of both Arizona and New Mexico, so that they could make the necessary legal, judicial, and constitutional adjustments necessary in a transition to statehood.[32] At last, on January 14, 1910, Representative Edward L. Hamilton of the House Committee on Territories introduced an enabling act, and though Beveridge held it up for two months in the Senate until a good school-lands clause was included, it passed both houses. Even then the measure was loaded with qualifications which revealed continued suspicion of Southwestern motives for statehood. Beveridge himself made a final attempt to add provisos that would forbid anyone who could not read or speak English to vote or hold office, and even Curry and Andrews — with their eyes on the Spanish-American vote in New Mexico — did not manage to have all language requirements deleted from the final bill.[33]

The Arizona and New Mexico admission fights demonstrated the familiar struggle of a region acting to resist outside authority which was attempting to standardize and force conformity. In this case the authority wanted adherence to national Republican and Progressive ideals. Though the federal government, by trying to make the two territories into one, was trying to be fair and achieve proportional

31. Maddox, pp. 103–08.
32. Richard E. Sloan, *Memories of an Arizona Judge* (Stanford, Cal., 1932), bears this out, as do the Official Papers and Letter Books of Governor T. B. Mills, NMSRC.
33. Curry to Andrews, February 16, 1910, Curry Papers.

representation in the national sense, it violated history, local political habits, and customs in a rather obtuse way. On the other hand, indignation over jointure helped make statehood a popular rather than a politician's cause.

The struggle for statehood also illustrates another classic pattern in American political history—how national issues and fads can so vitally affect local causes. Not only did admission become entangled in the prohibition issue and involved in the debates over women's rights and new ideas like the initiative and the referendum, but it was clouded by the free-silver controversy, war, conservation, land policies, feelings about the new immigration, and antisouthwestern attitudes. The regional struggle between East and West and the political struggle between conservative and insurgent Republicans in the 1910 Congress played vital roles as well. All in all, then, the admission debate mirrored American prejudices and preoccupations at the turn of the century and demonstrated how the concerns of the "metropolis" and the nation could affect the fortunes of the "province."

It has been traditional for Southwestern historians to blame Roosevelt, Taft, Beveridge, and Pinchot for holding up statehood. Yet many Arizonans and New Mexicans, first openly and later secretly, supported continued territorial status. More than once the influential New Mexican banker Jefferson Raynolds dashed off to Washington to oppose statehood. The Democrats in New Mexico opposed statehood throughout the last years before admission, for they felt it would perpetuate the Republicans and their Spanish-American supporters in power. Furthermore, neither state changed its traditional frontier attitudes toward land policy, conservation, lax elections, and public education enough to impress Congress. Indeed, Mark Smith spent most of his public career opposing federal land and water policies, and he continued to do so during the statehood crusade. William F. Andrews' correspondence with Governor Curry reveals that the former always wanted statehood for selfish and venal reasons and that Curry himself dreamed of a probusiness constitution. Thomas Catron tried at the last minute to defeat a fair water-rights clause in the New Mexican constitution, and Holm Bursum cynically used the whole statehood movement to establish a new Santa Fe Ring. At a crucial moment in 1909, Mark Smith did not hesitate to hold up the state-hood bill for two weeks until Arizona got a 600,000-acre grant of land.[34] It is not surprising therefore that Congress, Roosevelt, and Beveridge were so distrustful of the statehood movement.

What Congress, Roosevelt, and Taft did not realize, however, was that a large number of citizens in the Southwest had come to believe sincerely that territorial status was a terrible stigma and an insuffer-able mark of inferiority. They agreed with a remark made by Gov-ernor Prince in 1902 that "a Territory with bad officials is a despotism, and not a republic; it is ruled by men named by an authority 2,000 miles away, who are not responsible to any local instrument of power." Such men, he said, should be compared to Butcher Weyler in Cuba and the territory to "an East Indian State under Hastings."[35]

It was such sentiments, reminiscent of the assertions of local liberty in the thirteen colonies, that led the Arizona and New Mexico citizens to campaign for their own independence between 1900 and 1910. In so doing, they eventually forced Congress to observe the spirit of the Ordinance of 1787 rather than to pursue the imperial implications of Beveridge's New Nationalism. The nation had finally followed the flag into the Southwest.

The constitutional conventions of New Mexico and Arizona met at time when the nation stood at a political and social crossroads. Would they heed the cry of insurgents and Progressives for a "new freedom" and the "square deal," or would they stand pat with the conservatives now epitomized in President Taft? Not since the heyday of Populism had the country been so self-analytical or full of debate over the future.

The questioning and furor reached into the charming adobe city of Santa Fe in the fall of 1910, where 100 delegates gathered in the golden haze of September to write a state constitution for a region that had been a territory now for sixty-four years. Tremendous changes had overtaken the remote "provincia interna" of New Spain in the hundred years since Don Pedro Pino had begged for a new era in

34. Andrews to Curry, February 4, 1909, Curry Papers.
35. L. B. Prince, "Statehood Pamphlet," Otero Papers.

New Mexico. Yet American conquest still was an incomplete revolution. Although a thousand New Mexicans were to cast their votes for a Socialist candidate for delegate that year, the political patterns built by the Republican Party—using local customs—still remained; the patron system still worked; and there was still a clear cultural distinction between Spanish and Anglo-American habits and attitudes. As if to symbolize the necessary compromise, thirty-two of the delegates in the convention were Spanish-Americans while sixty-eight were Americans, although the observer might be justly confused by noting that the convention secretary was named George Washington Armijo.[36]

In stark contrast to the Arizona constitutional convention, the New Mexican one was Republican, cautious, and conservative. Led by Holm Bursum, Solomon Luna, Charles Springer, and Charles A. Spiess and with Thomas Catron playing an independent role, the members wrote a conservative document that denied women the vote, evaded the prohibition issue, and rejected most Progressive ideas. They made it virtually impossible to amend the new document. One scholar has observed it was a perfect 1810 model, while Arizona's was a 1910 one.[37]

Once completed, the constitution raised both a liberal and partisan storm. Eighteen Democratic members in the convention refused to sign it, and ex-delegate Harvey B. Fergusson, the dynamic Albuquerque lawyer, joined other Progressives in an attempt to defeat its ratification. Claiming that "it perpetuates in power the old ring which has misgoverned New Mexico as a territory so long," Fergusson toured the territory in a speech-making campaign and bombarded Democratic senators with letters urging them to defeat it.[38] But it was impossible to change the mood of a long-established, tradition-bound region overnight, so that a majority of the citizens, anxious to gain statehood, approved of the constitution.

36. See Miscellaneous Manuscripts and Documents Relating to the New Mexico Constitutional Convention of 1910, NMHS.

37. John R. Murdock, "Constitutional Development of Arizona" (Phoenix?, 1930), p. 30.

38. Fergusson to George E. Chamberlain, June 17, 1911; to A. A. Jones, June 19, 1911; to R. L. Owens, July 5, 1911; to W. J. Bryan, September 15, 1911, in H. B. Fergusson Statehood Letters, University of New Mexico Library, Albuquerque.

The conservative victory was not quite complete, however, for in the first state election W. C. McDonald, a Democrat, became governor when Progressive Republicans, among them ex-governor Hagerman, bolted their own party to support him. The New Mexico Democrats, with the support of Taft himself, also persuaded Congress to pass the Smith-Flood amendment, which required a change in the amending clause and provided a system of ratification by means of a "blue ballot" that would prevent fraud at the polls. With these changes and their ratification, Taft admitted New Mexico to the Union on Jan 6, 1912. As prominent New Mexicans crowded about the President, Taft remarked: " 'Well it is all over, I am glad to give you life.' " Then he smiled and added, " 'I hope you will be healthy.' " That year Thomas B. Catron, who had dreamed of a Senate seat since 1873, joined Albert B. Fall to represent his state in the national upper house, while ex-governor George Curry and Harvey B. Fergusson became New Mexico's first congressmen.

To the west, the Arizonans, also in convention, were "bursting out all over" with progressive ideas. This liberal spirit had expressed itself sporadically ever since "Bucky" O'Neill had run for Congress on a Populist antirailroad ticket in 1896 and 1898. Temperance and female suffrage crusades accounted for other outbursts, and the rise of labor unions in mining regions provided still other sources of radical discontent. In party terms, however, the liberal protest had become increasingly identified with an anti-Mark Smith wing of the Democratic Party, for Smith and his conservative law partner, Eugene S. Ives, were now obviously spending much time as legal counsel for railroad and copper companies and were now being called "Corporation Democrats."[39]

The acknowledged leader of the Arizona progressive and labor Democrats was George W. P. Hunt, a portly, balding, bespectacled businessman and publisher from Globe. The poker-faced Hunt was to prove one of the most capable and enduring public men in Arizona history, and once statehood was achieved, he was to serve as gov-

39. The correspondence between Smith and Ives in the Eugene S. Ives Letter Books, 1901–1913, in the University of Arizona Library, indicate this. See also Tucson *Citizen*, July 18, 1910.

ernor for fifteen years. Hunt's political success was based on the muckraker principle: a full exposure of every issue to the public. Fond of catch phrases and new crusades, he kept Arizona in a healthy ferment for three decades, and he gave to the state the liberal activist spirit that Frederick Jackson Turner so often identified as a frontier trait.[40]

In 1910 Hunt, as spokesman for the liberal statehood forces, began a campaign to "start in with a clean slate and a clean state," by which he meant the adoption of the initiative, the referendum and recall, and the direct election of senators. Hunt actually traveled to Oregon and California to study Progressive constitutions and measures and to talk with liberal leaders. Refusing to compromise with Republicans or the conservative Democrats, the liberals of Arizona captured the constitutional convention in 1910 and made Hunt its president. Of the forty-one Democrats and eleven Republicans, some nine were cattlemen, fourteen were lawyers, five were miners, and four were merchants. The others represented a scattering of occupations ranging from saloon keepers to ministers.[41]

Typically, Hunt announced that the convention itself would operate in the full glare of public view and that there would be no caucuses. In the days that followed, proposals for female suffrage and prohibition vied with the initiative, referendum, and recall for attention, while a labor delegate from Bisbee introduced pro-union and anti-Pinkerton clauses. Still other delegates proposed to restrain courts from granting labor injunctions. The *Daily Globe* at one point declared that the "crimping of corporations is proceeding merrily."[42]

Along with these more familiar items, other delegates advocated a clause forbidding capital punishment, openly discussed and voted down segregation in schools, and considered the problem of child labor and juvenile crime. As the conservatives watched in growing

40. "G. W. P. Hunt" in *DAB*.

41. *Daily Globe* (Globe, Arizona), July 19, August 6, 1910, in the G. W. P. Hunt Scrapbooks in the University of Arizona Library.

42. Clipping from *Daily Globe* (n.d.) in Hunt Scrapbooks. The convention proceedings are available in four massive quarto volumes entitled "Complete Verbatim Report of Arizona Constitutional Convention, 1910," University of Arizona Library, Tucson.

horror, the convention voted to adopt initiative, referendum, and recall and to make recall applicable to judges on the bench. This act led President Taft, who visited Phoenix in the fall of 1910, to warn them against the "crank constitution" that he felt Oklahoma now had. But the delegates went on from there to approve of female suffrage, direct primaries, and direct elections of senators.[43]

In the realm of business and government the convention passed antilobbying and corrupt practices clauses, created a corporation commission, and established a valuation system for fixing railroad rates. Labor legislation included an antichild-labor measure and employer liability for employees, and made the path of unions easier in Arizona. Similarly, in water-rights clauses they modified traditional common law rules to fit the needs of a state dependent upon irrigation.[44]

The excitement over the writing of the constitution was mild compared to the furious ratification campaign. The Republicans, both in Washington and in Arizona, so violently opposed it that the administration founded a paper in Tucson to defeat the document. Accusations flew back and forth that it was a Socialist constitution, while others called it a clever corporation measure, and still others dismissed it as a creature of the Western Federation of Miners. Mark Smith warned voters that it would never be approved by Congress or Taft, but 77 per cent of the voters endorsed the 1910 constitution. The *Arizona Gazette* caught the spirit of the times in the headlines: "POPULAR GOVERNMENT SUCCEEDS OLD REGIME: SPECIAL INTEREST DETHRONED."[45]

The election of the first state government was also a wide-open affair, but the liberals succeeded in electing Hunt to the governor's chair and sent the youthful Carl Hayden to Congress. When the first legislature met, young Henry F. Ashurst, the "Boy Orator of Bill Williams Mountain," was elected to the Senate. Out of respect for Mark Smith's own statehood efforts and because of his continuing great power, the legislature also elected the perennial Delegate to the Senate.

43. See clippings from September to December, 1910, same source as above. President Taft made his remark in Phoenix on October 13.
44. The Los Angeles *Recorder*, December 13, 1910.
45. Arizona *Gazette* (Phoenix), February 10, 1911, in the Hunt Scrapbooks.

Arizona exuberance over statehood was temporarily dimmed when Taft declared he would veto admission unless the provision for the recall of judges was omitted from the Arizona constitution. A new resolution including this amendment had been signed and ratified by December 1911, so that all obstacles were cleared. Two months later, on St. Valentine's Day, 1912, Taft signed the proclamation that admitted Arizona into the Union. But shortly thereafter a Democratic legislature reinserted the "recall of judges" clause, and in the fall of 1912 a Democratic electorate voted for Woodrow Wilson. The youngest state was now in the forefront of the Progressive march.

A long and colorful but often painful era of political apprenticeship had come to an end for the Spanish borderlands of the American Southwest. American habits, customs, and democratic institutions—such as the two-party system, public schools, elective office, county government, and secular courts—were now established there, for while Congress never had a real territorial policy, it had always set these conditions as a minimal requirement. Yet the immutable fact of a mountainous, semi-arid environment remained, and the institutional and cultural compromises born out of the meeting of Mormon, Anglo-American, Spanish-American, and Indian would live on for generations to come. The fact of statehood symbolized that a satisfactory "Americanization" had been achieved. But in the process the unique qualities of the Far Southwest and the long persistence of the frontier period there had greatly affected and enriched the unfolding chronicle of American history.

Bibliographical Essay

 The titles in the following essay represent a highly selective list of manuscripts, documents, books, and articles, but hopefully they are the ones most pertinent to the study. In many cases a document or title illustrative of a theme will be cited in place of a more general source.

Any investigation of the territorial periods of the Four Corners States must begin with two excellent expositions of federal policy: Max Farrand, *The Legislation of Congress for the Government of the Organized Territories of the United States, 1789–1895* (Newark, 1896), and Earl S. Pomeroy, *The Territories and the United States, 1861–1890* (Philadelphia, 1947). The voluminous details and day-to-day workings of the territorial system are recorded in the many thousands of manuscript letters, public documents, newspapers, and printed reports which comprise the Territorial Papers of the United States in the National Archives, Washington, D.C. Selections from the Territorial Papers have been in the process of publication since 1933, but none of the volumes published thus far deal with the Far Southwest. Microfilm copies of the Territorial Papers dealing with the political histories of Colorado, New Mexico, Arizona, and Utah are easily available, however, and are cited in the appropriate places below.

Essential to a study of territorial history are large collections in the H. H. Bancroft Library (Berkeley), the Henry E. Huntington Library (San Marino), and the Beinecke Rare Book and Manuscript Library of Yale University. Each state historical society and state archives contains vital manuscripts and records necessary for an understanding of the territorial period. Finally, the libraries of the universities of Arizona, Colorado, New Mexico, and Utah house papers and sources of great value. Philip M. Hamer, *A Guide to Archives and Manuscripts in the United States* (New Haven, 1961), provides specific information about the most important materials in the state and local archives. For this study the Territorial Papers cited below seemed most relevant:

Territorial Papers of the U.S. Senate, 1789–1873 (RG 46):
  New Mexico, 1840–54 (Roll 14)
  Utah, 1849–70 (Roll 15)
  Colorado, 1860–68 (Roll 17)
  Arizona, 1857–65 (Roll 18)
State Department Territorial Papers (RG 59):
  New Mexico Territorial Papers, 1851–72 (Rolls 1–4) T–17
  Colorado Territorial Papers, 1859–74 (Roll 1) M–3
  Utah Territorial Papers, 1853–73 (Rolls 1–2) M 12
  Arizona Territorial Papers, 1864–72 (Roll 1, to 1867) M 342
Interior Department Territorial Papers (RG 48):
  New Mexico, 1851–1914 (Rolls 1–15) M 364
  Colorado, 1868–85
  Utah, 1878–96
  Arizona, 1868–1907

Both the State and Interior Territorial Papers contain official correspondence, executive proceedings, and reports. Of particular interest in these sometime routine documents are the reports of Governor Connelly of New Mexico to Secretary Seward on the Confederate invasion of New Mexico. Later the letters of Governor Lew Wallace to Secretary Schurz on the Lincoln County War do much to clarify Wallace's part in the difficulties.

The Appointments Division (Letters of Application and Recommendation) of the Department of State, and the Appointments Division and Patents and Miscellaneous Records of the Department of the Interior contain revealing letters concerning the various applicants for territorial office. In addition, the Indian Division of the Interior Department has in its Letters Received, 1849–1906, and Letters Sent, 1849–1907, materials concerning Indian troubles in Colorado between 1861 and 1867 which were used. Similarly, the Letters Received, 1860–69, by the Indian Division of the War Department were consulted in connection with both Colorado and Arizona Indian difficulties. The records of the Departments of the Treasury (RG 56) and Justice (RG 60) and those of the Bureau of Indian Affairs (RG 75)—the latter containing the field records of the various territorial superintendents— bear upon this study but were not consulted in detail.

National debate and legislation concerning territorial matters may be followed in *The Congressional Globe* (Washington, 1851–73), *The Congressional Record* (Washington, 1874–1910), and the *U.S. Statutes at Large*. The *Annual Reports* of the territorial governors were usually printed in the *Annual Report of the Secretary of State* (Washington, 1851–73) and in the *Annual Report of the Secretary of the Interior* (Washington, 1873–1910), but they were usually so politically discreet that the most valuable information contained therein was statistical. The Interior Department *Reports* contain useful reports from the Commissioner of Indian Affairs and from the Land Office which are of some value.

NEW MEXICO

MANUSCRIPTS

Of central importance to this study is the extensive William G. Ritch Collection in HEH. A former newspaper editor from Oshkosh, Wisconsin, Ritch served as territorial secretary of New Mexico from 1876 to 1884, and during that time he began to collect the materials of New Mexican history from the time of conquest to his own day (1846–96). The Collection consists of some thirty-one boxes of manuscript letters, copies of memoirs, diaries, interviews and legal papers, and thirteen volumes of newspaper clippings covering the period 1865 to 1896. The Collection deals in detail with the 1846 conquest, military and civil government, the Civil War period, Carleton's Navajo campaigns, Indian affairs to 1876, the Lincoln County War, private land grants, and the fight over secular versus religious education.

For the period of conquest the Ritch Collection must be supplemented with the Letters of Charles Bent to Manuel Alvarez, December 1839 to June 1846, NMHS, in which the Bent–Martinez controversy is detailed. The vast operations of Bent's Fort are recalled in the Letters of George Bent to George Hyde, 1906–11, YWA. The early Letters of Donaciano Vigil, NMHS, are of limited value, but William Montgomery Boggs, Narrative Adventures in 1844 and 1845, YWA, captures the flavor of the times nicely.

Debate on the organization of New Mexico Territory, the Texas–New Mexico boundary question, and "statehood" in 1849 may be followed in the collection of congressional speeches, brochures, and documents in YWA. A similar collection concerning the events of 1847–49 is in the Bancroft Library.

The colorful political history of New Mexico Territory may be traced through the papers of various officials. Annie H. Abel, ed., *The Official Correspondence of James S. Calhoun* (Washington, D.C., 1915), and Ralph P. Bieber, ed., "The Letters of William Carr Lane, 1852–54," in NMHS, *Publications, 6* (Santa Fe, 1928), make these manuscript materials available in print. The Papers of Secretary W. W. H. Davis, 1846–57, YWA, reveal the workings of the political cliques in New Mexico from 1853–57 along with Davis' own considerable political and economic ambitions. Civil War troubles may be traced in part through the reports of Governor Connelly to Seward mentioned above.

Although scattered correspondence relating to various governors may be found in the Official Governors' Files of New Mexico in NMSRC, they are of limited value. The Papers of Governor Lew Wallace (1878–81) are disappointing. Governor Lionel A. Sheldon (1881–85) composed for H. H. Bancroft a manuscript autobiography which is now in the Bancroft Library. Twenty-four Letters from Colonel J. Francisco Chavez to General H. H. Heath, 1867–69, APHS, reveal much about New Mexican delegate politics in those years.

The first significant collection of gubernatorial papers is that of Edmund G. Ross (1885–89) which also contains pamphlets, newspaper clippings, and items about politics, mining, and immigration. Ross' successor, L. Bradford Prince (1889–93) was an amateur historian whose papers include many important documents relating to politics and the statehood movement between 1889 and 1902. The voluminous Official Papers of Governor M. A. Otero (1897–1905), while often devoted to routine matters, graphically depict the statehood activities of Delegate Rodey. The Official Papers of Governors H. J. Hagerman (1905–07) and George Curry (1907–10) are excellent for a coverage of the conflicts between federal and local policies in the final years before statehood.

Three major collections concerning political affairs are to be found in the University of New Mexico Library, Albuquerque. The Papers of Dr. Michael Steck, Indian Superintendent, cover Indian affairs in extraordinary detail for the 1860s. Even more impressive and more pertinent are the Papers of Thomas B. Catron. Because he was a key political figure in New Mexican politics for over fifty years, his letters provide a major source of information about Republican politics, land grants, and the economic development of New Mexico. Finally, the Statehood Letters of Harvey B. Ferguson, 1910–11 offer insights into the conservative and progressive debate about admission.

PRINTED DOCUMENTS AND CONTEMPORARY ACCOUNTS

Ralph E. Twitchell, *The Spanish Archives of New Mexico* (2 vols. Cedar Rapids, Iowa, 1914), provides a convenient documentary history for the years preceding the American occupation of New Mexico. Mexican New Mexico is described in Pedro B. Pino, *Exposicion sucincta y sencilla de la provincia del Nueva Mexico* (Cadiz, 1812), YWA. Antonio Barreiro, *Ojeada sobre Nueva Mexico* (1832) is also useful but borrows from Pino and other accounts.

The rise of the Santa Fe trade and the coming of the gringo to New Mexico is treated in Josiah Gregg's delightful *Commerce of the Prairies* (2 vols. New York, 1844; Dallas, 1933); James Josiah Webb, *Adventures in the Santa Fe Trade, 1844–47*, ed. Ralph P. Bieber (Glendale, Calif., 1931); Lewis H. Garrard, *Wah-To-Yah and the Taos Trail* (Cincinnati, 1850; Norman, Okla., 1955). George A. Ruxton's *Adventures in New Mexico and the Rocky Mountains* (New York, 1847) is less valuable.

Printed materials relating to the period of conquest may be found in a series of broadsides and pamphlets in HEH concerned with military and political affairs between 1846 and 1851. The *Laws of the Assembly of New Mexico, 1847* (Santa Fe, 1848), HEH, is also instructive. These may be supplemented with a set of public addresses, pamphlets, and the famous *Kearny Code* or *Laws of the Territory of New Mexico* (Santa Fe, October 7, 1846) in YWA. Still other relevant documents—and particularly the statehood "Petition of the People of New Mexico . . . December 13, 1848 (Santa Fe, 1848) may be found in the Bancroft Library.

A number of special reports to Washington helped shape the views of the Polk, Taylor, and Fillmore administrations: J. A. Abert, *Report and Map of the Examination of New Mexico* (Washington, 1848); George A. McCall, *Report of the Secretary of War on the State of New Mexico* (Washington, 1851); and James H. Simpson, *Journal of a Military Reconnaissance from Santa Fe . . . to the Navajo Country* (Philadelphia, 1852).

The first legislative proceedings after territorial organization in 1850 are in the *House and Council Journals of the Territory of New Mexico, 1851–52* (Santa Fe, 1852). The *House and Council Journals* of subsequent Assemblies to 1901 have been consulted but the titles and imprints vary. The *Annual Messages* of the governors of New Mexico are conveniently contained in the *Journals. The Laws of the Territory of New Mexico, 1851–52* (Santa Fe, 1852) and for subsequent years are useful in revealing the economic and political concerns of the day. Useful, too, are L. Bradford Prince, comp., *General Laws of New Mexico from the "Kearny Code of 1846" to 1880* (Albany, N.Y., 1880); C. Valdez, comp., *Compiled Laws of New Mexico to 1885* (Topeka, Kans., 1885); and Victor and Bartlett, comp., *Compiled Laws of New Mexico to 1897* (Santa Fe, 1897).

Two sets of public addresses and pamphlets located respectively in HEH and YWA help clarify the first New Mexican delegate election in which Reynolds and Weightman were the contestants. Of these *R. H. Weightman to the Congress of the United States* (Washington, 1851) is revealing, if biased.

Southern interest and influence in New Mexico during the 1850s is seen in *An Act to Provide for the Protection of Property in Slaves in this Territory* (Santa Fe, 1859), and the *Pacific Railroad Speech of Hon. M. A. Otero of New Mexico* (Washington, 1858). The coming of the Civil War to New Mexico and political affairs to 1872 are covered in a series of proclamations and addresses to be found in HEH, NMHS, and YWA. The continuing Indian menace is described in *Indian Disturbances in the Territory of New Mexico*, H. of R. Exec. Doc. No. 24, 36th Cong. 2d Sess. (1861).

After the war the economic potentialities of New Mexico were advertised in a series of addresses and propaganda brochures of which the following are representative: Charles P. Clever, *New Mexico, Her Necessities for Railroad Communication with the Atlantic and Pacific States* (Washington, 1868), HEH; W. F. M. Arny, *Interesting Items Regarding New Mexico* (Santa Fe, 1873); Elias Brevoort, *New Mexico, Her Natural Resources and Attractions* (Santa Fe, 1874); C. M. Chase, "The Editor's Run in New Mexico and Colorado" (Lyndon, Vt., 1882); New Mexico Bureau of Immigration: *The Mines of New Mexico* (Santa Fe, 1896). To the above may be added a series of pamphlets relating to New Mexican land grants in HEH, and the "New Mexican Miscellany" of pamphlets in the Bancroft Library which concern mining, railroad, and land grant issues.

NEWSPAPERS

The majority of the newspapers listed below are in the extensive Bancroft Library collections, but fugitive copies of minor papers are in the Ritch and Ross Collections. The Santa Fe *Gazette* and the *New Mexican* files were used at the New Mexico Historical Society, which in 1959 was still located in the Palace of the Governors, Santa Fe.

Albuquerque *Morning Democrat*, 1884–87
Albuquerque *Morning Journal*, 1883–85
Albuquerque *Daily Citizen*, 1889–90
(Chloride) *Black Range*, 1887–90
Cimarron *News and Press*, 1878–80 passim
Colfax County *Stockman*, 1889
Deming *Headlight*, January 1887–April 1889
Las Cruces *Borderer*, 1872–73
Las Vegas *Chronicle*, August 1886
Las Vegas *Optic*, 1885–90 passim
Las Vegas *Stockgrower*, February 11, 1888

Lincoln *Independent*, 1889–90
Lordsburg *Western Liberal*, 1889–94
Mesilla Valley *Independent*, April 1878–May 1879
(Mora) *Democrata de Mora*, 1889
Raton *Daily Independent*, 1889
Rio Grande *Republican*, 1887–90
Santa Fe *Gazette* (weekly and daily), 1853–94 passim
Santa Fe *New Mexican* (weekly and daily), 1864–84
Santa Fe *Weekly Post*, 1869
Santa Fe *Sentinel*, July 24, 1879
Silver City *Enterprise*, 1889–90
Silver City *Southwest Sentinel*, 1886–88
Socorro *Chieftain*, 1890
Springer *Banner*, July 1885–October 1890
Taos County *Herald*, 1884–88
(White Oaks) New Mexico *Interpreter*, 1889–90

BOOKS AND ARTICLES

Every Southwestern territory had a number of prominent citizens and public officials who showed their devotion to the region by writing massive narrative histories. Because of their richness of detail and because many episodes were based on interviews with the actual participants, these chronicles have also become major fonts of information. In New Mexico, Ralph Emerson Twitchell's *Leading Facts of New Mexican History* (6 vols. Cedar Rapids, Iowa, 1912) is a representative example of the chronicle-source which, though biased in favor of the Santa Fe ring and the Republican party, is extremely useful and informative. H. H. Bancroft, *History of Arizona and New Mexico, 1530–1888* (San Francisco, 1889) performs a similar function but is now dated and incorrect in places.

Also useful are: Charles F. Coan, *A History of New Mexico* (3 vols. Chicago, 1925); Benjamin M. Read, *Illustrated History of New Mexico* (Santa Fe, 1912), an account by a learned local scholar; Helen Haines, *History of New Mexico . . . 1530–1890* (New York, 1891), readable but limited; and Governor L. Bradford Prince, *A Concise History of*

New Mexico (Cedar Rapids, Iowa, 1912), a helpful if occasionally slanted summary.

Of the more recent books on New Mexico, G. P. Hammond and T. C. Donnelly, *The Story of New Mexico, Its History and Its Government* (Albuquerque, 1937), is a succinct, balanced, factual history. Paul F. Horgan's *Great River: The Rio Grande in North American History* (2 vols. New York, 1954) provides both a panoramic view of New Mexico from prehistoric times to the present as well as an impressive number of intelligent insights into southwestern history. Erna Fergusson's *New Mexico: A Pageant of Three Peoples* (New York, 1951) vividly catches the sense of contrast between the various New Mexican cultures.

Four textbook histories of the Southwest should be used to place the New Mexican story in context. They are Carl Coke Rister, *The Southwestern Frontier* (Glendale, Calif., 1928) ; Warren A. Beck, *New Mexico, A History of Four Centuries* (Norman, Okla., 1962); Eugene Hollon, *The Southwest Old and New* (New York, 1961); and Lynn I. Perrigo, *Our Spanish Southwest* (Dallas, 1960). Burl Noggle's outstanding article, "Anglo Observers of the Southwest Borderlands, 1825–1890: The Rise of a Concept," *Arizona and the West, 1* (Summer, 1959), traces the slowly emerging appreciation of the region by the Anglo-American.

By far the most comprehensive study of the Indian tribes of New Mexico, Arizona, and Northern Mexico is Edward E. Spicer's thoughtful *Cycles of Conquest: The Impact of Spain, Mexico, and the United States on the Indians of the Southwest, 1533–1960* (Tucson, 1962). Spicer's view of the Spanish impact on Apache-Navajo relations is challenged in Jack Forbes, *Apache, Navaho, and Spaniard* (Norman, Okla., 1960), which finds the Spanish a disrupting factor in the existing trade relations between the two tribes.

Indian-white relations during the American period have been treated in scores of studies. Particularly useful are: Averam B. Bender, *The March of Empire: Frontier Defense in the Southwest, 1848–1860* (Lawrence, Kans., 1952), and Frank D. Reeve, "Federal Indian Policy in New Mexico, 1858–1880," *NMHR, 12–14* (July 1937–June 1939). Annie H. Abel, ed., "The Journal of John Greiner," *Old Santa Fe,*

3 (July 1916) , pp. 189–243, depicts the experiences of an Indian official in New Mexico. A useful new study is Chris Emmett, *Fort Union and the Winning of the Southwest* (Norman, Okla., 1965), while post-Civil War relations are covered generally in Loring Benson Priest, *Uncle Sam's Stepchildren: The Reformation of the United States Indian Policy, 1865–1887* (New Brunswick, 1942).

The Spanish-American population of New Mexico still lacks a historian. Useful, however, is Lyle Saunders, *A Guide to Materials Bearing on Cultural Relations in New Mexico* (Albuquerque, 1944) , and George I. Sanchez' warm account of the contemporary Spanish-American, *Forgotten People: A Study of New Mexicans* (Albuquerque, 1940). Fray Angelico Chavez, *Origins of New Mexican Families* (Santa Fe, 1954) is technically a genealogical study, but it contains many insights. Sigurd Johansen, *Rural Social Organization in a Spanish-American Culture Area* (Albuquerque, 1948) , and John H. Burma, *Spanish-Speaking Groups in the United States* (Durham, N.C., 1954) are useful studies of contemporary Spanish-Americans with historical introductions.

Frank W. Blackmar, *Spanish Institutions of the Southwest* (Baltimore, 1891) , is a dated and disappointing institutional study of the pre-American period. Cleofas Jaramillo, *Shadows of the Past* (Santa Fe, 1941), provides a nostalgic history of a leading New Mexican family. Her brief account of Padre Martinez is more than supplemented by E. K. Francis' excellent "Padre Martinez: A New Mexican Myth," *NMHR, 21* (1956) .

Most accounts of the Santa Fe trade rest on Gregg, *Commerce of the Prairies,* but that romantic business has been intelligently reappraised in Max L. Moorhead, *New Mexico's Royal Road: Trade and Travel on the Chihuahua Trail* (Norman, Okla., 1958) . R. L. Duffus, *The Santa Fe Trail* (New York, 1930) , remains a standard account.

The Southwestern fur trade is well treated in Hiram M. Chittenden, *The American Fur Trade of the Far West* (2 vols. Stanford, Calif., 1954) , and Robert Glass Cleland, *This Reckless Breed of Men: The Trappers and Furtraders of the Southwest* (New York, 1952), which is a more thorough and readable up-to-date account. David Lavender, *Bent's Fort* (New York, 1954) , is an exceptionally well-written history of a major nerve center of the trade. A more prosaic study of the Bent empire is George B. Grinnell, "Bent's Old Fort and Its Builders," Kansas Historical Society, *Collections, 15* (1919–22). Ceran St. Vrain and Charles Beaubien still lack biographers, but many of their activities are mentioned in Edwin L. Sabin, *Kit Carson Days, 1809–1868* (Chicago, 1914), which also remains the standard biography of the famous scout and trapper.

The American conquest of New Mexico has been treated in numerous works. A readable contemporary history is J. M. Cutts, *Conquest of California and New Mexico* (Philadelphia, 1847). Justin Smith, *War With Mexico* (2 vols. Gloucester, Mass., 1919), is a standard general history. Ralph E. Twitchell, *The Military Occupation of New Mexico, 1846–1851* (Denver, 1909), covers the local events in detail. Sister Mary Loyola, "The American Occupation of New Mexico, 1821–1852," *NMHR, 14* (1939), sees the military occupation from a broader perspective.

Three useful contemporary accounts are James Josiah Webb, *Adventures in the Santa Fe Trade, 1844–47*, and George R. Gibson, *Journal of a Soldier Under Kearny and Doniphan, 1846–47*, which comprise vols. 1 and 3, respectively, in the Southwest Historical Series, Ralph P. Bieber, ed. (Glendale, 1931 and 1935); and Stella M. Drumm, ed., *Down the Santa Fe Trail and into Mexico: The Diary of Susan Shelby Magoffin, 1846–1847* (New Haven, 1926 and 1963). A sprightly report by one of the major participants is Philip St. George Cooke, *The Conquest of New Mexico and California* (Philadelphia, 1878). Dwight L. Clarke, *Stephen Watts Kearny: Soldier of the West* (Norman, Okla., 1961), is a needed biography of the conquering general, but it adds little to the known details of the New Mexican conquest.

The subsequent history of the American Army in the Southwest during the Mexican War period may be followed in John Taylor Hughes, *Doniphan's Expedition: An Account of the Conquest of New Mexico* (Washington, 1914), and W. E. Connelley, *Doniphan's Expedition* (Topeka, Kansas, 1907).

The role New Mexico played in the events surrounding the Compromise of 1850 is detailed in Loomis Morton Ganaway, *New Mexico and the Sectional Controversy, 1846–61* (Albuquerque, 1944), and more generally in Allan Nevins, *Ordeal of the Union, I* (2 vols. New York, 1947), and Robert J. Rayback, *Millard Fillmore: Biography of a President* (Buffalo, 1925). William Seward's role in the New Mexican statehood movement has yet to be treated, but it is mentioned in Frederic Bancroft, *The Life of W. H. Seward* (2 vols. New York, 1900).

The difficulties of establishing civil government are amply illustrated in Annie H. Abel, ed., *The Official Correspondence of James S. Calhoun* (Washington, D.C., 1915), and Ralph P. Bieber, ed., "The Letters of William Carr Lane, 1852–54," in NMHS, *Publications, 6* (Santa Fe, 1928) while W. W. H. Davis recorded a vivid if condescending picture of New Mexico during the 1850s in *El Gringo: Or New Mexico and Her People* (New York, 1857).

Archbishop Lamy's career in New Mexico is treated in Rev. James H. Defouri, *Historical Sketch of the Catholic Church in New Mexico* (Santa Fe, 1887), and briefly in Mary Zerwekh, C.S.J., "John Baptist Salpointe, 1825–1894," *NMHR, 37* (January 1962). J. B. Salpointe, *Soldiers of the Cross, Notes on the Ecclesiastical History of New Mexico, Arizona and Colorado* (Banning, Calif., 1898), is full of praise and piety. Although Louis H. Warner's *Archbishop Lamy: An Epoch Maker* (Santa Fe, 1936) is a more recent biography, the student should anticipate a forthcoming study by Paul F. Horgan. Two Protestant views of New Mexico are Charles R. Bliss, *The New West: New Mexico* (Boston, 1879), and Frederick G. Bohme, "Horatio Oliver Ladd: A New England Conscience for New Mexico," *Church History, 26* (June 1957), 143–55.

The Civil War in the Southwest is treated by William A. Keleher, *Turmoil in New Mexico, 1846–1868* (Santa Fe, 1952), and Ray C. Colton, *The Civil War in the Western Territories* (Norman, Okla., 1959). Max L. Heyman, Jr., *Prudent Soldier: A Biography of Major General E. R. S. Canby, 1813–1873* (Glendale, Calif., 1959), and Martin H. Hall, *Sibley's New Mexico Campaign* (Austin, 1960), treat the New Mexico events in detail. The feats of the Pike's Peakers are admiringly reported in Ovander J. Hollister, *Boldly They Rode* (Denver, 1949), and in William C. Whitford, *Colorado Volunteers in the*

Civil War: The New Mexico Campaign in 1862 (Denver, 1906). The central figure in New Mexico between 1862 and 1865 still lacks a definitive biography although Aurora Hunt, *Major General James Henry Carleton, 1814–1873* (Glendale, Calif., 1958), provides valuable factual data and a readable account. Charles S. Walker, "Causes of the Confederate Invasion of New Mexico," *NMHR, 8* (April 1933) is useful in revealing southern ideas about the Southwest.

The problem of governing New Mexico has received much attention. Besides Hammond and Donnelly, *The Story of New Mexico,* a useful introduction to the literature is Frederick C. Irion, "Selected and Annotated Bibliography of Politics in New Mexico" (Albuquerque July 1958, mimeographed). A lively and entertaining history of the territorial courts is Arie W. Poldervaart, *Black Robed Justice* (Santa Fe, 1948). William S. Wallace, ed., *A Journey Through New Mexico's First Judicial District in 1864* (Los Angeles, 1956), and Aurora Hunt, *Judge Kirby Benedict* (Glendale, Calif., 1961), give vivid accounts of the practical difficulties experienced by the early judges. Edward D. Tittmann, "The Last Legal Frontier," *NMHR, 2* (July 1927), 219–27, treats the important probate judgeship.

The Santa Fe ring was such an ever shifting amorphous group that it is virtually impossible to write a satisfactory history of its operations; however, William A. Keleher, *The Fabulous Frontier* (Santa Fe, 1945), explains its makeup and function briefly. Unfortunately Oscar D. Lambert's *Stephen B. Elkins* (Pittsburgh, Penn., 1955) does not stress the New Mexican period, and a life of Thomas B. Catron by Victor Westphall is still forthcoming. Since the ring was always associated with land grant schemes, studies of the grants are often helpful. William A. Keleher, *Maxwell Land Grant: A New Mexico Item* (Santa Fe, 1949), connects the ring and the grants in an entertaining and readable volume.

The most detailed history of the private land grants is Herbert O. Brayer, *William Blackmore: The Spanish-Mexican Land Grants of New Mexico and Colorado, 1863–1878. A Case Study in the Economic Development of the West, 1* (Denver, 1949). The federal government's role in the land grant schemes is well treated in Harold H. Dunham, *Government Handout, A Study in the Administration of Public Lands*

(New York, 1941). A recent study, Jim Berry Pearson, *The Maxwell Land Grant* (Norman, Okla., 1961), is an excellent account which traces the history of the grant down to the present time. Pearson's treatment of the squatter-settler conflict may be supplemented with F. Stanley, *The Grant that Maxwell Bought* (Denver, 1952).

The rise of the New Mexico cattle range industry and the subsequent Lincoln County troubles are covered in Miguel A. Otero, *The Real Billy the Kid* (New York, 1936); Ramon F. Adams, *A Fitting Death for Billy the Kid* (Norman, Okla., 1960); and C. L. Sonnichsen and William V. Morrison, *Alias Billy the Kid* (Albuquerque, 1955). The fantastic outpouring of printed matter on this subject is recorded in J. C. Dykes, *Billy the Kid, The Bibliography of a Legend* (Albuquerque, 1952). Irving McKee, *Ben-Hur Wallace: The Life of General Lew Wallace* (Berkeley, Calif., 1947) has chapters on his New Mexican governorship.

The story of mining in New Mexico still needs a historian, although the rush to the northeastern region is well covered in Pearson, *Maxwell Land Grant*. Rodman W. Paul, *The Mining Frontiers of the Far West, 1848–1880* (New York, 1963), summarizes New Mexican mining developments briefly. The coming of the railroad to New Mexico is traced in Glenn D. Bradley, *The Story of the Santa Fe* (Boston, 1920); William S. Greever, *Arid Domain: The Santa Fe Railway and its Western Land Grant* (Stanford, 1954); Ira G. Clark, *Then Came the Railroads: The Century from Steam to Diesel in the Southwest* (Norman, 1958); James Marshall, *The Railroad that Built an Empire* (New York, 1945); and L. L. Waters, *Steel Rails to Santa Fe* (Lawrence, Kans., 1950). Julius Grodinsky, *Transcontinental Railway Strategy, 1869–1893* (Philadelphia, 1962), sees the story in a larger perspective. The mercantile economy of New Mexico which the railroad was to replace is nicely epitomized in William J. Parish, *The Charles Ilfeld Company: A Study of the Rise and Decline of Mercantile Capitalism in New Mexico* (Cambridge, Mass., 1961), and in his "The German Jew and the Commercial Revolution in New Mexico," *New Mexican Quarterly, 29* (1959), 307–32.

The coming of the railroad was paralleled by attempted reforms in the political structure of the territory and by a rising interest in statehood. This transition period is treated in Miguel A. Otero, *My Life on the Frontier* (2 vols. New York, 1935), who was a participant; Howard R. Lamar, "Edmund G. Ross as Governor of New Mexico Territory: A Reappraisal," *NMHR, 36* (July 1961) ; George W. Julian, "Land Stealing in New Mexico," *North American Review* (July 1, 1887), pp. 20–25. The last fifteen years of territorial politics are partly covered in Miguel A. Otero, *My Nine Years as Governor of the Territory of New Mexico* (Albuquerque, 1940).

The history of the statehood movement is recorded by an ardent advocate in L. Bradford Prince, *New Mexico's Struggle for Statehood: Sixty Years of Effort to Obtain Self-government* (Santa Fe, 1910). Marion Dargan, "New Mexico's Fight for Statehood, 1895–1912," *NMHR, 14* (January–April 1939), 1–33, 121 ff.; *15* (1940), 133–87; *16* (1941), 70–103, 379–400, summarizes the movement concisely but is notably unsympathetic to the opponents of statehood in Washington.

UNPUBLISHED DISSERTATIONS

A number of masters and doctoral theses provide helpful insights into the history of the territorial period. Olen Leonard, "The Role of the Land Grant in the Social Organization and Social Processes of a Spanish-American Village in New Mexico" (Ph.D. dissertation, Louisiana State University, 1943), traces the social impact of the New Mexican land system, while Aristide B. Chavez, "The Use of the Personal Interview to Study Subjective Impacts of Culture Contacts" (Master's thesis, University of New Mexico, 1948), dramatically notes the increasing sense of helplessness the Spanish-American of today feels when confronted by an Anglo-American society.

John W. Caughey, "Early Federal Relations with New Mexico," (Master's thesis, University of California, Berkeley, 1926), is still a fine study of the problems facing the United States government in New Mexico between 1846 and the Civil War. Robert D. Helpler, "William Watts Hart Davis in New Mexico" (Master's thesis, University of New Mexico, 1941), depends heavily on Davis' letters to his hometown paper. Thomas J. McLaughlin, "History of Fort Union, New Mexico," (Master's thesis, University of New Mexico, 1952), points up the role of that important post in the subjection of the wild Indians.

William I. Waldrip, "New Mexico During the Civil War," (Master's thesis, University of New Mexico, Albuquerque, 1950) is a clear and useful summary of that turbulent period.

Aspects of New Mexican social and cultural history are traced in Ernest S. Stapleton, Jr., "The History of the Baptist Missions in New Mexico, 1849–1860," (Master's thesis, University of New Mexico, 1954); Frederick G. Bohme, "A History of Italians in New Mexico" (Ph.D. dissertation, University of New Mexico, 1958); Victor Westphall, "History of Albuquerque, 1870–1880" (Master's thesis, University of New Mexico, 1947); Bernice Ann Rebord, "A Social History of Albuquerque, 1880–1885" (Master's thesis, University of New Mexico, 1947); and Audry Thomas Tapy, Las Vegas, 1890–1900; "A Frontier Town Becomes Cosmopolitan" (Master's thesis, University of New Mexico, 1943).

The economic development of New Mexico is partially treated in two excellent studies: Ray Willoughby, "The Cattle Range Industry in New Mexico" (Master's thesis, University of New Mexico, 1933), and Jim F. Heath, "A Study of the Influence of the Atchison, Topeka, and Santa Fe Railroad Upon the Economy of New Mexico, 1878–1900" (Master's thesis, University of New Mexico, 1955).

The political history of New Mexico has been treated in a number of special studies. The important role of the probate judge is explained in William Lee Harper, "A History of New Mexican Election Laws" (Master's thesis, University of New Mexico, 1927). Mary Elizabeth Sluga, "The Political Life of Thomas B. Catron" (Master's thesis, University of New Mexico, 1941), and Vioalle Clark Hefferan, "Thomas B. Catron" (Master's thesis, University of New Mexico, 1940), are excellent and frank studies.

The students of the late Marion Dargan of the University of New Mexico have traced in great detail the history of the statehood movement in New Mexico in a series of Masters theses: Archie M. McDowell, "The Opposition to Statehood Within the Territory of New Mexico, 1888–1903" (1939), is supplemented by Beatrice A Cottrell, "Senate Action on the Omnibus Statehood Bill of 1902" (1938); Charles Edgar Maddox, "The Statehood Policy of Albert J. Beveridge, 1901–1911" (1938); Mary J. Masters, "New Mexico's Struggle for Statehood, 1903–1907" (1942); Donald B. Leopard, "Joint Statehood,

1906" (1958); and Dorothy E. Thomas, "The Final Years of New Mexico's Struggle for Statehood, 1907–1912" (1939); all these theses cover the final years of the statehood crusade. The role played by a Spanish-American political leader in these years is sensitively recorded in Alfred G. Cordova, "Octaviano A. Larrazolo: The Prophet of Transition in New Mexico" (Master's Thesis, University of New Mexico, 1950).

COLORADO

MANUSCRIPTS

The bulk of manuscript materials for territorial Colorado are to be found in the Colorado State Historical Society files, in the Colorado State Archives, and in the Department of Western History of the Denver Public Library.

In the CSHS, the "Scrapbook of N. L. Patterson" contained useful copies of the *Western Mountaineer*, 1859–60, while the "Gilpin File" and "Gilpin Miscellany" were helpful in illuminating the often cryptic career of this pioneer geopolitician and governor. Major Edward W. Wynkoop's "Unfinished Colorado History," provides an interesting anti-Chivington account of Sand Creek. Samuel H. Elbert "Public Men and Public Measures," though brief, has valuable observations about Colorado political attitudes. The earlier volumes of Thomas F. Dawson's "Scrapbooks" (62 vols.) point up the split between Henry M. Teller and Jerome B. Chaffee. As Teller's private secretary, Dawson was also to write two useful reminiscences: "The Personal Side of Senator Teller" and "Teller and Wolcott in Colorado Politics."

The CSA contain the colorful "John M. Francisco Papers," as well as those of his contemporary, Albert Henry Pfeiffer. The voluminous John H. Evans Collection, while extremely rewarding, seems to have had key letters deleted from its files. Boxes 11 and 12 containing material on Indian affairs and Colorado statehood were quite useful, however. The tangled history of the Colorado Spanish-Mexican land grants may be traced in the vast Blackmore Collection (microfilm), while other aspects of land grant history and colonization may be gleaned from the "William J. Palmer Papers, 1858–1874."

The career of the able William N. Byers, editor of the *Rocky Mountain News,* may be traced 'in the Diaries of Willian N. Byers, 1850–1902, and in the "William N. Byers Letterbooks, 1879–1883," which are in the Denver Public Library. The manuscript "Journal of John L. Dailey" catches the spirit of the "Hundred Day Volunteers." The informal and affectionate "Letters of [Territorial Secretary] Frank Hall to [his mother,] Emma Skidmore Law, 1857–1890," tell much about Colorado politics. The remarkably frank and often amusing "Letters of James B. Thompson, 1871–74" touch on the battles between Governor McCook and the Evans-Chaffee forces. All the above are to be found in the Denver Public Library.

A lively account of life in Denver and the diggings in the first years of the Gold Rush exist in the "Samuel Ryan Curtis Letters," YWA.

PRINTED DOCUMENTS AND CONTEMPORARY ACCOUNTS

The famous Pike's Peak Gold Rush has been well chronicled by hundreds of pioneer participants. The best of these observations have been edited by LeRoy R. Hafen in three excellent volumes for the Southwest Historical Series: *Pikes Peak Gold Rush Guide Books of 1859* (Glendale, 1941), *Overland Routes to the Gold Fields, 1859, from Contemporary Diaries* (Glendale, 1942), and *Colorado Gold Rush: Contemporary Letters and Reports, 1858–1859* (Glendale, Calif., 1941). One of the most famous of the contemporary reports is found in Henry Villard, *The Past and Present of the Pike's Peak Gold Regions,* ed. LeRoy R. Hafen (Princeton, N.J., 1932).

Individual guides and accounts in YWA which proved useful are: John W. Oliver, *Guide to the Gold Regions of Western Kansas and Nebraska* (New York, 1859); William B. Parsons, *The New Gold Mines of Kansas and Nebraska* (Cincinnati, 1859); O. B. Gunn, *New Map and Hand-book of Kansas and the Gold Mines* (Pittsburgh, 1859); Pratt and Hunt, *A Guide to the Gold Mines of Kansas* (Chicago, 1859); Luke D. Tierney, *History of the Gold Discoveries on the South Platt River* (Pacific City, Iowa, 1859); William N. Byers and John H. Kellom, *A Handbook to the Gold Fields of Nebraska and Kansas* (Chicago, 1859). Libeus Barney, *Early Letters from Auraria*

(Bennington, Vt., 1859-60), is amusing and skeptical, while Daniel Blue, *Thrilling Narrative of . . . Pike's Peak Gold Seekers* (Chicago, 1860), tells a tragic tale. A more ambitious account is William Gilpin, *The Central Gold Region . . .* (Philadelphia and St. Louis, 1860). An important pioneer recounts the early days in "Reminiscences of General William Larimer and of his Son, William H. Larimer" (Lancaster, Pa., 1918).

The official acts of the Jefferson government may be seen in *Provisional Laws and Joint Resolutions Passed at the First and Called Session of the General Assembly of Jefferson Territory* (Omaha, 1860), while the *Letter from the Delegate Elect from . . . Jefferson* (Washington, 1860) traces the arguments for organization.

The *House and Council Journals of the Legislative Assembly of the Territory of Colorado* (Denver, 1862 et seq.) between 1861 and 1874 not only include the annual messages of the governor but are useful for following the political issues of the day and the changing makeup of the Assembly itself. The development of mining law in Colorado may be seen in *Laws of the Eureka District, May 9, 1860* (Denver, 1860), *Laws of the Gregory District* (Denver, 1860), and *Revised Laws of the Spanish Bar District* (Denver, 1861), all in YWA. A useful summary is *Mining Laws Enacted by the Legislature of Colorado from the First to the Ninth Session . . . and the Laws of the United States* (Central City, 1873), as well as the *General Laws, Resolutions, Memorials, and Private Acts of the 1861 (et seq.) Assembly* (Denver, 1861, et seq.).

Railroad development in Colorado can be partially traced in William J. Palmer, *Report of Surveys Across the Continent in 1867–68 . . . for a Route Extending the Kansas Pacific Railway* (Philadelphia, 1869), *Report of the Board of Directors of the Colorado Central Railroad* (Golden, 1873), and *First Annual Report . . . of the Denver and Rio Grande Railway to the Stockholders* (Philadelphia, 1873) in YWA.

Promotional literature concerning Colorado land grants is epitomized in William Blackmore, "Colorado: Its Resources, Parks and Prosperity (London, 1869), and his "The Sangre de Cristo Grant" (n.d.), brochures in the Denver Public Library. A larger view of both

America's and Colorado's destiny is depicted in William Gilpin, *Mission of the North American People, Geographical, Social, and Political* (Philadelphia, 1874).

Proceedings of the Constitutional Convention . . . (Denver, 1907) traces in detail the writing of the Colorado state constitution.

NEWSPAPERS

The files of the *Rocky Mountain News,* located in CSHS, were used for the entire territorial period. Other newspapers used either at CSHS or the Bancroft Library were:

The Western Mountaineer, 1859–60
Central City *Register,* 1861
Colorado *Republican,* 1862
Black Hawk *Mining Journal,* 1864–65
(Denver) *The Commonwealth,* 1864
Golden City *Transcript,* 1867
Boulder *News,* 1872–74
(Georgetown) *The Colorado Miner,* 1873–74
Denver *Daily Tribune,* 1875–76

BOOKS AND ARTICLES

Like New Mexico, Colorado has its pioneer historians who have written praiseful accounts of the political and economic leaders of the territorial period. Secretary Frank Hall's *History of the State of Colorado* (4 vols. Chicago, 1889) is representative of this approach. William N. Byers, *Encyclopaedia Biography of Colorado* (2 vols. Chicago, 1901), takes a similar stand. Still another is Wilbur F. Stone, ed., *The History of Colorado* (5 vols. Chicago, 1918–19). Stone was a lawyer for the Denver and Rio Grande Railroad and served on the Colorado Supreme Court and on the Court of Private Land Claims. Alice Polk Hill, *Colorado Pioneers in Picture and Story* (Denver, 1915), contains useful observations. One of the best of the earlier works on Colorado is J. C. Smiley, *History of Denver* (Denver, 1903). H. H. Bancroft, *History of Nevada, Colorado, and Wyoming* (San Francisco, 1890), is now dated.

Three excellent summary histories of Colorado exist in LeRoy R. Hafen, *Colorado: The Story of a Western Commonwealth* (Denver, 1933); his *Colorado and Its People* (2 vols. New York, 1948), which contains articles by other Colorado scholars; and Percy S. Fritz, *Colorado, the Centennial State* (New York, 1941). A very readable and thoughtful summary of Colorado history may be found in Robert G. Athearn, *High Country Empire* (New York, 1960).

For the Pike's Peak rush, Hafen's *Colorado Gold Rush* is good, as is Ray A. Billington's *Far Western Frontier, 1830–1860* (New York, 1956), pp. 259–66. Rodman W. Paul, *The Mining Frontiers of the Far West, 1848–1880* (New York, 1963), is a model of balance and excellence, while his "Colorado as a Pioneer of Science in the Mining West," *MVHR, 47* (July 1960), is very thoughtful.

"Jefferson Territory" has received much attention, but it lacks a recent historian. The standard accounts are by Frederick Logan Paxson: "The Territory of Jefferson: A Spontaneous Commonwealth," University of Colorado, *Studies, 3* (November 1905), 15–18; "The Territory of Colorado," University of Colorado, *Studies, 4*, 63–76; and "The Territory of Colorado," *American Historial Review, 12* (October 1906), 53–65. A. J. Fynn, "Creating a Commonwealth," *CM, 1* (July 1924), 204–13, adds details.

Mining codes and law are treated in Paul, *Mining Frontiers*, and in James Grafton Rogers, "The Mining District Governments of the West: Their Interest and Literature," *Law Library Journal, 28* (1935), 247–59.

The difficulties of securing territorial status on the eve of the Civil War is summarized in David M. Potter, *Lincoln and His Party in the Secession Crisis* (New Haven, 1942), and briefly in Lamar, *Dakota Territory, 1861–1889* (New Haven, 1956), pp. 60–65.

Despite several biographical studies William Gilpin remains a cypher to the historian. H. H. Bancroft, *History of the Life of William Gilpin* (San Francisco, 1889), takes Gilpin own account of himself at face value. Henry Nash Smith, *Virgin Land: The American West as Symbol and Myth* (Cambridge, Mass., 1950), pp. 35–48, and Bernard DeVoto, "Geopolitics with the Dew On It," *Harper's Magazine, 188* (March 1944), 313–23, are far more discerning.

The Civil War in Colorado is covered in Ray C. Colton, *The Civil*

War in the Western Territories (Norman, Okla., 1959), Ovander J. Hollister, *Boldly They Rode*, (Denver, 1949), William C. Whitford, *Colorado Volunteers in the Civil War: The New Mexico Campaign in 1862* (Denver, 1906), and David Lavender, *Bent's Fort* (New York, 1954). James W. Covington, "Federal Relations with the Colorado Utes, 1861–65," *CM, 28* (October 1951), 257 ff., is useful. The Sand Creek Massacre has prompted much writing. The Indian side of the story is well told in George B. Grinnell, *The Fighting Cheyennes* (New York, 1915), and Lavender, *Bent's Fort*. Several recent books and articles throw new light and perspective on the tragedy: Stan Hoig, *The Sand Creek Massacre* (Norman, Okla., 1961); Michael Straight, *A Very Small Remnant* (New York, 1963); W. E. Unrau, "A Prelude to War," *CM, 41* (1964), 299–313; Raymond G. Cary, "The Puzzle of Sand Creek," and Janet LeCompte, "Sand Creek," *CM, 41* (1964), 315–35. Wartime politics and the 1864 statehood movement are treated in Edgar McMechan, *Life of Governor John Evans* (Denver, 1924).

Central to an understanding of the private land grants in Colorado is Herbert O. Brayer's study, *William Blackmore: The Spanish-Mexican Land Grants of New Mexico and Colorado,* and *Early Financing of the Denver and Rio Grande Railway* (2 vols. Denver, 1942). Studies of the New Mexico grants cited above are helpful, and Harold H. Dunham, *Government Handout* is quite good on Colorado. Briefer accounts are: LeRoy R. Hafen, "Mexican Land Grants in Colorado," *CM, 4* (May 1927); Ralph Carr, "Private Land Claims in Colorado," *CM, 25* (January 1948); and Edmond C. Van Diest, "Early History of Costilla County," *CM, 5* (August 1928); and Dunham, "Coloradans and the Maxwell Land Grant," *CM, 32* (1955).

Railroad building is partly covered in two biographies: George LeVerne Anderson, *General William J. Palmer: A Decade of Colorado, 1870–1880* (Colorado Springs, 1936), and John S. Fisher, *Builder of the West: The Life of General William Jackson Palmer* (Caldwell, Idaho, 1939). A fine history of the railroad itself exists in Robert G. Athearn, *Rebel of the Rockies: A History of the Denver and Rio Grande* (New Haven, Conn., 1962). Brayer, *Financing of the Denver and Rio Grande Railway,* traces in detail the economic history of the building period.

The Colorado cattle industry is well treated in O. B. Peake, *The Colorado Range Cattle Industry* (Glendale, 1939), but the expansion in this area of the economy came largely after statehood.

The rise of the statehood sentiment is traced in LeRoy R. Hafen, "Steps to Statehood in Colorado," *MC, 3* (August 1926), 97–110, and Elmer Ellis, "Colorado's First Fight for Statehood, 1865–1868," *CM, 8* (1931), 23–30. Colorado politics in the five years before admission are chronicled in Elmer Ellis, *Henry Moore Teller: Defender of the West* (Caldwell, Idaho, 1941). The constitution itself is discussed in Henry J. Hershey, "The Colorado Constitution," *CM, 3* (1928), 65–76, and in Colin B. Goodykoontz, "Some Controversial Questions Before the Colorado Constitutional Convention of 1876," *CM, 17* (January 1940), 1–17. Elmer H. Meyer, "The Constitution of Colorado," *Iowa Journal of History and Politics, 2* (1904), 256–74 is disappointing, but Dudley T. Cornish, "The First Five Years of Colorado's Statehood, 1876–1881," *CM, 25* (July-September 1948), 179–188, 220–232, is thoughtful.

UNPUBLISHED DISSERTATIONS

Bernard O. J. Linnevold, "A Study of the Attitudes on Public Questions of Colorado's Territorial Delegates, 1861–1876" (Master's thesis, University of Colorado, 1931), has patiently traced the voting records of the delegates. Donald Wayne Hensel, "A History of the Colorado Constitution in the Nineteenth Century" (Ph.D. dissertation, University of Colorado, 1957), is a good study. Leah M. Bird, "The History of Third Parties in Colorado" (Master's thesis, University of Denver, 1942), and J. O. Van Hook, "Settlement and Economic Development of the Arkansas Valley from Pueblo to the Colorado-Kansas Line, 1860–1900" (Ph.D. dissertation, University of Colorado, Boulder, 1933), were of limited use.

UTAH

MANUSCRIPTS

Other than materials in the National Archives, manuscript collections relating to territorial Utah are to be found in the Utah State Historical Society, the Utah State Archives, Brigham

Young University Library (Provo, Utah), the Henry E. Huntington Library, the Bancroft Library, and the Beinecke Rare Book and Manuscript Library, Yale University. The Church Historian's Office of the Latter-Day Saints in Salt Lake City contain materials about Utah politics, but many of these are not available to the non-Mormon scholar. Microfilm copies of some of the most pertinent materials on politics have been made available at the Utah State Historical Society, however, and were used there. Mormon scholars such as Leland Creer, Preston Nibley, Nels Anderson, S. George Ellsworth, and Leonard Arrington by using church sources have also established the major outlines in the Utah political narrative. Two major Church history sources that are available, however, are *The Journal of Discourses* (26 vols., Liverpool, 1854–1886), and Andrew Jenson, *Encyclopedic History of the Church of Jesus Christ of Latter-Day Saints* (Salt Lake City, 1941).

Among the USHS collections which proved helpful were newspaper materials dealing with the early church in New York, Ohio, and the Midwest collected by Dale E. Morgan. For the Utah settlement period the "Diary of Hosea Stout" (now published as Juanita Brooks, ed., *On the Mormon Frontier: The Diary of Hosea Stout, 1844–1861*, Salt Lake City, 1965) is an invaluable account of day-to-day events during the exciting fifties.

Insight into the political history of the territory may be gleaned from the John M. Bernhisel Scrapbooks; the "Letters of Brigham Young, 1858–64"; the "Journal of Elias Smith, 1859–1864"; the "Alfred E. Cumming Papers, 1857–1858" (microfilm of originals in Duke University Library); "Letters of Col. E. J. Steptoe and Lieutenant Sylvester Mowry," Records of the War Department, Office of the Adjutant General, 1855 (microfilm of original in NA); Records of the U.S. House of Representatives (RG 233) pertaining to Utah, 1854–73 (microfilm of original in NA); "Letters of John W. Dawson, 1861–62"; "Letters and Congressional Addresses of John T. Caine." The latter reveal the sense of crisis within the church during the anti-polygamy crusade of the 1880s, as do the "Letters of President Wilford Woodruff, 1885–1894."

The Utah State Archives contain the official Utah Executive Proceedings, vols. 1–4, 1850–1889, and the Executive Papers, 1851–1896, most of which concerns routine territorial business. The records and reports of the Utah Commission, 1882–96, on the other hand, help reconstruct the federal crusade against polygamy.

For the convenience of the researcher the Mormon materials in the Bancroft Library have been listed in S. George Ellsworth, "Guide to the Bancroft Manuscripts," *UHQ*, 22 (April and July 1954). Of particular interest are the "Letters of Grenville Dodge and General Patrick E. Connor" (originals in Historical, Memorial and Art Department of Iowa, Des Moines).

The life and thought of the Mormon pioneers may be gleaned from a number of diaries in the Huntington Library. Among the most useful are those of Allen J. Stout, John Pulsifer, John Lee Jones, Charles L. Walker, S. W. Richards, H. W. Bigler, and the Journal of Essaias Edwards. The Gentile's impressions of Utah during the 1870s and 1880s is vividly set down in the Papers of Jacob S. Boreman, and especially in his "Reminiscences of My Life in Utah," and "Curiosities of Early Utah Legislation," HEH.

In the Mormon collection housed in YWA, Mormon-federal difficulties and the events of the Utah war are detailed in the "Letters of Thomas Leiper Kane," and the "Letters of Brigham Young to William H. Hooper, 1853–1869." The latter illustrate the close liaison between the delegate and the leader of the Saints.

PRINTED DOCUMENTS AND CONTEMPORARY ACCOUNTS

Mormon-federal difficulties and Mormon attempts at self-government are disclosed in a number of documents. The *Report of the Commissioner of Indian Affairs on the Status of the Mormons Encamped on the Omaha Lands . . . April 21, 1847*, YWA, reveal the troubles they experienced as they fled Nauvoo. Popular sovereignty sentiments are obvious in the *Constitution of the State of Deseret with the Journal of the Convention Which Formed It* (Kanesville, 1849) , YWA. A spirited defense of the sect is Thomas L. Kane, *The Mormons: A Discourse Delivered Before the Historical Society of Pennsylvania* (Philadelphia, 1850).

Three finely edited volumes of documents and contemporary accounts give the scholar an unforgettable impression of Mormon life and difficulties: O. O. Winther, ed., *The Private Papers and Diary of*

Thomas L. Kane, A Friend of the Mormons (San Francisco, 1947) ;
William Mulder and A. Russell Mortensen, eds., *Among the Mormons:
Historic Accounts by Contemporary Observers* (New York, 1958) ; and
LeRoy R. Hafen and Ann W. Hafen, *The Utah Expedition, 1857–
1859: A Documentary Account* (Glendale, 1958), which is essential for
an understanding of the Mormon "war" of 1857–58.

The *House and Council Journals of Utah Territory, 1851* [et seq. to
1894] (Salt Lake City, 1851 et seq., title and imprint vary) contain
the messages of the governors. Of particular interest are the *Acts and
Resolutions of the Territorial Assembly of Utah, 1858–59* (Salt Lake
City, 1859). Since Utah came under such close surveillance after the
implementation of the Poland Act of 1874, the *Annual Reports* of the
governors of Utah from that year until 1896 are of great interest.
They may be found in the *Annual Report of the Secretary of the
Interior, 1874–1896* (Washington, 1875–1897). The *Reports of the
Utah Commission* (1883–96) are also of much value in tracing politi-
cal developments in the final decade of the territorial period. *The
Constitution of the State of Utah* (1882) and (1887) in YWA and
various broadsides in defense of the Mormons help explain the Mormon side of the statehood movement.

The *Utah Directory and Gazeteer for 1879–80* (Salt Lake City,
1880) gives an impression of the state of business enterprise in the
Great Basin.

NEWSPAPERS

The most valuable discussion of political events in
Utah is to be found in the powerful Mormon newspaper, the *Deseret
News*, whose issues, either in weekly or daily form, span the entire
territorial period. Nearly every issue and crisis was treated extensively
in its columns, and the church used the paper to persuade when necessary. The *Salt Lake City Tribune* (1871–96) conveniently mirrored
the Gentile view of Utah affairs, but its accounts of Mormon doings
were often so biased as to be of little use. Two early anti-Mormon
papers consulted were the *Valley Tan*, 1858–59 (YWA) and the
Union Vedette, 1863–64 (USHS).

BOOKS AND ARTICLES

Much of the historical literature concerning Mormon Utah is so bitter and partisan that it is of little use, but the lessening of animosities has allowed scholars to produce some excellent factual and dispassionate studies. Of the older historians of the church, Brigham H. Roberts, *A Comprehensive History of the Church of Jesus Christ of Latter-Day Saints, Century I*, (6 vols. Salt Lake City, 1930) is the most useful. Orson F. Whitney, *History of Utah* . . . , (4 vols. Salt Lake City, 1892–1904), is full of information. Andrew Jenson, *Latter-Day Saints Biographical Encyclopaedia* (4 vols. Salt Lake City, 1901–1936) is useful but often substitutes praise for facts. None of the early anti-Mormon works are worthy of notice, but John W. Gunnison, *The Mormons or Latter-Day Saints in the Valley of the Great Salt Lake* (Philadelphia, 1852) , and Benjamin G. Ferris, *Utah and the Mormons* (New York, 1854) , have some value as contemporary descriptions. H. H. Bancroft, *History of Utah, 1540–1886* (San Francisco, 1889) is surprisingly cautious in its evaluation of the Saints.

A useful summary of Utah history is Nels Anderson, *Desert Saints: The Mormon Frontier in Utah* (Chicago, 1942). Two sympathetic accounts are Gustive O. Larson, *Prelude to the Kingdom: Mormon Desert Conquest* (Francestown, N.H., 1947) , and Ray B. West, Jr., *Kingdom of the Saints: The Story of Brigham Young and the Mormons* (New York, 1957), but they contain little about politics. Leonard Arrington, *Great Basin Kingdom* (Cambridge, Mass., 1958) , while claiming to be primarily an economic history, is actually the most complete history of Utah and the Mormons extant. Utah history is placed in regional and cultural context in Earl S. Pomeroy, *The Pacific Slope* (New York, 1965) .

The most perceptive study of Joseph Smith and the early church is Fawn M. Brodie, *No Man Knows My History: The Life of Joseph Smith* (New York, 1945). To understand the ethical, social, and economic beliefs of the Saints, the following should also be consulted: E. E. Ericksen. *The Psychological and Ethical Aspects of Mormon Group Life* (Chicago, 1922) ; W. J. McNiff, *Heaven on Earth: A*

Planned Mormon Society (Oxford, Ohio, 1940) ; Thomas F. O'Dea, *The Mormons* (Chicago, 1957); West, *Kingdom of the Saints;* Lowry Nelson, *Mormon Village Life: A Pattern and Technique of Land Settlement* (Salt Lake City, 1952) ; Arrington, *Great Basin Kingdom*; and Milton R. Hunter, *Brigham Young, the Colonizer* (Independence, Mo., 1945). Land policies are discussed in Wallace Stegner, *Beyond the Hundredth Meridian* (Cambridge, Mass., 1954) , and George W. Rollins, "Land Policies of the U.S. as Applied to Utah, to 1910," *UHQ, 20* (July 1952) , 239–51. Polygamy is intelligently treated in Stanley S. Ivins, "Notes on Mormon Polygamy," *Western Humanities Review, 10* (Summer 1956) , 229–39.

No definitive biography of Brigham Young exists, but Morris R. Werner, *Brigham Young* (New York, 1925) is a balanced narrative. A more recent if highly sympathetic study is Preston Nibley, *Brigham Young: The Man and His Work* (Salt Lake City, 1936), which uses the "Journal History of the Church" extensively. Susa Y. Gates, *The Life Story of Brigham Young* (1930) , is by a daughter.

The establishment of the Mormon Kingdom in the Great Basin may be followed in: Herbert E. Bolton, "The Mormons in the Opening of the Great West," *Utah Genealogical Historical Magazine, 44* (Salt Lake City, 1926) ; Daniel Tyler, *A Concise History of the Mormon Battalion in the Mexican War* (Salt Lake City, 1881) ; Brigham H. Roberts, *The Mormon Battalion* (1919) ; and Hunter, *Brigham Young, the Colonizer.*

Early political organization in Utah is delineated in a superb article by Dale Morgan *et al.,* "The State of Deseret," *UHQ, 8* (April, July, and October 1940). The role of the local courts may be seen in W. W. Davis, "Western Justice: The Court at Fort Bridger, Utah," *UHQ, 23* (1955), 99–125. Political evolution is treated in Leland H. Creer, "The Evolution of Government in Early Utah," *UHQ, 26* (1958), 23–42; James R. Clark, "The Kingdom of God, The Council of Fifty, and the State of Deseret," *UHQ, 26* (1958), 131–148; and H. R. Lamar, "Political Patterns in New Mexico and Utah," *UHQ, 28* (1960), 363–387.

Mormon Indian policy is discussed in Dale Morgan, "The Administration of Indian Affairs in Utah, 1851–1858," *Pacific Historical Re-*

view, 17 (November 1948), 383–409. A good example of the achievements of Mormon Indian policy is symbolized in Leland H. Creer, "The Activities of Jacob Hamblin in the Region of the Colorado," University of Utah, *Anthropological Papers, 33* (1958). One should also consult P. H. Corbett, *Jacob Hamblin, The Peacemaker* (Salt Lake City, 1952), and Paul Bailey, *Buckskin Apostle* (Los Angeles, 1948).

The religious revival of the 1850s has been recently reviewed in Gustive O. Larson, "The Mormon Reformation," *UHQ, 26* (January 1958), 45–63; also of use is Richard D. Poll, "The Mormon Question Enters National Politics, 1850–1856," *UHQ, 25* (April 1957), 117–31. For the Mormon War one should consult Hafen and Hafen, *The Utah Expedition,* first. Leland Creer, *Utah and the Nation* (Seattle, 1929) is readable and accurate but very critical of federal policy. Norman Furniss, *The Mormon Conflict* (New Haven, 1960), is a good recent account. William P. MacKinnon, "The Buchanan Spoils System and the Utah Expedition," *UHQ, 31* (1963), 127–150, disagrees in part with Creer and Furniss after it analyzes the war from the point of view of Buchanan and his cabinet. Two books by Juanita Brooks, *The Mountain Meadows Massacre* (Norman, Okla., 1962) and *John Doyle Lee* (Glendale, Calif., 1962), comprise exhaustive and finely written studies of that tragic affair. William Preston Johnston, *The Life of General Albert Sidney Johnston* (New York, 1878), is stiff and laudatory, but conveys Johnston's hostility to the Mormons.

The Civil War period in Utah is only partly covered in Alice E. Smith, *James Duane Doty: Frontier Promoter* (Madison, Wis., 1954), and in Fred B. Rogers, *Soldiers of the Overland . . . General Conner and his Volunteers in the Old West* (San Francisco, 1938).

Continued immigration to Utah is nicely treated in William Mulder, *Homeward to Zion: The Mormon Migration from Scandinavia* (St. Paul, Minn., 1957), while the flavor of life in Utah is caught in Mulder and Mortensen, *Among the Mormons.*

The development of mining and the coming of the railroad to Utah is well covered in Arrington, *Great Basin Kingdom.* Special aspects of mining are treated in: Bernice Gibbs Anderson, "The Gentile City of Corinne," *UHQ, 9* (1941), 141–54; William T. Jackson, "The

Infamous Emma Mine," *UHQ, 23* (1955), 339–62; and Clark Spence, *British Investments and the American Mining Frontier, 1860–1901* (Ithaca, 1958). A splendid larger view of economic development in the Far Southwest is Leonard Arrington, *The Changing Structure of the Mountain West, 1850–1950,* Monograph Series 10 (Logan, Utah, 1963).

The rise of the anti-Mormon and antipolygamy crusade is detailed by a Gentile participant in R. N. Baskin, *Reminiscences of Early Utah* (Salt Lake City, 1914). Two prominent anti-Mormons express themselves briefly in George F. Edmunds, "Political Aspects of Mormonism," *Harper's Magazine, 64* (1882), 285–88; and in E. H. Tullidge, "The Reformation in Utah," *Harper's Magazine, 43* (1871), 602. G. H. Durham, "Development of Political Parties in Utah," *Western Humanities Review, 1* (April 1947), and Everett L. Cooley, "Carpetbag Rule: Territorial Government in Utah," *UHQ, 26* (April 1958) are useful. A full study is to be found in Robert J. Dwyer, *The Gentile Comes to Utah: A Study in Religious and Social Conflict, 1862–1890* (Washington, 1941). The efforts to be self-sufficient through the establishment of ZCMI and The United Order during these years are traced in Arrington, *Great Basin Kingdom,* and in his *Orderville, Utah: A Pioneer Mormon Experiment in Economic Organization,* Monograph Series 2 (Logan, Utah, 1954).

The coming of statehood and the changes in educational and political patterns are nicely handled in Frank Herman Jonas, "Utah: Sagebrush Democracy," in T. C. Donnelly, ed., *Rocky Mountain Politics* (Albuquerque, 1940); Stanley S. Ivins, "Free Schools Come to Utah," *UHQ, 21* (1954), 321–42; and Ivins, "A Constitution for Utah," *UHQ, 25* (April 1957), 95–116.

UNPUBLISHED DISSERTATIONS

An intensive study of the origins of Mormon economic thought is to be found in Mario S. DePillis, "The Development of Mormon Communitarianism, 1862–1846" (Ph.D. dissertation, Yale University, 1960). A series of Masters theses written at the University of Utah treat specific aspects of Utah political history: Robert H.

Sylvester, "Dr. John Milton Bernhisel, Utah's First Delegate to Congress" (1947); Everett L. Cooley, "The Utah War" (1947); V. G. Erickson, "The Liberal Party of Utah" (1947); Stanford O. Cazier, "The Life of William Henry Hooper, Merchant-Statesman" (1956); and Francis Edward Rogan, "Patrick Edward Connor: An Army Officer in Utah, 1862–1866" (1952).

Three Doctoral dissertations also aid in an understanding of territorial history: Therald N. Jensen, "Mormon Theory of Church and State" (Ph.D. dissertation, University of Chicago, 1938); Ellsworth E. Weaver, "The Evolution of Political Institutions in Utah" (Ph.D. dissertation, New York University, 1953), which uses the "Journal History"; and Stewart Lofgren Grow, "A Study of the Utah Commission, 1882–1896" (Ph.D. dissertation, University of Utah, 1954).

ARIZONA

MANUSCRIPTS

One of the main repositories of materials on the history of territorial Arizona is the Arizona Pioneers' Historical Society, Tucson. There manuscripts, printed items, and newspaper items relating to nearly every important political figure have been collected, cross-indexed, and filed. One may easily consult files, therefore, on such pioneers as Sylvester Mowry, Charles DeB. Poston, Granville and William Oury, and on all the governors and delegates. Since the individual files consulted have been indicated in the footnotes, they will not be repeated here.

These biographical files can be supplemented with the "Joseph Fish Manuscript History of Arizona" (typescript); C. C. Smith, "Some Unpublished History of the Southwest," and his "History of the Oury Family"; and the APHS "Miscellany."

The Arizona State Archives at Phoenix contain the "Letters of Jonathan Richmond, 1863–1865"; and "Territorial Papers concerning Indian Affairs, 1870–1887," in which are to be found letters to and from Delegate McCormick and Governor Safford, Delegate Caleb Bean, General George C. Crook, and John P. Clum, Governor Meyer Zulick, and others. From these an intriguing but only partial impression of the complexities of Arizona politics may be gained. Of particular interest is (1) McCormick to Safford, August 4, 1869, proposing that the two men cooperate politically; and (2) the telegrams and letters of Governor Zulick during the Indian outbreak of 1885–86. Also located in the ASA were the "Letter Press Books of the Governors of Arizona, 1892–1898," which were of limited use, and the "Official Record of Mark A. Smith (1887–1909)," (6 vols.) which allows one to trace his long career as delegate in some detail. Mulford Winsor's typescript "Arizona's Way to Statehood" (Phoenix, 1945) was helpful as well.

The Special Collections of the University of Arizona Library, Tucson, house the Journal of Alexander Bowman, 1861–65; the Pictures, Scrapbooks and Letters of John P. Clum; the Louis C. Hughes Letterbook, 1893–96, and "Scrapbooks," 3 vols.; the Private Letterbooks of Mark A. Smith, 1900–1905; and those of his partner, Eugene S. Ives, 1901–1913. The Library also holds the voluminous "Scrapbooks" of Governor G. W. P. Hunt as well as those of the late Senator Henry F. Ashurst. The extensive "Complete Verbatim Report of the Arizona Constitutional Convention, 1910" (4 vols.) is also there. Insight into local government may be grained from a perusal of the "Original Documents Pertaining to the Financial, Legal and Political Affairs of Pima County . . . 1864–1923" (53 vols.)

The "Correspondence and Papers of John Charles Fremont, 1862–1889" in the Bancroft Library leave much untold about Fremont's Arizona sojourn but are of some pertinence.

PRINTED DOCUMENTS, LEGISLATIVE PROCEEDINGS
AND CONTEMPORARY ACCOUNTS

Report from the Secretary of War Communicating . . . a Copy of the Official Journal of Lieutenant-Colonel Philip St. George Cooke . . . , 30th Cong., Spec. Sess., Sen. Exec. Doc. 2 (1849), covers Cooke's trip through southern Arizona. Early Arizona's bright prospects are portrayed in Sylvester Mowry, *Memoir of the Proposed Territory of Arizona* (Washington, 1857), and his *Arizona and Sonora* (New York, 1864); Capt. T. J. Cram, "Memoir Showing How to

Bring the Lead, Copper, Silver, and Gold of Arizona into the Marts of the World," (Troy, New York, 1858); *Report of Frederick Brunckow, Sonora Exploring and Mining Company* (Cincinnati, 1859); and John R. Bartlett, *Charter and By-Laws of the Sopori Land and Mining Company* (Providence, R.I., 1859). One of the most famous accounts of early Arizona is J. Ross Browne, *Adventures in the Apache Country* (New York, 1869).

The efforts to establish a separate government for Arizona may be traced sporadically in *Constitution and Schedule of the Provisional Government of the Territory of Arizona* (Tucson, 1860), and James M. Ashley, *Protection and Freedom in Arizona* (Washington, 1862), both pamphlets; and in the *Journal of the First Legislative Assembly of the Territory of Arizona, 1864* (Prescott, 1865). The history of subsequent assemblies may be followed in the *House and Council Journals* to 1909. The accomplishments of the first political pioneers may also be seen in the *Acts, Resolutions, and Memorials . . . of the First Legislative Assembly of . . . Arizona, 1864* (Prescott, 1865), and in the *Laws of Arizona Territory for . . . 1865*. A good summary of a later Assembly is James H. McClintock, *Nineteenth Legislature of Arizona, 1897"* (Phoenix, 1897), pamphlet.

The *Annual Report of the Secretary of the Interior for 1864* (and for subsequent years to 1900) carries the *Annual Reports* of the governors as well as information on Indian affairs.

Indian troubles in Arizona may be followed in part through the reminiscences of some of the participants: John G. Bourke, *On the Border with Crook* (New York, 1891); General O. O. Howard, *My Life and Experiences Among our Hostile Indians* (Hartford, 1907); General Nelson A Miles, *Personal Recollections* (Chicago and New York, 1897); and Martin F. Schmidt, ed., *General George Crook, His Autobiography* (Norman, Okla., 1946). For an instructive account of Indian troubles see the "Memorial and Affidavits Showing Outrages Perpetrated by the Apache Indians in . . . Arizona, 1869–70" (San Francisco, 1871), YWA.

The coming of the mining boom to Arizona is shown in T. R. Sorin, *Handbook of Tucson and Surroundings* (Tombstone ?), YWA; "The Private Journal of George Whitwell Parsons," Arizona Statewide

Archival and Records Project, WPA (Phoenix, 1936); and "Globe Gold and Silver Mines, Arizona" (Aurora, Ill., 1880), YWA.

Early efforts to gain statehood may be seen in *Constitution for the State of Arizona As Adopted by the Constitutional Convention . . . 1891* (Phoenix, 1891), and *Proceedings of the Arizona Convention for Statehood* (Phoenix, 1893), pamphlet, ASA.

NEWSPAPERS

Newspaper accounts in the San Francisco *Herald,* 1858–62, and the *Alta California,* July–December 1862, have been compiled in the Ida Reid Leonard Collection, APHS, and are helpful. The pioneering *Weekly Arizonian,* March 3, 1859 to July 14, 1859, and the Arizona newspaper files in the Bancroft Library were consulted. While no paper dominated the whole territorial period as did the *Rocky Mountain News,* the Arizona *Miner* (Prescott) and the Arizona *Citizen* (Tucson) were generally important and representative papers. The following papers were used:

Arizona *Citizen,* 1870–1910 (a weekly and daily which evolved through several name changes to become the Tucson *Daily Citizen*)

(Phoenix) Arizona *Democrat,* 1901–12

(Florence) Arizona *Enterprise,* September 26, 1891 and March 3, 1892

(Phoenix) Arizona *Gazette,* February 10, 1911

(Prescott) Arizona *Miner,* 1864–1900 (a weekly and daily which evolved through several name changes)

Arizona *Star* (and *Daily Star*), 1877–1910

Tombstone *Epitaph,* 1880–82

(Tucson) *Weekly Arizonian,* 1869–71

BOOKS AND ARTICLES

A definitive history of Arizona in the American period remains to be written. H. H. Bancroft, *History of Arizona and New Mexico, 1530–1888* (San Francisco, 1889), is dated and in need of corrections. A good textbook summary is Rufus K. Wyllys, *Arizona: The History of a Frontier State* (Phoenix, 1950). Eminently readable but now dated is Frank C. Lockwood, *Pioneer Days in Arizona* (New York, 1932). James H. McClintock, *Arizona, the Youngest State* (3 vols. Chicago, 1916) is still useful. Thomas J. Farish cites so many documents and sources *in toto* in his *History of Arizona* (8 vols. San Francisco, 1915–18) that it is a compendium rather than a true history.

Exploration of the Arizona area is covered in Ralph P. Bieber, *Exploring Southwestern Trails, 1846–1854* (Glendale, Calif., 1938). Cooke's career is revealed in his own *Conquest of New Mexico and California* (new ed. Oakland, Calif., 1952). Federal interest in the possibility of a transcontinental railroad across Arizona is brought out in Robert R. Russel, *Improvement of Communication with the Pacific as an Issue in American Politics, 1783–1864* (Cedar Rapids, Iowa, 1948), and in William H. Goetzmann, *Army Exploration in the American West, 1803–1863* (New Haven, 1959), which covers in detail the government explorations.

Paul Neff Garber, *The Gadsden Treaty* (Philadelphia, 1923), is a standard history of the Purchase, but it may be supplemented with Louis B. Schmidt, "Manifest Opportunity and the Gadsden Purchase," *Arizona and the West, 3* (Autumn 1961). James P. Shenton, *Robert J. Walker, A Politician from Jackson to Lincoln* (New York, 1961), explains the role of the "hundred million" company.

The federal organization of Arizona Territory has been carefully and accurately detailed in B. Sacks, *Be It Enacted: The Creation of the Territory of Arizona* (Phoenix, 1964). The first year of government is treated in Pauline Henson, *Founding A Wilderness Capital: Prescott, A.T. 1864* (Flagstaff, Ariz., 1965). Ray C. Colton, *The Civil War in the Western Territories,* summarizes the brief history of Confederate Arizona, as does Robert Lee Kirby, *The Confederate Invasion of New Mexico and Arizona, 1861–62* (Los Angeles, 1958), while Aurora Hunt, *Major General James Henry Carleton, 1814–1873* (Glendale, Calif., 1958), traces the march of the California Column across Arizona.

The war between the Apaches and the Americans has been treated in scores of books. Edward E. Spicer, *Cycles of Conquest: The Impact of Spain, Mexico, and the United States on the Indians of the Southwest, 1533–1960* (Tucson, 1962) is very good. Frank C. Lockwood, *The*

Apache Indians (New York, 1948), is readable, but Ralph C. Ogle, *Federal Control of the Western Apaches, 1848–1886* (Albuquerque, 1940), is more pertinent to the focus of this study. Sonia Bleeker, *The Apache Indians: Raiders of the Southwest* (New York, 1951), should be consulted as well. The extent of the Army's commitment to Arizona defense is suggested in Ray Brandes, "A Guide to the History of the U.S. Army Installations in Arizona, 1845–1886," *Arizona and the West, 1* (Spring 1959). James R. Hastings, "The Tragedy at Camp Grant in 1871," *Arizona and the West, 2* (Summer 1959), provides a much needed recent account of the massacre. Clum's career is narrated in Woodworth Clum, *Apache Agent: The Story of John P. Clum* (Boston, 1936).

A number of books and articles are helpful in piecing together the political history of Arizona Territory: Farish, *History of Arizona* gives lengthy details about men and events and tells the story from the point of view of the Democrats. The careers of the governors are briefly summarized in E. E. Williams, "The Territorial Governors of Arizona," *AHR, 6* and *7* (1935–36). Roscoe G. Wilson, "The Little Governor Does Well by Arizona," *Arizona Days and Ways Magazine* (March 30, 1958), is appreciative of Safford. Fremont's Arizona career is treated only briefly in Allan Nevins, *Fremont, Pathmarker of the West* (New York, 1939).

The Mormon experience in Arizona is revealed in two works: James H. McClintock, *Mormon Settlement in Arizona* (Phoenix, 1921); and David King Udall and Peal Udall Nelson, *David King Udall: Arizona Pioneer Mormon* (Tucson, 1959).

Outlines of the mineral development of Arizona may be followed in Wyllys, *Arizona*, in Anne M. Peck, *The March of Arizona History* (Tucson, 1962), and in Rodman W. Paul, *Mining Frontiers of the Far West, 1848–1880* (New York, 1963), but a definitive history of Arizona mining remains to be done. Copper mining is treated in Robert G. Cleland, *A History of Phelps-Dodge* (New York, 1952). The territorial railroad story still lacks a historian, but the story of the larger lines may be followed in Robert E. Riegel, *Story of the Western Railroads* (New York, 1926). Studies of the Santa Fe are listed above in the New Mexico section. Bert Haskett, "Early History of the Cattle

Industry in Arizona," *AHR, 6* (1935), traces the beginnings of the industry. The Reavis land fraud is covered in William A. Depuy, *Baron of the Colorados* (San Antonio, 1940).

The Arizona crusade for statehood is best followed in the series of unpublished theses listed in the New Mexico section, but for brief printed accounts see Lockwood, *Pioneer Days*, Wyllys, *Arizona*, and Richard E. Sloan, *Memoirs of An Arizona Judge* (Stanford, Calif., 1932). Sloan, the last territorial governor of Arizona, viewed the admission with amusement and detachment. Claude G. Bowers, *Beveridge and the Progressive Era* (New York, 1932), gives the senator's side of the story, while Waldemar Westergaard, "Senator Thomas R. Bard and the Arizona-New Mexico Controversy," *Annual Publication of the Historical Society of Southern California, 11* (Los Angeles, 1919) explains a specific case of hostility to statehood. George H. Kelly, *Arizona Legislative History, 1864–1912* (Phoenix, 1926), is of limited help.

UNPUBLISHED DISSERTATIONS

Annie M. Cox, "History of Bisbee, 1877 to 1937" (Master's thesis, University of Arizona, Tucson, 1938), is a good introduction to the social and economic structure of an Arizona border mining town. Robert L. Swor, "The Development of Prescott" (Master's thesis, Arizona State College, Tempe, 1952), is informative and understanding. Katherine Shepard, "The Miles-Crook Controversy" (Master's thesis, University of New Mexico, Albuquerque, 1936), is cautious. LeMoine Langston, "Arizona's Fight for Statehood in the Fifty-Seventh Congress" (Master's thesis, University of New Mexico, 1939), is quite good.

Index